An Archaeology of Tools

Hand Tools in History Series

An Archaeology of Tools

The Tool Collections
of the Davistown Museum

H. G. Brack

Davistown Museum Publication Series
Volume 9

© Davistown Museum 2013
ISBN 978-0-9829951-9-8

Copyright © 2013 by H. G. Brack
ISBN 13 978-0-9829951-9-8
ISBN-10: 0982995199

Davistown Museum

First Edition

Cover illustration: Main hall of the Davistown Museum

Cover design by Sett Balise

This publication was made possible by a donation from Barker Steel LLC.

Pennywheel Press
P.O. Box 144
Hulls Cove, ME 04644

Preface

Davistown Museum *Hand Tools in History*

One of the primary missions of the Davistown Museum is the recovery, preservation, interpretation, and display of the hand tools of the maritime culture of Maine and New England (1607-1900). The *Hand Tools in History* series, sponsored by the museum's Center for the Study of Early Tools, plays a vital role in achieving the museum mission by documenting and interpreting the history, science, and art of toolmaking. The Davistown Museum combines the *Hand Tools in History* publication series, its exhibition of hand tools, and bibliographic, library, and website resources to construct an historical overview of steel- and toolmaking strategies and techniques used by the edge toolmakers of New England's wooden age. Included in this overview are the roots of these strategies and techniques in the early Iron Age, their relationship with modern steelmaking technologies, and their culmination in the florescence of American hand tool manufacturing in the last half of the 19th century.

Background

During over 40 years of searching for New England's old woodworking tools for his Jonesport Wood Company stores, curator and series author H. G. Skip Brack collected a wide variety of different tool forms with numerous variations in metallurgical composition, many signed by their makers. The recurrent discovery of forge welded tools made in the 18th and 19th centuries provided the impetus for founding the museum and then researching and writing the *Hand Tools in History* publications. In studying the tools in the museum collection, Brack found that, in many cases, the tools seemed to contradict the popularly held belief that all shipwrights' tools and other edge tools used before the Civil War originated from Sheffield and other English tool-producing centers. In many cases, the tools that he recovered from New England tool chests and collections dating from before 1860 appeared to be American-made rather than imported from English tool-producing centers. Brack's observations and the questions that arose from them led him to research the topic and then to share his findings in the *Hand Tools in History* series.

Hand Tools in History Publications

- Volume 6: *Steel- and Toolmaking Strategies and Techniques before 1870* explores ancient and early modern steel- and toolmaking strategies and techniques, including those of early Iron Age, Roman, medieval, and Renaissance metallurgists and toolmakers. Also reviewed are the technological innovations of the Industrial

Revolution, the contributions of the English industrial revolutionaries to the evolution of the factory system of mass production with interchangeable parts, and the development of bulk steelmaking processes and alloy steel technologies in the latter half of the 19th century. Many of these technologies play a role in the florescence of American ironmongers and toolmakers in the 18th and 19th centuries. Author H. G. Skip Brack cites archaeometallurgists such as Barraclough, Tylecote, Tweedle, Smith, Wertime, Wayman, and many others as useful guides for a journey through the pyrotechnics of ancient and modern metallurgy. Volume 6 includes an extensive bibliography of resources pertaining to steel- and toolmaking techniques from the early Bronze Age to the beginning of bulk-processed steel production after 1870.

- Volume 7: *Art of the Edge Tool: The Ferrous Metallurgy of New England Shipsmiths and Toolmakers* explores the evolution of tool- and steelmaking techniques by New England's shipsmiths and edge toolmakers from 1607-1882. This volume uses the construction of Maine's first ship, the pinnace *Virginia*, at Fort St. George on the Kennebec River in Maine (1607-1608), as the iconic beginning of a critically important component of colonial and early American history. While there were hundreds of small shallops and pinnaces built in North and South America by French, English, Spanish, and other explorers before 1607, the construction of the *Virginia* symbolizes the very beginning of New England's three centuries of wooden shipbuilding. This volume explores the links between the construction of the *Virginia* and the later flowering of the colonial iron industry; the relationship of 17th, 18th, and 19th century edge toolmaking techniques to the steelmaking strategies of the Renaissance; and the roots of America's indigenous iron industry in the bog iron deposits of southeastern Massachusetts and the many forges and furnaces that were built there in the early colonial period. It explores and explains this milieu, which forms the context for the productivity of New England's many shipsmiths and edge toolmakers, including the final flowering of shipbuilding in Maine in the 19th century. Also included is a bibliography of sources cited in the text.

- Volume 8: *The Classic Period of American Toolmaking 1827-1930* considers the wide variety of toolmaking industries that arose after the colonial period and its robust tradition of edge toolmaking. It discusses the origins of the florescence of American toolmaking not only in English and continental traditions, which produced gorgeous hand tools in the 18th and 19th centuries, but also in the poorly documented and often unacknowledged work of New England shipsmiths, blacksmiths, and toolmakers. This volume explicates the success of the innovative American factory system, illustrated by an ever-expanding repertoire of iron- and steelmaking strategies and the widening variety of tools produced by this factory system. It traces the vigorous growth of an American hand toolmaking industry that was based on a rapidly expanding economy, the rich natural resources of North America, and continuous westward expansion until the late 19th century. It also includes a company by company synopsis of America's most important edge toolmakers working before 1900, an extensive bibliography of sources that deal with the Industrial Revolution in America, special topic bibliographies on a variety of trades, and a timeline of the most important developments in this toolmaking florescence.

- Volume 9: *An Archaeology of Tools* contains the ever-expanding list of tools in the Davistown Museum collection, which includes important tools from many sources. The tools in the museum exhibition and school loan program that are listed in Volume 9 serve as a primary resource for information about the diversity of tool- and steelmaking strategies and techniques and the locations of manufacturers of the tools used by American artisans from the colonial period until the late 19th century.

- Volume 10: *Registry of Maine Toolmakers* fulfills an important part of the mission of the Center for the Study of Early Tools, i.e. the documentation of the Maine toolmakers and planemakers working in Maine. It includes an introductory essay on the history and social context of toolmaking in Maine; an annotated list of Maine toolmakers; a bibliography of sources of information on Maine toolmakers; and appendices on shipbuilding in Maine, the metallurgy of edge tools in the museum collection, woodworking tools of the 17th and 18th centuries, and a listing of important New England and Canadian edge toolmakers working outside of Maine. This registry is available on the Davistown Museum website and can be accessed by those wishing to research the history of Maine tools in their possession. The author greatly appreciates receiving information about as yet undocumented Maine toolmakers working before 1900.

- Volume 11: *Handbook for Ironmongers: A Glossary of Ferrous Metallurgy Terms* provides definitions pertinent to the survey of the history of ferrous metallurgy in the preceding five volumes of the *Hand Tools in History* series. The glossary defines terminology relevant to the origins and history of ferrous metallurgy, ranging from ancient metallurgical techniques to the later developments in iron and steel production in America. It also contains definitions of modern steelmaking techniques and recent research on topics such as powdered metallurgy, high resolution electron microscopy, and superplasticity. It also defines terms pertaining to the growth and uncontrolled emissions of a pyrotechnic society that manufactured the hand tools that built the machines that now produce biomass-derived consumer products and their toxic chemical byproducts. It is followed by relevant appendices, a bibliography listing sources used to compile this glossary, and a general bibliography on metallurgy. The author also acknowledges and discusses issues of language and the interpretation of terminology used by ironworkers over a period of centuries. A compilation of the many definitions related to iron and steel and their changing meanings is an important component of our survey of the history of the steel- and toolmaking strategies and techniques and the relationship of these traditions to the accomplishments of New England shipsmiths and their offspring, the edge toolmakers who made shipbuilding tools.

- Volume 13 in the *Hand Tools in History* series explores the iconography (imagery) of early American hand tools as they evolve into the Industrial Revolution's increased diversity of tool forms. The hand tools illustrated in this volume were selected from the Davistown Museum collection, most of which are cataloged in *An Archaeology of Tools* (Volume 9 in *Hand Tools in History*), and from those acquired and often sold by Liberty Tool Company and affiliated stores, collected during 40+ years of "tool picking." Also included are important tools from the private collections of Liberty Tool Company customers and Davistown Museum supporters. Beginning with tools as simple machines, reviews are provided of the metallurgy and tools used by the multitasking blacksmith, shipsmith, and other early American artisans of the Wooden Age. The development of machine-made tools and the wide variety of tool forms that characterize the American factory system of tool production are also explored. The text includes over 800 photographs and illustrations and an appendix of the tool forms depicted in Diderot's *Encyclopedia*. This survey provides a guide to the hand tools and trades that played a key role in America's industrial renaissance. The iconography of American hand tools narrates the story of a cascading series of Industrial Revolutions that culminate in the Age of Information Technology.

The *Hand Tools in History* series is an ongoing project; new information, citations, and definitions are constantly being added as they are discovered or brought to the author's attention. These updates are posted weekly on the museum website and will appear in future editions. All volumes in the *Hand Tools in History* series are available as bound soft cover editions for sale at the Davistown Museum, Liberty Tool Co., local bookstores and museums, or by order from www.davistownmuseum.org/publications.html, Amazon.com, Amazon.co.uk, CreateSpace.com, Abebooks.com, and Albris.com.

Table of Contents

Preface to the Collection

The Davistown Museum exhibition *An Archaeology of Tools* interprets the European settlement of Maine and New England through the medium of hand tools, always for archaeologists among the most revealing of the accidental durable remnants of ancient peoples. Occasionally, interspersed within the tool collections recovered by the Liberty Tool Co. for the Davistown Museum are artifacts dating prior to the European settlement of North America. The history of the Ancient Dominions of Maine is the history of two cultures, the Native Americans who lived in Maine before 1600 and the Europeans who gradually cleared the landscape of these first inhabitants after 1600.

Historical Background

The mission of The Davistown Museum exhibition *An Archaeology of Tools* is the recovery, identification, evaluation, and display of the hand tools of the maritime culture of coastal New England from the first European visitors in the 16th century to the fluorescence of the Industrial Revolution. Particular emphasis is put on the display of hand tools characteristic of the maritime culture of Maine and New England, its shipbuilders and toolmakers, as well as the tools of the trades of the artisans of Davistown Plantation, later the towns of Montville and Liberty.

The many villages and mill sites of the Davistown Plantation evolved into a flourishing community of coopers by the third decade of the 19th century. These coopers, as well as other craftsmen and small manufacturer's establishments and water mills, produced a wide variety of woodenware, wood products, such as clapboards and house frames, and some tools that were then transported to the market and shipbuilding towns of coastal Maine including Belfast, Thomaston, Warren, and Waldoboro. The artifacts produced at mill sites such as Liberty, Kingdom Falls, South Liberty, Searsmont, Appleton, and Union played a key role in the evolution of the maritime culture of Maine including its Downeast cod fishery, West Indies and coasting trade, lime and granite industries, and flourishing lumber and cordwood exports. A study of the maritime history of Maine is incomplete without tracing the evolution of the infrastructure and industries that were the basis for its florescence from the end of the Indian Wars (1759) to the Industrial Revolution. The tool collection of The Davistown Museum – *An Archaeology of Tools* – reflects the evolution of toolmaking from Maine's first colonial dominion to the twilight years of its maritime culture during the late 19th century. Particular emphasis is placed on recovering tools and artifacts characteristic of the trades and mercantile activities of both the pre-Civil War communities of Liberty and Montville and the

Davistown Plantation which preceded them, as well as those characteristic of New England's early American industries and later machine age production, which now forms the bulk of the museum's collections .

A primary source of the tools on exhibit are those collected by the Jonesport Wood Co., Liberty Tool Co. (located across the street from the Museum), and the Hulls Cove Tool Barn since tool collecting began in 1970 in and near New England shipbuilding communities. Specific significant tools with special characteristics and/or tool manufacturer or maker's signatures collected during the last four decades were then loaned or donated to the Davistown Museum when it was founded in 1999 to form the core of its current collection. More recently, donations and loans from other collectors have allowed the collection of the Davistown Museum to become among the most important in the United States. Particular emphasis has been put on the chronological documentation of tool manufacturers in New England and Maine.

The collection of tools in the Davistown Museum is the result of the recovery of hand tools manufactured either in England, continental locations, or in the early forges, foundries, and factories of America during the settlement of New England by Europeans in the 17th, 18th, and 19th centuries. These tools are organized in chronological groupings and displayed in the Davistown Museum exhibition *An Archaeology of Tools*. The organization of the museum's tool exhibition expresses the history of the state of Maine and its peculiar anomalies (e.g. the depopulation of most areas of Maine east of Wells after 1676; coastal resettlement was gradual, if sporadic, until the fall of Quebec in 1759.) The historical schema used for the collation of these tools in the Museum collection expresses the rhythms of Maine's history – the ancient dominions of the old maritime cultures of Maine and the gradual impact of the Industrial Revolution on this culture. The study of early tools as material cultural artifacts helps us trace the gradual, at times tortuous, settlement of the Maine coast and its tidewater communities and the later penetration of European settlers into ever more inland locations. The tools used by European settlers in Maine prior to the Industrial Revolution illustrate their near total dependence on a resource-based economy based first and foremost on forest products, with shipbuilding as its most essential industry. The creative use of these forest products by the adept use of steel edged tools allowed the efficient exploitation of Maine's other major natural resource, its marine fisheries, as well as the manufacture of the wide variety of milled lumber and coopers' products that, along with fish, were the most important cargos on Maine's coasting and oceangoing ships.

Since some of the tools recovered by the Liberty Tool Co. in southern New England and Maine were manufactured during the historical interregnum (1676-1720), when no tools were being made in Maine. They are cataloged in Historic Maritime I if appearing to be made before 1700 (always a guess); otherwise they are listed in Maritime II. An example of this is the Jo Fuller (Providence, RI) rounding plane (ID: 31102T1).

Implicit in our attempt to explore the technological history of hand tools in Maine is a triad: forest products – woodworking tool kits – and the wooden ships they produced. This triad underlies the organizational plan of the museum exhibition, *An Archaeology of Tools*. The schema of this exhibition references the ebb and flow of a series of historical events, the details of which can be pursued and explored in the wealth of written literature on the manufacturing of hand tools and the history of technology. The historical background and related literature and research, which constitutes the essential background information for understanding and interpreting the exhibition *An Archaeology of Tools*, is contained in volumes 6 - 8 of the museum publication series, *Hand Tools in History*. The specifics of tool manufacturing in Maine are explored in volume 10 of this museum publication series, the *Registry of Maine Toolmakers*. Together these volumes explore the historical background, steelmaking strategies, and tool manufacturing history of New England's maritime era.

Our chronological examination of hand tools in Maine history begins with the following time frame.

- The first tidewater settlements in Maine (Maritime I, 1607 - 1676) and the scattering of most of these settlers during the French and Indian Wars
- The resurgence of European settlement in Maine beginning in the second decade of the 18th century and continuing through the early days of the Republic (Maritime II, 1720 - 1800)
- The boomtown years of coastal Maine and the dawn of the Industrial Revolution (Maritime III, 1800 - 1840)
- The early years of the Industrial Revolution and the impact of rapid technological change on the tool kits of Maine's artisans (Maritime IV, 1840 - 1865)
- The florescence of a full blown Industrial Revolution that forever changed the lifestyle of Mainers, New Englanders, and Americans after the Civil War (1865 forward)

This schema or historical timeline, as well as the various chronologies, which precede or follow it, provide a handy reference for Museum staff, visitors, and students to interpret the changes in technology essential to understanding Maine and American history.

An Archaeology of Tools: Exhibition Overview

The Museum displays illustrate the evolution of tool manufacturing in the United States from blacksmith-made hand-forged tools (circa 1600 - 1830) to the early years of the Industrial Revolution and the emergence of a vigorous American tool manufacturing industry. The history, manufacturing techniques, and products of American hand tool manufacturing industries before the Civil War are poorly documented. The many American-made tools, especially edge tools, surviving from this period help supplement the meager written literature on this subject. While finely made English tools, and to a lesser extent German tools, continued to be imported to the United States until after the Civil War, American tool manufacturing activities can be divided into four general categories. All are compatible with our interpretation of the maritime era of Maine's unique history, the overlap of steel producing strategies and technologies notwithstanding.

- Until the American Revolution all hand tools were hand-forged; many of the best tools were imported from England but a robust domestic toolmaking industry made its appearance along with the first blacksmiths in early colonial New England. Sources of steel used on edge tools during this period was first and foremost imported "German steel", most of it made in English furnaces, soon supplemented by both domestically-produced natural steel from the direct process bloomery and domestically-produced "German steel" from decarburized cast iron. Blister steel was produced in cementation furnaces in England after 1700, and soon in clandestine colonial furnaces. In the mid-17th century a robust but undocumented domestic hand tool production industry evolved centered near the extensive bog iron deposits of southeastern New England. By the mid-18th century, bloomery-derived natural steel, German steel, and cementation steel were beginning to be produced in western Connecticut (Litchfield) and especially to the west and southwest in Pennsylvania, New York, and New Jersey. High quality, imported English crucible steel became available to American toolmakers after 1780.
- After the Revolutionary War, a vigorous domestic edge tool manufacturing industry arose, making timber framing and shipwrights' tools utilizing imported German and English steel. While Sheffield-made cast steel, also called crucible steel, is the best known of the imported steels, the majority of edge tools were made with either imported or American-made blister and/or German steel. Numerous examples of high quality edge tools in the museum collection not marked "cast steel" attest to the wide availability and use of steel made by other techniques. The evolution of steelmaking technologies and strategies is explored in detail in the museum publication series *Hand Tools in History*.

After 1830, American toolmakers quickly adopted, implemented, and improved innovative English machine designs. American entrepreneurs combined originality, inventiveness, the open exchange of information, and the efficient organization of production and distribution to create a factory system that made America the leader in world production of most hand tools by the time of the Civil War.

During and after the Civil War, and with the help of a proliferating railroad system, westward expansion, and the discovery and use of extensive continental natural resources, especially iron ore, forest products, and coal, America began producing its own crucible steel, followed by large quantities of bulk process steel. It was during this time that the tradition of handmade hand tools was gradually subsumed by factory-made tools, many of great beauty and inventiveness. Between 1865 and 1930, what is now called the classic period of American machinist and patented plane production, achieved its famed excellence in hand tool production.

The museum tool exhibition is intended to illustrate the technological changes impacting the Davistown Plantation, the towns of Liberty and Montville, and the livelihood of local residents, and in a larger context, all the maritime rural and incipient industrial communities of late colonial and early America. The exhibits document the replacement of handmade tools with factory- and machine-made tools, and illustrate an Industrial Revolution that perfected the art of tool manufacturing at the same time that it bypassed the communities of coastal and back country Maine, which escaped both its benefits and the urban blight that is its legacy.

Historical Context for the Exhibition *An Archaeology of Tools*

The most important tools in the tool kits of the residents of the historical maritime cultures of Maine (1607 - 1865) were woodworking tools, especially those associated with shipbuilding, boat building, and construction of mills, buildings, and wharfs. Central among these primordial tools are the adz, broad ax, framing chisel, pit saw, drawknife, hewing ax, hand plane, and pod auger. As our exhibition *An Archaeology of Tools* has been collected and organized from the surviving remnants of the workshops and tool chests of 18th and 19th century New England, a series of questions naturally arise as to the origins and prototypes of the iron and steel tools used by the early settlers in New England.

In the late 18th century, what was a trickle of settlers moving into the back hill country of central coastal Maine became a virtual flood of immigrants seeking free land and new opportunities. The extensive network of rivers and streams that eventually led to the coastal tidewater shipbuilding towns of Thomaston and Warren (St. Georges River),

Waldoboro (Medomak River), Damariscotta and Boothbay (Davis Stream and Damariscotta River), and Wiscasset (Sheepscot River) provided numerous water mill sites for what was to be a vigorous forest-resource dependent network of coopers, woodsmen, sawyers, and millwrights. These newly arrived migrants from forest-resource starved southern New England often followed traditional seasonal patterns of labor to work in the tidewater shipyards or serve as crew for winter and early spring fishing expeditions. The forms (shapes, styles, and design characteristics), origins (place of manufacture), and manufacturing methods of the tools used by these settlers tell us more about their lives, technology, and social milieu than any other material cultural remnants except the written records they left for posterity.

Of particular importance for the newly established villages of the Davistown Plantation, always located at mill sites (The Kingdom, Liberty Village, South Montville, and South Liberty) as well as nearby Searsmont, Appleton, Palermo, and Union, was an already well established coastal shipbuilding industry. It was the needs of this shipbuilding industry for heavy timber, planking, and spars as well as for the ship cargos of cordwood, clapboards, house frames, and, especially, cooperage products (staves, trawl line tubs, water kegs, salt boxes, etc.) that enabled these back hill country mill towns to rapidly grow in the boomtown years of the first four decades of the 19th century. The hand tools utilized in the harvesting of timber resources and the manufacture of wooden products were, along with the essential skills necessary for the efficient use of these tools, the key to the success of these industries. The seasonal and itinerant nature of shipbuilding also meant that many of the same tools and skills used in the boom town years of the inland water mill towns were also the key ingredient in the success of Maine's booming shipyards. A comparison of the number of ships built in the Waldoboro customs district shows an almost exact correlation with mill town population levels in the early and mid-19th century.

As early as 1640, southern New England colonists, including many new artisans who had arrived in the great migration (1629-1645), had been forced to build their own fishing and trading vessels due to the disruption of shipping caused by the English Revolution, 1640 - 1660. With the return of peace after the disruption and uncertainties of the long Parliament and Cromwellian years, New England colonists began participating in, and soon became an important component of, an English-based polygon of transatlantic trade that included Newfoundland, New England, the West Indies, the Wine Islands (Madeira, etc.), and European and English ports. As southern New England depleted its forest resources, Maine soon became an important source of forest products. By the time of the American Revolution and the early years of the republic, coastal Maine had become an important shipbuilding center as well as a source for milled and raw timber products of every description. By the 1840s, Maine

6

had become the most important center of America's shipbuilding industry. Of particular significance for both the history of the Davistown Plantation and the formation of the museum is that by the late 1840s the Waldoboro Customs District, downstream from Liberty and Montville, was producing as much as 10% of all wooden ships built in the United States. This florescence of shipbuilding and associated need for cargo, supplies of woodenware, and agricultural products explains why local population levels as well as water mill-related manufacturing activities reached their peak levels in the 1840s. The third, fourth, and fifth decades of the 19th century thus provide a focus for the museum's tool collection, which begins with the earliest forged iron and imported English tools (Maritime I and II) and ends with the classic period of the Industrial Revolution.

After 1870, fewer but larger sailing vessels continued to be built in Maine, especially at Bath and at surviving larger shipyards at Thomaston, Waldoboro, Damariscotta, and elsewhere, but in the era of railroads and steamships, the small community-sponsored coasters and West Indies traders were fast disappearing. After the Civil War, the full rigged downeasters, and later, the huge bulk cargo schooners, the last wooden ships built in Maine, were transporting coal, ice, cotton, lime, and granite to the growing cities and mills along the Atlantic seaboard and elsewhere. This final florescence of wooden shipbuilding in Maine played an ironic role in ending the era of wooden ships and the decline of the mill towns located upstream from a now shrinking shipbuilding industry. The decline in wooden shipbuilding in many coastal Maine locations closely correlates with declining population levels and manufacturing activity in the mill towns of the central coastal Maine hill country, in contrast to growing industrial activity in southern New England cities and Maine mill towns such as Biddeford, Auburn, and Lewiston.

Inventory Key

The inventory list of the collections of the Davistown Museum is divided by the categories listed below.

The following abbreviations are used:

Status:

DTM	Owned by The Davistown Museum (donation or purchase)
DA	Deaccessioned
LPC	Loans from a Private Collection except for loans from artists
LA loans	Loans from the Artist; many of the works in the Annual Art Show are
	from the artist
BDTM	Bequest to the Museum from a Private Collection
GA	Gift from the artist; these are also part of the permanent collection but are differentiated from Museum purchases in order to acknowledge individual gifts.
LSS	Items Loaned for Special Shows
MAG	Maine Artists Guild item
NOM	Not Owned by the Museum
SOLD	Sold by MAG
WD	Withdrawn by the Artist

Location codes:

The letter codes correspond to those used on the Museum map.

MH	Main Exhibition Hall except display cases
MHC	Main Exhibition Hall, in the Cases (A-L)
	For example: MHC-K for Main Exhibition Hall Case K
RR	Reading Room (T) and display cases (R)
ESML	Elliot Sayward Memorial Library, second, third, and fourth floors
CP	Children's Room and Print Collection
CSA	Coffin Stream Assemblage (3)
CT	Captain Tinkham's Emporium, Searsport
MH3	Main Hall to DTHP connector (3)
DTHP	Davistown History Project room (U)
LTC	Liberty Tool Co., Davistown Museum Annex, second floor
P	Fourth floor Photography exhibit and stairwell (P, V)
Q	Bathroom (Q)

MAG	MAG Gallery on second floor (rooms 1 - 8)
YX	Stairwell and Entrance Hall (Y, X)
T	Reading room display case
TT	Tools Teach (Basement)
TT (pub)	Illustrated in *Tools Teach* and deaccessioned
OM	Outside the museum (at street level)
GWIS	Gallery, Great Wass Island Salvage Co., Hulls Cove
HC	Hulls Cove Office
SG	Hulls Cove Sculpture Garden
TB	Hulls Cove Tool Barn
UNK	Unable to locate or unknown

Photographs of the item and/or a biography of the maker are shown as web links in the format:

http://www.davistownmuseum.org/pics/... for photographs

http://www.davistownmuseum.org/bio... for biographies.

An Archaeology of Tools: Historical Overview

The tools in the collection of the Davistown Museum are organized and cataloged according to Maine's unique patterns of historical settlement. The King Philip's War in southern New England spread to Maine in 1677 and resulted in the great diaspora of English settlers living east of Wells, Maine, in the several decades after that date. The gradual return of settlers began in coastal areas in the 1720s. The fall of Quebec in 1759 and the Treaty of Paris in 1763 reopened much of central and eastern Maine for resettlement. Many of the tools in the museum collection were produced in southern New England during this period of political turmoil and uncertainty.

Historic Maritime I (1607-1676): The First Colonial Dominion

After the Popham Colony's unsuccessful attempt to establish a settlement in "North Virginia" at Fort St. George at the mouth of the Kennebec River, the first of a series of early settlements in the coastal tidewater areas of the Sheepscot and Georges rivers were established at Damariscove Island (1622), Cape Newagen (1623), and Pemaquid (1625). By the 1630s, settlements dotted the Maine coast from Machias (1631) to Kittery (1631). By the early 1670s, Maine's colonial era population was ±10,000 people. Blacksmiths and shipsmiths were known to be active at Pemaquid (John Brown, 1625) as well as at Arrowsic on Georgetown Island (The Clark and Lake Co., ±1650). Every 17th century coastal community in Maine would have required shipsmiths and toolmakers as a matter of survival. Hand-forged iron tools surviving from this era are difficult to date. Possibly some of the reforged steel rasps in the museum collection, along with a small number of items in the following listing, actually date from this period. Colonial era settlements along the Maine coast were brought to a quick halt by the onset of the French and Indian Wars, which began with King Philip's War in 1676. Within a year of the onset of this war, all of the English settlements east of Wells were burned or abandoned. In fact, only a few tools in the museum collections can be identified as dating from this first colonial dominion.

There are no surviving woodworking tools that can be identified as having been used by the first wave of European settlers in Maine. Most of the tools in the first display case were made in the 18th century. Nonetheless, they are similar to those that might have been found in the tool kits of the earliest settlers.

Historic Maritime II (1720-1800): The Second Colonial Dominion & the Early Republic

After the onset of the Indian wars of 1676, the Maine coast was essentially abandoned until settlers began returning to coastal Maine, starting in 1710. One of the earliest communities on the coast of Maine reoccupied after this interregnum (1676-1720) was the nearby settlement of Thomaston. What was, at first, tentative and isolated resettlement of the Maine coast east of Wells after 1710 became a flood of new immigrants after the fall of Quebec in 1759 and the Treaty of Paris in 1763. This treaty resulted in English control of Maine from the Piscataquis River to the St. Croix River opening up the previously dangerous inland environs of what was soon to become the Davistown Plantation and more distant eastern locations, such as Mount Desert Island and the Pleasant River settlements. The tools illustrated in this section of the museum collection are typical of those used by the second wave of settlers in Maine, including the early settlers of Davistown Plantation (1775). Shortly after resettlement, a vigorous timber harvesting and shipbuilding industry became the stimulus for a rapid growth in population, especially after the end of the American Revolution.

Historic Maritime III (1800-1840): Boomtown Years & the Dawn of the Industrial Revolution

The tools in this exhibit are typical of those that may have been used by the residents of Liberty and Montville in the early boomtown years of what was, until 1807, the Davistown Plantation. By 1800, the vigorous colonial iron- and toolmaking industries, which had evolved in southern New England before as well as during the Indian Wars (1675 - 1759), had spread to Maine. Shipsmiths and blacksmiths were again active in every coastal boatbuilding and shipbuilding community despite the lack of written documentation of their presence. It is, in fact, the surviving hand tools made by these artisans, often unsigned if not intended for resale in a market economy, that are the primary evidence of their existence. During the colonial period and well into the early 19th century, the majority of small edge tools and plane blades were imported from English toolmaking centers at Sheffield and Birmingham. Examples of these tools are included in the museum exhibitions. Nonetheless, a robust indigenous toolmaking industry, as detailed in the museum publication *Art of the Edge Tool*, had evolved in southern New England and, then, in Maine by the late 18th century. Most of the surviving larger edge tools used by New England's shipwrights, including broad axes, adzes, slicks, mast shaves, and timber framing tools, were made in New England by New England and Maine toolmakers. These tools were made with the help of a variety of steelmaking strategies, including the use of direct process bog-iron-derived natural steel, steel made from forged malleable iron bar stock, domestically-made or imported blister steel, German steel, or imported crucible steel. The forge-welding of steel cutting edges was the most common edge toolmaking technique, but not the only one. Please refer to the museum metallurgy guide for a listing of steelmaking strategies. (*Handbook for Ironmongers Appendix I* or online at http://www.davistownmuseum.org/PDFs/Vol11_Appendix_GuideToToolMetallurgy.pdf)

The boomtown atmosphere of Liberty and Montville in the early 19th century with its water-powered mills and coopers' shops was typical of many areas of New England where riverine resources provided a link between forest and a robust maritime economy. The development of the factory system in southern New England soon required larger water power sources (rivers) than were present in Liberty and Montville, whose population, as well as its manufacturing output, appears to have peaked between 1840 and 1850. Little information is available about the blacksmiths and small foundries with their water-powered trip hammers that produced tools, stoves, and other implements for the many villages of Liberty, Montville, and the surrounding area before 1850. In contrast, a significant amount of data is available about major New England toolmakers and some Maine toolmakers who supplied the bustling downstream shipyards of the period. For information on later toolmakers, mills, and tradesmen in Liberty and Montville, see the Davistown History Project at this webpage: http://www.davistownmuseum.org/publications/volume2.html.

Historic Maritime IV (1840-1865): The Early Industrial Revolution

The years between 1840 and the panic of 1857 witnessed the peak production of the shipyards downstream from Liberty and Montville. These years also saw the spread of railroads in southern New England, and then into Maine, as well as an amazing growth in American manufacturing, including water-powered textile mills, iron foundries, coal production, steam-powered equipment, and machinery for use in the newly evolving factory system of production utilizing interchangeable parts. Small Maine manufacturers and edge toolmakers participated in this early Industrial Revolution, which is reflected in the changing designs and expanding tool kits of the period.

Liberty and Montville achieved their peak population levels exactly as the Waldoboro customs district achieved its peak production of wooden ships. Their construction and their need for supplies, cargos, produce, and crews help explain the boomtown years of both the central coast and its back hill country mill towns. One or more foundries were operating in Liberty during this time, with many coopers making staves and other woodenware for the flourishing coasting trade. Other toolmakers continued production of axes and other implements. View the registry of the known 19th century Liberty and Montville toolmakers on the web here: http://www.davistownmuseum.org/history.html.

The Industrial Revolution (1865f.)

Hegemony of the New England Toolmakers

The period between 1840 and 1865 was a time of rapid industrial change that culminated in the Civil War. By the end of the Civil War the world of the toolmaker and the tool user had changed radically and would never be the same.

The routine production of malleable cast iron was well established by the 1850s, allowing tool makers, such as Leonard Bailey, and the patented plow makers documented by Roger Smith (1981-1992) to begin their innovative production of cast iron planes. Also well established was the use of the steam-powered rotary blowing engines and the steam hammer, greatly increasing the efficiency of iron and steel production. In 1850, Joseph Dixon invented high temperature resistant graphite crucibles of equal durability to the famed Stourbridge clay crucibles that were used for cast steel production in England since 1742.

When Thomas Witherby began making chisels in Millbury, MA, in 1849, it wasn't long before he began using domestically-produced cast steel equal in quality to that long produced in England. By 1860, the drop-forging rather than forge-welding of tools utilizing machinery rather than the hand of the multitasking blacksmith dominated tool production, including those with interchangeable parts. As a result of this ongoing Industrial Revolution, there was a vast increase in the variety of tools in the tool kits of the machinists and woodworkers who worked after the Civil War.

An important event in the evolution of the Industrial Revolution was the direct process production of steel by the Bessemer method, soon supplanted by the more flexible, modern Siemens open hearth method, which allowed quality control production of countless alloy steel variations. By 1870, both of these new steelmaking techniques began dominating American steel production. As a result, a variety of new tool steel variations, many of them secret, were introduced. Most important among these was the perfection of tempered alloy steels especially useful for the rapidly growing repertoire of machinist measuring tools.

The mass production of steel permitted the continued rapid growth of both railroads (iron rails soon become steel rails) and the factory system that supplanted and gradually made obsolete the small workshops of the mill towns of rural America, including Liberty and Montville. The final display area of the *Archaeology of Tools* exhibit is devoted to illustrating some of the tools typical of the new tool kits that began supplanting the implements produced by the blacksmiths and small forges in the earlier maritime culture of Maine and New England. The transitional and patented planes and the classic machinists' tools in the Museum exhibits are important historical artifacts illustrating the ongoing revolution in the factory system of mass production. They also are esthetically interesting sculpture objects.

Despite the full onslaught of the Industrial Revolution, shipbuilding continued in Maine, especially in the larger ports of Penobscot Bay, Waldoboro, Damariscotta, and Bath. A golden age of exquisitely designed and constructed schooners and downeasters supported a flourishing industry of Maine edge tool and agricultural equipment manufacturers, but the most important developments in manufacturing technology, including edge tool and hand plane production, occurred in southern New England, where the classic period of American toolmaking overlapped with Maine's lingering maritime culture.

The sojourn of America's first machinists in Maine, Darling, Bailey, and Schwartz, was brief. The florescence of the classic period of machinist tool manufacturing was in southern New England. The maritime culture of Maine was in decline. The final sections of the exhibition of the Davistown Museum's *Archaeology of Tools* illustrates the rapid emergence of new types of meticulously designed and constructed tools.

Martin Donnelly, in his introduction to the *Makers of American Machinist's Tools* (Cope 1994), provides this summary of machine tool production in the height of the Industrial Revolution; a final footnote to the hegemony of New England's maritime culture.

> The Classic Period of American machinist tools... [is] that period of time from shortly before the American Civil War to the beginning of the First World War when, in response to tremendous economic growth and technological advancement, there was an incredibly rapid increase in the number of manufacturers and marketers of machinist tools. A great number of companies and individuals, producing all manner of products, grew and prospered, marketing elaborately conceived and artistically machined hand tools for those skilled workers who manned the engines of industry. As the end of this Classic Period approached, the vicissitudes of the emerging economy, which brought periodic recessions or "panics", together with the need to compete on a national, rather than regional, scale, had served to eliminate nearly all of those many companies.
>
> Certain industry leaders, particularly the L.S. Starrett Company of Athol, Mass., and the Brown & Sharpe Mfg. Company of Providence, R.I., were the principal survivors, in many cases (particularly that of Starrett) buying out the other companies as the businesses of those companies foundered. As this Classic Period

came to an end, standardization of design and minimization of embellishment became the rule, largely as a result of the demands of mass production. In many cases, tools included in the Starrett product line at the end of this period continue to be produced in essentially the same form today.

The many tools in the museum collection dating after 1865 illustrate the vigorous growth and evolution of the classic period of American toolmaking, documented in volume 8 of the Davistown Museum's *Hand Tools in History* series.

A listing of the principal machinist tool manufacturers of the classic period is on the web at: http://www.davistownmuseum.org/TDMVtoolMfg.htm.

A Note on the Metallurgy of Tools Made After 1865

A number of observations need to be made about the metallurgy of many tools made after 1865 in the museum collection. After 1750, many of the highest quality edge tools, including plane blades, chisels, carving tools, and patternmakers' tools, were marked "cast steel", indicating that they were made from cast steel that was smelted in small crucibles. After 1870, Henry Bessemer perfected the production of low-carbon steel in blast furnaces by melting cast iron. Once he realized the necessity of adding manganese to produce strong and durable low-carbon steel, which could be used to fabricate steel rails and steel skyscrapers, a wide variety of equipment was made by casting this steel into molds in the shape of, for example, wheel axles, industrial equipment of all types, and certain types of tools. Objects made from modern bulk processed steel that was cast into molds was never labeled "cast steel". Any tool labeled "cast steel" in this catalog is either so marked, or our best guess of its constituency. After 1870, and especially, after 1900, a rapidly increasing variety of steel types were produced, many for the manufacture of hand tools that were either drop-forged or cast in molds of some kind. While the drop-forging method was more common than casting steel in molds for tools, the following classifications of steel and iron used to make tools had evolved. Extensive discussions of these technologies are available in the museum publication *Steel- and Toolmaking Strategies Before 1870* (Brack 2008) and *The Handbook for Ironmongers: A Glossary of Ferrous Metallurgy Terms* (Brack 2013), both of which contain information about steelmaking after 1870. Rapid advances had also been made in the technology of producing machinable cast iron, which was also used for hand tool production. Categories of iron and steel that were either drop-forged or cast in molds to make hand tools include the following:

- Carbon steels with a range of carbon content from 0.05 – 1.5% and a manganese content of < 1.65%, silicon 0.9%, and copper 0.6%.

- Alloy steels, which contain a similar amount of carbon but which also contain alloys, such as manganese above 1.65%, as well as tungsten, cobalt, vanadium, nickel, molybdenum, and chromium.
- Tool steels, which have a similar carbon content but contain alloys in excess of 4%. Tool steels are notable for their ability to cut steel at high speeds and are sometimes called high speed tool steel.
- Stainless steels, which did not appear until after 1914, have a minimum chromium content of 10%. Stainless steels are particularly notable for their resistance to corrosion due to the chromium content.
- Grey cast iron and soft grey cast iron, with a total carbon content of 3.4 – 3.5%. Grey cast iron was subject to a wide variety of heat treatment processes and is most well known as the constituent of Stanley plane bodies.
- Annealed malleable cast iron, with a carbon content of 2.75%. Both the grey cast irons and malleable cast iron are machinable and were often used for manufacturing drop-forged tools.

After 1870, new terminology for designating how tools were made included: "tempered alloy steel" and "drop-forged steel" and after 1900, occasional marks indicate the use of "alloy steels", "high speed tool steel," and "stainless steel". If not specifically marked, it's difficult to know exactly what kind of steel or iron was used to make the tools cataloged in the museum. In many cases, toolmakers would provide little or no information about what kind of iron or steel they were using. Tool quality varies widely depending on the wide variety of heat treatment techniques and varieties of carbon steel, alloy steel, tool steel, or stainless steel used in the production. In cataloging the tools in the museum collection made after 1865, the medium always includes the marking on the tool, e.g. "tempered alloy steel". Most tools, however, have no such markings and our designation of the medium, aside from obvious wood or brass components, is often our best guess. Many modern tool manufacturing processes use a combination of drop-forging and casting in molds. In general, the more modern the tool, the more complicated the manufacturing process. After 1930, the term "cast steel" no longer appeared on high quality edge tools, which are now made from steel produced in electric arc furnaces. Anyone perusing the museum's catalog of its tool collections please keep in mind the increasing complexity of tool manufacturing processes and the difficulty of exactly describing the metallurgy of modern hand tools.

Historic Maritime I (1607-1676): The First Colonial Dominion

Agricultural Implements

TAB1013   **Flax hatchel**   BDTM   MH

Wood (maple?), iron, 45" long, 16" wide, 34" high, unsigned.

It was made in Connecticut (?) in the late 17th or early 18th century and brought to Detroit, Maine by the first settlers. This is an essential tool for preparing flax for the weaver. After "breaking" the flax, it would be cleaned and sorted with the help of a scutching knife and board, ripple, and hatchel and then wound on a spinning jenny. For more information on this process, see the reprint on flax dressing available in the Museum files.

http://www.davistownmuseum.org/pics/tab1013.jpg

71903T4   **Grub hoe**   DTM   MHC-D

Forged iron and natural steel, 9 1/4" long, 4 2/3" wide cutting edge, unsigned.

This is a typical colonial era grub hoe with a poll-less socket for the handle. It is hand-forged with a three quarter inch natural steel cutting edge hand-welded on to the tool. It is probably made from refined wrought iron as silica inclusions are not visible.

TAB1011   **Grub hoe**   DTM   MHC-D

Hand-forged malleable iron, 4" wide, 6" high, unsigned, 17th or 18th century.

This is a generic gardening tool, with early forged rivets. It is typical of a gardening tool used by the first settlers in coastal Maine, but could also date from the 18th century.

http://www.davistownmuseum.org/pics/tab1011_p1.jpg
http://www.davistownmuseum.org/pics/tab1011_p21.jpg

TAB1009   **Hay cutter**   DTM   MH

Forged iron, 16 1/2" long with two blades with a 7" separation between the ends of the two blades, unsigned, 17th or 18th century.

http://www.davistownmuseum.org/pics/tab1009_p1.jpg
http://www.davistownmuseum.org/pics/tab1009_p21.jpg

Blacksmith, Farrier, and Metalworking Tools

42801T14   **Double calipers**   DTM   MH

Brass and forged iron, signed with initials "AWB".

These handmade calipers could be 17th or 18th century and are typical of those found in a blacksmith shop of this period.

Domestic Utensils

81801T2   **Cheese whisk**   LPC   MH

Forged iron and wood, 30 1/2" long, 7" wood handle, unsigned.

This is a colonial era variety for mixing the curds in whey in the cheese-making process.

http://www.davistownmuseum.org/pics/81801t2.jpg

Historic Maritime I (1607-1676): The First Colonial Dominion

Domestic Utensils

TAB2208   **Horn**   DTM   MH

Horn and wood, 6" long, 1 3/4" wide at bell, unsigned.

TK1003   **Loom**   DTM   LTC

Wood (beech or maple?), 5 1/2' wide, 6' long, 5' in height, unsigned, late 17th or early 18th c..

This loom was brought by the first settlers to Beals Island, Maine, from southern New England (Martha's Vineyard or Connecticut?) in the late 18th century. It was a most essential component of any colonial era farm. It is on display at the Davistown Museum Annex, second floor of the Liberty Tool Co.

81800-M   **Paint brush (4)**   DTM   MHC-D

Horsehair, leather, and twine, 4 1/2" x 2 1/4"; 4 1/2" x 3"; 5" x 2 1/4"; 5 1/2" x 2 1/4", unsigned.

Early settlers had no hardware stores to visit for brushes, they had to make their own from materials around the farm. What else would early settlers have used these brushes for?

TAB1014A   **Spoon**   DTM   MHC-D

Hand-forged wrought iron, 6 1/4" long, unsigned, 17th century.

This spoon is typical of the utensils used by Maine's first European settlers.

http://www.davistownmuseum.org/pics/tab1015a.jpg

81801T8   **Sugar tongs**   DTM   MH

Forged iron, 9 1/2" long, unsigned.

These elaborately decorated sugar tongs are typical of a tool that might have been brought to America by a well-to-do family during the great migration to Massachusetts, 1630 - 1650.

http://www.davistownmuseum.org/pics/81801t8.jpg

Fishing Implements

TAB1015A   **Fishing spear**   DTM   MHC-D

Forged iron, 6 1/2" long, unsigned, mid-17th century or earlier.

This is probably a French trade item.

http://www.davistownmuseum.org/pics/tab1015a.jpg

Hammers

TAB1003   **Claw hammer**   DTM   MH

Forged bog iron, 6" long, 1" square face, 10" wooden handle, unsigned.

The most primitive of the many claw hammers in the Museum collection, this particular claw hammer is exceptional because it shows the distinct layering characteristic of forged bog iron. It was farm-forged by the earliest settlers, probably in Massachusetts, c. 1650.

http://www.davistownmuseum.org/pics/tab1003_p1.jpg
http://www.davistownmuseum.org/pics/tab1003_p2.jpg

Historic Maritime I (1607-1676): The First Colonial Dominion

ID #   Status   Location

Hammers

11201T7   **Hammer**   DTM   MH

Forged bog iron and wood, 8" long, 3 2/8" x 1 3/4" x 1 1/2" head, unsigned.

This primitively wrought iron hammer could have been made by Vikings at L'Anse aux Meadows in Newfoundland or at any New England farm with a primitive open hearth forge and access to bog iron. Made directly from the bloom, this soft iron hammer shows evidence of both hand-forging and long years of use.

TAB1002   **Hammer**   DTM   MH

Wrought iron, 3" width, unsigned, c. 1720-1750.

The soft face of this hammer has been peened over from use. It is similar to hammers in use during the first colonial dominion.

Knives

011006T1   **Basket knife**   BDTM   MH

Hand-forged German steel, 6 7/8" long, 1/2" wide, unsigned, c. 1700.

This is a rare variation of the crooked knife and was solely used for splitting the wood for baskets of ash or other woods. This tool may be an excellent example of the use of cementation steel (blister steel - the blisters are clearly visible on the tool) for the production of steel edge tools and other trade items. This tool was almost certainly made in Europe and may have been specifically designed and produced to meet the needs of Native American basketmakers during the early days of contact with European traders.

http://www.davistownmuseum.org/pics/011006t1_p8.jpg

Logging Tools

TAB1005   **Bark spud**   DTM   MH

Hand-forged malleable iron, 10 1/4" to the end of the socket, unsigned, 17th or 18th century.

The bark spud is an essential component in the tool kit of the early settlers of the Davistown Plantation (ax, drawknife, sod cutter, spud, bowie knife, and frame saw).

http://www.davistownmuseum.org/pics/tab1005_p1.jpg
http://www.davistownmuseum.org/pics/tab1005_p2.jpg

Measuring Tools

72002T5   **Framing square**   DTM   MH

Forged iron, signed with a combination of Roman numerals and dots, +/-1650.

This is a most interesting example of a primitive backcountry farm-made tool.

Miscellaneous Forged Hardware

Historic Maritime I (1607-1676): The First Colonial Dominion

Miscellaneous Forged Hardware

92911T9   **Chain**   DTM   MH-D

Hand-forged and welded wrought iron, Seven links, each 4 1/2" long, 2 3/4" wide and one circle at the end, 6 1/2" diameter, unsigned.

This chain is made out of 1/2" diameter stock.

Other Tools

31012NOM1   **Unidentified tool**   NOM   UNK

Wood, 13" long, 6" wide, 5 1/2" high, unsigned.

This strange tool has channels leading to holes carved into its basin. It has very old patina with traces of pigment remaining. Courtesy of Mike Nelson.

913108T6   **Unidentified tool**   DTM   MHC-D

Malleable steel and wood, 4 7/8" long, 2 1/2" wide, 2 7/8" blade, unsigned.

Woodworking: Axes and Hatchets

72708T1   **Ax**   LPC   MHC-D

Forged steel, 6 3/4" long, 5 1/2" wide, unsigned.

This looks to be an early German ax.

111001T29   **Broad ax**   DTM   MH-D

Forged iron, 9 1/2" long, 8" blade, unsigned.

Distinctly and primitively forged, possibly from bog iron, this 17th century ax came in the Abiel Walker (Alna, ME) tool kit and was probably made and used by the earliest settlers in coastal Maine. See the Registry of Maine Toolmakers (Brack 2008) for more information on Abiel Walker.

http://www.davistownmuseum.org/pics/111001t29_p1.jpg
http://www.davistownmuseum.org/pics/111001t29_p2.jpg

102409T1   **Hatchet**   DTM   MH-D

Steel, iron, and wood, 13 1/2" long, 3 1/8" cutting edge, unsigned.

It has a forge-welded edge.

http://www.davistownmuseum.org/pics/102409T1web1.jpg
http://www.davistownmuseum.org/pics/102409T1web2.jpg

TAB1004   **Hatchet**   BDTM   MHC-D

Forged iron with wrought strapping, 5 1/2" long, notched blade, 3" wide with 4 3/8" strapping, signed with an obscured but mysterious oval touch mark.

It has the original rivets and handle. Is this an American tool from the first colonial dominion or from another culture?

http://www.davistownmuseum.org/pics/tab1004_p1.jpg
http://www.davistownmuseum.org/pics/tab1004_p2.jpg

Woodworking: Axes and Hatchets

102904T2   Hewing ax   DTM   MH

Forged iron and steel, wooden handle, 8" long, 7" wide cutting edge, 2" long and 1" wide poll, 31" long handle, unsigned.

This ax is typical of those imported from England in the 17th and early 18th centuries. With a lightweight poll, this type of ax soon proved impractical in the huge forests of North America and was supplanted by axes of American design with heavier polls. The Registry of Maine Toolmakers (Brack 2008) contains information about the similarly designed Wilson Museum Jonesport broad ax. These axes were typical in colonial era shipyards before 1740.

http://www.davistownmuseum.org/pics/102904t2.jpg
http://www.davistownmuseum.org/publications/volume10.html

102904T3   Mortising ax   DTM   MHC-D

Forged iron, natural steel, and wooden handle, 9 1/4" long, 15/16" wide cutting edge, 3 5/16" long and 1" wide poll, 24 1/2" long handle, signed with the mark "J254" on handle.

This edge tool has been torturously forged and shows a clearly hand-forged natural steel cutting edge. The mark on the handle indicates this tool might have once been in an institutional collection. It was found at a Massachusetts estate. This ax is typical of one that would be found in an early colonial shipyard. It has an obscured signature that suggests it was made by an enterprising colonial blacksmith for New England's shipbuilding industry.

http://www.davistownmuseum.org/pics/102904t3.jpg

111206T1   Tomahawk   DTM   MHC-D

Iron, weld steel with a wood handle, 8" long head, 2 1/4" wide edge, 16 1/4" long handle, unsigned, c. 1680-1750.

This is an everyday run-of-the-mill tomahawk with traditional weld steel forging and a more recent handle.

42607T5   Trade ax   DTM   MHC-D

German steel, 7 15/16" long, 4" wide blade, unsigned.

This 17th century felling ax has a curved light-weight poll characteristic of European-made axes. It shows no sign of a weld steel-iron interface. Highly pitted, the ax is probably made from one piece of German steel bar stock.

Woodworking: Boring Tools

111006T1   Auger   DTM   MH

Malleable iron and wood, 16" long with an 18" long handle, unsigned, c. 1650.

The wooden handle is probably a replacement. This is an unusual hand-forged auger with a curved cutting edge that is lipped and tapers from 3/4" down to an openly folded 1/3 curved and twisted iron bar stock about 1/8" thick.

http://www.davistownmuseum.org/pics/111006T1_p1.jpg
http://www.davistownmuseum.org/pics/111006T1_p3.jpg

Historic Maritime I (1607-1676): The First Colonial Dominion

Woodworking: Boring Tools

TAB1010   **Stone drill**   DTM   MH

Forged iron, 8 1/2" long, unsigned.

This stone drill has clearly been re-fashioned from a used blacksmith rasp. It was made in the 17th or 18th century. It is typical of the type of tool early settlers would have used to drill a mooring hole.

http://www.davistownmuseum.org/pics/tab1007.jpg

Woodworking: Edge Tools

100109T1   **Adz**   DTM   MH

German steel, 6" long, 1 1/2" wide, 3" wide cutting edge, signed with a complex of circles, lines, and arches.

An attached tag states: "16th - early 17th century pre-1640 French or Basque mfg iron adze. Recovered from the Quarry Cache/Site, Union, Maine in the 19th century. As of date, one of the earliest recovered European metal artifacts from Maine, only exception is a 16th century/very early 17th century Basque brass metal kettle, Maine State Museum, Augusta, Maine." Donated by Will West.

http://www.davistownmuseum.org/pics/100109T1web1.jpg
http://www.davistownmuseum.org/pics/100109T1web2.jpg

81101T9A   **Chisel**   DTM   MH

Forged iron, wood, and pewter ferrule, 10" long, 3/8" wide blade, unsigned.

This late 17th century (?) tool is clearly forged and typifies the more primitive edge tools that New England's first settlers would have used before the era of imported cast steel English tools.

42602T4   **Drawknife**   BDTM   MHC-D

Forged steel and leather, 10" wide, 4 1/2" wide blade, unsigned.

This hand-forged tool has been carefully refashioned from file steel. The short chubby handles are in the English style and are made of carefully cut and glued leather. This nifty tool is difficult to date; it is probably made in the 18th century. It is displayed in the Maritime I case because it is so typical of the homemade tools of the early colonial period. This tool is, in fact, exactly what a small drawshave in the tool kits of the first New England settlers could have looked like.

71903T1   **Gutter adz**   DTM   MH-O

Natural steel, 10 1/4" long, 3 1/2" wide mouth, 1 1/4" deep curved blade, unsigned.

Clearly manufactured by a blacksmith working directly from the bloom, this tool has the telltale silica inclusion of reworked bog iron. A distinct welded forged iron cutting edge extends 4 1/2" to a narrow flat polled body. It is a classic example of a rare form of a colonial era adz. It was probably used for making rain gutters and wooden drains. It was found in an old New England carpenters' tool chest c. 1885-1900, but is much older than that.

http://www.davistownmuseum.org/pics/71903t1_p1_LippedAdz.jpg

Historic Maritime I (1607-1676): The First Colonial Dominion

Woodworking: Edge Tools

102904T1   Slick   DTM   MH

Forged iron and steel, 39" long including an 11" long handle, 3" diameter ferrule, 4 1/4" wide, unsigned.

This clearly hand-forged slick has a hand chamfered wrought socket and appears to be late 17th or early 18th century. It was found in Massachusetts. It shows no sign of a weld steel cutting edge. It is used for cleaning up the sides of large mortises in construction and shipbuilding, and for leveling surfaces as on the deck of a ship. Slicks are particularly useful to shipwrights in areas that cannot be reached by an adz. They are often pushed by the shoulder, hence the swollen top of the wooden handle.

http://www.davistownmuseum.org/pics/102904t1_p1.jpg

Woodworking: Other Tools

TAB1006   Mallet   DTM   MHC-D

Wood burl, 2 1/3" wide, 2" high, length including handle 6", unsigned.

Ageless, but typical of a tool an early settler would own, possibly for a musket ball starter.

http://www.davistownmuseum.org/pics/tab1007.jpg

TAB1012   Shaving horse (bench)   BDTM   MH

Wood (maple), 57" wide, 17" tall, 4" wide clamp, unsigned.

This was a commonplace tool on any working farm in the 17th or 18th century. Used with a drawknife for shingle-making, the shaving bench was also used for many other tasks. This is probably 18th century but is of the same design as those used in the 17th century.

http://www.davistownmuseum.org/pics/tab1012.jpg

Woodworking: Planes

TBW1001   Adjustable plow plane   NOM   UNK

Wood (beech), 1" wide with 1 1/8" wide fence, signed "I. NICHOLSON LIVING IN WRENTHAM".

Pollak (2001) says this stamp was used between 1733 and 1740. This tool is amongst the rarest of early American tools, I. Nicholson tools being rarer than those of his father F. Nicholson. It is particularly noteworthy that Nicholson moved to Union, Maine, late in his life. There is no record of his making any tools while living in Union. (This tool is no longer in the museum collection as it was loaned only for our opening exhibition.)

http://www.davistownmuseum.org/pics/tbw1001.jpg
http://www.davistownmuseum.org/toolPloughPlane.html

81602T2   Beading plane   DTM   MH

Oak with forged iron blade, 10 5/8" long, 7/8" wide compound bead, signed with owner's initials.

Is this English or American?

Historic Maritime I (1607-1676): The First Colonial Dominion

Woodworking: Planes

50402T1   **Complex molding plane**   LPC   MHC-D

Wood, forged steel blade, 10 14" long, 2 5/8" wide, signed "Robert Wooding".

This late 17th century plane by one of England's earliest planemakers was found in Maine. Unsprung, this plane has to be worked at an angle and is more difficult and inefficient to use compared to later "sprung" planes, which could lie flat on a wood surface to work up a molding. This plane is heavily and erratically chamfered and lacks rounded chamfers at each end, making it more awkward to use -- but also easy to date as one of the earliest signed hand planes by a known English or American maker. Goodman (1993) states that Wooding worked as a joiner from 1693 to his death in May, 1727. Four of his apprentices also became significant planemakers (William Cogdell, John Jennion, Thomas Phillipson, and Robert Fitkin) (Goodman 1993, 464). This plane was formerly in the Bob Wheeler collection and is now loaned to the Museum by the current owner.

http://www.davistownmuseum.org/pics/50402t1_p1.jpg
http://www.davistownmuseum.org/pics/50402t1_p2.jpg

83102T1   **Molding plane**   DTM   MHC-D

Birch (?) with forged steel blade and a replaced wedge, 10 3/8" long, 1 3/4" wide, signed "JB" twice upside down in 17th or 18th century script.

This complex molding plane is heavily chamfered. A survivor from the 17th century, this tool has a southern New England provenance and is typical of a hand plane c. 1650.

TAB1014   **Plow plane**   BDTM   MHC-D

Tropic wood with brass stringers, hand forged iron depth adjustment, 8" long, 8 1/2" screws, unsigned.

This is a double wheeled screw-armed plow plane, no blade or wedge, probable European origin. The age of this plane is unknown, but a similar tool could have been in the tool chest of a coastal Maine carpenter during the first colonial dominion (1620-1676).

http://www.davistownmuseum.org/pics/tab1014.jpg

TAB1015   **Rabbet plane**   DTM   MH

Wood unknown (fruitwood?), 8 1/2" long, tapered to 1 5/8" width at base, unsigned.

This plane is representative of a typical homemade hand plane of the period.

Woodworking: Planes Made in Maine

TBW1010   **Adz**   DTM   MH

Forged iron and wood, 4 1/4" long with a 4 3/4" handle, 1" wide blade, unsigned.

This is a small hand adz; use unknown. The original handle has been replaced. This tool was found on the beach in Addison, Maine, and may have been made in Maine, though it has been speculated that it could have had a Viking origin. Formerly part of the Bob Wheeler collection.

http://www.davistownmuseum.org/pics/tbw1010.jpg
http://www.davistownmuseum.org/pics/tbw1010p2.jpg

Woodworking: Saws

Historic Maritime I (1607-1676): The First Colonial Dominion

Woodworking: Saws

TAB1001   **Hand saw**   DTM   MH

Forged iron and/or steel, 12" long, unsigned.

This saw has a distinctive 18th century handle, c. 1720. It could be as early as 1675 or as late as 1780.

http://www.davistownmuseum.org/pics/tab1001_p4.jpg
http://www.davistownmuseum.org/pics/tab1001_p5.jpg

Agricultural Implements

040103T4   **Bill hook**   DTM   MH

Forged iron and steel, wood handle with peen iron and brass rivets, 13 1/4" long including a 4" handle, signed with a cartouche of a crown and the capital letter M.

This handmade tool has clear signs of forging, filing, and other handwork. It is a generic18th century tool that appears even earlier in style than the bill hooks illustrated in the 18th century pattern book of R. Timmons & Sons (1976) "Tools for the Trades and Crafts".

42801T8   **Bill hook**   DTM   MH

Forged iron, steel, and wood, 13" long, 3 5/8" cutter, signed with an unidentifiable touchmark.

The nicely turned handle and early touchmark indicate this bill hook is late 18th century. It is similar to the fascines used by Revolutionary War soldiers to cut brush.

http://www.davistownmuseum.org/pics/42801t8.jpg

41302T6   **Corn dryer**   DTM   MH

Forged iron, 19 3/4" long with 9 tangs or barbs for drying the corn, unsigned.

102409T2   **Grafting froe**   DTM   MH

Hand-forged iron and steel, 13" long, 4" wide, 2 3/4" cutting edge, unsigned.

http://www.davistownmuseum.org/pics/102409T2web1.jpg
http://www.davistownmuseum.org/pics/102409T2web2.jpg

101400T1   **Grafting froe**   DTM   MH

Forged iron and steel, 12" long with a 3 1/2" long and 1/2" wide chisel and 2 3/8" wide block, unsigned.

This primitively forged 18th century tool was used for grafting fruit trees. The cutter makes the initial slot that is then deepened by the extended chisel.

913108T47A   **Grafting iron**   DTM   MH

Hand-forged recycled file or rasp, 9 1/2" long, 2 3/4" long blade, unsigned.

22813LTC1   **Grub hoe**   DA   TT (Pub)

Hand-forged steel and iron, wood (hickory), 32" long handle, 13" long head, 6" wide edge, signed "6GY".

31301T9   **Grub hoe**   DTM   MH

Forged iron and wood, 37" long with 11" long and 3 1/4" wide blade, unsigned.

This unique grub hoe has two ferrules, is distinctly hand forged, and has a unique 18th century appearance. Maine coastal provenance.

Agricultural Implements

TCR4000   **Hatchel**   DTM   MH

Forged iron and wood, 25 1/2" long x 4 3/4" wide, unsigned.

This flax puller has 108 combs. It is an essential component of the flax dressers' tool kit.

http://www.davistownmuseum.org/pics/tcr4000.jpg

101400T6   **Hatchel**   DTM   MH

Forged iron and wood, 13 3/8" long, 3 1/2" wide, unsigned.

This is an unusually small hatchel. It is a key component of the tool kit of a flax dresser.

102904T16   **Hay thief**   DTM   MH

Forged iron, wood handle, 34" long including 18" handle, unsigned, c. 1760 - 1820.

This hay thief has a gorgeous original twisted wood handle and a single prong, rather than a double prong. This tool is also known as a hay hook and was used for testing hay. Hay thiefs would characterize most any 18th century New England farmyard though most specimens would not be the spectacular sculpture object that this one is.

http://www.davistownmuseum.org/pics/102904t16.jpg

71903T3   **Mattock**   DTM   MH

Forged iron, 14 3/8" long, 3 3/4" wide edge, tapered peen pole, replaced handle, unsigned.

This mattock is hand-forged with a small welded forged steel cutting edge. The work of a bloomer who knew how to forge his own steel, then welded the carefully forged cutting edge to his tool. It is hard to date, 1675 - 1725?

102904T10   **Peat cutter**   DTM   MH

Hand-forged malleable iron, 16 5/8" long including 9 3/4" overlapped welded handle, 6 1/2" wide set of arms, unsigned.

The wooden handle is missing. The set of arms would be ideal for supporting the feet for leverage and pushing in cutting peat. It is completely hand wrought, a tool form not commonly encountered by the museum staff.

http://www.davistownmuseum.org/pics/102904t10.jpg

81801T3   **Peat cutter**   DTM   MH

Forged iron and wood, 28 3/4" long, 4 3/4" (replaced) wood handle, unsigned.

The original handle would have been much longer to facilitate cutting the peat in coastal salt marshes prior to draining for salt hay grazing.

81101T22   **Peat cutter**   DTM   MH

Forged iron and wood, 33" long, 17" long handle, unsigned.

The early colonists drained the salt marshes and bogs with tools similar to this one, cutting the ditches that can still be seen throughout coastal New England.

Historic Maritime II (1720-1800): The Second Colonial Dominion & the Early Republic

Agricultural Implements

TCK1001   **Pitchfork**   BDTM MH

Forged iron and wood, 38" high, unsigned, 18th century.

A three tined, hand forged tool with a Concord, MA provenance. This tool was in the family it was purchased from at the battle of Lexington-Concord. After the war ended and the person who used this tool died, the tool was put away and saved for over 200 years until purchased from the last descendent in the family in Wayland, MA, several years ago.

http://www.davistownmuseum.org/pics/tck1001.jpg

81801T1   **Scutch knife**   DTM   MH

Wood, 19" long with a 9" long and 2" wide wooden blade, unsigned.

It is used for cleaning flax on a scutching board after breaking the flax on a flax breaker. After removal of the husk by the tedious task of scutching, the flax was ready for hackling on a hatchel.

TCK1002   **Shovel**   BDTM MH

Forged iron and wood, 30 1/2" in height, 7" wide, signed "O. Ames", c. 1790-1810.

O. Ames is listed in DATM as working from 1779 - 1863. The Ames Shovel Co., North Easton, Mass., is still in business and has its own shovel museum in North Easton. This is a rare odd sized specimen of a small shovel and may be one of the earliest shovels produced by the Ames Co. Was this a specially made child's shovel? What was its purpose?

http://www.davistownmuseum.org/pics/TCK1002.jpg
http://www.davistownmuseum.org/bioAmesShovel.html

Blacksmith, Farrier, and Metalworking Tools

TBF3501   **Bench vise**   DTM   MH

Forged iron, 7" high, 2 1/2" wide, unsigned.

The hold down is made from a recycled farriers' rasp.

TBB1002   **Blacksmiths' hammer**   DTM   MH

Forged iron, 3" long, 1 5/16" wide face, unsigned, c. 1790-1800.

8312T1   **Bolt and nail header**   DTM   TT

Hand-forged natural steel, 9 3/4" long, 1" wide, 5/16" thick, 3/8" wide aperture, unsigned.

121805T2   **Bolt header**   DTM   MH

Forged iron, 12 1/2" long, 11/16" wide square head, and 3/8" diameter round head hole, unsigned.

http://www.davistownmuseum.org/pics/121805t2_121805t3.jpg

Historic Maritime II (1720-1800): The Second Colonial Dominion & the Early Republic

ID #   Status   Location

Blacksmith, Farrier, and Metalworking Tools

121805T3   Bolt header   DTM   MH

Forged iron (refined bog iron), 13" long, 3/16", and 9/16" diameter round head holes, unsigned.

These two bolt headers (121805T2 and T3) came from a Duxbury, MA, blacksmith shop which dates back to circa 1700. They are probably made of refined bog iron and indicate the sophistication of early colonial refinery techniques. They were used for making the bolts for ship construction to hold the frame of the ship together. For example, the ribs are made up of 5 or 6 futtocks and the bolts are used to hold the futtocks together to form the rib. Photographs of these are included in the History of Hand Tools Museum publication series, vol. 7.

http://www.davistownmuseum.org/pics/121805t2_121805t3.jpg

TBG1001   Calipers   DTM   MH

Forged iron, 7 1/4" long, unsigned.

032103T2   Die stock   DTM   MH

Forged iron, 16 7/8" long, 1 1/4" wide stock, unsigned.

This distinctive hand-forged die stock has 6 dies ranging in diameter from 3/4" to 1/8" cut into a narrow forged iron bar with a nicely wrought handle. It is a great example of a one-of-a-kind or very limited run blacksmith-made tool.

http://www.davistownmuseum.org/pics/032103t2_p1.jpg
http://www.davistownmuseum.org/pics/032103t2_p2.jpg

111406T3   Dinglestock (field anvil)   DTM   MH

Wrought iron with a low carbon steel anvil top, 8 1/2" long, 9/16" wide post with a 1 5/8" square anvil top, 2" footpad, unsigned.

The nicely wrought footpad is used to insert the item into the ground. Shows signs of wear.

TBB1001   Double calipers   BDTM   MH

Forged iron, 18" long, 6 " long adjustable wings, unsigned.

The generic design of this tool is characteristic of both the 18th and early 19th centuries. The initials inscribed on its handle are distinctly 18th century.

http://www.davistownmuseum.org/pics/tbf1001.jpg

43006T6   Drill bit   DTM   MH

Forge-welded German steel?, 7 3/4" long with a tapered end widening from 3/4" diameter to 1 5/16", unsigned.

2713T6   End cutters   DTM   TT

Forged steel, 5 1/4" long, 3/8" cutting edge, unsigned.

Historic Maritime II (1720-1800): The Second Colonial Dominion & the Early Republic

Blacksmith, Farrier, and Metalworking Tools

31501T8   Farriers' buttress   DTM   MH

Forged iron and wood, 21 1/2" long including an 11" wood handle, unsigned.

This is a typical blacksmith-made 18th or early 19th century farriers' tool for removing a horse's shoe. It has a Maine provenance.

TBD1004   Farriers' hammer   DTM   MH

Forged iron and steel, 4 3/8" long, 5/8" wide face, unsigned, c. 1800.

It is strongly beveled.

TBB1004A   Gunsmith tools   DTM   TT

Forged iron and steel, unsigned, c. 1740.

This collection (27) of early taps, dies, diestocks, and other tools in this 19th century toolbox are typical of those used by an 18th century blacksmith with skills in gunsmithing. The guns made by these tools predate the era of mass-produced guns with interchangeable parts. These tools have a southeastern Massachusetts origin, as does the box they were found in. (Note the Barnstable Mass notation on the lid of the box.) The blacksmith utilizing these tools may have specialized in gunsmithing, or as was more commonly the case, was skilled in a multitude of metalworking trades.

43006T2   Hacksaw   DTM   MH

Blister steel, saw steel, and wood, 17" long with a 4" wood handle, signed "AOES Co" on the iron ferrule.

This is a very unusual form, the saw, with a hand-forged looped end, appears to have a later factory-turned handle and ferrule with 19th century script. The tool itself appears much earlier than the handle, with a saw steel insert in a hand-forged and filed wrought iron and/or blister steel holder. Comments are solicited. No such manufacturer is listed in DATM (Nelson 1999). The A in the mark may be preceded by another obscured letter.

61601T4   Hacksaw   DTM   MH

Steel, brass, and wood, 11 3/8" long with a 5 1/4" blade, unsigned.

This saw is a classic example of a common 18th century tool probably made in Europe and brought to the U.S.

51201T5   Hacksaw   BDTM   MH

Steel, brass, and wood, 11 1/2" long, unsigned, c. 1800.

This brass framed saw is too coarse for a jeweler and too small for general purpose work. It has distinctly hand-forged blade attachments and frames.

http://www.davistownmuseum.org/pics/51201t5_p1.jpg
http://www.davistownmuseum.org/pics/51201t5_p4.jpg

Blacksmith, Farrier, and Metalworking Tools

101400T16   **Hand vise**   DTM   MHC-D

Forged iron, unsigned.

The distinctive ram's horn nut identifies this tool as 18th century.

92901T2   **Hot set**   DTM   MHC-J

Forged iron, 13" long, 1 1/2" wide and 3/8" long cutting wedge, unsigned.

A hot set is used for splitting forged iron prior to lapping and welding iron handles, strapping, or other iron hardware. This tool was once part of the tool kit of the boat builder and planemaker Abiel Walker of Alna, Maine (b. 1808) and was probably an antique when he came into possession of it.

12900T6   **Nippers**   DTM   MH

Forged iron, 12 3/8" long, 7/8" wide cutters, unsigned, c. 1790 - 1800.

This is a typical blacksmith horseshoe nail nipper of the period.

111001T37   **Pincers**   DTM   MHC-D

Forged iron, 7" long, unsigned.

These primitive pincers could be seventeenth or eighteenth century and are typical of the primitive forged iron tools used by the first settlers.

TBF1004   **Post vise**   DTM   MH

Forged iron, 5 1/2" long, 3" throat, unsigned.

TBC1002A   **Punch**   DTM   MH

Forged iron with signs of bog iron, 11" long, unsigned.

Unknown use.

3213T1   **Soldering iron**   DTM   TT

Forged iron, copper, 11 1/4" long, 2 3/8" tip, 2 3/8" wide, unsigned.

TBL5005   **Stone drill**   DTM   MH

Forged iron, 11 3/4" long, unsigned.

What's the use of this unusual tool?

111406T2   **Stump anvil**   DTM   MH

Malleable iron and steel, 2 5/8" by 1 7/8" with a 3 3/8" tang, unsigned.

072112T5   **Thread cutter**   DTM   TT

Forge-welded malleable iron, 7" long, 3/8" wide, unsigned.

Historic Maritime II (1720-1800): The Second Colonial Dominion & the Early Republic

Blacksmith, Farrier, and Metalworking Tools

61601T5   **Tin snips**   DTM   MH

Forged iron, 12 3/4" long, unsigned.

These are clearly reforged from a file. The first rolled tin dates to the early 18th century. This reforged smith-made tool is at least 200 years old.

TBB1003   **Tongs**   DTM   MH

Forged iron, 15 1/2" long, 9/16" wide jaw, unsigned.

This tool is difficult to date and could be late 18th century or early 19th century.

http://www.davistownmuseum.org/pics/tbf1001.jpg

Cobbler and Saddler Tools

51100T4   **Cobblers' hammer**   DTM   MH

Forged iron, 3 5/8" long head, 1 7/8" diameter face, unsigned.

31501T6   **Curriers' slick**   DTM   MH

Steel and wood, 16 3/8" long, 7 1/4" blade, unsigned.

The blade is made from a recycled smith-made saw blade. It is used in the preparation of leather for shoemaking, fishermens' aprons, etc.

62406T3   **Curriers' slick fleshing knife**   DTM   MH

Reforged steel, 6" long, 2" blade, unsigned.

It is forge-welded from a recycled rasp.

Coopers' Tools

62212T2   **Coopers' vise**   DTM   MHC-F

Forged iron, 4 1/4" long, 1/2" diameter bore, 3 5/8" wide handle, unsigned.

62212T1   **Hoop driver**   DTM   MHC-G

Forged iron, wood, 6" long, 3 1/4" wide edge, unsigned.

This tool is the wooden version of the form and is also known as a hoop set.

Domestic Utensils

11301T1   **Block knife**   DTM   MH

Forged iron and wood, 20 5/7" long with 15 3/4" chopping arm and 5" wide iron blade, unsigned.

The iron component of this food and/or tobacco chopper is made of a recycled farriers' file.

Historic Maritime II (1720-1800): The Second Colonial Dominion & the Early Republic

Domestic Utensils

TCR2203   **Box**   DTM   MH

Wood, 7" long, 4" wide, 4 3/4" high, unsigned.

This is an early box with a sliding lid.

TAB2209   **Box**   DTM   MHC-D

Wood with hinge, 3 5/8" long, 2 1/4" wide, 3/4" high, unsigned.

Early settlers might have used boxes similar to this one for storing flints.

52512LTC2   **Candle holder stake**   DA   TT (Pub)

Forged steel, 8 1/8" long, unsigned.

Courtesy of Liberty Tool Co.

TBF3000   **Cleaver**   DTM   MH

Forged iron, 8 3/8" long with a 2 1/2" blade, unsigned.

It was forged out of an old rasp.

51201T8   **Document box**   BDTM   MH

Brass, hide, wood, and iron, 12" long, 6 1/4" wide, unsigned, c. 1785 - 1800.

This domed hide document box was converted to a small tool box by Benjamin Willard or his sons and then used as a toolbox to hold the assorted tools and woodenware listed in the Simon Willard Group.

http://www.davistownmuseum.org/pics/51201t14_p3web.jpg
http://www.davistownmuseum.org/bioWillard.htm

072112T7   **Door latch**   DTM   TT

Wrought iron, 9" long, 2 1/8" wide, unsigned.

TCR3502   **Firkin**   DTM   MH

Wood with iron straps, 11 3/4" high, 9 3/4" top diameter, 12 1/2" bottom diameter, unsigned.

It has old red paint.

101400T12   **Food chopper**   DTM   MH

Forged or cast steel and wood, unsigned.

This is a generic late 18th or early 19th century food chopper. It needs a good trencher to accompany it.

30311T3   **Food chopper**   DTM   TT

Forged steel, 7 1/2" long, 6" wide, unsigned.

The handle is missing.

ID #		Status	Location

Domestic Utensils

9308T37	**Food chopper**	DTM	MAG

TBG1001A	**Forks (two)**	DTM	MH

Forged iron or steel, bone, wood, 6 1/2" with bone handle, 5 1/2" with wood handle, unsigned.

TBL5006	**Gudgeon**	DTM	MH

Forged iron, 10 1/2" long, 1 1/2" wide blade, unsigned.

It is used to hold a fireplace crane in place.

TAB1014B	**Hook**	DTM	MH

Forged iron, 2 1/4" height, signed with the mark "8".

This is a steelyard hook for a scale with a distinctive, delicate 18th century look.

22813LTC6	**Kettle crane**	DA	TT (Pub)

Forged iron, 33" x 23 1/2", unsigned.

41302P1	**Knife box**	DTM	MH

Wood, 11 1/4" wide base tapered outward to 12 3/4", 6 1/2" wide tapering up to 6 7/8", unsigned.

It is a typical dovetailed knife box of 18th century make with imported mahogany and several early nails used to reinforce the dovetails.

101400T7	**Peel**	BDTM	TT-wall

Forged iron, 30 1/4" long, 6 1/2" peel, unsigned.

It is used for removing bread from an oven.

http://www.davistownmuseum.org/pics/101400t7.jpg

TAB2210	**Pitcher**	DTM	MH

Pewter or Britanniaware, 4 5/8" high, 4 1/8" wide, unsigned.

It has a hinged lid.

12801T13	**Powder horn**	DTM	MH

Horn and wood, 13" long, unsigned.

This is a typical example of an 18th century or early 19th century powder horn.

TBF1005	**Pry**	DTM	MH

Forged iron, 5 1/2" long, unsigned.

It is typical of the handmade tools of this period.

Historic Maritime II (1720-1800): The Second Colonial Dominion & the Early Republic

Domestic Utensils

50402T0   **Shoe**   DTM   MHC-D

Leather, 9" long, unsigned.

This 18th century un-soled, un-sewn shoe comes from western Maine. It's an excellent example of an unfinished farm-made shoe typical of a New England backcountry frontier homestead.

TBF1301B   **Shuttle**   DTM   MH

Wood, 10 1/2" long, unsigned.

TBF1301A   **Shuttle**   DTM   MH

Wood, 11 1/2" long, signed "I.M." in an 18th century script.

This is typical of the shuttles used on the primitive looms on Maine farms.

30202T11   **Skewer**   DTM   MH

Forged iron, 4 3/4" long, unsigned.

An excellent example of the art of the blacksmith.

http://www.davistownmuseum.org/pics/30202t11.jpg

12900T10   **Wig blower (bellows)**   DTM   MH

Wood, leather, and tin, 6 5/8" long, 2" wide, 2 1/4" tall, unsigned.

http://www.davistownmuseum.org/pics/12900t10.jpg

7309P1   **Wooden bucket**   DTM   MH

Wood, 12 1/2" outside diameter, 7 1/4" high, unsigned.

This is a finely crafted wood container from the late 17th or early 18th century with a 1" hole in the bottom. Its use is unknown.

http://www.davistownmuseum.org/pics/7309p1web-1.jpg
http://www.davistownmuseum.org/pics/7309p2-web.jpg

Fishing Implements

112704T5   **Eel spear**   DTM   MH

Forged iron, 14 5/8" long, 8 5/8" wide, unsigned.

This spear has a central flat shaft and seven sharply curved tangs. One tang may have broken off. Found in an old fishing shed in Acushnet, Massachusetts, this eel spear is typical of the 18th and early 19th century implements used by the Native Americans and early settlers to catch one of the most nutritious and commonly encountered marine species of New England's coastal coves and estuaries. It's probably a colonist-forged tool or a trade item.

Historic Maritime II (1720-1800): The Second Colonial Dominion & the Early Republic

Fishing Implements

102005T1   **Fish or eel spear**   DTM   MH

Hand-forged malleable iron, 13 1/2" long, 8 1/4" wide, unsigned.

This spear has 4 prongs with short hooked ends and was probably used for fish as the prongs are somewhat wide for catching eels.

Hammers

TBD1002   **Claw hammer**   DTM   MH

Steel, 4 1/2" long, 3/4" face, unsigned, c. 1800.

This steel hammer lacks the hint of layering noted in the bog iron hammer, has less distinct beveling, and an unusual infill in the socket for the handle.

TBD1001   **Claw hammer**   DTM   MH

Forged iron, 4 1/2" with a 1" face, unsigned.

It has a replaced handle. It is a generic 18th c. hammer but of particular interest because it shows signs of the layering characteristic of forged bog iron, which was the constituent of the earliest blacksmith-made tools made in the United States.

TBD1005   **Stone hammer**   DTM   MH

Forged iron, 9" long with a 3/4" square face, unsigned.

91303T18   **Stone hammer**   DTM   MH

Forged iron with wooden handle, 10" long, 15" long handle, unsigned.

It is a primitively-forged wrought iron tool. The evidence of folded and molded wrought iron indicates it was made directly from a bloom and not drop-forged.

71401T10   **Tuning hammer**   DTM   MH

Cast steel and wood, 5 1/2" long, 4 3/4" long handle, unsigned.

This is known as a tuning hammer/lever/wrench or stringing hammer. It is used to turn the tuning pins on a piano. More modern tuning hammers have a longer lever allowing greater control, so this older model would now be primarily used for stringing. This tuning hammer has a rectangular hole reflecting the shape of older tuning pins. Modern tuning pins are square. The Museum wishes to thank an anonymous visitor for this information.

Knives

TCN1003   **Bowie knife**   DTM   MH

Forged steel with a bone handle and small leather scabbard, 8 1/6" long, 4" blade, 3 1/4" handle, signed with a buck carved into the handle, c. 1800.

Historic Maritime II (1720-1800): The Second Colonial Dominion & the Early Republic

Knives

81101T14　**Crooked knife**　　　　　　　　　　　　　DTM　　MHC

Wood and forged steel, 8 1/2" long, 3" blade, unsigned.

Crooked knives are especially common in northern New England where they were used by Native Americans and European settlers for many purposes including basket-making and working birch bark. This knife has been reforged from an old file or rasp, one of early American artisans' most important sources of recycled forged steel. The crosshatched carving on the nicely fashioned applewood (?) handle suggests a Native American user.

http://www.davistownmuseum.org/pics/81101t14.jpg

913108T36　**Crooked knife**　　　　　　　　　　　　DTM　　MH

Hand-forged steel, wood, and rope, 9 1/4" long with a 3 1/8" long blade, unsigned.

The handle of this knife has decorative sailor knot trim made from rope and the wooden handle is carved.

TCN1004　**Knife**　　　　　　　　　　　　　　　　DTM　　MH

Forged steel, brass, and bone, 7 1/8" long, 3" blade, 3 1/4" handle, 3 5/8" wide scabbard, unsigned.

The knife has an undecorated carved bone handle with a brass scabbard.

72801T12　**Oyster knife**　　　　　　　　　　　　　DTM　　MH

Forged iron, brass, and wood, 6 1/2" long, 4" blade, unsigned.

It has a nicely turned oak (?) handle. This is probably what an 18th century oyster knife imported from England looked like.

Logging Tools

1302T1　**Pit saw**　　　　　　　　　　　　　　　　DTM　　MH

Forged saw steel, wood, 62" long, 55" long and 14 1/2" wide blade, 20 1/2" long handles at each end, unsigned, 18th century.

This is a classic pit saw from the boomtown years of Maine lumbering. It is also known as a frame saw.

http://www.davistownmuseum.org/pics/1302t1_FrameSaw.jpg

42613T1　**Splitting wedge**　　　　　　　　　　　　LPC　　MH

Forged iron bar stock, 8 1/2" long, 2" wide, 2 1/8" edge, unsigned.

This splitting wedge is on loan from Will West. It is forged from four pieces of iron bar stock and was dug up in Liberty, Maine, near the mill sites on the bank of the St. George's River.

913108T49　**Spud**　　　　　　　　　　　　　　　　DTM　　MH

Hand-forged iron and recycled file and rasp, 8 1/2" long, 2" wide, unsigned.

Historic Maritime II (1720-1800): The Second Colonial Dominion & the Early Republic

Logging Tools

81101T21   Spud   DTM   MH

Forged iron and wood, 26" long, 17" long wood handle, unsigned.

This tool is probably late 18th century. The worm eaten handle looks original.

Measuring Tools

TBE3500   Adjustable calipers   DTM   MH

Forged iron, 11 1/4" long, 8 1/2" wide, unsigned.

101400T10   Calipers   DTM   MH

Forged iron, 13 1/4" long, unsigned, c. 1800.

TBE1001   Calipers   DTM   MH

Forged iron, 5" long, signed "E. H__LEY", clearly of 18th century manufacture.

It is lacking the thumb screw.

21201T7   Carpenters' square   DTM   MH

Wood, 12" x 12", unsigned.

This primitive small framing square is distinctive both in its simplicity and its mortised and pegged (wood) construction. This tool would have been owner-made anytime in the late 18th or early 19th centuries.

TBF1002   Circle cutter   DTM   MH

Forged iron, wood, and steel, 8 " long, 2 1/2" wide, unsigned, could be late 18th century or early 19th century.

The wooden thumb screws extend out another inch. It has a steel cutter and threaded wooden nuts for adjusting the diameter.

81101T17   Compass   DTM   MH

Cast steel, 6 3/16" long, signed "William Friedricks" with a touchmark, W in a heart with an F over it, all within a circle.

DATM (Nelson 1999) lists Friedricks as working in New York, circa 1790. If this is cast steel, was Friedricks reworking imported English cast steel at this early date?

111001T14   Dividers   DTM   MH

Forged iron, 4 7/8" long, signed "O. W." probably the owner's initials.

These early 18th century dividers are clearly smith-made. They are a classic example of a common 18th century tool, possibly seventeenth century.

Historic Maritime II (1720-1800): The Second Colonial Dominion & the Early Republic

Measuring Tools

33002T19   **Dividers**   DTM   MH

Forged iron, 7 1/2" long, unsigned.

This is a generic example of a late 18th century factory-made tool, probably English from the Sheffield region.

http://www.davistownmuseum.org/pics/33002t19.jpg

42801T13   **Dividers**   DTM   MH

Forged iron, brass, and wood, unsigned.

This primitive divider comes from an 18th century Martha's Vineyard shipyard and is typical of owner-made hand tools in the era prior to the factory systems of the Industrial Revolution.

TBE1001A   **Framing square**   DTM   MH

Forged iron, 24" long and 12" wide, signed "CUTTER", 18th century.

Hand stamped; this maker is not listed in DATM (Nelson 1999).

913108T14   **Framing square**   DTM   MH

Hand stamped wrought or malleable iron, 2' long and 1 1/2" wide x 1' long and 1" wide, unsigned.

This was probably made in 1800 or earlier.

81602T14   **Framing square**   DTM   MH

Forged iron, 24" x 12", signed "JBH".

This is a typical smith-made, hand-stamped framing square of the 18th century.

7800T14   **Gauge**   DTM   MHC-J

Forged iron and steel, signed with an obscure mark.

TBF3500   **Line reel**   DTM   MH

Wood and forged iron, 8" long, unsigned.

TBL5004   **Lumbermans' scribe**   DTM   MH

Forged iron, 9 7/8" long with a scribe at one end and a scribe on the side, unsigned.

81101T5   **Mortise gauge**   DTM   MH

Forged iron and wood, 10 1/4" long with double scribes, depth stops 13" and 9" long, signed with the mark "B" in 18th century script.

This tool is a colonial era coachmakers' instrument.

Historic Maritime II (1720-1800): The Second Colonial Dominion & the Early Republic

Measuring Tools

70701T4   Plumb bob   DTM   MH

Cast bronze with an iron tip, 2" high, 1 3/8" wide, unsigned.

This is a diminutive 18th century plumb bob.

111406T1   Rule   DTM   MH

Forged iron, 24" long, 2" wide, signed "F PERKS".

The mark is hand-stamped. DATM (Nelson 1999, 614) reports F. Perks as a square-maker circa 1800.

42801T11   Slitting gauge   DTM   MH

Wood and forged iron, 16 1/8" long, 6 1/4" wide gauge, unsigned.

This slitting gauge is probably from a late 18th century Martha's Vineyard area shipyard. A similar gauge fragment is on the hands-on display table and has a similar hand-forged gauge adjusting nut.

7602T4   Traveler   DTM   MH

Forged iron, brass ferrule, wooden handle, 14" long, 7 5/8" diameter wheel, 4 3/4" long handle, unsigned.

It can be used as a wagon wheel measuring tool by a wheelwright.

TBE3000   Traveler   DTM   MH

Forged iron, 13" long, 5 1/4" diameter wheel, unsigned.

http://www.davistownmuseum.org/pics/tbe3000.jpg

TBW1006   Wantage rule   BDTM   MHC-D

Boxwood and brass, 11 1/8" long box, rule is 10 1/4" long when folded and fitted into a box, signed "Made by Robert Merchant for Noah Emery, Berwick, [Maine], 1720" in script, dated 1720.

This tool, among the most historically significant pieces of Americana in any Maine or New England museum, is the earliest known signed and dated tool made in Maine. No earlier signed and dated tool has been located in the collections of the Smithsonian, Mercer, or Shelburne, VT museums. This tool is a six-fold rule and was used as a wantage rule for measuring quantities of wine, beer, and ale. The strong alcohol and tannin component of the liquids it measured has given this rule a mellow hue. Its gorgeous box is fitted so exactly to the folded rule that a ribbon is needed to remove it. Additional information about Noah Emery can be obtained by following the "bio" link. While we know something about the recipient of this tool, information about the maker of this rule, Robert Merchant, is not available. Bob Wheeler, the previous owner of this rule, speculates that Robert Merchant may have been a carpenter and toolmaker associated with the many Merchants of Portsmouth, NH. Anyone with additional information about who Robert Merchant was, please contact the Museum.

http://www.davistownmuseum.org/pics/tbw1006.jpg
http://www.davistownmuseum.org/bioEmery.htm

Historic Maritime II (1720-1800): The Second Colonial Dominion & the Early Republic

Measuring Tools

913108T17   **Wire gauge**   DTM   MH

Steel (possibly sheaf steel), 5" long, 1 1/8" wide, signed "STUBS".

http://www.davistownmuseum.org/pics/913108t17.jpg
http://www.davistownmuseum.org/bioStubs.htm

Miscellaneous Forged Hardware

12801T15   **Chain**   DTM   MH

Forged iron, 10' long, unsigned.

This is a typical smith-forged iron chain from the 18th century. Each component is tediously and laboriously forged, hopefully, not on a hot August day.

52603T4   **Door latch**   DTM   MH

Forged iron, wood, 2 15/16" long, 2 15/16" wide, unsigned.

It is hand-forged.

22601T7   **Hinge**   DTM   MH

Forged iron, 6" long, unsigned.

This is a typical blacksmith-made H hinge.

913108T8   **Hinges (2)**   DTM   MH

Hand-forged wrought or malleable iron, 12 3/4" long, unsigned.

32502T44   **Keys (2)**   BDTM   T

Iron, unsigned.

These are used for steel locks on the box lids.

http://www.davistownmuseum.org/bioEpstein.htm

TBW3000   **Strap hinge**   DTM   MH

Forged iron, 18" long, unsigned.

Miscellaneous Tools

Miscellaneous Tools

122302T1   Anchor   DTM   MH

Wrought iron and rope, unsigned.

Jack Schmelzer found this anchor and gave the following history: "This anchor was caught on our net 8 miles east of Boston in 1993 on a traditional cod fishing grounds. A knowledgeable anchor collector estimated its age as pre-1800 due to the shape of the stock where the wooden cross attached. Also, the ring is wrapped with rope which indicates pre-chain. Because of the location and size we surmised that it was from a fishing sloop of about 50 feet or more. Cod fishing was the major industry of Massachusetts Bay harbors and this was probably a prolific bottom then, as it is now. The area in which the anchor was caught, is now a closed area in the winter months due to its designation as a major spawning grounds."

TCG1002   Block   DTM   MH

Forged iron and wood, 11 1/2" long, 4" wide, unsigned, c. 1810.

This block has hand-forged strapping, hook, and tie down, lignum vitae shiv with rosehead clinchers.

http://www.davistownmuseum.org/pics/tcg1001.jpg

TK1001   Brickmakers' smoothing wheel   DTM   LTC

Wood (pine or spruce?) with leather strapping, 5 1/2' long, 22" wide with a 26" diameter smoothing wheel, unsigned, c. 1790 - 1820.

This primitive tool would be typical of that used by brickmakers during the boomtown years of the Davistown Plantation. Brickmakers closer to ports such as Belfast shipped their bricks to booming coastal cities such as Portland, Portsmouth, or Boston. Brickmakers in Davistown probably only serviced the local market for chimneys and the few brick homes in the area. For comparison, see the patent model of a brickmaking machine in The Davistown Museum main hall. This tool is on display at the Davistown Museum Liberty Tool Annex.

32708T57   Clamp   DTM   MH

Hand-forged malleable iron, 3 1/4" long, 2 1/2" wide, unsigned.

http://www.davistownmuseum.org/pics/32708t57-1.jpg

4713T3   Nail   DTM   MH

Hand-forged iron, 3" long, 1 3/8" x 1 1/2" head., unsigned.

40501T4   Pry bar   DTM   MH

Forged iron and reforged steel, 21 3/4" long, unsigned.

Refashioned from an old rasp, this rip is a classic example of recycling a dull rasp. With a nicely forged rattail hanger, this tool is probably late 18th century.

102212T2   T-handle wood threading tap   DTM   MH

Forged malleable iron, 10 1/2" long handle, 6" long, 5/8" wide bit, signed "N HARRIS".

Historic Maritime II (1720-1800): The Second Colonial Dominion & the Early Republic

Miscellaneous Tools

32502T30   **Wheels (64)**   BDTM   T

Cast steel, 1/2" to 1" in diameter, unsigned.

All the wheels have different patterns with no shaft or tooling.

http://www.davistownmuseum.org/bioEpstein.htm

TBF1003   **Whetstone**   DTM   MH

Arkansas stone and wood, 7 3/4" long, set in a 9 1/2" wood case, signed with an owner's signature "R S DAVIS".

This generic Arkansas type whetstone, too old to have come from Arkansas, has a distinctly carved 18th century owner's signature in the wood. It came from coastal Maine; is there any relationship with the Davis clan of Davistown?

Patternmakers' Tools

21013T2   **Patternmakers' molding tool**   DTM   MH

Forged iron, wood (boxwood), 14 1/2" long, 1 1/4" wide, 4 1/2" long handle, unsigned.

Shipwrights', Sailmakers', and Mariners' Tools

121805T23   **Caulking iron**   DTM   MH

Hand-forged iron and steel, 6 1/4" long, 2 1/2" wide, unsigned.

This early hand-forged iron caulking iron could be 18th century or from the Roman Empire vis a vis its forge welding, i.e. steeled forged iron.

http://www.davistownmuseum.org/pics/121805t23_p2.jpg

7800-T2   **Maritime gauge (fragment)**   DTM   MHC-J

Wood with a forged iron screw, 5 1/2" wide, 2" wide screw, unsigned, 1780.

This is a typical shipyard measuring tool with a hand-forged screw.

100400T14   **Marlin spike**   DTM   MHC-K

Cast steel, 17 1/2" long, 1 1/4" diameter, unsigned.

http://www.davistownmuseum.org/pics/100400t14.jpg

61612T5   **Mast shave**   DTM   TT

Forged steel with welded edge, wooden handles, 21" long, 16" cutting edge, 5" and 7" long handles, signed "N: JENNINGS".

This tool was found in the central Maine region and almost certainly is a previously unlisted Maine toolmaker.

Historic Maritime II (1720-1800): The Second Colonial Dominion & the Early Republic

Shipwrights', Sailmakers', and Mariners' Tools

72801T10   **Nail header**   DTM   TT

Forged iron, 14 1/2" long with a 3/4" x 3/8" pritchel or header hole, signed "LX" in 18th century script.

Was this nail header used for heading spikes for shipbuilding? It is very early -- possibly 17th century?

31212T7   **Ship pulley**   DTM   TT

Tropical wood, 10" long, 6 1/2" wide, 4" high, unsigned.

This pulley is from a ships' block and tackle and has a rather old looking dark patina. Courtesy of Liberty Tool Co.

Unidentified Tools

11301T6   **Unidentified tool**   DTM   MH

Forged iron, 19" long with a 5" hook, unsigned.

What was this tool used for?

71401T15   **Unidentified tool**   DTM   MH

Forged iron, 13" long, unsigned.

This nicely wrought tool is 18th century. What is its use?

71401T22   **Unidentified tool**   DTM   MH

Forged iron, 8 1/2" long, unsigned.

This is a smith-made implement. What is its use? Is this the tip of a cant hook?

63001T7A   **Unidentified tool (plier-like)**   DTM   MH

Cast steel or German steel, unsigned, 18th century (?).

Is it imported from France? What is its use?

Watchmakers, Jewelers, and Silversmiths' Tools

32502T29   **Adjustable clamp**   BDTM T

Cast steel with broken forged iron wing adjustment nut, 3 3/4" long, 5/8" wide jaws, unsigned.

This is a typical model adjustable clamp.

http://www.davistownmuseum.org/bioEpstein.htm

32502T27   **Adjustable clamp**   BDTM T

Cast steel (?) and brass, 5" long, 1 1/2" wide sliding side clamp with brass screws, unsigned.

This has an unusual and uncommon form.

http://www.davistownmuseum.org/bioEpstein.htm

ID #		Status	Location

Watchmakers, Jewelers, and Silversmiths' Tools

32502T45   **Awl**   BDTM   T

Bone and steel, 3 1/2" long including broken 3/4" long bone handle, 1/12" diameter, unsigned.

http://www.davistownmuseum.org/bioEpstein.htm

32502T43   **Bowl pin auger handle**   BDTM   T

Cast steel (?), 1 13/16" long, unsigned.

http://www.davistownmuseum.org/bioEpstein.htm

32502T39   **Brush**   BDTM   T

Wood and hair, 8 3/4" long , most of the hair or bristles are worn off, signed "Masters Late St London".

http://www.davistownmuseum.org/bioEpstein.htm

32502T38   **Calipers**   BDTM   T

Cast steel and brass, 2 3/4" long, 1 3/4" wide when closed, unsigned.

http://www.davistownmuseum.org/bioEpstein.htm

12900T8   **Draw plate**   DTM   MH

Cast steel, signed "Latapd" and hand stamped "1-13".

This is an early imported jewelers' tool, probably French.

32502T6   **Draw plate (2)**   BDTM   T

Cast steel, 4" long, 1 1/2" wide, 5/16" thick and 4 9/16" long, 1 1/16" wide, 1/8" thick, signed on the larger one "B H & Co 33 - 46".

The smaller also has smaller square holes.

http://www.davistownmuseum.org/bioEpstein.htm

32502T7   **Fragments from tiny jewelers' laths (4)**   BDTM   T

Brass, wood, one with wood pulley 5/8" diameter, unsigned.

It has two tracks for a belt.

http://www.davistownmuseum.org/bioEpstein.htm

32502T28   **Handles**   BDTM   T

Bone, 3 1/16" long and 2 3/8" long, unsigned.

These bone handles have no tool with them.

http://www.davistownmuseum.org/bioEpstein.htm

Historic Maritime II (1720-1800): The Second Colonial Dominion & the Early Republic

Watchmakers, Jewelers, and Silversmiths' Tools

32502T26   Jewelers' _____   BDTM   T

Cast steel, unsigned.

It has an adjustable slide.

http://www.davistownmuseum.org/bioEpstein.htm

31713LTC1   Jewelers' hack saw   DA   TT (Pub)

Forged steel, wood (cocobolo), brass, 11" long, 5" long cutting edge, signed "T. MOON" "J GREEN".

Thomas Moon worked in London from around 1795 to 1821.

81101T15   Jewelers' saw   DTM   MH

Cast steel, wood, and brass, 6 1/4" long frame with an adjustable sliding handle for various blade lengths, unsigned.

This saw has no blades. It is probably an English import pre-dating American production of cast steel tools (1820 and after).

32502T8   Jig   BDTM   T

Brass and steel, 1 3/4" long including adjustable steel pin, unsigned.

This is some sort of 18th century jewelers' precision measuring tool. It has finely made tiny knobs on the side and on the adjusting steel leg. A most unusual tool.

http://www.davistownmuseum.org/bioEpstein.htm

32502T31   Tweezers (8)   BDTM   T

Cast steel, 3 1/4" to 5 7/8" long, signed with unidentified touchmarks.

http://www.davistownmuseum.org/bioEpstein.htm

Woodworking: Axes and Hatchets

91303T2   Belt ax   DTM   MH

Reforged iron and steel with a wooden handle, 3" long, 2" wide head, 8 1/4" long handle, unsigned.

This tiny tomahawk or hatchet is clearly made of forged iron and steel. All surfaces show evidence of hand filing after the forged iron was bent and fashioned into a miniature edge tool and then forged again into steel. A very unusual form.

http://www.davistownmuseum.org/pics/91303t2.jpg

61204T14   Belt ax   DTM   MH

Forged iron, steel and wood, 7 1/2" long handle, 2 1/2" wide, 2 5/16" cutting edge, unsigned, c. 1700 - 1800.

This is an exquisite miniature belt (?) hatchet possibly used for hunting or light woodworking; a very unusual form.

http://www.davistownmuseum.org/pics/61204T14.jpg

Woodworking: Axes and Hatchets

091608T1   **Hatchet**   DTM   MH-O

German steel (?), 5" long, 2 5/8" wide blade, 1/2" square poll, unsigned.

This miniature hatchet is particularly interesting because it is completely forge-welded with file marks on all surfaces, including the cutting edge. There is a hint of a welded steel-iron interface on one side, which could also be evidence of further heat treatment rather than the welded steel-iron interface. The relatively uniform appearance of the edge tool suggests that it is probably a German steel rather than blister steel edge tool.

111006T2   **Hewing ax**   DTM   MH

German or blister steel, 9" long, 5 1/2" long blade, signed with the mark "20", c. 1700 - 1800.

The ax blade shows signs of later heat treatment of the cutting edge. A large 18th century trade ax in the continental style, probably French.

http://www.davistownmuseum.org/pics/111006t2.jpg
http://www.davistownmuseum.org/pics/111006T2_p2.jpg

TBC1003   **Hewing ax**   BDTM   MH

Forged iron and steel, 5" rounded blade, 19" handle, signed "I H", "HARRISON", and "N:4", c. 1750 (?).

This tool is made by John Harrison, Instone Mills, Dronfield, Sheffield UK (http://swingleydev.com/archive/get.php?message_id=95422&submit_thread=1).

http://www.davistownmuseum.org/pics/tbc1003.jpg
http://www.davistownmuseum.org/pics/TBC1003_p2.jpg

81411T1   **Incomplete trade ax**   DTM   TT-O

Forged iron and steel, 5 1/4" long, 3 3/4" wide, 2" high, unsigned.

This is a half-finished trade ax with the piece of metal intended to become a forge-welded edge attached but not yet hammered into shape.

http://www.davistownmuseum.org/pics/81411t1web2.jpg
http://www.davistownmuseum.org/pics/81411t1web3.jpg

102612T13   **Mortising ax head**   LPC   MH

Malleable iron, 10" long, 4" wide, unsigned.

There is no indication of steeling on this ax head.

33013T1   **Mortising tool**   DTM   HC

Hand-forged natural steel, 10" long, 2 1/2" cutting edge, 1 3/4" tall, unsigned.

61204T4   **Sod ax**   DTM   MH

Forged iron and wood handle, 33" long, 3" poll, curved 8 1/2" blade, unsigned.

This is clearly made by a blacksmith with no signs of a weld steel cutting edge.

http://www.davistownmuseum.org/pics/61204T4_p1.jpg

Historic Maritime II (1720-1800): The Second Colonial Dominion & the Early Republic

Woodworking: Axes and Hatchets

32708T65   **Spike-shaped tomahawk**   DTM   MH

Forged iron and steel, 5 3/4" long, 7/8" wide, unsigned.

http://www.davistownmuseum.org/pics/32708t65-1.jpg
http://www.davistownmuseum.org/pics/32708t65-2.jpg

62813T1   **Trade ax**   LPC   MH

Natural steel, 8" long, 3 3/4" cutting edge, 2 1/4" wide, unsigned.

This ax head is on loan from Will West. Its design is typical of the crude axes used as trade items in the American Northwest, with a round eye obviously formed by wrapping a piece of metal around a mandrel and forming it onto the rest of the bit, the shape of which is obvious on this particular specimen.

41203T11   **Trade ax**   DTM   MH

Forged iron and German steel, 7 5/8" long, 3 1/2" blade, signed "_M".

This ax was apparently broken in two and then re-welded. This partially obscured the maker's mark on it. It has the typical form of a trade ax with its light poll. It is difficult to date, but probably 18th century. It has only a slight hint of a weld steel cutting edge.

http://www.davistownmuseum.org/pics/41203t11.jpg

Woodworking: Boring Tools

TBA1002   **Auger**   DTM   MH

Forged iron, 14" long, 5/8" wide cutter, signed "ALDEN" and also inscribed "2 1/2" in eighteenth century script.

DATM (Nelson 1999, 18) lists E. Alden as a maker of augers without a date or location.

41801T4   **Augers (2)**   DTM   MH

Forged iron, 9" long, 1 7/17" diameter and 8 3/4" long, 3/4" diameter, unsigned, c. 1780 - 1800?.

These are typical blacksmith-made wood augers with distinctly forged shafts.

21201T10   **Countersink**   DTM   MH

Cast steel (?), 5" long, unsigned.

This distinctly beveled tool has a relatively stubby and slightly bent shaft and appears to have been designed to fit in a primitive brace.

72801T11   **Gimlet auger**   DTM   MH

Forged iron, 1' long, unsigned.

It is distinctly hand-forged.

Woodworking: Boring Tools

81801T5   **Lipped pod auger**   DTM   MH

Forged iron and wood, 17 1/2" long wood handle, 5 1/2" long and 1 1/2" wide pod, signed "N.° Smith I".

No N. Smith is listed in DATM (Nelson 1999).

070907T3   **Pod auger**   DTM   MH

Forged iron, 23 3/4" long, 1 5/8" wide pod, unsigned.

The typical kind of pod auger used before they invented the screw auger for cutting the holes for the trunnels.

http://www.davistownmuseum.org/pics/070907t3_3.jpg
http://www.davistownmuseum.org/pics/070907t3_1.jpg

TBA1004   **Pod auger**   DTM   MH

Forged iron, 26" long, unsigned, 18th century.

This pod auger was used in the creation of wooden water pipes.

http://www.davistownmuseum.org/pics/tba1004.jpg

TBA1003   **Pod auger**   DTM   MH

Forged iron, 6 3/8" long, handle 4 1/4" wide, unsigned, 18th century.

81801T4   **Pod auger**   DTM   MH

Forged iron, 24 1/2" long, maximum width 11", 1 7/8" wide pod, unsigned.

This auger was used in shipbuilding and post and beam construction for cleaning out mortises and trammels. Similar tools were used as axle reamers.

TBA1001   **Pod auger**   DTM   MH

Forged iron, 6 1/2" long, 7 3/4" long handle, unsigned, distinctly 18th century.

72712T1   **Ring auger**   DTM   MAG-4

Hand-forged steel, wood, 21 1/2" long, 1 1/2" diameter, 12 5/8" long handle, signed "T SNELL 9".

This ring or eye auger has been carefully hand-welded together from three distinct pieces of steel. T. Snell is probably Thomas Snell of Ware, Massachusetts, who worked from circa 1790 to 1854. His connection, if any, to the Snells who also made augers in Sturbridge is unknown.

102800T4   **Screw auger**   DTM   MH

Forged iron, wooden handle, 16" long, 1 1/4" diameter, 12" long handle, signed "D Bisbee Kingston".

Two David Bisbee's were known to have lived in Kingston, MA, a toolmaking center and home to the famous Drew Co. This auger is also marked with a "5" in 18th century script indicating its diameter as 5/4 of an inch. In the late 18th century, screw augers began supplementing, then replacing, the forged folded-over pod augers used by shipyards since the early Iron Age.

Historic Maritime II (1720-1800): The Second Colonial Dominion & the Early Republic

Woodworking: Boring Tools

81101T10   Screw auger   DTM   MH

Forged iron and wood, 15" long, 1 1/8" diameter, 14 7/8" long handle, signed "Perkins 5" in 18th century script.

It has a nice early forged and peened handle crimp. No 18th century Perkins is listed in DATM (Nelson 1999). This colonial era tool has a southern NH provenance (Portsmouth or Newburyport, MA?)

42604T7   Screw box   DTM   MH

Forged iron and wood, 6 5/8" long, 4 1/2" wide handle, 3" x 1 7/8" screw box, unsigned.

21013T1   Screwtip auger bit   DTM   MH

Forged iron, 9" long, 1 1/2" diameter, unsigned.

TJR1301   Turn screw   DTM   MH

Forged iron or steel, wood, and a brass ferrule, 12 1/2" long, 3 1/2" handle, unsigned, c. 1800.

This shows the typical recycling of used rasps.

31602T2   Turn screw   DTM   MH

Forged iron and steel, wood, 19 1/2" long with 15" long and 5/8" wide blade, unsigned.

It has a nicely turned handle with a recycled iron ferrule. A recycled file has been used as the turn screw. An unusual hole has been wrought and drilled in the turn screw center.

TBF1005A   Turn screw   DTM   MH

9 1/8" long, 5 1/2" blade, unsigned.

TBF1001   Water pipe auger   DTM   MH

Forged iron, 13 1/2" long, wooden handle 16 3/4" long, unsigned, c. 1750-1800.

It was used for cleaning out the ends of a long wooden water pipe. See Goodman (1993) for an illustration of a water pipe auger that would be worked through a log to make a water pipe.

http://www.davistownmuseum.org/pics/tbf1001.jpg

Woodworking: Edge Tools

43006T3   Adz   DTM   MH

Hand-forged natural steel, 6 5/16" long, 3 1/2" wide cutting edge, 2 3/8" wide x 1 1/4" deep block end, 1" x 1 1/4" block shaft, unsigned.

It is clearly forge-welded with no sign of steeling. Almost certainly it was bloomery-derived. This adz has an unusual early form that is one-of-a-kind.

Historic Maritime II (1720-1800): The Second Colonial Dominion & the Early Republic

Woodworking: Edge Tools

42604T1   **Adz**   DTM   MH

Natural steel, 9" long, 4" wide, unsigned.

It is distinctly hand-forged.

90908T1   **Bowl adz**   DTM   MAG-4

Forged iron and steel, wood, 9 3/4" long handle, 6" long blade, 6 1/2" cutting edge, unsigned.

TBC1004   **Clapboard slick**   BDTM   MH

Forged iron and steel, 16 1/4" long including the tang, 3 7/8" wide blade, with a 9" long distinctly beveled handle, signed "W. ROGERS".

DATM (Nelson 1999) lists a W. Rogers that is a planemaker circa 1800. This tanged slick is difficult to date and could be late 18th century or early 19th century.

http://www.davistownmuseum.org/pics/TBC1004.jpg
http://www.davistownmuseum.org/pics/TBC1004_sig.jpg

102904T11   **Corner chisel**   DTM   MH

Hand-forged iron and weld steel, 6 1/4" long, 1" x 1" chisel, unsigned.

This primitively wrought woodworking tool has the remains of a broken off wooden handle and an obscured maker's mark in 18th century script. It has an unusual construction with a squared-off solid socket above the corner chisel. It is clearly all handmade with a weld steel construction.

http://www.davistownmuseum.org/pics/102904t11.jpg

32412T2   **Drawknife**   DTM   TT-32

Reforged steel file, hardwood handles, brass ferrules, wood, 14" long, 8 1/2" long blade, unsigned.

This drawknife is crudely welded together from a file and two separate pieces of steel. Courtesy of Liberty Tool Co.

31702T2   **Drawknife**   DTM   MH

Forged steel, 10 1/2" wide, 5 5/8" blade, unsigned, probably late 18th century.

This is an excellent example of an edge tool made out of recycled file steel with English style handles.

81801T11   **Drawknife**   DTM   MHC-D

Forged iron and steel with wood handles, 6" long, 3 1/4" blade, unsigned.

This carefully wrought shave is made from the recycled steel of a rasp or file and predates the patternmakers' drawknives that it resembles. Its use is unknown.

Historic Maritime II (1720-1800): The Second Colonial Dominion & the Early Republic

Woodworking: Edge Tools

6212LTC1   Drawknife
DA   TT (Pub)

Forge-welded steel, wooden handles, 21 1/2" long, 17 1/2" long cutting edge, 4" long handles, signed "L. Rogers".

This drawknife has a long, thin blade and is obviously of 18th century origin. The maker's mark belongs to an unknown maker not listed in the DATM (Nelson 1999). Courtesy of Sett Balise.

913108T50   Drawshave
DTM   MH

Forged iron and German steel with a wood handle, 22 1/8" long, 13 9/16" long blade, signed "VESEY" in a square in two places and "ES" in dots on the middle of the blade.

This is possibly Italian in origin or made by an immigrant toolmaker.

http://www.davistownmuseum.org/pics/913108t50-1web.jpg
http://www.davistownmuseum.org/pics/913108t50-2web.jpg

TBC1005   Drawshave
DTM   MH

Forged iron and steel, 11 5/16" long blade, 15 1/2" wide, unsigned.

It has a clearly forged blade edge characteristic of the drawshaves a blacksmith made. This is what a drawshave would look like prior to the era of cast steel tools. The 18th century appearance is typical of a tool used by the early settlers of the Davistown Plantation.

T81700   Drawshave
DTM   MH

Forged iron and steel, 20" long, unsigned.

This tool provides a graphic illustration of a blacksmith-forged edge tool. On the back of the shave the transition from the forged iron to the forged steel component of the shave is clearly illustrated by the line running the full length of the tool. Since this tool is located outside the display cases and on the hands-on workbench, turn the tool over to see the workmanship characteristic of hand-forged edge tools. Be careful, it's sharp!

913108T41   Drawshave
DTM   MH

Iron with weld steel and wooden handle, 16 3/4" long, 10" blade, signed "Wm FISS" on the blade and "_E. LAUBER" on a band on the handle.

Neither mark is listed in DATM (Nelson 1999).

913108T39   Drawshave
DTM   MH

Steel and brass, 20 3/4" long, 7 3/4" blade, unsigned.

This shave is made from a recycled rasp or file.

81700T1   Drawshave
DTM   MH

Forged iron and steel, wood (beech), 20" long, 4 1/4" handles, unsigned.

This drawshave has a clearly steeled cutting edge.

ID #   Status   Location

Woodworking: Edge Tools

100400T11   Froe   DTM   MH

Forged iron or steel and wood, 17 1/4" long, unsigned.

This is an extra heavy duty specimen for cutting shakes.

http://www.davistownmuseum.org/pics/100400t11.jpg

10407T5   Gouge   DTM   MH

Forged iron and natural steel, 8" long, 1 1/4" diameter, unsigned.

http://www.davistownmuseum.org/pics/10407t5.jpg

30801T3   Gouge   DTM   MH

Forged iron and steel, 15" long with nicely wrought 6 3/4" ferrule, 1 1/2" wide gouge, unsigned.

This is a typical 18th century edge tool.

42904T8   Gouge   DTM   MH

Hand-forged iron and steel, 10 3/4" long, 1 3/16" wide, unsigned.

This is an early example of a blacksmith-made natural steel edge tool with no sign of a weld steel construction.

61204T11   Gouge   DTM   MH

Forged iron and steel, 8 1/4" long, 1 1/2" wide, signed "W GREAVES & SONS", c. 1720 - 1750.

This is an interesting example of an imported edge tool made by an important English edge tool manufacturer just prior to the era of English cast steel edge tools.

http://www.davistownmuseum.org/pics/61204T11_p1.jpg

72812T4   Inside bevel gouge   DTM   MH

Forged steel, wood (hickory), 14 1/2" long, 1 1/4" wide cutting edge, unsigned.

080907T1   Mortising chisel   DTM   MH

Natural steel, 17 1/4" long, 4" long handle, 9/16" thick blade, 5/8" wide cutting edge, signed "KIMPTON" with a backwards N and a scalloped edge around the imprint, there is a first initial that might be "I" or "J".

http://www.davistownmuseum.org/pics/080907t1_p1.jpg
http://www.davistownmuseum.org/pics/080907t1_sig_Kimpton Chisel.jpg

Historic Maritime II (1720-1800): The Second Colonial Dominion & the Early Republic

ID #   Status   Location

Woodworking: Edge Tools

71401T7   Mortising chisel   DTM   MH

Cast steel and wood, 12" long, 6" blade, 1/8" wide, signed "W" and "P" with crossed hammers over an anvil.

This c. 1800 chisel is typical of imported English tools used by American woodworkers before the domestic production of cast steel edge tools began in earnest after 1850.

http://www.davistownmuseum.org/pics/71401t7-2.jpg
http://www.davistownmuseum.org/pics/71401t7-1.jpg

81801T12A   Shovel-makers' drawknife   DTM   MH

Forged iron and steel, oak handles, 11 3/4" long, 1 3/4" wide deeply curved shave, unsigned.

This 18th century tool is finely wrought with a New Hampshire area provenance.

http://www.davistownmuseum.org/pics/81801t12a_p2.jpg
http://www.davistownmuseum.org/pics/81801t12a_p1.jpg

121805T6   Socket chisel   DTM   MH

Hand-forged natural steel, iron, and wood, 6 3/4" long including a 5 3/4" handle, 1 1/2" wide, signed "C KALER" with an obscured mark.

The turned wooden handle appears late 19th century, the forge-welded framing chisel looks mid- or early 18th century and appears to be steeled. This tool was once much longer yet still retains a sharp cutting edge.

http://www.davistownmuseum.org/pics/121805t6_web.jpg

41907T1   Socket chisel   DTM   MH

Natural steel, 9 1/4" long, 15/16" wide, with a 3 3/4" long handle, unsigned.

The handle has been replaced. An excellent example of a direct process forged steel tool, this chisel is made entirely of natural steel with obvious slag and iron inclusions, and also shows evidence of additional steeling, with a welded steel bit on the lower half of the cutting edge, extending at least 3/4 of an inch into the body of the tool. Heavily filed, this tool has a southern New England provenance.

http://www.davistownmuseum.org/pics/41907t1_p2.jpg

TBC1001   Socket chisel   DTM   MH

Forged iron and German steel, 12" long, 2" wide, signed with an 18 c. style touch mark "J.W." in a circle with triangles around the edge and dots in between the triangles.

It has no handle. This tool has a clearly defined welded iron-steel interface.

42604T6   Socket chisel   DTM   MH

Forged iron and weld steel with wooden handle, 12 1/2 " long plus a 4" long handle with an iron ferrule, 1" wide blade, signed "W. ASH&Co.".

William Ash is a Sheffield edge toolmaker, however the signature and the tool construction do not appear to be English, but rather the mark of an 18th century American edge toolmaker.

54

Historic Maritime II (1720-1800): The Second Colonial Dominion & the Early Republic

Woodworking: Edge Tools

| 8312T4 | **Socket firmer chisel** | DTM | TT |

Hand forged natural steel, 9 3/4" long, 13/16" wide cutting edge, unsigned.

| 8312T3 | **Socket framing chisel** | DTM | TT |

Natural steel, 10" long, 1 7/8" wide cutting edge, unsigned.

| 4105T4 | **Socket gouge** | DTM | MH |

Forged iron and steel, 9" long, 8 1/8" handle, signed but the maker's mark is not legible, c. 1780 - 1800.

This is clearly forged-welded and steeled with the look of a German steel cutting edge. It is from a southeast Massachusetts barn; the iron component is probably refined bog iron.

| 61204T6 | **Socket gouge** | DTM | MH |

Forged iron and weld steel with iron ferrules and wooden handle, 14 5/8" long including 3 3/4" long handle, unsigned, c. 1750 - 1800.

This is a classic example of a blacksmith forge-welded steel edge tool.

http://www.davistownmuseum.org/pics/61204T6.jpg

| 111001T21 | **Toothed chisel** | DTM | MHC-D |

Reworked forged steel, 3 7/16" long, 2" cutting head with 17 teeth, unsigned.

This is an excellent example of recycling file steel. Its use is unknown; it is too delicate for stone facing.

Woodworking: Other Tools

| 81801T6 | **Gentlemans' brace** | DTM | MH |

Forged iron and wood, 15 1/2" long, knob is 4" long, 3" wide, unsigned.

It is without any bits. This is what a blacksmith-made brace would have looked like 200 years ago.

| 21201T6 | **Iron brace** | DTM | MH |

Forged iron with wooden handle, 11 3/4" by 8" with 3 1/2" wide handle, unsigned, c. 1800.

This variation of a common iron brace has a hand-forged wing nut to hold in the bit. It is a typical woodworkers' brace.

| 32802T12 | **Nail puller** | DTM | MH |

Forged iron, 19" long, unsigned.

This is a nice example of a blacksmith-made tool of the 18th century. The large jaws suggest a shipyard use for spikes in timbers.

http://www.davistownmuseum.org/pics/32802t6a.jpg

Historic Maritime II (1720-1800): The Second Colonial Dominion & the Early Republic

Woodworking: Other Tools

TBJ1001   Planemakers' float   DTM   MH

Forged iron, 8" long blade, 6" long handle, unsigned, distinctly 18th century.

It is used for cutting out the throat of a plane.

TBJ3500   Saw set   DTM   MH

Forged iron, 12 1/4" long, 2" wide, unsigned.

This set has three set holes.

62406T1   Screw box and screw   DTM   MH

Wood and forged steel, 14 1/8" long, 3" wide screw box; 11 1/2" long, 1 1/4" wide screw, unsigned.

This is a typical 18th century wood screw and clamp-making tool.

81101T2   Threader   DTM   MH

Forged steel and wood, 7 1/4" long, 10" handle, signed "N. Harris" on the handle.

This nicely wrought tool for cutting wood threads for screw clamps pre-dates any factory made screw clamps. No such toolmaker is listed in DATM (Nelson 1999).

12801T4   Wimble   DTM   MH

Forged iron with brass handle, 14" high, 11" swing arm with 6 1/2" lower arm extending from outer end, unsigned.

It is distinctly forged and filed (nut etc.) An uncommon survivor from an 18th century New England shipyard. See pg. 75 of Sellens' (2002) "Dictionary of American Hand Tools" for a photograph of a much more recent wimble, also noted by Sellens as being used on large "bridge" timbers.

Woodworking: Planes

42607T1   Adjustable grooving plane   DTM   MH

Birch with replaced wedge, steel blade and fence guide, forged iron screw, 5/16" wide blade, unsigned, c. 1790.

This is a special purpose (tongue) and groove plane with an adjustable steel and wood fence and three nicely decorated carved wooden adjustment screws. The steel fence and blade guide are forge-welded natural or German steel. The blade is unsigned. The plane is unsigned and is in the basic form of the adjustable plow pane. A nice late 18th century (or early 19th century) woodworking tool.

Woodworking: Planes

33013T3   Angled molding or jointing plane   LPC   MH

Wood (beech), cast steel, 8 3/8" long, 3 3/4" and 2 3/4" wide sides, signed "L TINKHAM" "C C GRIFFITH" "F.C.S".

This unusual triangular plane cuts a curved profile. It came from the Watts boat shop and might have a function in making edges of hull planks join together in such a way that they don't come apart when the wood expands and contracts.

http://www.davistownmuseum.org/bioTinkham.htm

TBH1001   Beading plane   BDTM   MH

Wood (beech?), 5 1/2" long, signed "K Hornberger", 18th c..

This plane is similar in age and design to those that might have been imported to Waldoboro, Maine, by the early (c. 1750) German immigrants who settled there in the 18th century.

33002T2L   Beading plane   DTM   TT

Wood, 8 9/16" long, unsigned, c. 1790 - 1800.

The bead is damaged. This plane is from the Abiel Walker hoard, Alna, Maine. It has the same wedge profile as the three other late 18th century planes in Walker's tool kit. Its length is unusually short.

81602T6   Beading plane   DTM   MH

Birch with forged steel blade, 10" long, 1" wide including fence, bead is 5/16" wide, signed "S. DOGGETT DEDHAM".

Probably this is S. Doggett Jr. (b. 1751, Dedham, d. 1831). Pollak (2001, 124-5) states Samuel Doggett Sr. began making planes as early as 1747. This mark is probably that of his son.

42801T12   Beading plane   DTM   MH

Wood with steel blade, 10" long, 5/16" wide cutter, signed "H Goss".

Goss is not listed in Pollack (2001), Goodman (1993), or DATM (Nelson 1999) so is a previously unidentified planemaker of the late 18th or early 19th century. The wedge is distinctively 18th century.

51703T3   Carriage-makers' plane   LPC   MH

Cast iron, steel blade, wood wedge, 4 1/4" long, 1 7/8" wide, 6 5/8" overall length with extended handle, unsigned.

This exquisite hand-forged, hand-filed plane is probably late 18th century.

81101T12   Coachmakers' router   DTM   MH

Wood and reforged steel, 13 3/8" wide, 7/16" wide cutter, unsigned, c. 1780 - 1810.

This once common 18th century tool shows indications of being refashioned from an old file or rasp.

Woodworking: Planes

80102T1   Complex molding plane   DTM   MHC-D

Wood (beech), steel blade, 9 1/4" long, 2" wide, 1/4" flat chamfers, signed "L·LITTLE" on plane.

Pollack (2001, 232) states "Levi Little, 1770-1802, was a Boston, MA, housewright, tool dealer, and planemaker. Born in Newbury, MA, in 1770, son of John Little and Hannah Noyes and brother of Noah Little, he married Mary Lovering in 1794, and died in 1802. Little made planes of both beech and birch; they range from 9 1/2" to 10" long, and have 1/4" flat chamfers. They are occasionally found with irons by Sheffield makers. He was first listed in the Boston Directory in 1796 as a carpenter at S. Bennet Street; then as a carpenters' toolmaker in 1798 and 1800 on Orange Street. The house he occupied in 1798, which included his workshop, was described as two-storied, 936 sq. ft., 11 windows, and was valued at $900."

31102T1   Double beading plane   BDTM   MHC-E

Wood (maple), 10" long, 1 3/16" wide cutting blade, signed "JO. FULLER PROVIDENCE".

This plane was made by Joseph Fuller of Providence, RI (Pollack 2001). It is one of the most important planes in the Museum collection and a classic example of the 18th century florescence of planemakers in southern New England.

http://www.davistownmuseum.org/pics/31102t1_p1.jpg
http://www.davistownmuseum.org/pics/31102t1_p2.jpg

81912T1   Fillet and cove molding plane   DTM   MH

Wood (beech), steel cutter, 9 3/4" long, 1 1/2" wide, 3 1/4" tall without cutter, 7/8" cutting edge, unsigned.

The wood on this plane has a dark patina typical of beechwood lubricated with mutton grease.

12801T3   Fillister plane   BDTM   MH

Wood with steel blade, 9 9/16" long, signed "Ar. Ritchie" also marked "Stewart" in a smaller font, probably an owner's mark.

This narrow adjustable fillister is unusual in its slightly angled bottom. The Ritchie signature is not listed in Pollak (2001) or Goodman (1993).

TBH1003   Fore plane   DTM   MH-J

Wood (apple wood or beech?), 16 " long, unsigned.

This plane has no blade, is beveled, shows early repairs, and has amazing patina. It has a characteristic 18 c. handle which is not offset. This tool shows signs of generations of use; an extraordinary testament to the stubborn persistence of the early settlers of New England.

http://www.davistownmuseum.org/pics/tbh1003.jpg

Woodworking: Planes

TBH3000   **Fore plane**   BDTM MH-J

Wood (beech), cast steel blade, 16 1/4" long, 2 3/8" wide, 1 7/8" wide blade, signed on blade "W. BUTCHER CAST STEEL WARRANTED" and the plane is unsigned.

This run-of-the-mill fore plane is undistinguished except for its distinctly 18th century handle, which is offset as were most plane handles up to about 1800. The blade is the typical English import made by one of the largest of the Sheffield steel manufacturers, W. Butcher. This tool is typical of those that might have been used by the early settlers of the Davistown Plantation.

42801T9   **Gutter plane**   DTM MH

Wood, 14 1/4" long, 2" wide throat, unsigned.

There is no blade or wedge. This strongly chamfered plane comes from Martha's Vineyard. It has a nicely wood pinned 18th century style handle, c. 1720 - 1750. It is a great hands-on tool for the children visiting the Museum.

33013T5   **Hollow plane**   DTM MH

Wood (beech), cast steel, 12 3/4" long, 2" wide, 5 1/2" tall, signed "G D" "C C GRIFFITH".

The G D mark belongs to Gideon Davenport, who worked in Newport, RI in the late 1700's.

6405T3   **Jack plane**   DTM MH

Wood with a steel blade, 12 1/2" long, 2 1/4" wide, 1 5/8" wide blade, 4 1/2" long rear handle, unsigned, c. 1720.

This is a typical 17th or 18th century imported Dutch or French plane with a characteristic curved design on the front of the plane and a trunneled rear handle in lieu of a rear tote. The wedge is replaced, the steel blade is probably not original, and the blade holder is a trunneled peg. It was found in the Bath, Maine, area.

101801T7   **Molding plane**   BDTM MH

Mahogany, 9 1/2" long, signed "AFW" for Abiel F. Walker, owner.

http://www.davistownmuseum.org/publications/volume10.html

7800T9   **Molding plane**   BDTM MH-D

Wood with steel blade, 9 5/8" long, unsigned, c. 1790 - 1810.

The heavily chamfered sides and distinctive wedge are characteristic of the late 18th century planes. Possibly it was used for door moldings.

12801T2   **Molding plane (Ogee bead)**   BDTM MH

Wood with steel blade, 9 11/16" long, signed "London".

It is strongly beveled. London appears to be a manufacturer's signature rather than the location of manufacture. No London, however, is listed in Goodman (1993), Pollak (2001), or DATM (Nelson 1999) as a planemaker. This is probably another imported plane of the late 18th century.

Historic Maritime II (1720-1800): The Second Colonial Dominion & the Early Republic

Woodworking: Planes

12801T1   Molding plane (reverse Ogee)   BDTM   MH

Wood with steel blade, 9 7/16" long, signed "WATSONS Leeds".

Watsons was an English maker, 1792-1798 (Goodman 1993). This plane also has multiple owner's marks: "J FAIRBANK" over stamped "I. WILSON". It is a good example of the typical imported molding planes of a c. 1800 southern New England carpenters' tool kit. It is only slightly, not strongly beveled. Perhaps Watson's working dates extended into the early 19th century?

51713LTC1   Moving filletster plane   DA   DA

Wood (beech), cast steel, 15" long, 2 1/4" wide, 1 15/16" wide blade, 6 3/4" tall, signed "J. DARLING" "J GREAVES & SONS WARRANTED CAST STEEL" on blade.

4613T1   Panel raising plane   DTM   MH

Wood (rosewood), cast steel, 14" long, 2 1/4" wide, 6 1/2" tall, signed "C.C. GRIFFITH" "L*T; E*CLARK MIDDLEBORO" and "BENNET" on blade.

The L*T signature is probably Levi Tinkham. E. Clark is Elisha Clark. The Bennet mark is probably N. Bennet, a smith in Middleboro, MA. Pollack (2001) notes some connection between Clark and Tinkham; the DATM (Nelson 1999) notes that Bennett is known to have made irons for Clark.

http://www.davistownmuseum.org/bioTinkham.htm

4106T8   Panel razee plane   DTM   MH

Wood, forged iron and steel blade, 14" long, 2 1/4" wide, signed with obscured initials.

This 18th century plane was found in Maine. It has the traditional offset handle and pegged wood handle of an early plane. It is slightly beveled at the front, rear, and on one side of the body with a primitive iron and steel blade, probably made by a local blacksmith. The handle may be beech or birch.

101900T1   Plow plane   DTM   MHC-D

Birch with an ash wedge, forged steel blade, and forged iron fence and bolts, 9 1/2" long, 8 1/2" arms, 3/16" wide blade, signed "H. R. WEBB" on the side of the plane.

This plane was possibly made by a cooper; coopers often signed their tools with large letters on the sides. The chamfering, wooden arm wedges, and hand-forged ironwork clearly indicate this is an 18th century tool. It was found in Maine and donated to the Museum by Bob Wheeler, Oct. 18, 2000. See our essay in the Hand Tools in History section for more photographs and a discussion of this type of plane (click the info link).

http://www.davistownmuseum.org/pics/101900T1_p5.jpg
http://www.davistownmuseum.org/toolPloughPlane.html

Historic Maritime II (1720-1800): The Second Colonial Dominion & the Early Republic

Woodworking: Planes

40501T3   Plow plane   DTM   MH

Wood (beech), steel blade, iron rivets, brass depth stop, 9" long, unsigned.

This is the prototypical Yankee plow plane with wooden screws for the fence slide stops. English plow planes of the same period and design use wooden wedges for the fence stops. This is probably an owner-made plane. It is slightly damaged and dates from either the end of the 18th or beginning of the 19th century.

http://www.davistownmuseum.org/toolPloughPlane.html

1302T4   Rabbet plane   BDTM   MH

Wood with steel blade, 10" long, signed "Darbey".

Goodman (1993) lists the Darbey family as making planes in Birmingham, England, 1750 - 1794. This is a typical example of a plane found in a late 18th century carpenters' tool kit.

81602T1   Rabbet plane   DTM   MH

Birch with oak wedge and cast steel blade, 12" long, 1 3/8" wide, unsigned, c. 1780.

TBW1008   Rabbet plane   DTM   MHC-D

Wood (beech), steel blade, 10 7/8" long, 1" wide, signed but the signature is obscured.

http://www.davistownmuseum.org/pics/tbw1008.jpg
http://www.davistownmuseum.org/pics/tbw1008p2.jpg

TBH1004   Rounding plane   DTM   MH

Birch with a very distinctive mahogany wedge, 9 1/2" long, 5/8" diameter, signed "H·S", early 18th c., probably c. 1720.

There is no blade. This maker is not listed in Pollak (2001). H·S may be an owner's mark; the owner may also have made this plane.

81602T15   Rounding plane   DTM   MH

Wood, no blade, 10 1/8" long, 1 1/2" wide, unsigned.

This generic molding plane with its heavy chamfers and robust shoulder moldings is probably a late 18th century European import that would typify the working tool kit of a c. 1820 woodworker.

http://www.davistownmuseum.org/pics/81602t15_p1.jpg
http://www.davistownmuseum.org/pics/81602t15_p4.jpg

Woodworking: Planes

100400T4   Sash plane   BDTM   MHC-D

Birch with a cast steel blade, 10" long, 1 3/4" wide with a 7 1/2" blade, signed "I: B: WALTONS IN READING" on the wood.

Pollack (2001, 391) has this comment on I B Walton: "John Walton (1744-1823) of Reading, MA, until 1771 and Cambridge, MA, thereafter; and Benjamin Walton, his brother. Planes signed I:B:Waltons were probably made before 1771, when John Walton moved to Cambridge to work as a housewright. Some of the brothers' planes are fruitwood, others birch. Though they had their own name stamp, they used their father's location stamp IN READING.". This is another treasure of the Museum's tool collection.

42801T10   Sash plane   DTM   MH

Curly maple with iron spline, no blade or wedge, 10 3/4" long, unsigned.

This is a beautiful and unusual specimen of an early 18th century plane. It has a Martha's Vineyard provenance. Another great specimen for hands-on inspection.

33013T2   Sliding fence plow plane   LPC   MH

Wood (beech), cast steel, 9 3/4" long, 9" tall, 7 1/2" wide, signed "L. TINKHAM" "C.C. GRIFFITH" "F C S".

http://www.davistownmuseum.org/bioTinkham.htm

111001T7   Tongue and groove plane   DTM   MH

Wood with steel blade, forged iron fence screws, 10 1/4" long, 1 3/16" wide including a 3/8" wide fence, 3/8" wide groove, unsigned.

This is a typical owner-made 18th century plane.

81606T3   Tongue and groove plane   DTM   MH

Wood (beech), 11 1/4" long, 1 3/8" wide, 3 3/8" tall without peg, unsigned.

This plane has no cutter.

81602T5   Tongue and groove plane   DTM   MH

Wood, no blade, 9 1/2" long, 1 3/4" wide with a 5/16" wide groove, signed "J TABER".

Pollack (2001, 403-4) reports three other J. Taber planes: a crown molder, a boxed complex molder, and a 1/4" halving plane. How was J. Taber related to the Taber family and, especially, to N. Taber who made planes in New Bedford and Falmouth, MA, 1785 - 1820, and was the father of the prolific G. M. Taber?

81602T3   Tongue and groove plane   DTM   MH

Wood, no blade, 11 3/8" long, 7/16" wide groove, unsigned.

This plane is European in origin and completely different in style from American and English planes of the 18th century. Is it German, French, or Dutch?

Historic Maritime II (1720-1800): The Second Colonial Dominion & the Early Republic

Woodworking: Planes

32313T5   **Toted match plane**   LPC   MH

Wood (maple), steel, 10 3/8" long, 2 1/8" wide, 7" tall, signed "W" "I HATCH" on blade and "C.C. GRIFFITH".

The "W" appears to be the maker's mark.

51213T1   **Wheelwrights' outside compass plane**   LPC   MH

Wood (beech), cast steel, 7 1/2" long, 2 5/8" wide, 2" wide blade, signed "NEWBOULD" on blade "L TINKHAM" "C C GRIFFITH CCG" on body.

The blade was probably made by Thomas Newbould or Samuel Newbould and Co. of Sheffield, England (http://www.gracesguide.co.uk/Samuel_Newbould_and_Co).

http://www.davistownmuseum.org/bioTinkham.htm

Woodworking: Planes Made in Maine

71504T3   **Complex molding plane**   LPC   MHC-D

Wood (yellow birch), steel blade, 9 1/2" long, 1 1/2" wide, signed "JOHNFLYN".

Could John Flyn be Maine's earliest known planemaker? He worked in Warren, Maine circa 1780 - 1800.

http://www.davistownmuseum.org/pics/71504T3_p3.jpg
http://www.davistownmuseum.org/publications/volume10.html

TBW1002   **Panel raising plane with adjustable fence**   BDTM   MHC-L

Wood (beech), steel blade, 14" long, 3 1/2" wide including the adjustable fence, 2" wide blade, signed "T. WATERMAN" on plane and "JAMES CAM SHEFFIELD WARRANTED CAST STEEL" on blade.

This is currently the earliest signed hand plane known to have been made in the state of Maine. The Waterman signature is distinctly 18th century. The plane was probably made in the last years of the 18th century. James Cam, the prolific Sheffield, England edge tool manufacturer made the blade for this plane. Many Cam blades and tools were imported to America during this time. The biography links for Waterman and Cam go to pages that include photographs of this plane.

http://www.davistownmuseum.org/bioJamesCam.htm
http://www.davistownmuseum.org/publications/volume10.html

71504T1   **Plow plane**   LPC   MHC-D

Wood (beech), steel blade, rosewood fence, and one rosewood thumbscrew, 9" long with a 9 5/8" fence, 5/16" flat chamfers, signed "C·GOVE".

The plane was found in Eliot, Maine. It was originally in the collection of Ben Blumenberg. It is possibly made by Charles C. Gove of Kittery, Maine.

http://www.davistownmuseum.org/pics/71504T1_p1.jpg
http://www.davistownmuseum.org/publications/volume10.html

ID #   Status   Location

Woodworking: Planes Made in Maine

TBW1009   **Rabbet plane**   DTM   MHC-D

Wood (beech), steel, 10 13/16" long, 5/8" wide, signed "J. METCALF".

This plane was made by Joseph Metcalf of Winthrop, ME. The style and the wedge is distinctly 18th century. Joseph Metcalf was Maine's earliest documented planemaker, working slightly earlier than Thomas Waterman. This late 18th century example may have been made in Massachusetts before Metcalf moved to Winthrop, Maine, in 1789. The style and wedges are distinctly 18th century. Joseph was born in Medway, MA, in 1756, and apprenticed to his brother Luther. He went to Hallowell, Maine, by oxcart, for reasons unknown in 1789, and in the same year went to Winthrop, Maine, where he immediately began to build a workshop, finishing it that same year. His simple center chimney Georgian home was completed in 1792.

http://www.davistownmuseum.org/pics/tbw1009.jpg
http://www.davistownmuseum.org/bioMetcalf.htm

71504T2   **Rounding plane**   LPC   MHC-D

Birch with a steel blade, 11" long, 3/4" wide, signed "J. METCALF".

http://www.davistownmuseum.org/bioMetcalf.htm

50402T2   **Skew plane**   LPC   MH

Wood, no blade, 13 1/4" long, 2 3/8" wide, signed "J. C. Larrabee" with owner's initials "C.J.S." over stamped on the mark, partially obscuring it.

Larrabee is an up-to-now unlisted Brunswick-area Maine planemaker. The plane is heavily chamfered with the offset handle and handle profile characteristic of 18th century planes. This tool may predate the Waterman and Metcalf planes in the Museum collection. His working dates are as yet unknown. This plane was formerly in the Bob Wheeler collection and is now loaned to the Museum by the current owner.

http://www.davistownmuseum.org/pics/50402t2_p1.jpg
http://www.davistownmuseum.org/publications/volume10.html

111104T1   **Yankee plow plane**   DTM   MH

Birch, 9 1/2" long, 8" wide, 6" high, 1/4" wide cutting edge, signed "S.KING" and also "A H" owner's mark.

The plane has a wedge arm lock, wood depth stop, flat chamfers, and is screw locked. S. King is possibly one of Maine's earliest planemakers.

Woodworking: Saws

ID #   Status   Location

Woodworking: Saws

TCB3000   **Backsaw**   BDTM   MH

Sheaf steel, wood, and brass, 23 1/4" long with a 9 1/4" long blade, signed "S*J", "LLOYD DAVIES" with a crown touchmark. It is also stamped "GERMAN STEEL", c. 1800.

This small backsaw has a crown touchmark, a distinctly 18th century style handle, solid brass nuts, and is typical of the tools imported into the United States from England in the late 18th century and early 19th century. This saw is unusual in being stamped "German Steel." The mark indicates this was made by Spear and Jackson of Sheffield, England, from refined and reforged cementation steel. For a detailed explanation of sheaf steel as refined cementation steel and not German steel (despite the mark), see the chapter "Sheaf Steel and the Search for Quality" in "Steel- and Toolmaking Techniques and Strategies Before 1870 (Brack 2008, 68-70).

http://www.davistownmuseum.org/pics/TCB3000-2.jpg
http://www.davistownmuseum.org/pics/TCB3000-1.jpg

83102T6   **Buck saw**   DTM   MH

Forged iron, forged steel blades, and wood frame, 31" wide, 27" height, unsigned.

The exquisitely formed ram's horn adjustment screws date this primitive blacksmith-made buck saw to the 17th or early 18th century. With a southern New England provenance, this saw is a rare survivor from the colonial era.

101400T8   **Hand saw**   DTM   MH

Forged steel, wood, and brass, 20 1/2" long, unsigned.

Probably a tool used in a shipyard, this saw is distinguished by its 18th century handle and shape.

032203T1   **Hand saw**   DTM   MH

Steel, wood, and brass, 30" long, 25 7/8" blade, unsigned.

This is a typical late 18th century or early 19th century hand saw with peened brass rivets on the handle and the characteristic horizontal design of the lower handle grip of 18th century hand saws. By 1820, this saw was probably 25 or 50 years old -- a typical used tool found in any tool box of the era.

http://www.davistownmuseum.org/pics/032203t1_p1.jpg
http://www.davistownmuseum.org/pics/032203t1_p2.jpg

111206T3   **Hand saw**   DTM   MH

Cast steel, brass, and wood, 21 1/2" long, signed "G. Biggin & Co. S.B. Sheffield cast steel" with a crown touchmark, c. 1780-1840.

The saw has three solid brasses. The center brass replicates the signature and has a more ornate crown to signify licensed production permission from the king.

71401T1   **Hand saw**   DTM   MH

Forged steel, iron, and wood, 17" long, 13" blade, unsigned.

This is a typical late 18th century or early 19th century smith-made rip saw.

Historic Maritime II (1720-1800): The Second Colonial Dominion & the Early Republic

Woodworking: Saws

121805T22   **Keyhole saw**   DTM   MH

Saw steel, brass, and wood, 20 1/8" long, unsigned.

Primitive saw brasses, handle, and saw steel suggest this saw dates from the late 18th or early 19th century.

http://www.davistownmuseum.org/pics/121805t22_p2.jpg

72002T3   **Keyhole saw**   DTM   MH-E

Steel, wood, brass, 11" long, 5 1/2" blade, signed "MAWSALL", c. 1800.

This keyhole saw has all the characteristics of a late 18th century tool. DATM (Nelson 1999) lists a John Mawsall as a rule-maker working in Philadelphia c. 1813, who also made umbrellas. Could he also have been one of Philadelphia's early saw makers?

TBJ1002   **Keyhole saw**   DTM   MH

Saw steel, wood, 12 1/2" long with a 6 1/4" blade, unsigned, c. 1780 - 1800.

TBF1007   **Pad saw**   DTM   MH

Forged iron, 9 1/4" long, unsigned.

It has three unidentified touchmarks.

51201T7   **Rip saw**   DTM   MH

Sheaf steel, wood, 27 13/16" long, signed "Browne German Steel", c. 1690 - 1740.

No Browne is listed in DATM (Nelson 1999). This is a perfect example of an 18th century saw: It has forged iron rivets instead of brasses in the handle, a distinctly 18th century style handle with flattened lower grip, and the mark German steel, which indicates that the steel is carefully reforged blister steel, which was a significant source of saw steel for a few decades before and after 1700. At this time, a few German ironmongers were living in Newcastle and Sheffield and had perfected the art of reforging blister steel before the advent of Benjamin Huntsman's cast steel. The use of the mark German Steel (in English) is confusing in that German steel made from partially decarburized cast iron was the main source of imported steel for Sheffield toolmakers in the 16th to early 18th centuries. Any English-made tool marked "German steel" is almost certainly made from sheaf steel; tools made from the more commonplace German steel are not labeled as such. This saw is a classic tool from the Ancient Dominions of Maine.

31602T11   **Tenon saw**   DTM   MH

Steel, wood, and brass nuts, 14 7/8" long, blade 9 7/8" long, signed "____ & Sellars & Grayson's improved Sheffield CAST STEEL".

This is a typical imported late 18th century tenon saw with solid brass mats.

31012NOM2 **Two-man crosscut saw**   NOM   UNK

Saw steel, 50" long, 6" wide, unsigned.

Courtesy of Mike Nelson.

ID #		Status	Location

Wrenches

32103T4   **Adjustable wrench**   DTM   MH-O

Forged iron, 13 1/4" long, 3 1/4" wide, unsigned.

Allegedly an English-made coach wrench, c. 1825, the Davistown Museum believes this is a late colonial era or early Republic all-purpose axle wrench, possibly blacksmith-made in or near Boston. This wrench lacks the beveled handle and sophisticated workmanship of the typical English coach wrench and its primitive forged construction suggests an 18th century origin. It is the fourth in our series of Boston wrenches (follow the bio link for more discussion).

http://www.davistownmuseum.org/pics/32103t4_p2.jpg
http://www.davistownmuseum.org/bioBostonWrench.htm

TBK1002   **Adjustable wrench**   BDTM   MH

Forged iron, 8 1/2" long, signed "Mathieson Glasgow".

One of four unusual early wrenches of similar design, it has a strongly beveled handle and is part of the Boston wrench group.

http://www.davistownmuseum.org/pics/tbk1001.jpg
http://www.davistownmuseum.org/bioBostonWrench.htm

TBK1003   **Adjustable wrench**   BDTM   MH

Forged iron, 13 1/4" long, unsigned.

It has a slightly beveled handle. These late eighteenth or early nineteenth century wrenches keep turning up in the Boston area. Use the biography link to see our information file on the Boston wrenches.

http://www.davistownmuseum.org/pics/tbk1001.jpg
http://www.davistownmuseum.org/bioBostonWrench.htm

TBK1001   **Adjustable wrench**   BDTM   MH

Forged iron, 11 1/8" long, unsigned, 18th c..

It is a member of the Boston wrench group and has a beveled handle.

http://www.davistownmuseum.org/pics/tbk1001.jpg
http://www.davistownmuseum.org/bioBostonWrench.htm

102100T21   **Auger wrench**   DTM   MH

Forged iron, 6 1/2" long, unsigned, c. 1800?.

What was this distinctly smith- made socket-tool used for?

TBK1004   **Open ended wrench**   DTM   MH

Forged iron, 15" long, 1 1/2" and 1 7/16" wide ends, unsigned, c. 1780 - 1800.

8912T3   **S-curve open box wrench**   DTM   TT

Natural steel, 7 1/8" long, 3/16" thick, 11/16" and 1/2" ends, unsigned.

This wrench is made to fit square nuts.

Historic Maritime II (1720-1800): The Second Colonial Dominion & the Early Republic

Wrenches

8912T4   **S-curve open box wrench**   DTM   TT

Cast iron, 6" long, 3/16" thick, 1 3/16" and 1 1/8" ends, unsigned.

121805T10   **Tap wrench**   DTM   MH

Forged natural steel and/or iron with a natural steel insert, 9 5/8" long, 3/8" square tap hole, unsigned.

This is a nice example of a primitive 18th century American forge-welded natural steel tool made directly from a bloom of natural steel.

http://www.davistownmuseum.org/pics/121805t10.jpg

71401T6   **Tap wrench**   DTM   MH

Forged iron, wrought iron screws, and wood, 5 7/8" long, 6" handle, unsigned.

This is a typical 18th century tool for threading wood for small wood screw clamps.

43006T4   **Wagon wrench**   DTM   MH

Forged iron and/or natural steel, 3/4" and 13/16" wide wrench openings, unsigned.

It is a curved wrench, forge-welded and hand-filed from a handmade rasp. It is a nice example of an 18th century wagon wrench.

42801T15   **Wagon wrench**   DTM   MH

Forged iron, 9 5/8" long, unsigned.

This is a very early wagon wrench from the mid-18th century.

71401T23   **Wrench**   DTM   MH

Forged iron, wood, and brass, 4" long, 2 1/4" wood handle, signed with the initials "F. W." in 18th century script.

What was this simple wrench used for?

Historic Maritime III (1800-1840): Boomtown Years & the Dawn of the Industrial Revolution

Agricultural Implements

100208T1   Brush scythe   DTM   MH

Forged malleable iron and steel, 20" long, 18" blade, unsigned.

This heavy duty scythe is clearly hand-forged with a distinct weld steel-iron interface and numerous markings from cold hand hammering. Formerly in the collection of Ed Shaw.

http://www.davistownmuseum.org/publications/volume10.html

TCR1008   Dibble   DTM   MH

Forged steel and wood (beech?), 9" long, 4 3/4" point, unsigned.

This tool has a nicely turned handle. This tool is difficult to date, but is probably late 18th or early 19th century.

http://www.davistownmuseum.org/pics/tcr1008.jpg

TH1001   Dibble   DTM   MH

Forged iron or natural steel and wood, 10 1/2" long, 5" dibble, unsigned.

A dibble is used for planting seeds.

TCK1004   Fork with three prongs   DTM   MH

Forged iron, 9 3/4" long including handle, 4 1/2" wide, unsigned, c. 1800.

http://www.davistownmuseum.org/pics/TCK1004.jpg

TCR1001A   Grafting froe   DTM   MH

Forged iron, 8 5/8" long with a 3 1/4" blade, unsigned.

This tool is refashioned from an old file or rasp. It was a basic necessity for Davistown residents maintaining orchards in the 19th century.

http://www.davistownmuseum.org/pics/tcz1006.jpg
http://www.davistownmuseum.org/pics/tcr1001a.jpg

42405P2   Grain bucket   DTM   MH

Wood with iron bail, 10" high, 6 3/8" diameter top, 5 1/2" diameter bottom, 1 1/4" wooden handle holders, unsigned.

This bucket looks identical to 42405P1, but is smaller.

42405P1   Grain bucket   DTM   MH

Wood with iron bail, 10 3/4" high, 6 1/4" diameter top, 5 1/2" diameter bottom, 1 1/2" wooden handle holders, unsigned.

This grain bucket came from a New Hampshire farm and has a red stain. It may have been handmade in a farm workshop by a cooper during a typical winter work session. It looks identical to 42405P2, but is larger. Compare these to the factory-made pork barrel (102503P3).

Historic Maritime III (1800-1840): Boomtown Years & the Dawn of the Industrial Revolution

Agricultural Implements

51606T2   Hay cutter   DTM   MH

Forged iron and welded steel, 16 3/8" long, 6 1/4" wide, 1 3/16" diameter socket, signed "STINSON".

This early 19th century tool has the basic form of a hay cutter but may also be for trimming the flesh of a large fish, e.g. a flensing tool. Comments are welcomed. Three Stinson edge toolmakers are listed in the Registry of Maine Toolmakers, two in Bath. Is this a fisheries-related tool? See ID 31811T30.

TCK1301   Hay knife   DTM   MH

Forged iron and steel, wood, 16" blade, 18" handle, unsigned.

72312T1   Hay knife   DTM   MH

Forged iron and steel, wooden (oak) handle, 23" long blade, 8" long handle, unsigned.

TCK3000   Hoe   DTM   MH

Forged iron and wood, 9 3/4" long, 4 1/2" wide hoe, 4" long prongs, unsigned.

This is a typical early 19th century blacksmith-made garden tool.

101701T10   Oxen shoe   DTM   MH

Forged iron, 5 3/8" long, unsigned.

This smith-made shoe is unmarked and difficult to date.

81602T13   Oxen shoes   DTM   MH

Forged iron, 4" long, unsigned.

These are typical farrier-made small sized oxen shoes, essential for maximizing the efficiency of the long work days of the typical ox.

101701T3   Sheep shears   DTM   MH

Steel, 12 1/2" long, signed "Shear Steel W. Wilkinson".

This appears to be an imported English shear. No W. Wilkinson is listed in either DATM (Nelson 1999) or W. L. Goodman's (1993) index of British plane iron makers in "British Plane Makers from 1700". Shear steel is reworked blister steel and of a higher quality.

31811T30   Sod cutter (?)   DTM   TT

Hand-forged malleable iron, 17" long, "Y" shaped end 4 3/4" long and 6 1/4" wide, signed "STINSON".

This is an unusual configuration for a tool, which has been hand-forged and welded, perhaps for a special use. It could also be a hay cutter. See ID# 51606T2.

70

Historic Maritime III (1800-1840): Boomtown Years & the Dawn of the Industrial Revolution

Agricultural Implements

| 83102T7 | **Trowel** | DTM | MH |

Cast steel, brass ferrule, and wood handle, 7 1/4" long, 4" long blade, signed "C Monk".

This is an exquisite heart shaped trowel. DATM (Nelson 1999) lists a C. M. Monk making molders' tools, c. 1894. This tool appears significantly older. Another C. Monk is also listed in Brooklyn, NY without any tools associated with his work.

| TKD3000 | **Yoke** | DTM | MH |

Wood with forged iron ferrules, 24" long, unsigned.

One of the many artifacts that Kenneth Lynch brought back from Europe in his collecting days in the 1930s and 1940s.

http://www.davistownmuseum.org/bioLynch.htm

| 32802T9 | **Yoke puller** | DTM | MH |

Forged iron, 10 3/8" long, unsigned.

See Richardson (1978) "Practical Blacksmithing" volume II, pg. 16, Fig. 19.

http://www.davistownmuseum.org/pics/32802t9.jpg

Blacksmith, Farrier, and Metalworking Tools

| 31808PC1 | **Blacksmiths' double calipers** | DTM | MH |

Hand-forged malleable iron, 14" long, signed on the end of the handle with a decorative heart shape that mimics the shape of the caliper.

| 72812LTC1 | **Blacksmiths' double calipers** | DA | TT (Pub) |

Forged steel, 16" long, 5 3/4" wide, unsigned.

Courtesy of Liberty Tool Company.

| 10700T2 | **Blacksmiths' fluted tongs** | DTM | MH |

Forged iron, 15" long, unsigned.

| 4106T10 | **Blacksmiths' leg vise** | DTM | MH |

Forged iron, 37 3/4" high, 4 1/4" wide jaw, unsigned.

This traditional tool is completely hand-forged and is probably early 19th century or possibly late 18th century. Found in almost every barn workshop in the 19th century, this tool predates the era of the drop-forged bench vise.

http://www.davistownmuseum.org/pics/4106t10_p1_small.jpg
http://www.davistownmuseum.org/pics/4106t10_p2_small.jpg

ID #   Status   Location

Blacksmith, Farrier, and Metalworking Tools

5412LTC1   **Blacksmiths' pointed lip tongs**   DA   TT (Pub)

Forged iron, 15 5/8" long, 9/16" jaw, unsigned.

Courtesy of Liberty Tool Co.

71801T8   **Blacksmiths' straight lip tongs**   DTM   TT

Forged iron, unsigned.

913108T53   **Blacksmiths' tap**   DTM   MH

Forged iron or steel, 4 7/8" long, unsigned.

42405T4   **Blacksmiths' tongs**   DTM   MH

Forged wrought iron, 27 5/8" long, 1" wide jaws, unsigned.

These are an excellent example of an 18th or early 19th century smith-made tongs. Found in Massachusetts, the distinct presence of siliceous slag inclusions indicates this tool was made from unfined bog iron, probably at one of the many forges in the swampy lowlands of southeastern Massachusetts.

913108T7   **Blacksmiths' tongs**   DTM   MH

Reforged steel rasp or file, 13" long, unsigned.

913108T37   **Blacksmiths' tools (5)**   DTM   MH

Reforged steel rasps and files, A) 2 1/2"; B) 9 1/4"; C) 6 1/2"; D) 1 3/4"; E) 7 3/4", unsigned.

This is a set of tools a blacksmith may have made for his own use. They consist of: B) grafting tool, C) spud, D) wedge, and two farriers' hoof cutters A) and E).

TCF1001   **Blacksmiths' tools (8)**   DTM   MH

Forged iron, unsigned.

These eight small tools were found together and represent a mixture of late 18th century and early 19th century blacksmith taps and other tools.

31611T6   **Bolt header**   DTM   TT

Forge-welded malleable iron, 8 1/2" long, 1 1/8" wide, unsigned.

It is handmade.

TCF3000   **Butteris**   DTM   MH

Forged iron, steel, and wood, 16 1/2" long, 1 15/16" wide blade, unsigned.

This tool is used by a farrier for paring a horses' hoof. The long handle rests against the shoulder. It is operated with a thrusting movement.

http://www.davistownmuseum.org/pics/tcf3000.jpg

ID #   Status   Location

Blacksmith, Farrier, and Metalworking Tools

| 021812T4 | **Clinch cutter** | DTM | TT |

Reforged steel, unsigned.

This is a farriers' tool rendered out of a recycled rasp or file.

| 72712LTC10 | **Coal tongs** | DA | TT (Pub) |

Forged iron, 13 1/2" long, 1 3/4" wide, 3 3/4" tall, unsigned.

These tongs show significant signs of fire-related oxidation. Courtesy of the Liberty Tool Company.

| 81200T7 | **Farriers' burnisher** | DTM | MHC-J |

Wood, 16 1/4" long, unsigned, c. 1820 - 1840.

| 61612T6 | **Farriers' butteris** | DTM | TT |

Forged malleable iron and steel, wooden handle, 14" long, 1 3/4" cutting edge, 4 7/8" long handle, unsigned.

| 032103T3 | **Farriers' chisel** | DTM | MH |

Forged iron and steel, 7 3/8" long, 2" long cutter, unsigned.

This is an excellent example of recycled steel. Originally a steel rasp, worn out rasps were saved and reworked into other useful edge tools. The peened top cutting edge reflects the transition from forged iron to a hammered steel cutting edge.

http://www.davistownmuseum.org/pics/032103t3_p1.jpg
http://www.davistownmuseum.org/pics/032103t3_p2.jpg

| 102911T1 | **File** | DTM | TT |

Cast steel, 21 3/4" long, signed "WARRANTED CAST STEEL".

This handmade tool has some indecipherable markings.

| 51201T12 | **File** | DTM | MH |

Steel, 10 1/2" long, signed "P S Stubs".

This file is from the Simon Willard toolbox.

http://www.davistownmuseum.org/pics/51201T12.jpg
http://www.davistownmuseum.org/bioStubs.htm

| TCR1302 | **Hand vise** | DTM | MH |

Forged iron or steel, 3 1/2" long, signed "G. KIPP".

This maker is not listed in DATM (Nelson 1999); who was G. Kipp? This tool looks very similar to a Stub hand vise, but is probably German in origin.

ID #   Status   Location

Blacksmith, Farrier, and Metalworking Tools

TCR1301   **Hand vise**   DTM   MH

Forged iron and steel, 4" long, signed "STUBS" also signed "K. MAIER".

This is another example of the fine quality imported tools of the Stubs Company in Lancashire, England. The signature K. Maier is probably an owner's signature.

http://www.davistownmuseum.org/bioStubs.htm

TCR1011   **Hand vise**   DTM   MH

Forged iron and steel, 4 1/2" long, 1 5/16" wide jaw, signed "P. S. STUBBS".

http://www.davistownmuseum.org/bioStubs.htm

102800M10   **Hand vise**   DTM   MH

Forged iron and steel, 4 5/" long, 1 1/2" wide jaw, signed "P S Stubs" and by owner "W.F. Blake".

This was found in the machinists' tool box on display with the W. F. Blake tools. Peter Stubs was the prolific Lancashire file and toolmaker (Dane 1973; Brack 2008).

http://www.davistownmuseum.org/bioKnoxEngine.htm
http://www.davistownmuseum.org/bioStubs.htm

62406T7   **Hand vise**   DTM   MH

Iron and forged steel, 6 1/2" long, 2 13/16" wide jaws, 3 3/8" long nut, signed with the characteristic P Stubs mark.

This is a highly unusual variation of a common hand vise due to an ornate forge-welded ram's horn nut.

http://www.davistownmuseum.org/bioStubs.htm

83102T2   **Horseshoe**   DTM   TT

Hand-forged iron, 5" high, 4 1/2" wide, unsigned.

This is a nicely forged example of a farrier-made horseshoe.

TCF1002   **Nail header**   DTM   MH

Forged iron, 10" long, unsigned, c. 1820 (?).

This is a typical tool utilized for nail-making.

TCF2201   **Nail header**   DTM   MH

Forged iron, 11" long with 1 7/8" wide head, unsigned.

072112T12   **Nail or bolt header**   DTM   TT

Malleable iron, 5" long, 1/2" wide, unsigned.

ID #   Status   Location

Blacksmith, Farrier, and Metalworking Tools

072112T6   **Nail or bolt header**   DTM   TT

Malleable iron, 10 5/8" long, 1 1/4" wide, unsigned.

102100T6   **Nippers**   DTM   MH

Forged iron and steel, 5 5/8" long, 1/2" wide jaw, unsigned.

101701T11   **Pincers**   DTM   MH

Forged iron, 6 1/8" long, 5/8" jaw, unsigned.

This is distinctly hand wrought with clear signs of filing; a generic 19th century tool in a small size.

TCR1002   **Pliers**   DTM   MH

Forged iron, 7 15/16" long, unsigned, probably c. 1820.

These primitive hand-forged pliers are hard to date and have no maker's signature.

TG1010   **Punch**   DTM   MH

Forged iron, 5 1/4" long, unsigned.

121600T3   **Punch**   DTM   MH

Forged iron, 5 1/2" long, signed "G. Platte".

This tool shows distinct evidence of hand work. No Platte is listed in DATM (Nelson 1999).

102904T15   **Ratchet bit**   DTM   MH

Forged iron, 8 3/4" long, 1 3/8" wide cutter, unsigned.

This bit is clearly hand-forged by a smith and has beveling characteristic of an 18th century tool. The cutting end is flared wide and angled. This bit, designed for use in a ratchet drill, is probably an early form of sheet metal cutter.

http://www.davistownmuseum.org/pics/102904t15.jpg

22411T19   **Shears**   DTM   TT

Forged steel, 12" long with a 3" blade, signed "P S Stubs".

http://www.davistownmuseum.org/bioStubs.htm

51311T1   **Silversmith's hammer head**   DTM   TT

Cast steel, 4 1/2" long, 9/16" edge, 1/2" face, unsigned.

33002T15   **Snips**   DTM   MH

Cast steel, 5 1/4" long, 1 3/16" long cutting blades, signed "Brown Germany Cast Steel".

Who was Brown, why did he work in Germany and when did he work?

ID # Status Location

Blacksmith, Farrier, and Metalworking Tools

33002T17 **Snips** DTM MH

Forged iron with welded steel blades, 8 3/8" long, 2" blades, signed with the mark "T-8".

This appears to be a generic early 19th century tin snips with a distinctly smith peened rivet.

http://www.davistownmuseum.org/pics/33002t17.jpg

72801T8 **Square file** DTM MH

Forged or cast steel, 17 1/4" long, 1/2" square, signed "A Prior".

No A. Prior is listed in DATM (Nelson 1999). Who was this smith, where and when did he work?

51610T1 **Stump anvil** DTM MH

Forged iron and steel, wood base, 40" tall, signed "1838".

This was used as a wagon anvil.

http://www.davistownmuseum.org/pics/51610t1web1.jpg
http://www.davistownmuseum.org/pics/51610t1web3.jpg

81200T16 **Thread cutter** DTM MH

Wood and forged steel, 3 3/8" long cutter, 1/2" diameter thread, unsigned.

This is a typical blacksmith-made primitive of the early 19th century. Donated by David McLaughlin.

111001T31 **Tin snips** DTM MH

Cast steel, 5" long, 1 3/8" cutting blade, signed "P. S. Stubs".

This is another example of an imported English tool.

http://www.davistownmuseum.org/bioStubs.htm

121805T18 **Tin snips** DTM MH

German steel, 12" long, 3 3/4" wide at widest handle loop when closed, signed "_USESTAHL" and "___ STEEL" and "F W BRANT" with a sun stamp..

These have a universal handle design.

http://www.davistownmuseum.org/pics/121805t18.jpg

090508T8 **Tin snips** DTM MH

German steel, 15" long, 3 3/8" long cutting blade, signed with a trefoil mark.

TCO1001 **Wedge** DTM MH

Forged iron, 6 3/8" long, 3" wide, unsigned.

It is typical of a small blacksmith-made wedge. One of the most essential items in the tool kits of a Davistown or other frontier settler.

ID #   Status   Location

Blacksmith, Farrier, and Metalworking Tools

021812T6   **Wedge**   DTM   TT

Reforged steel, 3" long, 1 1/4" wide, unsigned.

This is possibly a farriers' or blacksmiths' tool made from a recycled rasp or file. It has a hand-drilled hole of 1/4" diameter that might be used for a handle.

102100T14   **Whitesmiths' shears**   DTM   MH

Forged iron and steel, 14 1/2" long, 3" cutter, 3" stake extension, signed "P S STUBS".

This is an unusual adaptation of common shears to use in a whitesmiths' staking plate.

http://www.davistownmuseum.org/bioStubs.htm

10700T4   **Whitesmiths' shears**   DTM   MH

Forged iron and steel, 14 1/2" long with a 3" long cutter, signed "P S STUBS".

These small whitesmith shears are fitted with a vertical 5/8" square leg for use in a stake plate.

http://www.davistownmuseum.org/bioStubs.htm

Cast Iron Tools and Artifacts

10700CI-1   **Fire company insignia**   BDTM   MH

Cast iron, 12" diameter, signed "F. I. Co".

http://www.davistownmuseum.org/pics/fico.jpg
http://www.davistownmuseum.org/pics/10700CI-1.jpg

TCR3510   **Gluing press (?)**   DTM   MH

Wood and cast iron, 7" long, 4 1/4" wide, unsigned.

TCR3511   **Jig**   DTM   MH

Cast iron and steel, 8" long, 3" wide, unsigned.

The use of this jig is unknown.

TTCI3500   **Pot with three legs**   DTM   MH

Cast iron, 10 3/8" long, 6 1/2" high, unsigned.

TTCI3001   **Sinker mold**   DTM   MH

Cast iron, 5 1/4" long, 2 1/2" wide, unsigned.

TTCI3002   **Steelyard weight**   DTM   MH

Cast iron with a forged iron link, 1 3/4" high, 1 1/2" diameter, unsigned.

An essential component of any general store, steelyards are primitive scales used for weighing flour, sugar, and other foodstuffs.

ID #   Status   Location

Cobbler and Saddler Tools

102904T9   Burnisher   DTM   MH

Forged iron, wooden handle, 10 1/2" long, 1 3/4" diameter, unsigned.

The handle extends through the eye of the ball. This tool is similar in appearance to early cobblers' burnishers and smoothing hammers. If it is not for this use, then what is its function?

http://www.davistownmuseum.org/pics/102904t9.jpg

32802T7   Burnisher   DTM   MH

Steel and wood, 12 1/2" long, 2 3/8" long burnisher, unsigned, c. 1820 (?).

It was probably used by a currier for creasing and burnishing. This tool is extremely uncommon. This is a tentative identification.

http://www.davistownmuseum.org/pics/32802t7.jpg

51201T4   Burnisher   DTM   MH

Wood, 7" long, 13/16" wide, unsigned.

A typical shoemakers' creasing tool, it was also used by upholsterers and other producers of finished leather products.

TCR3002   Burnishing tool   DTM   MH

Steel, brass, and wood, 9" long, unsigned, c. 1820 - 1840.

TCR1013   Burnishing tool   DTM   MH

Steel and wood, 5 5/8" long, 1 3/4" blade, unsigned.

What would have this burnishing tool been used for, if not for leather burnishing?

TCH1005   Cobbler's corrugated burnisher   DTM   MH

Steel, brass ferrule, wood (beech), unsigned.

70701T7   Cobblers' pliers   DTM   MH

Forged and filed iron, signed with the marks "6" and "LS" with a star insignia.

This is a typical early 19th century home shop tool.

TCH1003   Cobblers' slitting cutter (?)   DTM   MH

Forged iron and steel, 6 1/4' long, 1/2" wide blade, signed "BARNETT 37".

DATM (Nelson 1999) lists a Barnett in Attleboro Falls as a manufacturer of Jewelers' tools, 1820.

ID #   Status   Location

Cobbler and Saddler Tools

62406T2   **Curriers' fleshing knife**   DTM   MH

Forged iron and steel, brass ferrule, wood handle, 19 3/4" long with a 11 1/8" burnishing knife, signed "D TOMLINSON PATENT".

Tomlinson worked in Brookfield, CT, 1820 - 1845 and had a July 2, 1820 patent for a curriers' fleshing knife (DATM 1999, 792).

http://www.davistownmuseum.org/pics/62406T2-3.jpg

81200T4   **Curriers' knife**   DTM   MH

Forged steel, brass, and wood, 9 1/2" long, unsigned.

This is a commonplace smallish knife for cutting leather.

TCH1003B   **Group of 7 cobblers' tools**   DTM   MH

Steel, wood, and brass, unsigned.

TCH1004   **Hammer**   DTM   MH

Forged iron, steel, and wood, 2 1/2" long, 2" diameter face, 6" long handle with leather strapping, unsigned.

111001T35   **Leather chamfer tool**   DTM   MH

Wood, brass, steel, 6" long, 1 3/4" blade, signed with an obscure signature.

913108T22   **Leather cutter**   DTM   MH

Hand-forged and hand-filed malleable iron and steel, 5 9/16" long, 3 3/4" wide head, unsigned.

This tool was used for cutting a heart shape in leather or for some other unknown purpose.

TCR1003   **Pliers**   DTM   MH

Cast steel, 11 1/4" long, signed "HUBER TOOL WORKS 5 PHILADA" and on the reverse side of the handle marked "C. STEEL".

DATM (Nelson 1999) lists an H. Huber as a maker of leather tools, Philadelphia, 1836 and English & Huber, Philadelphia, 1834-1842.

7800-T21   **Saddlers' vise**   DTM   MH

Wood, 30" high, 4 1/2" mouth, unsigned, c. 1840.

70701T1   **Shoemakers' box lot**   DTM   MH

Wood, forged iron, and leather, 15 1/4" x 13 1/4", unsigned.

Odd tools, shims, and fragments, all are remnants from an early 19th century shoemakers' home or farm workshop.

ID #		Status	Location

Cobbler and Saddler Tools

TCQ3000   **Tack pry**   DTM   MH

Forged iron and wood, 7 1/4" long, unsigned.

This mundane blacksmith-made tack pry has a replaced handle and is typical of smith-made tools used before the mass production of tack prys in the late 19th century.

TG1007   **Tack pry**   DTM   MH

Forged iron, 11 3/8" long, unsigned.

It is made from a file.

TCH1002   **Tack puller**   DTM   MH

Forged or cast iron, 6 1/2", unsigned, c. 1840.

http://www.davistownmuseum.org/pics/tcp1005a.jpg

Coopers' Tools

81101T6   **Barrel shave**   DTM   MH

Cast steel and wood, 13 1/8" long, 7" curved blade, unsigned, c. 1800 - 1820.

The iron ferrules on this curved shave appear English.

100400T13   **Chamfer knife**   DTM   MHC-G

Wood and cast steel, 17" long with a 9" handle, unsigned.

This type of knife is also called a jigger.

http://www.davistownmuseum.org/pics/100400t13.jpg

81801T13A   **Coopers' _____?**   DTM   MH

Wood, steel, with brass ferrule, 6" long, 4" angle extension, unsigned.

This tool is characterized by the same grooved crease found in all coopers' hammers, though slightly narrower (1/8") than the crease in 81801T13 (1/4"). It is clearly refashioned from recycled file steel and is very unusual. A specific identification is welcomed.

092409T3   **Coopers' adz**   DTM   MH

Reforged steel rasp and wood, 9 1/3" long, 1" wide with a 12" long handle, unsigned.

http://www.davistownmuseum.org/pics/092409T3web2.jpg
http://www.davistownmuseum.org/pics/092409T3web4.jpg

72812T3   **Coopers' adz**   DTM   MH

Forged steel, wood (hickory), 8 3/8" long, 7 1/2" long and 2 1/2" wide head, unsigned.

ID #   Status   Location

Coopers' Tools

TCJ1002   **Coopers' adz**   DTM   MH

Forged iron with steel face and blade, 7" long, 1 1/4" square face, 2 1/2" blade, signed partially obscured "WHITE 1837", mid-19th century.

This was made by L. and I. J. White Co., Buffalo, a prolific New York maker of both edge tools and coopers' tools, 1837f.

http://www.davistownmuseum.org/pics/tcj1002.jpg

7309T1   **Coopers' adz**   LPC   MH

Forged iron and steel, wooden handle, 10" long, 3 1/4" wide blade, 12" long handle, signed "FAXON".

This adz has a southern New Hampshire Merrimack River provenance (S. Pelham) and must have been made by the Faxon clan of Braintree, MA.

http://www.davistownmuseum.org/pics/7309t1web-1.jpg
http://www.davistownmuseum.org/pics/7309t1web-2.jpg

100400T17   **Coopers' auger**   DTM   MH

Forged iron and steel, wood, 14 1/2" long, 17 1/2" handle, signed "2 1/2" indicating the diameter of the auger.

A cooper would use this auger for boring bung holes.

http://www.davistownmuseum.org/pics/100400-17.jpg

101400T5   **Coopers' broad ax**   BDTM   MH

Cast steel and wood, 11 1/2" long, 3 1/2" poll, signed "Roxbury _____ EVRETT CAST STEEL".

No Evrett is listed in DATM (Nelson 1999). This is a typical coopers' broad ax used for trimming staves, etc.

http://www.davistownmuseum.org/pics/101400t5.jpg

TCJ2001A   **Coopers' bung**   DTM   MH

Wood, 6" long, unsigned.

Bungs are used for setting the hoops used on the barrels and casks manufactured in coastal mill towns such as Liberty and Montville.

TCJ2002A   **Coopers' bung**   DTM   MH

Wood and forged iron, 6 1/2" long by 3 1/4" wide with 4" wide strap, unsigned.

It has a blunted end.

72801T6   **Coopers' bung mallet**   DTM   MH

Wood, 1' long, 5 1/2" x 15/16" head, unsigned.

This is an unusually small coopers' bung mallet.

Coopers' Tools

100400T19   Coopers' hammer   DTM   MHC-K

Forged iron and steel (?), 4 1/2" long, 1 5/8" blade, unsigned.

Coopers' hammers can be distinguished by their peculiar narrow concave face. In this example, the face is only 3/4" wide and long years of use have flattened out the concave surface, which was used to work the rims of the barrels.

51100T12   Coopers' hammer   DTM   MH

Cast steel and wood, 5 1/8" long, 1 1/2" wide face, 13" long wood handle, unsigned.

72812T6   Coopers' jigger   DTM   MH

Forged steel with welded edge, 8" long, 2 3/8" wide cutting edge, unsigned.

111900TX1   Coopers' jointer plane   DTM   MH

Wood with a cast steel blade, 75 1/2" long, 4 1/4" wide, 26 1/2" long tapered leg, 3 3/8" wide blade, signed "RYING" on the leg and an illegible signature on the blade.

Is Rying a maker's signature?

TCJ1007   Coopers' mallet   DTM   MH

Wood, 11 3/4" long, 4 1/2" tapered width, domed face 3" wide, unsigned.

TCJ1006   Coopers' plane   DTM   MH

Wood, 12 5/8" long, 2 3/4" wide, unsigned.

It has no blade or wedge and appears unused.

http://www.davistownmuseum.org/pics/tcj1006.jpg#

TCJ1001   Coopers' plane   DTM   MH

Wood with a forged or cast steel blade, 8 1/4" long, 4 1/4" wide, 2 3/8" blade, signed on the blade "2 KENYON SHEFFIELD" with a mark "IK" to the side.

http://www.davistownmuseum.org/pics/tcj1001.jpg

31602T10   Coopers' shave   DTM   MH

Wood and cast steel, 14" long, 3/16" curved cutting edge, signed "L Hardy CAST STEEL".

L. Hardy is not listed in DATM (Nelson 1999). This is probably Ephraim L. Hardy of Brookline, NH.

32412T3   Coopers' spokeshave   DTM   TT-38

Forged malleable iron and steel, 17" long, 2 1/8" blade, unsigned.

The iron body on this tool has evidence of extensive filing and hand-finishing. Courtesy of Liberty Tool Co.

ID #   Status   Location

Coopers' Tools

100400T7   **Croze**   DTM   MHC-K

Wood, cast steel, and forged iron, 14 3/4" long, 4" high, unsigned.

TCJ1003   **Croze**   DTM   MH

Wood and forged iron, 13" long, 2 3/8" wide, unsigned.

This tool is missing its cutter, but it's particularly interesting because it utilizes the discarded blades of a reaper and has nice handmade nails. It is a good example of mid-19th century recycling.

TCJ1005   **Croze**   DTM   MH

Wood with a steel blade, 16" wide, unsigned.

The original blade has been replaced by a Stanley No. 3 smooth plane blade dating from the late 19th c.

TCJ3500   **Howell (chiv)**   DTM   MH

Wood (beech) and cast steel with two iron screws, 10" long, 3 5/8" wide, signed "MORTON ARNOLD" on blade.

There is no Morton Arnold listed in DATM (Nelson 1999). This is a heavy duty coopers' tool used for making wet casks for beer and spirits, also called a beer howell in the US.

http://www.davistownmuseum.org/pics/tcj3500.jpg

81801T7   **Howell (chiv)**   DTM   MH

Wood, forged iron, and cast steel blade, 15 1/2" long, 7 1/4" wide including handle and adjustable screws, signed "H.S.T.   H.N.S" and on the blade "Hand Cast Steel".

It is from southern New Hampshire.

http://www.davistownmuseum.org/pics/81801t7_p1.jpg
http://www.davistownmuseum.org/pics/81801t7_p2.jpg

TCJ1004   **Howell (chiv)**   DTM   MHC-L

Wood (beech), 11 1/2" long, 2 3/4" wide, with room for a skew cutter 1 1/4" wide, signed "B. FARLEY" on the side of the plane and "G. B URGE" on the top.

It is lacking the wedge and blade. DATM (Nelson 1999) reports a Benjamin Farley, Hollis, NH, as a manufacturer of coopers' and edge tools, c.1849. Burge is probably an owner's mark.

81101T7   **Howell (chiv)**   DTM   MH

Cast steel, iron wedge nut, and wood (beech), 12 3/4" diameter, 3 3/8" wide, 1 1/2" curved blade, unsigned.

This is an excellent example of a coopers' tool used to get a barrel ready for the croze.

ID #   Status   Location

Coopers' Tools

100400T6   Leveling plane (sun plane)   DTM   MHC-K

Wood, cast steel blades, 14" long, 3" wide, 2" wide blade, signed with an obscure signature on the blade, probably WHITE 1837.

This is a typical coopers' tool used for barrel-making, it is also called a topping plane. Sun planes are curved in shape. A sun plane is used for leveling the ends of staves after they have been beveled with a coopers' adz. The narrow ledge created by the sun plane serves to hold first the chiv and later the croze to cut the groves on the inside of the staves to hold the cask heads.

http://www.davistownmuseum.org/pics/100400t6.jpg

81101T20   Leveling plane (sun plane)   DTM   MH

Applewood (?) and cast steel, 14 7/8" long, 1 13/16" wide blade, signed "W. Butcher Warranted Cast Steel" on blade, plane marked "SSH" and "SST".

This is an American-made tool with an English cast steel blade.

81101T4   Leveling plane (sun plane)   DTM   MH

Cast steel and applewood, 19 3/4" long, 4" wide, 2 1/8" wide blade, signed "Ward" on blade, plane unsigned.

This is an interesting and uncommon coopers' plane with a Portsmouth, NH, provenance. The blade is English.

TCJ3501   Mallet   DTM   MH

Wood and iron, 5 1/2" diameter with a 10" diameter grapple, unsigned.

It has a replaced handle and an iron grapple.

100400T5   Spokeshave   BDTM   MHC-K

Wood, cast steel, and brass, 19" long, 5 1/2" blade, 5 1/2" brass plate, unsigned.

This Maine-made unsigned spokeshave is the largest ever noted by this editor. With a Lubec shipyard provenance, this shave was likely originally constructed for use by a cooper. When found this tool was associated with other coopers' tools.

Domestic Utensils

30201T3   Bathtub   DTM   LTC

Tin, aprox. 46" in diameter, unsigned.

This is what you used before the era of cast iron bathtubs and running water. It is on display at the Davistown Museum Liberty Tool Annex across the street from the Museum, on the second floor. This tub was apparently made in the Midwest (Minnesota?) and brought east to Maine.

ID #   Status   Location

Domestic Utensils

91303C1   Bean pot   DTM   MH

Red earthenware, 5" high, 5" diameter, unsigned.

This is a typical kitchen utensil of a working family or farm anywhere in New England in the early or mid-nineteenth century. It is similar to redware produced at Woolwich, ME, and numerous other New England locations.

TCR3501   Bench   DTM   MH

Wood (spruce), 24" long, 9" wide, unsigned.

82512T2   Butter knife   DTM   TT

Shear steel, stag horn, 9 7/8" long with 6" blade, signed "SANDERSON SHEAR STEEL".

This knife was originally part of a collection that belonged to Oliver Wendell Holmes. There were many Sandersons in Sheffield, England that made knives.

TAB3001   Butter spoon   DTM   MH

Maple, 3 7/8" wide, unsigned.

121805T24   Cheese auger (?)   DTM   MH

Drop forged steel or iron, 22 1/4" long, 1/2" wide, handle is 2 5/8" wide oval, unsigned.

Possibly this is a cheese tester? Look for it in the unidentified tool area.

http://www.davistownmuseum.org/pics/121805t24_p2.jpg

43006T1   Cheese cutter   DTM   MH

Wood, forged iron, and steel wire, 21 5/8" long, 18 5/8" wide, including a 6" handle, unsigned.

This is a nicely forged and very rare large early 19th century implement.

5303PR1   Cribbage board   LPC   MH

Wood and brass, 31 7/8" long, 4 1/2" wide, unsigned.

A spar salvaged from a transpacific China trade vessel wreck, c. 1820, was made into a cribbage board and used for the lifetime of the unidentified salvage vessel (another China trader), which made a number of trips around Cape Horn. It is from a Chelsea, MA, seamans' collection via the Liberty Tool Co., around 1985.

102100T27   Crimper   DTM   MH

Wood with copper coin, unsigned.

The purpose of this crimper is unknown. Note the use of an old coin or token as the cutter. The words "Victory Del Grat__" are visible on the side of the coin. A woman's head can be seen in the center of the coin.

ID #   Status   Location

Domestic Utensils

52512T1 **Curling iron**   DTM   MH

Forged steel, 4 1/2" long, 7/8" wide, signed "JOSEPH LINGARD REGISTERED TRADEMARK" with a knife and tweezers logo.

Courtesy of Liberty Tool Co.

111001T41 **Doll's dress**   DTM   MH

Hand woven flax with wool trim, 14" high, unsigned.

This is from Abiel Walker's attic in Alna, Maine. The date of production is unknown.

22601P1 **Firkin**   DTM   MH

Wood, 22 1/4" high, 14 1/4" top diameter, 16 1/2" bottom diameter, unsigned.

913108T37A **Food chopper**   DTM   MH

Recycled file, forged iron, and wooden handle, 6 1/2" long, 7 3/8" wide blade, unsigned.

41801T3 **Ladle**   DTM   MH

Forged iron, 14" long, 2 3/8" diameter ladle, signed with the mark "3".

This is a typical blacksmith-made tool of the early 19th century.

92911T13 **Mortar and pestle**   DTM   TT

Wood, wrought iron, and leather, 9" tall, 6" diameter mortar; 14" long, 1 3/4" diameter tapering pestle, unsigned.

The mortar is made from a log that was hollowed out and has a blackened bottom to seal the end grain. There is a hand-forged iron ring on the bottom of the mortar. The mortar has a leather handle. The pestle is wooden with a leather braid fastened about 1/4 of the way up from the working end. This might have had a maritime use for mixing caulking.

TAB1302 **Pestle**   DTM   MH

Wood, 31" long, 4" diameter pestle, unsigned.

This was probably used for grinding up grain.

CER3500 **Pitcher**   DTM   MH

Earthenware, 7 3/8" high, 4 1/2" diameter, unsigned.

It has a cracked handle.

CER3501 **Plate**   DTM   MH

Earthenware, floblue, 8 3/4" diameter, signed "The Temple".

ID #   Status   Location

Domestic Utensils

7800-T20   **Potty chair**   DTM   MH

Wood, 21 1/2" high, 12 1/2" wide, unsigned, c. 1820.

51100T5   **Scissors**   DTM   MH

Cast steel, 12" long, signed "Jonathan Crookes".

Jonathan Crookes and Son worked in Sheffield, England from 1827-1910.

TCC3006   **Scissors**   DTM   MH

Forged steel, 10" long, 4 1/2" blade, unsigned, c. 1810, could be 18th century.

These are generic forged steel scissors

121805T11   **Shears**   DTM   MH

Wrought iron, 9 7/8" long, unsigned.

This is an unusual smith-forged shear made entirely of wrought iron with no thought of steeling. It is a totally useless but unique tool.

http://www.davistownmuseum.org/pics/121805t11_p2.jpg

TCH1301   **Shoes (pair)**   DTM   MH

Leather, 8" long, unsigned.

42602T8   **Skates**   DTM   MH

Forged steel, curly maple, leather thongs, forged iron heel holders, 5" diameter arch, signed with an obscured mark "___W WIRTES IN ___MSCREID".

These are probably imported German steel blades manufactured into skates in the United States with American grown curly maple. Not all imported steel came from Sheffield. These skates have the look of early skates (c. 1800) with their sharply curved front runners.

33002T5   **Spatula**   DTM   MH

Forged iron, 6 1/4" long, 1" wide, unsigned.

It is nicely forged by a blacksmith. With traces of old lead paint, this is probably a precursor of a putty knife used for glazing windows.

http://www.davistownmuseum.org/pics/33002t5.jpg

TCR3512   **Stool**   DTM   MH

Wood, 18" long, 9 3/4" wide, 8 3/4" high, unsigned.

TAB3502   **Table**   DTM   MH

Wood, 10 3/8" long, 6 1/8" wide, unsigned.

One of a number of small benches and tables used by the museum for display.

ID #   Status   Location

Domestic Utensils

3912LTC3 **Taper candle mold**   DA   TT (Pub)

Tin, 10" long, 4" wide, 4" high, unsigned.

This is a mold for pouring wax candles. Courtesy of Liberty Tool Co.

TAB1016 **Tapered wooden box**   DTM   MH

Wood with square nails, 11 3/4" x 11 3/4", unsigned.

TBB1004D **Tool box**   DTM   MH

Wood with forged iron handles, 22" long, 1' wide, 9 1/2" high, signed "L_ I_ JONES West Barnsta" (ble), c. 1820 - 1840.

This toolbox contains blacksmith and gunsmith tools of the 18th century that were in it when it was found in southern Massachusetts. The box dates to a later period than most of the tools.

TCR1022 **Turned burl**   DTM   MH

Wood, 3 1/2" high, 3 1/2" wide, unsigned.

70701T10 **Tweezers**   DTM   MH

Cast steel, signed "Joseph Lisaro Sheffield England" and "Jos. F. McCoy Co.".

McCoy is not listed in DATM (Nelson 1999), he probably is a vendor.

31602T14 **Weights (collection)**   BDTM   T

Bronze, 3 1/2", 2" and 1 13/16" wide, unsigned except for troy weight descriptions.

Three crucibles with three different varieties of weights.

http://www.davistownmuseum.org/bioEpstein.htm

7800-T15 **Whale oil lamp**   BDTM   MHC-G

Tin, 4 1/4" high, unsigned, c. 1820.

This is an excellent example of the work of a whitesmith.

Files

TCL1001 **Rasp**   DTM   MH

Forged steel, 6" long with a 4 1/2" long handle, signed "J. DAY & CO.".

DATM (Nelson 1999) lists James Day of Gloucester, MA, as a maker of planes, c. 1780. The manufacturer's signature on this is distinctly 19th century in style. This tool is notable because it came from the tool chest of David Livingston, which was purchased by the Jonesport Wood Co. around 1980. Livingston worked as a woodcarver in the Boston area and his tool chest contained a large number of edge tools and a great Davis level. More biographical information is wanted about the life and work of David Livingston.

Historic Maritime III (1800-1840): Boomtown Years & the Dawn of the Industrial Revolution

Files

22411T29   **Triangular file**   DTM   TT

Hand cut German or cast steel, 14 3/4" long, 12" x 13/16" cutting surface, signed "GENUINE" "P S STUBS" "ENGLAND".

http://www.davistownmuseum.org/bioStubs.htm

Fishing Implements

30311T1   **Eel spear**   DTM   TT

Hand-forged iron, 18" long, 4" wide, unsigned.

This spear originally had 8 tines, one is missing.

7309T3   **Eel spear**   LPC   MH

Malleable iron and wood, 15 7/8" long, 6 1/2" wide, 78" long wooden handle, unsigned.

This tool is clearly forge-welded. It was found mixed with an assortment of farm tools in the Merrimack River drainage area (S. Pelham, NH).

http://www.davistownmuseum.org/pics/7309t3web-1.jpg

21201T8   **Mackerel plow**   DTM   MH

Iron, slate, lead, brass, steel, and wood, 6 3/4" long, 4" handle, 1 5/8" curved blade and a brass ferrule, unsigned.

This unusual tool has a steel shank fitted with a 2" curved lead tip into which is inserted a steel cutting blade. This is a tool that would have been commonly encountered on the decks of Maine's 19th century mackerel fleet. A mackerel plow is made of wood and slate rather than wood and iron or steel to prevent rusting on the open ocean. The form has an appearance that is similar to Native American implements such as the crooked knife suggesting the possibility that this tool is Native American in origin, design, and perhaps manufacture. It is also called a fish gut. Two additional examples of a mackerel plow may be seen at the Penobscot Maritime Museum in Searsport and the Maine Maritime Museum in Bath. The die.net online dictionary says a mackerel plow is "an instrument for creasing the sides of lean mackerel to improve their appearance." A further description is given on www.lostatsea.ca/mackplow.htm: "When the fish has been thrown from the seine to the schooner's deck, men split them down the back with large knives, the operation being performed with one sweep of the hand. The plow is then picked up and in two or three deft slashes less than an eighth of an inch deep parallel to the backbone opens the flesh in such a manner that it looks as if superabundance of fat had burst the mackerel just as it does his more corpulent fellow. " Thus the fish looks as a fatter one would. "Everybody connected with the industry knows that a fat mackerel will break open on pressure of the hand after it has been split down the back in process of cleaning."

102212T1   **Mackerel plow**   DTM   TT

Wood (beech), steel, 7 1/4" long, 3/4" wide, 1" cutting edge, unsigned.

ID #   Status   Location

Fishing Implements

TAB1007   **Mackerel plow**   DTM   MH

Curved wood handle with a slate cutter, 7 5/8" long handle, 13/16" cutter, unsigned.

http://www.davistownmuseum.org/pics/tab1007.jpg
http://www.davistownmuseum.org/pics/tab1007_p2.jpg

102503P2   **Net menders (2)**   DTM   MH

Wood, unsigned.

This pair of net menders have a coastal Maine provenance and were used to mend seine nets and other fishing gear.

Hammers

041505T10   **Ball peen hammer**   DTM   MH

Forged iron and forged steel (?), 6 1/4" long, 1 3/8" diameter face, 7/8" diameter peen, unsigned.

This hand-forged blacksmith-made hammer is made from wrought iron and/or low carbon steel. Its face shows the wear characteristic of a used tool with low carbon content and with ductile characteristics. It is on the far right of the photograph.

http://www.davistownmuseum.org/pics/041505t10.jpg

071704T6   **Carriage-makers' tack hammer**   DTM   MH

Forged iron, wood, 6 3/4" long, 7/16" diameter head, unsigned, c. 1820.

This tool is distinctly hand-forged with a new wooden handle.

TCN1002   **Claw hammer**   DTM   MH

Forged iron and/or steel, 5 1/4" long with a 1" square face, signed "G LINDLEY", c. 1820.

No G. Lindley is listed in DATM (Nelson 1999).

http://www.davistownmuseum.org/pics/tcz1006.jpg

TCM1004   **Claw hammer**   DTM   MH

Forged iron and/or steel, 2 1/2" long, 1/2" circular face, unsigned.

What would such a small hammer be used for?

TBD1003   **Claw hammer**   DTM   MH

Forged iron, 5" long, 15/16" face, signed "TACONY 2".

The Tacony Edge Tool and Hammer Factory was located in the greater Philadelphia area and was owned by C. Hammond. The Tacony factory can be found illustrated here in a plate from 1877: http://www.philageohistory.org/rdic-images/view-image.cfm/HGSv13.1189

5413T1   **Claw hammer**   DTM   TT

Forged steel, 7" long handle, 4 3/4" long head, 1" face, signed "S.S." "3".

Historic Maritime III (1800-1840): Boomtown Years & the Dawn of the Industrial Revolution

Hammers

82500T1   Claw hammer   DTM   MH

Forged iron and wood, 12" long, 4 1/2" long head, 4 1/4" long straps, unsigned.

This is a typical early 19th century hammer.

52603T21   Claw hammer   DTM   MH

Forged iron, 1 1/4" long, 4 1/2" head, unsigned.

71401T5   Cobblestone hammer   DTM   MH

Forged steel and wood, 13 1/16" long, unsigned.

This is an elegant example of the common cobblestone hammer of the 18th and early 19th centuries. It was probably manufactured after 1800.

http://www.davistownmuseum.org/pics/71401t5.jpg

102012T1   Fence post maul   DTM   HC

Wood (oak?), 40" long, 11" wide head, 8 1/2" diameter face, unsigned.

TCM1003   Hammer   DTM   MH

Forged iron and steel, 5 3/8" long, unsigned.

It is clearly forged with many bevels and the use is unknown.

TCM1005A   Hammer   DTM   MH

Forged iron and steel, 4" long, 11/16" square face with 1 1/4" straps, signed "H M CHRISTENSEN BROCKTON MASS", c. 1840 (?).

DATM (Nelson 1999) lists Christen & Son as making hammers in Brockton, MA with no dates. It is also marked "WALSH."

TCY1002   Hammer   DTM   MH

Forged or cast steel, 6" long including the head, unsigned.

It has an unusual pointed head and unknown use.

112400T2   Hammer   DTM   MH

Cast steel and wood, 10 5/8" long handle, 3 3/4" long head, 5/8" square face, signed "R.A. FISH".

No R. A. Fish is listed in DATM (Nelson 1999).

22411T8   Hammer head   DTM   TT

Hand-forged iron and steel, 5" long, 1 1/8" x 1 1/8" head, 3 1/2" long handle brackets, unsigned.

This is a claw hammer with forge-welded brackets used to secure the handle.

Historic Maritime III (1800-1840): Boomtown Years & the Dawn of the Industrial Revolution

Hammers

913108T20   **Hammer head**   DTM   MH

Hand-forged malleable iron, 9 1/2" long, unsigned.

041505T18   **Hammer heads (6)**   DTM   MH

Drop-forged or cast steel, Not measured, signed on one cross peen "WARNER & NOBLE" "CAST STEEL" and two claws "HAND MADE".

This hammer study group consists of three claw, two cross peen, and one anomalous hammer head, circa 1800 - 1920. The two claw hammers marked handmade are drop-forged with later hand filing on them. According to DATM (Nelson 1999) Warner & Noble made tools c. 1894, location unknown. The other cross peen is an early looking (c. 1820 - 1840) upholsterers' hammer. The unique hammer with an extended claw is forged iron, c. 1800 - 1840. What was its use?

http://www.davistownmuseum.org/pics/041505t18.jpg

31602T12   **Mallet**   DTM   MH

Oak handle with ironwood burl striking head, 11 1/2" long, 4" diameter and 3 1/8" high head, unsigned.

Three smith-made (?) screws attach the handle to the head.

041505T11   **Miniature hammer**   DTM   MH

Cast or forged steel with a wooden handle, 6" long including handle, 2 1/2" head, 1/2" diameter face, unsigned.

This tiny hammer is an uncommon form and may have been used by a jeweler or metalsmith. It is in the center of the photograph.

http://www.davistownmuseum.org/pics/041505t10.jpg

041505T7   **Sledge hammer**   DTM   MH

Forged iron and steel, wooden handle, 8 1/2" long including the handle, 4 1/4" long head, 1 1/2" and 2 2/4" faces, unsigned.

This rather primitive looking sledge hammer was possibly made as a one-of-a-kind sledge by a blacksmith. There is some hint of "steeling" on the faces, was it reworked and re-tapered after casting? It is in the top left of the photograph. This hammer is part of the hammer study group.

http://www.davistownmuseum.org/pics/041505t7.jpg

102800T3   **Sledge hammer**   DTM   MH

Forged steel, 5 1/8" long, 1 15/16" square face, signed "G KITTREDGE", 1840 or earlier.

With a New Hampshire provenance, this hammer is probably related to the Jonathan Kittredge hammer-making enterprises of Canaan, NH. This 5 lb (?) sledge is also marked with an owner's signature, "Seth C. Patten".

ID #   Status   Location

Hammers

72801T7   **Sledge hammer**   DTM   MH

Forged iron, 5 1/8" long, 1 5/8" square face, unsigned.

This primitively-forged sledge hammer appears to have been made with many impurities and defects. How old is this hammer and who made it?

913108T19   **Sledge hammer head**   DTM   MH

Hand-forged malleable iron or low carbon steel, 3 3/4" long, unsigned.

This small sledge hammer was made from direct process bloomery iron or natural steel

TCM1005   **Snowball hammer**   DTM   MH

Forged iron, 9 1/2" long, iron handle 4 1/2" long, 1/2" round face, unsigned.

Also called a snowshoe hammer or snow knocker, this is a prototypical tool used for removing ice and snow from the shoes of horses. See Eric Sloane's (1964) "A Museum of Early American Tools" for an illustration of another snowball hammer.

http://www.davistownmuseum.org/pics/tcm1005.jpg

032203T3   **Snowball hammer**   DTM   MH

Reforged steel rasp, 8 3/4" long, 2 3/16" cutter at one end, unsigned.

This is a typical example of a late 18th century or early 19th century recycling of a precious forged steel rasp. After becoming dull, this rasp was reshaped into a tool for knocking the snow and ice from a shoed horse. What was the cutting edge used for? Notice that the malleable wrought iron top edge of the tool has been bent over from use, whereas the steel cutting edge shows no evidence of wear. This illustrates the varying amount of carbon in different sections of this tool.

http://www.davistownmuseum.org/pics/032203t3_p1.jpg
http://www.davistownmuseum.org/pics/032203t3_p2.jpg

51201T6   **Stone hammer**   DTM   MH

Forged iron and steel, 7 1/2" long, unsigned, c. 1840 (?).

This is a smith-made double ended splitting maul.

42405T7   **Upholsterers' hammer**   DTM   MH

Forged iron and steel with wooden handle, 5 1/4" long, 5/8" diameter head, 10" long handle, unsigned.

This is a nice example of a smith-made hand-forged strapped hammer, possibly used for carriage interiors.

Ice Tools

ID #   Status   Location

Ice Tools

101400T14   **Ice tongs**   DTM   MH

Forged iron, 16" long, unsigned.

These are a particularly graphic example of blacksmith-made ice tongs. Note the distinct marks of hand-forging just below the handles.

Knives

TCR1006   **Cleaver or block knife**   DTM   MH

Cast steel, 12" long, 5 5/8" blade, signed with a small obscure signature on the blade that is no longer legible.

It is probably a block knife with one piece construction. It has a hole in the handle for convenient hanging.

913108T15   **Crooked knife**   DTM   MH

Recycled file blade, copper wire, and wood, 8 1/2" long, 3/4" long blade, unsigned.

This is typical of the forge-welded crooked knife used by the settlers of North America for basketmaking and other uses.

TG1009   **Knife**   DTM   MH

Forged steel and wood, 9 1/2" long, 3 3/8" handle, unsigned.

TCN1001A   **Knife**   DTM   MH

Forged iron or steel, 8 1/2" long with a 4" blade, unsigned.

It is made from a recycled saw blade?

TCR1007   **Knife**   DTM   MH

Forged iron and steel, wood handle, 17" long, 9 3/4" blade, unsigned.

The blade is distinctly hand-forged, with a handmade handle. What is the purpose of this tool -- was it used for skinning?

121805T20   **Knife**   DTM   MH

Steel with a tropical wood handle, 16 1/4" long including a 5" handle, signed "JC _____ F", too obscure to read.

This knife appears hand-forged, hand-finished, and is probably pattern welded.

http://www.davistownmuseum.org/pics/121805t20.jpg

72801T13   **Knife**   DTM   MH

Cast steel, wood handle, signed "J Ward & Co. Riverside Mass".

J Ward & Co. is an unlisted in DATM (Nelson 1999), Boston knife maker. This is a common kitchen knife.

ID #   Status   Location

Knives

93011T19   **Knife**   DTM   TT

Cast steel and wooden handle, 9" long, 3/4" wide, signed "J. WARD & CO." "RIVERSIDE, MASS".

913108T40   **Knife**   DTM   MH

Steel, brass, and wood, 5" long, signed with a circle touchmark containing 5 dots.

This knife has hand-forged notches and an unusual serrated pattern on the top of the blade. The blade is deeply scored on each side.

81200T14   **Knife**   DTM   MHC

Steel, rosewood, and lead, 9 1/2" long, signed "J Ward Riverside Mass", c. 1840.

It has an early lead inlaid handle.

TCN1002A   **Oyster knife**   DTM   MH

Forged iron or steel with copper rivets, 5 1/2" long, 2 1/2" blade, unsigned, c. 1820.

TCN1001   **Oyster knife (?)**   DTM   MH

Forged iron or steel, 7 3/4" long; the blade has a maximum width of 3/4", signed with the touchmark "D".

What other use could this knife have?

102100T20   **Palette knife**   DTM   MH

Rosewood and cast steel, 6 1/4" long, 3 5/8" handle, signed "FWD & Co".

100400T11A   **Putty knife**   DTM   MHC-G

Cast steel, brass, and rosewood handle, 7" long, 1 3/8" wide blade, signed "J. RUSSELL & CO GREEN RIVER WORKS", c. 1836 - 1840.

Working first in Deerfield in 1832 utilizing this name, John Russell moved to Greenfield in 1836. The knives and cutlery bearing this imprint are among the best ever made in the United States. Many later important tool companies with the name Russell descend from this, the original Green River Works (Nelson 1999, 679-80).

http://www.davistownmuseum.org/bioRussel.html

Logging Tools

TCO1002   **Bark spud**   DTM   MH

Forged iron, 25" long, 2 1/2" diameter, unsigned, c. 1820-1840.

It has a beveled iron shaft. This is among the most essential tools in the first tool kits of the Davistown settlers. Its purpose is the removal of bark from logs prior to the milling of lumber. It is also used to remove hemlock bark for use in a tannery.

ID #   Status   Location

Logging Tools

31808PC6   **Bark spud**   DTM   MH

Malleable iron and steel, wood, 27 1/2" long, 9 1/2" long blade, unsigned.

7309T7   **Cant dog**   DTM   MH

Forged malleable iron, wood handle, 52 1/2" long, 14 1/4" long cant dog, unsigned.

This is what a cant dog looked like before Mr. Peavey came along. It is a typical early 19th century log rolling tool.

http://www.davistownmuseum.org/pics/7309t7web-1.jpg

101900T3   **Peavey**   DTM   MH

Forged and cast iron, 13 1/4" long, unsigned.

This is a generic peavey, but with a clearly hand-forged handle casing.

http://www.davistownmuseum.org/pics/101900t3.jpg

121412T17   **Pickaroon**   DTM   TT

Forged steel, wood (rosewood), 10" long, 8 1/2" long handle, 6 1/2" long head, unsigned.

102904T5   **Pickaroon**   DTM   MH

Forged iron and natural steel, wood, 28 1/2" long including 26 1/4" handle, 7" from poll to point, unsigned.

This tool was formed out of bar stock and pounded into its generic form by a blacksmith at his forge. The tip is natural steel; it has some indications of hand filing. Pickaroons are among the essential tools of the timber harvester; after felling trees and trimming off the branches, the pickaroon would be used by the woodsman to pull away the branches prior to the tree being dragged out of the woods and into the nearest river for transport to a water mill. It then would be used for maneuvering the smaller logs.

http://www.davistownmuseum.org/pics/102904t5.jpg

101400T17   **Race knife (timber scribe)**   DTM   MH

Cast or forged steel and wood, 5 3/4" long with a 2" slitter, unsigned.

It is used to mark the ends of planks and logs.

http://www.davistownmuseum.org/pics/101400T17.jpg

100400T18   **Race knife (timber scribe)**   DTM   MHC-F

Cast steel and wood, 6 1/2" long, unsigned.

This is a typical lumbermans' tool for marking and identifying the trees cut by loggers before they would be floated down to the sawmills. It has a leather pouch for storage.

http://www.davistownmuseum.org/pics/100400t18.jpg
http://www.davistownmuseum.org/pics/100400t18-3.jpg

Historic Maritime III (1800-1840): Boomtown Years & the Dawn of the Industrial Revolution

Logging Tools

012812T9   **Scraper**   DTM   MH

Reforged steel, 12 1/2" long, 2 1/4" wide, unsigned.

This curved scraping tool could be for bark and is made from a reforged file or rasp.

31901T1   **Tho-shot**   DTM   MH

Wood (spruce), 30" long, 3 1/2" diameter end knurl, unsigned.

It may also be spelled thorough-short or thorough-shot. A tho-shot is the wooden pin used to secure log booms for the spring log drives. The tho-shot in the Davistown Museum had been for sale for about 25 years, first at the Jonesport Wood Co. in West Jonesport and then at the Hulls Cove Tool Barn for $16.00. There were no buyers during this period for this unidentified wood primitive. On March 2, 2001, Robert Lawrence was visiting the Davistown Museum for the specific purpose of loaning his tho-shot to the Museum collection when he spotted our (as yet unidentified) specimen next to the flax breaker in the main hall. For more information on the history of the tho-shot, click on the bio link.

http://www.davistownmuseum.org/pics/31901t1.jpg
http://www.davistownmuseum.org/bioThoShot.htm

50101T3   **Tho-shot**   DTM   MH

Wood, 3' high, 5 1/2" diameter end knurl, unsigned.

This tho-shot is broken off at the notch. It was donated to the Davistown Museum by Robert Lawrence.

http://www.davistownmuseum.org/bioThoShot.htm

Measuring Tools

032203T5   **Adjustable bevel**   DTM   MH

Rosewood, brass, and steel, 7 3/4" long handle, 12" blade, signed "C G PINKHAM" possibly an owner's mark.

This nicely made adjustable bevel was probably manufactured in England and then imported to the U.S. in the early 19th century. The design of the set back brass adjustment nut appears English. The handle is made of high quality rosewood. A check of English tool pattern catalogs might locate the specific design.

http://www.davistownmuseum.org/pics/032203t5_p2.jpg

81101T19   **Adjustable calipers**   DTM   MH

Cast steel, 5" long, signed "P. S. Stubs".

This finely cast caliper is another fine example of the Stubs empire of tool manufacturing.

http://www.davistownmuseum.org/bioStubs.htm

ID #   Status   Location

Measuring Tools

111002T4   Adjustable dividers   DTM   MH

Forged iron, 1' 7 3/4" long, unsigned.

These are a nice example of blacksmith-made dividers of the early 19th century. These were probably used either by a shipwright or wagon-maker.

72712LTC2   Bevel   DA   TT (Pub)

Wood (rosewood), 11 1/2" long handle, 10 1/4" long blade, 1 1/8" wide, unsigned.

Courtesy of the Liberty Tool Company.

81212LTC11   Brass body steel point divider   NOM   TT (Pub)

Cast brass, steel, body is 5 1/2" long, 1 3/4" wide when closed, steel point is 6 1/4" long, signed "AMALO".

101701T12   Calipers   DTM   MH

Cast steel, 6 5/8" long, signed "P. S. Stubbs".

This is a clear example of an English pattern that was later copied by American companies such as T. Stevens, Chicopee Falls, MA, 1844 - 1903. Also using the same pattern was the Boker Co., which DATM (Nelson 1999, 98) indicates was a German manufacturer exporting tools in the 19th century. This tool is also marked with numerous stars -- probably an owner's mark. Stevens as well as Boker copied the English style of adjustable calipers, which were originally European in origin. Did English toolmakers who emigrated from Sheffield bring this prototype with them?

http://www.davistownmuseum.org/bioStubs.htm

111001T15   Calipers   DTM   MH

Cast steel, 4 5/16" long, signed "Cast Steel".

Probably an early 19th century tool, these calipers show signs of hand work and careful filing. Are they an English import or an unsigned American tool?

31012T1   Circular wire gauge   DTM   MH

German or sheaf steel, 3 1/8" diameter, signed "PS Stubbs".

http://www.davistownmuseum.org/bioStubs.htm

11301T4   Dividers   BDTM   MH

Forged iron and steel, 18" long, signed "I Wilson" with another mark of "H Wilson" in a larger font.

Possibly this is Increase Wilson (b. 1785, d. 1861), New London, CT. Wilson made a wide variety of hand tools beginning in 1815. This is the finest pair of dividers in the Museum collection with nicely wrought and peened joints, nuts, arms, and legs. It has beveled central leg shafts. It is an early 19th century masterpiece of forged iron and steel. The transition to steel tips on the legs is distinctly visible.

Historic Maritime III (1800-1840): Boomtown Years & the Dawn of the Industrial Revolution

ID #   Status   Location

Measuring Tools

83102T8   **Dividers**   DTM   MH

Forged iron, 12" long, signed "W H Hale".

No W H Hale is listed in DATM (Nelson 1999).

914108T5   **Dividers**   DTM   MH

Steel, 8" long, signed "G. BUCK".

111001T26   **Double calipers**   DTM   MH

Cast steel, 4" long, signed "E. A. Belcher".

DATM (Nelson 1999) lists many Belchers as making rules and bevels in New York and Providence, RI as early as 1825, but no listing for E. A. Belcher.

61204T10   **Folding rule**   DTM   MH

Boxwood and brass, 24" long, signed "RICHARDSON & CO" and "MIDDLETON".

Asa Richardson worked in Middleton, Connecticut from 1820 - 1838.

http://www.davistownmuseum.org/pics/61204T10_p1.jpg

TCQ1001   **Framing square**   DTM   MH

Forged iron, signed "J. F. Brown", c. 1820.

The square is hand-stamped. This maker is not listed in DATM (Nelson 1999). It is an American made form. Who was J. F. Brown and where did he work?

121906T1   **Framing square**   DTM   MH

Forged iron or steel, 12" x 24 ", signed "S. HAWS PATENTED WARRANTED STEEL".

This square is clearly hand-stamped, with increments of inches on one side and a complex numeration of board rule (?) on the other. Of particular interest is the notation "STEEL"; though clearly not cast steel, this mark may suggest the use of either blister steel or puddled steel. Alternatively, it may suggest an awareness that malleable iron, having a carbon content greater than wrought iron, is a form of low carbon steel and is so marked. The hand-stamping on the square suggests it was made prior to 1850, pre-dating the use of the dividing machine for marking squares as well as the availability of domestically made cast steel. Whatever "steel" was used in this square was most likely made in Vermont, which at this time had not only cementation furnaces for making blister steel but also reverbatory furnaces for decarburizing or fining cast iron, in which the knowledgeable forge-masters could halt the decarburization process to produce puddled steel -- a surprisingly common form of steel before the Civil War.

http://www.davistownmuseum.org/bioEagleSq.htm

30801T1   **Framing square**   BDTM   MH

Cast steel, 18" x 24", signed "CAST STEEL J. ESSEX WARRANTED NO I".

DATM (Nelson 1999) lists J. Essex as working in Bennington, VT, 1830 - 1859 and then merging with the Eagle Sq. Co. This is an historic American tool.

Measuring Tools

102100T15   Framing square   DTM   MH

Forged iron, 24" long, 12" wide, unsigned.

This is a typical example of a mid-19th century blacksmith hand-stamped framing square made just prior to their mass production.

040103T9   Framing square   DTM   MH

Forged iron, 24" by 15", signed "HAWES Patent 1825" "$3.50" with owner's mark "Charles Scot".

DATM (Nelson 1999) indicates Silas Hawes made squares in Shaftsbury, VT, 1814 - 1828, but that several other local makers also marked their squares "HAWES PAT". These were predecessors to the famous Eagle Square Co. organized in 1859. This is a fine example of a used hand-forged, hand-stamped square of the early days of the republic.

http://www.davistownmuseum.org/pics/040103t9_p1.jpg
http://www.davistownmuseum.org/bioEagleSq.htm

41203T9   Framing square   DTM   MH

Forged iron, 13 1/2" by 12", signed "M Hildick".

DATM (Nelson 1999) notes M. Hildick worked in Walsall, which is in the UK. This is another hand-forged, hand-stamped, framing square.

63001T1   Framing square   DTM   MH

Forged iron, 12" x 24", signed with a hand stamped "J Walker".

This tool has a Maine origin and may be the product of J. Walker of Scarborough, Maine, 1831f. Or it could be from the workshop of J. Walker of W. Hampton, NH, no date available, listed in DATM (Nelson 1999).

http://www.davistownmuseum.org/publications/volume10.html

41203T10   Framing square   DTM   MH

Forged iron, 23" by 12", unsigned.

This typical hand-forged, hand-stamped square is interesting in that the short edge has broken off and been entirely replaced by a newly produced, welded, and peened section. It is a great example of Yankee thrift.

63001T2   Framing square   DTM   MH

Forged iron, 12" x 24", signed "W Smallwood".

DATM (Nelson 1999) lists Smallwood as a maker of squares with no date or location. This tool has a central Maine origin and was probably made in Maine, but where?

http://www.davistownmuseum.org/publications/volume10.html

TBE1003   Level   DTM   MH

Brass, 2 1/2" long, 7/16" wide, unsigned, c. 1820.

This is an example of a user-made tool.

ID #   Status   Location

Measuring Tools

TCQ2201   **Navigational rule**   DTM   MHC-D

Wood, 24" long, 1 3/4" wide, 1/4" deep, unsigned.

040103T8   **Parallel rule**   DTM   MH

Rosewood and brass, 15" long, 2 1/4" wide, 5 1/4" wide when fully opened, unsigned.

This nicely made parallel rule was recovered with the mariners' rule (040103T3). Also used by architects and draftsmen, this rule was probably used for navigation.

http://www.davistownmuseum.org/pics/040103t8_p1.jpg
http://www.davistownmuseum.org/pics/040103t8_p3.jpg

91303T14   **Parallel rule**   DTM   MH

Brass and ebony, 6" long, unsigned.

Navigators and architects often used parallel rules. This one is the smallest size normally made.

71401T18   **Plumb bob**   LPC   MH

Cast brass, 4 3/4" long, unsigned.

This is probably an early product of the Stanley Tool Co. and an excellent example of the most sought after of 19th century plumb bobs.

http://www.davistownmuseum.org/pics/71401t18.jpg

51201T9   **Screw clamp**   DTM   MH

Wood, 3 7/8" wide with 5" long wooden screws, signed with the mark "5".

This clamp is from the Simon Willard toolbox.

http://www.davistownmuseum.org/pics/51201T9.jpg
http://www.davistownmuseum.org/bioWillard.htm

81101T16   **Screw plate**   DTM   MH

Cast steel, 10 1/8" long, 3 5/8" handle, signed "P. S. Stubs H".

This is an exquisite example of a Stubs tool. This screw plate is used to make clock and gun screws.

http://www.davistownmuseum.org/bioStubs.htm

32708T51   **Trammel point**   DTM   MH

Bronze and oak, 14" long, points 5" from screw to tip, unsigned.

http://www.davistownmuseum.org/pics/32708t51-1.jpg

TCP1002   **Try square**   DTM   MH

Forged iron and wood, 7 5/8" long, 3 7/8" wide, unsigned.

This is a typical shop-made tool used on site by its maker.

Historic Maritime III (1800-1840): Boomtown Years & the Dawn of the Industrial Revolution

Measuring Tools

100400T8   Try square
DTM   MHC-K

Malleable iron or steel, brass, rosewood, 7 1/2" long, 5 1/4" wide, signed "S A JONES & CO HARTFORD CON".

DATM (Nelson 1999, 430) lists Solomon A. Jones & Co. in Hartford, CT, 1838-1841 as making bevels, marking gauges, rules, and squares.

http://www.davistownmuseum.org/bioSAJones.html

71401T12   Try square
DTM   MH

Cast steel, brass, and wood, 6 1/4" long, 3 5/8" handle, signed "Ridgewell Middletown CONN".

This try square is American-made but reflects the influence of Sheffield, England prototypes.

71401T11   Try square
DTM   MH

Cast steel, brass, and wood, 4 3/8" long, 3 5/16" handle, signed "Walters Co Sollyworks Sheffield".

This is a typical c. 1800 imported English tool and is very similar to ID# 71401T12.

102100T11   Violin makers' gauge
DTM   MH

Wood and brass, 8 1/4" long, unsigned.

81200T   Whitesmith caliper
DTM   MHC-F

Forged iron, 26 1/2" long, 2 1/2" wide, unsigned, 1825 (?).

31311T9   Wing dividers
DTM   TT

Cast steel, 20" long, 3/4" wide, unsigned.

Miscellaneous Items

31811T7   Arrowhead
DTM   TT

Natural steel, 4" long, 1/2" wide, 1/8" thick, unsigned.
It is hand-forged.

70701T11   Carriage-wheel hub
DTM   MH

Cast iron, 8" high, 4 1/2" diameter spoke holder, unsigned, c. 1820 - 50.
It is from a Searsport, Maine, wheelwrights' shop.

Historic Maritime III (1800-1840): Boomtown Years & the Dawn of the Industrial Revolution

Miscellaneous Items

70701T2   **Carriage-wheel hubs (3)**   DTM   MH

Wood with steel ferrules, 6 3/4" high, 4" dia.; 6 3/4" high, 4 5/8" dia.; 7" high, 5 1/8" dia., unsigned, c. 1820 - 50.

These oak hubs are probably patterns or prototypes for a wheelwright, Searsport, Maine, origin. Also see the wheelwrights' balance at the Davistown Museum annex on the second floor of Liberty Tool Co. across the street.

TGB2207   **Owl figurine**   DTM   MH

Cast bronze (?), 4 1/2" long, 1 3/8" wide, unsigned.

Miscellaneous Tools

102100T10   **Awl**   DTM   MH

Forged iron or steel, 6 1/8" long, unsigned.

TBF1007A   **Awls (3)**   DTM   MH

Forged iron or steel and wood, unsigned.

51100T1   **Block**   DTM   MH

Wood, rope, and iron, 12" high, 8 3/8" wide, 8" diameter, signed "D ADAMS MAKER BOSTON".

The block has boxwood shives. There is no D. Adams listed in DATM (Nelson 1999).

40501T5   **Block**   DTM   MH

Wood, forged iron, and rope, 11" long excluding hook, unsigned.

This is a classic coasters' block with wood shives, typical of Maine coasting vessels of the 19th century.

TCR1004   **Box hook**   DTM   MH

Forged iron and wood, 8" in length, unsigned, c. 1820.

This hook is nicely forged, with distinct beveling. These were often used for unloading boxes and crates from ships.

063012T1   **Box hook**   DTM   TT

Iron and steel, baleen handle, 6 1/2" long hook, 5 1/2" long, 1 1/8" wide handle, unsigned.

TG1006   **Brick chisel**   DTM   MH

Reforged steel, 5 3/4" long, 1 1/2" wide, unsigned.

It does not have a handle.

Historic Maritime III (1800-1840): Boomtown Years & the Dawn of the Industrial Revolution

ID #   Status   Location

Miscellaneous Tools

TCR1014   **Brick chisel (?)**   DTM   MH

Forged iron, 7" long, 2 1/8" blade, unsigned.

TKD3501   **Carved flower**   DTM   MH

Wood, 10 1/2" high, 4 1/2" wide, unsigned.

This flower is European in origin, 17th or 18th century. It may have been a pattern fragment in a casting, or may have served a decorative function in an unknown context. It is another gem from the collection of Kenneth Lynch, who brought this item from Europe with the numerous tools he imported.

http://www.davistownmuseum.org/bioLynch.htm

102100T25   **Chalk line**   DTM   MH

Wood, 6 1/4" long, unsigned.

This is a nicely turned example of a common 19th century tool.

040103T10   **Clamp**   DTM   MH

Forged iron, 12 1/2" closed, unsigned.

What was this clamp used for?

TAB1301   **Clamp**   DTM   MH

Wood, 30" high, 5" long and 5 1/4" wide base, unsigned.

We are not sure what the use of this tool would have been. Comments and opinions are solicited.

913108T5   **Clamp**   DTM   MH

Hand-forged wrought or malleable iron, 3 1/2" by 2 7/8" clamp with a 3" long screw, unsigned.

51606T7   **Clamp**   DTM   MH

Forged iron, 11" long, unsigned.

The exact function of this hand-wrought and hand-filed tool is unknown.

072112T10   **Grafting iron (?)**   DTM   TT

Drop-forged malleable iron, 11 1/8" long, 1 3/4" wide, unsigned.

This tool is similar to a grafting iron but could have been used by a cooper or blacksmith.

TAB3500   **Icons (2)**   LPC   MH

Limestone (?), 7" high, 5" wide and 7" high, 3 1/2" wide, unsigned.

The age and function of these are unknown.

Historic Maritime III (1800-1840): Boomtown Years & the Dawn of the Industrial Revolution

Miscellaneous Tools

10407T8   Iron ship fitting   DTM   MH

Forged iron, 13 1/2" long, 6" wide, 2" high, unsigned.

It is made from the typical forged iron of the shipsmith, but what was it used for? It was found along the New England coast.

http://www.davistownmuseum.org/pics/10407t8_p2.jpg

32802T5   Lathing staff   DTM   MH

Forged iron, 11" long, 5 9/16" cant, unsigned.

Joseph Moxon's "Mechanick Exercises" (1703) shows a lathing staff of iron on the plate of bricklayers' gear. It looks very similar to this tool. Joseph Gwilt mentions this tool in his "Encyclopedia of Architecture" (1826). We believe the lathing refers to tilers working with roofing tile. [Information courtesy of Elliot Sayward.] This tool was donated by Chris Harvey.

http://www.davistownmuseum.org/pics/32802t5.jpg

51201T14   Lot of 21 tools   DTM   MH

Steel or wood, unsigned.

Eight steel tools (files, punches) and 13 wood items (handles, shims, and three wood balls used for measuring diameters). These are all from the Simon Willard toolbox.

http://www.davistownmuseum.org/pics/51201t14_p1web.jpg
http://www.davistownmuseum.org/bioWillard.htm

TCR1018A   Nail set   DTM   MH

Forged iron, 4 1/8" long, 3/16" diameter set, unsigned, c. 1820.

Distinctly hand-forged, this is a typical notched, blacksmith-made nail set. The notches on the edge of the nail set are a tip off that this tool dates before the era of industrial mass production of drop-forged nail sets.

TCP1006   Number stamps   DTM   MH

Forged iron, 2 1/4" long with 1/8" numbers, unsigned.

Eight hand-forged number stamps and also the letter "P", 5/16" high.

81200T3   Oil stone   DTM   MH

Arkansas stone (?) with a wood case, 7 7/8" long, 1 1/4" wide, unsigned.

33002T21   Oil stone   DTM   TT

Arkansas stone (?) and wood, 9 7/8" long, frame 10 1/16" long, unsigned.

ID #   Status   Location

Miscellaneous Tools

TKD3500   **Pattern**   DTM   MH

Wood, 9 1/2" high, 9 1/4" wide, unsigned.

It is European, from the 16th or 17th century; another of the interesting accidental durable remnants in the Kenneth Lynch collection.

http://www.davistownmuseum.org/bioLynch.htm

TKD2001   **Pattern**   DTM   MH

Brass and wood, 9 1/2" long, 2 1/4" wide, unsigned.

This tool is part of the Kenneth Lynch Collection.

http://www.davistownmuseum.org/bioLynch.htm

TKD2003   **Pattern of Greek warriors in combat**   DTM   MH

Wood, 11" high, 21" wide, unsigned.

This wooden pattern is of two Greek soldiers fighting. It was found at the Lynch foundry in Wilton, CT, but was originally discovered in Europe and brought to America by Lynch while amassing his huge tool collection. It's age is unknown.

http://www.davistownmuseum.org/bioLynch.htm

TAB3501   **Patterns (2)**   DTM   MH

Wood and plaster, 5 7/8" long, 2 1/4" wide and 7 3/8" long, 3 1/2" wide, unsigned.

These are patterns used for fret work repairs by creating plaster models of fret work on classical revival furniture.

52603T28   **Pry bar**   DTM   MH

Forged iron, 9 1/2" long, unsigned.

TCR3500   **Screwdriver**   DTM   MH

Wood and cast steel, 7 1/4" long, unsigned.

102904T4   **Screwdriver**   DTM   MH

Steel, wood, brass, 32" long including an 8 3/4" handle, unsigned.

This extra large screwdriver has a turned wooden handle with a brass ferrule.

http://www.davistownmuseum.org/pics/102904t4.jpg

913108T34   **Screwdriver**   DTM   MH

Hand-forged malleable iron, 5" long, unsigned.

ID #		Status	Location

Miscellaneous Tools

51100T3   **Screwdriver**   DTM   MH

Cast steel, brass, and rosewood, 23 3/8" long, signed "J. W. Ferren".

No J. W. Ferren is listed in DATM (Nelson 1999); could this be an owner's mark?

TCR2204   **Sharpening stone**   DTM   MH

Unknown stone, 9" long, unsigned.

81101T8   **Slaters' rip**   DTM   MH

Forged iron, brass ferrules, and wood handle, 15 7/8" long, 10 1/8" blade, unsigned.

41801T14   **Socket extension**   DTM   MH

Forged iron, 7 1/2" long, unsigned.

This fits an early form of a bit brace. What was its use?

81200T8   **Soldering iron**   DTM   MH

Forged iron and copper, 16 1/4" long, unsigned, c. 1820 - 1840.

This is typical of soldering irons used to solder copper plating on a ships' hull.

3312T12   **Spear head**   DTM   TT

Hand-forged malleable iron, 11 1/4" long, unsigned.

Courtesy of Liberty Tool Co.

52603T25   **Straight razor in box**   DTM   MH

German steel, 6 1/2" long, signed "BROEKER BROS. ANCHOR SOLINGEN Germany" and on the box "PYRAMID BRAND Geneva Cutlery Corp. Geneva, N.Y. USA".

51201T13   **Stroup**   DTM   MH

Leather and wood, 10 5/8" long, 1 5/16" wide, unsigned.

A stroup is used for keeping a fine edge on gouges by removing burrs.

http://www.davistownmuseum.org/pics/51201T13.jpg
http://www.davistownmuseum.org/bioWillard.htm

072112T9   **Tack**   DTM   TT

Forge-welded malleable iron, 3" long, 2 1/2" wide head, unsigned.

TCK1006   **Tool carrier**   DTM   MH

Wood, 22 1/4" long, 12 5/8" wide, unsigned.

Historic Maritime III (1800-1840): Boomtown Years & the Dawn of the Industrial Revolution

Miscellaneous Tools

TCR1010   **Turnscrew**   DTM   MH

Forged iron and wood, 8" long, unsigned, probably made 1820-1840.

This blacksmith-made turnscrew has a strongly beveled shaft.

111001T39   **Turnscrew**   DTM   MH

Wood, brass, and forged steel, 6 3/4" long, 3" handle, unsigned.

81200T2   **Turnscrew**   DTM   MH

Wood, brass, and forged iron and steel, 24 1/2" long, signed with owner's initials "C.B.N." on the wood handle, c. 1820 - 1840.

http://www.davistownmuseum.org/pics/81200t2.jpg

TG1008   **Unidentified tool**   DTM   MH

Wood and reforged steel, 16" long, 14" wood handle, unsigned.

71401T4   **Unidentified tool**   DTM   MH

Forged steel, 22" long, unsigned.

82500T2   **Wrecking bar**   DTM   MH

Forged iron, 26" long, 2 1/4" wide pry, unsigned, c. 1820 - 1840.

This is a blacksmith-forged wrecking bar with an exceptionally wide claw.

Quarrying Tools

81602T11   **Granite facing tool**   DTM   MH

Cast steel, 9 5/16" long, 5/8" wide five toothed cutting edge, unsigned.

This elegantly chamfered hand-filed tool probably dates from the early years of the 19th century.

121112T7   **Rock chisel**   DTM   MH

Forged iron and steel, 7 3/8" long, 7/16" wide cutting edge, signed "P. Devlin".

No toolmaker with this name is listed in DATM (Nelson 1999).

TCU1004   **Square faced stone hammer**   DTM   MH

Cast iron, 5 5/8" long, 1 3/4" square faces, signed with an obscure maker's sign.

TCU3000   **Stone chisel**   DTM   MH

Forged iron and steel, 9 1/4" long, 1 11/16" diameter forged steel cutter in a cross pattern, unsigned.

ID #   Status   Location

Quarrying Tools

101900T2   **Stone chisel**   DTM   MH

Forged steel (?), 4 1/4" long, 1 1/2" wide, unsigned.

This is a nicely beveled quarrymans' finishing chisel.

41212T8   **Stone chisel**   DTM   TT

Malleable iron, 10" long, 1 3/4" wide cutting edge, unsigned.

The hammering surface of this tool has mushroomed in little strips and the edge is very rough and chipped. Courtesy of Liberty Tool Co.

TCR1018B   **Stone drill**   DTM   MH

Forged iron, 7" long, unsigned, c. 1820 (?).

TCU1007   **Stone drill**   DTM   MH

Forged iron, 8 1/2" long, 1/8" wide drill point, unsigned.

This primitive hand-forged drill is hard to date and could be 18th or 19th century.

TCU1001   **Stone hammer**   DTM   MH

Forged iron and steel, 5 1/8" long, 15/16" square peen, signed "H.C. Briggs" on the handle, c. 1820-1840.

This hammer is made of forged iron with the typical layering of steel at the peen as well as at the face. There is no H.C. Briggs in DATM (Nelson 1999).

32802T6A   **Stone hammer**   DTM   MH

Forged iron and wood, 1 1/2" x 2 1/2" faces, signed "JOHN HALLAHAN BOSTON,MASS.".

This is a two-faced rectangular stone hammer, probably used for chipping.

http://www.davistownmuseum.org/pics/32802t6a.jpg

93011T15   **Stonemakers' chisel**   DTM   TT

Malleable iron, 5 1/2" long, 2" wide, signed "J. BACKES" four times, possibly an owner's mark.

TCU1005   **Toothed stone chisel**   DTM   MH

Forged steel, 5" long, 1 1/8" wide, signed "T. GRANGER", c. 1840.

It has seven teeth. This maker is not listed in DATM (Nelson 1999).

TCU1003   **Toothed stone chisel**   DTM   MH

Forged iron or steel, 6" long, 1 1/4" wide, signed "J. GERM" with a second illegible signature.

It has six teeth. Five of the six distinctly beveled sides are signed; at least three signatures are J. Germ. This maker is not listed in DATM (Nelson 1999). Would Germ be an owner-maker?

ID #   Status   Location

Quarrying Tools

TCU1008   **Wedge**   DTM   MH

Forged iron and steel, 10 1/2" long, unsigned.

http://www.davistownmuseum.org/pics/tcp1005a.jpg

Shipwrights', Sailmakers', and Mariners' Tools

TCV1301   **Awl**   DTM   MH

Forged steel, brass, and wood with a leather scabbard, 9 1/2" long with a 1 1/16" brass ferrule and a 6 1/2" scabbard, unsigned.

41302T13   **Awl**   DTM   MH

Steel, brass, and rosewood, 4 1/8" long, unsigned.

This exquisite sailors' awl has a beautiful rosewood handle and would be typical of a seamans' tool chest, 1800 - 1840.

7800T-1   **Awl with case**   DTM   MHC-F

Wood, rope, and cast or forged steel, unsigned.

81212LTC15 **Bodkin**   NOM   TT (Pub)

Wood (ebony), forged steel, brass ferrule, 14 1/8" long, 10 3/8" blade, unsigned.

102100T19   **Compass**   DTM   MH

Forged steel, 5" long, unsigned.

This is a generic ships' navigators' compass used throughout the 18th and 19th centuries on charts.

100400T9   **Deadeye (3)**   DTM   MHC-K

Lignum vitae (?), one is 4" diameter; the other two are 3" diameter, unsigned.

TCV1001   **Fid**   DTM   MH

Wood, unsigned.

A fid is used to loosen the strands of rope when splicing two pieces of rope together. They look like wooden Marlin spikes and are used by sailmakers.

102911T2   **Fid**   DTM   MH-O

Rosewood, 14" long, 2" diameter at hand end, signed "M" owners mark.

This is from the early 19th century - most likely used on a large sailing schooner due to its large diameter. We are not sure of the rope composition on the turkshead.

Historic Maritime III (1800-1840): Boomtown Years & the Dawn of the Industrial Revolution

Shipwrights', Sailmakers', and Mariners' Tools

TCV3000   **Harpoon (?)**   DTM   MH

Bronze, 4 3/4" long, unsigned.

012705T2   **Hawsing iron**   DTM   MH-O

Forged iron and steel, 21 1/2" long handle, 5 7/8" long and 3 3/4" wide curved blade, unsigned.

040103T7   **Mariners' rule**   LPC   MH

Boxwood, 2' long, 1 3/4" wide, unsigned.

The rule is marked in great detail on both sides: Log, Rhumb, M Log, Chord, S Rhumb, T Rhumb, Number, Sine, W. Sine, Tangent, Meridian, Continent, eg2 Parts. Each designation is accompanied by numerical inscriptions the length of the rule. It is a most intriguing rule for navigation the old fashioned way. Rule 040103T8 was found with this rule.

http://www.davistownmuseum.org/pics/040103t7_p1.jpg
http://www.davistownmuseum.org/pics/040103t7_p2.jpg

TCV1002   **Marlin spike**   DTM   MH

Forged or cast steel, unsigned.

93011T16   **Marlin spike**   DTM   TT

Malleable iron, 6" long, 5/8" diameter tapered, unsigned.

It has a hole at the end for threading the rope.

41412LTC3   **Parallel folding rule**   DA   TT (Pub)

Ebony wood, brass, 6" long, 1 5/16" wide, unsigned.

These are often used by mariners for sailing chart calculations. Courtesy of Liberty Tool Co.

30202T10   **Parallels**   DTM   MH

Rosewood and brass, 6" long, unsigned.

This is a typical example of a mariners' parallel except for the diminutive size.

http://www.davistownmuseum.org/pics/30202t10.jpg

012705T4   **Reefing iron**   DTM   MH

Forged iron and steel, 35 1/2" long handle, 7 1/4" long and 2 1/2" wide triangular blade, unsigned.

101701T19   **Sailors' awl case**   DTM   MH

Wood and rope, 5" long, unsigned.

Who made this wooden case with its finely woven cover? It is an excellent whatsit.

ID #   Status   Location

Shipwrights', Sailmakers', and Mariners' Tools

TCV3500   **Sailors' whimsey**   DTM   MH

Rope, 3" diameter, unsigned.

102503P1   **Sculling oar**   LPC   MH

Wood, 75" long, 4 1/2" wide, unsigned.

The wood shows evidence of canvas slips. The provenance of this oar is Merrymeeting Bay, Maine. It was used for early 19th century scalloping and shellfishing -- essentially, the early form of an oar.

61404T15   **Seam rubber**   DTM   MH

Wood, 5 5/16" long, 2 1/16" wide, unsigned.

A seam rubber is used to flatten the seams and creases in a sail.

http://www.davistownmuseum.org/pics/61404T15.jpg

TCV1004   **Serving tool**   DTM   MH

Wood, 5 3/8" long, 1 3/4" wide server, unsigned.

Serving tools were used to guide the ropes when raising or lowering the sails.

TCV1003   **Serving tool**   DTM   MH

Wood, 11 1/4" long, 2 3/8" wide, unsigned.

TEV1006   **Serving tool**   DTM   MH

Wood, 8 5/8" long, 1 3/4" wide, unsigned.

42604T10   **Serving tool**   DTM   MH

Wood, 4 4/4" long including 3 1/8" handle, 3 1/3" wide, 1 1/4" diameter serving surface, unsigned.

41302T9   **Ship carpenters' bevel**   DTM   MH

Wood, iron, brass, and copper, 10 3/8" long with 3 bevels, unsigned.

It is handmade with mahogany from the West Indies. This is the traditional bevel of a ships' carpenter commonly used prior to the era of factory made bevels (after 1850).

Historic Maritime III (1800-1840): Boomtown Years & the Dawn of the Industrial Revolution

ID #   Status   Location

Shipwrights', Sailmakers', and Mariners' Tools

TCC2005   Shipwrights' slick   LPC   MH

Cast steel with wood handle, 14 1/2" long, 3 1/2" wide, 10" handle, signed "WARRANTED CAST STEEL" and "_. TINKHAM".

Other than "warranted cast steel," this tool has no manufacturer's touch mark. The slick has an owner's sign (?) "Tinkham" and is part of our collection of Tinkham artifacts and papers that are on display in the Museum. This slick came from a ship carpenters' tool box discovered in Foxboro, MA, several years ago and was undoubtedly used by one of the Tinkham clan, probably in the shipyards of New Bedford, Fairhaven, or Mattapoisset, MA. C. 1810 - 1850. This slick is similar to signed specimens produced by the prolific Underhill clan of Nashua, NH.

http://www.davistownmuseum.org/pics/tcc2005.jpg
http://www.davistownmuseum.org/bioTinkham.htm

TCV1005   Shuttles   DTM   MH

Wood, 1' long, unsigned.

A shuttle is used in net or sail making.

040904T2   Tanged slick or French chisel   DTM   MH

Forged weld steel (German?) and iron, wooden handle, 12 1/2" long with a nicely turned wood handle with iron ferrule 6 1/4" long, 2 1/2" wide, signed "FERDIN" "RUBENS" with a bell shaped touchmark.

This forge-welded edge tool is from a Mt. Desert Island boatyard. It is European in style and was probably brought to Maine from France sometime in the early 19th century. It is used for cleaning up the sides of large mortises in and for leveling surfaces such as on the deck of a ship. Slicks are particularly useful to shipwrights in areas that cannot be reached by an adz. They are often pushed by the shoulder, hence the swollen top of the wooden handle.

http://www.davistownmuseum.org/pics/040904t2_p3.jpg

TBG1002   Turned net weight   DTM   MH

Lead (?) interior, 1 5/8" diameter, unsigned.

Unidentified Tools

22601T6   Unidentified tool   DTM   MH

Wood and stone, 5" long with a 3" sandstone burnisher, unsigned.
Could this tool be a burnisher?

040103T11   Unidentified tool   DTM   MH

Forged iron, 13 1/2" long, 2 1/2" lower jaw, 3" upper jaw, unsigned.
The jaws on this unusual tool do not meet. What would its use have been?

Historic Maritime III (1800-1840): Boomtown Years & the Dawn of the Industrial Revolution

ID #   Status   Location

Unidentified Tools

92901T3   **Unidentified tool**   DTM   MH

Wood, 15" long with a 10" breast plate similar to that of a breast drill, unsigned.

This tools use is unknown.

70701T3   **Unidentified tool**   DTM   MH

Wood, cast steel, and brass, 10" long, 1/2" x 3/4" serrated cutting attachment, signed "SFL".

Watchmakers, Jewelers, and Silversmiths' Tools

32502T46   **Anvil**   BDTM   T

Cast steel, 3" long including tang for pritchel, unsigned.

http://www.davistownmuseum.org/bioEpstein.htm

32502T1   **Box**   BDTM   T

Walnut with brass hardware, 13 3/4" x 12 3/4" x 4 1/8" high with two hinged lids, signed "BERTIE FAXON Brookville #4 c. 1800" on a brass label on the box.

This box contains the Norman Epstein hoard of jewelers and watchmakers tools. Does Bertie Faxon have any relationship to Richard Faxon edge toolmaker of Braintree, MA, c. 1795? The Liberty Tool Co. recycled at least five of his edge tools (broad axes, draw knifes) in the 1970s.

http://www.davistownmuseum.org/bioEpstein.htm

32502T40   **Burnisher**   BDTM   T

Cast steel, unsigned.

It has no handle.

http://www.davistownmuseum.org/bioEpstein.htm

32502T10   **Chasing tools (3)**   BDTM   T

Cast steel, 2 1/2" to 3 1/2" long, signed with unknown touchmarks.

http://www.davistownmuseum.org/bioEpstein.htm

TCP1003   **Draw plate**   DTM   MH

Cast steel, 6 1/8" long, 3" wide, unsigned.

It has numbers on it indicating the hole diameters.

3405T1B   **Draw plate**   DTM   MH

Steel, 4 7/8" long, 1 5/8" wide, 1/2 oval holes, signed "Perelet France Garantie" and "L3L".

It is also numerated 1 - 20.

ID #   Status   Location

Watchmakers, Jewelers, and Silversmiths' Tools

3405T1A   **Draw plate**   DTM   MH

Steel, 4 1/16" long, 1 1/4" wide, square holes, signed "Perelet France Garantie" and "L24".

It is also numerated 1 - 20. The two drawplates signed Perelet and the two signed Joubert are nice examples of 19th century German steel tools used by a jeweler for wire drawing. They are French toolmakers, working dates are not available.

3405T1C   **Draw plate**   DTM   MH

Steel, 4 1/2" long, 1 3/16" wide, circular holes, signed "Joubert France Garantie" and "B" with a crown touchmark.

It is also numerated 1 - 20.

3405T1D   **Draw plate**   DTM   MH

Steel, 4" long, 1 3/16" wide, circular holes, signed "Joubert France Garantie" and "A" with a crown touchmark.

It is also numerated 1 - 20.

3405T4   **Draw plate**   DTM   MH

Steel, 3 13/16" long tapering to 15/16" wide, signed "MARTIN", "FITA", "GARANITIE", "36", "L" and numbered 0 - 14 including four zero sizes.

Fourteen is the smallest diameter mark. This is an interesting example of an early 19th century French jewelers' drawplate.

32502T9   **Etching and scribing tools (5)**   BDTM   T

Wood handles, 3 rosewood, 2 unknown tropical wood with brass ferrules, 4 1/2" to 6" long, unsigned.

One has a steel file and one a diamond cutter with a diamond tip. The other three have steel, brass, or iron tips.

http://www.davistownmuseum.org/bioEpstein.htm

32502T12   **Float**   BDTM   T

Cast steel, 3" long with 1" float surface, unsigned.

The long end is a fine filing surface.

http://www.davistownmuseum.org/bioEpstein.htm

31011T7   **Hammer head**   DTM   TT

Cast steel, 2" long, 3/8" wide, 1/4" diameter round head, straight closed claw, signed "P S STUBS" "1".

http://www.davistownmuseum.org/bioStubs.htm

Watchmakers, Jewelers, and Silversmiths' Tools

32502T24   Hand spindles (3)   BDTM   T

Cast steel, brass, and wood, 5 1/16", 4 3/4", and 3 3/8" long, unsigned.

http://www.davistownmuseum.org/bioEpstein.htm

32502T25   Jewelers' anvils (2)   BDTM   T

Bronze, 3 11/32" long, 3/4" wide and 3 3/8" long, 5/8" wide, unsigned.

One is more highly finished than the other.

http://www.davistownmuseum.org/bioEpstein.htm

32502T4   Jewelers' files   BDTM   T

Cast steel, various lengths, signed "Graves & Sons" "W Greaves" "Lord & Co." "Triumph Smart & Child Co." "J. M. Martin" (2) "P. Ashton" (2) "Martin CS" "RS Sanders" (2) "Spanale" "RAINE".

"R M Cock" "Grobet" (2) "Friely". This Epstein hoard file lot illustrates the wide variety of European sources for steel files: English, German, French, and Italian.

http://www.davistownmuseum.org/bioEpstein.htm

32502T2   Jewelers' files (30)   BDTM   T

Cast steel or iron, 3" to 6" long, signed with obscure marks or no mark.

http://www.davistownmuseum.org/bioEpstein.htm

32502T3   Jewelers' files (7)   BDTM   T

Cast steel, 3 1/4" to 6 3/4" long, signed "Stubs".

http://www.davistownmuseum.org/bioEpstein.htm

TJG3000   Jewelers' hammer   DTM   MH

Cast steel and wood, 9 1/4" long including the handle, 2 3/16" long head with a 5/8" diameter face, signed with an obscured signature.

TST3000   Jewelers' wire snips   DTM   MH

Cast steel and iron, 5 3/8" long, signed "P S STUBS".

This is another of Stubs finely made imported tools.

http://www.davistownmuseum.org/bioStubs.htm

32502T18   Ladle   BDTM   T

Cast iron, bronze, and wood, 6" long, unsigned.

http://www.davistownmuseum.org/bioEpstein.htm

ID #   Status   Location

Watchmakers, Jewelers, and Silversmiths' Tools

32502T47   **Ring sizer**   BDTM   T

Wood, 11 7/8" long, 3/4" maximum diameter at head of taper, unsigned.

This is used for measuring ring diameters.

http://www.davistownmuseum.org/bioEpstein.htm

32502T22   **Scale level**   BDTM   T

Brass, 3 1/4" long, 1 1/16" wide, signed "PR" (by the owner) and marked "1 - 18".

http://www.davistownmuseum.org/bioEpstein.htm

32502T21   **Scale level**   BDTM   T

Brass, 5 3/4" long, tapered, unsigned.

It is marked "1 - 32" for measuring.

http://www.davistownmuseum.org/bioEpstein.htm

32502T23   **Scale level**   BDTM   T

Brass, 5 5/8" long, 13/16" wide, signed "Sussfeld Lousch & Co New York", "Lepine", "Lever" with scale 000 to 30 and 1 - 27.

http://www.davistownmuseum.org/bioEpstein.htm

111001T6   **Screw plate**   DTM   MH

Cast steel, 9" long, signed "P.S. Stubs" and marked "19".

Screw plates are used by jewelers and watchmakers for threading fine brass and steel wire to make screws.

http://www.davistownmuseum.org/bioStubs.htm

32502T42   **Screwdriver**   BDTM   T

Brass, 3 15/16" long, unsigned.

http://www.davistownmuseum.org/bioEpstein.htm

041505T28   **Spinning tool**   DTM   MH

Pewter, steel, and wood, 15" long including a 14" wood handle, 2 1/2" long pewter ferrule, unsigned.

The wood handle holds the tanged steel chisel. This cutting tool is clearly made of recycled file steel. It is an uncommon tool from a long lost trade.

41801T11   **Tongs**   DTM   MH

Forged iron, 16 1/4" long, jaws are 1 5/8" long, 7/32" wide, unsigned.

This is the smallest, most delicate pair of jewelers' tongs in the Museum collection.

Historic Maritime III (1800-1840): Boomtown Years & the Dawn of the Industrial Revolution

Watchmakers, Jewelers, and Silversmiths' Tools

32502T20   **Width and depth gauges (set of 8)**   BDTM   T

Brass, the marks don't match the apparent sizes, unsigned.

They are marked "1/4", "1/8", and "1".

http://www.davistownmuseum.org/bioEpstein.htm

32502T41   **Wrenches (2)**   BDTM   T

Cast steel, unsigned.

http://www.davistownmuseum.org/bioEpstein.htm

Woodworking: Axes and Hatchets

913108T47   **Ax**   DTM   MH

Malleable iron with a steel cutting edge, wooden handle, 17 3/4" long, 10 5/8" wide blade, signed "MORGAN" "THOMAS" "CAST STEEL".

This is most likely Thomas Morgan of Rochester, NY, working dates 1820 - 1828 (Nelson 1999). Axes with this mark are not commonly found in New England tool chests.

52603T33   **Belt ax**   DTM

Forge-welded steel, wooden handle (hickory), 13 1/2" long, 4 1/2" wide head, 2 1/4" long cutting edge, unsigned.

032203T4   **Broad ax**   DTM   MH

Forged iron and weld steel, wood handle, 12 1/2" long blade, 8 3/4" wide from poll to blade, 19" handle includes a 4 1/2" insert, unsigned any marks on the insert are no longer visible.

This heavily pitted generic 19th century broad ax was found in the woods near Portland, ME, and is the typical broad ax used by shipbuilders to rough out large beams and keels. A tool of this design would have been found in the shipyards of Maine at any time during the 19th century, but is certainly typical of those edge tools used ca. 1820. This tool was donated to The Davistown Museum by Bob Wheeler.

http://www.davistownmuseum.org/pics/032203t4_p2.jpg
http://www.davistownmuseum.org/pics/032203t4_p1.jpg

100400T15   **Broad ax**   DTM   MH-O

Cast steel and wood, 19 1/2" handle, 9" wide blade with 3 1/2" poll, unsigned.

http://www.davistownmuseum.org/pics/100400T15.jpg

42604T3   **Broad ax**   DTM   MH

Forged iron, weld cast steel, wood, 11 1/4" long and 6 1/2" wide blade, 2 1/2" poll, 32" wooden handle, signed "UNDERHILL" "EDGETOOLCo" "WARRANTED" "CAST STEEL".

ID #   Status   Location

Woodworking: Axes and Hatchets

111001T17   Felling ax   DTM   MH

Iron and steel, 6 1/2" long head, 4 3/8" wide cutting edge, unsigned.

A classic example of the ax makers trade: the steel blade is clearly welded onto the iron casing. It predates the era of the one piece cast steel or drop-forged steel ax.

TCC3005   Hatchet   DTM   MH

Forged iron and steel, 3 1/4" wide blade, signed "Gray's", with "0" above the touch mark.

DATM (Nelson 1999) lists a Gray (no dates) as an ax maker in Kingston, MA.

42607T6   Hatchet   DTM   MH

Cast steel, 4 3/4" long, 1 15/16" wide blade with a 1" square poll, unsigned.

This small hatchet appears to be one piece all cast steel.

914108T8   Hatchet   DTM   MH

Malleable iron with a weld steel cutting edge, wooden handle, 6 1/4" long and 3 1/3" wide blade, 10 1/4" long handle, signed "E. COB".

TCC3000   Hatchet   DTM   MH

Cast steel and wood, 3 3/8" long with a 1 7/16" blade, signed "L. OLSEN".

100400T12   Hewing ax   DTM   MH

Forged iron and steel, wood, 28" long, with a 9 1/2" long and 6" wide head, signed with an obscure signature.

http://www.davistownmuseum.org/pics/100400t12.jpg

040904T5   Hewing ax   DTM   MH

Forged iron and steel, 10 1/4" long, 7 15/16" wide, signed "T. ROGERS".

T. Rogers is not listed in DATM (Nelson 1999). This is another undocumented New England edge toolmaker, probably from interior N.H. or Maine.

http://www.davistownmuseum.org/pics/040904t5_p4.jpg
http://www.davistownmuseum.org/pics/040904t5_sig.jpg

111001T1   Hewing ax   DTM   MH

Cast steel, 6 1/4" wide blade, signed "J. Hatch CAST STEEL".

No J. Hatch is listed in DATM (Nelson 1999). This is a second example of the work of the unidentified J. Hatch.

Woodworking: Axes and Hatchets

12801T5   Hewing ax   DTM   MH

Forged iron with steel cutting edge and nicely offset handle, 10 3/4" long, 6" wide cutting edge, 29 3/4" long handle, signed "A HIGHT SCARBORO".

The Registry of Maine Toolmakers (Brack 2008) lists Amos Hight as working between 1832-56. Perhaps he was related to George Hight of Gorham, also making edge tools and knives as early as 1815. This ax was located by Dana Phillippi of Liberty, Maine.

http://www.davistownmuseum.org/pics/12801t5_p3.jpg
http://www.davistownmuseum.org/publications/volume10.html

111002T2   Hewing ax   DTM   MH

Forged iron and steel, 30" long, blade 5 1/2" wide and 8" long, signed "I H. Harrison No 4".

This tool is made by John Harrison, Instone Mills, Dronfield, Sheffield UK (http://swingleydev.com/archive/get.php?message_id=95422&submit_thread=1). There is no evidence of an iron-steel interface. The poll has an unusual hand punched (?) triangle decoration on all sides ranging in size from 3/4" to 3/16" high. The poll also shows distinct signs of hand filing.

http://www.davistownmuseum.org/pics/111002t2_pic1.jpg
http://www.davistownmuseum.org/pics/111002t2_sig.jpg

12801T6   Hewing ax   DTM   MH

Cast steel, wood handle not original, 10 7/16" long, 6 3/4" wide cutting blade, signed "J HATCH CAST STEEL".

No Hatch ax makers are listed in DATM (Nelson 1999).

http://www.davistownmuseum.org/pics/12801t6_p2.jpg
http://www.davistownmuseum.org/pics/12801t6_p3.jpg

TCC2006   Hewing ax   DTM   MH

Cast steel, 12" long, 5 5/8" blade, signed "J. EMERY" "CAST STEEL WATERHOUSE", c. 1820.

DATM (Nelson 1999, 830) lists W. H. Waterhouse of Gardiner, Maine as making axes in 1869. Jeremiah W. Emery of Newfield, Maine made farm tools from 1871 to 1885. Finally, from 1871 to 1894, there was a hardware company in Portland, ME that marked planes with variations of "WATERHOUSE EMERY & CO". It is unknown if this mark was used by any of them.

ID #   Status   Location

Woodworking: Axes and Hatchets

TAX3500   **Hewing ax**   DTM   TT

Forged iron and steel, 6" long with 4 1/4" blade, signed with an obscured manufacturer's sign and with a number "3".

This 19th century ax is an excellent example of the American designed ax, which was substituted for the lighter in weight English trade axes that the first settlers brought to America. The lighter English axes with their lack of a poll were impractical for cutting the large tracts of forested land in New England. In the late 18th century American blacksmiths' designed new heavier axes that were much more practical to use in cutting and clearing the forests of New England and the eastern United States. This ax is the best example in the museum collection of this new type of ax with its heavier poll, which played such an important role in frontier communities. The transition from the steel blade to the forged iron poll is clearly visible in this specimen.

http://www.davistownmuseum.org/pics/tax3500.jpg

72801T2   **Mast ax**   DTM   MH-O

Forged iron and steel, wood handle, 10 3/4" long, 7" wide blade, 28" handle, signed "PAYSON".

Payson is not listed in DATM (Nelson 1999); there are three different Payson's in the Registry of Maine Toolmakers. This ax has a Portsmouth, NH, area origin and illustrates the Kent pattern.

http://www.davistownmuseum.org/pics/72801t2.jpg
http://www.davistownmuseum.org/publications/volume10.html

72206T3   **Mortising ax**   DTM   MH

Iron and forged steel with a clearly welded steel interface, 10" long, 1 5/8" vertical cutting blade, unsigned.

This early 19th century ax was probably used for cutting holes for shipwrights' treenails (trunnels). Compare it to mortising ax ID# 72206T2; this ax has a shorter reach and may have been used on smaller coasting vessels.

72206T2   **Mortising ax**   DTM   TT

Forge-welded iron and steel, 12 3/4" long, 1 1/4" wide, unsigned.

The body of the tool is wrought iron with a clearly scarfed wedge of welded, forged, probably blister steel as the cutting edge. It is from the early 19th or possibly late 18th century. It has a horizontal cutting blade and is a typical shipsmith product, used by a shipwright to cut the hole for a treenail (trunnel).

7309T2   **Offset angle hewing ax**   LPC   MH

Forged iron, steel, and wood handle, 8 1/2" long, 6 3/4" wide cutting blade, 46" handle, signed "FAXON".

There is no hint of a welded steel cutting edge. This tool is too sharp to be a grub hoe. It is one of several edge tools in the collection that are made by the Faxon clan of Braintree, MA.

http://www.davistownmuseum.org/pics/7309t2web-2.jpg
http://www.davistownmuseum.org/pics/7309t2web-1.jpg

ID #   Status   Location

Woodworking: Axes and Hatchets

81602T9   Offset mast ax (small broad ax)   DTM   MH

Cast steel (?), 10 1/2" long, 6 15/16" wide blade, signed "BROAD ST. JOHN NB".

Broad is one of many edge toolmakers in the important shipbuilding and toolmaking community of St. John, New Brunswick, Canada. Just up the Bay of Fundy from coastal New England, St. John toolmakers, including John Fowler, supplied high quality tools to the shipwrights living west of St. John throughout the 19th century. Possibly this mark is that of H. Broad (see the bio link).

http://www.davistownmuseum.org/pics/81602t9_pic2.jpg
http://www.davistownmuseum.org/publications/volume10.html

Woodworking: Axes and Hatchets Made in Maine

100605T3   Broad ax   DTM   TB

Cast steel with wooden handle, 11" long, 7 3/4" wide blade, new 30" long handle, signed "C. HUNTER BINGHAM" " CAST STEEL WARRANTED".

This ax was found in Maine and was possibly made in Bingham. The initial C. in the mark is hard to read and may be something else.

http://www.davistownmuseum.org/pics/100605t3.jpg
http://www.davistownmuseum.org/publications/volume10.html

21201T1   Hewing ax   DTM   MH

Cast or forged steel, 10 3/8" long, 7 5/8" wide blade, 3 1/4" poll, signed "B GRAVES SOLON".

This Maine ax maker is not listed in either DATM (Nelson 1999) or Yeaton's (2000) "Axe Makers of Maine". This important Maine tool by a previously unidentified Maine toolmaker was a gift to the Davistown Museum from Rick Floyd of Newport, ME.

http://www.davistownmuseum.org/pics/21201t1.jpg
http://www.davistownmuseum.org/publications/volume10.html

21201T2   Hewing ax   DTM   MH

Forged iron and natural steel (?), 10 3/4" long, 7 5/8" blade, 3" poll, signed "WHORFF MADISON".

This tool has no clearly delineated welded steel-iron interface nor any mark suggesting it is cast steel. The ax is not obviously forge-welded, raising the intriguing question: was this tool drop-forged (then hand stamped) from puddled or German steel, one of the alternative steelmaking strategies of the mid-19th century, before the era of bulk processed steel, which was not suitable for edge tool production. A gift to the Davistown Museum from Rick Floyd of Newport, ME. More information on Whorff is available in the Registry of Maine Toolmakers (Brack 2008).

http://www.davistownmuseum.org/pics/21201t2.jpg
http://www.davistownmuseum.org/bioWhorff.html

Woodworking: Boring Tools

Woodworking: Boring Tools

102904T7   Auger   DTM   MH

Forged iron, wooden handle, 15 3/4" long with a 17 5/8" long handle, 1 3/4" wide cutter, signed "HAYER T HAYER" and "8".

This auger has clearly been hand wrought with beveling on its handle. No T. Hayer is listed in DATM (Nelson 1999). The 8 mark suggests a 2" cutting dimension. It is of New England origin and represents another unknown New England Toolmaker.

http://www.davistownmuseum.org/pics/102904t7_p2.jpg

TCE1003F6   Auger bit   DTM   MH

Forged iron, 1 1/4" double notched bit, signed "TOWNE SNELL 5".

Towne Snell is listed in DATM (Nelson 1999) without a date or location. This was a predecessor to the famous Snell Mfg. Co.

TCE1003E5   Auger bit   DTM   MH

Forged iron, 9/16" diameter cutter, signed with a tiny touchmark.

TCE1003G7   Auger bit   DTM   MH

Forged iron, 3/8" diameter cutter, signed "T. DAVIS & CO No 6".

This maker is not listed in DATM (Nelson 1999).

TCE1003A1   Auger bit   DTM   MH

Forged iron, wood, signed "J T Pugh Phila PA 16".

This maker is listed in DATM (Nelson 1999) without any data. Job T. Pugh of Philadelphia had an auger bit patent (967,055) from August 9, 1910. It is known there were earlier Pughs: "Job T. Pugh's Auger Works (Pugh Alley, west of 30th Street) established in 1774, was one of the many metalworking companies in West Philadelphia and remained active into the twentieth century." (http://www.workshopoftheworld.com/west_phila/west_phila.html).

TCE1003D4   Auger bit   DTM   MH

Forged iron, 1" diameter cutter, signed "LG HALL 16".

This maker is not listed in DATM (Nelson 1999).

TCE1003C3   Auger bit   DTM   MH

Forged iron, 1/2" diameter cutter, signed with the mark "No 8", c. 1820 - 1840.

This is a typical notched auger bit.

TCC3011   Burin   DTM   MH

Cast steel and wood, 4" long, unsigned.

This commonplace tool is refashioned out of an old file and has a beautifully turned handle.

Woodworking: Boring Tools

TCE1004   Carpenters' nut auger   DTM   MH

Forged iron, 15 3/4" long, signed with an obscured signature and "5" with a superscript "2".

It has no handle.

70701T8   Center bit   DTM   MH

Cast steel, 4 1/2" long, 9/16" diameter cutter, signed "Melhuish Fetler Lane".

This is a very unusual manufacturer's signature; probably from Sheffield, England. Additional information wanted.

41203T31   Center bit   DTM   MH

Cast steel, 4 1/4" long, 19/32" diameter, signed "J. BEE CAST STEEL".

DATM (Nelson 1999, 993) indicates James Bee, 1814, is a foreign maker of braces and bits.

102100T7   Countersink   DTM   MH

Cast steel, 4" long, signed "IBBOTSON & CO CAST STEEL".

An imported tool from one of Sheffield's most prolific forges.

72801T14   Countersink   DTM   MH

Cast steel, 4 7/8" long, signed "R M Diton Hermitage Works Sheffield".

This notched countersink is for a gentlemans' brace. It is an excellent example of an imported English tool of the early 19th century. This is not a common signature.

TCE3000   Pod auger   DTM   MH

Forged iron or steel, 5 1/4" long, unsigned.

TCE1002   Pod auger   DTM   MH

Forged iron, 8 3/8" long, 5 1/4" wide handle, signed "HARRESON".

DATM (Nelson 1999) has 6 entries for Harrison, all working during the 19th century, but no Harreson.

102100T23   Pod augers (4)   DTM   TT

Cast steel, 8 3/8" long, 7 1/2" long, 7 3/8" long, 6" long, signed "IBBOTSON & Co CAST STEEL".

These are imported English tools made by one of England's more prolific edge toolmakers. They were made for the American trade.

111412T2   Spade bit   DTM   MH

Wrought or malleable iron, 5" long, 1 3/4" diameter, unsigned.

This bit is hand-forged.

Historic Maritime III (1800-1840): Boomtown Years & the Dawn of the Industrial Revolution

Woodworking: Boring Tools

913108T30   **Tap**   DTM   MH

Steel and wood, 3 1/2" long with a 2 5/8" long metal end, 3" wide handle, unsigned.

This is a wooden tap for making a hole in a piece of wood.

TCE1001   **Tap borer**   DTM   MH

Forged iron and steel, wood, 13 1/2" long, 15" handle, signed with an obscure maker's sign.

31602T5   **Taper bit**   DTM   MH

Cast steel, 12 1/4" long, 2" wide at top, signed "F. Walker Sheffield".

The most depth at the shoulder is 7/8".

Woodworking: Edge Tools

041505T1   **Adz**   DTM   MH

Forged steel, iron, and wood, 9 1/2" long, 4 1/4" wide blade, 9 1/4" long handle, signed "No 2" with a distinct hallmark.

This adz is the typical style of European hand adzes used for centuries. It was brought to the Fall River, Massachusetts area by a Portuguese immigrant in the late 19th or early 20th century. Its hallmark and nicely carved hooped wooden handle date it to the early 19th century.

http://www.davistownmuseum.org/pics/041505t1.jpg

22612T3   **Cabinet scraper**   DTM   TT

Cast bronze body, steel blade, malleable iron cap, 10" long, 2" long blade, signed "TORRTS" owners' mark.

This tool is hand-forged and typical in design and materials of scrapers that were made as early as the Roman empire. The British Museum has a similar specimen, date unknown.

31811T18   **Chisel**   DTM   TT

Hand-forged iron and steel, 9 1/12" long, 1/2" wide, signed obscured in a forge fold, might be "SHAW".

6703T1   **Corner chisel**   DTM   MH

Forged steel, 11 3/8" long, 7/8" edges, signed "G. SHELDON".

This socket chisel looks like it was cast and then finished by hand. DATM (Nelson 1999, 711) states that both the name G. Sheldan and Sheldon Mfg. Co. have also been reported for gouges and chisels. There is no known location or dates.

ID #   Status   Location

Woodworking: Edge Tools

22311T18   Drawknife   DTM   TT

Forged wrought iron and steel with a wood handle, 18 1/2" long, 12 1/2" long blade, unsigned.

This drawknife is handmade and hand-forged with a steel cutting edge. Part of the Robert Sullivan Collection donation.

041505T21   Drawknife   DTM   MH

Forged iron and steel, wood handles, brass ferrules, 11" long, 6 1/2" wide cutting edge, 4 1/2" long handles, signed "J. Windly".

This is an American-made tool. Windly is not listed in DATM (Nelson 1999).

http://www.davistownmuseum.org/pics/041505t21.jpg

21201T5   Drawknife   DTM   MH

Forged iron and steel with a wood handle, 16 3/4" long, 11 1/4" blade, 4 3/4" handle, signed "Hardy" followed by a hatchet touchmark.

Possibly this is Ephraim L. Hardy of Brookline and Hollis, NH, working after 1821, died 1870. "All tools marked with this last name are not necessarily his." (DATM 1999, 354).

http://www.davistownmuseum.org/pics/21201t5.jpg

22411T3   Drawknife   DTM   TT

Forge welded steel with brass ferrules, 15 1/2" long, 6 1/2" wide, 10" long blade, unsigned.

This drawknife is handmade from a file.

12812T4   Drawknife   DTM   TT

Forged iron and steel with laminated edge, brass, wood (rosewood) handles, 10 1/2" long, 4" handles, 5 3/4" cutting edge, signed "J.T. COFFIN & SON".

DATM (Nelson 1999, 177) notes John T. Coffin (b.1881 d.1892) of Center Harbor, NH, worked as John T. Coffin and Son from 1884 to 1886 making edge tools.

50402T5   Drawknife   DTM   MH

Hand-forged steel, wood handle, brass ferrules, 14" wide, 8 1/2" blade, unsigned.

Distinctly hand-forged, this drawknife's uniqueness lies in two molding profiles carefully worked into the forged steel blade making this tool very useful for making moldings 5/8" and 7/8" wide. A one-of-a-kind adaptation for a drawknife, this adaptation has not previously been noted.

http://www.davistownmuseum.org/pics/50402t5_p1.jpg
http://www.davistownmuseum.org/pics/50402t5_p2.jpg

ID #   Status   Location

Woodworking: Edge Tools

51606T6   **Drawknife**   DTM   MH

Forged welded iron and steel with wooden handles, 18" long with a 11 3/8" cutting blade, signed "J. MATLACK".

J. Matlack is another unknown and unlisted New England edge toolmaker. The handmade handles with peened tangs attest to the affect of this tool.

http://www.davistownmuseum.org/pics/51606t6.jpg
http://www.davistownmuseum.org/pics/51606t6_sig.jpg

913108T23   **Drawknife**   DTM   MH

Recycled steel file, wood handle, 12" long, 7 3/4" long blade, unsigned.

TG1004   **Drawshave**   DTM   MH

Cast steel (?), 13 5/8" long, 9 1/2" blades, unsigned.

It has no handles.

102800T1   **Drawshave**   DTM   MH

Forged iron and cast steel, signed "J. Taylor Cast Steel".

This tool was found in a tool chest with a southern NH - western Massachusetts provenance and is either late 18th or early 19th century. It is unusual in that the forged iron handles are obviously welded onto the clearly marked cast steel blade, with both letters "s" inverted during stamping. John Taylor of Liverpool, England, worked 1816 - 1849 and may have made this tool.

10407T4   **Drawshave**   DTM   MH

Steel, wood, brass ferrules, 10 1/2" wide with a 7" cutting edge, unsigned.

The handles are handmade and it is obviously forged from an old file. It is a typical edge tool utilizing the strategy of recycling a high quality (probably English or German) steel file.

http://www.davistownmuseum.org/pics/10407t4.jpg

913108T32   **Drawshave**   DTM   MH

Iron with a welded steel cutting edge, wood, 19 1/4" long, 13" blade, signed "HIGGINS", c. 1835-40?.

42904T3   **Framing chisel**   DTM   MH

Forged iron and weld steel, 10 9/16" long, 2" wide cutting edge, unsigned.

It has no handle.

TCS1001   **Froe**   DTM   TT

Forged iron and steel, 17 1/2" long, 15" cutting edge, unsigned.

A froe is an essential woodworking tool utilized for shingle-making and one of the basic tools in a settlers' tool kit.

ID #   Status   Location

Woodworking: Edge Tools

090109T3   Gouge   DTM   MH

Forged iron, steel, and wood, 16" long including a 4 1/4" long wood and iron handle, 1 1/4" wide, signed "HORTON" and "NEW YORK".

William Horton made adzes, axes, and chisels in New York from 1837-1853 and used this signature. He was earlier part of Horton & Morris and later of Horton & Arnold (Nelson 1999, 398).

http://www.davistownmuseum.org/pics/090109T3web1.jpg
http://www.davistownmuseum.org/pics/090109T3web2.jpg

090109T1   Gouge   DTM   MH

Blister steel, iron, and wood, 15 1/4" long including a 2 1/2" long wooden handle, 1 7/8" wide cutting edge, unsigned.

http://www.davistownmuseum.org/pics/090109T1web1.jpg
http://www.davistownmuseum.org/pics/090109T1web3.jpg

TCC3002   Gouge   DTM   MH

Cast or forged steel with wood handle, 8 1/2" long including handle, 1/2" wide, signed "F. Stones".

Stones is listed in DATM (Nelson 1999, 761) but his location is unknown. We have two gouges by this maker; who is F. Stones and where did he work?

41907T2   Gouge   DTM   MH

Forged iron and German steel, 9 7/8" long, 1 1/4" wide with a later 3 3/4" long wooden handle, signed "Weldon".

DATM (Nelson 1999, 839) lists Weldon as a maker of plane irons and saws with no location or date. Forge welding is clearly evident on the socket of this tool, which also shows evidence of additional forging of its cutting edge. No obvious steel bit insert is evident. The tool body appears to be one piece of steel welded onto the iron socket.

31808PC8   Mortising chisel   DTM   MH

Steel and wood, 13 1/8" long, 1 1/2" wide blade, signed with a partially obscured "D. W_____WAY" and "DA___WICH" and perpendicular "LSISSON".

Possibly the mark on the tool is "Hathaway" who was a New Bedford, MA, edge toolmaker.

31808PC7   Mortising gouge   DTM   MH-O

Hand-forged natural steel, 12" long, 2 1/4" wide, unsigned.

http://www.davistownmuseum.org/pics/31808pc7.jpg

TCC3004   Scorp   DTM   MH

Forged iron and steel, 7 1/4" diameter, unsigned, c. 1840.

This is a multiple purpose woodworking tool used for bowl- and shave-making.

Woodworking: Edge Tools

32113T1   **Slick**

Forged iron and steel, brass ferrule, wooden handle, 22" long, 16" long blade, 2 3/4" wide cutting edge, signed "D BABCOCK & Co".

Oliver and Daniel Babcock formed this company in 1824 in Potter Hill, CT (http://dcodriscoll.pbworks.com/w/page/9955123/Babcock_(I)).

121412T5   **Slick**

Forge-welded steel, wood (oak), 21 1/2" long, 8 1/2" handle, unsigned.

071704T2   **Socket chisel**

Forged steel and wood, 7" long including a 3 3/4" wood handle, signed "Weldon".

Weldon is listed in DATM (Nelson 1999) without working locations or dates.

090109T2   **Socket chisel**

Forged iron and steel, wood, 15 1/4" long with a 3 3/4" long wood and iron handle, 1 1/2" wide cutting edge, signed "UNDERHILL", "& GEORGE", "BOSTON" with a flower cartouche.

George Washington Underhill worked in Boston with a brother (thought to be Samuel G.) before returning to Nashua, NH, in 1839. He later was a founder of the Underhill Edge Tool Co. This exact mark is not reported in DATM (Nelson 1999).

http://www.davistownmuseum.org/pics/090109T2web-3.jpg
http://www.davistownmuseum.org/bio#bioUnderhill.html

071704T7   **Socket chisel**

Forged iron and steel, 16" long, 1 5/16" wide cutting edge, signed "W. Beatty".

W. Beatty is the patriarch of a whole clan of Pennsylvania edge toolmakers who worked in the Springfield area throughout the 19th century. W. Beatty's working dates are: 1806-1829 - Waterville, PA, after 1829 he worked in Springfield, PA. W. Beatty's tools often include the touchmark of a figure of a cow, which can be barely seen on this tool. Unusual in its long length, this edge tool was almost certainly used for mortising.

http://www.davistownmuseum.org/bioBeatyson.html

121805T16   **Socket chisel**

Forged iron and German or blister steel, 13 5/8" long including 4" handle, 1 1/2" wide, unsigned.

This chisel is forge-welded with a lap and no clear iron-steel interface. It has an iron ferrule on the wood handle and an early 19th or late 18th century appearance.

http://www.davistownmuseum.org/pics/121805t16_p2.jpg

ID #   Status   Location

Woodworking: Edge Tools

4105T3   Socket chisel   DTM   MH

Forged iron and steel, wood handle, 16" long including a 5 3/4" long handle with iron ferrule, 1 15/16" wide, signed "R&HPORTER", c. 1810.

No R & H Porter is listed in DATM (Nelson 1999). This has the appearance of an early 19th century forge-welded tool with a handmade, not factory turned, handle. Only the slightest hint of the steel - iron interface is visible.

http://www.davistownmuseum.org/pics/4105t3.jpg
http://www.davistownmuseum.org/pics/4105t3_sig.jpg

42912LTC1   Spokeshave with bone sole   DA   TT (Pub)

Forged steel, bone, hardwood, 11" long wooden handle, 4" wide cutting edge, unsigned.

Courtesy of Liberty Tool Co.

32113T2   Timber framing chisel   LPC   MH

Forged iron and steel, steel ferrule, wooden handle, 16 1/2" long, 11 3/4" long blade, 2" wide cutting edge, signed "DEAN & SAWYER".

041505T22   Wheelwrights' shave   DTM   MH

Forged iron, weld steel, and wood handles, 11" long, 2" sharply curved cutting blade, 2 7/8" long handles, peened forged iron handle holders, unsigned.

This may also have been a shovel handle makers' shave. It is hand-forged and filed.

http://www.davistownmuseum.org/pics/041505t22.jpg

10407T3   Wheelwrights' shave   DTM   MH

Malleable iron or German steel, wooden handles, 12" long, 1 12/16" wide and 7/8" deeply curved cutting edge, unsigned.

Previously described as a coopers' shave and shown on the Martha Stewart show, this shave shows no evidence of a steeled cutting edge, but is made of one piece of high quality malleable iron or German steel with significant evidence of hand filing and peened iron handle ends, typical of handmade tools of the period (1800 - 1840).

http://www.davistownmuseum.org/pics/10407t3.jpg
http://www.davistownmuseum.org/pics/10407t3_pic1.jpg

Woodworking: Edge Tools - American Made Cast Steel

TCC2011   Claw hatchet   BDTM   TT

Cast steel with wood handle, 12" long with a 2 7/8" blade, signed "JOEL HOWE PATENT".

DATM (1999) lists Joel Howe as a manufacturer of hammers and hatchets, Medford, MA, 1834. The pattern of this tool echoes mid-18th century English designs. See Diderot (1964). Did Howe learn his trade in Sheffield and then emigrate to the United States as did many other toolmakers? This is one of the finest as well as most enigmatic tools in the Museum's Archaeology of Tools.

http://www.davistownmuseum.org/pics/tcc2011.jpg

Woodworking: Edge Tools - American Made Cast Steel

111001T2   **Corner chisel**   DTM   MH

Cast steel and wood, 5" handle, 1 1/16" x 1 1/16" cutting edges, signed "J.GRAY" and "CAST.STEEL".

DATM (Nelson 1999) lists John Gray as working in Kingston, MA, c. 1840. This chisel was associated with a Marshfield, MA boatbuilders' tools which included one Tolman plane.

http://www.davistownmuseum.org/pics/111001t2_p1.jpg
http://www.davistownmuseum.org/pics/111001t2_p2.jpg

TCC2008   **Corner chisel**   DTM   MH

Cast steel, 16 3/4" long, 11/16" wide, unsigned, c. 1820.

This unusual tool is a one-of-a-kind and utilizes cast steel billets. It is typical of a blacksmith shop-made edge tool.

101701T1   **Drawknife**   DTM   MH

Cast steel with wood handle, 17 3/8" wide, 12" blade, signed "LAVERY CAST STEEL", c. 1820.

One wood handle is missing. DATM (Nelson 1999) does not list any Lavery as a maker of edge tools. This appears to be American. Who was Lavery and where did he work?

TCC2001   **Drawknife**   DTM   MH

Cast steel, brass, with wood handle, 18 1/2" length, 12" blade, signed "BROWN & WALKER WARRANTED CAST STEEL".

The maker is not listed in DATM (Nelson 1999). Where did Brown & Walker manufacture their tools?

http://www.davistownmuseum.org/pics/TCC2001.jpg
http://www.davistownmuseum.org/pics/TCC2001_sig2.jpg

51100T8   **Drawknife**   DTM   MII

Cast steel and wood, 10 1/4" long, 6" blade, signed "R. Dickinson Warrented".

DATM (Nelson 1999) lists an F. Dickinson Warranted mark used by chisel-maker Friend Dickinson of Higganum, CT, in 1849.

913108T51   **Drawshave**   DTM   MH

Malleable iron, welded cast steel, and wood, 15 1/2" long, 9 1/4" long blade, signed "CAST" and "STEEL" in a box and "I.POPE" in a box.

The signature is of a late 18th century style.

31212T15   **Framing gouge**   DTM   TT

Cast steel, iron ferrule, hickory handle, 20" long, 1 1/2" wide edge, signed "J. GRAY CAST STEEL".

This inside bevel gouge is obviously hand-forged, as is the iron ferrule on the butt. John Gray worked out of Kingston, Massachusetts circa 1840s, but local historical records of his existence are scant at best. (http://www.numismalink.com/drew.note17.html). Courtesy of Liberty Tool Co.

ID #   Status   Location

Woodworking: Edge Tools - American Made Cast Steel

102100T26   Gouge   DTM   MH

Cast steel, wood, brass, 9 5/8" long with a 4" long and 3/8" wide blade, signed "Charles Buck CAST STEEL".

He is among the most famous of all American edge toolmakers.

http://www.davistownmuseum.org/bioBuckBrothers.html

10700T5   Gouge   DTM   MH

Cast steel, brass, and wood, 10" long, 1/2" wide, signed "Tremont Co".

There is no Tremont listed in DATM (Nelson 1999). There was a cotton mill named Tremont Co. in Lowell, MA, in 1835 (White, 1836, "Memoir of Samuel Slater").

TCC3001   Gouge   DTM   MH

Cast steel with wood handle, 7 5/8" long, 3/8" wide blade, signed "F. Stones".

It has a strongly beveled handle. DATM (Nelson 1999, 761) lists F. Stones as a maker of chisels and plane irons (no location or dates.)

31212T16   Inside bevel gouge   DTM   TT

Cast steel, wood (hickory), 15 1/8" long, 1" wide edge, signed "J. GRAY CAST STEEL".

This gouge is obviously hand-forged. John Gray worked out of Kingston, Massachusetts circa 1840s, but local historical records of his existence are scant at best. Courtesy of Liberty Tool Co.

100400T16   Peen adz   DTM   MH

Weld - cast steel, 9 1/4" long, 4 1/8" wide blade, signed "HOLLAND CAST STEEL" with 4 small suns and an oval with a keyhole inside it.

DATM (Nelson 1999) lists a Holland as a maker of drawknives, no date or location. This tool has a New England provenance - who made it and where? While the date of manufacture of this peg poll adz is uncertain, it could typify the working tool box of any shipwright working in Maine, c. 1840. This tool raises the question of when, even if in small quantities, cast steel tools were made in America. Was the cast steel in this tool imported from England before being transformed by a small American workshop into this edge tool? Or did "Holland" have his own foundry and manufacture the cast steel used for this tool from wrought iron now readily available from US puddling (reverbatory) furnaces?

http://www.davistownmuseum.org/pics/100400-16.jpg

TCR1005   Scraper   DTM   MH

Cast steel and wood, 9" long, 2 3/4" wide blade, signed "H. M. INMAN".

This maker is not listed in DATM (Nelson 1999). Is this the manufacturer's signature or the owner's signature? What was this old scraper used for? This tool was found in a ship carpenters' tool chest.

ID #   Status   Location

Woodworking: Edge Tools - American Made Cast Steel

6712LTC2   **Slick**   DA   TT (Pub)

Forged cast steel, rosewood, 32" long, 6" wide, 4 5/8" long cutting edge, signed "CAST STEEL COBB & THAYER".

Courtesy of Frank Kosmerl. According to him, Cobb & Thayer first advertised in the local Rochester, NY, paper in Dec. of 1820. They announced dissolution of the partnership in Dec. of 1821.

TCC2003   **Socket chisel**   DTM   MH

Cast steel, forged iron, and wood, 1 1/2" width, 13 3/4" length, signed with multiple signatures "B.D. Hathaway" "J. F. Marbel".

B.D. Hathaway is listed in DATM (Nelson 1999) as a New Bedford MA, edge toolmaker, 1836 f. The second signature, within an 18th century cartouche, is "J. F. Marbel" and is not listed in DATM. This tool was probably used in shipyard work in New Bedford during the florescence of the whaling industry. The handle has a forged ferrule and the socket shows clear signs of hand forging. It is an interesting example of the adaptation of cast steel manufacturing process at an early date by a U.S. manufacturer. Since the touchmark is earlier than the later manufacturer's signature (Hathaway), could this tool have originally been manufactured in England and then brought to the United States for finish work? Or was this tool made in two stages by American makers? Who is J.F. Marbel? Please contact the Museum if you believe any of these maker's marks are those of Sheffield toolmakers.

http://www.davistownmuseum.org/pics/TCC2003.jpg
http://www.davistownmuseum.org/pics/TCC2003_sig.jpg

TCC2004   **Socket chisel**   DTM   MH

Malleable iron and cast steel, wood, 2 1/2" wide, 17 3/4" long, signed "J. BRIGGS" "CAST-STEEL" and "#" on the opposite side, c. 1800.

The handle has a forged ferrule. This tool has a distinctly forged socket. It is not specifically listed in DATM (Nelson 1999) but many Briggs are noted as toolmakers.

http://www.davistownmuseum.org/pics/tcc2004.jpg

42602T5   **Socket chisel**   DTM   MH

Cast steel, 6 3/4" long, 5/16" wide, signed "S. W. DROWN CAST STEEL".

DATM (Nelson 1999) lists a Drown & Walker as chisel makers, no date or location. Who was S. W. Drown and when and where did he work? One of the many mysteries in the collection of The Davistown Museum. Information is welcomed.

TCC2011A   **Socket chisel**   DTM   MH

Cast steel, 9" long and 1/4" wide, signed "TILTON & WHEELWRIGHT MANUFG. CO. WARRANTED CAST STEEL".

This maker is not listed in DATM (Nelson 1999). Who was Tilton & Wheelwright and where did they manufacture their tools?

Woodworking: Edge Tools - American Made Cast Steel

TCC2010   **Socket chisel**   DTM   MH

Cast steel, 9" long, 1/2" wide, signed "SALISBURY & ALDEN STAFFORD CT CAST STEEL" with an eagle mark.

The company is listed in DATM (Nelson 1999) without a date.

8312T2   **Socket firmer chisel**   DTM   TT

Cast steel with forge-welded laminated edge, 11 3/4" long, 1 1/2" wide cutting edge, signed "UNDERHILL EDGE TOOL CO. WARRANTED CAST STEEL".

http://www.davistownmuseum.org/bioUnderhill.html

102904T13   **Socket gouge**   DTM   MH

Forged iron and welded cast steel, wooden handle, iron ferrule, 15 2/8" long including 4 3/4" long handle, 5/8" wide, signed "J. GRAY CAST STEEL".

J. Gray is from Kingston, MA, c. 1849. He made edge tools used by the Rochester, MA, shipbuilders to create the New Bedford whaling ships. Did he use imported English cast steel or a local source of slightly inferior American cast steel? The primitive hand-forged appearance of this gouge suggests that it may have been made prior to the working dates listed by DATM -- was there more than one J. Gray working in Kingston, MA, which was a center of edge tool production utilizing local bog iron beginning at least as early as the mid-18th century?

http://www.davistownmuseum.org/pics/102904t13_p1.jpg

52603T2   **Tang chisel**   DTM   MH

Cast steel with brass handle, 10 1/4" long, 4" head, unsigned.

Woodworking: Edge Tools - Imported Cast Steel

090508T11   **Chisel**   DTM   MH

Cast steel and wood, 13 3/4" long, 7" long and 1/4" wide blade, signed "WM ASH & CO" and "CAST STEEL".

William Ash is first listed in the 1825 Sheffield directory as a joiners' toolmaker, and then, from 1828 to 1841 as William Ash & Co.

TCC1008   **Chisel**   DTM   MH

Cast or forged steel, 4 1/8" long, 3/4" wide, signed "Stubs".

It is made from one of Stub's recycled files.

http://www.davistownmuseum.org/bioStubs.htm

TCC1005   **Chisel**   DTM   MH

Cast steel, 7 5/8" long including handle, 1/4" wide blade, signed "W.N. Greaves & Son Cast Steel" and marked "Sheafworks" on the reverse side.

"Sheafworks" clearly identifies this as an imported tool from Sheffield, England.

ID #   Status   Location

Woodworking: Edge Tools - Imported Cast Steel

33002T20   **Chisel**   DTM   TT

Cast steel, wood, with brass ferrule, 9" long including 5 1/6" handle, signed "Moulson Brothers Cast Steel".

81200T15   **Chisel**   DTM   MHC

Cast steel and wood, 8" long with a 4" blade, signed "____ Jackson Sheffield" with KIM's cartouche. Owner's stamp on handle "H.M. INMAN".

TCC1004   **Chisel**   DTM   MH

Cast steel with wood handle, 8 1/4" long, skewed blade that is 3/4" wide, signed "W.N. Greaves & Son Cast Steel" and marked "Sheafworks" on the reverse side.

It has a beveled handle.

TCC1003   **Chisel**   DTM   MH

Cast steel with oak handle, 9 1/2" long including handle, blade 1 3/4" wide, signed "James Cam cast steel".

The handle is strongly beveled. James Cam was one of the most prolific Sheffield edge tool manufacturers.

http://www.davistownmuseum.org/bioJamesCam.htm

111002T3   **Drawknife**   DTM   MH

Cast steel, brass ferrules, wood handle with iron rivets, 17 1/2" long, 10 1/4" long blade, signed "JAMES CAM CAST STEEL".

This is a very fine example of a quality English edge tool.

112704T4   **Drawknife**   DTM   MH

Cast steel, Forged iron, and wood handle, 17 3/4" wide, 10 1/2" long blade, 5" long turned handles, signed "SPEAR & JACKSON CAST STEEL" "10 inch" and a cartouche "S*J".

This edge tool typifies the high quality of imported English edge tools of the early and mid-19th century. If an American craftsman was not using a hand-wrought American drawknife, this would be his rather expensive alternative.

http://www.davistownmuseum.org/pics/112704t4.jpg
http://www.davistownmuseum.org/pics/112704t4_sig.jpg

135

ID #   Status   Location

Woodworking: Edge Tools - Imported Cast Steel

63001T6   **Drawknife**   DTM   MH

Cast steel, wood, and iron ferrules, 15 1/4" long, 9" blade, signed "W BUTCHER WARRANTED CASTSTEEL" with the initials "W.B" and "9".

A classic example of a late 18th century or early 19th century quality English Sheffield-made cast steel tool imported to the US just before the rise of American cast steel and malleable cast iron manufacturing processes.

http://www.davistownmuseum.org/pics/63001t6_p1.jpg
http://www.davistownmuseum.org/pics/63001t6_p3.jpg

32313LTC5   **Firmer chisel**   DA   TT (Pub)

Cast steel, forged steel, wood (hickory), brass, 16 1/2" long, 5 1/2" long handle, 1" cutting edge, signed "W. ASH & CO" "BDH".

121911T1   **Gouge**   DTM   TT

Crystallized cast steel and wood, 9 3/4" long handle, 3" long, 1" wide cutting edge, signed "T. TILLOTSON SHEFFIELD" "patent crystallized cast steel" and 3 touchmarks.

111001T16   **Gouge**   DTM   MH

Wood, brass, and cast steel, 6 3/4" long, 3 3/16" wood handle, signed "Groves & Son Cast Steel".

Made by one of the more prolific of English cast steel tool manufacturers.

TCC1009   **Gouge**   DTM   MH

Cast steel, 6 5/8" long, 5/16" wide, signed "J. CAM".

http://www.davistownmuseum.org/bioJamesCam.htm

51201T10   **Gouge**   DTM   MH

Cast steel and wood, 9 1/2" long with 5 1/2" wood handle, 13/64" wide gouge, signed "Butcher".

This gouge is from the Simon Willard toolbox.

http://www.davistownmuseum.org/pics/51201T10.jpg
http://www.davistownmuseum.org/bioWillard.htm

42904T10   **Gouge**   DTM   MH

Cast steel and wood, 11 1/8" long including 4 1/8" wooden handle, 1 1/2" wide, signed "SPEAR &" "JACKSON" "IMPROVED" on front and "WARRANTED CAST STEEL" on front.

Made by a Sheffield, England manufacturer.

Woodworking: Edge Tools - Imported Cast Steel

TCC2002   Gouge   DTM   MH

Cast steel, 14" long, gouge 2" in diameter, signed "Holland & Turner, cast steel".

"Holland & Turner, steel and file manfrs. 12 Bower spring" is the listing in the 1852 Directory of the Borough and Parish of Sheffield [UK] (http://www.genuki.org.uk/big/eng/YKS/Misc/Transcriptions/WRY/Sheffield1852AlphaG-J.html). They are also listed as steel converters and refiners on Sussex St. in the 1857 Sheffield Directory (http://freepages.history.rootsweb.ancestry.com/~claycross/964-980.htm).

TCC1002   Gouge   DTM   MH

Cast steel with wood handle, 9 3/4" long including handle, blade 13/16" wide, signed "Mottran Cast Steel".

51201T11   Gouge   DTM   MH

Cast steel and wood, 10 1/4" long, 5 7/8" wooden handle, signed "J. CAM".

This gouge is from the Simon Willard toolbox.

http://www.davistownmuseum.org/pics/51201T11.jpg
http://www.davistownmuseum.org/bioWillard.htm

TCC1007   Gouge   DTM   MH

Cast steel, 7 1/2" long, 3/16" wide blade, signed "P. STUBBS CAST STEEL".

http://www.davistownmuseum.org/bioStubs.htm

33002T18   Gouge   DTM   MH

Cast steel, 10" long, 1 9/16" wide, signed "W. Greaves & Son Cast Steel".

This gouge is typical of the 19th century woodworking tools imported from Sheffield, England.

http://www.davistownmuseum.org/pics/33002t18.jpg

31212T18   Mortising chisel   DTM   TT

Malleable iron and cast steel, 6" long, signed "JAMES HOWARTH CAST STEEL".

James Howarth was a Sheffield, UK, edge toolmaker (http://www.popularwoodworking.com/woodworking-blogs/editors-blog/james-howarth-19th-century-toolmaker). This crudely cast chisel shows signs of hand-forging. Courtesy of Liberty Tool Co.

Historic Maritime III (1800-1840): Boomtown Years & the Dawn of the Industrial Revolution

Woodworking: Edge Tools - Imported Cast Steel

102904T12   Socket chisel   DTM   MH

Cast steel, brass ferrule, 15 1/4" long including 5" long handle, 7/8" wide, signed "J. L. WHELPLEY" "BOSTON, MASS." "WARD CAST STEEL" and various touchmarks and cartouches.

The owner's signature (Whelpley) is in a more modern (c. 1870) style. Several other Whelpley signed tools accompanied this one in a Wells, Maine, tool chest, including a Steer's patented plane and several interesting calipers. This socket chisel is clearly stamped with a prominent English edge toolmakers' hallmark, accompanied by numerous touchmarks, including one indicating Ward was licensed by the crown to produce tools, possibly for export. At the same time that this English woodworking tool was being exported to the United States, numerous American foundries were gearing up their production of high quality edge tools, also utilizing imported English cast steel. Who was Mr. Whelpley and what did he make with his tools?

http://www.davistownmuseum.org/pics/102904t12_p3.jpg

041505T3   Socket chisel   DTM   MH

Malleable iron, cast steel, wooden handle, iron ferrule, 13 1/4" long, 1 7/16" wide blade, signed "CAST STEEL" and an obscured maker's mark.

This is an excellent example of an early forged and weld steel edge tool. The cast steel in this primitively forged tool is almost certainly imported from England.

http://www.davistownmuseum.org/pics/041505t3_p1.jpg

TCC1006   Tanged gouge   DTM   MH

Cast steel with wood handle, 9 1/2" long, 1" wide blade, signed "Groves & Son Cast Steel".

It has a replaced handle. DATM (Nelson 1999, 1021) lists Richard Groves & Son as a foreign maker of chisels and saws dating from 1770 - 1892.

TCC3010   Wood chisel   DTM   MH

Cast steel with replaced handle and ferrule, 7 3/8" long, 7/16" wide blade, signed "A. ARTHUR CAST STEEL".

This mundane looking chisel is unusual in that it's the only tool we've ever encountered with this signature. Was A. Arthur an obscure Sheffield maker or an unlisted American maker?

Woodworking: Edge Tools Made in Maine

12801T10   Chisel   DTM   MH

Forged iron and steel, 10 5/8" long, 1/2" wide blade, signed very crisply "G. B. RICKER" and "B.G.F" probably an owner's mark.

http://www.davistownmuseum.org/pics/12801t10_p5.jpg
http://www.davistownmuseum.org/publications/volume10.html

Historic Maritime III (1800-1840): Boomtown Years & the Dawn of the Industrial Revolution

ID #   Status   Location

Woodworking: Edge Tools Made in Maine

12801T9   **Chisel**   DTM   MH

Forged iron and steel, 11 1/4" long, 1 15/16" wide, signed "G. B. RICKER" "CHERRYFIELD".

This timber framing chisel dates from the heyday of the Cherryfield and Down East shipbuilding era (1820 - 1850) when hundreds of ships were built in Cherryfield, Addison, Columbia Falls, Jonesport, and other Down East communities for the cod fishery.

http://www.davistownmuseum.org/pics/12801t9_p5.jpg
http://www.davistownmuseum.org/publications/volume10.html

111001T13   **Drawshave**   DTM   UNK

Cast steel and wood, 14 1/2" long, 8 1/4" blade, signed "Wilson Lewiston" with an 8 point asterisk touchmark.

DATM (Nelson 1999) does not list a Wilson of Lewiston. It is early 19th century in appearance.

http://www.davistownmuseum.org/publications/volume10.html

032203T2   **Framing chisel**   DTM   TT

Forged iron and cast steel, 14 1/2" long including 3" long handle, 2" wide, signed "MAL_ETT CAST STEEL".

The underside of this framing chisel shows distinct evidence of hand-forging, especially at the junction of the socket and body. No obvious weld steel edge is visible; therefore, this tool may be a direct process smith-forged tool. This is probably a product of the workshops of either James Mallett of Warren or John Mallett of Rockland.

http://www.davistownmuseum.org/pics/032203t2_p2.jpg
http://www.davistownmuseum.org/pics/032203t2_p3.jpg

40501T2   **Gouge**   DTM   UNK

Forged iron and weld steel, 12 1/2" long, 1 7/8" wide, signed "G. B. RICKER" "CHERRYFIELD".

Ricker is Down East Maine's most famous edge toolmaker. A gift to the Museum by Rick Floyd.

http://www.davistownmuseum.org/pics/40501t2_p5.jpg
http://www.davistownmuseum.org/publications/volume10.html

100108T3   **Socket chisel**   DTM   MH

Cast steel, wood, and forged iron, 14 1/4" long, 1 1/4" wide, signed "MALLET" "CAST STEEL" "WARRANTED" and "WARREN ME".

This hand-forged chisel has a primitive iron ferrule and is clearly steeled. The spelling of Mallet raises the question, is this John Mallet of Rockland, earlier working in Warren, his father, or did he sometimes spell his name Mallett? It was formerly in the collection of Ed Shaw.

http://www.davistownmuseum.org/publications/volume10.html

Woodworking: Edge Tools Made in Maine

81602T17   **Socket chisel**   DTM   MH

Cast steel, 14 1/4" long including a 4 3/8" ferruled handle, signed "BILLINGS." "CAST STEEL" "CHINA" "CAST STEEL" "WARRANTED".

This chisel appears to be earlier than other tools made by the Billings clan, except possibly John Billings of Clinton, ME (1825-1881). Did he also work in China, or is this an unrelated Billings? This is a previously unrecorded mark on a clearly handmade tool. It was donated to the Museum by Rick Floyd.

http://www.davistownmuseum.org/pics/81602t17_p1.jpg
http://www.davistownmuseum.org/publications/volume10.html

Woodworking: Other Tools

12801T8   **Bit brace**   DTM   MH

Forged iron, signed "Taylor's Patent", also marked "I Wilson".

DATM (Nelson 1999) lists J. M. Taylor as being issued a patent for a brace on June 30, 1836 in Hebron, CT. It also lists Increase Wilson as working in New London, CT, 1818 to 1855 (d. 1861) and as the manufacturer of Taylor's braces. Could this be an unmarked cast steel tool or forged malleable iron?

31501T1   **Brace and bits (3)**   DTM   MH

Cast steel and wood, one 4" and two 3 1/2" bits, 9 1/2" long brace with 3 3/4" swing, signed "CAST STEEL" on bits.

These were mounted by a previous collector on wood; any manufacturer's signature is not visible. It is a typical bit and brace set of the early 19th century, prior to the mass production of patented braces.

TAB3000   **Carving mallet**   DTM   MH

Maple, 10" high, 5 1/2" diameter, unsigned.

TG1003   **Center punch**   DTM   MH

Forged steel, 3 1/2" wide, unsigned.

32708T56   **Gentlemans' brace**   DTM   MH

Brass and wood, 14 7/8" wide, 5" high, signed "A & W" "JINKIMSON" "SHEFFIELD" on a brass plate and "S. HART" on the other side.

http://www.davistownmuseum.org/pics/32708t56-4.jpg
http://www.davistownmuseum.org/pics/32708t56-3.jpg

10700-T3   **Gimlet**   DTM   MH

Forged iron and wood, 10 3/4" long with 7" long handle, unsigned.

ID #   Status   Location

Woodworking: Other Tools

101312T16   Gutter hand adz   DTM   TT

Forged steel, wood (hickory), 15" long, 4 3/4" cutting edge, signed "I * F" in a heart.

The mark could belong to Ivory Foss of Freedom, NH; Isaac Fitch of Lebanon, CT; or Isaac Field of Trenton, NJ and Providence, RI.

102100T13   Log dog   DTM   MH

Forged iron, 4" long single wedge leg, 3 1/8" long double wedge leg, unsigned.

A log dog is used to hold wood together during gluing.

041505T23   Log dog   DTM   MH

Forged iron, 12 3/8" long, unsigned.

This is one of the essential iron components of a timber framed barn, house, or wharf. It is smith-forged and difficult to date. It is also called a barn dog.

http://www.davistownmuseum.org/pics/041505t23.jpg

TCR1019   Mallet   DTM   MH

Wood, 6" long, unsigned.

This is a generic tool typical of a carpenters' tool box of the mid-19th century.

http://www.davistownmuseum.org/pics/tcr1021.jpg

TCS1002   Marking gauge   DTM   MH

Fruitwood, 1' long, 3" wide, unsigned, c. 1820.

This is a depth measuring tool with a threaded screw; common to all carpenters' tool kits.

43006T7   Marking gauge   DTM   TT

Forged iron or steel, 11 3/4" long, 9/16" square with a single 3 1/8" adjustable depth marker, signed "W. R. Stone".

The signature is not listed in DATM (Nelson 1999); it is almost certainly owner-made.

82500T5   Mortise cleaner   DTM   MH

Forged iron, 23 1/3" long, signed with an illegible signature.

This delicate tool is probably early 19th century. It is displayed with our collection of mortising tools.

42012T3   Rasp   DTM   TT

Forge-welded German steel, 12 5/16" long, 1" wide, signed with an English touchmark.

This is a typical imported English file. Courtesy of Liberty Tool Co.

TCR3000   Saw set   DTM   MH

Drop-forged iron, 5 1/8" long, 1 5/16" wide, signed "BORUEAU PARIS".

141

ID #   Status   Location

Woodworking: Other Tools

041505T29   **Saw set**   DTM   MH

Forged iron and steel, signed "S. C. BEMIS", c. 1838.

It is made by Stephen C. Bemis, probably of Springfield, MA. Bemis later founded Bemis & Call H & T Co. of Springfield, 1844-1910.

http://www.davistownmuseum.org/pics/041505t29.jpg
http://www.davistownmuseum.org/bioBemis.html

3405T7   **Saw set**   DTM   MH

Cast steel and boxwood, 8" long including a 4 1/8" long wooden handle, signed "W & C WYNN H.22 CAST STEEL" and signed on verso by the owner "D C Stetson".

DATM (Nelson 1999, 884) lists W. & C. Wynn with no location or date. This nicely made saw set appears to be early 19th century.

42405T8   **Saw set**   DTM   MH

Drop-forged iron and steel with a brass nut, 8 3/8" long, signed "J. Gladding Deep River CT".

DATM (Nelson 1999) lists J. Gladding, Jr. as a Saybrook, CT, planemaker circa 1835, his father, "J" of Deep River, CT, as a maker of dividers and trammel points, no dates. This is the first time we have observed this rare maker's mark.

52603T36   **Saw set**   DTM   MH

Drop-forged iron, 8 3/16" long, unsigned.

TCR1019A   **Saw set (?)**   DTM   MH

Drop-forged iron or steel, 9 5/8" long, unsigned.

This saw set is unusual due to its elegant wing shaped handles.

81101T11   **Shake mallet**   DTM   MH

Wood, 15 1/2" long, unsigned.

This is a typical farm mallet probably used with a froe to make shakes and shingles.

TCR1009   **Turnscrew**   DTM   MH

Reforged iron or steel and wood, 12 1/2" long, 8 3/8" long blade, unsigned, c. 1800.

This tool has been refashioned out of an old file.

TG1015   **Wedge**   DTM   MH

Forged iron, 2 3/8" wide, unsigned.

Historic Maritime III (1800-1840): Boomtown Years & the Dawn of the Industrial Revolution

Woodworking: Other Tools

TG1005   **Wedge**   DTM   MH

Forged iron, 1 3/4" wide, unsigned.

TG1011   **Wedge**   DTM   MH

Forged iron, 4 5/8" long, 2 5/16" wide, unsigned.

30201T2   **Wheelwrights' stand**   DTM   LTC

Wood, aprox. 28" high, 26" wide, unsigned.

This tool was used to balance and repair broken carriage wheels. It is on display at the Davistown Museum Liberty Tool Annex.

Woodworking: Planes

101801T8   **Beading plane**   BDTM   MH

Mahogany with steel blade, 10 3/8" long, signed by owner "AFW" for Abiel F. Walker.

http://www.davistownmuseum.org/publications/volume10.html

101801T6   **Beading plane**   BDTM   MH

Mahogany with steel blade, 8 5/8" long, signed by owner "AFW" for Abiel F. Walker.

http://www.davistownmuseum.org/publications/volume10.html

121311T4   **Beading plane**   DTM   TT

signed "GABRIEL" "SHELLEY" "D MAXTED".

The Gabriel clan were English toolmakers (1770 - 1822). This tool is likely to be a later Gabriel (Goodman 1993, 240). There are 3 owners marks: Shelley, D. Maxted, and a third one that is indecipherable, possibly a re-sellers stamp.

81602T4   **Beading plane**   DTM   MH

Wood (beech), steel blade, 9 1/2" long, 1 1/4" wide, 1/2" bead, signed "I Eastman".

Pollack (2001) reports two other I. Eastman boxed side beading planes. Who was I. Eastman and when did he make planes?

91303T4   **Beading plane**   DTM   TT

Wood with a steel blade, 9 1/2" long, 1" bead, unsigned.

This is a generic run of the mill hand plane typical of a 19th century tool box. The slight chamfering suggests an early to mid-19th century date.

Woodworking: Planes

TCD1006   Beading plane   DTM   MH

Wood, 8 1/2" long, signed "OLR".

This plane is unsigned but has the owner's initials OLR burned into the top.

TCD1003   Bench (fore) plane   LPC   MH

Wood (birch), 21 1/2" long, signed very faintly "Levi Tinkham", c. 1840.

Tinkham lived from 1766 - 1857 and worked in Middleboro, MA. The plane has a replaced wedge. This plane is typical of the many thousands of generic bench planes that have survived through the 20th century. It was a gift to The Davistown Museum from Bob Wheeler of Pepperell, MA.

http://www.davistownmuseum.org/pics/tcd1003.jpg
http://www.davistownmuseum.org/bioTinkham.htm

TJE1301   Block plane   DTM   MH

Wood (mahogany?), cast steel blade, 7" long, 3" wide with 2 1/8" wide blade, signed "IS" on the plane face and "HUMPHREYSVILLE (TOOL?) CO WARRANTED CAST STEEL" on blade.

18th century style owner's signature. The blade signature is a 19th century style, in script.

22512T4   Block plane   DTM   TT

Cast bronze with cast steel blade, 9" long, 1 1/2" wide blade, signed "EC LUCAS" owner's mark.

Courtesy of Liberty Tool Co.

72801T16   Block plane   DTM   MH

Cast steel and wood, 9 5/8" long with a wide blade, signed "E. French", blade unmarked.

No E. French planemaker is listed in DATM (Nelson 1999); this mark is probably that of the owner. It is a typical owner-made low angle boat carpenters' plane of the 19th century.

62202T5   Block plane   DTM   MH

Boxwood with cast steel blade, 9 5/16" long, 1 1/4" wide, 1" wide blade, signed "Moulson Brothers" on the partially cut down blade and "D. Lewis" on the plane.

DATM (Nelson 1999) notes only a D. B. Lewis of Groton (MA?). This tool was probably used by a patternmaker though it was found in the collection of an East Boston caulker who last worked in the late 19th century.

http://www.davistownmuseum.org/pics/62202t5.jpg

TCD1005   Carriage-makers' bead plane   DTM   MH

Wood (beech?), 5 3/4" long, 5/8" bead, unsigned.

There is no maker's sign but the wedge appears professionally made.

ID #   Status   Location

Woodworking: Planes

51703T1   Carriage-makers' plane   DTM   MH

Wood with steel blade, 4 1/4" long, 1" wide, unsigned.

A nice example of an early 19th century carriage-makers' plane used for close-in work. The sharp beveling on the plane suggests a c. 1820 date.

http://www.davistownmuseum.org/pics/51703T1.jpg

72206T1   Carriage-makers' plane   DTM   MH

Beach, ivory, with a steel blade, 7 3/8" long, 3/4" wide, unsigned.

The blade appears to have been cut and trimmed from a larger beading plane blade. The plane was associated with an Amesbury, MA, carriage-maker shop active in the 1840s and 50s and was found in a collection of tools dispensed from this source.

81101T3   Carriage-makers' skew panel plane   DTM   MH

Cast steel, wood, and forged iron fittings, 21" long plus extension skew blade 3" wide, signed "H. Ward Warranted Cast Steel" on blade, plane unsigned, 1810 - 1830 (?).

This is an uncommon early 19th century American tool with an English blade.

81801T10   Coffin plane   DTM   MH

Rosewood and maple with cast steel blade, 8 1/4" long, 1 7/8" wide blade, signed on the blade "Moulson" and with the plane owner's signature "E. French" on the body.

This fine rosewood plane has a maple wedge and steel blade.

81801T9   Complex spar plane   DTM   MH

Wood with cast steel blade, 9 1/2" long, 1 1/2" convex blade, signed "TR Johnson. Hanover Mass 2" and on blade "Moulson Brothers Warrented Cast Steel Improved Welded". Owner signature "J.A. Junkins", c. 1820.

This unusual curved spar plane also has a longitudinal convex curve. T.R. Johnson was a 19th century American spar planemaker. This may be one of Johnson's earlier planes showing the continuing use of English steel blades.

http://www.davistownmuseum.org/pics/81801t9.jpg
http://www.davistownmuseum.org/pics/81801t9-2.jpg

81602T8   Convex rabbet plane   DTM   MH

Wood (beech), steel blade, 11 7/16" long, 1 3/8" wide, signed by owner "W. A. Jordan".

This plane looks and feels like one typical of J. R. Tolman's workshop in Hanover, MA (1820 - 1860). The plane, though having the distinctive wedge of the prolific Tolman shipbuilders' workshop planes, is marked only by the owner. It is a remnant of the legacy of New England's maritime heritage.

81212LTC13 Core box plane   NOM   TT (Pub)

Cast bronze, wood (rosewood), steel cutter, 9" long, 5" tall, 2 3/4" wide, 3/4" cutting edge, unsigned.

Historic Maritime III (1800-1840): Boomtown Years & the Dawn of the Industrial Revolution

Woodworking: Planes

TBH1002   Dado plane   BDTM   MH

Wood with forged steel blade, 9 3/8" long, signed "Marsh & Winn" and "J. Ho___".

It lacks a front blade. Marsh & Winn are not listed in Pollak (2001) or Goodman (1993). DATM (Nelson 1999) lists them as a foreign planemaker with the date 1807. It is also marked J. Ho___, possibly J. Holmes who is listed in Pollak (2001,195) without further identification. The distinct beveling is characteristic of an 18th century plane.

TCD3000   Fore plane   DTM   MH

Wood with a cast steel blade, 20 1/2" long including the overhanging handle, unsigned.

This highly decorated plane is distinctly European in appearance and contrasts sharply with the simpler designs of the American made planes of the period.

111001T9   Gutter plane   DTM   MH

Wood with cast steel blade, 15 1/2" long, 2" wide, 1 3/4" wide blade, signed "Roberts & Ash" on blade with a clover leaf touchmark to the right of Ash, plane marked "DM".

Goodman's (1993) "British Plane Makers" does not list Roberts & Ash as blade makers. He does list a William G. Ash. DATM (Nelson 1999, 664) lists Roberts & Ash as leather tool makers, no date or location.

http://www.davistownmuseum.org/pics/111001t9.jpg

63001T9   Hand plane   DTM   MH

Wood with steel blade, 8 1/2" long, unsigned.

Another example of the ubiquitous unsigned owner-made planes of New England workshops of the 18th, 19th, and 20th century.

63001T8   Hand plane   DTM   MH

Wood, steel, and brass, 7 3/4" long, unsigned.

This is an excellent example of the ubiquitous unsigned owner-made planes of New England workshops of the 18th, 19th, and 20th centuries. It is a reminder that most planes were made by their owners.

81212LTC16   Hand router   NOM   TT (Pub)

Cast bronze, steel cutter, 7 1/2" long, 3 1/2" wide, 2 1/4" tall, 3/8" edge, unsigned.

7800-T8   Jack plane   DTM   MHC-J

Wood (beech), steel blade, 14 5/8" long, 2 1/2" wide, signed on the blade "W. Greaves & Son Cast Steel".

This is a typical homemade plane with an imported English blade, a type that would have been used by the residents of Davistown Plantation c. 1810 - 1830.

ID #   Status   Location

Woodworking: Planes

92911T1   Jointer plane   LPC   MH

Wood with shear steel blade, 29" long, 3 1/4" wide, 2 3/4" high, blade 7" long, 2 1/2" wide, signed "L. TINKHAM" "MIDDLEBORO" and on blade "F. STONES" "SHEAR.STEEL".

Pollak (2001) in "American Wooden Planes" indicates this is thought to be Levi Tinkham. DATM (Nelson 1999) lists F. Stones as a maker of plane irons with no dates or location.

http://www.davistownmuseum.org/bioTinkham.htm

TCD1002   Low angle block plane   BDTM   MH

Rosewood, 10" long, signed "L.O. Tappan" (probably the owner's signature), c. 1830-50 (?).

It has a Newburyport, MA, shipyard provenance and was probably used for interior cabin finish work.

72801T17   Molding plane   DTM   MH

Wood with steel blade and runner, 10" long, unsigned.

An owner-made plane typical of the 19th century but with an unusual center runner for cutting a V groove. It is a one of a kind plane that is unlisted in plane guide descriptions.

33002T1L   Molding plane   DTM   TT

Wood with steel blade, 10 1/2" long, 11/16" wide concave cutter, unsigned, c. 1810.

This is a typical generic homemade molding plane.

72002T1   Molding plane   LPC   MHC-D

Wood (beech) with steel blade, 9 1/2" long, 1 7/16" wide, signed "JO FULLER PROVIDENCE" with the imprint "D-2", 1805 - 1808.

This is a fine example of a complex beading plane by one of colonial America's most important planemakers. DATM (Nelson 1999) lists Fuller as working 1773 - 1808. Pollack (2001) notes "In later years when he adopted the standard 9 1/2 length, his chamfers became rounded and the fluting disappeared. The wood he used evolved from yellow birch to beech with a few maple examples, and his wedge profiles became relieved after his early period then rounded." This is a crisp clear example of one of his last planes.

040904T3   Plane blade wedge   DTM   MH

Wood, 11" long, 4 3/4" wide, unsigned.

This coopers' jointer plane wedge was found independently of the plane it once belonged to and it is the largest blade wedge we have ever seen. It is a curious accidental durable remnant of the ancient maritime culture of the past.

http://www.davistownmuseum.org/pics/040904t3_p2.jpg

ID #   Status   Location

Woodworking: Planes

30202T4   **Rabbet plane**   DTM   TT

Wood with steel blade, 17 3/8" long, 7/8" wide blade, signed "J.R. Tolman Hanover Mass".

DATM (Nelson 1999) indicates Tolman was born in 1787 and was making planes in S. Scituate, MA, by the 1820s. Tolman made planes specifically for the shipbuilding industries and was one of New England's most prolific planemakers specializing in spar planes during this era.

http://www.davistownmuseum.org/pics/30202t4.jpg

81212LTC14   **Rabbet plane**   NOM   TT (Pub)

Cast bronze, steel cutter, 5 5/8" long, 5/8" wide, 1 5/8" tall, unsigned.

32708T53   **Rabbet plane**   DTM   MH

Metal and oak, 11" long with a 6 3/8" by 1" blade, signed with a cross made of tilde-like marks on the side of the plane.

http://www.davistownmuseum.org/pics/32708t53-1.jpg
http://www.davistownmuseum.org/pics/32708t53-2.jpg

91303T1   **Rabbet plane**   LPC   MH

Cast steel with rosewood infill and wedges, 9 1/8" long, 5/8" wide, signed "Wards Cast Steel" on blades, plane unsigned, c. 1800 - 1820.

The wedges have an owner's signature "G. R. Oliver". This is a most unusual double rabbet plane. It is obviously English and was found in New England. Its use is unknown.

http://www.davistownmuseum.org/pics/91303t1_p1.jpg
http://www.davistownmuseum.org/pics/91303t1_p3.jpg

32802T8   **Rabbet plane**   BDTM   MH

Lignum vitae with an oak wedge and a steel blade, 9 15/16" long, 2 15/16" high, 1 9/16" maximum width at middle, tapers to 1 1/4" bottom, 1 1/8" top, unsigned, c. 1820 (?).

This is a special purpose boat builders' plane.

http://www.davistownmuseum.org/pics/32802t8.jpg

62202T1   **Rabbet plane**   DTM   MH

Bronze with ebony infill and steel blade, 8" long, 1 1/2" wide, 7/8" wide blade, signed "W. J. Foote", probably an owner.

This exquisite tool was formerly in the collection of Joel Pontz, formerly a staff member, woodworking consultant, and trader for Plimouth Plantation. This shoulder plane is typical of an early to mid-19th century joiners' tool kit.

http://www.davistownmuseum.org/pics/62202t1.jpg

ID #   Status   Location

Woodworking: Planes

22411T14   **Razee-style rabbet plane**   DTM   TT

Wood with cast steel blade, 10" long, 2 1/2" x 2 1/2", signed "MOULSON BROTHERS" "WARRENTED" and "CAST STEEL" on the blade; "Wm ASH & Co" and "CAST STEEL" on the cap iron; "J. L. LEE" on body, probably an owner.

31602T7   **Rounding plane**   DTM   MH

Wood with a concave steel blade, 9 1/2" long, 1 1/4" wide, signed "BROWN & BARNARD".

Goodman states that it is felt that this was a partnership of Henry Brown and Thomas Barnard working in Birmingham, England, between 1800 and 1803. Before and after these dates, these two individuals are listed separately.

81602T7   **Rounding plane**   DTM   MH

Wood (beech), steel blade, 12" long, 15/16" wide, signed by the owner.

A nice example of an early 19th century owner-made and signed plane. Unusual in its long length, this plane must have had a special purpose in a single workshop situation.

81801T12   **Router**   DTM   MH

Wood with iron fittings and steel blade, 10 1/8" wide, 3/16" wide blade, unsigned, c. 1800 - 1820.

This tool was used for routing a groove - but in what context?

100400T3   **Smooth plane**   BDTM   MHC-K

Cast steel, cast iron, and wood, 9 1/8" long, 2 1/2" wide with a 2" blade, signed on the blade "MOULSON BROTHERS WARRANTED CAST STEEL".

This is an interesting early cast iron plane, its maker's location is unknown. It has a typical English imported blade and is an early example of the transitional planes in this case. This is probably the earliest cast iron (or steel) plane in our collection and foreshadows the innovative design of the later patented and transitional metallic planes with which it is displayed. This is an example of a special purpose alloy-steel tool.

TCD1008   **Spar plane**   BDTM   MH

Wood (beech), 9 1/2" long, 2 1/4" wide, blade 1 9/16" wide, signed "L.O. Tappan" (probably the owner), blade signed "Moulson", c. 1840.

This plane is from a Newburyport, MA shipyard. It is typical of spar planes produced by the Tolman workshop of Hanover, MA. This is an American-made plane with the usual English blade of the period.

http://www.davistownmuseum.org/pics/tcd1008.jpg

TCD1004   **Spar plane**   DTM   MH

Wood (maple or beech), 17" long, 1 11/16" wide, signed "S T. Livingston".

It has a smith-made blade. Livingston is not listed in Pollak (2001) or Goodman (1993). This tool is typical of a mid-19th century New England shipyard.

ID #   Status   Location

Woodworking: Planes

33013T4   Tongue and groove plane   DTM   MH

Wood (beech), cast steel, 12 3/8" long, 2 1/4" wide, 7" tall, signed "J W" "C C G".

The JW mark belongs to Thomas J. Wood who owned Wood's Tool Store in New York City in the 1830's to 1850's.

32313T1   Toted double cutter door plane   LPC   MH

Wood (beech), steel, 13 1/2" long, 1 3/4" wide, 6 1/2" tall, 11/16" and 1/2" cutters, signed "L. TINKHAM" "C.C. GRIFFITH" "F.G.S.".

Levi Tinkham made planes, working in Middleboro, MA.

http://www.davistownmuseum.org/bioTinkham.htm

Woodworking: Planes Made in Maine

92001T1   Double sash plane   DTM   MH

Oak and steel, 10 3/4" long, signed "AFW".

Abiel F. Walker was a very small producer of hand planes, making them only for himself and area craftsmen. These are typical of those produced by a skilled boat carpenter and housewright who would make his own tools. The Davistown Museum obtained a collection of Abiel Walker's planes directly from the attic of the house in which he spent most of his life. For additional information about Abiel Walker's plane collection and its significance see his listing in the Registry of Maine Toolmakers (Brack 2008) and the essay on Walker in the Registry introduction.

http://www.davistownmuseum.org/publications/volume10.html

101801T1   Molding plane   DTM   MH

Wood (beech), 9 3/4" long, signed "AFW".

http://www.davistownmuseum.org/publications/volume10.html

61601T3   Molding plane   BDTM   UNK

Wood (beech), steel blade, 9 3/8" long, 1" wide blade, signed "B. MORRILL" "BANGOR".

Pollack (2001) indicates Morrill is known to have been making planes in Bangor, ME, as early as 1832. This plane is a classic relic of the boomtown era of coastal Maine, with a prolific Maine maker's mark and an unusual profile. It is among the most important Maine-made tools in the collection.

http://www.davistownmuseum.org/pics/61601t3_p2.jpg
http://www.davistownmuseum.org/publications/volume10.html

92001T2   Panel raising plane   DTM   MH

Wood (beech), cast steel blade, 13 1/2" long, 2" wide blade, signed "AFW".

This plane was made by Abiel F. Walker.

http://www.davistownmuseum.org/publications/volume10.html

ID #   Status   Location

Woodworking: Planes Made in Maine

TBW1003   Panel raising plane   DTM   MH

Wood (beech), 9 1/2" long, 3" wide, signed "T. WATERMAN".

This is an example of one of Maine's first toolmakers, Thomas Waterman of Waldoboro.

http://www.davistownmuseum.org/pics/tbw1003.jpg
http://www.davistownmuseum.org/pics/tbw1003p2.jpg

TBW1004   Plane   DTM   MH

Wood (beech), steel, 9 3/8" long, 2 1/2" wide, 1 1/2" wide blade, 3/8" slitter on one side, signed "T. WATERMAN".

We don't know the proper name of this plane. It has a slightly convex blade and was a shipwrights' tool. Pollak (2001) lists T. Waterman as being born c. 1775 and still alive in 1850. Waterman was one of the many planemakers of the boomtown years of the Waldoboro, Warren, and Thomaston shipbuilding era.

http://www.davistownmuseum.org/pics/tbw1004.jpg
http://www.davistownmuseum.org/pics/tbw1004p2.jpg

42602T1   Plow plane   DTM   MH

Birch with beach wedge and fence, steel blade, forged iron fence guide and screws, 8 3/4" long, 1 5/8" wide body, 9" wide fence arms, signed "T & W Sorby" on blade, c. 1835 - 1840.

The plane was made by Abiel Walker, Alna, ME, following English prototypes. The blade was made by I & W Sorby of Sheffield, UK (http://www.robert-sorby.co.uk/company_info.htm).

http://www.davistownmuseum.org/pics/42602t1_p3.jpg
http://www.davistownmuseum.org/publications/volume10.html

50402T4   Rounding plane   DTM   MH

Wood, 10" long, 1 1/8" wide convex profile, signed "I HOLMES" plus "C REED" and "C.R" owner's marks.

Pollack (2001) lists a J. Holmes mark with no location. All the J. Holmes planes listed by Pollak are shorter than this plane, which more closely matches their listing of a 10 inch beech molder with flat chamfers, the only known plane of I. P. Holmes of Berwick, Maine. Is there a relationship between the two makers? Is I. Holmes a third Holmes? Is he from the Berwick area? Could J. Holmes be from the Berwick area? Comments and information welcomed. This plane was purchased by Bob Wheeler a decade ago from the Liberty Tool Co., resold, and is now owned by the Museum.

http://www.davistownmuseum.org/pics/50402t4_p1.jpg
http://www.davistownmuseum.org/publications/volume10.html

42607T2   Sash plane   DTM   MH

Boxwood, 9 3/8" long, 2 1/8" wide with 3/4" right blade and 1/2" left blade, signed "J. C. Jewett Waterville Me".

This sash plane is double bladed. J. C. Jewett worked circa 1820 - 1850. It has a nice crisp signature by an important central Maine planemaker of the mid-19th century.

http://www.davistownmuseum.org/publications/volume10.html

ID #   Status   Location

Woodworking: Planes Made in Maine

92001T3   **Skew panel plane**   DTM   MH

Wood (beech), brass and cast steel, 15 7/8" long, 1 3/4" wide blade, signed "AFW", blade signed "MOULSON BROTHERS WARRANTED CAST STEEL".

Abiel F. Walker is the maker, the blade comes from England

http://www.davistownmuseum.org/publications/volume10.html

101801T2   **Tongue and groove planes (matched pair)**   DTM   MH

Oak and brass, 11 7/16" long, signed "AFW".

These both have a brass lower plate instead of the characteristic iron plate of the factory-made tongue and groove planes.

http://www.davistownmuseum.org/publications/volume10.html

50402T3   **Yankee plow plane**   LPC   MH

Wood with brass, forged steel blade, and iron rivets, 8 3/8" long, 7 3/4" wide fence, signed "W. H. Cary".

The plane has atypical brass depth stops. This plane was probably made in Maine after Cary moved from New Salem, MA. As noted in DATM (Nelson 1999), the Cary family made farm tools and plows in Houlton later in the 19th century (-1869 - 71-); his son, J. H. Cary stayed in New Salem as a rule and caliper maker. The 4th Edition of Pollack (2001) agrees with Trevor Robinson (see bio link) that Cary never made any planes after moving to Houlton. This information is disputed by Bob Wheeler who formerly owned it; it is now loaned to the Museum by the current owner.

http://www.davistownmuseum.org/pics/50402t3_p2.jpg
http://www.davistownmuseum.org/bioCary.htm

Woodworking: Saws

TCW1301   **Backsaw**   DTM   MH

Cast steel, brass, and wood, 13 7/8" long blade, 6 1/2" long handle, signed "WELCH & GRIFFITHS" "CAST STEEL" "BOSTON" and "WARRANTED".

The saw has the typical solid brasses of the period. Welch & Griffiths is listed in DATM (Nelson 1999, 839). The following information is from a great great grandchild (lsteneck65@earthlink.net): "Welch and Griffiths Saw Manufacturing Co. began about 1830 and went out of business about 1844. My g.g.grandfather, Joseph Woodrough, worked for Welch & Griffiths after he arrived in this country from England. Following the demise of the company, Joseph Woodrough and William Clemson (who also worked for W & G) started their own saw manufactory called Woodrough & Clemson."

http://www.davistownmuseum.org/pics/tcw1301.jpg
http://www.davistownmuseum.org/pics/TCW1301-bw300-1.jpg

TCW1003   **Backsaw**   DTM   MH

Cast steel with solid brasses, 14 3/4" long, 11 3/8" blade, signed "T TILLOTSON SHEFFIELD (FIN)EST REFINED CAST STEEL SPRINGTEMPER WARRANTED", 1800 - 1820.

The unusual markings also include a crown touchmark and brasses.

Historic Maritime III (1800-1840): Boomtown Years & the Dawn of the Industrial Revolution

Woodworking: Saws

111001T8   Backsaw   DTM   MH

Cast steel and brass, 19" long, 14 5/16" blade, signed "S. Biggin & Sons Sheffield Cast Steel Warranted Gauged".

The handle has solid brass nuts and a signed brass nut emblem. Both the saw and the brass have the characteristic English crown mark. This is a typical Sheffield imported tool of the early 19th century.

100605T1   Backsaw   DTM   TB

German steel, solid brass nuts, and wooden handle, 18 1/2" long including 14" blade, signed "BARBER & GENN GERMAN STEEL".

The handle is characteristic of saws made before 1820. Barber & Genn are listed in DATM (Nelson 1999) with a possible working date of 1870 and no known location. However, they are a Sheffield partnership starting around 1781. See this online discussion for more information: http://www.backsaw.net/index.php?option=com_jfusion&Itemid=58&jfile=showthread.php&t=154.

J/TCW2202   Backsaw   DTM   MH

Cast steel, 20 3/4" long with 15 7/8" blade, signed "US".

71401T13   Backsaw   DTM   MH

Steel, brass and wood, 6 1/2" long, 3 1/8" handle, signed "Stillman Patent".

DATM (Nelson 1999) lists Stillman of Herkimer Co. with working dates of 1837 - 48. Where is Herkimer County? This is a tool from the early days of the florescence of American toolmakers.

61601T2   Backsaw   DTM   MH

Cast steel and wood, 18 5/8" long with a 13 3/4" blade, signed "Sheffield Wheatman & Smith Russell Works Cast Steel Solid Brass".

This is a classic example of an imported English cast steel tool with a rare maker's mark.

914108T16   Backsaw   DTM   MH

Metal, brass ferrule, and wooden handle, 11 1/4" long, 8" long blade, signed "ABRIE".

Part of the maker's mark may be completely worn off. This saw appears to be homemade.

7309T6   Buck saw   DTM   MH

Wood, steel, rope, leather, 46" wide, 35" long blade, unsigned.

This is a finely crafted gentlemans' buck saw of the early 18th century, probably made by a domestic toolmaker as one of a kind.

http://www.davistownmuseum.org/pics/7309t6BW300ppi-6.jpg

ID #   Status   Location

Woodworking: Saws

7309T4   Chisel-edged pruning saw   DTM   MH

Cast iron, malleable iron, and steel, 17 1/2" long, 3 1/2" wide grafting end, 11" long saw blade, and 72" long handle, unsigned.

This is an early 19th century model of an orchard masters' grafting and pruning tool.

http://www.davistownmuseum.org/pics/7309t4BW_web.jpg

TCW1001   Fret saw   DTM   MH

Forged iron and steel, 4 1/4" long, unsigned.

This saw is homemade.

111001T11   Hacksaw   DTM   MH

Wood, steel and brass, 13" long, 4" wood handle, no blade, signed "T Smith & Co" with a touchmark of a $ within two circles.

DATM (Nelson 1999, 727) lists T Smith & Co. as making dividers, with no location or date. This saw appears to be early 19th century though it has an 18th century hacksaw form.

072112T2   Hand saw   DTM   TT

Cast steel, solid brass, wooden handle, 22" long, 5 1/4" wide, 7/8" thick, signed "B. BIGGIN & SONS" curved over a crown, under the same crown "S.B." "AMERICA WORKS" "Sheffield" "CAST STEEL".

12900T5   Hand saw   DTM   MH

Cast steel, brass, and wood, 13 7/8" long blade, unsigned.

This is a typical early 19th century tool with solid brasses, probably imported from England.

4105T1   Hand saw   DTM   MH

Cast steel, wood, and brass, 26 3/4" long, 22" long blade, signed "Groves & Sons USI Sheffield" on blade, "Established 1770" on brass, c. 1820.

This is a typical example of a fine imported English finish saw.

7309T5   Hand saw   DTM   MH

Cast steel, brass, and wood, 31" long, 8" handle, signed "R. GROVES & SONS" with the Queen's insignia.

This is a typical example of a finely made imported English crucible steel tool.

http://www.davistownmuseum.org/pics/7309t5web-1.jpg

32412T1   Keyhole saw   DTM   TT-33

Forged steel, beech, 14 1/2" long, unsigned.

Courtesy of Liberty Tool Co.

Historic Maritime III (1800-1840): Boomtown Years & the Dawn of the Industrial Revolution

Woodworking: Saws

TCW1002   **Pad saw**   DTM   MH

Reforged steel, 9 5/8" long, 5 1/2" blade, unsigned.

This pad saw is difficult to date and could be late 18th or early 19th century. This saw is typical of one that might be found in the tool chest of an early resident of Davistown Plantation.

Wrenches

101900T6   **Adjustable wrench**   DTM   MH

Cast or forged steel, 9 1/2" long, unsigned.

This is a one-of-a-kind early 19th century wrench pre-dating most or all patented wrenches (1835f).

http://www.davistownmuseum.org/pics/101900t5.jpg

TCZ1005   **Bed wrench**   DTM   MH

Forged iron, 5 3/4" long, 5/8" socket, handle 6 1/8" wide, unsigned.

This tool is difficult to date but could be late 18th century or early 19th century. If this is not a bed wrench, what is it?

TBF6003   **Bed wrench**   DTM   MH

Cast iron, 5" long with 4" handle, unsigned.

This is a generic tool commonplace in households in the eighteenth and early nineteenth centuries. A bed wrench was used with an old feather bed. This type of bed would have a wooden frame. The frame did not hold a box spring or wooden cross boards as a more modern bed does. Instead, the bottom of the bed was rope. The long rope would loop through holes drilled in the frame and go back and forth across the opening in the center. This creates a crisscrossed appearance. Bedding such as a straw tic would then go on top of that. The ropes eventually will stretch. The bed wrench is used to tighten the rope.

http://www.davistownmuseum.org/pics/tbf6003.jpg

32502T34   **Closed socket wrench**   BDTM   T

Forged steel, 2 7/8" long, 1/7" thick, 1/4" square socket, unsigned.

http://www.davistownmuseum.org/bioEpstein.htm

ID #   Status   Location

Wrenches

62406T6   **Monkey wrench**   DTM   MH

Drop-forged iron, wood (rosewood), 10" long closed including a 3" long wood handle, signed "S. MERRICK'S PATENT" plus owner signature "Wm E. SIBLEY".

DATM (Nelson 1999) lists Solymon Merrick as having both an 18 April 1834 and an August 1835 patent for a monkey wrench, but indicates a connection with P Merrick is unknown at that time. More recently, Herb Page notes the Bemis Co. of Springfield manufactured a Merrick wrench that inspired the Coes Brothers to design their improved No. 1 & 2 Coes patent wrenches after having difficulty adjusting the older model Merrick wrench, which required two hands to adjust. Page illustrates the Merrick patent on pg. 20 of his text on the Coes Co. noting "substantially the same as the old Springfield or Merrick wrench, which were issued as a cheaper No. 3 Railroad Wrench", very similar in design to this predecessor patent.

http://www.davistownmuseum.org/pics/62406t6_p2.jpg
http://www.davistownmuseum.org/pics/62406t6_p3.jpg

32802T4   **Pipe wrench**   DTM   MH

Drop-forged iron, brass, and wood, 10" long, unsigned.

This unusual pipe wrench has no maker's mark; the remains of two letters are visible on the jaw arm in 18th century script, "T S"? As yet, unidentified, Museum wrench references have not been consulted.

http://www.davistownmuseum.org/pics/32802t4.jpg

TG1002   **Wrench**   DTM   MH

Drop-forged iron, 8" long, 3/4" and 5/8" wide open ends, unsigned.

TG1001   **Wrench**   DTM   MH

Drop-forged iron, 13 1/2" long, 9/16" and 1 3/14" open ends, unsigned.

Historic Maritime IV (1840-1865): The Early Industrial Revolution

Agricultural Implements

| 102612T5 | **Brush cutter** | LPC | MH |

Steel, wooden handle, 35" long, 9" long and 5" wide head, unsigned.

| 33013LTC2 | **Bush hook** | DA | TT (Pub) |

Forged steel, wood (hickory), 43 1/2" long, 8 1/4" long head, 5" wide head, unsigned.

| 31808PC12 | **Oxen shoes (2)** | DTM | MH |

Malleable iron or steel, 5" long, signed "No 30" on each one.

Many other shoes were drop-forged or forge-welded by hand from high-carbon malleable iron. The "No 30" indicates these were made by drop-forging.

| 43805T1 | **Pig skinner** | DTM | MH |

Steel, wire, and wood, 4 5/8" long hardwood handle, 21" long from base of handle to the wire, and 18 1/2" long wire, unsigned.

http://www.davistownmuseum.org/pics/43805t1.jpg

| 32313T4 | **Pitchfork** | DTM | MH |

Forged steel, wood (hickory), 47" long, 31 1/2" long handle, 8 1/4" wide head, unsigned.

This unusual fork has a two pronged, winged head.

| 32802T6 | **Pruning shears** | DTM | MH |

Forged iron or steel, 9 1/4" long, unsigned.

This distinctly hand-forged tool appears to be made entirely of forged malleable iron and steel. They were donated by Chris Harvey.

http://www.davistownmuseum.org/pics/32802t6.jpg
http://www.davistownmuseum.org/pics/32802t6_p2.jpg

| TCK1005 | **Pruning shears** | DTM | MH |

Forged iron and steel, 10 1/2" long, 2 3/8" wide blade, signed "J.F. FOX PELHAM N.H".

Josiah F. Fox is listed in DATM (Nelson 1999) as working 1853 - 1877. He specialized in making pruning shears.

| 090508T1A | **Sod cutter** | DTM | MH |

Malleable iron, wood, 81" long, 7" long blade, unsigned.

This was made on an island off the coast of England.

Agricultural Implements

102612T3   Turf ax   LPC   MH

Steel, wooden handle, 36" long, 9" long and 8 1/2" wide head, signed "JOSEPH BRECK & CO" "BOSTON MASS".

Joseph Breck was a toolmaker and later a dealer whose company was in Boston from 1838 to 1905. The "& Co" is not always on the mark and there is a report of the mark "& Son" (Nelson 1999, 110).

Blacksmith, Farrier, and Metalworking Tools

92911T10   Bar stock   DTM   MH

Malleable iron, 36" long, 1" wide, 1" high, unsigned.

This is a product of a finery, which produced bloomery or puddling furnace-derived malleable iron bar stock for blacksmiths of many trades, often for hand tool production.

22512LTC11   Blacksmiths' curved concave hardy   DA   TT (Pub)

Cast or forged steel, 3 3/8" long, 1 3/4" wide, 6" high, unsigned.

This is a curved bottom tool or hardy used for forging a rounded edge. It has a square shank for insertion into an anvil or swage block. Courtesy of Liberty Tool Co.

22512LTC10   Blacksmiths' curved convex hardy   DA   TT (Pub)

Cast or forged steel, 3" long, 4 1/2" wide, 1 3/8" high, unsigned.

This is a curved bottom tool or hardy used for forging a smooth, rounded object. It has a square shank for insertion into an anvil or swage block. Courtesy of Liberty Tool Co.

42405T3   Blacksmiths' double calipers   DTM   MH

Forged steel or iron, 16 1/8" long, 6 5/8" wide when closed, signed with the owner's initials "HJK".

This is a typical smith-made pair of calipers for shop use; probably one of a kind.

22512LTC3   Blacksmiths' horned anvil   DA   TT (Pub)

Cast steel, 28 3/4" high, 10" x 8.5" wide, unsigned.

 Courtesy of Liberty Tool Co.

102904T17   Blacksmiths' punch   DTM   MH

Forged iron, 12" long, unsigned.

This is a nicely fashioned smith-made special purpose punch, possibly for sheet metal work.

http://www.davistownmuseum.org/pics/102904t17.jpg

5412LTC4   Blacksmiths' straight lip tongs   DA   TT (Pub)

Forged iron, 21" long, 3/4" jaw, unsigned.

Courtesy of Liberty Tool Co.

Blacksmith, Farrier, and Metalworking Tools

5412LTC3   **Blacksmiths' straight lip tongs**   DA   TT (Pub)

Forged iron, 23" long, 1" jaw, unsigned.

Courtesy of Liberty Tool Co.

111412T18   **Blacksmiths' tongs**   DTM   MH

Forged malleable iron, 14" long, unsigned.

5412LTC2   **Blacksmiths' tongs**   DA   TT (Pub)

Forged iron, 27 1/4" long, 1/2" jaw, unsigned.

These tongs are not illustrated in Sellens (2002). Courtesy of Liberty Tool Co.

31811T27   **Bolt header**   DTM   TT

Hand-forge-welded malleable iron, 12 1/2" long, 1 3/4" x 7/8" head with a 3/4" hole, unsigned.

31811T28   **Bolt header**   DTM   TT

Hand-forge-welded malleable iron, 12 1/2" long, 1 7/8" round double-head with square holes 1/2" and 5/8"., unsigned.

041709T1   **Chasing tools (11)**   DTM   MH

Forged steel, 2" to 3" long, 1/4" to 1" wide, signed "W. Jessop & Sons", 1832-1900 (?).

This group of tools is an example from a larger collection of such chasing and die sinking equipment used by blacksmiths and jewelers, all acquired from the estate of Leon Robbins. The marking "W. Jessop & Sons" on some of the pieces indicates that they were made by William Jessop & Sons, a Sheffield, England company that took up the name in 1832 and eventually became Jessop Saville & Company. The size of the designs on the stamps ranges from an inch to less than 1/32 of an inch. 11 tools total.

72801T9   **Chisel**   DTM   MH

Forged iron and steel, signed "Trafton Brothers" with other obscured markings.

DATM (Nelson 1999) reports the Trafton Brothers as Portsmouth, NH area blacksmiths working c. 1860.

913108T37C **Farrier's buffer**   DTM   MH

Reforged steel, 6 1/4" long, 1 5/8" wide, 3/8" thick, unsigned.

This farrier's tool is made from a reforged rasp.

61612T4   **Farriers' butteris**   DTM   TT

Forged malleable iron, wooden handle, 17" x 4 1/2" x 1 3/4", unsigned.

Historic Maritime IV (1840-1865): The Early Industrial Revolution

Blacksmith, Farrier, and Metalworking Tools

31212T20   Farriers' shoeing hammer

DTM   TT

Drop-forged steel, hickory handle, 14" long, 4" long head, unsigned.

This tool has evidence of hand filing on the head. Courtesy of Liberty Tool Co.

5412LTC5   Farriers' tongs

DA   TT (Pub)

Forged steel, 14 1/2" long, 3/4" jaw, unsigned.

Courtesy of Liberty Tool Co.

121805T25   File

DTM   MH

Cast steel, 13 1/4" long, 9/16" diameter, signed "6 granobs" and "cuss stahl".

This file is entirely handmade and hand cut in the traditional file-making manner. Stahl is steel in German and cusseisen is cast iron.

http://www.davistownmuseum.org/pics/121805t25.jpg

TCR1016   Hand vise

DTM   MH

Forged iron and steel, 6" long, 1 5/8" throat, signed "G. W. DANIELS WALTHAM MA NO.2".

DATM (Nelson 1999) lists a George Washington Daniels as a maker of dividers, vises, and other tools, working in Waltham, MA with working dates between 1850 -1886 (born 1830, died 1886). This vise is a variant of a common hand vise, with a small square anvil on a heart shaped hold down. The bottom nut appears to be a replacement.

22411T21   Hand vise

DTM   TT

Cast steel or German steel, 6" long and 2" wide head, signed "P S STUBS".

http://www.davistownmuseum.org/bioStubs.htm

3405T6   Hand vise

DTM   MH

Steel, 3 1/8" long, 1" wide jaw, signed "Heile and Quack".

No Heile and Quack are listed in DATM (Nelson 1999). This is probably an example of a German-made tool using German steel.

42801T21   Hand vise

DA   UNK

Drop-forged iron or steel, signed "Smith & Co.".

DATM (Nelson 1999) lists Smith & Co. with no dates. Many Smiths made tools -- who was Smith & Co. and where did they make hand vises?

TCF1002A   Nail header

DTM   MH

Drop-forged iron, 8 3/4" long with 3 heads, 3/4" sq., 5/8" sq., and 3/16" sq., signed "P.S. CRONIN", c. 1850.

The maker is not listed in DATM (Nelson 1999).

Historic Maritime IV (1840-1865): The Early Industrial Revolution

Blacksmith, Farrier, and Metalworking Tools

33002T4   **Nail header**   DTM   MH

Tempered alloy steel, 11 3/4" long, 9/16" square head socket, signed "F. E. Streeter".

This maker is not in DATM (Nelson 1999). Any relationship to A. W. Streeter of Shelburne Falls, MA, c. 1855?

090109T8   **Nippers**   DTM   MH

Drop-forged iron and steel, 10 3/4" long, 4 1/2" wide when open, 2" wide cutting edge, unsigned.

32912T7   **Ox shoe**   DTM   TT-46

Drop forged steel, 4 1/2" long, signed "L".

Courtesy of Liberty Tool Co.

TCR1021A   **Pliers**   DTM   MH

Drop-forged steel (?), 5 1/2" long, signed "_. NISSEL".

This maker is not listed in DATM (Nelson 1999).

TCR1020   **Pliers**   DTM   MH

Forged iron, 6" long with 13/16" wide jaws, signed "Fletcher".

Fletcher may be a New Hampshire toolmaker. Increased use of larger and larger water-driven hammers preceded the large equipment necessary for drop-forging malleable iron. Is this an unmarked example of drop-forging?

http://www.davistownmuseum.org/pics/tcr1021.jpg

31011T4   **Punch**   DTM   MH3-D3

Cast steel, 5 5/8" long, 1/2" wide, signed "C. DREW & CO." "CAST STEEL".

http://www.davistownmuseum.org/bioDrew.htm

121805T21   **Rasp**   DTM   MH

Cast or German steel, 12 1/4" long, 1 5/16" wide, signed "Grover & Son" with a touchmark, c. 1850.

This is a typical Sheffield, England, cast steel handmade rasp or shaver. Each notch was cut by an English file-maker by hand.

http://www.davistownmuseum.org/pics/121805t21.jpg

TCL1002   **Selection of files**   DTM   MHC-H

Forged steel, unsigned.

This selection of files illustrates the transition from the imported steel files c. 1800 to the c. 1900 mass-produced files.

Historic Maritime IV (1840-1865): The Early Industrial Revolution

Blacksmith, Farrier, and Metalworking Tools

914108T6   **Spoon**   DTM   MH

German steel, 8 1/4" long, signed "BERTOCCHI".

This tool is shaped like a punch or chisel with the end curved into a spoon shape. Possibly it was used in a foundry.

Cast Iron Tools and Artifacts

111001T32   **Awl**   DTM   MH

Cast iron, 7" long, unsigned.

This is another tool from the age of cast iron (1840 - 1865).

TCR1018   **Block**   DTM   MH

Cast iron, 10" height, with a 5" diameter iron shive, signed "Clayville Iron Works NY".

No Clayville is listed in DATM (Nelson 1999). This factory-produced tool is typical of the blocks that would have been brought to and used in the mills of Liberty and Montville after the Civil War when mass-produced tools supplanted the handmade and hand-forged wooden blocks characteristic of the earlier stages of the historic maritime culture of coastal Maine and New England.

TGB2205   **Crucifix**   DTM   MH

Cast iron, 6 1/2" long, 5 1/2" wide, unsigned.

TTCR1001   **Doorknob patterns**   DTM   MH

Cast iron, 5 3/4" long, unsigned.

If these were not cast by a patternmaker for molds for ceramic doorknobs, what are they? Most patterns are wood, not cast iron. Comments are solicited.

111001T30   **Harness-makers' vise**   DTM   MH

Cast iron, 5 1/2" wide, 3 1/2" wide jaw, unsigned.

This is a common 19th century tool; in the 21st century, just another whatsit?

111001T33   **Insignia**   DTM   MH

Cast iron, 5 1/4" diameter, signed with a 4" high "1".

This is another artifact from the age of cast iron. What was its use?

Cobbler and Saddler Tools

041505T40   **Burnisher**   DTM   MH

Lignum vitae, 15 1/2" long, 1 1/2" wide, unsigned.

This is a leather burnisher made from a tropical wood - a nice example of a tool from long ago.

http://www.davistownmuseum.org/pics/041505t40_p2.jpg

Cobbler and Saddler Tools

102800T5   Burnisher (slitted)   DTM   MH

Drop-forged steel and wood, 3 3/8" long, 1 1/4" wide, unsigned.

913108T29   Chamfering tool   DTM   MH

Iron, brass, and wood, 4 1/2" long curved wooden handle, 3 1/2" long brass portion, unsigned.

This tool is used for leather work.

33002T8   Cobblers' clamp   DTM   MH

Drop-forged iron or steel, 8 3/8" long, 3 5/8" adjustable jaw, unsigned.

This tool has a specific name -- what is it?

http://www.davistownmuseum.org/pics/33002t8.jpg

101900T4   Cobblers' hammer   DTM   MH

Drop-forged steel and wood, 9 1/2" long, 1 3/8" diameter face, unsigned.

This is a typical cobblers' hammer that was used in the mid-nineteenth century Liberty and Montville cobblers' shops.

http://www.davistownmuseum.org/pics/101900t4.jpg

42405T9   Cobblers' hammer   DTM   MH

Drop-forged steel, wood handle, leather strap holding the head in place, 3 1/8" long, 1 3/8" diameter face, 1 3/4" square and oval face, 6 1/4" long handle, unsigned, c. 1850.

This hammer shows signs of drop-forging.

52603T9   Cobblers' sling cutter   DTM   MH

5 " long, unsigned.

102904T8   Curriers' slick   DTM   MH

Forged steel, iron ferrules, wooden handle, 26 1/4" long, 16" long and 1 1/3" wide blade, signed "C J KIMBALL & SON".

Caleb Jewett Kimball worked in Milford and Bennington, NH. The Kimballs are famous for their high quality drawknives, which were produced in sufficient quantities to be frequently encountered today. The curriers' slick is less common; it is used for smoothing leather.

http://www.davistownmuseum.org/pics/102904t8_p2.jpg
http://www.davistownmuseum.org/bioKimball.html

51606T12   Curriers' slick   DTM   MH

Steel, iron, and wood, 11 3/4" long, 5 1/2" wide double-edged blade, unsigned.

This is a transitional tool showing evidence of handwork (hand-filed surfaces, oak (?) pegs trunneled into one handle for strength) and machined components (factory-made screws and a second machine-made handle.) This is the smallest curriers' slick we have seen.

Historic Maritime IV (1840-1865): The Early Industrial Revolution

Cobbler and Saddler Tools

102100T17   **Eyelet punch**   DTM   MH

Drop-forged steel, 6 3/8" long, signed "W F BINGHAM".

No Bingham with these initials is listed in DATM (Nelson 1999), but these might have been made by the Bingham Toolmakers of Norwich, CT, c. 1857-58.

92112T9   **French pattern cobblers' hammer**   DTM   TT

Cast steel, 6 3/8" long, 1 5/8" diameter face, 1 1/2" edge, signed with a lion touchmark.

111001T36   **Leather cutter**   DTM   MH

Drop-forged steel, 4 1/4" long, 7/8" diameter serrated cutting edge, signed with the mark "7/8".

61204T9   **Leather slitter**   DTM   MH

Brass, steel, iron screws, and wood handle, 7" long, brass slitter 1 3/4" wide, steel slitter 2 3/8" long, unsigned.

http://www.davistownmuseum.org/pics/61204T9.jpg

TCH1004A   **Leather stretcher**   DTM   MH

Drop-forged iron with a wood handle, 10 1/4" long with a 1/2" wide mouth, 5 1/4" long handle, unsigned.

30202T1   **Shoemakers' lasting pliers**   DTM   MH

Drop-forged iron, 8 1/2" long, 1" wide jaws, signed "L. B. Richardson Athol Mass Patented Oct 11, 1859".

http://www.davistownmuseum.org/pics/30202t1.jpg

TCH1001   **Tack pry**   DTM   MH

Cast steel with rosewood handle, 7 1/4" long, 3 7/8" handle, signed "C.S. OSBORNE & CO. STEEL", c. 1850.

DATM (Nelson 1999) lists the C.S. Osborne Co. as located in Newark, NJ, as early as 1826. The C.S. Osborne Co. is still in business; many of its tools have been sold over the last 25 years by the Liberty Tool Co. across the street from the Museum. Www.csosborne.com

http://www.davistownmuseum.org/bioOsborne.html

Coopers' Tools

22311T19   **Chamfer knife**   DTM   TT

Drop-forged iron and steel, 15" long, 5" long blade, signed "L. & I. J. WHITE" "BUFFALO, N.Y." in an oval shape with "1837" in the center, "5" above the trademark, and "A" on the inner handle.

This is also called a howelling knife. Part of the Robert Sullivan Collection donation.

Coopers' Tools

41203T6   Chamfer knife   DTM   MH

Drop-forged iron and steel, wood, 15" long, 5 1/2" long cutting blade, 8" long handle, signed "L. & I. J. White 1837 Buffalo NY" and "5 1/2".

DATM (Nelson 1999) notes this famous and prolific maker of coopers' tools and other edge tools worked from 1837 to 1928. Almost all of their tools have the founding date of 1837 marked on them. This is an essential tool for both wet and dry coopers.

http://www.davistownmuseum.org/pics/41203t6_p1.jpg
http://www.davistownmuseum.org/pics/41203t6_p2.jpg

12801T7   Coopers' adz   DTM   MH

Malleable iron and steel, 8" long, 1 1/4" square striking face, 2 9/16" wide blade, signed "VAUGHAN" "PARDOE & COX" "UNION" WARRANTED".

This tool shows some evidence of hand work, including hand filing and hand-forged beveling at the handle socket, which protrudes from the adz's body. An essential and commonly encountered tool in a coopers' workshop, it was used to construct the barrels, kegs, and casks of Maine and New England's fishing and commercial industries and the West Indies and Wine Island trades. This is the first tool in our Vaughan & Pardoe collection with Cox as part of the signature. Donated to the Museum by Rick Floyd.

http://www.davistownmuseum.org/pics/12801t7_p7.jpg
http://www.davistownmuseum.org/bioVaughn.htm

81212NOM1 Coopers' adz   NOM   TT (Pub)

Forged steel, wood (hickory), 7 1/2" long, 6" long handle, 8" long head with a 2 3/4" cutting edge and a 1 1/4" x 1 1/4" face, signed "HIGGINS".

The signature on this adz probably belongs to the Higgins working in Portland and Bangor Maine, circa 1850's. Courtesy of Sett Balise.

7602T3   Coopers' adz   LPC   MH

Malleable iron and steel with wood handle, 9" long, 3" wide blade, 10" long handle, signed with an obscure "KING New York".

This large coopers' adz came with the H. A. W. King coopers' broad ax (7602T2) and appears to be of the same vintage.

11301T5   Coopers' broad ax   DTM   MH

Malleable iron and steel, wood, 9" long blade, 4 1/2" maximum width of blade, 3 1/8" long pole, signed "Beardsley & Tyler".

Beardsley and Tyler is not listed in DATM (Nelson 1999), but there was a B. R. Beardsley making axes and edge tools in Elmira, NY, c. 1859.

Coopers' Tools

7602T2   Coopers' broad ax   LPC   MH

Forged iron and weld steel with wood handle, 17 1/2" long, 9 3/4" blade, signed "H. A. W. KING" "LEWIS STNY" (?).

DATM (Nelson 1999) lists an H. & J. W. King as working in New York in 1856, making bits, braces, drawknives, and planes. No other information is available on a King as a maker of coopers' tools. William Horton of New York stamped his tools "121 LEWIS ST N.Y." This coopers' ax is typical of those found in a shipyard at any time in the 19th century. However, even as late as 1868, working coopers played an essential role in supplying vessels of every description with casks and kegs for water, rum, lime, and other liquids, as well as dry cooperage for salt, flour, rope, etc. By 1880 the twilight of the era of the cooper had arrived.

http://www.davistownmuseum.org/pics/7602t2_p5.jpg

111412T14   Coopers' bung   DTM   MH

Forged iron, wooden handle, 6 1/4" long, 4" wide, unsigned.

121805T17   Coopers' bung   DTM   MH

Wood with leather header, 5 1/2" long, 4 7/8" wide, unsigned, c. 1850.

This is a typical coopers' bung for closing kegs and securing staves; a ubiquitous tool found in every workshop at that date.

http://www.davistownmuseum.org/pics/121805t17.jpg

913108T45   Coopers' bung   DTM   MH

Recycled steel with a wooden handle, 7 3/4" long, 3 3/4" long blade, unsigned.

It is unusual to see a coopers' bung used for a handle attached to a curved blade.

4713T4   Coopers' curved drawknife   DTM   MH

Cast steel, wood (rosewood), 16 1/2" long, 7 1/8" cutting edge, 5" handles, unsigned.

102612T12   Coopers' flagging iron   LPC   MH

Malleable iron and steel, 21" long, 4 1/4" wide, unsigned.

It is used for spreading barrel staves before caulking.

42801T7   Coopers' howell   DTM   MH

Wood (tiger maple), steel, 13 7/8" long, 1 9/16" wide blade, unsigned.

121311T1   Coopers' side ax   DTM   TT

Malleable iron and steel, wood, 17 1/2" long handle, 9" long and 6" wide blade, signed "J. F. Staples".

This broad ax shows distinct evidence of iron steeling. James Forest Staples worked in Portland, ME, 1849 - 1856.

Historic Maritime IV (1840-1865): The Early Industrial Revolution

Coopers' Tools

30301T1   Coopers' stove   DTM   LTC

Sheet metal and cast iron, aprox. 38" high, 16" diameter, unsigned.

This stove was made in Liberty and was used in the 19th century by the dry coopers to heat the metal rings for the barrels. It is on display at the Davistown Museum Liberty Tool Annex.

111412T15   Coopers' vise   DTM   MH

Drop-forged steel, 4" long, 3" wide, unsigned.

This tool is a screw with a curved handle.

31808PC10   Croze   DTM   MH

Steel, copper trim, brass screws, and wood, 13 3/4" long, 1/4" cutter, signed with an 1850 woman's profile and 4 stars over her head plus three decorative copper coins.

120907T3   Drawshave   DTM   TT

Malleable iron, forged steel, and wood, 15" long, 1 5/8" long blade, and 4 1/2" handles, signed "L & T WHITE" "18*7" and "BUFFALO N.Y." in an oblong oval with "6" on the other side.

This coopers' shave shows evidence of either a weld or a differential temper line on the backside.

31808SLP28   End shave   DTM   TT

Steel and wood, 7 1/2" long, 4 5/8" wide, unsigned.

http://www.davistownmuseum.org/pics/31808slp28-1.jpg
http://www.davistownmuseum.org/pics/31808slp28-2.jpg

100605T2   Hoop driver   DTM   MH

Steel with wooden handle, 5 1/8" long head with 1 1/2" drive, 12 1/2" long handle, signed "A. G. MORSE&CO" "BOSTON".

This is an undistinguished example of a coopers' driver, also known as a hoop set, with a previously unrecorded maker's sign. This tool was found in a barn in Washington, Maine.

51606T10   Hoop driver   DTM   MH

Puddled steel and wood, 9 1/4" long including an 8" wood handle, 1 1/2" head, unsigned.

The maker's mark is obscured by a heavily peened head showing many years of intensive use.

81801T13   Hoop driver   DTM   MH

Cast steel with wood handle, 4 5/8" long head, 1 5/8" long groove, signed "C. Drew & Co. Cast Steel".

This is a rare Drew tool.

http://www.davistownmuseum.org/pics/81801t13.jpg
http://www.davistownmuseum.org/bioDrew.htm

Coopers' Tools

51201T3   **Hoop driver**   DTM   MH

Steel, iron, and wood, 7 3/4" long including a 4 3/8" handle, 2 5/8" wide driver, unsigned.

An iron ferrule is at the end of the wood handle. This is an excellent example of a coopers' hoop driver or bung with a provenance from a New Bedford cooperage, c. 1860.

http://www.davistownmuseum.org/pics/51201t3.jpg

31808SLP29 **Shave**   DTM   TT

Steel and wood, 11 1/2" long, 4" long blade, unsigned.

http://www.davistownmuseum.org/pics/31808slp29-1.jpg
http://www.davistownmuseum.org/pics/31808slp29-2.jpg

121311T2   **Shingle knife**   DTM   TT

Puddled or German steel, wood handle, 8 3/4" long, 2 3/4" wide, signed "Higgins & Libby" "8" "Portland".

It is likely to be made of local forged puddled or German steel. Higgins & Libby worked in Portland, ME, in 1856.

http://www.davistownmuseum.org/publications/volume10.html

Domestic Utensils

112303P1   **Apple corer (?)**   DTM   MH

Wood, 10 1/4" high, 10 1/2" wide, 7" by 2 1/4" footing, mounted on 15" by 8" base, unsigned.

This is a typical homemade primitive of the 19th century. Was this used as an apple corer or a yarn winder?

TCP10040   **Button hole cutter**   DTM   MHC

Cast steel, 3 1/2" long, 3/8" thick handle, 15/16" wide cutting edge, signed "W.N. SEYMOUR & Co NEW YORK".

William N. Seymour & Co. operated circa 1828 to 1861. After 1842 they were listed as a hardware company (Nelson 1999, 707).

31701T1   **Candlewick cutter**   DTM   MH

German (?) steel with cast iron handles, 5 3/4" long, signed "W_BANNA_ PATD _ 25th ____".

No such maker is listed in DATM (Nelson 1999). This is a generic 19th century tool with a mysterious maker's mark.

Domestic Utensils

61601T1   **Cleaver**   DTM   MH

Cast steel, 15 5/8" long, 10 1/4" blade, signed "BILLINGS" "CAST STEEL" "AUGUSTA".

This tool is intriguing because its steel cutting surface is welded to a steel, not iron, body. Is the body of the cleaver "cast steel" or a lower quality puddled or blister steel? Many Billings are listed in the Registry of Maine Toolmakers as working in N. Monmouth, Clinton, and Saco. John P. Billings and his son George made axes in Clinton from about 1860 to 1909. Other members of the Billings clan are listed as making tools as early as the 1840s.

When making this cleaver (as well as the clapboard slick also in the collection of The Davistown Museum) did Billings utilize imported English cast steel or American made cast steel (1865 f.)?

http://www.davistownmuseum.org/pics/61601t1_p2.jpg
http://www.davistownmuseum.org/publications/volume10.html

30106T1   **Earthen redware pot**   DTM   MH

Redware, 5 1/2" diameter top, 3 1/4" diameter bottom, 5" high, unsigned.

It has an incised one inch band with black stain at top and a brown drip glaze interior.

111001T22   **Graining tools (set of 11)**   DTM   MH

Cast steel, 3 1/2" high, widths vary from 3/4" to 4", unsigned.

These are used for grain patterning painted surfaces, especially on blanket chests and other Victorian style cottage furniture.

http://www.davistownmuseum.org/pics/111001t22.jpg

101701T8   **Gun powder flask**   DTM   MH

Brass and leather, 7 1/2" long, 2 1/2" brass nozzle with closure, unsigned.

This is a generic Civil War era gunpowder container with hand sewn leather.

72002C1   **Ink bottle**   DTM   T-R

Ceramic stoneware, 7 1/2" high, 3" diameter, unsigned.

Liberty Tool Company recovered several hundred of these ink bottles from a Boston resident who had dug them up from a school (?) dump. Around the Civil War era, these were used to hold ink for the public schools before the changeover to glass ink bottles.

92001T7   **Milk bowl**   LPC   MH

redware, unsigned.

It was made by John Corliss's pottery at Days Ferry, ME, just across the Kennebec River from Bath.

71401T16   **Pinching iron**   DTM   MH

Drop-forged iron, 10 3/8" long, unsigned.

This is a typical 19th century pinching iron, used for straightening hair.

http://www.davistownmuseum.org/pics/71401t16.jpg

Historic Maritime IV (1840-1865): The Early Industrial Revolution

Domestic Utensils

121805T4   Scissors

DTM   MH

Steel, 10" long, signed "SUPREMO", c. 1850-60.

These are a nice example of Italian scissors of the early Industrial Revolution - i.e. an early example of drop-forging.

http://www.davistownmuseum.org/pics/121805t4_p2.jpg

914108T14   Scissors

DTM   MH

Drop-forged steel, brass screws, 4 1/6" long, signed "BARCLAY".

Possibly this is Barclay & Co. of Newark, NJ, who made leather tools circa 1875 - 1885. These scissors have a special notch cut out of the blades.

41801T6   Shears

DTM   MH

Malleable iron and steel, 12 1/2" long, 6 1/2" long blades, signed "P H Hahn NY".

It could be signed Harn? No makers with this mark are listed in DATM (Nelson 1999). This tool is difficult to date (1840 - 1880?) but has a clearly defined steel cutting edge welded to the iron blade similar to many axes made during this period.

50402P1   Tintype in a reliquary with a bible

NOM

Ivory and tin, 13/16" wide, 1" high tintype; 1 5/8" wide, 2" high reliquary; 1" high, 1/2" wide bible, signed "H Ramsdell, Lubec, Oct 1 1863" on ivory.

The tintype is a photograph of a Civil War soldier who perhaps died on or near the date. The reliquary and bible have been polychromed. The reliquary is made of ivory scrimshawed in colored ink with flags, tent, weeping willow, and three guns. The bible is scrimshawed with flowers. Henry Ramsdell of Lubec was in the 15th Infantry, Maine Volunteers. Born circa 1843, he was at Harper's Ferry and Louisiana battles during the Civil War. More information about Ramsdell is welcomed. These pieces were loaned to the Museum by Robert Wheeler for the 2002 exhibit and have now been returned.

http://www.davistownmuseum.org/pics/50402p1_p1.jpg
http://www.davistownmuseum.org/TDMnewAcquisitions.html

Files

913108T24   File

DTM   MH

Medium carbon steel and wood, 7 3/4" long, unsigned.

The use of this tool is unknown. It looks similar to a planemakers' float but originated with a collection of leatherworking tools in Merrimac, MA, in 2008. The uniformity of the grooves, which are only on one side, suggests it is machine-made.

Fishing Implements

112704T3   Frost fish spear

DTM   MH

Forged iron, wood handle, iron ferrule, 6 spears, 6 3/8" long, 2 3/8" wide, 4 1/2" long ferrule, 38" long handle, unsigned.

See the description of this type of tool under tool #112704T2.

Historic Maritime IV (1840-1865): The Early Industrial Revolution

Fishing Implements

112704T2 **Frost fish spear**   DTM   MH

Forged iron, wood handle, 8 spears, 4 1/2" long, 2 3/4" wide, 38 1/4" long handle, unsigned.

Found in an Achusnet, MA, fishing shed, this hand-forged fishing spear and a second one (112704T3) are difficult to date and may be early 19th century or possibly late 18th century. These tools were used in the tradition of Native Americans to spear fish from shore which, especially on cold nights of the first fall frosts, swarm to the sandy shallows and mudflats of New England coves and estuaries. Frost fish were especially common in the warmer water of Buzzards and Narragansett Bays, but are also a tradition in Maine rivers and inland bays.

10910T1 **Swordfish harpoon head**   DTM   MHC-G

Brass, 6" long, 1 5/8" wide, unsigned, c. 1865-1900's.

http://www.davistownmuseum.org/pics/10910t1web2.jpg
http://www.davistownmuseum.org/pics/10910t1web1.jpg

Hammers

52603T18 **Ball peen hammer**   DTM   MH

Drop-forged iron or steel, wood, 10 1/4" long, 3 1/2" head, unsigned.

TTCR1002 **Ball peen hammer patterns (2)**   DTM   MH

Forged iron or steel, 9 1/2", unsigned.

This curious artifact is probably two ball peen hammers rejected as seconds prior to drop-forging. Do they represent the early stages of drop-forge production? Comments are solicited.

33002T16 **Claw hammer**   DTM   MH

Forged iron and steel, 5 3/8" long, 1" square face, signed "C. BARNARD".

Barnard is not listed in DATM (Nelson 1999); another unregistered American (?) toolmaker of the 19th century.

http://www.davistownmuseum.org/pics/33002t16.jpg

TCM1001 **Cobblestone hammer**   DTM   MH

Forged iron and steel, 12" long, 1 1/8" round face, signed "COCKRHYMES & CO" on one side and "J.T. & CO" on the reverse side.

It has distinct beveling on the head; the prototypical tool used to construct the cobblestone streets of Portland, Boston, and other Atlantic coastal cities. It may have been drop-forged.

http://www.davistownmuseum.org/pics/TCM1001.jpg
http://www.davistownmuseum.org/pics/TCM1001-2.jpg

913108T10 **Granite hammer**   DTM   MH

Iron and steel, 5" long, 4 3/4" diameter, unsigned.

One end of the hammer head is in a star shape and is used to break up granite.

ID #   Status   Location

Hammers

32802T14   Gristmill stone hammer (?)   DTM   MH

Forged iron and steel, 8 7/8" long, 1 3/8" cutting edge, signed "JOHN HARTMAN Boston Mass".
DATM (Nelson 1999) does not list this hammer-maker.

http://www.davistownmuseum.org/pics/32802t6a.jpg

121805T13   Hammer   DTM   MH

Forged iron and steel, wood, 10 3/4" long including wooden handle, 4 9/16" wide, 1" diameter head, unsigned.

This is an incomplete example of one of America's first patented hammers. One piece below the looped claws is missing.

http://www.davistownmuseum.org/pics/121805t13_p2.jpg

041505T17   Hammer   DTM   MH

Forged iron and steel with wood handle, 14 3/8" long handle, 5 7/8" long face, 2 faces both 1" diameter, unsigned.

This old hammer shows evidence of hand-forging and filing, but was probably drop-forged before it was reworked by hand. It is part of the hammer study group. It is the hammer on the left of the photograph.

http://www.davistownmuseum.org/pics/041505t11.jpg

041505T12   Hammer   DTM   MH

Forged iron and steel, wood handle, 9 3/4" long including handle, 4 1/2" head, 1/2" wide hatchet-like cutting edge, 15/16" diameter face, unsigned.

Clearly made of hand-filed steel, this hammer is difficult to date and of unknown use. It is part of the hammer study group. It is the hammer on the far right of the photograph with its handle pointing upward.

http://www.davistownmuseum.org/pics/041505t4.jpg

123012T2   Hammer head casting   DTM   TT

Cast iron, 6 1/2" long, 1 1/2" wide, 1" face, signed "5".

This appears to be a half-finished hammer head casting.

31602T4   Millstone facing hammer   DTM   MH

Iron, steel, and wood, 9 1/2" long, 4 1/2" long head, 1 3/8" wide steel faces, unsigned.

041505T14   Sledge hammer   DTM   MH

Forged iron and steel, wood handle, 23 1/2" long handle, 7 1/4" long head, 1 1/2" square peen and 3/4" square face, unsigned.

This old sledge shows evidence of hand-forging and filing. It is probably smith-made in the mid-19th century.

http://www.davistownmuseum.org/pics/041505t14.jpg

Historic Maritime IV (1840-1865): The Early Industrial Revolution

Hammers

TCM1006   Stone hammer   DTM   MH

Forged iron and steel with wood handle, 10" long, head 2 1/2" long and 1/2" wide, signed with the touchmark "AHEW" (in a triangle).

The handle has a twist design at the grip.

TML1003   Tack hammer   DTM   MH

Drop-forged steel, 4 5/8" long, 1/2" diameter, signed "C. DREW & CO".

Drew hammers are rare; this one has a split face.

http://www.davistownmuseum.org/bioDrew.htm

TCM1002   Tack hammer   DTM   MH

Drop-forged iron and steel, wood, 13 3/4" long, 2 5/8" long head, 5/8" diameter face, unsigned.

It was probably used in the carriage-making trade.

090109T6   Tack hammer   DTM   MH

Tool steel and wood, 3 1/2" long, 9/16" wide head, 6 1/2" long wooden handle, signed "E.LIBBY".

TBL1003   Tack hammer head   DTM   MH

Drop-forged steel, 4 1/2" long, signed "C. DREW & CO.".

http://www.davistownmuseum.org/pics/51100t6.jpg
http://www.davistownmuseum.org/bioDrew.htm

Ice Tools

040904T4   Ice ax   DTM   MH

Iron and weld steel, 11 1/4" long, 2 3/4" wide blade, signed possibly "DERNELL & Co" "ATHENS NY".

This is a generic ice ax. The signature is partly obscured and appears to have the letters above. The Village of Athens, 1896 Greene County Directory lists: "Frederick F. Dernell (H. F. Dernell & Co.)---res. Washington St. near Third St." [on the web at: http://www.rootsweb.com/~nygreen2/1896_village_of_athens.htm]. DATM (Nelson 1999, 222) lists H. F. Dernell & Co. in Athens, NY, with working dates from 1854-1917.

http://www.davistownmuseum.org/pics/040904t4_p1.jpg

71903T2   Ice saw   DTM   MH

Steel with cast iron and wood handle, 45 1/2" long. 7 3/4" wide at widest point, unsigned.

This double sided ice saw has an atypical form -- smaller than most ice saws. This may have been a limited production saw from a small foundry. It has a Maine provenance.

12713T2   Two man ice crosscut saw   DTM   MH

Spring steel, iron, wood (beech), 52" long, 5 1/2" at widest, 42" long cutting edge, 10 1/4" long handles, unsigned.

Historic Maritime IV (1840-1865): The Early Industrial Revolution

Ice Tools

12713T1   **Two man ice saw**   DTM   MH

Spring steel, iron, wood (beech), 52 1/2" long, 4 3/8" at widest, 41" long cutting edge, 8 1/4" long handles, unsigned.

Knives

71401T19   **Banana knife**   DTM   MH

Drop-forged steel, wood, and brass, 10" long, 3 1/8" wood handle, unsigned.

This is an example of a now forgotten tool, the banana knife.

41801T2   **Oyster knife**   DTM   MH

Wood, steel and brass, 6 3/4" long, 3 5/8" blade, signed "TUCK".

It is sometimes also called a clam knife. This Brockton Massachusetts company was established from 1852 until 1915, and made prolific quantities of hand tools including screwdrivers. The Davistown Museum is seeking more information on this toolmaker

51606T14   **Putty knife**   DTM   MH

Steel and rosewood, 7 1/8" long including a 3 1/2" oval handle, signed "J Russell & Co. Green River Works".

This is a mundane tool made by one of America's most important toolmakers, the John Russell Mfg. Co.

http://www.davistownmuseum.org/bioRussel.html

31808PC11   **Trappers' knife**   DTM   MH

Steel, copper trim, and wood, 9" long, 4 7/8" blade, signed "RUSSELL & CO." and "GREEN RIVER WORKS" on the blade.

John Russell & Co. was located in Deerfield and Greenfield, Massachusetts from 1832 - 1865.

http://www.davistownmuseum.org/bioRussel.html

Logging Tools

71903T7   **Log rule**   DTM   MH

Wood, 48" long, unsigned.

Clearly hand stamped, this logging rule may predate the era of the factory-made Lufkin logging rule.

4105T6   **Peavey**   DTM   MH

Malleable iron, 9 1/4" long, unsigned.

This hand wrought peavey point is nicely forge-welded and could also be early 19th century. It is a nice example of the craft of the blacksmith and the beauty and ductility of malleable iron.

Historic Maritime IV (1840-1865): The Early Industrial Revolution

Logging Tools

913108T13A   **Peavey**   DTM   MH

Malleable iron, 12 1/2" long, signed "WILLARD", the first initial is obscured.

This tool is also known as a cant dog spike.

913108T12   **Spike**   DTM   MH

Hand-forged malleable iron, 11 6/8" long, signed "J. H. PEAVEY" "_ANGOR, ME".

This is the spike end from a cant hook or peavey. DATM (Nelson 1999) believes that James Henry Peavey of Bangor, Maine, was probably part of the Peavey Tool Co.

http://www.davistownmuseum.org/bioPeavey.htm

61204T8   **Spud**   DTM   MH

Forged iron and steel, 19" long including 5 5/8" long handle, signed "_____ Brewer Maine".

This tool is made of forge-welded iron and steel with a distinctive forge-welded iron socket. This is a classic example of a 19th century spud used to remove the bark from a log, either for preparing the log for the mill or removing the bark (e.g. Hemlock) for the tannery. Part of the signature is not legible. Could this be an early forge-welded Snow & Nealley tool?

http://www.davistownmuseum.org/pics/61204T8.jpg

4713T2   **Timber scribe**   DTM   MH

Wood (rosewood), hand-forged steel, 5" long, 1 1/4" tall, 5/8" wide, 1 1/2" long cutting blade, unsigned.

42112LTC1   **Timber scribe knife**   DA   TT (Pub)

Forged steel, brass, 3 1/2" long handle, 2 1/2" long blade, unsigned.

Courtesy of Liberty Tool Co.

Machinists' Tools

TCQ1001A   **Calipers**   DTM   MH

Malleable iron or steel, brass rivet, 13 1/2" long, unsigned.

121805T5   **Calipers**   DTM   MH

Tempered alloy steel, 12 1/2" long, signed "H. C. Perry" and "H.C.P.", c. 1850.

No H. C. Perry is listed in the Directory of American Toolmakers (Nelson 1999). These exquisitely made cast steel calipers are almost certainly American-made by the owner of a small machine shop. A gorgeous finely made specimen from the classic period of the florescence of American toolmakers.

http://www.davistownmuseum.org/pics/121805t5_p2.jpg

Machinists' Tools

41203T5   Depth gauge

Tempered alloy steel, 4" depth gauge on a 3 3/8" long, 15/32" wide japanned base, signed "D & S".

D & S is the mark on the very rare tools of Darling & Schwartz, Bangor, ME, 1854 - 1866. This is the only known example of this tool -- a treasure from the boomtown years of Bangor, by one of America's finest machinist toolmakers.

http://www.davistownmuseum.org/pics/41203t5_p3.jpg

http://www.davistownmuseum.org/publications/volume10.html

TCP1005A   Dividers

Cast steel, 6 7/16" long, signed "H.A. PAGE CAST STEEL", c. 1840 (?).

This maker is not listed in DATM (Nelson 1999). It is similar in style to both Boker and Stevens calipers. Boker tools were imported from Germany and Stevens manufactured calipers of this style in Holyoke, MA.

http://www.davistownmuseum.org/pics/tcp1005a.jpg

TCP1004A   Dividers

Forged iron, 7 3/4" long, signed "W.D.EVANS".

DATM lists a William B. Evans as an ax maker of Compton, NH, c. 1884. This divider appears older than that.

http://www.davistownmuseum.org/pics/tcp1005a.jpg

041505T37   Double calipers

Malleable iron or steel, signed "PAT APL'D FOR" "J.P. BARNES".

No J. P. Barnes is listed in DATM (Nelson 1999).

http://www.davistownmuseum.org/pics/041505t37_p2.jpg

2713LTC1   Fay calipers

Hand-finished cast steel, 5 1/4" long, 2 3/8" wide, signed "PS STUBS".

http://www.davistownmuseum.org/bioStubs.htm

50402T6   Height gauge

Tempered alloy steel, 3 5/8" long with 1 5/8" diameter base, unsigned.

This exquisite shop-made machinist tool was probably made just prior to the appearance of factory made surface gauges in the classic period of American machinists' tools (1865 - 1900).

22411T24   Inside/outside calipers

Cast steel or German steel with brass knob and copper rivet, 5" long and 2" wide closed, signed "P S STUBS".

http://www.davistownmuseum.org/bioStubs.htm

Historic Maritime IV (1840-1865): The Early Industrial Revolution

Machinists' Tools

33002T6   Knurling tool   DTM   MH

Steel, 5 1/2" long handles, 3 13/16" wide, 4 1/2" diameter knurling cutters, signed "55" for 1855 (?).

It is typical of the shop produced machinists' hand tools of the pre-mass production era.

http://www.davistownmuseum.org/pics/33002t6.jpg

TJG1002A   Level   DTM   MH

Brass and drop-forged iron, 7 3/4" long, 7/8" wide, signed with the mark "1862".

Who made this level? Probably it is a user-made or at least a locally produced tool.

TCP1001   Level   DTM   MH

Cast iron, 8 1/4" long, 7/8" wide, 1 5/16" high, unsigned.

This 19th century tool comes from southern New England. It is typical of a tool manufactured at the location the tool was used, probably by the person who made it.

71908T1   Level   DA   MH

Wood and brass, 24" long, 2 5/8" wide, and 1 1/2" deep, signed "O. Little" and also has a paper label "SPIRIT LEVEL", "OF ALL KINDS," "MADE AND WARRANTED BY" and "___ McCOSKRIE".

DATM (Nelson 1999, 525) lists James McCoskrie of East Cambridge, MA as a maker of levels in 1848-1850. This name matches the partially legible label, which also states "Camb" on the torn bottom line. O. Little was the owner.

http://www.davistownmuseum.org/pics/71908t1-3.jpg

21201T9   Machinists' level   DTM   MH

Tempered alloy steel, 9" long, 13/16" wide, unsigned.

This is an elegant owner-made shop tool dating from an era (1840 - 1860) where machinists often made their own tools.

41203T2D   Machinists' pry bar   DTM   MH

Forged steel, 15 1/2" long, signed "C. Drew & Co. No 75".

http://www.davistownmuseum.org/bioDrew.htm

040103T5   Marking gauge   DTM   MH

Tool steel, 12 1/4" long with 4" sliding gauge, signed "D. Cummings".

No D. Cummings is listed in DATM (Nelson 1999). The sliding gauge is attached to the middle of the rule by an adjustable nut. The unusually odd design of this early machinists' tool and its perplexing signature make this an intriguing example of either a one-of-a-kind tool or one made in very limited quantities. Who was D. Cummings and where and when did he work?

http://www.davistownmuseum.org/pics/040103t5_p1.jpg
http://www.davistownmuseum.org/pics/040103t5_p2.jpg

Machinists' Tools

71903T6   Rule   DTM   MH

Tool steel, 24", signed "D & B Bangor Me USA Stnd.".

One of the rarest of all marks, Darling & Bailey made machinist rules in Bangor, Maine, for only one year before becoming Darling & Sharpe (1854), the precursors of the famous Brown & Sharpe Company. This rule is also marked "Shr" for shrunk on one side with increments in tenths of inches.

http://www.davistownmuseum.org/publications/volume10.html

14302T16   Screw plate   DTM   MH

Tool steel, 10 1/4" long, unsigned.

This is a typical machinist tool of the mid-19th century.

TCP1004B   Set of boxed precision ground bearings   DTM   MH

Tool steel, 8" long, 2 3/4" wide, unsigned.

The sizes are all hand stamped.

52603T7   Spring calipers   DTM   MH

Tempered alloy steel, 3 6/16" long, unsigned.

52603T6   Spring calipers   DTM   MH

Tempered alloy steel or tool steel, 3" long, signed "F. TROMRLEV".

Perhaps the signature is Trombley?

111001T38   Surface gauge   DTM   MH

Malleable iron and steel, 4 1/8" long, 4" high, unsigned.

This is a finely constructed tool; ornate in form with a carefully filed surface. It is typical of a shop-made tool from the beginning of the Industrial Revolution.

111001T20   Surface gauge   DTM   MH

Malleable iron and steel, 6" high, unsigned.

This is a typical shop-made tool of the era.

22512LTC6   Tap and die set   DA   TT (Pub)

Drop-forged tempered alloy steel, drop-forged steel bits, 8 1/2" x 5 1/2" x 1 1/2", signed "GREENFIELD" "GERMANY" "GTD".

The set includes 9 dies, 12 taps, and a T Handle from various manufacturers. Courtesy of Liberty Tool Co.

Measuring Tools

Measuring Tools

42012T4   Calipered wire gauge   DTM   TT

Cast steel, 8 5/16" long, 4" wide, signed "PARTRIDGE, MAKER, MARLASTON".

This unusual tool was made by George Partridge & Sons of Darlastown, England. They operated circa 1816 to 1950 (http://blackcountryhistory.org/collections/getrecord/GB149_D-SSW_2_GP/). Courtesy of Liberty Tool Co.

81212LTC2   Ivory folding carpenters' rule   DA   TT (Pub)

Ivory, German silver, 2' unfolded, 1/2" wide, 1/8" thick, signed "No 83 STEPHENS & CO. RIVERTON CT".

Stephens & Co. is listed as working from 1828 to 1901 by the DATM (Nelson 1999). His full name was Lorenzo Case Stephens. Courtesy of Liberty Tool Company.

102503T2   Outside firm-lock calipers   DTM   MH

Steel, 9 1/8 " long, signed "D. E. LYMAN".

There is no D. Lyman listed in DATM (Nelson 1999). This heavy duty caliper -- the steel is unusually thick -- is almost certainly made by its owner for his own shop use. It predates the era of factory made tools -- its quality would not be practical to duplicate in a large production.

31611T3   Try square   DTM   TT

Steel and rosewood, 6" long, 2" blade, 4 1/4" wooden leg, signed "W. MARPLE".

William Marples is listed in DATM (Nelson 1999) as a wooden planemaker, 1828-1856. William Marples & Sons, 1833 - 1983 made planes, edge tools, and files. It is unknown if this tool was made by them, it could be an owner signature.

12812LTC1   Walking wheel caliper   DA   TT (Pub)

Wood, brass, 48" long, 18" diameter wheel, signed With wood board graduations.

This tool has been the subject of numerous improvised repairs, including a .40 caliber brass handgun cartridge and a sink fitting. Courtesy of Liberty Tool Company.

121805T28   Wire gauge   DTM   MH

Steel, 4 1/2" long, signed "No. 1 DISSTON STANDARD PHILA.U.S.A." and then with sizes 1 - 26.

This is a rare Disston gauge for "measuring sheet stock used in making saws. I believe this gage goes back to the time when there were no national standards for sheet, requiring individual companies to establish their own standards." (Ray Larsen).

http://www.davistownmuseum.org/pics/121805t28_p2.jpg
http://www.davistownmuseum.org/bio#bioDisston.htm

Measuring Tools (Except Machinist Tools)

11301T9   Adjustable calipers   DTM   MH

Tool steel, 5" long, signed "W. D. Smith PAT Sep 24 67".

There is no W. D. Smith listed in DATM (Nelson 1999). Who was he and where did he make calipers?

Measuring Tools (Except Machinist Tools)

12801T14   Bevel square   DTM   MH

Wood, forged iron, and brass, 12" blade with 7 3/8" long handle, signed "Tidgewell & Co. Middletown Ct".

DATM (Nelson 1999) lists Tidgewell as working c. 1850. This is an uncommon signature and one of America's earliest manufacturers of carpenters' measuring tools. This is the only Tidgewell seen by the Liberty Tool Co. in 31 years, but we may not have looked as carefully as we should have for these often difficult to see signatures (located on the wood handle, not on the iron or steel blade.)

TCP1004   Compass   DTM   MH

Malleable iron or steel, 6" long, signed "THEWLIS & GRIFFITH".

Worrall's directory of Warrington, Wigan, St. Helens [England] (1876, 27) lists Thewlis & Griffith as file and tool manufacturers, Phoenix Works, Mercy St., indicating Thewlis Shaw as one of the principals.

82709T1   Cordage rule   DTM   MH

Boxwood and brass, 4 3/4" long, 1 7/8" wide, and 3/16" thick, signed on one edge, "KERBY & BRO. N.Y." The back of the rule is marked "JOHN A. ROEBLING'S SONS CO.", "MFR'S OF WIRE ROPE", and "TRENTON, N.J.".

John A. Roebling's Sons Co. was a wire rope manufacturer with one of its locations in Trenton, New Jersey. The company began operating around 1842 and was sold in 1952 (http://www.inventionfactory.com/history/main.html). Kerby & Bro. was a 51 Fulton St., NY, NY, maker that specialized in rules, operating from as early as 1860 (http://home.att.net/~philcannon/makers.htm#K). This rule, made by Kerby, is advertising the Roebling's wire rope.

http://www.davistownmuseum.org/pics/82709t1-2.jpg
http://www.davistownmuseum.org/pics/82709t1-1.jpg

Measuring Tools (Except Machinist Tools)

42602T2   **Cordage rule**   DTM   MH

Boxwood and brass, 6 5/8" long, 2 1/2" wide, signed on the edge of the rule "KERBY & BRO." and "_____ CORDAGE CO PLYMOUTH _____".

It is also marked "Estimated Weight of Rope" with four columns marked: "CIR. INCHES", "DIA INCHES", WEIGHT ONE FATH MANILA", and "WEIGHT ONE FATH TAND HEMP". This Kerby cordage rule is also typical of the rules made by Stanley Rule and Level Co. for wharf men and skippers. See Philip Stanley's (1984) "Boxwood and Ivory" for additional information about this type of tool. DATM (Nelson 1999, 446) lists Kerby & Bro. in New York City. Phil Platt states "Kerby & Bro were reported as rulemakers at 51 Fulton St., NY and 90 Fulton St. NY. The Kerby in both firms has always been considered the same person or of the same family. Unfortunately, I do not have any better dates to indicate which firm came first. However, I do have one barrel head gauge that carries the imprint of Kerby & Davidson makers 95 Bowery NY. The 'imprint' is very well done and impressive -- judging on that basis I would guess that Kerby & Davidson is the later or successor firm. Also 'Bowery' begins about 6 blocks north of Fulton St. and runs north (Fulton is E-W). If memory serves me 1883 saw the opening of the Brooklyn Bridge -- which probably spurred land development north of the Manhattan end of the bridge (Fulton St. is 3 blocks south of the bridge entrance). H. Davidson is listed in DATM as working 1885 forward, I have two pieces carrying the H. Davidson mark at 95 Bowery."

http://www.davistownmuseum.org/pics/42602t2_p1.jpg
http://www.davistownmuseum.org/pics/42602t2_p2.jpg

42801T6   **Dividers**   DTM   MH

Cast steel, signed "S H F Bingham Cast Steel".

No SHF Bingham is listed in DATM (Nelson 1999) or in Cope's (1993) American Machinists' Tools; probably a heretofore unrecorded American toolmaker. Was there an English manufacturer with this name?

TCP1002A   **Folding rule**   BDTM   MH

Wood and brass, 12" long, signed "J. WATTS BOSTON".

DATM (Nelson 1999) lists a Joseph Watts as a manufacturer of rules, bevels, gauges, scales, dress squares, and log calipers, c. 1849. This is the only J. Watts rule the curator has seen in over 30 years in the tool business. Phil Platt states "Joseph Watts' working dates were 1834 - 1849 (D.A.T.) He apparently worked at rule making, making gauges and squares in Charlestown, MA.; but, marked at least the rules 'BOSTON'. There are many Watts' family members in and around the city of Boston. Don and Anne Wing, Marion, MA (EAIA) are currently doing research on J. Watts and trying to connect him back to English rule makers. See: Milt Bacheller (2000) 'American Marking Gages' for an extensive write up on the Watts family."

http://www.davistownmuseum.org/pics/tcp1002A_p2.jpg
http://www.davistownmuseum.org/bioWatts.html

Measuring Tools (Except Machinist Tools)

TCQ3500   **Framing square**   DTM   MH

Cast steel, signed "H A WEST PATENTED WARRANTED ___?___ STEEL" AND "B HARMON".

DATM (Nelson 1999) doesn't list any H. A. West as a maker of squares but it does list B. Harmon and Company as a square-maker in N. Bennington, Vt, c. 1850. Under the heading Harmon and Fay, DATM also notes that Bronson Harmon made squares in N. Bennington, Vt, c. 1848 (Nelson 1999, 134).

090508T1   **Framing square**   DTM   MH

Steel, 24" x 16", signed "D. J. GEORGE" "WARRANTEED STEEL".

Dennis J. George of Shaftsbury, Vermont worked from 1846 - 1859 and then merged into Eagle Square.

http://www.davistownmuseum.org/bioEagleSq.htm

090508T3   **Framing square**   DTM   MH

Metal, 4 12/16" x 3", signed "HOWELL TOOL CO." "ORANGE, MASS" and "U.S.A." with owner's mark "J.D." on the short end.

This company made machinists' squares around 1900 and might be connected to F. L. Turner & Co. of Ohio (Nelson 1999).

63001T3   **Framing square**   DTM   MH

Cast steel, 12" x 24", signed "J. Essex CAST STEEL WARRANTED No 1".

DATM (Nelson 1999) lists Jeremiah Essex as making squares in Bennington, Vermont, 1830 - 59 before merging with the Eagle Square Co. in 1859. The variety of numeration on this square reflects the increasing complexity of construction techniques in the early years of the Industrial Revolution and may reflect changing measurement needs for constructing newly introduced balloon frame buildings.

http://www.davistownmuseum.org/bioEagleSq.htm

102503T3   **Line level**   LPC   MH

Drop-forged steel, signed "H. B. BROWN".

DATM (Nelson 1999, 119) lists H. B. Brown & Co. of New Haven, CT, 1887, as making "other" tools, including bolt and pipe cutters. This tool came directly out of a c. 1850 tool chest in southern New Hampshire.

TCP1003A   **Plumb bob**   DTM   MH

Cast iron, 3 3/4" long, 2 1/4" wide, unsigned.

TCQ1003   **Plumb bob**   DTM   MH

Cast iron, 3 5/8" long, 2 1/8" wide, unsigned.

This is a generic mid-19th century plumb bob.

ID #   Status   Location

Measuring Tools (Except Machinist Tools)

121401T1   Rule   DTM   MH

Drop-forged iron or steel, 24" long, 1 3/4" wide, signed "Revere", marked with hand stamped numerals, dated "11 17 1847".

DATM (Nelson 1999) lists only one tool, a caliper, "1780" as being marked Revere. Paul Revere died in 1818. Who is Revere and when did he work? Was this once a framing square that was cut down? The rule is exactly 24" long, the last measurement marking reads only 2.

041505T36   Rule   DTM   MH

Tool steel, 6" long, signed "D. & S." "BANGOR Me." "U. S. Stnd.".

A famous Bangor, Maine, toolmaker, Darling & Schwartz worked from 1854 - 1866.

http://www.davistownmuseum.org/pics/041505t36_p1.jpg
http://www.davistownmuseum.org/publications/volume10.html

052107T1   Square   DTM   MH

German steel, signed "TURNER & _____" and "GERMAN STEEL".

This square is probably made from reforged blister steel (shear steel also called sheaf steel) rather than decarburized cast iron (German steel). When written in English, the term "German steel" usually refers to shear (sheaf) steel, the manufacture of which was perfected by German steelmakers working at Shotley Bridge on the Derwent River sometime after 1686. Production of sheer steel continued into the 19th century despite the widespread appearance of cast steel in the late 1760s. See the chapter on sheaf steel in "Steel- and Toolmaking Strategies and Techniques Before 1870" (Brack 2008). The maker may be English, there were many Turners in Sheffield, UK.

http://www.davistownmuseum.org/pics/052107t1_p4.jpg
http://www.davistownmuseum.org/pics/052107t1_p6.jpg

22612T6   Tenon gauge   DTM   TT

Cast brass, hardwood, 8" long, 5/8" square track, 2 3/8" by 1" block, signed "*WATTS Boston*".

Joseph Watts made marking gauges in Charleston, MA and marked them Boston from 1834 to 1849 (Nelson 1999, 833).

http://www.davistownmuseum.org/bioWatts.html

32708T43   Traveler wheel   DTM   MH

Malleable iron, 11 7/8" long, 9 1/4" long handle, 7 3/4" diameter, unsigned.

http://www.davistownmuseum.org/pics/32708t43-2.jpg
http://www.davistownmuseum.org/pics/32708t43-1.jpg

32708T44   Traveler wheel   DTM   MH

Malleable iron, wood, 13" long, 7 7/8" diameter, 9 1/4" long handle, signed "WILEY & RUSSELL MFG CO. GREENFIELD MASS." and on the back "THE GREEN RIVER TIRE WHEEL".

Wiley & Russell's working dates are from 1872 - 1912. They used "Green River" and "Lightning" as brand names.

http://www.davistownmuseum.org/pics/32708t44-2.jpg
http://www.davistownmuseum.org/pics/32708t44-3.jpg

Historic Maritime IV (1840-1865): The Early Industrial Revolution

Measuring Tools (Except Machinist Tools)

71401T14   **Try square**   DTM   MH

Malleable iron or steel, 7 1/4" long, unsigned.

The numeration on this tool appears hand stamped. This tool reflects the transition from blacksmith-made tools to the factory system.

81101T18   **Try square**   DTM   MH

Tempered alloy steel, 2", signed "DISSTON" and "A. MORSE", probably the owner.

Henry Disston (1819 - 1878) was making saws in Philadelphia as early as 1840. See DATM (Nelson 1999, 227-9) for a complete listing of the Disston clan and their tool manufacturing operations.

http://www.davistownmuseum.org/bioDisston.htm

51100T7   **Vernier calipers**   DTM   MH

Tool steel, 9 1/4" long, 3 3/4" wide jaw, signed "E. F. Sibley", 1840 - 1860.

Was Sibley an owner-maker?

http://www.davistownmuseum.org/pics/51100t6.jpg

3405T2   **Wire gauge**   DTM   MH

Tool steel, 3 3/4" long, signed "LACENE Mfg. Co Manchester NH" also numerated 2 -12.

It is hand stamped with numerals. Lacene is not listed in DATM (Nelson 1999).

3405T5   **Wire gauge**   DTM   MH

Tool steel, 3" diameter, signed "C TOLLNER WARRENTED STEEL".

Charles Tollner is listed as a Bower, New York City planemaker and hardware dealer working from 1851 - 1861. He later became a partner of the famous Albert Hammacher, the New York City hardware dealer (1864 - 1884). Is this an example of either German or puddled steel?

83102T4   **Wire gauge**   DTM   MH

German (?) steel, signed "CARANTIE" and marked 1 to 60.

The size of the gauge index for 1 to 60 is less than the United States standard gauge and doesn't seem to match Stubs steel or iron wire gauges. Could this be a Roebling or a Washburn and Moen's gauge?

50402T7   **Wire gauge**   DTM   MH

Tool steel, 3 1/4" diameter, signed "J. R. Brown & Sharpe Providence R.I. standard wire gauge 0 - 30".

Joseph R. Brown and Lucian Sharpe worked together from 1853 to 1866, before the formation of Darling, Brown and Sharpe in 1866. This mark, however, was used after this date (Nelson 1999, 120).

http://www.davistownmuseum.org/bioBrownSharpe.htm

Miscellaneous Forged Hardware

Miscellaneous Forged Hardware

22813T2   **Shovel**   DA   TT (Pub)

Forged steel, wood (hickory), cast iron, 51" long, 31 1/2" long handle, unsigned.

This shovel has two slots in the blade. Its purpose is unknown.

Miscellaneous Items

4713T5   **Chimney cap**   DTM   MH

Cast iron, 6 1/2" diameter, 1/2" thick, signed "9".

This chimney cap is from Ellis, South Carver, Massachusetts.

TJR3501   **Cupboard**   DTM   MH

Wood and glass, 12" long, 6" wide, unsigned.

31811T34   **Eyelet**   DTM   TT

Forged malleable iron, 4 3/4" long, 1 7/8" diameter, signed "16" and "27".

It is tapered so it can be driven into wood.

33002T7   **Horseshoe**   DTM   MH

Forged iron, 4 1/2" long, 4 1/2" wide, unsigned.

This shoe was made by a farrier for a small horse or pony.

http://www.davistownmuseum.org/pics/33002t7.jpg

93011T2   **Iron pyrite**   DTM   TT

Stone, 1 1/4" diameter, unsigned.

A note indicates this sample was gathered at Sutter Creek.

41203T14   **Lightening rod**   LPC   MH

Bronze, the longest of the 5 points is 8 1/2", unsigned.

This is a typical example of one of the many forms of 19th century lightning rods; a true sculpture object.

http://www.davistownmuseum.org/pics/41203t14.jpg

102100T8   **Nail set**   DTM   MH

Drop-forged steel, 3 5/8" long, signed "Tuck & Co".

Tuck manufactured bits, chisels, knives, and screwdrivers in Brockton, MA, 1852 - 1915. What relationship is Tuck & Co. to S. V. Tuck who manufactured edge tools in Bridgewater, MA, c. 1870?

Historic Maritime IV (1840-1865): The Early Industrial Revolution

Miscellaneous Items

111001T19   Oil can

DTM   MH

Brass, copper, and tin solder, 12 3/4" high, unsigned, c. 1850.

This is an oil can from the early days of the Industrial Revolution. Are there any known examples of oilers in tool kits that predate the Industrial Revolution other than those in watchmakers' kits?

10402T1   Ships' clock

LPC   MH

Brass, steel, and silver, 7" diameter, signed "Seth Thomas".

This clock came from the Harvey Mills, a West Indies trader out of Thomaston, Maine. It is loaned to the Museum with Blunt's "The American Pilot," which is inscribed with the Captain's name: A. F. SPEAR Thomaston, Maine.

21805T24   Tropical wood specimens (5)

DTM   HC

Lignum vitae (1), cocobolo (2), rosewood (3), mahogany (4), and ironwood (5), (1) 9 1/2" x 1 7/8" x 2 3/8, (2) 9 1/2" x 2 1/4" x 2", (3) 5 7/16" x 3 3/16 diameter, unsigned.

(4) 12 1/2" x 2 1/8" x 2 1/4", (5) 14 3/8" x 2 3/16" x 2 1/2". These specimens are from four plane bodies and one mallet head typical of tropical woods found on coasting traders headed for New England's boat shop plane construction early to mid-19th century.

Miscellaneous Tools

21812LTC3   Bench roller with clamp and crankshaft handle

DA   TT (Pub)

Drop-forged steel, 24" tall, 12" wide, 7" handle, 6" rolling surface, signed "PEXTO" (in a circle) "PECK STOW & WILCOX CO SOUTHINGTON CONN." "945".

This is a tool commonly encountered in a sheet metal shop. The handle on the clamp is broken off. Courtesy of Liberty Tool Company.

http://www.davistownmuseum.org/bioPeck.html

112704T7   Blocks (2)

DTM   MH

Wood, rope, and malleable cast iron, First 6 1/2" long, 5" wide; second 6" long, both 4 7/8" wide with 3 1/4" diameter shives, unsigned, c. 1840.

These blocks with their homemade rope bindings are typical of mid-19th century coasting vessels. Made in small shops or factories, the cast iron sheaves have now replaced the typical wood sheave of a slightly earlier period.

TCG1001   Blocks (matched pair)

DTM   MH

Wood (mahogany), forged iron, and malleable cast iron, 7 1/4" high, 2 3/4" wide, with 2 1/2" shives, unsigned.

These blocks are typical of tools that might have had their wooden components manufactured in coastal mill towns such as Liberty or Montville for use on coastal traders. The eyelets holding the blocks are distinctly hand-forged and the blocks themselves are distinctly handmade, but the shives appear to be factory cast.

http://www.davistownmuseum.org/pics/tcg1001.jpg

Historic Maritime IV (1840-1865): The Early Industrial Revolution

Miscellaneous Tools

31501T3   **Box hook**   DTM   MH

Cast steel and wood, 9" long, 5" wide handle, signed "S PURDY MAKER".

DATM (Nelson 1999) lists an S. Purdy as a maker of edge tools, Rome, NY, 1850. This tool is also called a Longshoremans' hook.

41203T2G   **Brick chisel**   DTM   MH

Forged steel, 6 7/8" long, 2 7/8" wide, signed "C. Drew & Co.".

http://www.davistownmuseum.org/bioDrew.htm

TCR1017   **C-clamp**   DTM   MH

Cast iron, 6 3/4" long, 3 1/2" throat, signed with the mark "W's No 1".

This C clamp has a winged screw typical of an early 19th century tool and represents a transition between hand-forged blacksmith-made tools and the mass-produced drop-forged C clamps of the late 19th century. Is this cast iron or drop forged iron?

TCR1001   **C-clamp**   DTM   MH

Forged iron, 2 1/4" wide throat, 3 1/2" deep, unsigned.

This tool has a beautiful forged ram's horn bolt. The threads look fairly modern. How early is this tool?

TCR1012   **Clamp**   DTM   MH

Cast or drop-forged iron, 5" long including the lever and thumbscrew with a 2" throat, signed "KNOTT BOSTON".

DATM (Nelson 1999, 457) lists a L. E. Knott Apparatus Company in Boston, MA that made school science lab items. What was the function of this strange clamp?

http://www.davistownmuseum.org/pics/51100t6.jpg

TCR1021   **Gasket cutter**   DTM   MH

Dropped forged iron and steel, 9 7/8" long and 5 7/8" wide, unsigned, c. 1850.

http://www.davistownmuseum.org/pics/tcr1021.jpg

101400T3   **Grave diggers' shovel**   DTM   MH

Drop-forged iron and wood, 84 1/8" long with a 9 1/4" blade, unsigned.

http://www.davistownmuseum.org/pics/101400t3_p1.jpg
http://www.davistownmuseum.org/pics/101400t3_p2.jpg

103104T2   **Pry bar**   DTM   MH

Drop-forged iron, 2' long, 2 1/4" wide, unsigned.

This tool is also called a wrecking iron.

ID #   Status   Location

Miscellaneous Tools

41203T2A   **Pry bar**   DTM   MH

Forged steel, 15 1/4" long, signed "C. Drew and Company".

http://www.davistownmuseum.org/bioDrew.htm

43006T8   **Push screwdriver**   DTM   MH

Brass and rosewood with a steel driver, 12 3/8" long including 3 3/8" wood handle and 2 11/16" bit with a capacity of 8 inserted bits, unsigned.

This is an example of an early factory-made push screwdriver, but who made this 1850 - 1875 tool?

111412T17   **Saw set**   DTM   MH

Drop-forged iron, brass ferrule, wooden handle, 6 1/2" long, signed "A. STILLMAN'S" "PATENT. 1848".

Patent 5,810 belonged to Abel Stillman of Poland, NY: http://www.datamp.org/patents/advance.php?pn=5810&id=12180&set=8.

14302T20   **Screwdriver**   DTM   MH

Malleable steel, size unknown, unsigned.

This three pronged driver is nicely beveled.

41203T7   **Screwdriver**   DTM   MH

Wrought and malleable iron, brass, and wood, 20 1/2" long with a 7 1/4" long handle and ferrule, unsigned.

This is an excellent example of a smith-made screwdriver. The long iron blade has several artful twists indicating it's made of wrought iron. It also has signs of hand filing and a nicely turned handle.

http://www.davistownmuseum.org/pics/41203t7_p1.jpg
http://www.davistownmuseum.org/pics/41203t7_p2.jpg

41203T20   **Screwdriver**   DTM   MH

Forged steel, 9" long, signed "C. Drew & Co.".

http://www.davistownmuseum.org/bioDrew.htm

31501T7   **Slaters' rip**   DTM   MH

Malleable iron and steel, 31 1/4" long, signed with an obscured signature "_____ JR. _____ VT".

41203T2B   **Small wrecking bar**   DTM   MH

Forged steel, 12" long, signed "Drew No. 12".

http://www.davistownmuseum.org/bioDrew.htm

103104T1   **Soldering iron**   DTM   MH

Wrought iron, brass, and copper, 16 1/4" long, unsigned.

Historic Maritime IV (1840-1865): The Early Industrial Revolution

Miscellaneous Tools

TEE5005   **Unidentified tool**   DTM   MH-H

Cast steel, brass, and wood, 8 1/2" long, unsigned, 19th century.

http://www.davistownmuseum.org/pics/tee5005.jpg

12713T3   **Wooden ringed maul**   DTM   CT

Wood (oak, hickory), forged iron rings, 38" long, 12" long head, 7" diameter faces, unsigned.

Patternmakers' Tools

TCT1005   **Bodkin**   DTM   MH

Bronze handle and forged iron point, 5 3/8" long, unsigned.

This tool came in a patternmakers' tool chest.

TCT1002   **Gouge**   DTM   MH

Cast steel, 8" long, 1" wide, signed "S.J. ADDIS CAST STEEL" on the blade back with an unusual touchmark; "ENGLAND" on the blade front.

Importing of high quality Sheffield steel tools continued well into the 20th century.

TCT1007   **Lifter**   DTM   MH

Drop-forged iron, 9 1/4" long, unsigned.

Lifters are used for shaping the interiors and bottom of molds for casting.

102112T3   **Molders' hand tool**   DTM   MH

Cast brass, 9" long, 1 1/2" ends, 5/8" wide, unsigned.

TCT1301   **Molders' slick and oval spoon**   DTM   MH

Cast steel, 7 3/4" long, signed with an obscured touchmark.

TCT1008   **Molding tool**   DTM   MH

Drop-forged steel, unsigned.

It is used for smoothing the sand cast prior to pouring the molten metal into the cast.

TCT1003   **Patternmakers' slick**   DTM   MH

Bronze, 7" long, unsigned.

A slick is used for shaping and smoothing sand casts. Patternmakers' slicks should not be confused with the large slicks used by shipwrights (an edge tool).

http://www.davistownmuseum.org/pics/tct1003.jpg

TCT1004   **Patternmakers' slick**   DTM   MH

Drop-forged iron, 5" long, signed with an obscured signature.

Patternmakers' Tools

TCT1006   **Patternmakers' slick**   DTM   MH

Bronze, 4 1/2" long, signed "C.H.P." (probably the manufacturer's sign), also has other letters and touchmarks.

62202T9   **Patternmakers' slicks (2)**   DTM   MH

Cast bronze, one 5 1/2" long and the other 4 3/4" long with 2 round smoothing globes at each end, unsigned.

These are typical slicks found in a patternmakers' tool kit.

http://www.davistownmuseum.org/pics/62202t6.jpg

TCT1001   **Spokeshave**   DTM   MH

Bronze, 7 1/2" long, 1 3/16" blade, unsigned.

Patternmakers' Tools - H A Cobbett Group

42801T5   **Rule**   BDTM   MH

Tool steel, signed "D & S Bangor Me. U.S. Stnd" with owner signatures "Chris K. Farmer" in script and "H A Cobbett".

The Farmer signature probably predates Cobbett as the Darling & Schwartz working dates in DATM (Nelson 1999, 210) are 1854 - 1866, and Cobbett as a patternmaker appears to have worked later in the 19th century. DATM has this to say about D & S: "Samuel Darling and Michael Schwartz (who succeeded Darling & Bailey) made squares with 1852 (possibly Nathan Ames' 6 July 1852) and 6 Oct. 1857 (Darling) patents and circular iron planes patented by George F. Evans in 1862 and 1864. The 1857 patent square was later made by Darling, Brown & Sharpe after Darling joined J. R. Brown & Sharpe in 1866. Schwartz worked otherwise as a Bangor saw maker and hardware dealer and did not join the new company." The rest of the Cobbett group are in the Industrial Revolution section.

http://www.davistownmuseum.org/publications/volume10.html

Quarrying Tools

TCU1002   **Brick chisel**   DTM   MH

Forged iron, 7 1/4" long, 3/16" wide, signed "SHEARER" in two different places, also marked "SCF".

This chisel is characterized by 8 beveled surfaces. The quarrying tools in this display are difficult to date but range from 1820 to 1880.

81200T11   **Cold chisel**   DTM   MHC

Forged iron, 5" long, 1 1/4" wide peen, signed "M Fognaty".

This maker is not listed in DATM (Nelson 1999). This is a typical small quarry chisel.

ID #   Status   Location

Quarrying Tools

914108T12   Cold chisel   DTM   MH

Hand-forged malleable iron and steel, 8 1/4" long, signed "E. MILLER MS" and on the other side "S.W.T".

This chisel was probably used by stone workers.

81602T10   Feathers (2) and wedge   DTM   MH

Forged malleable iron, 11 1/2" long, 1 5/16" wide wedge; 12" long, 1 1/4" wide feathers, unsigned.

These are the largest set of feathers and wedge ever noted by the curator. These are used for really heavy cutting and splitting, probably in the coastal granite quarries.

41302T8   Feathers and wedges (lot of 12)   DTM   MH

Iron, 9 feathers that are 3 3/4" long, 3 wedges that are 3 5/8" long, unsigned.

These are the traditional tools used by Maine quarrymen for splitting granite.

1302T2   Quarry grapple   DTM   MH

Forged iron, 10" long, 2 1/2" x 1 1/8" wide jaws, signed "B".

This unusual tool is shaped like a very chunky pair of pliers. It comes with a shackle for lifting.

Shipwrights', Sailmakers', and Mariners' Tools

51100T6   Adjustable calipers   DTM   MH

Puddled steel, 9 1/4" long, signed "E. F. Sibley", 1840 - 1860.

No E. F. Sibley is listed in DATM (Nelson 1999), however the Sibley Scythe Co. was a partnership of Ezra Taft Sibley and his son Frank Arthur Sibley of Northville, NH. Ezra was known to also work on his own. This tool probably predates the mass production of machinist measuring tools that became widespread after the Civil War. This is an outside caliper, used to measure the outside diameter of a round or cylindrical object. It has curved legs with rounded tips that come together at the center.

http://www.davistownmuseum.org/pics/51100t6.jpg

TCV1007   Awl   DTM   MH

Steel (?), 5 3/4" long, signed "GEO. LAUTE BOSTON.".

This maker is not listed in DATM (Nelson 1999). What would this awl be used for?

TKD1301   Blubber cutter (?)   DTM   UNK

Forged iron or steel, 18" long with an 8" diameter cutter, signed "VAUGHAN" and "PARDOE & Co UNION WARRANTED".

Working dates for this company are 1844-1868. This tool was available for hands on perusal at the workbench in the main hall and is now missing.

http://www.davistownmuseum.org/bioVaughn.htm

Shipwrights', Sailmakers', and Mariners' Tools

120907T6   Caulk remover   DTM   TT

Forged steel, 13" long, 2" wide, unsigned.

This is a heavy hooked implement for removing caulk from ships.

TCX1002   Caulking iron   DTM   MH

Cast steel, 6" long, 2 1/2" wide, signed "C. DREW & CO. CAST STEEL".

http://www.davistownmuseum.org/pics/TCX1002_small.jpg
http://www.davistownmuseum.org/bioDrew.htm

041505T2   Caulking iron   DTM   MH

Steel, 8" long, 2" wide blade, signed "J.STOR".

Stor is not listed in DATM (Nelson 1999). A not uncommon mark on caulking irons, this is a German import made of German steel.

http://www.davistownmuseum.org/pics/041505t2_p1.jpg

41302T10   Caulking iron   DTM   MH

Malleable iron and steel, 6 1/4" long, 2 1/4" wide, signed "H Reed".

H. Reed is listed in DATM (Nelson 1999) with no location or date. The following information is from Andrew Pollock: "See page 6 of the C. DREW reprint catalogue No. 34, for a listing of H. REED caulking irons. These were actually made by C. DREW & CO. for clients who wanted to pay less than what C. DREW irons would cost, and who were willing to accept somewhat lower quality."

http://www.davistownmuseum.org/bioDrew.htm

3405T3   Caulking iron   DTM   MH

Malleable iron and steel, 5" long, 1 3/4" wide, signed "H. Reed".

The Kingston, Massachusetts: Tool Encyclopedia states: "H. REED was a mark used by C. DREW & Co. on some of the tools they manufactured. 'H. REED' tools were less expensive than those marked 'C. DREW' and by inference were probably somewhat lower in quality."

http://www.davistownmuseum.org/bioDrew.htm

120907T8   Caulking iron (2)   DTM   TT

Cast steel, 7" long, 2" wide and 6" long, 1" wide, signed "C. DREW & CO" and "CAST STEEL".

http://www.davistownmuseum.org/bioDrew.htm

120907T10   Caulking iron (3)   DTM   TT

Steel, 5 1/2" long, 1 1/2" wide; 7" long, 2 1/4" wide; and 5 5/8" long, 1 1/2" wide, signed "J.STORTZ".

This is a set of three fairly standard steel caulking irons. The medium-sized one shows significant evidence of heat treating. John Stortz worked in Philadelphia, PA starting in 1853 and later added "& Son" to the company name (Nelson 1999, 762).

Historic Maritime IV (1840-1865): The Early Industrial Revolution

Shipwrights', Sailmakers', and Mariners' Tools

120907T5   **Caulking mallet**   DTM   TT

Wood with iron bands, 13" long, 11 1/4" wide, unsigned.

This is a typical shipbuilders' caulking mallet.

120907T7   **Caulking wheel**   DTM   TT

Drop-forged steel, 8" long, 2 1/4" wide, unsigned.

This tool is used to finish caulking work on a ship.

102911T3   **Chisel**   DTM   TT

Cast steel, signed "HOMER" "CAST STEEL", 1850.

The term cast steel only describes the forge-welded "steeled cutting" edge, which is clearly visible. Also visible is the forged weld socket. It is made by Benjamin H. Homer & David C. Homer, Bucksport, Maine, 1850.

121311T5   **Deck chisel**   DTM   TT-D17

German steel, malleable iron, and wood, 11" long, 1" wide, 4 3/4" long handle, signed "HIGGINS & LIBBY" "Portland".

This is also known as a ships' carpenters' chisel. Higgins & Libby were Portland, ME, toolmakers in 1856. It is hand-forged, and while not signed cast steel, is likely to be locally forged German steel. There is no evidence of laminated steel construction. It appears to be all steel extending up to a malleable iron socket.

http://www.davistownmuseum.org/publications/volume10.html

TCX1001   **Early ships' caulking tools (set)**   BDTM   MHC-K

Puddled or German steel and wood, signed "E. A. DEXTER".

The set includes 13 caulking irons, a caulking mallet inventoried separately (second mallet has been stolen,) a carrying case and folding stool. It was last used to repair the U.S.S. Constitution. The maker is not listed in DATM (Nelson 1999). The demise of the cod fishery due to the withdrawal of government subsidies, the spread of railroads after the Civil War, and the depletion of forest resources all played a role in the decline of shipbuilding in the ports south and east of Liberty and Montville (Thomaston, Warren, Boothbay, Waldoboro, and Wiscasset.) In the boomtown years of Liberty and Montville, a number of ships' caulkers lived in this area and would have used tools similar to these as itinerant caulkers visiting area shipyards as needed.

http://www.davistownmuseum.org/pics/tcx1001_p3.jpg
http://www.davistownmuseum.org/pics/tcx1001combo.jpg

12900T4   **Fid**   DTM   MH

Wood, 15 1/2" long, 2 5/8" maximum diameter, unsigned.

A fid is used to loosen the strands of rope when splicing two pieces of rope together.

http://www.davistownmuseum.org/pics/12900t4.jpg

ID #   Status   Location

Shipwrights', Sailmakers', and Mariners' Tools

81212T1   Fid   DTM   TT

Cast steel, brass ferrule, hardwood handle (ebony?), ivory butt, 13 1/2" long, 8" long spike, signed "R.D. Wiley Boston. 1858.".

81212LTC3   Fid   NOM   TT (Pub)

Hardwood (apple?), 10 1/4" long, 1" diameter, unsigned.

Courtesy of Liberty Tool Company.

81212LTC5   Fid   DA   TT (Pub)

Hardwood (beech), 11" long, 3/4" diameter, unsigned.

Courtesy of Liberty Tool Company.

61204T12   Fid   DTM   MH

Wood, 18 1/4" long, 2 1/4" diameter, unsigned.

This is a classic example of a hand fid used by a sailor for splicing rope on a ships' rigging.

http://www.davistownmuseum.org/pics/61204T12.jpg

81212LTC4   Fid   DA   TT (Pub)

Cast steel, brass ferrule, wood handle (mahogany), ivory inset, 6 1/8" long, 2" blade, unsigned.

Courtesy of Liberty Tool Company.

040610T1   Harpoon point   DTM   MH

Forge-welded malleable iron and steel, 29 1/4" long, 6" long cutting edge on the spear point, unsigned.

This harpoon point was found in a Camden, Maine area antique shop in 1962. The maritime curator at the New Bedford Whaling Museum said, "The one thing outstanding thing about that harpoon is the workmanship. It is quite good workmanship. The steel, however, is completely wrong for an actual whaling harpoon which was made entirely of malleable iron. Shanks were long and (more or less) thin and made to bend, even twist if necessary. Harpoons were made to be used once. If a harpoon was slightly damaged at its first use, it could be employed as a 'second iron,' that is, a backup harpoon in case the first 'live iron' pulled loose. It is an interesting piece of metal work but it is not an actual whaling harpoon." It is very similar to the earliest harpoon on display at the Mystic Seaport Museum. Additional comments are solicited.

http://www.davistownmuseum.org/pics/040610t1web1.jpg
http://www.davistownmuseum.org/pics/040610t1web3.jpg

012705T1   Hawsing iron   DTM   MH-O

Forged iron and weld steel, 25 1/4" long handle, 7 5/8" long and 3 1/8" wide blade, unsigned.

012705T3   Hawsing iron   DTM   MH-O

Forged iron and weld steel, 24" long handle, 5 5/8" long and 3 1/2" wide blade, unsigned.

Historic Maritime IV (1840-1865): The Early Industrial Revolution

Shipwrights', Sailmakers', and Mariners' Tools

TCX1004   Lipped peen adz   DTM   MH

Cast steel, 11 3/8" long, 4 1/4" wide blade, signed "Albertson & Co., Po'kpsy, NY".

Albertson & Co. is listed in DATM (Nelson 1999, 17) as a Poughkeepsie, New York, edge toolmaker, working dates 1867-1871. This type of adz is among the most essential tools in a New England shipyard.

913108T56   Marlin spike   DTM   MH

Steel, 17 3/4" long, signed "C. DREW & CO." and "MADE IN U.S.A.".

The Stoney Brook Ironworks was on the same Kingston, MA, site as this company. They made edge tools and some ship-related tools.

http://www.davistownmuseum.org/bioDrew.htm

81212LTC7   Marlin spike   DA   TT (Pub)

Forged steel, 13 1/2" long, 1 3/8" diameter at widest, signed "B.D. WILEY".

Courtesy of Liberty Tool Company.

12613T3   Mast rings   DTM   MAG-8

Forged steel and iron, 11 3/4" diameter, 1" thick, unsigned.

TCX1006   Mast shave   DTM   MH

Malleable iron, cast steel, and wood, 18" wide with 8" blade, signed with an obscure mark similar to White, NY, c. 1840 - 1860.

http://www.davistownmuseum.org/pics/TCX1006_p1.jpg

120907T4   Mast shave   DTM   TT

Malleable iron, forged steel, and wood, 25" long, 2" wide blade, 5 1/2" handles, signed "L & T WHITE" "18*7" "BUFFALO N.Y." and "6" on the other side.

This mast shave shows a very obvious weld line running parallel to the blade on its back side.

032203T14   Mast shave   DTM   MH

Forged iron and steel, 20" wide, 10" blade, signed "L. & I.J WHITE BUFFALO" "10".

White made coopers' tools and drawknives in Buffalo, NY, from 1837 to 1928. This large shave could have been used by a cooper or as a spar or mast shave. It is another of the high quality American-made tools signaling the florescence of the domestic tool manufacturing industry in the late 19th century.

http://www.davistownmuseum.org/pics/032203t14_p2.jpg

Shipwrights', Sailmakers', and Mariners' Tools

72801T1   Mast shave   BDTM   MH

Cast steel, wood, and brass, 22 1/2" long, 15 3/4" blade, signed "MALLET CAST STEEL" "WARRANTED WARREN ME".

The uniformity of grain structure combined with the appearance and mark (cast steel) suggests a one piece construction from domestic-made cast steel. Most American-made cast steel was made in Pittsburg after 1865 and transported east by train and coasting vessels. The sharp edges of the nearly square shave extensions suggests the possibility of drop-forging using machinery now becoming readily available to most toolmakers at this time. DATM (Nelson 1999) lists James Mallet as working in Warren from 1856 - 1871. For more information see the Registry of Maine Toolmakers (2008).

http://www.davistownmuseum.org/pics/72801t1_p3.jpg
http://www.davistownmuseum.org/publications/volume10.html

51100T2   Mast shave   DTM   MHC-F

Malleable iron, forged steel and wood, 24" long, 14" blade, 4 1/2" handles, signed "L & I J WHITE" "BUFFALO, NY" "1837" inside an oval and also stamped "14".

White made adzes, chisels, and drawknives, 1837f.; a most prolific maker of coopers' jiggers, drawknives, and other edge tools (Nelson 1999). Many an L. White tool has been recycled to Maine woodworkers in the last 30 years by the Liberty Tool Co.

http://www.davistownmuseum.org/pics/51100t2.jpg
http://www.davistownmuseum.org/pics/51100t2_p1.jpg

070705T3   Mast shave (?)   DTM   TB

Forged iron and steel with wooden handles, 19" long with a 12 3/8" long and 2" wide cutting blade, 5 1/4" handles, signed "M.BABCOCK".

This drawshave was found in a coastal Maine workshop and the maker is not listed in DATM (Nelson 1999). It is characterized by a heavy cutting blade, welded steel construction with evidence of heavy filing, and appears to be from 1840 - 1860. It is uncertain if this is a heavy duty coopers' shave, or as is more likely, a mast shave. If not of Maine origin, it is most certainly a New England-made edge tool.

913108T1   Mending needle   DTM   MH

Wood, 9" long, unsigned.

This needle is used by fishermen for mending nets.

111900TX2   Outside calipers   DTM   MH

Forged malleable iron, unsigned.

These large calipers have the provenance of being used on the keels and ribbing in a Maine shipyard (Lubec).

31112T3   Sail-makers' bodkin   DTM   TT-D27

Rosewood, cast steel, brass ferrule, 7 1/2" long, 1 1/2" wide, unsigned.

Courtesy of Liberty Tool Co.

Historic Maritime IV (1840-1865): The Early Industrial Revolution

Shipwrights', Sailmakers', and Mariners' Tools

42012T6   Sailmakers' kit   DTM   TT

Cast steel, wood, leather, paper, cotton twine, signed "Patent" "FORGED" "Cast Steel" "SAIL NEEDLES No 14"
and an image of an anchor.

The kit contains: 3 paper packs of needles tied together with twine, 38 loose needles, 2 sailmakers (thimble) palms, and 1 wooden needle case with miscellaneous needles and thread inside. Courtesy of Liberty Tool Co.

TCX1001A   Ship caulkers' mallet   BDTM   MHC-K

Malleable iron and wood, unsigned.

This caulking mallet is part of the ships' caulkers tool set in case K; last used to repair the U.S.S. Constitution.

http://www.davistownmuseum.org/pics/tcx1001_p4.jpg
http://www.davistownmuseum.org/pics/tcx1001combo.jpg

52403T1   Shipbuilders' adz   LPC   MH

Tool steel, wood handle, 10" long, 5" wide cutting edge, 2 3/4" peen, 31" long handle, signed "T C Jackson Stinson Bath".

T. C. Jackson is believed to be a Bath, Maine, maker of edge tools, c. 1869. He is also listed as a Maine ax-maker, 1832 - 64 by Yeaton (2000). Also see The Registry of Maine Toolmakers (Brack 2008).

http://www.davistownmuseum.org/pics/52403t1_p1.jpg
http://www.davistownmuseum.org/publications/volume10.html

TCX1003   Ships' caulking iron   DTM   MH

Malleable iron and steel, 5 3/4" long, 2" wide, signed "C.B. Timpson & Tucker".

There is no listing for Timpson &Tucker in DATM (Nelson 1999), but there is a listing for C. B. Timpson with no location or date. This is an unrecorded 19th century seacoast New England ships' caulking tool manufacturing company. This and the other caulking tools in the Davistown Museum collection are typical of the caulking tools so essential in the shipbuilding trades of coastal Maine and New England in the early to mid-19th century. Some of these ships caulkers resided in Liberty and Montville.

102012T2   Shipwrights' maul   DA   TT (Pub)

Forged malleable iron, wood (ash, hickory), 34" long, 10" long head, 5" diameter face, unsigned.

20712T1   Slick   DTM   TT

Forged steel, 14" long, 2" wide cutting edge, 5/8" bevel, signed "E. BROAD BANGOR" "N.J. MARDEN'.

This ship carpenters' edge tool has a forge weld clearly visible at the edge. N. J. Marden may possibly be an owners mark. Elisha Broad of Bangor is listed in the 1855 Maine Business Directory as an edge toolmaker (Brack 2008, "Registry of Maine Toolmakers").

Historic Maritime IV (1840-1865): The Early Industrial Revolution

Unidentified Tools

42602T7   **Unidentified tool**   DTM   MH

Cast steel and baleen, 6 3/4" long, two 15/16" disks for trimming or cutting, 3 3/4" long baleen handle, signed "Rodgers Culters to his Majesty" with 2 cartouches and on reverse side "England".

Was this used for sharpening knives? It is a great whatsit. Rodgers Cutlers to His Majesty was located at No 6 Norfolk Street, Sheffield, England and made knives.

91303T19   **Unidentified tool**   DTM   MH

Forged steel, 5 1/2" long, 1 3/8" wide at the top, 5/8" wide curved burnishing surface at the top, unsigned.

The bottom of this tool is shaped into a slitting cutter; the top a curved burnisher. Was this a leather working tool?

81801T16   **Unidentified tool**   DTM   MH

Drop-forged steel, 7 1/4" long, signed "PATENT PENDING".

This spring controlled tool combines characteristics of pliers, chain cutters, and tubing benders. What is its use?

Watchmakers, Jewelers, and Silversmiths' Tools

32502T11   **Awl**   BDTM   T

Steel, wood, and brass, 3 1/2" long, unsigned.

http://www.davistownmuseum.org/bioEpstein.htm

32502T15   **Burins (3)**   BDTM   T

Cast steel, wood handles, unsigned.

http://www.davistownmuseum.org/bioEpstein.htm

32502T37   **Dividers**   BDTM   T

Forged steel, 3 3/8" long, signed with an obscure mark.

http://www.davistownmuseum.org/bioEpstein.htm

TCY1003   **Hammer**   DTM   MH

Drop-forged steel, 9 3/4" long, 2 1/2" round head, unsigned.

Is this for metalworking? Its use is unknown.

TCY1004   **Jewelers' hammer**   DTM   MH

Forged or cast steel, 2 1/4" long, 3/8" square face, signed with an obscured mark.

32502T13   **Jewelers' hammer**   BDTM   T

Cast steel, 1" long handle, 3 1/2" wide with 1/2" square chamfered face, unsigned.

http://www.davistownmuseum.org/bioEpstein.htm

Watchmakers, Jewelers, and Silversmiths' Tools

102100T9   **Pin vise**   DTM   MH

Cast steel, 4 5/16" long, 3/8" wide jaw, signed "C HAMACHER".

No C. Hamacher is listed in DATM, but several other Hamachers were making tools in New York city in the mid- to late 19th century (1864f.)

32502T5   **Punch**   BDTM   T

Cast steel, 4 1/4" long, signed "C. HARLTON CAST STEEL" and "6".

http://www.davistownmuseum.org/bioEpstein.htm

TCY1001   **Tongs (3)**   DTM   MH

Forged iron, 6 1/2", 6 1/2", 8 3/4" long, unsigned.

These three tools were found together; what was their use? They are unusual in their diminutive size.

32502T17   **Tweezer - clamp**   BDTM   T

Steel with whale bone handle, 4 5/8" long including the 2 5/8" long handle, unsigned.

http://www.davistownmuseum.org/bioEpstein.htm

Woodworking: Axes and Hatchets

914108T10   **Ax**   DTM   MH

Cast steel and a broken wooden handle, 4 1/2" long, 2 3/8" wide, signed "C. MAMM" "PHILAD" and "CAST STEEL".

More information is sought on this obscure maker.

22411T7   **Box hatchet**   DTM   TT

Hand-forged iron and steel, 14" long, 5" x 1" head, unsigned.

It is also known as a barrel hatchet.

062603T1   **Broad ax**   DTM   MH

Forged iron and natural (?) steel with wooden handle, 9" long, 7 1/2" wide head, 21" long handle, signed "H.BRAGG CORNVILLE.".

http://www.davistownmuseum.org/pics/062603t1_p1.jpg
http://www.davistownmuseum.org/publications/volume10.html

42710T1   **Broad ax**   DTM   MH

Forged iron and steel, 30 1/2" long, 10 1/4" wide head, 6 3/4" cutting edge, signed "JOSIAH FOWLER CO. LTD" with an F in a triangle.

http://www.davistownmuseum.org/pics/072410t1web4.jpg
http://www.davistownmuseum.org/bioFowler.html

Woodworking: Axes and Hatchets

41203T13   **Broad ax**   DTM   MH

Forged iron and steel, 9" wide blade, signed with the distinctive touchmark of J Fowler of St. Johns, New Brunswick.

This is an excellent example of a forged ax with a weld steel cutting edge. Did Fowler use cast steel as his weld steel? Probably, yes.

http://www.davistownmuseum.org/pics/41203t13_p6.jpg
http://www.davistownmuseum.org/bioFowler.html

41907T3   **Broad ax**   DTM   MH

Blister steel (?), 10" long, 6 7/8" wide blade, 3 1/4" long poll, signed "S. AVERY" and "WHORF CAST".

S. Avery is a Wallingford, CT, edge toolmaker working circa 1849. The interesting second mark opposite S. Avery of WHORF CAST has no hint of or room for "steel" after cast. This tool appears to be a one piece blister or German steel ax due to its many imperfections. The cutting edge appears to have been subject to additional forging, but no obvious welded steel bit is evident. Numerous hammer marks can still be seen on this ax, which has the usual evidence of the folding and welding at the eye (haft hole) cheek (body) interface.

http://www.davistownmuseum.org/pics/41907t3.jpg

31811T13   **Broad ax head**   DTM   TT

Forged iron and cast steel, 10 1/4" long, 7 1/4" wide, signed "J EMERY" and "C STEEL".

An H. Emery is listed as an edge toolmaker in Buxton, ME, 1849 (Nelson 1999, 260).

72801T3   **Double bitted ax**   DTM   MH

Forged iron, steel, and wood, 8 3/4" long blade, 3 3/4" wide, 31 1/2" handle, signed with an obscure signature, only "Oakland" is visible along with "S.S." who might be the owner..

This is a classic example of a Maine-made double bitted ax, which appears to not have been made before 1820. Unless clearly marked, many axes from this era are difficult to identify and date.

040103T3   **Felling ax**   DTM   MH

Forged iron and steel, 6 7/8" long, 5 1/8" wide cutting blade, unsigned.

This felling ax is typical of the American style felling axes produced after 1750 and would characterize the tool kit of a woodworker or shipbuilder anytime during the 19th century. The heavy poll makes this ax much more efficient than earlier English trade axes. The obvious weld steel cutting edge means that this ax predates the ubiquitous all cast steel or drop-forged steel axes of the late 19th and 20th centuries.

http://www.davistownmuseum.org/pics/040103t3_p1.jpg
http://www.davistownmuseum.org/pics/040103t3_p2.jpg

Woodworking: Axes and Hatchets

81812T1   Felling ax   DTM   MH

Forged steel, wood (hickory), 35" long, 6 1/2" wide cutting edge, 11" long head, signed "ELWELL FORGE WEDNESBURY SOLID CAST STEEL WARRANTED 376369".

Elwell Forge operated in Wednesbury, England, from 1817 until the 1970s. This area has been a hot-spot of the iron industry from at least the 1500s (http://www.scribd.com/doc/55843847/Wednesbury-Forge-Excavations).

111900T2   Hatchet   DTM   MH

Steel and wood, 9 1/2" long, 1 1/4" wide blade, unsigned.

This is a miniature hatchet of unknown use; one of two in the Museum exhibits.

914108T15   Hatchet   DTM   MH

Cast steel and wooden handle, 12 3/4" long, 3" long blade, signed "AMOSKEAG AX" "CAST-STEEL" and "REYNOLDS. AG".

The Amoskeag Mfg. Co. was located in Manchester, NH, from the 1830s to the 1930s and made textiles and heavy machinery. They are listed as making tools only from 1849 - 56. Henry C. Reynolds of Manchester, NH, worked for Amoskeag from 1855 - 1877. He may have been the inventor of a combination hatchet they sold.

42604T4   Hatchet   DTM   MH

Forged iron and steel, 6 3/8" long, 3 5/8" wide, 1 1/4" diameter poll, unsigned.

The lower side of the hatchet has a notch and the poll end is beveled.

51100T11   Hatchet   DTM   MH

Cast steel and wood, 6" long, 3 3/4" blade, signed "BLODGETT EDGE TOOL MFG." and with "2".

DATM (Nelson 1999) states that the Blodgett Edge Tool Mfg. Co. was in Manchester, NH, from 1853 - 1862. It became the Amoskeag Ax Co. in 1862. They made adzes, axes, edge tools, hatchets, and shaves.

TCC3003   Hatchet   DTM   MH

Forged iron and steel with wood handle, 5 3/4" long, 3/4" blade, 1" six sided peen, signed "1 UNDERHILL EDGE Tool Co.", probably dates 1850 to 1860.

DATM (Nelson 1999) lists the Underhill Edge Tool Co. as Boston c. 1870-1871, however, the Underhill clan of edge toolmakers began production by 1813 or earlier (DATM lists 24 separate Underhill names 1813-1890), with tool production beginning in Boston c. 1825. Much of the Underhill activity was centered around Nashua, NH.

22411T27   Hatchet head   DTM   TT

Cast steel, 5" long, 3" wide, signed "__NDLEY MORSE" "WARRANTED" "CAST STEEL".

This hatchet has a claw design. DATM (Nelson 1999, 484) lists Lindley & Morse making adzes, axes, and hatches in Douglas, MA in 1855.

Woodworking: Axes and Hatchets

072112T3   Hewing ax   DTM   TT

Iron and steel, wood, 8 1/2" long, 6" wide head, 24 1/2" long handle, signed "W. GRIFFEN".

There is no obvious weld iron/steel interface. Is it late enough to be drop-forged? DATM (Nelson 1999, 335) lists a W. Griffen as a maker of wooden planes with no other information about him.

100208T2   Hewing ax   DTM   MH

Forged iron and steel, 7 5/8" long, 5" blade, unsigned.

This hand-forged ax is unique in its distinctive welded steel bit, exactly and uniformly 2 5/8" wide on both sides of the blade.

http://www.davistownmuseum.org/publications/volume10.html

91303T20   Hewing ax   DTM   MH

Cast steel, 11 3/4" long and 7" wide blade, 3" long and 1 3/8" wide rectangular poll, 34" long new handle, signed "THAXTER PORTLAND CAST STEEL WARRENTED".

This is a previously seen but unnoted Portland ax-maker, not listed in DATM (Nelson 1999). It has a probable shipyard use as a mast ax. For more information see the Registry of Maine Toolmakers (Brack 2008).

http://www.davistownmuseum.org/pics/91303t20.jpg
http://www.davistownmuseum.org/publications/volume10.html

42604T5   Hewing ax   DTM   MH

Forged iron and steel, wood handle, wood and leather blade cover, 4 1/8" long, 6" wide blade, 2 3/4" pole, signed "JP.BILLINGS" "CLINTON" "MAINE" "556".

http://www.davistownmuseum.org/pics/42604t5_p3.jpg
http://www.davistownmuseum.org/publications/volume10.html

090508T9   Lathing hatchet   DTM   MH

Forged steel, 6 3/4" long, 2" wide blade, signed "UNDERHILL" and "EDGE TOOL Co".

http://www.davistownmuseum.org/bioUnderhill.html

41203T8   Lathing hatchet   DTM   MH

Forged steel, 6 7/8" long, 2 1/8" wide cutting blade, 12" long wooden handle, signed "US PAT OFFICE UNDERHILL BOSTON TRADEMARK".

This is a typical forged steel tool from the prolific Underhill clan. Some tools marked Boston may have been made elsewhere and marketed in Boston.

http://www.davistownmuseum.org/pics/41203t8_p4.jpg
http://www.davistownmuseum.org/pics/41203t8_p1.jpg

Historic Maritime IV (1840-1865): The Early Industrial Revolution

Woodworking: Axes and Hatchets

091909T1   **Mast ax**   DTM   MH

Cast steel and wood, 27" long, 11 1/2" wide, 6" cutting edge, signed "UNDERHILL", "EDGE TOOL CO.", "WARRANTED", and "CAST STEEL".

This ax was acquired from a 19th century Deer Isle, ME, boat shop.

http://www.davistownmuseum.org/pics/091909t1web2.jpg
http://www.davistownmuseum.org/pics/091909t1web1.jpg

22411T26   **Shingling hatchet**   DTM   TT

Forged steel with a wooden handle, 12" long, 2 1/2" x 4 1/4" head, unsigned.

This is a small size for this type of hatchet

102612T1   **Yankee pattern broad ax**   LPC   MH

Steel, wooden handle, 34 1/2" long, 10 1/2" long and 6 1/4" wide head, signed "T. C. JACKSON" "BATH ME".

T. C. Jackson worked in Bath, ME from 1855 to 1869.

102612T2   **Yankee pattern mast ax**   LPC   MH

Cast steel, wooden handle, 28" long, 12 1/2" long and 6" wide head, signed "UNDERHILL" "EDGE TOOL CO" "WARRENTED" "CAST STEEL" and an owner's mark "B. G. PRATT" on the handle.

http://www.davistownmuseum.org/bioUnderhill.html

Woodworking: Axes and Hatchets Made in Maine

110611T4   **Broad ax**   DTM   TT

Forged iron and steel with ash wood handle, 9 3/4" long blade, 9 1/2" cutting edge, 2' long handle, signed "S. EASTMAN BANGOR".

The 1882 Maine business directory lists S. Eastman making axes and knives in both Bradford and N. Bradford Maine. This is the first Eastman edge tool in the Museum collection. For more information, see the Registry of Maine Toolmakers (Brack 2008).

http://www.davistownmuseum.org/publications/volume10.html

51113T1   **Hewing ax**   LPC   MH

Forged steel, wood (hickory), 30" long overall, head is 10" long with a 6 1/2" edge, signed "I.L. DUNTON LIBERTY WARRANTED".

The Registry of Maine Toolmakers lists Isaac L. Dunton as an ax-maker in Liberty in 1862-1869. It is unknown if he was part of Dunton, Copp & Co.

121805T27   **Mast ax**   DTM   MH

Forged iron and steel, signed "B Kelley & Co. Belfast".

The working dates of this company were from 1855 - 1881. The origin of the steel is uncertain.

http://www.davistownmuseum.org/pics/121805t27.jpg
http://www.davistownmuseum.org/publications/volume10.html

Historic Maritime IV (1840-1865): The Early Industrial Revolution

Woodworking: Axes and Hatchets Made in Maine

100208T4   Mast ax   DTM   MH

Forged iron and steel, 10" long, 6" wide blade, 2 5/8" long and 15/16" wide poll, signed "PAYSON _O_" and "SO HOPE, ME. WARRANT__".

The mark is possibly Payson & Son, another variant of the marks of the Payson clan of Hope and Appleton, Maine. The Payson forge was probably located at the privilege at the drainage of Fish Pond in South Hope near Harts Mill. Courtesy of Liberty Tool Co.

http://www.davistownmuseum.org/publications/volume10.html

Woodworking: Boring Tools

111002T1   Auger   DTM   MH

Forged iron and steel, wood handle, 20 1/2" long, 2" diameter, 16" handle, signed "8 C. Drew & Co. Kingston".

http://www.davistownmuseum.org/bioDrew.htm

TCE3001   Auger   DTM   MH

Forged iron and steel, 16 1/2" long, 15/16" diameter, signed "N. C. SANFORD & CO 15 PATENT MAR071840".

DATM (Nelson 1999, 688) lists Nathaniel C. Sanford & Co. working in Meridan, CT, manufacturing augers in 1851.

TCE1003B2   Auger bit   DTM   MH

Forged iron and steel, 7/16" diameter cutter, signed "New Haven Copper Co. No 7".

The "No 7" indicates the size. DATM (Nelson 1999, 571) lists this company as located in Seymour, CT, 1848, maker of augers and bits.

41203T3J   Center bit   DTM   MH

Steel, signed "Spears & Jackson".

This is made by another well known Sheffield, England, manufacturer.

41203T3H   Center bit   DTM   MH

Steel, signed "W. Greaves & Sons Steel Works".

This is made by a famous and prolific Sheffield, England, manufacturer.

41203T3G   Center bit   DTM   MH

Cast steel, signed "__ Wells & Co Cast Steel".

DATM (Nelson 1999) lists a T. E. Wells with working dates from 1850 - 1854 in Philadelphia, PA.

41203T3A   Center bit   DTM   MH

Drop-forged steel, signed "J Booth & Son".

DATM (Nelson 1999) lists this company's working dates from 1850 - 1854 in Philadelphia, PA.

Woodworking: Boring Tools

63012LTC1 **Center bit set**   DA   TT (Pub)

Cast steel, 3 3/4" to 5 1/2" long, 5/32 to 1 3/4" wide, signed "H HAWKE CAST STEEL" "F. WALTER CO CAST STEEL" "BOWER CAST STEEL" "MARSDEN BROTHERS SHEFFIELD" "P. WALTER & Co CAST STEEL" "BROWN & FLATHER CAST STEEL.

This set contains 12 bits total. These auger drill bits are for use with a gentleman's bit brace. Courtesy of Liberty Tool Company.

41203T3 **Center bits (10)**   DTM   MH

Cast steel, unsigned.

This collection is intriguing because, though coming from the same tool chest, they all have different manufacturer's marks. They are an amazing example of the wide variety of sources for cast steel center bits in the mid-19th century, with a surprising number of Philadelphia makers. Perhaps the tool chest these were found in originated in Philadelphia. Follow the bio link to see a listing of these bits.

http://www.davistownmuseum.org/pics/41203t3_p1.jpg

http://www.davistownmuseum.org/Inventoryofpictures/WebInfoCenterBits.html

913108T46B **Countersink**   DTM   MH

Steel, 4" long, signed "MORRISON & PARKER".

This is an English maker, the name shows up in the "Official Descriptive and Illustrated Catalogue of the Great Exhibition of 1851" (books.google.com). They are listed as located on Rockinghamshire St, Sheffield and as making carpenters' braces and center bits, spirit levels, gauges, saw pads, augers, and other tools. The countersink is notched, suggesting that it goes in a gentlemans' brace.

31811T33 **Drill bit**   DTM   TT

Drop-forged steel, 2 1/2" long, 3/8" diameter, signed but it is too worn to read, it might say "1855".

It appears to be a Jennings type bit.

090508T6 **Expansion bit**   DTM   MH

Steel, 9" long, signed "__ GIBBS" "NY" "PATENT" "JUNE 17 1855" and also stamped "H. M. WILSON" on the side.

The initials on the mark on this tool are obscured. It is L. H. Gibbs who received this patent. At the time, he was living in Washington, DC. It is unclear if he made the bit or if he moved to NY (Nelson 1999).

http://www.davistownmuseum.org/pics/090508t6-bw-4_web.jpg

http://www.davistownmuseum.org/pics/090508t6-bw-1-web.jpg

42012T5 **Expansion bit**   DTM   TT

Steel, 9 1/8" long, 1" wide, signed "I H GIBBS" "NY" "PATENT" "June 17, 1855".

DATM (Nelson 1999, 312) lists L. H. Gibbs of Washington, DC and NY, NY as holder of a patent for expansive bits, but the stamped date is invalid. This is one of the earliest expansion bit designs. Courtesy of Liberty Tool Co.

Historic Maritime IV (1840-1865): The Early Industrial Revolution

Woodworking: Boring Tools

101008T1   Rafting auger   DTM   MH

Malleable iron and low carbon steel, 37 1/2" long, 6" diameter auger, signed "MFG. CO." "MASS" and "USA" the rest is obscured.

There is a fair amount of hang-forging noticeable, especially in the application of the handle. There is no spiral tip on the end.

22813T1   T-handle nut auger   DTM   MH

Forged steel, wood (oak), 6 5/8" handle, 15" long bit, 1 3/4" diameter, unsigned.

Woodworking: Edge Tools

12812T1   Adz   DTM   TT

Drop-forged steel, 10 1/2" long, 2" tall, 3 1/2" cutting edge, signed "HARWOOD 3" "HARWOOD TOOL CO".

This maker is not in DATM (Nelson 1999).

31908PC4   Adz   DTM   MH

Steel and wood, 30" long, 5" wide blade, signed "JOSIAH FOWLER CO. LT." and "ST. JOHN N.B.".

Josiah Fowler was a St. John, New Brunswick, Canada, edge toolmaker from 1864 to 1920.

http://www.davistownmuseum.org/pics/31808pc4p1.jpg
http://www.davistownmuseum.org/bioFowler.html

31908T19   Bevel edge firmer chisel   DTM   MH

Forged iron and steel, wood, 16 1/2" long, 8 1/2" long blade, 1 1/2" wide, signed "GI. MIX & Co" "YALE" and "EX".

It is possibly made with German steel that was made in the US by decarburizing cast iron. The maker might be Mix & Co., a chisel and drawknife maker in Cheshire, Connecticut.

http://www.davistownmuseum.org/pics/31908t19.jpg
http://www.davistownmuseum.org/pics/31908t19-2.jpg

040103T12   Block poll adz   DTM   MH

Forged steel, 8" long, 4 3/8" wide blade, signed with what appears to be the touchmark of Josiah Fowler.

A hefty and finely made block adz, this tool seems to be all forged steel with no evidence of a weld steel lap.

http://www.davistownmuseum.org/pics/040103t12_p1.jpg
http://www.davistownmuseum.org/bioFowler.html

ID #   Status   Location

Woodworking: Edge Tools

32412T5   Carpenters' socket gouge   DTM   TT

Drop-forged steel, 9" long, 11/16" wide cutting edge, 13/16" diameter socket, signed "A.W. CROSSMAN".

The mark belongs to Amory W. Crossman, who worked out of West Warren, Massachusetts, circa 1850-1866.

31908T30   Carving chisel   DTM   MH

Steel and wood, 8 5/8" long, 2 1/2" long blade, signed "WARD".

This is most likely made by W. P. Ward, listed by DATM (Nelson 1999, 825) with no dates or location.

31808SLP30   Chisel   DTM   TT

Steel and wood, 12" long, 6 1/2" long blade, signed "2" on both sides of the blade.

http://www.davistownmuseum.org/pics/31808slp30.jpg

913108T46A   Chisel   DTM   MH

Forged iron and steel, brass ferrule, wood handle, 15 3/4" long, 7 1/2" long blade, signed "G. H. TUCKER".

This maker is not listed in DATM (Nelson 1999); perhaps it is English-made.

http://www.davistownmuseum.org/pics/913108t46A_p2.jpg

70701T9   Cold chisel   DTM   MH

Steel, 6" long, 1/2" wide, signed "C Drew & Co".

http://www.davistownmuseum.org/bioDrew.htm

41203T2J   Cold chisels and punches (12)   DTM   MH

Steel, from 4 1/2" to 8 1/4" long, signed "C. Drew & Co.".

http://www.davistownmuseum.org/pics/41203t2_p4.jpg
http://www.davistownmuseum.org/bioDrew.htm

22311T15   Drawknife   DTM   TT

Forged iron and steel with a wood handle, 14" long, 8" long blade, signed "P. MERRILL & CO" "8" and owner's mark "ULCE".

DATM (Nelson 1999) states that this is probably Pliny Merrill of Hinsdale, NH, c. 1856. It is part of the Robert Sullivan Collection donation.

071704T4   Drawknife   DTM   MH

Forged iron and steel, wood handles, 13" long, 6 1/2" long blade, signed "George", c. 1850.

This drawknife was made by Currier George, Danville, NH and has a clearly welded steel cutting edge.

Woodworking: Edge Tools

22311T17   **Drawknife**   DTM   TT

Forged iron and steel, brass ferrules, and a wood handle, 16" long, 8" long blade, signed "JAS".

This drawknife is handmade with a unique straight extended handle on the left side. The blade has a tool steel cutting edge hand-forged to the malleable iron body. Part of the Robert Sullivan Collection donation.

100605T4   **Drawknife**   DTM   TB-O

Forged iron and steel with wooden handles, 17 3/4" wide including a 11 5/8" cutting edge, signed "W. FARNHAM".

This tool was made by William Farnham of Richmond, Maine and has a clearly welded steel cutting edge. For more information see the Registry of Maine Toolmakers (Brack 2008).

http://www.davistownmuseum.org/publications/volume10.html

22411T16   **Drawknife**   DTM   TT

Forged steel, brass ferrules, and wooden handles, 8" long, 4" wide, 5" blade, unsigned.

It is hand-forged from an old file.

72812T5   **Drawknife**   DTM   MH

Forged steel with welded edge, wood (rosewood), 18 1/2" long, 12" wide cutting edge, 5 1/2" long handles, signed "J.P. BILLINGS".

This maker operated out of Clinton, Maine circa 1837 to 1887. For more information see the Registry of Maine Toolmakers (Brack 2008).

913108T26   **Drawknife**   DTM   MH

Forged iron and steel with wood handle, 12 1/2" long, 8" blade, signed "A. WHITTEMORE".

Amos Whittemore & Co. made cutlery, edge tools, knives, and leatherworking tools in Bennington, NH, 1855 - 1860. This tool's cutting edge is clearly welded steel. It has an uncommon New England maker's mark.

http://www.davistownmuseum.org/bioWhittemore.html

63001T7   **Drawknife**   DTM   MH

Forged iron, steel, wood, and brass ferrules, 13" long, 7" blade, signed "Wm Beatty & Son Chester PA 7".

A prolific maker of edge tools, DATM (Nelson 1999) lists Wm Beatty as working as early as 1839.

http://www.davistownmuseum.org/bioBeatyson.html

42801T17   **Drawknife**   DTM   MH

Forged iron, steel and wood, 11 1/2" long, 6 1/8" wide blade, signed "TH Witherby Razor blade".

This is an excellent example of one of America's most famous manufacturers of edge tools. T. H. Witherby's working dates begin in 1849. He later became Witherby Tool Co. and then Winsted Edge Tool Works (Nelson 1999, 873).

http://www.davistownmuseum.org/bioWitherby.html

ID #   Status   Location

Woodworking: Edge Tools

31908T26   Drawshave   DTM   MH

Forged iron, steel, brass ferrules, and wood, 14 1/2" wide, 9" long blade, signed "S. BALDWIN" on blade and "EMB" on handle.

Samuel Baldwin of Bennington, NH, had working dates from 1826 to 1870. He made axes, cutlery, drawknives, knives, leather tools, screwdrivers, and shaves.

051310T1   Drawshave   DTM   MH-O

Forged iron and steel, brass, and wood, 15" long, 4 1/2" wide, signed "H. E. Abbott" with two arrows, one on either side of the name, both pointing towards the name.

This maker is not in DATM (Nelson 1999). It has a clearly welded steel cutting edge.

121805T1   Drawshave   DTM   MH

Forged iron and steel, wood handles, brass ferrules, 12" wide, 7 3/16" long cutting blade, signed "G. BARNAR__".

This is probably G Barnard of Watertown, NY (DATM 1999, 58).

http://www.davistownmuseum.org/pics/121805T1_p2.jpg

61204T3   Drawshave   DTM   MH

Forged iron, steel, wood handle, 18" wide, 9 3/8" long blade, signed "HIGGINS & LIBBY" "PORTLAND" "5_".

They were prolific Maine toolmakers. For more information see the Registry of Maine Toolmakers (Brack 2008).

http://www.davistownmuseum.org/pics/61204t3_p1.jpg
http://www.davistownmuseum.org/publications/volume10.html

42604T8   Framing chisel   DTM   MH

Forged iron and steel, 11 3/4" long, 2" wide, signed "T. H. WITHERBY" "WARRANTED".

This tool has an obvious welded steel cutting edge.

http://www.davistownmuseum.org/bioWitherby.html

52907T4   Framing chisel   DTM   MH

Forged iron and steel, wood handle with an iron tang, 14 7/8" long with a 4 1/2" handle, 1 15/16" wide, unsigned.

This unmarked socket type edge tool is significant in that as a damaged tool with a broken off cutting edge, it clearly shows the common technique of welding steel to the bottom of a forged malleable iron body. The steel iron interface is clearly visible on the bottom of the tool, but not on the top surface, which appears to be all steel. The fracture of the break clearly illustrates the lower quality of the iron body of the chisel.

http://www.davistownmuseum.org/pics/52907t4_pic1.jpg
http://www.davistownmuseum.org/pics/52907t4_pic2.jpg

Woodworking: Edge Tools

14302T15   Gouge   DTM   MH

Forged iron, steel, brass, and wood, 9 1/2" long, 4 1/2" long handle, signed "IH" and "J. Harrison Warranted".

This tool is made by John Harrison, Instone Mills, Dronfield, Sheffield UK (http://swingleydev.com/archive/get.php?message_id=95422&submit_thread=1).

42607T4   Gouge   DTM   MH

Forged iron and steel, iron ferrules, wooden handle, 11 5/8" long including a 5 1/8" long handle and 1 5/16" wide blade, signed "PEUGEOT FRERES" with a man in the moon hallmark.

It is almost certainly forged from German steel.

81101T9   Gouge   DTM   MH

Forged iron and steel, wood, 14 7/8" long, 2" blade, signed "J.M. SHEFFIELD 141 AVE. CNY SOLD BY A. S. MORSE BOSTON MASS".

DATM (Nelson 1999) lists Sheffield as working in New York City, dates unknown and Stamford, CT, 1849 - 1859. This gouge was used by the Wheeler Boat Shop in Gloucester, MA. It dates from the early years of America's cast steel manufacturing.

http://www.davistownmuseum.org/pics/81101T9_p1.jpg
http://www.davistownmuseum.org/pics/81101T9_p2.jpg

121112T2   Gutter adz   LPC   MH

Forged steel and iron, wooden handle, 9 3/4" long, 2 1/2" peen, 2 3/4" long severely curved cutting edge, signed "Jim Sheffield 141 Ave C N. Y.".

This adz has a clearly steeled cutting edge. James M. Sheffield later became part of Watts & Sheffield around 1841 (Nelson 1999, 710, 833).

090105T1   Gutter adz   DTM   TB

Forged iron and steel, wood, 9 5/8" long, 4" wide head, 2 3/4" poll, 32 1/4" handle, signed "G.FLOYD" and owner's marks "J.B.L" and "R.T.W.".

This edge tool has a distinctly welded steel cutting edge, with evidence of use of file steel. DATM (Nelson 1999) states that G. Floyd made adzes. We believe this to be the same as Floyd of Portland, Maine who made adzes and axes circa 1850 and the Floyd & Stanwood edge toolmakers of Portland, ME of 1855-56 (Brack 2008). This is a rare mark.

http://www.davistownmuseum.org/pics/090105t1_p2.jpg
http://www.davistownmuseum.org/publications/volume10.html

31602T9   Mortising chisel   DTM   MH

Forged iron, steel, wood, brass ferrule, 10 3/8" long, 5/16" wide blade, signed "T. SHAW".

Goodman's "British planemakers" (1993) lists a Thomas Shaw who was a partner in the firm Martin & Shaw of Birmingham, England, from 1843f. Could he be this T. Shaw? DATM (Nelson 1999, 710) lists T. Shaw as making shaves with no location or dates.

Woodworking: Edge Tools

3213T3   **Mortising chisel**   DTM   MH

Cast steel, wood (hickory), 13 3/4" long, 9 1/2" blade, 5/8" edge, signed "J. RUSSELL & CO CAST STEEL".

http://www.davistownmuseum.org/bioRussel.html

041505T24   **Mortising chisel**   DTM   MH

Forged iron and steel, 10 7/8" long, signed "UNDERHILL" "EDGE TOOL Co.".

The Underhill Edge Tool Co. operated in Nashua, NH, 1852 - 1890. This is a particularly interesting specimen of an edge tool. The Underhills made some of the finest steel edge tools made in the US. This particular tool is not cast steel, but forged iron and weld steel. What is unusual is the appearance, in the iron component above the weld, of the tell tale inclusion of wrought iron illustrating that this particular tool was made of relatively unrefined wrought iron. The lower quality iron resulted in an irregular (but obvious) weld, in an unusual anomaly for a company that usually made the finest edge tools. In this case, was this bog iron from a local source? If so, it is unusual for this late date (c. 1855).

http://www.davistownmuseum.org/pics/041505t24_p2.jpg
http://www.davistownmuseum.org/pics/041505t24.jpg

111412T8   **Mortising chisel**   DTM   MH

Forged iron and steel, 9 3/4" long, 3/8" wide, unsigned.

This is a socket chisel with the handle missing. It provides a nice example of a clearly steeled cutting edge.

40107T1   **Mortising chisel**   DTM   MH

Forged iron and steel, 13 1/2" long, 1/2" wide including a 1 3/4" wood handle and iron ferrule, signed "HOWAR_".

It was probably made by a predecessor to the Howard Mfg. Co. of Belfast. This is a typical weld steel edge tool made of malleable iron with clearly visible alloy inclusions and the traditional welded steel cutting edge on the bottom of the chisel, angling towards the top of the chisel from mid-tool to the cutting edge.

http://www.davistownmuseum.org/pics/40107t1_pic1.jpg
http://www.davistownmuseum.org/pics/40107t1_sig.jpg

111412T9   **Paring chisel**   DTM   MH

Forged German steel, 10" long, unsigned.

This chisel's handle is missing.

12712T2   **Peen adz**   DTM   TT

Forged iron and steel, wooden handle, 10 7/8" long, 4 1/4" wide blade, 2 3/4" long and 3/4" wide 8-sided peen, signed "J STUART" and other obscured markings.

No J. Stuart is noted in DATM (Nelson 1999).

Historic Maritime IV (1840-1865): The Early Industrial Revolution

Woodworking: Edge Tools

3312T16   Putty knife (scraper)   DTM   TT

Drop-forged malleable iron or steel blade, rosewood handle, 8" long, 4" wide blade, signed "RUSSELL" "GREEN RIVER WORKS" and stamped on the handle "535" and "4".

John Russell & Co. was located in Greenfield and Deerfield, MA, from 1832 to 1865 (Nelson 1999). Courtesy of Liberty Tool Co.

http://www.davistownmuseum.org/bioRussel.html

31011T2   Reamer   DTM   TT

Forged malleable iron and steel, 7" long, 3" x 1" cutting area, unsigned.

This is a handmade tapered convex-shaped reamer.

71401T9   Scraper   DTM   MH

Forged iron, steel, wood, 15" long, 2 1/4" wide, 1 1/2" cutting edge, signed "L M Hildreth New Haven CONN PAT Applied For".

Hildreth is not listed in DATM (Nelson 1999).

102804T2   Slick   LPC   MH

Forged iron and steel, wood, signed "P. MERRILL & CO.".

DATM(Nelson 1999) states that this is probably Pliny Merrill of Hinsdale, NH, c. 1856. He later worked with his nephew George S. Wilder under the name MERRILL & WILDER around 1860.

62202T3   Slick   DTM   MH

Forged iron and steel with birch handle, 28 1/4" long, 2" wide, 9" long nicely turned handle, unsigned.

This tool is an exquisite example of a finely forged edge tool, date and location of manufacture unknown. Joel Pontz of the Plimouth Plantation (Plymouth, MA) purchased this tool at a yard sale many years ago for one dollar.

http://www.davistownmuseum.org/pics/62202t3.jpg

TCS1003   Socket chisel   BDTM   MH

Forged iron and steel, 7 1/4" long, signed "J Fowler St John NB".

http://www.davistownmuseum.org/bioFowler.html

63001T4   Socket chisel   DTM   MH

Forged iron and steel, 11 3/8" long, 1 1/2" wide, signed "T H Witherby Warranted".

This is an extra long example of the work of one of the most important American edge tool manufacturers of the early and classic periods of the Industrial Revolution. Thomas H. Witherby began making tools in Millbury, Mass., in 1849 and later became the Witherby Tool Co., c. 1868 and around 1890 the Winsted Edge Tool Works (Nelson 1999, 871 - 873).

http://www.davistownmuseum.org/bioWitherby.html

Woodworking: Edge Tools

TCC2007   Socket chisel
DTM   MH

Forged iron and steel, 10 5/8" long without handle, 7/16" wide, signed "Buck Brothers, Millbury, MA".

The touchmark on this chisel is probably the early mark of the Buck Brothers. While Buck tools are ubiquitous, Buck Brothers tools with this mark are very uncommon. This steel chisel signals the evolution of the factory system of mass production of hand tools that had evolved by the middle of the 19th century.

http://www.davistownmuseum.org/bioBuckBrothers.html

4106T7   Socket gouge
DTM   MH

Forged iron and steel, 6" long, 1 3/4" wide, signed "D. R. Barton 1832" with Barton's traditional hallmark.

This tool is hand-forged and may represent the transition from forge welded steeling to drop-forging. What kind of steel is this tool made from? D. R. Barton was a prolific Rochester, NY, edge and coopers' tool manufacturer.

http://www.davistownmuseum.org/pics/4106t7_p3.jpg
http://www.davistownmuseum.org/bioBarton.html

71401T17   Spokeshave
BDTM   MH

Cast grey iron, steel, and brass, 10 1/4" long, 2 1/4" wide blade, signed on the brass nut holding the blade "Bailey's Pat. July 13 58".

This is an excellent example of Leonard Bailey's tools before he joined in partnership with Augustus Stanley to form the Stanley Tool Co. For more information see Roger Smith's (1960) "Patented Transitional and Metallic Planes" Vol. I pg. 41 - 58 and Vol. II pg. 21 - 38.

http://www.davistownmuseum.org/pics/71401t17.jpg
http://www.davistownmuseum.org/bioBaily.html

TCC2009   Tang chisel
DTM   MH

Forged iron and steel, 5" long, 7/8" wide, signed "Buck Brothers Made of American Steel".

This is another unusual Buck Brothers' touchmark.

http://www.davistownmuseum.org/bioBuckBrothers.html

31908T24   Tanged framing chisel
DTM   MH

German steel, 4 1/2" long blade, 1 1/4" wide, signed "BERG. STAHL" "IND.GES" on front of the blade and "GUSSTAHL" on the back with a crossed sword mark.

It has no handle. This is a typical German steel edge tool.

32707T1   Timber framing chisel
DTM   MH

Steel with a forge-welded edge, wood (hickory), iron ferrule, 15 1/4" long including 5" long handle, 1 1/2" wide cutting edge, signed "UNDERHILL" and "EDGE TOOL CO" on chisel with owner mark "O T HAINES" on wood handle.

The Underhill Edge Tool Co. operated in Nashua, NH, 1852 - 1890.

http://www.davistownmuseum.org/pics/032707t1_p1.jpg
http://www.davistownmuseum.org/pics/032707t1_p2.jpg

Woodworking: Edge Tools

22512LTC13 Timber framing chisel   DA   TT (Pub)

Malleable iron, steel, with forge-welded laminated steel, 24 1/2" long, 3" wide, 9" long handle, signed "G.I. MIX & CO No. 1.EX.".

DATM (Nelson 1999) lists a Mix & Co., a chisel and drawknife maker in Cheshire, Connecticut. There is a 1901drawknife patent made by G.I. Mix & Co. of Yalesville, CT. According to the Directory of American Tool and Machinery Patents, the company was owned by Gary I. Mix whose son-in-law had the rights to that patent. A website listing silverplate marks (http://www.sterlingflatwarefashions.com/SPMfgs/SPM2.html) indicates this company made flatware from 1857 to 1903. Note that Chesire is only 5.5 miles away from Yalesville and both are considered part of Wallingford, CT. Courtesy of Liberty Tool Co.

81200T13   Wood chisel   DTM   MHC-J

Forged iron and steel, wood, lead, 10 1/2" long with a 6" blade, 5/8" wide, signed "Chas Mellor", 1850 (?).

It has an early lead inlaid handle. The only Mellor in DATM (Nelson 1999) is from Sedalia, MO.

Woodworking: Edge Tools - American Made Cast Steel

31811T29   Chisel   DTM   TT

Cast steel and wood, 14 1/2" long, 7" long and 1" wide blade, 7 1/2" long handle, signed "UNDERHILL" "BROWN" "LEIGHTON" "CAST STEEL".

DATM (Nelson 1999) indicates that "Nathaniel and/or John Sleeper Brown were probably part of this partnership which preceded Underhill & Brown in Auburn and Underhill & Leighton in Manchester. The Leighton was William W." The working date was 1849 in Auburn, NH.

http://www.davistownmuseum.org/bioUnderhillandbrown.html

31811T17   Chisel   DTM   TT-D9

Cast steel, 12 1/12" long, 3/4" wide, signed "J. BOWLIN" "CAST STEEL".

It has no handle.

914108T4   Chisel   DTM   MH

Cast steel, 9" long, signed "J. WADSWORTH" and "CAST STEEL".

62207T1   Chisel   DTM   MH

Cast steel, wood, 1 3/8" long including a 7 3/4" long handle, 1 15/16" wide, 1" iron ferrule, signed "THAMESVILLECo" "CAST STEEL".

This is probably an American-made tool but is the English style of a tanged chisel.

http://www.davistownmuseum.org/pics/062207t1_p1.jpg
http://www.davistownmuseum.org/pics/062207t1_sig.jpg

Woodworking: Edge Tools - American Made Cast Steel

72801T5   Complex spokeshave   DTM   MH

Cast iron with cast steel blades, 7 3/4" long, 1/2" curved blade and a 1 3/4" straight blade, signed "S. Smith & Son Cast Steel".

DATM (Nelson 1999, 728) lists Seymour Smith & Son as using this mark. They worked in Oakville, CT, 1854-1905 and made shaves, axes, and saw tools. Is this tool cast iron or drop forged iron? Were these blades imported from England?

31811T1   Drawknife   DTM   TT

Forged iron, cast steel, wooden handles, 21" long, 5" long handles, 13" long and 1 7/8" wide blade, signed "UNDERHILL BROWN & LEIGHTON CAST-STEEL".

DATM (Nelson 1999) indicates that "Nathaniel and/or John Sleeper Brown were probably part of this partnership which preceded Underhill & Brown in Auburn and Underhill & Leighton in Manchester. The Leighton was William W." The working date was 1849 in Auburn, NH.

http://www.davistownmuseum.org/bioUnderhillandbrown.html

071704T5   Drawknife   DTM   MH

Forged iron, cast steel, wood, 16 1/2" long, 8 7/8" long blade, signed "A.G.WOOD" and "CAST-STEEL".

Almost certainly this is a New England-made tool; there is no A. G. Wood listed in DATM (Nelson 1999).

http://www.davistownmuseum.org/pics/071704t5-2.jpg
http://www.davistownmuseum.org/pics/071704t5-2.jpg

71401T3   Drawknife   DTM   MH

Forged iron, cast steel, brass, and wood, signed "Underwood & Brown Warranted Cast Steel".

DATM (Nelson 1999) lists Underwood and Brown in Auburn, NH, 1850 - 56. One of the Underwood clan joined in business with a Nathaniel or John Sleeper Brown.

31808PC15   Drawshave   DTM   MH

Forged iron, cast steel, brass ferrules, and wood, 13 5/8" long, 8 3/4" long blade, signed "UNDERHILL" "& BROWN" "AUBURN N.H." "CAST STEEL" "WARRANTE" "8 1/2" and upside down "J. T. RICH", an owner's signature.

Underhill & Brown worked in Auburn, NH, from 1850 - 1856.

http://www.davistownmuseum.org/bioUnderhillandbrown.html

42405T6   Drawshave   DTM   MH

Forged iron, cast steel, iron ferrules, wood handles, 14 3/8" long, 8 1/2" cutting edge, signed "M & AM DARLING CAST STEEL WARRANTED".

This is a previously unrecorded maker's mark, almost certainly American. Is there any relationship to Samuel Darling of Darling, Brown & Sharpe or other New England Darling toolmakers?

Historic Maritime IV (1840-1865): The Early Industrial Revolution

Woodworking: Edge Tools - American Made Cast Steel

032203T13   Framing chisel   DTM   MH

Cast steel with a wood handle, 12 1/2" long including a 4" handle, signed "BUCK BROS" "CAST STEEL" with a bucks head touchmark.

This is a socket chisel.

http://www.davistownmuseum.org/pics/032203t10_p1.jpg
http://www.davistownmuseum.org/bioBuckBrothers.html

032203T10   Framing chisel   DTM   MH

Forged iron and cast steel, 16" long including a 4 3/8" handle, signed "TH WITHERBY" " Warranted".

Thomas H. Witherby began the manufacture of edge tools in Millbury, MA, in 1849, and along with the Buck Brothers and the Underhill clan, was one of the preeminent manufacturers of American-made edge tools after the Civil War. The Witherby Tool Co., and later the Winsted Edge Tool Co., continued using its founder's mark until as late as 1890.

http://www.davistownmuseum.org/pics/032203t13_p3.jpg
http://www.davistownmuseum.org/bioWitherby.html

101312LTC1 Framing chisel   DA   TT (Pub)

Cast steel, 10" long, 1 3/4" edge, signed "ISAAC.GREAVES CAST STEEL".

Isaac Greaves worked out of Basking Ridge, NY circa 1850. His relation, if any, to W. Greaves is unknown.

913108T42   Framing chisel   DTM   MH

Cast steel, 11 1/2" long, 7 1/2" long blade, signed "F. DICKINSON" "CAST STEEL" and "WARRANTED".

This was made by chisel-maker Friend Dickinson, Higganum, Connecticut who started working in 1849 (Nelson 1999).

http://www.davistownmuseum.org/pics/913108t42_p2.jpg

51100T10   Mortising chisel   DTM   MH

Forged iron and cast steel, 11 1/4" long, 11/16" wide, signed "UNDERHILL & LEIGHTON MANCHESTER CAST STEEL" with a owner's signature of "J.W. Benway".

DATM (Nelson 1999) states that this is thought to be a partnership of Hazen R. Underhill and William W. Leighton, both working in the Manchester, NH, area c. 1852. They were makers of chisels and edge tools. Underhill is the most prolific of all 19th century American edge toolmakers; this is a very rare mark. Hazen is only one of many toolmakers in the Underhill clan.

http://www.davistownmuseum.org/pics/51100t10.jpg
http://www.davistownmuseum.org/pics/51100t10_sig.jpg

42904T6   Mortising chisel   DTM   MH

Forged iron and cast steel with wooden handle, 10 3/8" long with additional 3 1/4" handle, 3/8" wide, signed "UNDERHILL" "& BROWN" "CAST STEEL" and on the other side "WARRANTED" "AUBURN.N.Y." and "JC" owner's mark, 1850 - 1856.

This is an excellent example of the florescence of American toolmakers.

Historic Maritime IV (1840-1865): The Early Industrial Revolution

Woodworking: Edge Tools - American Made Cast Steel

112303T2   Mortising gouge   DTM   MH

Hand-forged cast steel, 13 7/8" long, 3 1/8" wide, signed "UNDERHILL" "CAST STEEL" and on the underside "BOSTON", also "TH" made with small dots, probably an owner's mark.

This is the largest gouge we have ever seen. It was discovered in conjunction with a Buck Brothers slick and other timber framing tools in an 18th century barn in Hanson, MA. Probably, it was once used in the heyday of shipbuilding on the North River at Scituate, Norwell, and Hanover.

http://www.davistownmuseum.org/pics/112303t2_p1.jpg
http://www.davistownmuseum.org/pics/112303t2_p4.jpg

12900T2   Peen adz   DTM   MH

Forged iron and cast steel, 10 1/2" long, 2 1/2" tall, 4 1/2" wide cutting edge, signed "J. Gray Kingston" "CAST-STEEL".

DATM (Nelson 1999) lists John Gray as an edge toolmaker, Kingston, MA, c. 1849. What was his association with his famous neighbor, Christopher Drew?

72801T4   Peen adz   DTM   MH

Forged iron, cast steel, wood, 10 1/2" long, 4 1/4" wide blade, 31 1/4" handle, signed "Boston Arnold".

No Arnold of Boston is listed in DATM (Nelson 1999). Who was this manufacturer of edge tools?

http://www.davistownmuseum.org/pics/72801t4.jpg

030505T1   Slick   DTM   MH-O

Forged iron, cast steel, wood, 29 1/2" long including the wooden handle, 15 1/2" long blade that is 4" wide tapering to 1.5", signed "C. STILLER" "ST. JOHN" "CAST STEEL WARRANTED".

This slick is unusual; instead of being flat across, it has a central ridge with slightly slanted sides but no beveling. It came from a Brookline, MA, collector and was forged by an important Canadian edge toolmaker.

http://www.davistownmuseum.org/pics/030505t1_p1.jpg

81101T13   Socket chisel   DTM   MH

Forged iron and cast steel, 8 15/16" long, 1 1/2" wide, signed "F Dickinson cast steel warranted".

DATM (Nelson 1999) lists Friend Dickinson as working in Higganum, CT, 1849. Was this "cast steel" produced in Pittsburgh, PA, or imported from England?

31908T22   Timber framing chisel   DTM   MH

Forged iron, cast steel, wood, 14 1/4" long, 6 1/2" blade, signed "THE" "R E RIFLEWORKS" "CAST STEEL" and "WARRANTED", Rifleworks is in an arch shape.

This toolmaker is not listed in DATM (Nelson 1999).

Woodworking: Edge Tools - American Made Cast Steel

31908T20   Timber framing chisel   DTM   MH

Forged iron, cast steel, wood, 16 1/2" long with an 8" long blade, 2" wide, signed "CAST STEEL" and a partially obscured "BL_".

The signature is possibly Buck Brothers.

http://www.davistownmuseum.org/pics/31908t20.jpg
http://www.davistownmuseum.org/pics/31908t20-3.jpg

42405T5   Wood chisel   DTM   MH

Forged iron, cast steel, wood handle, 13 1/4" long including a 7 3/8" long handle, 1 1/2" wide, signed "Thamesville Co. Cast Steel".

This is a run of the mill edge tool except for its mark, which is not listed in DATM (Nelson 1999). It does list a Thames Tool Co. in Connecticut, but no dates for it. This mark has not been previously observed. There is a Thamesville, CT and a Thamesville, Ontario, Canada. Almost certainly, it is an obscure Connecticut toolmaker.

Woodworking: Edge Tools - Imported Cast Steel

31908T25   Carving tool   DTM   MH

Forged iron and cast steel (?), wood, 2 5/8" long curved blade, signed "HERRING BROS" and "LONDON".

091309T1   Chisel   DTM   MH

Cast steel and wood, 11 1/2" long, 1 1/4" wide, 5/16" cutting edge, signed "I. & H. Sorby".

"John Sorby was the brother of Thomas and hence uncle of Robert [Sorby]. He too was engaged in the manufacture of edge tools, joiners tools, saws, sheep shears, files and followed the family tradition by being appointed Master Cutler in 1806. After his retirement his two sons, John and Henry, continued the business and started to use the trade mark 'I & H Sorby'. Although John Sorby & Sons was acquired first in 1849 by Lockwood Brothers - cousins of the family - and later by both Turner, Naylor and Co and William Marples, the 'I and H Sorby' mark was still used well into the twentieth century." (http://www.robert-sorby.co.uk/company_info.htm).

Woodworking: Edge Tools - Imported Cast Steel

31908T34   Drawknife   DTM   MH

Steel and wood, 5 1/2" long blade, 13" wide, signed "PEUGEOT FRERES" "TOUT ACIER FONDU ANGLAIS".

The stamp translates to "all molten steel English", which suggest the company was using English cast steel. "Jean-Jacques Peugeot was a miller in 1725. One of his sons, Jean-Pierre, was a weaver. By leaving his inheritors the Sous-Cratet flour mill at Hérimoncourt, this son was the catalyst for the industrial orientation of the family. In 1810, Jean-Pierre's sons, Jean-Pierre II and Jean-Frédéric, joined forces with Jacques Maillard-Salins (who was a member of the well-known Japy family of watchmakers) to found the Peugeot Brothers and Maillard-Salins company. The company was a specialist manufacturer of laminated steel and tools. The requirement for the necessary capital to achieve growth led the company to form partnerships with new associates. It became Peugeot-Frères et Compagnie in 1819. Jean-Pierre II and Jean-Frédéric regained their independence in 1832 with the company Peugeot Frères Aînés. This company underwent a crisis in 1851. Jules and Emile, the two sons of Jean-Pierre II, entered a partnership with a nephew to create Peugeot Frères, with its head office in Valentigney." (http://www.peugeot.com/en/history/the-lion's-story/a-family-saga.aspx).

102904T14   Framing chisel   DTM   MH

Forged iron, steel, 11 5/8" long, 2" wide, signed "W. BROOKES & SONS".

It has no handle. It has clear evidence of hand filing. W. Brookes & Sons is not listed in DATM (Nelson 1999). The signature is very clear and not obscured. This chisel is a typical 19th century timber framing tool. A Sheffield Trades listing from 1857 gives: "Brookes W. & Sons, Carlisle st" as makers of edge tools, cutlery, razors, etc.

http://www.davistownmuseum.org/pics/102904t14_p1.jpg

090109T5   Gouge   DTM   MH

Cast steel, brass, and rosewood, 12" long including a 4 1/2" long handle, 1" wide cutting edge, signed "KNOWLES" and 'SHEFFIELD".

The mark may be "KNOWLES & Co", the last part is obscured.

http://www.davistownmuseum.org/pics/090109T5web2.jpg
http://www.davistownmuseum.org/pics/090109T5web3.jpg

913108T44   Gouge   DTM   MH

Forged iron and steel with a wooden handle, 15" long, 10" long blade, signed "ASKHAM & MOSFORTH".

This gouge was made by John Askham and Thomas Mosforth, 57 Broad Lane, Sheffield, England. It would have been made between 1852 and 1855. They also made chisels, and knives of various designs - table knives, pocket knives, spring bladed knives etc. They did have an office in New York, and Askham was there for some years as he carried on the business when the Askham and Mosforth partnership was dissolved in 1855. The company was then called 'Askham'. Thomas Mosforth died in 1857 at the age of 36. the Askham and Mosforth company was originally Frost, Askham and Mosforth 1850-1852 (Frost retired in 1852). This information courtesy of Thomas Mosforth's great, great, great niece.

http://www.davistownmuseum.org/biopics/Askham_letterhead.jpg
http://www.davistownmuseum.org/biopics/BroadLaneWorks.jpg

Woodworking: Edge Tools - Imported Cast Steel

71401T21   Gouge   DTM   MH

Forged iron and steel, 8 1/2" long, 3 1/2" handle, signed "Schroder & Arete".

This is an unusual signature of an as yet unidentified European manufacturer, which is almost certainly made of German steel.

51703T2   Tanged firmer chisel   DTM   MH

Cast steel, brass ferrule, and wood handle, 10 1/2" long, includes a 6" long handle, 5/8" wide cutting edge, signed "W. Butcher Cast Steel".

The Butcher cartouche is clearly imprinted on the reverse side of the chisel shoulder. Butcher was one of the most prolific Sheffield edge toolmakers and their tools were imported to the colonies and the republic until the late 19th century.

041505T27   Turning tool   DTM   MH

Cast steel, iron ferrule, and wood handle, 15" long including a 6 5/8" handle, 1 1/2" wide, signed "R GROVER & SON" "CAST STEEL" with crown hallmark.

This is a typical mid-19th century import from one of Sheffield's foremost edge toolmakers.

http://www.davistownmuseum.org/pics/041505t27.jpg

Woodworking: Edge Tools Made in Maine

121906T2   Adz   DTM   MH-O

Steel, wooden handle, 31 1/4" long handle, 2 7/8" long handle shaft, 9 7/8" including 2 1/2" peen on head, 5 7/16" wide, signed "J P BILLINGS CLINTON MAINE".

This adz is the only known example of a J. P. Billings shipwrights' adz. This adz has the lip of the Yankee pattern adz, the most popular adz for New England's shipwrights. Surprisingly, the tool, obviously of high quality steel is not marked cast steel, again raising the question of the type of steel used by New England edge toolmakers before the Civil War. Also of interest is the extent to which Billings and other Waterville area shipsmiths and edge toolmakers supplied the bustling shipyards downstream at Richmond, Dresden, and Bath (etc.) on the Kennebec River. Was Billings also a shipsmith producing some of the ironware needed by the sailing ships being built in the lower Kennebec, or was he only an edge toolmaker? J. P. Billings was one of many members of the Billings clan of blacksmiths and edge toolmakers whose activities date at least to the early 19th century and extend almost to the 20th century. More information about this obviously important edge toolmaker and his relationship to the booming shipbuilding towns on the lower Kennebec would be greatly appreciated.

http://www.davistownmuseum.org/pics/121906T2_p1.jpg
http://www.davistownmuseum.org/publications/volume10.html

33011T2   Adz   DTM   TT

Forged iron and steel with oak handle, 8 1/2" long, 4" wide head and 36" long handle, signed "VAUGHN" "_____" "WARRAN__" and "UNION".

This adz has a spike head. The signature is difficult to read but appears to be Vaughn and Pardoe of Union, ME. For more information see the Registry of Maine Toolmakers (Brack 2008).

http://www.davistownmuseum.org/bioVaughn.htm

Woodworking: Edge Tools Made in Maine

41212T1   **Adz**   DTM   MH

Forged iron and steel, wooden handle, 30 1/2" long, 4 1/4" wide cutting edge, signed "MOWRY".

This adz was probably made by M.H. Mowry of Union, ME, circa 1862. Courtesy of Liberty Tool Co.

40107T2   **Block adz**   DTM   MH

Forged iron and cast steel, 8 1/2" long, 4 3/8" wide cutting blade, 2" wide block end, signed "J. THAXTER" "PORTLAND" and "CAST STEEL".

This slightly defective block adz is interesting as an example of a welded steel or steeled adz with clear defects in the body of the rather wide cutting blade. On the block a late weld (1920s?) suggests it may have had a peen, yet its haft and breadth suggests a railroad adz.

http://www.davistownmuseum.org/pics/40107t2.jpg
http://www.davistownmuseum.org/publications/volume10.html

062603T2   **Clapboard slick**   DTM   MH

Forged iron and steel with a wooden handle, 34 3/8" total length, 15 3/4" handle, 4" wide blade, signed "VAUGHAN PARDOE & Co UNION WARRANTED".

http://www.davistownmuseum.org/pics/062603t2_p1.jpg
http://www.davistownmuseum.org/bioVaughn.htm

21201T3   **Clapboard slick**   DTM   MH

Forged iron and steel, 29 3/4" long including a 7" handle, 2 3/16" wide blade, signed "_UGHAN & PARDO_ UNION WARRANTEED".

This is made by Vaughan & Pardoe of Union, Maine. Working dates for this company are 1844-1868. It is a gift to The Davistown Museum from Rick Floyd of Newport, ME.

http://www.davistownmuseum.org/pics/21201t3_p3.jpg
http://www.davistownmuseum.org/bioVaughn.htm

52403T3   **Clapboard slick**   LPC   MH

Forged iron and steel, wood handle, 21 1/2" long, 4 3/4" wide cutting edge, 14 1/2" beveled steel handle, 4 3/4" long turned wood handle, signed "BILLINGS AUGUSTA".

Another fine production of the Billings clan -- this one is by the Augusta drawknife maker, first name and date of manufacture are not yet available. For more information see the Registry of Maine Toolmakers (Brack 2008).

http://www.davistownmuseum.org/pics/52403t3_p3.jpg
http://www.davistownmuseum.org/publications/volume10.html

Historic Maritime IV (1840-1865): The Early Industrial Revolution

Woodworking: Edge Tools Made in Maine

30801T2   Drawknife   DTM   MH

Forged iron and steel, wood handles, 19" wide, 13 3/4" blade, signed "J M DENNIS EAST NEW-PORTLAND".

The steel-iron interface in this edge tool has been made nearly invisible by careful forge-welding. Only one or two other J. M. Dennis tools are known to exist. The Directory of American Toolmakers (DATM 1999) lists Dennis as an ax and edge toolmaker, c. 1856. The Davistown Museum is looking for more information on this toolmaker. Donated by Roger K. Smith.

http://www.davistownmuseum.org/pics/30801t2_p3.jpg
http://www.davistownmuseum.org/publications/volume10.html

62504T1   Drawknife   DTM   MH

Forged iron and steel, wood, 15 3/4" long, 10 1/4" blade, signed "G.B. RICKER" "CHERRYFIELD".

This is a nicely made steeled drawknife in the English style, made by one of Downeast Maine's most prolific toolmakers. Question: where was the steel in this tool made?

http://www.davistownmuseum.org/pics/62504t1_p3.jpg
http://www.davistownmuseum.org/publications/volume10.html

31908T33   Drawshave   DTM   MH

Forged iron and steel, wood, 18" wide, 12" long blade, signed "B.R.MOWRY".

Bradley R. Mowry of Union, Maine worked from 1820 - 1860 making adzes and edge tools.

http://www.davistownmuseum.org/pics/31908t33p2.jpg
http://www.davistownmuseum.org/publications/volume10.html

51606T1   Framing chisel   DTM   MH

Forged iron and steel, 11" long, 1 7/16" wide, signed "A. SMART".

This is probably Alfred Smart of Pittston, ME, listed in the 1856 business directory. This is the only recorded edge tool with this mark. It was donated to the Davistown Museum by Chris of Belfast, Maine. For more information see the Registry of Maine Toolmakers (Brack 2008).

http://www.davistownmuseum.org/pics/51606t1.jpg
http://www.davistownmuseum.org/publications/volume10.html

91501T1   Framing chisel   DTM   MH

Forged iron and natural with wood handle, 15 3/4" long including 4" long handle, signed "C. LOVEJOY" "CHESTERVILLE".

DATM (Nelson 1999, 495) lists Leonard R. Lovejoy of Chesterville, ME as an ax-maker, 1869-1878. Possibly this is a relative? Clearly hand-forged, this is an excellent example of a small production forge banging out a natural steel edge tool. If a steel-iron interface exists, it is not visible. The most likely manufacturing strategy for this tool is that its cutting edge was subject to additional mechanical (hammering) and heat (tempering) treatment during forge welding making a functional edge tool out of a raw steel bloom.

http://www.davistownmuseum.org/pics/91501t1_p4.jpg
http://www.davistownmuseum.org/publications/volume10.html

Woodworking: Edge Tools Made in Maine

32103T1   Froe   DTM   MH

Forged iron and steel, wood handle, 14" long, 11" long cutting edge, 12 1/2" long handle, signed "W. M. WINN CLINTON WARRANTED".

No clear iron-steel interface is visible on this tool, but imperfections on the cutting edge, especially on the back (not visible) suggest the possibility of direct process forge-welding of a carburized bloom of malleable iron, or alternatively, the forge-welding of a piece of puddled, blister, or German steel. This is a newly discovered Maine edge toolmaker, courtesy of Rick Floyd. A large H marked next to the maker's stamp is probably the owner's mark.

http://www.davistownmuseum.org/pics/032103t1_p1.jpg
http://www.davistownmuseum.org/publications/volume10.html

31501T5   Gouge   DTM   MH

Forged iron and steel, 9 1/16" long, 1 1/8" wide blade, signed "VAUGHN" "TO__ & Co" " WARRANTED WARRANTED".

This is another example of the work of Vaughan & Pardoe of Union, ME.

http://www.davistownmuseum.org/bioVaughn.htm

111001T3   Gouge   DTM   MH

Forged iron and steel, wood, 14" long with 4 1/2" handle, 1 1/4" wide cutting edge, signed "Vaughan Pardoe & Co Warranted Union".

The working dates for this company are 1844-1868.

http://www.davistownmuseum.org/pics/111001t3_p2.jpg
http://www.davistownmuseum.org/bioVaughn.htm

TBC1002   Gouge   DTM   MH

Forged iron and steel, wood, 1 3/4" diameter, 13 3/4" long, with 6" handle and hand forged ferrule, signed "HIGGINS & LIBBY".

This company is listed in DATM (Nelson 1999) as a Portland ax and chisel maker, 1856, one of the most prolific of Maine's edge toolmakers.

http://www.davistownmuseum.org/pics/TBC1002_p3.jpg
http://www.davistownmuseum.org/publications/volume10.html

Woodworking: Edge Tools Made in Maine

61204T17   Gouge   DTM   MH

Forged iron and weld steel, wood, 22" long including 11" handle, 2 9/16" wide, signed "HIGGINS & LIBBY" "PORTLAND".

This gouge has a clearly hand-forged iron socket, but evidence of a welded iron-steel interface has been obliterated by forge welding of the highest quality. It is a finely wrought slick-like gouge from the golden age of Maine's shipbuilding era made by a major Maine edge toolmaker. It is of the quality of cast steel, but not marked as such. This forged steel edge tool shows how good Maine blacksmiths' were at making steel edge tools during the florescence of Maine's shipbuilding era; the quality of this edge tool suggests Higgins & Libby had perfected the art of piling and forging blister steel into shear steel, in the tradition of the German immigrants at Shotley Bridge and elsewhere in England, who perfected the art of reforging blister steel in the very late 17th and early 18th century.

http://www.davistownmuseum.org/pics/61204T17_p1.jpg
http://www.davistownmuseum.org/publications/volume10.html

61204T2   Gutter adz   DTM   MH

Forged iron and weld steel and wood, 10 3/4" long, 2 1/2" wide, 2 1/2" diameter adz, 16" wood handle, signed "VAUGHN & PARDOE UNION".

A welded steel-iron interface is clearly visible on this tool, which also shows extensive evidence of forge welding. The mark is partially obscured. Vaughn & Pardoe was a prolific Union, Maine, edge toolmaker working in the mid-19th century.

http://www.davistownmuseum.org/pics/61204t2_p12.jpg
http://www.davistownmuseum.org/bioVaughn.htm

31908T16   Mortising gouge   DTM   MH

Forged iron and steel, wooden handle, 17 5/8" long, 8" long blade, signed "VAUGHAN" " & PARDOE" "UNION" and "WARRANTED".

http://www.davistownmuseum.org/pics/31908t16p1.jpg
http://www.davistownmuseum.org/bioVaughn.htm

020807T1   Peen adz   DTM   MH

Forged iron and steel, wooden handle, 10" long, 4 1/8" wide adz head, 2 1/4" long, 3/4" diameter beveled peen, 28" long handle, signed "J. F. AMES" and "PE__RKING", probably an owner's mark.

J. F. Ames made edge tools in Richmond, Maine, c. 1855.

http://www.davistownmuseum.org/pics/020807T1_p3.jpg
http://www.davistownmuseum.org/bio#publications/volume10.html

Woodworking: Edge Tools Made in Maine

10606T1   Peen adz   DTM   MH

Forged iron and steel, 9" long, 3 1/2" cutting edge, 3/4" diameter, signed "Thaxter Portlan_", the last letter is illegible.

This run-of-the-mill peen adz is clearly by the same Portland, Maine, edge toolmaker as the hewing ax marked "Thaxter" in the Davistown Museum collection (ID # 91303T-20). As with many tools of this era, +/- 1850 - 70, the steel in the cutting edge of this adz is of a higher quality than the puddled steel body of this tool. This tool exhibits the mix of machine forming (drop-forging) and hand work (forge welding, as in the forge-welded peen) that characterizes many of the hand tools manufactured just prior to the era of factory-made tools.

http://www.davistownmuseum.org/pics/10606t1_p2.jpg
http://www.davistownmuseum.org/publications/volume10.html

121112T1   Slick   LPC   MH

Forged iron and steel, 15 1/4" long, 3 7/16" wide, 1 11/16" diameter socket, signed "T C Jackson Bath".

This slick has a clearly steeled cutting edge. Jackson was a Bath, ME, edge toolmaker working from 1832 into the 1860s.

040904T1   Slick   DTM   MH

Forged steel, 16 1/2" long, 6 7/8" long body with a 3 11/16" wide blade, signed "B. KELLEY & CO" "BELFAST" with owner's mark "HOMER N D G".

This tool appears to be all steel, with a higher quality cutting edge welded to the steel body. This slick is from the Spear Estate, Warren, Maine. It is an important and rare example of a prominent Belfast, Maine, edge toolmaker. It is used for cleaning up the sides of large mortises in construction and shipbuilding, and for leveling surfaces as on the deck of a ship. Slicks are particularly useful to shipwrights in areas that cannot be reached by an adz. They are often pushed by the shoulder, hence the swollen top of the wooden handle.

http://www.davistownmuseum.org/pics/040904t1_p1.jpg
http://www.davistownmuseum.org/publications/volume10.html

42604T2   Socket chisel   DTM   MH

Forged iron and welded steel, 8 1/4" long, 1 1/2" wide, signed "LIBBY & BOLTON".

Iron and steel with the welded iron steel interface clearly visible, this mundane edge tool is typical of those found in the workshops and boatyards of mid-19th century Maine, but has the signature of one of Maine's most important edge toolmakers. It was made in Portland, Maine, probably in the late 1850s.

http://www.davistownmuseum.org/pics/42604t2_p5.jpg
http://www.davistownmuseum.org/publications/volume10.html

Historic Maritime IV (1840-1865): The Early Industrial Revolution

Woodworking: Edge Tools Made in Maine

41801T7   **Socket chisel**   DTM   MH

Forged iron and steel with wood handle, 12" long, 5" wood handle, signed "VAUGHAN & PARDOE UNION WARRANTED".

Working dates for this company are 1844-1868. This was a gift to The Davistown Museum from Rick Floyd of Newport, Maine.

http://www.davistownmuseum.org/bioVaughn.htm

100108T1   **Wheelwrights' shave**   DTM   MH

Forged malleable iron and natural steel (?), 13" long, 2 1/2" wide semicircular cutter, signed "J.J.MORRILL".

http://www.davistownmuseum.org/publications/volume10.html

Woodworking: Other Tools

33002T3   **Bit brace**   DTM   MH

Forged iron and steel, brass washer, 11 1/16" long, 11/32" square socket with adjustable screw stop, signed "A. W. Streeter _____ Falls Mass PAT ___ 23, 1855 & March 31, 1857".

DATM (Nelson 1999) indicates Streeter worked in Shelburne Falls, MA, 1855 - 1871.

http://www.davistownmuseum.org/pics/33002t3.jpg

41203T2F   **Cat's paw**   DTM   MH

Forged steel, 10 1/2" long, signed "C. Drew CAT'S PAW - 277".

http://www.davistownmuseum.org/bioDrew.htm

31212T14   **Float cut or wagon-makers' file**   DTM   TT

Cast steel, wood, 18" long, 1 1/2" wide, unsigned.

Courtesy of Liberty Tool Co.

http://www.davistownmuseum.org/bioHellerBros.html

102100T12   **Gimlet**   DTM   MH

Forged steel, 5 3/4" long, unsigned.

This is a generic style steel gimlet common in the 19th century.

81212LTC12 **Hand scraper**   NOM   TT (Pub)

Cast bronze, steel edge, 11 1/2" long, 3" wide, 2 1/2" tall, 2 3/4" wide edge, unsigned.

121112T6   **Hand vise**   DTM   TT

Drop-forged iron or steel, 5 1/2" long, 1 1/4" wide jaw, signed "W&C Wynn".

DATM (Nelson 1999, 884) lists this toolmaker with no known location or dates of operation.

226

Historic Maritime IV (1840-1865): The Early Industrial Revolution

Woodworking: Other Tools

41203T2   Lot of hand tools (21)   DTM   MH

Forged iron and steel, signed with C. Drew signatures on each tool.

This collection of mid-20th century C. Drew tools indicates that Drew branched out to produce a wide variety of common hand tools ranging from screwdrivers and wrenches to hand chisels. They are more well known for their caulking irons, cat's paws, trunk chisels, and cold chisels. The two chisels, screwdriver, and wrench are the only Drew produced tools of this common type ever seen at Liberty Tool Co. Their production, unlike that of cat's paws, must have been extremely limited. These tools came from a Kingston, MA, workshop just down the street from the old Drew factory location and were all stored together in one metal box. A number of Goldblatt tools and one Osborne brick chuck were also in this hoard.

http://www.davistownmuseum.org/pics/41203t2_p2.jpg
http://www.davistownmuseum.org/bioDrew.htm

81200T5   Nail puller   DTM   MH

Drop-forged iron, wood, and brass, 16 3/4" long, unsigned, c. 1840 - 1860.

121805T7   Planemakers' float   DTM   MH

Cast steel, brass ferrule, and wood, 12 1/2" long including 3 1/2" long handle, 2" wide, signed "H" inscribed on handle in 18th century script.

This is a late 18th century planemakers' float. It is used to file out the inside of the plane to make it flat where the blade will be inserted.

http://www.davistownmuseum.org/pics/121805t7-web1.jpg
http://www.davistownmuseum.org/pics/121805t7-web2.jpg

30202T2   Saw set   DTM   MH

Drop-forged steel with hardened steel jaws, 7 1/2" long, signed "Bemis & Call".

Bemis & Call was opened by Stephen C. Bemis and Amos Call in 1844 in Springfield, MA. They are known for their wide variety of wrenches. They also made calipers, race knives, steelyards, and other tools (Nelson 1999, 78). This saw set has no patent date.

http://www.davistownmuseum.org/pics/30202t2.jpg

72801T18   Saw set   DTM   MH

Drop-forged steel, 5" long, signed "P _ Hopkins".

No P. Hopkins is listed in DATM (Nelson 1999); an unknown 19th century New England toolmaker.

31808SLP8   Sliding T bevel   DTM   TT

Steel, brass, and rosewood, 10 1/4" long blade, 6" long handle, signed "J G NICHOLAS".

DATM (Nelson 1999) lists Joseph Nicholas as making saws and squares in Philadelphia from approximately 1837 to 1857.

http://www.davistownmuseum.org/pics/31808slp8-2.jpg
http://www.davistownmuseum.org/pics/31808slp8-1.jpg

Historic Maritime IV (1840-1865): The Early Industrial Revolution

Woodworking: Other Tools

22211T5   **Spirit level**   DTM   TT

Mahogany with brass vial cover, 29 1/2" long, 3 3/16" x 1 3/8", signed "LAMBERT MILLIKEN," " & " "STACKPOLE" "BOSTON, MASS" with an American Eagle w/shield.

DATM (Nelson 1999) lists Lambert, Milliken, & Stackpole as working in Boston from 1859 to 1899. Part of the Robert Sullivan Collection donation.

Woodworking: Planes

1302T5   **Beading plane**   DTM   MH

Wood (beech), steel blade, 9 1/2" long, 1/2" wide blade, signed "P M Peckham Fall River".

This is an uncommon mark of a whaling era planemaker who worked from 1850 - 1860.

42602T3   **Beading plane**   DTM   TT

Wood (beech), steel blade, boxwood spline, 9 3/8" long, 3/8" wide bead, signed "Cox & Luckman" on plane, blade has an obscured mark "_____TH".

This is a typical imported English-made plane of the 19th century.

32802T11   **Bench plane**   DTM   TT

Wood (beech), cast steel blade, 7 3/4" long, 2 9/16" wide, 2" wide cast steel blade, signed on blade "ROBTSORBY", plane unmarked.

This plane is typical of the run of the mill smoothing planes of the mid-19th century; it might be found in any carpenters' tool kit. Robert Sorby is a well known Sheffield manufacturer of plane blades.

http://www.davistownmuseum.org/pics/32802t11_p1.jpg
http://www.davistownmuseum.org/pics/32802t11_p2.jpg

040103T1   **Block plane**   LPC   MH

Cast iron and steel, 5 1/4" wide, 1 3/8" wide blade, signed on blade "Birmingham Conn Plane Mfg. Co.".

The Birmingham Plane Co. made planes from 1855 - 1891. The unique designs of their planes made them among the most distinctive and sought after of the 19th century patented American planemakers. The rapid growth of American steel plane manufacturers after 1850 signaled the (coming) domination of this market by American planemakers after the Civil War.

http://www.davistownmuseum.org/pics/040103t1_p1.jpg
http://www.davistownmuseum.org/pics/040103t1_p2.jpg

31112T1   **Block plane blade**   DTM   TT-D28

Forged steel, 6 1/2" long, 2 1/4" wide, signed "SHAW&Co".

DATM (Nelson 1999) lists this signature as a foreign maker of plane irons. Courtesy of Liberty Tool Co.

Woodworking: Planes

092409T2   Carriage-makers' molding plane   DTM   MH-O

Wood (beech), steel blade, whale bone bottom, 4" long, 3 3/4" tall, blade is 7 1/4" long and 3/8" wide, unsigned.

It is from a Middlesex county, MA, carriage shop.

http://www.davistownmuseum.org/pics/092409T2web1.jpg
http://www.davistownmuseum.org/pics/092409T2web2.jpg

092409T1   Carriage-makers' router plane   DTM   MH

Wood (beech), iron and steel blade, steel bottom, 6 1/2" long, 5 3/4" tall, 1 5/8" wide blade, unsigned.

From a Middlesex county, MA, carriage shop.

http://www.davistownmuseum.org/pics/092409T1web1.jpg
http://www.davistownmuseum.org/pics/092409T1web5.jpg

913108T46   Compass plane   DTM   MH

Wood (beech), cast steel blade, 7 3/8" long, 1 3/6" wide blade, signed "J R TOLMAN HAN MASS" on the wood and "MOULSON BOTHERS" "WARRANTED" "CAST STEEL" and a trademark on the blade.

Joseph Robinson Tolman (b. 1787, d. 1864) started making planes in S. Scituate, MA, in the 1820s and 30s. He was in Boston in 1841 and Hanover, MA, by 1849 (Nelson 1999, 791). The plane blade is English.

32313T2   Complex molding plane   DA   TT (Pub)

Wood (beech), cast steel, 16" long, 4 5/8" wide, 7" tall, signed "W. KING" "C.C. GRIFFITH" "F.C.S.".

This badly damaged plane is a bevel and lying ogee opposite bevel and lying ogee molding plane (Whelan 1993).

32313LTC9   Complex molding plane   DA   TT (Pub)

Wood (beech), cast steel, 9 1/2" long, 3 1/8" wide, 3 1/4" tall, signed "H.M. Allen" "JOHN ***TABLE NEW BEDFORD" "B C".

101801T3   Complex molding plane   DTM   MH

Wood (beech), cast steel blade, 9 3/4" long, signed "J. T. Jones Philadelphia" with owner signature "AFW".

Pollak (2001) lists J. T. Jones as working in Philadelphia between 1831 and 1846.

http://www.davistownmuseum.org/publications/volume10.html

82312LTC1   Core box plane   DA   TT (Pub)

Brass, wood handles (rosewood), steel cutter, 9" long, 5" tall, 2 3/4" wide, 3/4" cutting edge, unsigned.

Historic Maritime IV (1840-1865): The Early Industrial Revolution

Woodworking: Planes

12900T3   Dado plane   DTM   MH

Wood (beech), steel blade, 9 1/2" long, 1/2" skewed blade, signed "Auburn Tool Co Albany NY" and by owner "J D McLellan".

The Auburn Tool Co. utilized convicts from the NY State Prison to mass produce planes, c. 1864 - 1869.

http://www.davistownmuseum.org/bioAuburn.html

913108T4   Float   DTM   MH

Steel, wood (beech), and brass, 3 1/4" long blade, 3 5/8" long handle, signed "HWINSUGGLES".

The first four characters of the signature are obscured and appear like "HWIN". This float is used by a planemaker for smoothing the throat to hold the blade.

6912LTC1   Floor plane   DA   TT (Pub)

Cast bronze, forged steel blade, 10 3/4" long, 2" wide blade, signed "N DEROIN" on the plane.

DeRoin is not listed in DATM (Nelson 1999), possibly it is an owner's mark. Courtesy of Liberty Tool Co.

6912LTC2   Floor plane   DA   TT (Pub)

Cast bronze, forged steel blade, 10" long, 2 3/4" wide blade, unsigned.

Courtesy of Liberty Tool Co.

72002T9   Gutter plane   DTM   MH

Wood (beech), steel blade, 16" long, 2" wide, signed "A CUMINGS BOSTON" with owner signature "F. A. Smith", blade marked "Wights Fre___ Warranted".

DATM (Nelson 1999) lists Allen Cumings as working in Boston from 1848 - 1854. He was one of Boston's more prolific planemakers.

072112T1   Hollowing plane   DTM   MH

Wood, steel, 9 1/2" long, 1 3/4" wide, 3 5/16" high, signed "J.F. BENNETT, WILLIS".

111106T1   Holly plane   DTM   MH

Malleable iron, cast steel, and wood (beech), 9 1/4" long, 2 1/8" wide blade, signed on blade "Moulson Bros.".

The plane is unmarked. Nonetheless, it is a Holly's patent plane c. 1852. See Roger Smith (1960, 39) "Patented transitional & metallic planes in America 1827 - 1927" Vol.1.

http://www.davistownmuseum.org/pics/111106t1.jpg

Historic Maritime IV (1840-1865): The Early Industrial Revolution

Woodworking: Planes

101801T4   Molding plane   DTM   MH

Wood (beech), cast steel blade, boxwood spline, 9 3/8" long, signed "Union Factory H. Chapin".

Pollak lists the H. Chapin, Union Factory dates as 1828 - 1860. It was one of the more prolific early factory period manufacturers.

http://www.davistownmuseum.org/bioHermonChapin.html

51606T13   Plane blade   DTM   MH

Cast steel, 8 1/8" long, 2 7/16" wide, signed "T Tillotson Refined Cast Steel" and an elaborate cartouche typical of English edge toolmakers.

This is typical imported English Sheffield steel plane blade by a prominent English maker.

63001T11   Plane blade   DTM   MH

Cast steel, 2 1/2" wide, signed "Baldwin Tool Co made from Butchers CAST STEEL WARRANTED".

DATM (Nelson 1999) indicates Baldwin Tool began business in Middletown, CT, in 1841 (to 1857). This mark on their early plane irons indicates they were still importing quality English cast steel blades in the period before the Civil War. This is another prolific early factory period manufacturer.

32313LTC2   Plow plane   DA   TT (Pub)

Wood (beech, boxwood), steel, 8 1/4" long, 10 1/2" wide, 6" tall, signed "A.B. SEMPLE & BRo LOUISVILLE. K.Y.".

32313LTC3   Plow plane   DA   TT (Pub)

Wood (beech, boxwood), steel, brass, 11" x 9 1/2" x 7", signed "A.B. SEMPLE & B__" cut off and "LOUIVILLE, K.Y.".

A.B. Semple & Brothers were dealers who marked tools from 1848 to 1859.

TCD1007   Plow plane   DTM   MH

Wood (beech), steel blade, 8" long, 9 1/4" fence, signed "J. Kellogg", c. 1845.

It was made by J. Kellogg (1835-1867), Amherst, MA. It is a typical example of a factory made plow plane that might have been found in the working carpenters' tool box in Liberty or Montville. This manufacturer's signature is mentioned in Pollak as frequently found (ff - B mark) (2001, 213); Kellogg was one of the most prolific of all planemakers, probably surpassed only by Greenfield Tool Co. in Massachusetts' output of planes.

http://www.davistownmuseum.org/pics/tcd1007_p1.jpg
http://www.davistownmuseum.org/pics/tcd1007_p2.jpg

72002T10   Rabbet plane   DTM   MH

Wood (beech), steel blade, 19 1/2" long, 7/8" wide, signed "T Swett" and "Wm True", both owner's signatures.

This is a nice example of a mid-19th century boatyard tool used for?

Historic Maritime IV (1840-1865): The Early Industrial Revolution

Woodworking: Planes

6405T1   Razee plane   DTM   MH

Mahogany, steel blade, 17 3/4" long, 2 3/16" wide, 5" high, signed "MOULSON BROTHERS WARRANTED CAST STEEL" on blade.

This plane was found in the Bath, Maine, area. It is a typical owner-made razee plane of the mid-19th century.

http://www.davistownmuseum.org/pics/6405T1_p1.jpg

42405T1   Razee plane   DTM   MH

Lignum vitae, cast steel blade, 15 7/8" long, 2 1/8" wide, signed "Buck Bros Warranted Cast Steel" on blade.

The handle has been replaced. It is a typical run of the mill Maine owner-made boat shop plane of the mid-19th century.

101801T5   Remaining planes in Abiel Walker's toolkit   DTM   MH

Wood (beech), cast steel blades, signed "AFW" on some.

Two more Union Factory planes, a quarter round molding plane signed with "AFW", a small sash plane signed with "AFW", and a number of undistinguished later molding planes.

http://www.davistownmuseum.org/publications/volume10.html

04505T8   Shipwrights' plane bodies (2)   DTM   MH

Tropical wood, unsigned.

These plane bodies are accompanied by four pieces of wood (see ID 21805T24).

http://www.davistownmuseum.org/pics/041505t8_p2.jpg

110404T1   Smooth plane   LPC   MH

Lignum vitae, cast steel blade, 9" long, 2 1/2" wide, 2 1/8" high body, 1 7/8" wide blade, signed "E.R.KING" "MAKER" "E. BOSTON" on nose, "CHARLES BUCK" "CAST STEEL" "WARRANTED" on blade, "MOULSON BROTHERS" "M B" "WARRANTED" "STEEL" on curling iron.

This tool was found in a Brookline, MA, private collection in late October of 2004. It also has a faint mark on the other end of the plane: "G. L. D." that might be an owner's mark. It appears to be a plane made during the heyday of the east Boston shipyards. Buck Brothers began making plane blades in Worcester, MA, as early as 1856. They moved to Millbury in 1864. The Buck blade suggests the plane was made after 1856, but probably before the Civil War as the 1850s represent the high point of production of the east Boston shipyards. No E.R. King hallmark is listed in either Pollak's 4th edition or DATM (Nelson 1999). The Davistown Museum solicits further information about this East Boston maker.

http://www.davistownmuseum.org/pics/110404t1_p6.jpg
http://www.davistownmuseum.org/pics/110404t1_p1.jpg

Historic Maritime IV (1840-1865): The Early Industrial Revolution

Woodworking: Planes

42405T2 Smooth plane   DTM MH

Lignum vitae, cast steel blade, 9 3/4" long, 2 1/8" wide at throat, 5" high, 1 3/4" wide blade, signed "MOULSON BROTHERS WARRANTED CAST STEEL" on blade.

This is a typical owner-made boat shop plane of the mid-19th century but with an imported English blade.

http://www.davistownmuseum.org/pics/42405T2.jpg

TCD1001 Spar plane   DTM MH

Wood (beech), 10 5/8" long with a 1 1/2" "Graves & Son" blade, signed "G. Walker", c. 1840?.

DATM (Nelson 1999, 820) lists Gustavus Walker, a hardware dealer in Concord, NH, from 1855-83, who usually marked planes "GUS WALKER". It is unknown if this mark was also used by him. This plane probably had an American maker. It utilizes an imported English blade.

42904T7 Spar plane   DTM MH

Wood (beech), cast steel blade, 9 1/2" long, 1 1/2" wide, signed "J. R. TOLMAN" "HANOVER" "MASS" on nose with "W.H. F" owner's mark and "WILLIAM ASH & CO" "WARRANTED" "CAST STEEL" on the blade.

Tolman worked from 1830 to 1860 and was known to be very productive in Hanover, MA in the 1840s.

61204T7 Spar plane   DTM MH

Wood (beech), cast steel blade, 9 3/8" long, 1 15/16" wide, 1 3/8" wide convex blade, signed "Gladwin & Appleton. Boston" on the plane; "Moulson Brothers Warrented Cast Steel" on the blade with cartouche.

This plane is similar in style to Tolman's spar planes and has the usual imported English cast steel blade.

http://www.davistownmuseum.org/pics/61204T7.jpg

91303T5 Spar plane   DTM MH

Wood (beech), cast steel blade, 9 5/8" long, 1 7/8" wide, 1 1/2" wide blade, signed "A Cummings Boston" and "William Ash" on the blade.

This nearly unused spar plane has a common Boston makers sign. Allen Cummings is listed as working in Boston from 1848 to 1854 (Nelson 1999, 202). William Ash was a Sheffield, England maker of plane blades.

72312LTC4 Transitional wood bottom jointer plane   DA TT (Pub)

Wood (beech) body and handles, cast iron fittings, 22" long, 3" wide, 2 3/8" wide cutting edge, signed "THE BIRMINGHAM PLANE MFG. CO. CONN.".

Courtesy of Liberty Tool Company.

Woodworking: Planes Made in Maine

Woodworking: Planes Made in Maine

111001T12   Block plane   DTM   UNK

Lignum vitae, 9" long, no blade or wedge, signed "J. P. Storer Brunswick".

Storer made planes in Brunswick, Maine, 1854 - 1873 (see the bio link to the Registry of Maine Toolmakers). He frequently used exotic tropical woods for his planes.

http://www.davistownmuseum.org/publications/volume10.html

32708T58   Curved beading plane   DTM   MH

Wood (beech), cast steel blade, 9 1/2" long, 2 3/8" wide, 1 1/2" wide blade, signed "L. S. SOULE" "WALDOBORO" "ME." and on the blades "Wm ASH & CO." in an arc with "WARRANTED" "CAST STEEL" below it.

Lewis S. Soule worked in Waldoboro from 1849 - 1854.

http://www.davistownmuseum.org/pics/32708t58-1.jpg
http://www.davistownmuseum.org/publications/volume10.html

81101T1   Double sash plane   BDTM   MH

Wood (beech), cast steel blades, 9 1/2" long, 5/8" wide blades, signed on plane "B Morrill Bangor" and blades signed "James Cam".

The Registry of Maine Toolmakers (2008) lists Morrill as working in Bangor as early as 1832. (See the Dec. 4 minutes of the Bangor Mechanic's Association.) Morrill also served in the state legislature. Morrill's planes are considered rare -- this is the only known specimen of a Morrill double sash and its crisp signature and mint condition make it an important artifact from the boomtown years of Bangor. This plane also illustrates the reliance on English cast steel as late as the 1830s.

http://www.davistownmuseum.org/bioJamesCam.htm
http://www.davistownmuseum.org/publications/volume10.html

032203T11   Molding plane   DTM   MH

Wood (beech), cast steel blade, 9 1/2" long, 1 5/7" wide concave blade, signed "B.MORRILL BANGOR".

Though Morrill manufactured hand planes between 1832 and 1851 in Bangor, his molding planes wouldn't have been unexpected in a c. 1880 carpenters' tool box in Portland, Maine, the provenance of this plane.

http://www.davistownmuseum.org/pics/032203t11.jpg
http://www.davistownmuseum.org/publications/volume10.html

061905T1   Plane   DTM   MH

Wood (beech), cast steel blade, 7 3/4" long, 2 1/4" wide at one end tapering to 1 1/2"wide, signed "D. FULLER" and "B" on the end. "A. WALDRON" "B.G. ROBINSON" on the other end. The blade is marked "Hallorhan" "SHEFFIELD" and "CAST STEEL".

D. Fuller is a Maine planemaker from Gardiner. The other marks are from owners. The blade is English.

http://www.davistownmuseum.org/publications/volume10.html

Woodworking: Planes Made in Maine

6405T2   Rabbet plane   DTM   MH

Wood (beech), steel blade, 14 1/4" long, 7/8" wide, 5 1/2" high, 1" wide double blades, signed "A. WALDRON" and on label "D. Fuller, Gardiner".

David Fuller, b. 1795, made planes beginning in 1829 and was particularly active in West Gardiner, ME, in the mid-1850s. A. Waldron is an owner's mark and is stamped twice on the top, twice on one end, and once on the other end. This is a typical boat shop rabbet plane by a prolific Maine maker.

http://www.davistownmuseum.org/pics/6405T2.jpg
http://www.davistownmuseum.org/publications/volume10.html

080704T1   Razee plane   LSS   MHC-D

Wood (beech), cast steel blade, 22 1/2" long, 2 1/2" wide, 6" high, signed "C A Spear" on plane with a Masonic symbol, "Moulson Brothers Warranted Cast Steel" on blade.

C. A. Spear was a local planemaker, probably in Warren, ME. This is a generic general purpose ships' joiner fore plane typical of 19th century Maine shipyards. Note the imported English blade. It is on loan to the museum from James Hill.

http://www.davistownmuseum.org/pics/080704t1_p1.jpg
http://www.davistownmuseum.org/pics/080704t1_p2.jpg

6405T4   Rounding plane   DTM   MH

Wood (beech), steel blades, 9" long, 1 1/4" wide with two 1 1/4" wide convex blades, signed "I. Spear".

Possibly, this plane was made by a member of the Spear family of Thomaston and Warren, Maine. Pollak (2001) lists an M. Spear center bead, c. 1840 - 1850 with a similar wedge profile.

http://www.davistownmuseum.org/publications/volume10.html

TBW1005   Spar plane   DTM   MH

Wood (beech), 9 7/16" long, 2 1/4" wide, signed "L.S. SOULE WALDOBORO ME." also signed "J.R.B. BULL" in much smaller print.

It has no blade and a replaced wedge. Pollack (2001) lists L. S. Soule, born 1813, as working 1849-54 in Waldoboro, ME. We are not sure what the correct name of this plane is. This convex plane also has a chamfer on one side, but it appears to have been used for making spars or rails.

http://www.davistownmuseum.org/pics/tbw1005.jpg
http://www.davistownmuseum.org/pics/tbw1005p2.jpg

070705T1   Tongue and groove plane   DTM   TB

Wood (beech), cast steel blade, 15 3/4" long, 3 1/2" wide, 7" high, 2 1/4" wide blade, signed "LSHOREY"; "WILLIAM ASH & Co" "WARRANTED" and "CAST STEEL" on blade.

This plane was found in a Bath, Maine area Kennebec River boatyard (Leon Robbins Collection). The wedge has been replaced. L. Shorey is not listed in DATM (Nelson 1999).

Woodworking: Saws

ID #   Status   Location

Woodworking: Saws

10700T1 **Backsaw**   DTM   MH

Spring steel, brass, and wood, 15 3/4" long with 12" blade, signed "NOOLE STANIFORTH & CO. SHEFFIELD" and "DOUBLE REFINED SPRING WARRANTED" with the brass signed "H. DISSTON & SONS PHILADA".

English-made spring steel has been processed by Henry Disston & Co. into a saw. The marks on this saw are a puzzle because H. Disston & Sons is a later signature and by this time Disston was producing his own cast and spring steel.

http://www.davistownmuseum.org/pics/10700t1_p2.jpg
http://www.davistownmuseum.org/bioDisston.htm

913108T34A **Backsaw**   DTM   MH

Cast steel, solid brass ferrule, and wood, 10 1/8" long, signed "BEARDSHAW" "& SON" "CAST STEEL".

This is a company that was located in Sheffield, England.

913108T45A **Backsaw**   DTM   MH

Malleable iron frame, steel cutting blade, iron ferrule, and rosewood handle, 13 1/2" long, 5" long handle, signed "CH WILLARD" on top of "D (T) BATES".

It is possible these are owner's marks on the saw. DATM (Nelson 1999, 862) lists a C. H. Willard 2nd of Townsend, VT, 1884-1886 as a rake-maker.

4105T2 **Backsaw**   DTM   MH

Shear steel, wood, and brass, 17" long, 12" blade, signed "BARBER & GENN" and "German steel".

A nice example of an English backsaw; the solid brass nut suggests it is mid-19th century. German ironmongers who immigrated to England (Bertram, etc.) perfected the art of making shear steel from bundled blister steel in the late 17th century. All saws and other tools marked German steel in English are made of English shear steel. True German steel is made from firing or decarburizing cast iron, also known as the "continental" method of making steel (Barraclough 1984), and is never marked "German" steel.

http://www.davistownmuseum.org/pics/4105t2.jpg

72801T15 **Hand saw**   DTM   MH

Cast steel and brass, 23 5/8" long, 19 5/8" 8 point (to the inch) blade, signed "F Dowst Boston Warrented Cast Steel".

No Dowst is listed in DATM (Nelson 1999). Was he a Boston hardware dealer who imported English saws and put his own mark on them? The brass medallion is an eagle, marked "Warranted Superior". Is this an unmarked Henry Disston saw?

71908T2 **Hand saw**   DA   UNK

Steel, brass, and wood, 10.5" long, 5" wide, signed "Henry Disston & Sons" in a curve, "Cast steel Philad'a Warranted", and faintly "A.J.Wilkinson & Co.".

http://www.davistownmuseum.org/bioWilkinson.html
http://www.davistownmuseum.org/bioDisston.htm

Historic Maritime IV (1840-1865): The Early Industrial Revolution

Woodworking: Saws

TJD1003   Keyhole saw   DTM   MH

Saw steel and wood, 10 1/2" long, signed "HARVEY W. PEACE BROOKLYN NY" on the saw brass with an arm and a hammer insignia.

DATM (Nelson 1999) lists Peace as being a saw and ice saw-maker c. 1870. Saws with his mark resurface frequently.

121112T5   Keyhole saw   DTM   TT

Cast steel, brass, wood, 18 1/2" long, 14 1/2" long blade, signed "Wm McNiece Philad" "Cast steel".

This saw was probably made pre-1865 given the solid brass attachment nuts and the "cast steel" mark. DATM (Nelson 1999, 530) lists McNiece as working from 1859 to 1882.

TJD1007   Pad saw   DTM   MH

Reforged steel, 8 3/4" long, blade 3 1/2" long, unsigned, c. 1860.

The blade is made from a recycled hack saw blade.

TCW3000   Pad saw   DTM   MH

Steel, brass, and wood, 9 1/4" long including the handle, unsigned.

Is the delicate blade on this pad saw blacksmith-made?

81602T12   Rip saw   DTM   MH

Cast steel with applewood (?) handle and solid brasses, 31 5/8" long, 28" blade, signed "Chas Grass & Sons St. Phillips Works Sheffield Improved Patent Wonder Spring".

The signature is repeated on the brass. The blade has a detailed fleur de lie underlined by TAY. The owner has signed it "F HEANEY". Perhaps it was brought to New England by an Irish immigrant. This is a classic example of an English-made and imported tool of the best quality.

71401T2   Rip saw   DTM   MH

Steel, wood, and brass, signed with the telltale eagle medallion of an early factory-made Henry Disston saw.

http://www.davistownmuseum.org/bioDisston.htm

8912LTC1   Tenon saw   DA   TT (Pub)

Cast steel, brass, wood (beech), 15" long, 10" cutting edge, 2 1/4" tall blade, 10 teeth per inch, signed "R. GROVES & SONS SHEFFIELD" "Cast Steel ELASTIC STEEL TEMPER WARRANTED".

This tenon or back saw has an unusual mark.

2213T1   Virginia pattern crosscut saw   DTM   MH

Spring steel, cast iron, wood (rosewood), 51" long, 7" long handles, unsigned.

Wrenches

Wrenches

102904T6   Adjustable wrench   DTM   MH

Drop-forged iron and steel, 13 1/4" long, 3 3/4" long and 1 1/8" wide jaws, signed "R".

This mid-19th century factory-made wrench is one of the largest and most sculptural of the twisted handled wrenches first made by the Owsley Bros & Marble (Cope 1993, 172, 191), patented in 1883 by Frederick Seymour. Later these Acme style wrenches were made by George Marble himself, 1887-88; then Capitol Wrench Co. until 1893; and by Whitman & Barnes after 1893. All of these Acme style wrenches, however, were signed by their makers, have clearly serrated adjustable nuts, and are smaller in size than this monster. This wrench has only the one "R" mark and shows more hand-work than the typical factory-made Acme, a not uncommon tool. It suggests a smith-made prototype, which then would have been patented and manufactured in a more sophisticated version by George Marble in Chicago in 1883. Did he find a wrench like this back in New England and bring it west?

http://www.davistownmuseum.org/pics/102904t6.jpg

22311T8   Carriage spoke wrench   DTM   TT

Drop-forged malleable iron with a wooden handle, 5 1/2" long, signed "FORGED" "PORTLAND ME.".

The trademark is obscured. Part of the Robert Sullivan Collection donation.

TCZ3000   Monkey wrench   DTM   MH

Drop-forged iron, wood handle, 11 7/8" long, signed "L. COES PATEN__" (date obscured) and on the second side "____ BOSTON & WORCESTER", probably c. 1835 - 1840.

This wrench appears to be one of the earliest versions of the famous Coes monkey wrench; Loring Coes patented his first wrench on April 16, 1841. The wrench has characteristics of the late 18th century or early 19th century hand-forged wrenches in the Davistown Museum collection, particularly in the way the handle is manufactured. According to Herb Page <mroldwrench@mchsi.com> "During the period of 1848 to 1852 the firm of L & A.G. Coes contracted with the firm of Ruggles, Nourse & Mason on a 5 year term to market the entire production of wrenches produced by this fledgling firm. R.N.& M. had branches in both Worcester & Boston and the wrenches produced during this time period were stamped with 1) "L. Coes Patent", 2) "Ruggles, Nourse & Mason" if space permitted, depending on size of wrench and 3) "Boston & Worcester" indicating the sales outlets of the marketing firm. These wrenches were manufactured in Worcester at the firm of L & A. G. Coes and the particular marking referred to is indicative of early production during the above mentioned dates. These are quite rare and have a distinctive circular insert in the working face of the lower jaw which is in line with the adjusting screw. Coes wrenches of this era are quite rare and desirable among antique wrench collectors."

http://www.davistownmuseum.org/bioCoes.htm

11301T12   Monkey wrench   BDTM   MH

Drop-forged iron and wood, 4 5/8" long, signed "L Coes & Co Pat Mar 29 1868".

Loring and his brother Aury Gates Coes had been in the wool machine business until 1839. This is the highly sought-after smallest size of the many Coes wrenches.

http://www.davistownmuseum.org/pics/11301t12.jpg
http://www.davistownmuseum.org/bioCoes.htm

Historic Maritime IV (1840-1865): The Early Industrial Revolution

Wrenches

8912T9   **Offset open box wrench**   DTM   TT

Cast iron, 9 7/8" long, 5/16" thick, 1" and 1 3/16" ends, signed "W.C. HASLAM".

The mark probably belongs to an owner. This tool has obvious signs of file-finishing and forging.

TCZ1008   **Open ended wrench**   DTM   MH

Forged iron, 7 1/2" long, 5/8" and 3/4" ends, signed "YORK M. Co", c. 1850 - 1860.

This maker is not listed in DATM (Nelson 1999).

41203T2H   **Open ended wrench**   DTM   MH

Forged steel, 3/4", signed "<-- 3/4 C. Drew & Co. 3/4 -->".

http://www.davistownmuseum.org/bioDrew.htm

52603T16   **Open ended wrench**   DTM   MH

Drop-forged iron, 6 10/16" long, signed "YORK Co.".

TCZ1006A   **Open ended wrenches (8)**   DTM   MH

Drop-forged iron, signed "W. C. HASLAM" on two of them, 1840 - 1875.

Eight open ended wrenches typical of mid-19th century mills and workshops.

http://www.davistownmuseum.org/pics/tcz1006a.jpg

7602T6   **Screw adjusted locking nut wrench**   DTM   MH

Cast steel, 6 1/2" long, 2 1/8" wide, 1/2" thick, unsigned.

8912T2   **S-curve open box wrench**   DTM   TT

Cast steel, 8 3/4" long, 3/8" thick, 5/8" and 11/16" ends, signed "G. EDGCUMBE".

No Edgcumbe is listed in DATM (Nelson 1999).

31811T32   **Tap wrench**   DTM   TT

Forged malleable iron, 19 1/4" long, 1/2" square hole in the center, unsigned.

This handmade tool could be a bolt header, but more likely was used as a wrench.

31811T8   **Tap wrench**   DTM   TT

Forged malleable iron, 6" long, 5/16" wide, the center is flattened to 1" x 1" with a 1/4" square hole, unsigned.

It was hand-forged.

Historic Maritime IV (1840-1865): The Early Industrial Revolution

Wrenches

31501T2   **Wrench**   DTM   MH

Drop-forged steel, 14" long, signed "E RIPLEY'S PATENT APRIL 7, 1857".

DATM (Nelson 1999) lists E. Ripley as working from prior to 1857 to 1865, location unknown. This may be the only known specimen of this wrench. Ripley's patent may be seen here: http://www.google.com/patents/US16997?printsec=drawing&dq=apr+7+1857+ripley&ei=JY50T46vF6 Ol0AWHu7n6Dw#v=onepage&q=apr%207%201857%20ripley&f=false

090109T7   **Wrench**   DTM   MH

Drop-forged steel and wood, 11 3/4" long closed, 2 3/8" wide head, unsigned.

ID #   Status   Location

Machinists' Tools

52712LTC3   **Combination adjustable plumb and level**   DA   TT (Pub)

Grey cast iron, steel, nickel plating, japanned finish, 12" long, 2 1/4" x 13/16", signed "STANLEY No 36 PAT'D.8-486-23.96".

Courtesy of Liberty Tool Co.

041505T38   **Die**   DTM   MH

Steel, 2 5/16" by 2 5/16" top, 2 3/4" high, signed "G. S. PAGET" "CO." "-BOSTON-" and "WOOD.".

The die stamps: "ALBEMARLE" "GOLF CLUB" "INCORPORATED 1800" and has a thistle mark. There is no Paget listed in DATM (Nelson 1999). This die was formerly owned by C. D. Evans Co. of Allston, MA, a button maker from Boston. Our curator grew up just down the street from the Albemarle golf course in Newtonville, MA.

http://www.davistownmuseum.org/pics/041505T38_p2.jpg
http://www.davistownmuseum.org/pics/041505T38_p1.jpg

33112T1   **Die stock**   DTM   TT

Cast steel, 7 3/4" long, 2 1/2" wide, signed "Wiley and Russell, MFG, CO." "Greenfield, MASS." "PAT. Aug 5, 1884" and "7/16, 1/32, 14".

The working dates for this company are from 1872 - 1912. Then they became part of the Greenfield Tap and Die Corp. This patent was assigned to them by Albert J. Smart of Greenfield. It may be viewed at:
http://www.google.com/patents?id=LWZAAAAAEBAJ&pg=PA2&dq=Aug+5,+1884+die+stock&hl=en&sa=X&ei=g6SZT7PxCMeZ0QWz_oDmBQ&ved=0CDIQ6AEwAA#v=onepage&q=Aug%205%2C%201884%20die%20stock&f=false.

http://www.davistownmuseum.org/bioRussel.html

30202T7   **Machinists' jack**   DTM   MH

Steel, 4 7/8" long, extends to 8", unsigned.

Probably this tool was made in a home shop.

30202T13   **Tapping stock**   DTM   MH

Steel, 5 1/2" long, signed "Card US No 0".

This diminutive tool is a product of one of New England's most important late classic period manufacturers of taps, dies, and related tools. DATM (Nelson 1999) lists S. W. Card Mfg. Co., which was located in Mansfield, MA, as operating between 1874 - 1908 before being bought out by the Union Twist Drill Co. of Athol. The factory building in Mansfield still stands.

http://www.davistownmuseum.org/pics/30202t13.jpg
http://www.davistownmuseum.org/bioCard.htm

11301T10   **Tapping stock**   DTM   MH

Cast steel, 4 1/2" long, signed "S. W. Card Mansfield Mass".

http://www.davistownmuseum.org/bioCard.htm

The Industrial Revolution (1865f.): Classic Period of American Machinists' Tools

Machinists' Tools

62202T7   **V block**   DTM   MH

Steel and brass, 1 1/2" long, 1" wide, unsigned.

This is a fine example of the work of a tool and die maker who needed a tiny V block for work on miniatures. It was made by a machinist for a specific use.

http://www.davistownmuseum.org/pics/62202t6.jpg

Measuring Tools

10910T2   **Adjustable calipers**   DTM   MH

Tempered alloy steel, 5" long, 2 3/4" wide, signed "PAT.FEB. 14, 1888" "STEVENS A. & T. CO. ****
FALLS, MA" and "F.A. SKELTON" (owner's mark), c. 1888.

The unreadable portion of the signature should be "Chicopee Falls". Donated by the Swenson family.

http://www.davistownmuseum.org/pics/10910t2web2.jpg
http://www.davistownmuseum.org/pics/10910t2web1.jpg

10910T3   **Adjustable calipers**   DTM   MH

Tempered alloy steel, 3 1/8" long, 2" wide, signed "PAT'D. FEB 14, 1888" "J. STEVENS A. & T. Co. CHICOPEE FALLS, MASS", c. 1888.

Donated by the Swenson family.

http://www.davistownmuseum.org/pics/10910t3web1.jpg
http://www.davistownmuseum.org/pics/10910t3web2.jpg

21201T11   **Adjustable calipers**   DTM   MH

Tempered alloy steel, 6 1/8" long, signed "J. Steven A & T Co. Chicopee Falls Mass".

This signature is one of three variations listed in DATM (Nelson 1999, 757) for this prolific maker of bits, calipers, dividers, levels, machinist tools, and guns, 1864 - 1903. In 1903 they were bought out by L.S. Starrett.

TJS1301   **Adjustable calipers (3)**   DTM   MH

Tempered alloy steel, 3 1/4" long, signed "US 48610568" on wrench.

http://www.davistownmuseum.org/pics/tjs1301.jpg

101701T16   **Adjustable die stock**   DTM   MH

Drop-forged steel, 13 5/8" long, signed "J. M. King & Co. Waterford NY No 42".

DATM (Nelson 1999) lists this company in Waterford from 1887 - 1910. They made dies, pliers, and taps; these tools are encountered frequently.

51100T14A   **Adjustable die stocks (2)**   DTM   MH

Drop-forged steel, 10 7/8" and 14 3/8" long, signed "J. M. King & Co. Waterford, NY".

The Industrial Revolution (1865f.): Classic Period of American Machinists' Tools

Measuring Tools

83102T9   **Adjustable dividers**   DTM   MH

Tempered alloy steel, 7" long, signed " L W POND" and "WORCESTER MASS PAT'd Sept'26 1867".

Lucius W Pond made calipers, dividers, and machinists' tools from 1859 - 1884. This caliper is a very uncommon tool. It was patented by Edward Wright and also later made by the Wright Machine Co. of Worcester. Pond's primary products were large machine tools, primarily planers (Nelson 1999, 627).

42602T6   **Adjustable dividers**   DTM   MH

Tempered alloy steel, 8" long, signed "J Stevens A & T Co Chicopee Falls Mass USA".

Formerly the J Stevens & Company, they changed their name to Stevens Arms & Tool Co. in 1886. Always a prolific maker of guns, their hand tools are sought after examples of the classic period of American machinists' tools.

81101T18A   **Adjustable dividers**   DTM   MH

Tempered alloy steel, brass, 5 3/4" long, signed "Peck Stow & Wilcox" and "6".

Peck, Stow & Wilcox Co. began operations in Southington, CT, in 1870 (to 1950). For details on their predecessors and history, see DATM (Nelson 1999, 610). This is an excellent example of the quality of a major producer of tools during the florescence of the classic period of American machinists' tools.

http://www.davistownmuseum.org/bioPeck.html

2713LTC4   **Angle divider**   DA   TT (Pub)

Grey cast iron, steel, nickel finish, 5" blade, 7 1/4" handle, 7/8" wide, signed "30" "PAT'D - OCT - 27 - 1903".

22211T19   **Architects' scale**   DTM   TT

Boxwood, 12 3/4" long, 7/8" wide, signed "U.S. ST'D".

The mark "U.S. ST'D" refers to United States standard measurements and may indicate this was foreign-made. Part of the Robert Sullivan Collection donation.

22211T23   **Architects' scale**   DTM   TT

Boxwood, 6" long, 1" wide, 1/4" thick, signed "KEUFFEL" "& BESSER CO." "N.Y." in a circle, "1419" and a winged griffin trademark.

This rule has a metric scale and is one meter long. The Keuffel & Esser Co. was located in New York City from 1867 to 1962 (Nelson 1999, 447). Part of the Robert Sullivan Collection donation.

102100T4   **Bevel**   DTM   MH

Tempered alloy steel, 3 1/8" long, unsigned.

The Industrial Revolution (1865f.): Classic Period of American Machinists' Tools

Measuring Tools

30202T6   **Bevel square**   DTM   MH

Steel, 6 1/2" blade, 7" blade guide with 2" adjustable nut, signed "Alworth Bevel Square Rule _ _ _ as made by Stark W_ _ _ _ss USA PATENTED Aug 7, 1888".

DATM (Nelson 1999) lists a Stark Tool Co. in Waltham, Mass, operating between 1862 - 1902. They were issued a patent for a spring chuck jewelers' lathe and their lathes turn up occasionally in the Boston area. Neither Cope (1993) nor DATM list an Alworth. This particular design for a bevel square and this maker's mark have not been seen before by the curator.

http://www.davistownmuseum.org/pics/30202t6.jpg

52512T2   **Caliper gauge set**   DTM   MH

Drop-forged steel, 2 1/4" long, 1 1/8" to 1 3/8" wide, signed "P.&W. CO St'd"; the four gauges are marked 3/16, 1/4, 1/8, and 5/16.

TJR3001   **Calipers**   DTM   MH

Drop-forged iron or steel, 10 1/2" long, unsigned.

102800M2   **Calipers**   DTM   MH

Steel, 13 1/2" long, unsigned.

102800M3   **Calipers**   DTM   MHC-K

Steel, 11 3/4" long, signed by owner "W.F. Blake".

http://www.davistownmuseum.org/bioKnoxEngine.htm

102800M4   **Calipers**   DTM   MHC-K

Steel, 9 1/4" long, signed by owner "W.F. Blake".

http://www.davistownmuseum.org/bioKnoxEngine.htm

102800M5   **Calipers**   DTM   MHC-K

Steel, 6" inside, signed by owner "W.F. Blake".

http://www.davistownmuseum.org/bioKnoxEngine.htm

102800M6   **Calipers**   DTM   MHC-K

Steel, 6" outside, signed by owner "W.F. Blake".

http://www.davistownmuseum.org/bioKnoxEngine.htm

102800M7   **Calipers**   DTM   MHC-K

Steel, 6" long, signed by owner "W.F. Blake".

http://www.davistownmuseum.org/bioKnoxEngine.htm

The Industrial Revolution (1865f.): Classic Period of American Machinists' Tools

Measuring Tools

121805T26   **Calipers**   DTM   MH

Steel, 4 7/8" long, signed "E R Wharton".

No E. R. Wharton is listed in DATM (Nelson 1999).

http://www.davistownmuseum.org/pics/121805t26_p2.jpg

102100T3   **Calipers**   DTM   MH

Steel, brass, 3" long, unsigned.

032203T9   **Calipers**   DTM   MH

Tempered alloy steel, brass, 3" long, signed "J. STEVENS A & T, CO." "FEALDEN", c. 1886.

This is an exquisite example of the fine work of J. Stevens Co.

http://www.davistownmuseum.org/pics/032203t9_p2.jpg

102800M8   **Calipers**   DTM   MHC-K

Steel, 5" long, signed by owner "W.F. Blake".

http://www.davistownmuseum.org/bioKnoxEngine.htm

102100T2   **Calipers**   DTM   MH

Steel, 6" long, signed "Boker".

DATM (Nelson 1999) lists an H. Boker & Co., but does not list it as using only Boker as the mark. The working dates are 1837-1969. It was the US affiliate of a German company and imported most of its tools until purchasing the Valley Forge Cutlery Co. in 1899.

http://www.davistownmuseum.org/pics/51100t6.jpg

090508T4A   **Calipers**   DTM   MH

Steel, 5 1/2" long, signed "GEO. PLUMPTON" with an X trademark.

111001T4   **Calipers**   DTM   MH

Steel, 4 7/8" long, signed "L. W. Pond Worcester Mass PAT. Sept 24, 1867".

DATM (Nelson 1999) lists this maker as Lucius W. of the Pond Machine Co., who made larger machine tools, primarily planes. This is an exceedingly rare signature on a caliper.

111900T14   **Center finder**   DTM   MH

Tempered alloy steel, 6 5/8" long with a 6" pivoting arm, signed "The L S Starrett Co Athol Mass USA".

DATM (Nelson 1999, 751) contains historical information on L. S. Starrett Co.

http://www.davistownmuseum.org/bioStarrett.htm

The Industrial Revolution (1865f.): Classic Period of American Machinists' Tools

Measuring Tools

42912LTC17 Center gauge   DA   TT (Pub)

Tempered alloy steel, 2 1/4" long, 3/4" wide, signed "THE L.S. STARRETT CO. ATHOL, MASS. U.S.A. NO. C391" "DOUBLE DEPTH OF AMER. NAT. THREAD" "ANGLES 60 TEMPERED MADE IN U.S.A".

Courtesy of Liberty Tool Co.

41212T3   Center gauge   DTM   TT

Tool steel, 2 1/4" long, 3/4" wide, signed "Darling, Brown & Sharpe Providence, R.I." and "P.H. MAY" owner's mark.

This machinists' tool bears a rare, early mark. Courtesy of Liberty Tool Co.

http://www.davistownmuseum.org/bioBrownSharpe.htm

92212LTC1   Combination square   DA   TT (Pub)

Cast iron, drop-forged steel, 12" long, 1" wide rule, 5" x 3 1/8" x 13/16" head, signed "GOODELL-PRATT CO. GREENFIELD MASS TEMPERED MADE IN U.S.A." on rule.

This is O.R. Chaplin's 1880 patent combination square. The rule itself is not original and one head is missing.

22512LTC4   Combination square with center head and reversible   DA   TT (Pub)
protractor head

Drop-forged tempered alloy steel, glass, satin and japanned finish, 18" long, signed "BROWN & SHARPE PROVIDENCE R.I. TEMPERED NO. 4" and on center head "PATENT 2085481".

Courtesy of Liberty Tool Co.

http://www.davistownmuseum.org/bioBrownSharpe.htm

32912T1   Combination square with square head   DTM   TT-44

Drop-forged steel rule, cast iron head, 10 1/4" long, signed "DAVIS THE HARDWARE MAN BOSTON".

Davis the Hardware Man is mentioned as a vendor operating on the corner of Portland and Sudbury streets in Boston in the April, 1905 issue of Hardware Dealers' Magazine. This rule is graduated in 64ths of an inch. Courtesy of Liberty Tool Co.

TCP1005   Compass   DTM   MH

Steel, 5 1/2" long, signed "THEWLIS & CO" and "BOOTH BROTHERS DUBLIN".

DATM (Nelson 1999, 782) lists Thewlis & Co. as a maker of a small machinists' square, Boston, 1885. This compass has an 18th century English pattern with a later style manufacturer's signature.

22311T2   Compass   DTM   TT

Drop-forged tempered alloy steel, 7 1/2" long, signed in a circle "W. SCHOLLHORN NEW HAVEN, CT." and "PAT. APPLD. FOR" "3" on one leg and owner mark "G.A.O." on other leg.

Part of the Robert Sullivan Collection donation.

The Industrial Revolution (1865f.): Classic Period of American Machinists' Tools

Measuring Tools

091608T2   Compass   DTM   MH

Steel, 10 1/2" long including the two adjustable 2" long extensions, signed "SULLIVAN'S PAT" "MAR 9, 1880".

The angle of the legs can be changed by two locking mechanisms at the ends. The markings on this tool are particularly crisp and clear; the tool is in fine condition. We haven't seen this model of calipers before; this is an uncommonly encountered tool as evidenced by the fact that it is listed in DATM (Nelson 1999) without location, dates of operation, or the first name of Sullivan. DATM also notes obviously incorrect dates of 1980 as well as 1890 on previously reported specimens. Further information on the identity of Sullivan would be greatly appreciated.

32708T46   Compass   DTM   MH

Tempered alloy steel, 7 1/2" long, 8" wide, signed "THE L S STARRETT Co" and "ATHOL MASS U.S.A.".

Laroy S. Starrett Co.'s working dates were from 1880 to the present day.

http://www.davistownmuseum.org/pics/32708t46-1.jpg
http://www.davistownmuseum.org/bioStarrett.htm

22512LTC9   Depth gauge micrometer   DA   TT (Pub)

Drop-forged tempered alloy steel, 4" long, 4" wide, 1/2" high, signed "Starrett" "No. 445".

This was found in a case with 3 of the original 6 attachments and tuning wrench. Courtesy of Liberty Tool Co.

http://www.davistownmuseum.org/bioStarrett.htm

31811T11   Dividers   DTM   TT

Drop-forged tempered alloy steel, 9" long, 5/16" wide, signed "OLDENBURG" and the James Swan trademark..

http://www.davistownmuseum.org/bioSwan.html

121201T2   Dividers   DTM   MH

Tempered alloy steel, 6 3/8" long, signed "P S & W co.".

This is the mark of the famous Peck, Stow & Wilcox Co. of Southington, CT, which was organized in 1870 through the merger of a variety of companies. It was a major manufacturer of fine hand tools during and after the classic period of American tool manufacturing. DATM (Nelson 1999, 610) contains extensive historical information on this company.

http://www.davistownmuseum.org/bioPeck.html

111900T7   Dividers   DTM   MH

Tempered alloy steel, 3 3/8" long, signed "B.S. Mfg Co Prov. R.I. USA".

This is made by Brown & Sharpe, a major competitor of Laroy Starrett in Athol, MA. The first mass-produced micrometer was designed by J. R. Brown in 1856.

http://www.davistownmuseum.org/bioBrownSharpe.htm

The Industrial Revolution (1865f.): Classic Period of American Machinists' Tools

Measuring Tools

1302T3   Dividers   DTM   MH

Tempered alloy steel, 5 1/2" long, signed "Mfg by Charles P. Fay Springfield Mass USA".

Prior to starting his own company, Fay worked for Steven Arms & Tool Co., J. Stevens & Co., and L S Starrett. "Fay assigned a number of patents to both Starrett and Stevens while working for them." DATM (Nelson 1999, 274). He had his own company from 1884 - 1887 then sold his business to L. S. Starrett.

http://www.davistownmuseum.org/bioFayCharles.html

111900T12   Dividers   DTM   MH

Tempered alloy steel, 3 13/16" long, signed "Starrett Athol Mass".

DATM (Nelson 1999, 751) contains historical information on L. S. Starrett Co.

http://www.davistownmuseum.org/bioStarrett.htm

122002T1   Dividers   DTM   MH

Tempered alloy steel, 4" long, signed "Stevens & Co.".

DATM (Nelson 1999, 757) contains historical information on Joshua Stevens & Co.

032203T8   Dividers   DTM   MH

Tempered alloy steel, brass, 9 3/4" long, signed "J STEVENS A & T CO. Chicopee Falls Mass USA".

J. Stevens began making calipers and dividers in 1864. They changed their name to J. Stevens Arms & Tool Co. in 1886. These high quality American-made dividers are typical of American-made tools appearing in tool kits at this time.

http://www.davistownmuseum.org/pics/032203t8_p2.jpg

32912T5   Dividers   DTM   TT-46

Tempered alloy steel, 9 1/2" long, signed "J. STEVENS A. & T. CO. CHICOPEE FALLS, MASS. U.S.A.".

These dividers have sliding steel points. The maker's mark indicates that these were made by Joshua Stevens Arms and Tool Company, 1864-1886. Courtesy of Liberty Tool Co.

041505T32   Double calipers   DTM   MH

Steel, 8" long, 3 1/2" wide, signed "J. HOOD".

DATM (Nelson 1999) lists a John Hood Co. of Boston as a maker of farriers' hoof levels. There is a William J. Hood Mfg. Co. of Rhode Island, circa 1889, that made hand and bench screws. We have not previously seen any J. Hood measuring tools.

http://www.davistownmuseum.org/pics/041505t32.jpg

The Industrial Revolution (1865f.): Classic Period of American Machinists' Tools

Measuring Tools

111900T9   Double square   DTM   MH

Tempered alloy steel, 4" rule, signed "No 13", "The L.S.S. CO.", and "HARDENED NO 1".

The accompanying bevel blade is not available. DATM (Nelson 1999, 751) contains historical information on L. S. Starrett Co. of Athol, MA.

http://www.davistownmuseum.org/pics/111900T9.jpg
http://www.davistownmuseum.org/bioStarrett.htm

22512LTC8   Drill and wire gauge   DA   TT (Pub)

Drop-forged tempered alloy steel, 6 1/4" long, 2 5/16" wide, signed "TIME SAVER. DRILL & WIRE GAUGE. CHART FOR MACHINE SCREW TAPS. THE L.S. STARRETT CO. ATHOL, MASS. U.S.A. No. 186".

Courtesy of Liberty Tool Co.

http://www.davistownmuseum.org/bioStarrett.htm

22603T1   Engine rule   DA   UNK

Steel, 36" long, 10" wide, 8" high, signed "DAVID W MANN COMPANY" and "102" on a paper label.

Follow the bio link to see the photographs of this tool. It is located in the Banks Garage, ask the person on duty for directions to find the tool and also the documentation in the CSET library.

http://www.davistownmuseum.org/BioPics/Mann2.JPG
http://www.davistownmuseum.org/bioMann.html

62112LTC1   Firm joint hermaphrodite calipers   DA   TT (Pub)

Tool steel, 6 1/4" long, signed "THE L.L.S. STARRETT CO. ATHOL, MASS. U.S.A. No. 248".

Courtesy of Liberty Tool Co.

22211T22   Folding rule   DTM   TT

Boxwood, 39.37" long, 5/8" wide, 3/32" thick, unsigned.

This rule has a metric scale and is one meter long. Part of the Robert Sullivan Collection donation.

22211T9   Folding rule   DTM   TT

Silver plated plastic composite, 12" long (extended), 3" long (folded), 5/16" wide, 1/8" thick, unsigned.

The body is a plastic composite made to mimic ivory. The metal is brass plated. Part of the Robert Sullivan Collection donation.

22211T11   Folding rule   DTM   TT

Boxwood and brass, 12" long (extended), 3" long (folded), 5/16" wide, 1/8" thick, signed "No 70" on both sides.

This is a Stanley No. 70 rule. Part of the Robert Sullivan Collection donation.

http://www.davistownmuseum.org/bioStanley.html

ID #   Status   Location

Measuring Tools

22211T16   Folding rule   DTM   TT

Boxwood and brass, 24" long (extended), 6" long (folded), 1/2" wide, 1/8" thick, signed "STANLEY No 62" "STANLEY RULE" "& LEVEL CO." "NEW BRITAIN, CONN." "USA" "WARRENTED" "BOXWOOD".

This is a Stanley No. 62 rule. Part of the Robert Sullivan Collection donation.

http://www.davistownmuseum.org/bioStanley.html

22211T10   Folding rule   DTM   TT

Boxwood and brass, 12" long (extended), 3" long (folded), 5/16" wide, 1/8" thick, signed "No 65" on both sides.

This is a Stanley No. 65 rule. Part of the Robert Sullivan Collection donation.

http://www.davistownmuseum.org/bioStanley.html

22211T12   Folding rule   DTM   TT

Boxwood and brass, 24" long (extended), 6" long (folded), 5/8" wide, 1/8" thick, signed "STANLEY" "NEW BRITAIN" "CONN. U.S.A." and "No 7" on both sides.

This is a Stanley No. 7 rule. Part of the Robert Sullivan Collection donation.

http://www.davistownmuseum.org/bioStanley.html

31908T35   Framing square   DTM   MH

Steel, 24" long, 14" wide, signed "S. HAYES" "PATENT" "WARRANTED" and "STEEL".

There is no S. Hayes in DATM (Nelson, 1999).

83102T5   Gauge guide   DTM   MH

Paper mounted on board, unsigned.

This gauge guide is printed on two sides and lists the following standards: USG (United States Standard Gauge), TDG (Twist Drill & Steel Wire Gauge), SWG (Stubs Wire Gauge), B&S (Brown & Sharpe or American Standard Wire Gauge), BWG (Birmingham or Stubs Iron Wire Gauge), NWG (National or Roebling or Washburn & Moen Gauge) and MWG (Music Wire Gauge).

30101T1   Gear tooth vernier caliper   LPC   MHC

Tempered alloy steel in leather box, 4 1/15" long, 4 1/4" high, signed "Brown & Sharpe Mfg. Co. Providence RI USA 20.2DP".

This tool is representative of the florescence of the New England toolmaker and is made by L. S. Starrett's principal 20th century competitor. The English measure caliper is an uncommon Brown & Sharpe product.

http://www.davistownmuseum.org/pics/30101t1.jpg
http://www.davistownmuseum.org/bioBrownSharpe.htm

The Industrial Revolution (1865f.): Classic Period of American Machinists' Tools

Measuring Tools

71912LTC1   Go nogo inspection gauges

DA   TT (Pub)

Drop-forged steel, japanned finish, signed "BROWN & SHARPE MFG. CO. PROVIDENCE, R.I. U.S.A.".

The set includes a 1 11/16" long, 0.6865" wide tool; a 1 1/4", 0.874" wide tool; a 3 5/8" long, 1.499" wide tool; a 4" long, 1.749" wide tool; a 4" long, 1.750" wide tool; and a 4 1/2" long, 3.000" wide tool. The Brown & Sharpe catalogs show these tools as being available made-to-order in a variety of precise sizes. Courtesy of Liberty Tool Company.

http://www.davistownmuseum.org/bioBrownSharpe.htm

72002T4   Height gauge

LPC   MH-I

Steel, 10" high, 6" scale, signed "L S Starrett Co. Athol Mass USA" "Athol Mass" "Made in USA" "No 354", 1900.

This is a fine boxed example of a late classic period machinist tool formerly owned by the Raytheon Co.

http://www.davistownmuseum.org/bioStarrett.htm

30911T4   Hermaphrodite dividers

DTM   TT

Drop-forged tempered alloy steel, 6" long, signed "W. C. HOWATT" a hand-stamped owner's mark.

102501T1   Inclinometer level

LPC   MH

Drop-forged iron and steel, brass, 6" long, 14/16" wide, 2 1/2" high, 2" diameter meter, signed "DAVIS LEVEL & TOOL Co" and "PAT.SEP 17, 1867" with owner's signature "J.F. McCABE".

This tool is also referred to as a mantle clock level. DATM (Nelson 1999, 214) has historical information on this company.

http://www.davistownmuseum.org/pics/102501t1_p3.jpg
http://www.davistownmuseum.org/bioDavis.htm

111900T5   Inside calipers

DTM   MH

Tempered alloy steel, 5" long, signed "STARRETT ATHOL MASS USA".

DATM (Nelson 1999, 751) contains historical information on L. S. Starrett Co.

http://www.davistownmuseum.org/bioStarrett.htm

111900T6   Inside calipers

DTM   MH

Tempered alloy steel, 2 3/4" long, signed "B.S. Mfg Co Prov. R.I. USA".

Inside calipers are used to measure the diameter of a cylindrical hole. They have rounded tips that are bent away from each other.

http://www.davistownmuseum.org/bioBrownSharpe.htm

The Industrial Revolution (1865f.): Classic Period of American Machinists' Tools

Measuring Tools

41302T11   Inside calipers   DTM   MH

Tempered alloy steel, 3 1/2" long, 1 3/8" wide when closed, signed "J. Stevens A & T Co. Chicopee Falls Mass PAT March 9 1886".

These are finely made beveled spring calipers. Joshua Stevens, one of the principal tool manufacturers of the classic period, worked in Chicopee, MA, from 1864 to 1903. Numerous patents are listed. They changed their name to Stevens Arms & Tool Co. in 1886. This company had a close association with the Davis Level & Tool Co. of Springfield, MA (1875 - 1892) with respect to the R. Hathaway patented square (4 Dec. 1866). (Nelson 1999, 757, 214).

62202T8   Inside calipers   DTM   MH

Drop-forged steel, 3 7/8" long, signed "Murphy".

No Murphy is listed by DATM (Nelson 1999) as a maker of calipers. Who was Murphy? Where and when did he make calipers? The style of the calipers is mid- to late 19th century.

http://www.davistownmuseum.org/pics/62202t6.jpg

22712LTC1   Inside micrometer calipers   DA   TT (Pub)

Drop-forged tempered alloy steel, 4 3/4" long, 1 1/4" wide, 4 3/4" high, signed "THE L.S. STARRETT CO. ATHOL, MASS. U.S.A.".

This is the No. 124 set. Courtesy of Liberty Tool Co.

http://www.davistownmuseum.org/bioStarrett.htm

TJG1001   Lathe tool holder   DTM   MH

Drop-forged iron with steel cutter, 6" long with 2" long 1/4" cutter, signed "MACHINISTS TOOL CO PROV. R.I. PATENTED MAY 26, 1868".

This machine-made tool is characteristic of the arrival of the era of mass-produced hand tools.

http://www.davistownmuseum.org/bioMachinistool.html

22311T1   Level   DTM   TT

Drop-forged tempered alloy steel, 12 1/4" long, 2 3/4" wide, 1 1/2" deep, signed "THE L.S.STARRETT Co" "ATHOL, MASS. U.S.A." with a border.

Part of the Robert Sullivan Collection donation.

http://www.davistownmuseum.org/bioStarrett.html

041712T1   Level   DTM   TT

Tempered alloy steel, glass, 12" long, 3/4" wide, 1 7/8" high, signed "THE L.S.S. Co. ATHOL MASS U.S.A.".

This machinists' level dates from 1940 - 1950.

http://www.davistownmuseum.org/bioStarrett.htm

The Industrial Revolution (1865f.): Classic Period of American Machinists' Tools

Measuring Tools

120907T2   **Level**   DTM   TT

Drop-forged iron and steel, brass, 24" long, 2 3/4" wide, signed "DAVIS LEVEL & TOOL Co" and "PAT SEP 17, 1867".

It has an intricately worked body and an adjustable dial with 90 degrees of movement. Davis' patent 68961 may be viewed here: http://www.google.com/patents?id=do4AAAAAEBAJ&printsec=frontcover&dq=68961&hl=en&sa=X&ei =s-nZT97ZO4fFswbP0tn6Bw&ved=0CDcQ6AEwAA

http://www.davistownmuseum.org/pics/120907t2_p2.jpg
http://www.davistownmuseum.org/bioDavis.htm

13102T1   **Level**   DTM   MH

Wood (rosewood), brass, 8" long, 1 " wide, signed "STRATTON BROTHERS GREENFIELD MASS" and "PATENTED JULY 16 1872 OCT 4 1887" and "No 10" on the end.

Edwin and Charles Stratton's patents may be viewed here: http://www.google.com/patents?id=L3BBAAAAEBAJ&pg=PA2&dq=JULY+16++1872+level&hl=en&sa =X&ei=IOrZT4- 3HsPetAakoeCLCA&ved=0CDoQ6AEwAQ#v=onepage&q=JULY%2016%20%201872%20level&f=fal se

http://www.davistownmuseum.org/pics/13102t1-3.jpg
http://www.davistownmuseum.org/bioStratton.html

92911T8   **Level**   DTM   MH

Rosewood and brass, 26 1/4" long, 3" wide, 1 1/4" high, signed "STRATTON BROTHERS" "GREENFIELD, MASS" "PATENTED July 16, 1872" and with an eagle mark.

Edwin A. and Charles M. Stratton began their level business in 1869 (DATM 1999).

http://www.davistownmuseum.org/bioStratton.html

71903T9   **Level**   DTM   MH

Drop-forged iron, brass, 9" long, signed "L. S. Starrett & Co Athol Mass Pat Applied For".

This appears to be the first model of this particular size level.

http://www.davistownmuseum.org/bioStarrett.htm

52408T4   **Level**   DTM   MH-O

Wood, glass, brass, 2 9/16" long, 1 1/2" wide, 3" high, unsigned.

This is a small circular level. It was made by Leon Robbins of Bath, ME.

http://www.davistownmuseum.org/bioLeon.html

The Industrial Revolution (1865f.): Classic Period of American Machinists' Tools

Measuring Tools

72002T2   **Level**   DTM   MH

Wood (cherry?), 12" long, 1" wide, signed "E. T. BURROWES CO." "PORTLAND, ME." on brass plate, 1910 (?).

This is a mundane late example of an everyday household tool made by one of Maine's most prolific toolmakers.

http://www.davistownmuseum.org/pics/72002t2_p1.jpg
http://www.davistownmuseum.org/publications/volume10.html

92911T7   **Level**   DTM   MH

Rosewood and brass, 32" long, 3 1/2" wide, 1 1/2" high, signed "MCFERNALD" owner stamp on the brass ends.

One spirit bubble.

92911T3   **Level**   DTM   MH

Rosewood and brass, 30" long, 3 3/8" wide, 1 3/8" high, signed "J. W. HARMON 65 HAVERHILL ST" in a circle with "BOSTON MASS." inside the circle.

It has two spirit bubbles. DATM (Nelson 1999, 355) indicates that John W. Harmon made levels and rules from 1860 to 1907. He had two patents.

92911T5   **Level**   DTM   MH

Rosewood with brass, 28" long, 3 3/8" wide, 1 5/16" high, signed "MILLIKEN & STACKPOLE" "BOSTON, MASS".

There are two spirit bubbles.

92911T6   **Level**   DTM   MH

Rosewood and brass, 24" long, 3 1/2" wide, 1 1/2" high, signed "H. M. POOL" "EASTON, MASS" and with an eagle and USA style shield.

Horace Minot Pool of Easton, MA was born July 9, 1803. He made levels and other scientific instruments from 1838 until his death on Nov. 1, 1878. He also worked with his brother, John, signing tools "J. & H. M. POOL" and later with other brothers, Nahum and Harrison, as "Horace Minot Pool & Bros". (DATM 1999).

92911T4   **Level**   DTM   MH

Mahogany with brass ends, 30 1/4" long, 3 1/8" wide, 1 1/4" high, signed "STANLEY RULE & LEVEL CO" "NEW BRITAIN, CONN USA" "PAT FEB 18.90".

There are two spirit bubbles with adjustments and an adjusting screw.

http://www.davistownmuseum.org/bioStanley.htm

The Industrial Revolution (1865f.): Classic Period of American Machinists' Tools

Measuring Tools

71412LTC1 **Level with adjustable inclinometer**	DA	TT (Pub)

Cast steel, japanned finish, glass vials, 10" long, 15/16" wide, 2 1/4" high, signed "THE L.S.S. CO., ATHOL, MASS. U.S.A.".

This is the Starrett No. 133. Courtesy of Liberty Tool Company.

http://www.davistownmuseum.org/bioStarrett.htm

41203T1 **Line level**	LPC	MH

Cast iron and brass, 3 1/2" long, signed "MANUFACTURED BY L.L. DAVIS SPRINGFIELD MASS" and "37 1/2".

Leonard L. Davis made levels and planes in Springfield, MA, 1867-1875, before changing the name of his company to Davis Level & Tool Co. (1875 - 92). This is an excellent example of one of the most sought after pocket or line levels by one of the most distinguished manufacturers of the classic period of American machinists' tools.

http://www.davistownmuseum.org/pics/41203t1_p2.jpg
http://www.davistownmuseum.org/bioDavis.htm

31808SLP23 **Marking gauge**	DTM	TT

Mahogany with brass inlay, 9" long, signed "PAT. AUG. 5, 1873".

http://www.davistownmuseum.org/pics/31808slp23-3.jpg
http://www.davistownmuseum.org/pics/31808slp23-1.jpg

32708T62 **Marking gauge**	DTM	MH

Brass, rosewood, and metal plate, 7" long, unsigned.

http://www.davistownmuseum.org/pics/32708t62-1.jpg

41801T10 **Marking gauge**	DTM	MH

Steel, 2 11/16" long, unsigned.

This tiny machinists' gauge is highly unusual in its diminutive size. Probably it was owner-made.

31808SLP7 **Miter square**	DTM	TT

Steel, brass, wood, signed with obscured mark "____YN" and "____NE" and "CFW" on the handle.

http://www.davistownmuseum.org/pics/31808slp7-1.jpg
http://www.davistownmuseum.org/pics/31808slp7-2.jpg

31808SLP27 **Mortising gauge**	DTM	TT

Wood and brass, 8" long, 7" long gauge, unsigned.

http://www.davistownmuseum.org/pics/31808slp27-1.jpg
http://www.davistownmuseum.org/pics/31808slp27-2.jpg

The Industrial Revolution (1865f.): Classic Period of American Machinists' Tools

Measuring Tools

TJS1302   **Multiple angle drill gauge**   DTM   MH

Drop-forged steel, 2 1/4" long, 1 1/2" wide, signed "COFFIN & LEIGHTON SYRACUSE NY".

DATM (Nelson 1999, 177) lists Coffin & Leighton as located in Syracuse, NY from 1885 - 1901. Herbert Leighton patented a combination vernier, bevel, and square 17 Jan. 1893 and a machinists' rule 25 Aug 1885 by both he and John Coffin. In 1902 they sold their business to the Goodell Pratt Co.

111900T8   **Outside calipers**   DTM   MH

Tempered alloy steel, 2 3/4" long, signed "B.S. Mfg Co Prov. R.I. USA".

http://www.davistownmuseum.org/bioBrownSharpe.htm

041505T35   **Outside calipers**   DTM   MH

Steel, 8 5/8" closed, signed "H. A. ELLIS" and "J. P.".

There is no H. A. Ellis in DATM (Nelson 1999). Possibly these are signed by the owner.

http://www.davistownmuseum.org/pics/041505t35.jpg

111900T4   **Outside calipers**   DTM   MH

Tempered alloy steel, 5" long, signed "L S S Co. ATHOL MASS USA" with an owner's signature "M. E. Weed".

DATM (Nelson 1999, 751) contains historical information on L. S. Starrett Co.

http://www.davistownmuseum.org/bioStarrett.htm

41801T1   **Outside calipers**   DTM   MH

Steel, 4 1/2" long, signed "Athol Machine Co. Athol Mass. U.S.A.".

Originally formed by Laroy Starrett in 1868, he sold Athol in 1878. It became a competitor to L.S. Starrett Co. and he purchased it back in 1905. In "about 1882 they [Athol] either bought or founded the Standard Tool Co. as an integral division making machinist tools." DATM (Nelson 1999, 40).

http://www.davistownmuseum.org/bioStarrett.htm

92911T2   **Outside calipers**   DTM   MH

Drop-forged tempered alloy steel, 24" long, signed "H BRINTON & CO".

32802T10   **Outside calipers**   DTM   MH

Steel, 6" long, signed "W. E. TRUFANT Whitman Mass PAT Apr 18 03".

This unusual caliper includes a small 4" scale welded to the casing. It is an extremely rare late classic period machinists' tool. The patent is 726,287 of April 28, 1903, assigned to Walter E. Trufant by Frank A. Hatch of Hanson, MA. Http://www.google.com/patents?id=0X9aAAAAEBAJ&pg=PA2&dq=trufant+apr++caliper&hl=en&sa=X &ei=vMF0T_ngNoyt8QPR0OxD&sqi=2&ved=0CDIQ6AEwAA#v=onepage&q=trufant%20apr%20%20 caliper&f=false

http://www.davistownmuseum.org/pics/32802t10.jpg

The Industrial Revolution (1865f.): Classic Period of American Machinists' Tools

Measuring Tools

32802T1   **Outside calipers**   DTM   MH

Steel, 4" long, signed "Pat. Jan 4 1887" with obscured maker's mark.

The maker's mark would probably be: Davis Level & Tool Co. Springfield, Mass. It might be patent 355,430
http://www.google.com/patents?id=w1BmAAAAEBAJ&pg=PA2&dq=jan+4+1887+caliper&hl=en&sa=X
&ei=Fb90T6PtOOrU0QX1kcnyAQ&ved=0CD0Q6AEwAw#v=onepage&q=jan%204%201887%20calip
er&f=false

http://www.davistownmuseum.org/pics/32802t10.jpg
http://www.davistownmuseum.org/bioDavis.htm

111001T40   **Parallels**   DTM   MH

Steel, 2 1/2" long, unsigned.

This is a precision tool set from the classic period (or later) of the Industrial Revolution.

30911T1   **Parting tool**   DTM   TT

Tool steel, brass ferrule, and wood handle, 13" long, 6" blade, signed "J. M. McPHAIL" "1889".

A parting tool is used to cut grooves in a spindle while it is turning. It gets its name from the tool's ability to remove finished "parts".

102800T7   **Pencil compass**   DTM   MH

Drop-forged steel, 6 5/8" long, signed "WT. ATHERHEAD PATENT. REISSUED FEB 18 187?".

Patent 5,290 issued to O. E. Weatherhead in 1873 for an improvement in dividers may be viewed here:
http://www.google.com/patents?id=rNweAAAAEBAJ&pg=PA1&dq=weatherhead+dividers&hl=en&sa=
X&ei=RPHZT4jJJsratAbYovDDCA&ved=0CDUQ6AEwAA#v=onepage&q=weatherhead%20dividers&f
=false

http://www.davistownmuseum.org/pics/51100t6.jpg

32912T6   **Pencil compass**   DTM   TT-44

Tempered alloy steel, 8 1/4" long, signed "S COPELAND PAT. MAY 24, 1887".

The first letter of the maker's mark is very faint, but the patent date identifies this tool as the product of Copeland & Chamberlain, working out of Worcester, Massachusetts, from circa 1872 to 1901. The company name was changed to Copeland Hardware Mfg. Co. In 1901 (Nelson 1999, 190). Salem Copeland's patent may be viewed here:
http://www.google.com/patents?id=8dE_AAAAEBAJ&printsec=frontcover&dq=363600&hl=en&sa=X&
ei=PBC1T5nVG4GI-gaYhqX0DQ&ved=0CD0Q6AEwAg. Courtesy of Liberty Tool Co.

The Industrial Revolution (1865f.): Classic Period of American Machinists' Tools

Measuring Tools

102904T21   Radius gauge   DTM   MH

Steel, 10 1/2" wide, 6" diameter swivel, 7 1/2" high gauge on 5 1/2" x 3" raised platform, signed "VINCOTOOL CO." "DETROIT MICH." "PAT. JUNE 5-1934" "PAT. NO. 1961242" "Set diamond from this face" on gauge post.

This is an interesting and rare sculpture object from the post-classic period of the Industrial Revolution. It is one of the most modern tools in the museum's collection.

http://www.davistownmuseum.org/pics/102904t21_p1.jpg

111900T1   Rule   DTM   MH

Tempered alloy steel, 12" long, signed "L.S. STARRETT ATHOL MASS USA TEMPERED No 4".

DATM (Nelson 1999, 751) contains historical information on L. S. Starrett Co.

http://www.davistownmuseum.org/bioStarrett.htm

102100T18   Rule   DTM   MH

Steel, 6" long, signed "J. R. BROWN & SHARPE PROVIDENCE R. I. U,S, ST'D".

This signature precedes the later B S Mfg. Co. (Brown and Sharpe).

http://www.davistownmuseum.org/bioBrownSharpe.htm

041505T31   Rule   DTM   MH

Steel, 6", signed "Fleming" in script and "U. S. A." and "Fleming Machine Co." "Worcester, Mass" and "No. 1334".

Black & Decker purchased Fleming Machine Co. of Worcester in 1929 (http://www.fundinguniverse.com/company-histories/The-Black-amp;-Decker-Corporation-Company-History.html).

http://www.davistownmuseum.org/pics/041505t31_p1.jpg
http://www.davistownmuseum.org/pics/041505t31_p2.jpg

111001T5   Rule   DTM   MH

Steel, 12" long, signed "Tool Co" with a star and also marked "Spring Steel".

The star is the touchmark of the Star Tool Co. DATM (Nelson 1999) lists Star Tool Co. in Middletown, CT, 1867-1883 with another location in Providence, Rhode Island (1870-71). It manufactured bevels, levels, marking gauges, and squares. Spring steel was produced from cementation (blister) steel.

102800M11   Rule   DTM   MHC-K

Steel, signed "DB&S" and by owners "W.F. Blake" and "W. Cross".

http://www.davistownmuseum.org/bioKnoxEngine.htm

The Industrial Revolution (1865f.): Classic Period of American Machinists' Tools

Measuring Tools

41801T13   **Rule**   DTM   MH

Tool steel, 2 15/16" long, signed "HOPE & Co. PROV. R.I." on one side and "SPRING STEEL" on the other.

DATM (Nelson 1999) lists Hope & Co. as making engraving machines in 1868. No mention is made of making any other tools. This is a rare find from the early years of the Industrial Revolution.

http://www.davistownmuseum.org/bioHope.html

52603T3   **Ruler**   DTM   MH

Tempered alloy steel, 4" long, signed "UNION CALIPER. Co" "Orange Mass" "Tempered No. 4".

DATM (Nelson 1999) lists this company's working dates as 1908-1916, manufacturing machinist's tools.

30311T10   **Scale**   DTM   TT

Tool steel, 10 1/2" long, 11/16" wide, 1/8" high, signed "Brown & Sharpe Mfg Co" "Providence, R.I. U.S.A." and with their trademark LBS.

http://www.davistownmuseum.org/bioBrownSharpe.htm

3912LTC2   **Scale set**   DA   TT (Pub)

Stainless steel blades, tempered alloy steel handle, 4" long handle, 1" long and 3/4" long blades, unsigned.

This handle and set of small ruler blades is used for making precise measurements in a confined space. Courtesy of Liberty Tool Co.

22512LTC1   **Set of 3 calipers (inside, outside, and dividers)**   DA   TT (Pub)

Drop-forged tempered alloy steel, 9" long (all three), signed "THE L.S. STARRETT CO. ATHOL, MASS. U.S.A.".

This set includes inside and outside diameter measurement calipers and one set of dividers. Courtesy of Liberty Tool Co.

http://www.davistownmuseum.org/bioStarrett.htm

5412LTC6   **Shrinkage rule**   DA   TT (Pub)

Boxwood and brass, 24 1/4" long unfolded, 1 15/16" wide, signed "STANLEY RULE & LEVEL Co NEW BRITAIN CONN." "No 31.".

Courtesy of Liberty Tool Co.

http://www.davistownmuseum.org/bioStanley.htm

31808SLP18   **Sliding T bevel**   DTM   TT

Steel blade, brass trim, and lacquered rosewood handle, 10" long, 6 5/8" long handle, signed "STANLEY" "RULE & LEVEL Co" "NEW BRITAIN. CONN" "U.S.A." and "PAT. 9-6-04".

http://www.davistownmuseum.org/pics/31808slp18-1.jpg
http://www.davistownmuseum.org/bioStanley.htm

The Industrial Revolution (1865f.): Classic Period of American Machinists' Tools

Measuring Tools

31808SLP19   Sliding T bevel   DTM   TT

Steel blade, brass trim, and rosewood handle, 6" long, 4 1/2" long handle, signed "MADE IN U.S.A.".

http://www.davistownmuseum.org/pics/31808slp19-1.jpg
http://www.davistownmuseum.org/pics/31808slp19-2.jpg

22512LTC7   Small hole gage gauges   DA   TT (Pub)

Drop-forged tempered alloy steel, vinyl pouch, 2" long, signed "Starrett NO. S830F SMALL HOLE GAGES" "THE L.S. STARRETT CO. ATHOL, MASS. U.S.A.".

This is a set of 5 small hole gauges in a red vinyl pouch that measure from 0.125" to 0.500". Courtesy of Liberty Tool Co.

http://www.davistownmuseum.org/bioStarrett.htm

052611T1   Speed indicator   DTM   TT

Drop-forged nickel plated steel, 5" long, signed "L. S. STARRETT CO." "ATHOL MASS".

Speed indicators are used for measuring the turning speed of machinery such as lathes.

http://www.davistownmuseum.org/bioStarrett.htm

22311T21   Spirit level   DTM   TT

____NEED MEDIUM _____, 30" long, 3 1/2" wide, 1 1/4" thick, signed "MANUFACTURED BY L. L. DAVIS" "SPRINGFIELD, MASS." "PAT. MARCH 17, 1867".

Part of the Robert Sullivan Collection donation.

http://www.davistownmuseum.org/bioDavis.htm

52603T35   Spring calipers   DTM   MH

Steel, 5 3/16" long, 4" wide, signed "SAWYER".

This might be Sawyer Tool Co. of Athol, Fitchburg, and Ashburnham, Massachusetts, working dates 1894-1915.

http://www.davistownmuseum.org/bioSawyer.html

111412T6   Spring dividers   DTM   MH

Alloy steel, 4" long, signed "S. T. Co." "ATHOL, MASS." on one leg and "THE BOSS" on the other leg.

The Standard Tool Company used "BOSS" as a brand. They were located in Athol, MA from 1880 to 1905 (Nelson 1999, 748).

111412T5   Spring outside dividers   DTM   MH

Tempered alloy steel, 3" long, signed "THE L. S. S. Co." "ATHOL, MASS." "PAT JUN. 2: 85".

Charles P. Fay's patent 319,215 can be viewed here:
http://www.datamp.org/patents/search/advance.php?pn=319215&id=12736&set=6.

http://www.davistownmuseum.org/bioStarrett.htm

The Industrial Revolution (1865f.): Classic Period of American Machinists' Tools

Measuring Tools

TJR2203   **Square**   DTM   MH

Malleable iron or steel, 12" x 8", signed with an obscured signature.

11301T3   **Square**   DTM   MH

Steel, 15 5/8" long, 1 7/8" wide with a 7 1/2" arm extended to 8 1/4" wide at blade joint, signed "J B Jopson".

No J. B. Jopson is listed in DATM (Nelson 1999). Could this be an owner's mark?

31611T4   **Square**   DTM   TT

Drop-forged tempered alloy steel, 12" long by 7" long, 1/8" wide, signed "'SAFFORD".

The blades are tapered. The longer one is stamped with numbers.

72812T1   **Square**   DTM   MH

Cast steel, 12" long, 8" wide, signed "WARRANTED STEEL No 2".

JTS1001   **Square**   DTM   MH

Drop-forged steel, 3" by 1 1/2", signed with the touchmark "JHM".

63001T12   **Square**   DTM   MH

Steel, 2 5/8" long, 2 1/8" blade, signed "The LSS Co Athol Mass No 20".

This is a classic example of Starrett's finest product. DATM (Nelson 1999, 751) contains historical information on L. S. Starrett Co.

http://www.davistownmuseum.org/bioStarrett.htm

42912LTC6   **Stair gauges**   DA   TT (Pub)

Drop-forged steel, 1 1/4" long, 1 3/4" wide, signed "THE L.S.S. CO. ATHOL, MASS. U.S.A. No. 111".

Courtesy of Liberty Tool Co.

Measuring Tools

21201T12   Surface gauge

DTM   MH

Steel, 1 1/2" long, 1 9/16" wide, 1 3/8" high, signed "V Oby".

Veikko Arne Oby (b. Worcester, MA 1916, d. 2/25, 2000), of Finnish descent, worked in Whitinsville, MA, and the Watertown Arsenal. This satin steel surface gauge, though not signed by its manufacturer, is similar to L.S. Starrett Toolmaker's surface gauge model 56A with 4" spindles. A contemporary L.S. Starrett catalog indicates this tool "is used in layout work for scribing lines on vertical or horizontal surfaces. A groove in the base adapts it for use on cylindrical as well as flat surfaces." This exquisite tool is a late example of the florescence of the classic period of American machinists' tools and is indicative of a proud machinists' careful use of a finely crafted Starrett tool or his meticulous reproduction of the same tool -- a possibility since Starrett surface gauges are rarely unsigned. Every hand tool has its own inscrutable history of manufacture and use.

http://www.davistownmuseum.org/pics/21201t12.jpg
http://www.davistownmuseum.org/bioOby.htm

101610T1   Surface gauge

DTM   MH

Steel, 3 5/8" long, 3 1/4" wide, 11 3/8" long gauge rod, signed "W. Anderson" owner's mark, c. 1910.

Donated by the Swenson family.

111900T3   Surface gauge

DTM   MH

Steel, 2 1/8" x 1 7/16" base, 4 3/8" arm, unsigned.

This is an essential component of the tool kit of the tool and die maker, constructor of the machines that then made other tools.

41203T4   Surface gauge

LPC   MH

Steel, 4 1/8" long arm with a 1 7/16" wide by 2 3/8" long bar, signed "J. Stevens A & T Co" "Chicopee Falls Mass USA".

This is a classic example of the exquisite workmanship of the classic period of American machinist tools.

http://www.davistownmuseum.org/pics/41203t4_p3.jpg

102503T1   Swivel gauge

DTM   MH

Steel, 7 3/8" long, with an 8" long velvet and leather case, signed "Boulet's Fine Tool Works Sebago Lakes Maine" "PAT OCT 2 1900 SEPT 10 1901 FEB 25 04".

It also has an owner's mark in script "T. Keech". It is accompanied by three small attachments whose purpose is not clear.

http://www.davistownmuseum.org/pics/102503t1a.jpg
http://www.davistownmuseum.org/publications/volume10.html

The Industrial Revolution (1865f.): Classic Period of American Machinists' Tools

Measuring Tools

111006T3   Swivel gauge   DTM   MH

Cast steel and leather box, 7 1/4" long with an 8" long box, signed "BOULET'S FINE TOOL WORKS, INC." "SEBAGO LAKE MAINE" "PAT.OCT.2.1900" "PAT.SEPT.10.1901" and "PAT.FEB.23 04".

http://www.davistownmuseum.org/pics/111006T3_p1.jpg
http://www.davistownmuseum.org/pics/111006T3_p3.jpg

041505T33   T square   DTM   MH

Steel and brass, 7 1/2" long, 3 1/2" wide, signed "C. EGGE".

Maker C. Egge was a Boston toolmaker and inventor of die engineering equipment, c. 1880s. He is not listed in DATM (Nelson 1999). This tool was purchased in Worcester, MA, by Liberty Tool Co. in March, 2005, from a descendent of one of his customers for die engineering equipment (C. D. Evan Co, Allston, MA) who fondly recalled the man who made this one-of-a-kind tool.

http://www.davistownmuseum.org/pics/041505t33.jpg

101701T7   Tap drill gauge   DTM   MH

Steel, 4 1/2" long, signed "Made by STERLING ELLIOTT NEWTON, MASS, USA", 1890 - 1910.

No such company is listed in DATM (Nelson 1999) but it does list "Elliott" as the maker of a tap drill gauge with a date of 1895 and no other information. The curator was born in Newton, MA, and after 30+ years in the tool business, has never seen this marking before. It is a very rare signature. The sizes 2 - 24 appear hand-stamped, they are slightly off center.

41302T5   Tapered gauge   DTM   TT

Tempered alloy steel, 6 1/8" long, 7/16" wide, signed "N. 270 The L. S. Starrett Co. Athol, Mass USA".

It is calibrated in millimeters and in hundredths of an inch. The maximum thickness this gauge measures is 0.150 inches. DATM (Nelson 1999, 751) contains historical information on L. S. Starrett Co.

http://www.davistownmuseum.org/bioStarrett.htm

914108T2   Thickness gauge   DTM   MH

Steel, 6 1/2" long, 6" long blades, signed "EINAR HANSON" "-TOOLS-" "WORCHESTER. MASS" and owner's mark "F. W. PAGE".

Folded inside are 8 blades marked: 2, 3, 4, 6, 8, 10, 12, and 18. Einar B. Hanson was superintendent of the factory established by his brother, H. L. Hanson (b. 1881) who rented a room and some machinery at No. 54 Hermon street, Worcester, MA, where he began the manufacture of piano hardware. He expanded and moved to No. 25 Union street. Mr. Hanson was the originator of many taps and dies (Nutt, Charles. History of Worcester and its people, Vol. 3).

41801T15   Tool and die-makers' jig   DTM   MH

Steel, unsigned.

Was this owner made? It was acquired along with the marking gauge (41801T10).

The Industrial Revolution (1865f.): Classic Period of American Machinists' Tools

Measuring Tools

101701T15   Tool and die-makers' square

Steel, 1 1/2" long, signed "Sawyer Tool Mfg Co Fitchburg Mass USA Hand", between 1894 - 1912.

This exquisite tool was made before this company moved to Ashburnham, MA in 1912. They later became the Almond Mfg. Co. in 1915 (Nelson 1999, 692). This tool illustrates the beauty and durability of hardened case steel.

http://www.davistownmuseum.org/bioSawyer.html

TJG1003   Toolmakers' buttons

Steel, 4 1/2" long, signed "STARRETT ATHOL MASS NO. 494-D".

The buttons are "used for precision location of holes in a work piece. The hole is roughly located by normal layout methods, drilled and tapped, and the button installed and snugged down. The button is then shifted to its precise location by measuring from other reference points with the precision required. This procedure is usually done on a surface plate. It is then set up in the machine, usually a lathe or boring machine, indicated, and final hole is bored. Frequently several holes would be bored in one piece, hence the need for several buttons."
(http://bbs.homeshopmachinist.net/showthread.php?t=9261)

http://www.davistownmuseum.org/bioStarrett.htm

111900T13   Toolmakers' buttons

Steel, 2 5/16" long, signed "Starrett Athol Mass USA No 494.B".

DATM (Nelson 1999, 751) contains historical information on L. S. Starrett Co.

http://www.davistownmuseum.org/bioStarrett.htm

8512T1   Toolmakers' buttons

Tool steel, 2 3/8" long, 3/4" wide, 1 1/16" high, signed "STARRETT ATHOL, MASS. U.S.A. NO 494" "PAT. JAN. 11 1921".

http://www.davistownmuseum.org/bioStarrett.htm

22512LTC12   Toolmakers' universal surface gauge

Drop-forged tempered alloy steel, 4" long, 4" wide, 1/2" high, signed "THE L.S. STARRETT CO. ATHOL, MASS. U.S.A." "STARRETT No. 56A With 4 inch Spindle TOOLMAKERS' UNIVERSAL SURFACE GAGE 1".

Also signed "ONLY THE L.S. STARRETT CO. Athol, Mass. U.S.A." It is designed so a variety of dial and probe attachments may be used to determine exact heights and distances on three dimensional objects. Courtesy of Liberty Tool Co.

http://www.davistownmuseum.org/bioStarrett.htm

22311T14   Try square

Steel scale, brass, rosewood handle, 6" long, 4" wide, signed "WINCHESTER" "TRADE MARK" "MADE IN U.S.A." and "9715".

Part of the Robert Sullivan Collection donation.

http://www.davistownmuseum.org/bioWinchester.html

The Industrial Revolution (1865f.): Classic Period of American Machinists' Tools

Measuring Tools

121112T4   Try square

Tempered alloy steel, brass, wood, 6" long, 3 1/2" long and 1 1/2" wide handle, signed "Disston & Morrs" "Philada Warrented".

This square includes a brass sidebar and blade attachment. DATM (Nelson 1999, 227) lists Disston & Morrs as working from 1867 to 1900 as a subdivision of Henry Disston and Sons. Joab Morrs died around 1886.

http://www.davistownmuseum.org/bioDisston.htm

3312T14   Try square

Drop-forged tempered alloy steel, brass, rosewood, 4 1/2" long, 3" wide, signed "PATENTED JUNE 20 '09" with a scratched in owner's mark "JOS".

This type of try square was used by a cabinetmaker. Courtesy of Liberty Tool Co.

22512LTC5   Wiggler center finder set

Drop-forged tempered alloy steel, vinyl pouch, 2 1/2" long pieces, signed "THE L.S. STARRETT CO. ATHOL, MASS. U.S.A. NO 828".

This set includes the handle and four attachments for finding centers in a red vinyl pouch. Courtesy of Liberty Tool Co.

http://www.davistownmuseum.org/bioStarrett.htm

5412LTC7   Wing calipers

Forged steel, 5" long, signed "BEMIS & CALL".

Courtesy of Liberty Tool Co.

31908T29   Wing dividers

Steel, 7 1/2" long, signed "C DELSTEN & SON" and "C & S".

81602T16   Wing dividers

Drop-forged steel, 14 1/4" long, signed "P. PETERS. NATICK MASS.".

The letters of the name are difficult to read. DATM (Nelson 1999) lists Patrick F. Peter (or Peters) in Natick as having a Jan. 22, 1878 patent for a cobblers' last hammer.

http://www.davistownmuseum.org/pics/81602T16_p2.jpg
http://www.davistownmuseum.org/pics/81602T16_p3.jpg

111412T4   Winged dividers

Iron and cast steel, 9" long, signed "HARRINGTON" "WESTON" "MASS" "CAST-STEEL" and with owner's marks "F R. KEGLER" and "W. H. SOUTHHARD".

DATM (Nelson 1999) lists sixteen different toolmakers named Harrington working in Southridge, MA, Philadelphia, and other locations, but none in Weston. None of them are listed as manufacturers of measuring tools.

The Industrial Revolution (1865f.): Classic Period of American Machinists' Tools

Measuring Tools

22411T23   Winged outside calipers   DTM   TT

Tempered alloy steel, 9" long, 4 1/2" wide when closed, signed "J. M. PARKHURST".

This appears to be an owner's mark and not a maker's mark.

TJS2201   Wire gauge   DTM   MH

Steel, 4 5/8" long, signed "STALL & ATHERTON BROCKTON, MASS".

Perhaps this mark is Snell & Atherton who made leather tools in Brockton, MA?

10910T4   Wire gauge   DTM   MH

Steel, 4" long, 1" wide, signed B. & S. STANDARD WIRE GAUGE; THE BLODGETT MF'G CO. ROCHESTER, N.Y., c. 1900.

The Blodgett Manufacturing Company was located in Rochester, NY from 1896 to 1905. Donated by the Swenson family.

http://www.davistownmuseum.org/pics/10910t4web1.jpg

22411T28   Wire gauge   DTM   TT

Drop-forged tempered alloy steel, 5 1/4" long, 1 5/8" wide, signed "E. W. SIMMONS".

It appears to be hand-stamped. DATM (Nelson 1999) does not list an E. W. Simmons or a Simmons that made wire gauges.

22412LTC1   Wire gauge   DA   TT (Pub)

Drop-forged tempered alloy steel, 3 3/16" diameter, signed "J.R. BROWN & SHARPE PROVIDENCE R.I. STANDARD WIRE GAUGE".

This is a circular wire gauge used for determining thickness. It is graduated from 0 to 36. Courtesy of Liberty Tool Company.

http://www.davistownmuseum.org/bioBrownSharpe.htm

10910T5   Wire gauge   DTM   MH

Steel, 5 1/4" long, 1 5/8" wide, signed "TWIST DRILL & STEEL WIRE GAUGE" "Morse Twist Drill & Mch. Co. New Bedford Mass.", c.1890.

Donated by the Swenson family.

http://www.davistownmuseum.org/pics/10910t5web2.jpg
http://www.davistownmuseum.org/bioMorseTwist.html

The Industrial Revolution (1865f.): Classic Period of American Machinists' Tools

Measuring Tools

032203T7   Wire gauge   DTM   MH

Steel, 3 1/2" diameter, signed "J. R. BROWN & SHARPE" "PROVIDENCE R.I." "STANDARD WIRE GAUGE" with bird trademark and "BS TRADE MARK".

The Directory of American Toolmakers (Nelson 1999) lists J. R. Brown, a predecessor of Brown & Sharpe, as working from 1853 - 1866, but continuing to use this mark after that date on some tools. This is a typical tool in the increasingly complex tool kit of a c. 1880 shipyard worker.

http://www.davistownmuseum.org/pics/032203T7_p3.jpg
http://www.davistownmuseum.org/bioBrownSharpe.htm

72002T8   Wire gauge   DTM   MH-I

Tempered alloy steel, signed "Lacene Mfg Co. Manchester NH".

Was this wire gauge made after 1900? If not a wire gauge, what is it?

Miscellaneous Tools

102800M   Machinists' tool box   DTM   MH-K

Wood, brass and steel, 22 3/4" long, 12 1/2" wide, 10 3/4" high, signed by owner "W.F. Blake".

A piece of Maine history, this tool box was formerly owned by Ken Milliken, Lincolnville, ME. Blake was once one of the chief machinists for the Knox Engine Co.

http://www.davistownmuseum.org/bioKnoxEngine.htm

111900T10   Pocket screwdriver   DTM   MH

Steel and rosewood, 4 1/4" long, signed "L S Starrett Co Athol Mass USA".

http://www.davistownmuseum.org/bioStarrett.htm

3912LTC1   Tinsmiths' compound levered shears   DA   TT (Pub)

Drop-forged tempered alloy steel, 14 1/4" long, 4 3/8" wide, signed "8896" "PAT. OCT. 12 NOV. 30 1909".

These shears were produced by Detroit Shear Company. The November 30 patent belongs to J.R. Searight and covers the levered design. Courtesy of Liberty Tool Co.

The Industrial Revolution (1865f.): Other Factory Made Tools

Agricultural Implements

121312LTC   Bee smoker
DA   TT (Pub)

Sheet steel, wood, leather, 10" x 9" x 4 3/4", signed "ROOT QUALITY BEE SUPPLIES" "MANUFACTURED BY THE A.I. ROOT COMPANY MEDINA OHIO U.S.A.".

Amos Ives Root (b. 1839 d. 1923) developed innovative beekeeping techniques in the United States during the mid-19th century. He founded the company in 1869 and it made beekeeping supplies until they were phased out in 1928 (http://en.wikipedia.org/wiki/Amos_Root).

100108T2   Brush cutter
DTM   MH

Steel, wooden handle, 11 1/4" long, 5 1/2" diameter cutting blade, signed ".W.T.CO" on the metal with a paper label "Champion Bus___" "NORTH WAYNE T__" and "HALLOWELL, M_".

The paper label is partially missing.

http://www.davistownmuseum.org/publications/volume10.html

72612LTC2   Brush hook
DA   TT (Pub)

Cast steel, wood (hickory), 40 1/2" long, 10" wide cutting edge, signed "OOLFMAN BROS. INC".

Courtesy of the Liberty Tool Company.

32708T45   Bull nose puller
DTM   MH

Malleable iron, 8 1/2" long, unsigned.

This is also called an oxen guide. It is used to walk a bull with no ring in the nose.

http://www.davistownmuseum.org/pics/32708t45.jpg

121412T3   Cargo hook
DTM   TT

Malleable iron and steel, wood (rosewood), 11" long, 5" long handle, 5 1/2" wide, signed "SNOW & NEALLEY CO. BANGOR MAINE".

101312T17   Crease nail puller
DTM   TT

Cast steel, 11 3/4" long, 1 1/2" wide, signed "DIAMOND NP12 U.S.A.".

101701T5   Fence puller
DTM   MH

Steel and wood, 16 1/4" long, 4" wood handle located in the middle of the tool, unsigned.

This is an excellent whatsit.

102211T3   Folding sickle
DTM   TT

Stamped steel, wood (pine), 11" cutting edge, 13" long handle, signed "LAWN RAZOR NO. WAYNE TOOL CO. OAKLAND, ME. U.S.A.".

http://www.davistownmuseum.org/bioNorthWayne.html

The Industrial Revolution (1865f.): Other Factory Made Tools

Agricultural Implements

30911T11   Garden rake   DTM   TT

Forged malleable iron, 4" long handle attachment, 7" x 4" tines, unsigned.

It is hand-forged with 4 tines. The handle attaching piece and two inner tines are forged to the body.

22411T11   Garden shears   DTM   TT

Drop-forged tempered alloy steel, 8 1/2" long, 2" wide, signed "J. T. HENRY" "HAMDEN, CT." and "49".

These feature a locking handle. DATM (1999) lists Henry's working dates as 1882 - 1894.

41212T5   Grain sickle   DTM   TT

Drop-forged steel, wooden handle, 17" long, signed "NOLIN NORTH WAYNE TOOL CO. OAKLAND, ME. U.S.A.".

It is a mid-twentieth century example of a tool made by a prolific Maine toolmaker. Courtesy of Liberty Tool Co.

http://www.davistownmuseum.org/bioNorthWayne.html

42912LTC8   Grain sickle   DA   TT (Pub)

Steel, rosewood handle, 16" long, unsigned.

Courtesy of Liberty Tool Co.

061813T2   Grass hook   DTM   MH

Drop-forged steel, wooden handle, cardboard box, 13" long, 1 3/4" wide blade, 12" long handle, signed "LITTLE GIANT" "NORTH WAYNE TOOL CO." "OAKLAND, MAINE U.S.A." on the handle.

This is a second grass hook, identical to ID# 061813T1. Donated by the Brockton Fire Department.

http://www.davistownmuseum.org/bioNorthWayne.html

061813T1   Grass hook   DTM   MH

Drop-forged steel, wooden handle, cardboard box, 13" long, 1 3/4" wide blade, 12" long handle, signed "LITTLE GIANT" "NORTH WAYNE TOOL CO." "OAKLAND, MAINE U.S.A." on the handle.

On the box it also says: "GRASS LITTLE GIANT HOOK" "No. 9" "MANUFACTURED BY THE" "NORTH WAYNE TOOL CO." "OAKLAND, MAINE U.S.A." "MAKER OF THE LITTLE GIANT LINE" "3 WAY ADJUSTABLE". Donated by the Brockton Fire Department.

http://www.davistownmuseum.org/bioNorthWayne.html

42912LTC9   Grass hook   DA   TT (Pub)

Steel, rosewood, 14" long, unsigned.

Courtesy of Liberty Tool Co.

61612T3   Grub hoe   DTM   TT

Forged iron, 5" x 4" x 2", unsigned.

269

The Industrial Revolution (1865f.): Other Factory Made Tools

Agricultural Implements

81812T2   Hay fork   DTM   MH

Cast steel, wood (hickory), 35" long, 12" long and 10" wide fork, unsigned.

Courtesy of the Davistown Museum tool shed.

72312LTC3   Hay fork   DA   TT (Pub)

Forged steel, wooden handle, 56" long, 7" wide, 12" long fork, unsigned.

Courtesy of Liberty Tool Company.

22612T1   Hay hook   DTM   MH3-D3

Drop-forged steel, wood handle, 9" long, 1/2" diameter, 5" long handle, signed "C DREW &CO. KINGSTON MASS.".

This tool is also known as a bale hook.

http://www.davistownmuseum.org/bioDrew.htm

102211T1   Hoe   DTM   TT

Forged steel, 9 1/2" long, 6" cutting edge, 2 1/4" high, signed "KLEIN LOGAN Co".

Klein, Logan & Co. worked out of Pittsburg, PA from 1868 to 1899.

3912NOM1   Mushroom doweling drill bit   DA   TT (Pub)

Tool steel, 6" long, 5/8" wide, depth stop is 3/4" diameter, unsigned.

This twist drill bit with a depth stop is specifically designed for drilling holes into damp hardwood for the insertion of wood dowels inoculated with mushroom spawn into logs for agricultural purposes. Courtesy of Liberty Tool Co.

101312T31   Ox shoes   DTM   TT

Cast steel, 4 3/4" long, 1 3/4" wide, signed "No 20" "ATWATER 2".

The Atwater Manufacturing Company of Southington, CT, was involved in a patent suit over an 1873 patent for improved dies for forging ox shoes. (http://bulk.resource.org/courts.gov/c/F1/0025/0025.f1.0101.pdf).

101400T9   Pig skinner   DTM   MH

Forged steel and wood, 11 1/4" wide with a 9 5/8" diameter scoop, unsigned, c. 1860 - 80.

This is the universal pig skinning jig.

TKD3001   Pitchfork   DTM   MH

Forged iron, 26" long, 4 7/8" wide, unsigned.

It is of European origin.

http://www.davistownmuseum.org/bioLynch.htm

The Industrial Revolution (1865f.): Other Factory Made Tools

Agricultural Implements

31212T17   Planters' dibble   DTM   TT

Drop-forged steel with red painted wooden handle, 11" long, 1 1/8" diameter, unsigned.

102800T6   Pruning shears   DTM   MH

Drop-forged steel, 10 1/2" long, 2 3/8" long cutters, signed "D. Bowers".

No D. Bowers is listed in DATM (Nelson 1999).

100208T3   Scythe blade (A) plus pieces of steel (B) and iron (C)   DTM   MH

Malleable iron and steel, A) 33 1/2" long, 1 7/8" wide, 28 3/4" blade; B) 33 3/4" long; C) 33" long, 1 5/8" wide 28 1/2" blade, unsigned.

This unique grouping from the North Wayne Scythe Co. illustrates the components of a late 19th century or early 20th century drop-forged scythe. A piece of high carbon steel bar stock (B) is forged onto a partially forged and shaped piece of malleable iron (A). After further drop-forging and hand hammering, (C) represents the final product prior to additional filing, shaping, and sharpening. It is a unique relic from the heyday of Maine's edge tool manufacturing era. From the collection of Ed Shaw.

http://www.davistownmuseum.org/publications/volume10.html

31908T37   Sheep shears   DTM   MH

Steel, 13 5/8" long, 6 1/2" long blade, signed "BURGON & BALL" "PATENT" "NO" "294(2)" in a trademark, also "B.B" "ENGLAND".

Burgon & Ball is still making manufacturing tools. They started in 1730 in Sheffield, England.

http://www.davistownmuseum.org/pics/31908t37p1.jpg
http://www.davistownmuseum.org/pics/31908t37p2.jpg

101701T4   Sheep shears   DTM   TT

Steel, 12 1/4" long, signed with an interesting cartouche illustrating the function of this tool: a farmer shearing a sheep with the mark "clipaway".

This is probably a 20th century tool and is an excellent specimen for in-class demonstration.

102211T2   Sickle   DTM   TT

Drop-forged steel, wooden handle painted black, 17" long, 5" handle, 9" wide, signed "North Wayne Tool Co., Oakland, ME USA" and an owners signature nearly obscured : "M__OLIN".

This sickle is used for cutting grass and probably is an early 20th century product.

http://www.davistownmuseum.org/bioNorthWayne.html

42912LTC14 Valve lifter   DA   TT (Pub)

Drop-forged malleable iron, 12 1/4" long, unsigned.

This tool is often used for fencing as it is ideal for working with barbed wire. It is also used as a valve lifter (Sellens 2003, 505). Courtesy of Liberty Tool Co.

Blacksmith, Farrier, and Metalworking Tools

The Industrial Revolution (1865f.): Other Factory Made Tools

Blacksmith, Farrier, and Metalworking Tools

22601T2   Adjustable jaw cut nipper   DTM   MH

Steel with carbide tipped jaw, 7" long, signed "L S Starrett Co. Athol Mass USA No 1- 7 IN".

It is for use in wire mills, piano tuning, and by telephone workers for wire cutting. The removable jaws may be reground, repaired, or replaced.

http://www.davistownmuseum.org/bioStarrett.htm

2713T3   Anvil bottom tool   DTM   TT

Forged steel, 17 1/2" long, 2 1/2" at widest, 1 1/8" anvil mounting shaft, signed "ANCHOR".

This tool is used for shaping.

101412T1   Anvil dolly hammer   DTM   TT

Cast steel, wood (maple), 19" long, 2 1/2" diameter face with a 3/4" long pin, 5 1/2" long head, signed "ATHA" with a horseshoe and A.

This tool is used for sharpening rock drills. This particular design has a pin in the middle, presumably to accommodate hollow drill bits.

http://www.davistownmuseum.org/bioAtha.html

3213T2   Bench hack saw   DTM   MH

Cast iron, steel, wood (rosewood), 17" long, 10" tall, 4" wide, signed "GOODELL PRATT" "PAT. JUNE 20, 1899 GREENFIELD, MASS. U.S.A.".

The patent belongs to Henry E. Goodell and Herbert D. Lanfair. This was sold as their "No. 1 Bench Hack Saw" with 9" blades.

http://www.davistownmuseum.org/bioGoodelpratt.html

62213LTC1   Blacksmiths' blower   DA   TT (Pub)

Cast iron, steel, 4 1/2 feet tall, signed "CHAMPION BLOWER & FORGE CO.".

102512T6   Blacksmiths' chipping hammer   DTM   TT

Steel, wooden handle, 14" long, 5 3/4" long head, signed "A" on the underside of the head.

Courtesy of Liberty Tool Co.

102512T4   Blacksmiths' chipping hammer   DTM   TT

Steel, wooden handle, 13" long, 5 1/2" long head, signed "B & M.R.R.".

It is signed by a railroad company, however, there are several different companies that used B & M, such as Boston & Maine and Burlington & Missouri. Courtesy of Liberty Tool Co.

93012LTC4   Blacksmiths' cross peen hammer   DA   TT (Pub)

Cast steel, wood (hickory), 17 1/2" long, 6 1/4" wide head, 2" wide edges, signed "H".

The Industrial Revolution (1865f.): Other Factory Made Tools

Blacksmith, Farrier, and Metalworking Tools

31212T1   Blacksmiths' end cutters
DTM   TT

Drop-forged iron and steel, 14" long, 1" wide cutting edge, signed "J-I-C. HELLER BRO'S.CO.U.S.A.".

Heller & Brothers worked in Newark, NJ from 1866-1899 (Nelson 1999). Courtesy of Liberty Tool Co.

http://www.davistownmuseum.org/bioHellerBros.html

102512T5   Blacksmiths' peen hammer
DTM   TT

Steel, wooden handle, 18 1/2" long, 5 1/2" long head, signed "MANUF'R" "H.H. HARVEY" "AUGUSTA. ME".

H. H. Harvey & Company was in Augusta, Maine, from 1872 to 1914. Courtesy of Liberty Tool Co.

102512T8   Blacksmiths' raising hammer
DTM   TT

Steel, wood, 12 3/4" long, 3 3/4" long head, signed by owners "S. SELDON + J. S. SELDON" twice.

Courtesy of Liberty Tool Co.

TJD1006   Blacksmiths' rasp
DTM   MH

Drop-forged steel, 15 11/16" long, 1 5/8" wide, signed "HELLER BROS NEWARK NJ" with its famous horse and farrier 4 touchmark.

This tool is unusual because it shows little sign of wear. Heller Brothers was one of the great late 19th century tool manufacturing companies. Rather than being a blacksmith-made rasp, this tool is a product of the factory system that arose during and after the Civil War. DATM (Nelson 1999) lists Heller as c. 1870 f.

http://www.davistownmuseum.org/bioHellerBros.html

102512T10   Blacksmiths' straight peen hammer
DTM   TT

Steel, wooden handle, 14 1/2" long, 4 3/4" long head, signed "1854" and "G".

Courtesy of Liberty Tool Co.

50402T9   Blacksmiths' tap
DTM   MH

Drop-forged steel, 3 1/2" long, signed "J M KING" and "14".

J. M. King is an early mark of J. M. King & Co., Waterford, NY (1887 - 1910), maker of dies, pliers, and taps (Nelson 1999, 151-2).

22411T4   Blacksmiths' tongs
DTM   TT

Drop-forged steel, 3 5/8" long, 1 1/8" wide, unsigned.

These miniature tongs were possibly a salesmans' sample or a design model.

3213LTC2   Blowhorn stake
DA   TT (Pub)

Cast and forged steel, 8" mount, 23 1/2" long, 4 3/4" wide, 3" deep, unsigned.

ID #   Status   Location

Blacksmith, Farrier, and Metalworking Tools

31611T5   Bolt header   DTM   TT

Drop-forged malleable iron and steel, 14 1/2" long, 3/8" x 1 3/16" working area, signed "C. J. Bradury". This is factory-made; Bradury is probably an owner.

8912T6   Center punch   DTM   TT

Cast steel, 3 5/8" long, 3/8" wide, signed "R.C. CLAY".
No R. Clay is listed in DATM (Nelson 1999).

8912LTC6   Center punch   DTM   TT (Pub)

Cast steel, unsigned.

091611T2   Channel swaging hammer   DTM   MH

Drop-forged cast (?) steel with wood handle, 14" long handle, 5" x 1 1/8" head, signed "A. B. MORES & CO." "BOSTON" "HAWKINS PATTERN".

A. B. Mores & Co. is not listed in DATM (Nelson 1999).

091611T1   Channel swaging hammer   DTM   MH

Drop-forged cast steel with wood handle, 19" long handle, 4 1/4" x 1 1/2" head, 3/8" diameter swage, signed "ATHA TOOL CO" "CAST STEEL" and "3/8".

The Atha Tool Co., started in 1884, was purchased by the Stanley Tool Co. in 1913.

http://www.davistownmuseum.org/bioAtha.html

101312T11   Clean claw farriers' hammer   DTM   TT

Cast steel, wood (hickory), 15" long, 4 1/2" long head, 3/4" diameter face, signed "HELLER BROS. CO PON".

http://www.davistownmuseum.org/bioHellerBros.html

72712LTC11 Coal tongs   DA   TT (Pub)

Cast steel, 8 1/2" long, 2 1/4" wide, jaws are 1/4" apart when closed all the way, unsigned.
Courtesy of the Liberty Tool Company.

31112T10   Cold chisel   DTM   MH3-D2

Drop-forged steel, 5 5/8" long, 1/2" wide cutting edge, signed "C. DREW & CO.".
Courtesy of Liberty Tool Co.
http://www.davistownmuseum.org/bioDrew.htm

31112T11   Cold chisel   DTM   MH3-D2

Drop-forged steel, 5 5/8" long, 1/2" wide cutting edge, signed "2173 C. DREW Kingston, MA".
Courtesy of Liberty Tool Co.
http://www.davistownmuseum.org/bioDrew.htm

Blacksmith, Farrier, and Metalworking Tools

31811T10   **Cold chisel**   DTM   TT

Drop-forged German steel, 5 3/4" long, signed "A" "G&U" and "PRODUKT" in a diamond, "TEMPERED STEEL" and "GERMANY".

31112T14   **Cold chisel**   DTM   MH3-D2

Drop-forged steel, 8 1/8" long, 3/8" wide cutting edge, signed "C. DREW & CO.".

Courtesy of Liberty Tool Co.

http://www.davistownmuseum.org/bioDrew.htm

31112T13   **Cold chisel**   DTM   MH3-D2

Drop-forged steel, 4 5/8" long, 3/8" wide cutting edge, signed "DREW-2302-1/8".

Courtesy of Liberty Tool Co.

http://www.davistownmuseum.org/bioDrew.htm

31112T8   **Cold chisel**   DTM   MH3-D2

Drop-forged steel, 7 1/8" long, 7/8" wide cutting edge, signed "C. DREW & CO.".

Courtesy of Liberty Tool Co.

http://www.davistownmuseum.org/bioDrew.htm

31112T12   **Cold chisel**   DTM   MH3-D2

Drop-forged steel, 4 1/2" long, 3/8" wide cutting edge, signed "DREW-230-D.T.".

Courtesy of Liberty Tool Co.

http://www.davistownmuseum.org/bioDrew.htm

111001T26A **Cold chisel**   DTM   MH

Drop-forged steel, 5 1/2" long, 7/16" blade, signed "Stanley Atha 16(?) 3-8 Made in USA".

http://www.davistownmuseum.org/bioStanley.htm

31112T9   **Cold chisel**   DTM   MH3-D2

Drop-forged steel, 6 1/2" long, 1/2" wide cutting edge, signed "C. DREW & CO.".

Courtesy of Liberty Tool Co.

http://www.davistownmuseum.org/bioDrew.htm

101701T14   **Cold chisel**   DTM   MH

Drop-forged steel, 5 3/16" long, signed "Miller's Falls Co Made in USA. No 1190".

Miller's Falls merged with Godell Pratt Co. in 1931 but retained their own name on some tools (Nelson 1999, 544).

http://www.davistownmuseum.org/bioMillersFalls.htm

The Industrial Revolution (1865f.): Other Factory Made Tools

Blacksmith, Farrier, and Metalworking Tools

TBL1002   Cold chisel   DTM   MH

Cast steel, 6 1/4" long, 5/8" cutter, signed "2173 C DREW KINGSTON MASS", c. 1920.

http://www.davistownmuseum.org/bioDrew.htm

TJD1008   Cold chisels (2)   DTM   MH

Forged alloy steel, 5 1/2" long, 9/16" wide, signed "SILICO MANGANESE STEEL", c. 1880 - 1900.

These illustrate the invention and use of steel alloys for special purpose tools.

12813LTC1   Cold cut hammer   DA   TT (Pub)

Cast steel, wood (hickory), 24 1/2" long, 5 3/4" long head, 1 1/2" cutting edge, 1 1/8" diameter face, unsigned.

102512T9   Coppersmiths' bumping hammer   DTM   TT

Steel, wooden handle, 11 1/2" long, 8 1/2" long head, unsigned.

Courtesy of Liberty Tool Co.

81200T12   Cross peen hammer   DTM   MHC

Drop-forged steel, 5" long, 1 1/4" wide peen, 1 3/8" long head, unsigned.

This is a typical late 19th century factory-made blacksmiths' cross peen.

41412LTC2   End cutting nippers   DA   TT (Pub)

Forged iron and steel, 2" long, 1" wide, 1" high, unsigned.

Courtesy of Liberty Tool Co.

31811T6   Engravers' tool   DTM   TT

Cast steel, 5 1/2" long, 1/2" wide, signed "AH".

It has a spiral (shell) pattern.

22411T30   Engraving stamp   DTM   TT

Drop-forged steel, 4 1/2" long, 1" wide, the letters are 1 5/" x 3/8", signed "S. M. SPENCER MFG. CO." "BOSTON, MASS.".

The stamp is used to mark "ROCKLAND". DATM (Nelson 1999, 741) lists this company as a die maker in Boston with unknown dates. S. M. Spencer was listed working in Brattleboro, VT, in 1867 and 1872.

102512T17   Farriers' buffer   DTM   TT

Steel, 5 3/4" long, 2 1/2" wide, signed "HELLER BROS".

Courtesy of Liberty Tool Co.

http://www.davistownmuseum.org/bioHellerBros.html

Blacksmith, Farrier, and Metalworking Tools

22813LTC9   Farriers' creasing hammer   DA   TT (Pub)

Cast steel, wood (hickory), 10 3/4" handle, 3 3/8" long head, 1" face and peen, signed "H.H. HARVEY MANUF'R. AUGUSTA ME".

This type of hammer is used to make the groove in horseshoes in which the nails are recessed.

http://www.davistownmuseum.org/bioHarvey.html

8512LTC2   Farriers' curved jaw nail clincher   DA   TT (Pub)

Drop-forged steel, 14 1/2" long, 1/2" wide jaws, signed "GE".

Courtesy of Liberty Tool Company.

21201T4   Farriers' hammer   DTM   MH

Drop-forged steel, wooden handle, 11 5/8" long, 9 5/8" handle, 4 3/8" wide, 5/8" octagonal face, signed "Atha Tool" with the distinctive horseshoe touchmark.

DATM (Nelson 1999) indicates the famous and prolific Atha Tool Co. may have been producing tools as early as 1875 in Newark, NJ. Buying out many competing tool and hammer-makers, they were purchased by the Stanley Rule & Level Co. in 1913, who retained their touchmark. "They were especially noted for farrier tools and also made mining tools." (Nelson 1999, 39).

http://www.davistownmuseum.org/bioStanley.htm

8512LTC3   Farriers' hoof nipper   DA   TT (Pub)

Drop-forged steel, 15" long, 1 1/8" wide cutting edge, signed "GE".

This is GE's "Easy Hoof Nipper." Courtesy of Liberty Tool Company.

101312T24   Farriers' hoof nippers   DTM   TT

Cast iron, cast steel, 14" long, 1" cutting edge, signed "CHAMPION DEARMENT OUR PRIDE BALL BEARING PATENTED JAN. 5, 1908".

101312T28   Farriers' hoof parer   DTM   TT

Cast iron, cast steel, signed "CHAMPION TOOL CO MEADVILLE, PA".

Champion Tool Company moved from Evansburg, PA to Meadville in 1904 (Nelson 1999).

32912T2   Farriers' hoof shears   DTM   TT-46

Drop-forged iron, steel cutter, 14" long, signed "OUR PRIDE BALL BEARING PATENTED JAN. 5, 1909 CHAMPION DEARMENT MEADVILLE, PA.".

The January 5, 1909 patent is owned by G. B. DeArment for hoof shears. Courtesy of Liberty Tool Co.

12812T5   Farriers' horse nail clinch tongs   DTM   TT

Forged malleable iron, 14" long, 3/4" wide jaw, signed "CHAMPION".

Made by Champion-DeArment, now known as Channellock.

The Industrial Revolution (1865f.): Other Factory Made Tools

Blacksmith, Farrier, and Metalworking Tools

111412T3   Farriers' knife   DTM   MH

Steel blade, drop-forged iron handle, 8" long, 1/2" wide blade, signed "HELLER BROS. CO. NEWARK, N.J. U.S.A." on handle with a horse touchmark on the blade.

http://www.davistownmuseum.org/bioHellerBros.html

32412T6   Farriers' knife   DTM   TT-34

Malleable iron handle, steel blade, 9" long, 4 1/4" long blade, unsigned.

This iron handled knife is the design of T. J. Pope (though this particular example bears no maker's mark). He made farriers' hoof knives from 1890-1913. Courtesy of Liberty Tool Co.

52603T22   Farriers' knife   DTM   MH

Malleable iron and steel, wooden handle, 11" long, 5 3/4" long blade, signed "S. W. Helway".

12613T1   Farriers' rasp   DTM   MH

Cast steel, wood (rosewood), cloth tape, 19 1/2" long, 1 3/4" wide, 3/16" thick, signed "NICHOLSON U.S.A. MADE IN U.S.A. 31-78".

http://www.davistownmuseum.org/bionicholson.html

81200T9   Farriers' shoe hammer   DTM   MH

Drop-forged steel, 5 3/8" long, signed "Champion Tool Co. Meadville PA", c. 1885.

071704T1   Farriers' tool kit   DTM   MH

Wood, 20 3/4" long, 12 1/2" wide, unsigned.

This wooden tool kit contains a selection of farriers' tools including: 3 rasps, tongs, 2 clinchers, pliers, 2 farriers' hammers, trimming tool, apron, and steel horseshoe nails.

101312T25   Fuller hammer   DTM   TT

Cast steel, wood (maple), 17" long, 5 1/2" long and 2 3/4" wide head, signed "1 1/2" "W CO" in a circle.

101312T9   Fuller hammer   DTM   TT

Cast steel, wood (maple), 21" long, 2 5/8" wide edge, 5 1/2" long head, signed "BICKNELL MFG" with "FRP" slogan with an anchor on the head.

93012LTC3   Fuller hammer   DA   TT (Pub)

Cast steel, wood (hickory), 13 3/4" long, 6" long head, 1 1/4" wide edges, unsigned.

This fuller hammer is probably a scaling hammer for working on boilers.

Blacksmith, Farrier, and Metalworking Tools

TJD1001   **Hammer**   DTM   MH

Drop-forged steel, 12 3/4" long, 7/32" square face, signed "MADE IN USA" with "H" as a touchmark.

This is an unusual blacksmiths' hammer; the stamped mark indicates it was made late in the 19th century.

121201T1   **Hand vise**   DTM   MH

Drop-forged malleable iron and steel, 3 1/2" long, 1 1/4" wide jaw, signed "IMHOFF & LANGE".

DATM (1999, 1030) indicates Imhoff & Lange is a foreign company that made bits. This maker's mark has never been seen before by the Liberty Tool Co. These smaller sized vises often appear in watchmaker toolkits.

42912LTC2   **Hand vise**   DA   TT (Pub)

Forged steel, brass ferrule, wood (cocobolo), 6 5/8" long, unsigned.

This hand vise has a hollow handle with a threaded wooden butt cap designed to hold a variety of bits and drivers which lock into it. For an illustration see Sellens (2002, 508). Courtesy of Liberty Tool Co.

41203T12   **Hand vise**   DTM   MH

Drop-forged steel, 5" long, 1 11/16" wide jaw, signed "Billings & Edmands Mfg. Co. Rocky Hill CONN" and "DROP FORGED OF BAR STEEL".

This tool has a most unusual designation of manufacturing process, not noted on any other tool; DATM (Nelson 1999) lists Billings & Edmands working dates as 1884 to 1899. It is a typical hand tool that would be found in any toolmaker or tool repair workshop. All drop-forged tools were made either from malleable iron bar stock or steel bar stock.

http://www.davistownmuseum.org/pics/41203t12_p1.jpg
http://www.davistownmuseum.org/pics/41203t12_p2.jpg

61612T2   **Hand vise**   DTM   TT

Cast steel, 3 1/2" x 1 7/8" x 15/16", signed "SMITH & CO".

No Smith & Co. is listed in DATM (Nelson 1999) as a maker of vises.

41412LTC1   **Hardy**   DA   TT (Pub)

Forged steel, 2" long, 1" wide, 1" high, unsigned.

This is a typical blacksmith's anvil cutting tool. Courtesy of Liberty Tool Co.

32313LTC1   **Horn anvil**   DA   TT (Pub)

Iron, forge-welded steel, 7" x 9" x 15 1/2", unsigned.

101312T6   **Hot set hammer**   DTM   TT

Cast steel, wood (hickory), 17 3/4" long, 7" long head, 1 1/2" wide edge, signed "VULCAN" in a diamond.

Blacksmith, Farrier, and Metalworking Tools

4713T1   **Iron bar stock**   DTM   TT

Malleable iron, 12 3/4" long x 1" x 1", unsigned.

12813LTC2   **Leg vise**   DA   TT (Pub)

Forged steel and iron, 42 1/2" long, 6" wide jaws, 16 1/4" tall, unsigned.

101312T8   **Long reach cross peen hammer**   DTM   TT

Cast steel, wood (hickory), 14 1/4" long, 7" long head, 1 1/4" wide edge, 1 1/8" diameter face, unsigned.

22813LTC10 **Mandrel**   DA   TT (Pub)

Cast steel, 10" long, 1 7/16" at base, tapers to 1/2", unsigned.

111001T28   **Nail holder**   DTM   MH

Drop-forged iron, 6" long, signed "Williams Nail Holder & Guide Patent 1688446".

This is a very uncommon tool. DATM (Nelson 1999) notes Williams only as a maker of lemon squeezes and rules with no mention of nail holders.

102612T10   **Pipe tongs**   LPC   MH

Steel, signed "JARECKI MFG. Co" "PAT APR 22 1870" "ERIE, PA" and "1" on the other handle.

Jarecki Manufacturing Company was formed in 1872 by brothers Henry and Charles Jarecki and was located at 149 East 9th St. in Erie, Pennsylvania (http://oldtimeerie.blogspot.com/2012/10/jarecki-manufacturing-company-east-9th.html).

914108T11   **Punch**   DTM   MH

Drop-forged malleable iron, 4" long, signed "WILLIAMS & PAGE" and "BOSTON".

The "Twelfth Exhibition of the Massachusetts Charitable Mechanic Association at Faneuil and Quincy Halls, Boston" in 1874 (books.google.com) lists this company name as a maker of railroad supplies. There is an auction listing for a kerosene lamp made by them that was dated 1865.

32502T35   **Punches (3)**   BDTM   T

Tempered alloy steel, 3" to 3 1/2" long, signed "L S Starret" on one, c. 1920.

http://www.davistownmuseum.org/bioStarrett.htm
http://www.davistownmuseum.org/bioEpstein.htm

Blacksmith, Farrier, and Metalworking Tools

31602T13   Rasp   DTM   MH

Steel, 18" long, 1 9/16" maximum width, signed "Carver File Co USA".

"The Carver File Co. of Philadelphia, with a fully paid in
capital of $100,000; has been incorporated under the laws of Pennsylvania and the new plant will
include two buildings each 40 x 170 ft., with a capacity of 900 dozen files per day. In the formation of
the company the plant of the D. B. Murphy File Co., of Camden, N. J., was absorbed and will
continue independent operation on special light files, all other grades being made at the new plant."
(The Iron Trade Review, June 1, 1905, pg. 39). The Hardware Dealers' Magazine of October, 1906
makes mention of "The Carver File Co., known also as the Delta File Works, 3227 Frankford avenue
[Philadelphia]".

80802T1   Ring pliers   DTM   MH

Drop-forged steel, 8" long, signed "FOR BETTER RING JOBS SPEEDY TOOL SALES LOS
ANGELES 42 CALIF. MADE IN USA".

http://www.davistownmuseum.org/pics/80802t1.jpg

101312T21   Round eye punch hammer   DTM   TT

Cast steel, wood (hickory), 14 1/2" long, 7 1/2" wide head, 1/2" diameter punch, 1 1/8" wide face,
signed "2".

12613T2   Scotch pattern farriers' shoeing hammer   DTM   MH

Cast steel, wood (hickory), 10" long overall, 4 1/2" long head, 7/8" diameter face, signed "HELLER
BROS CO." with a horse insignia.

http://www.davistownmuseum.org/bioHellerBros.html

31011T1   Screw plate   DTM   TT

Cast steel, 6 1/4" long, 1 1/8" wide, signed "BLECKMANN" in a circle with two unidentifiable letters
underneath it in script.

This is a thread cutting adjustable die used by a blacksmith. DATM (Nelson 1999, 93) lists
Bleckmann with no information on working dates or location.

21812LTC4   Sheet metal crimper   DA   TT (Pub)

Drop-forged steel, rosewood grip, 8 1/2" long, 4" deep, 7 1/4" wide, 7" long handle, signed "No 545
SMALL TURNING" "707" "708".

Courtesy of the Liberty Tool Company.

102512T2   Silversmiths' raising hammer   DTM   TT

Cast steel, wood (hickory), 12" long, 5 1/2" long head, unsigned.

Courtesy of Liberty Tool Co.

93012LTC2   Swage hammer   DA   TT (Pub)

Cast steel, wood (hickory), 16 1/2" long, 5" long head, 2" x 2 1/2" face with 7/8" fuller, signed "7/8".

Blacksmith, Farrier, and Metalworking Tools

914108T1   Tap wrench   DTM   MH

Steel, 7 3/4" long, 1" wide, signed "W. F. PAGE" and "NO. 1.".

Possibly W. F. Page is the owner of this tool and not the maker. The name is stamped on it in 3 places.

102100T5   Tapping stock   DTM   MH

Drop-forged steel, 7 1/4" long, unsigned.

10407T7   Tin snips   DTM   MH

German steel, 11 3/4" long, signed "MATEA".

Probably German- or Italian-made around the turn of the century (1900) of drop-forged German steel and then heavily polished. The steel in this relatively modern tool (1890 - 1910) would be the traditional German steel or an open hearth bulk process furnace steel commonly found after 1875.

102100T16   Tin snips   DTM   MH

Drop-forged iron and steel, 11 3/4" long, 2 7/8" blade, signed "Peak, Stow & Wilcox West Berlin Ct 9".

This is an early example of one of the most prolific toolmakers of the Industrial Revolution (1870f.) This specimen clearly illustrates the junction of the steel cutting components with the drop-forged sections of the blades. In more modern tin snips, this junction is no longer visible.

51606T8   Tin snips   DTM   MH

Forged iron and steel, 10 1/8" long, signed "Goldenberg" and "ACIER FONDU".

This is a nice example of a French-made late 19th century tool made with a weld steel cutting edge and hand-filed steel or iron handles. This tool has a modern appearance (post 1860) but still shows evidence of extensive handwork. Acier fondu is French for "molten steel".

93011T20   Tin snips   DTM   TT

Drop-forged steel, 10 1/2" long, signed "FORGED STEEL" on both handles.

22512T5   Tinsmiths' crimping tool   DTM   TT

Drop-forged steel, 10" long, signed "L.L.ROWE BOSTON" "PAT.DEC 21 1886".

L. Leroy Rowe received this patent No. 354,657 for an improvement to a device for crimping the ends of stove or other sheet metal pipe. http://www.google.com/patents/US354657. Courtesy of Liberty Tool Co.

5212LTC2   Tinsmiths' hand punch   DA   TT (Pub)

Drop-forged iron and steel, 7 1/4" long, unsigned.

Courtesy of Liberty Tool Co.

The Industrial Revolution (1865f.): Other Factory Made Tools

Blacksmith, Farrier, and Metalworking Tools

31611T10   **Tongs**   DTM   TT

Drop- and hand-forged malleable iron, 9" long, 1" nippers, unsigned.

The head of the tongs is convex in shape for holding round stock. It has an unusual configuration with one handle bent and extending 6 inches at a right angle.

12900T9   **Tubing cutter**   DTM   MH

Die cast nickeled alloy steel, signed "Imperial Brass, Chicago" and "94-F PAT. D-99190".

August C. Dobrick of Chicago, IL assigned his patent to Imperial Brass in 1935. http://www.google.com/patents?id=iHFpAAAAEBAJ&pg=PA2&dq=imperial+brass+99190&hl=en&sa=X&ei=vbXgT562N47dsgbMptjgCA&ved=0CDUQ6AEwAA#v=onepage&q=imperial%20brass%20999190&f=false

http://www.davistownmuseum.org/pics/51100t6.jpg

5212LTC3   **Turning sledge**   DA   TT (Pub)

Drop-forged steel, 6" long, 2 3/8" diameter face, signed "MEXICO".

Courtesy of Liberty Tool Co.

072112T11   **Unidentified tool**   DTM   TT

Steel, 14 1/4" long, 3/4" wide, signed "E.W. HAYNES".

This is a metalworking tool; its use is unknown. E. W. Haynes is not listed in DATM (Nelson 1999).

913108T31   **Wire-cutting pliers**   DTM   MH

Drop-forged steel, 5 1/2" long, signed "KRAEUTER U.S.A." including the quotation marks inside a rectangle with < > ends and "1821 5 1/2".

Kraeuter & Co. were located in Newark, NJ from 1879 - 1931 and made calipers, chisels, hammers, leather tools, machinist tools, pliers, and wrenches. This is a nice example of a turn of the century tool made by one of America's premier toolmakers.

40408DTM3   **Zigzag rule**   DTM   MH

Stainless steel, wrapped in wax and paper, 36" long in 12" sections, 3/4" wide, signed "No. 753 GENERAL HDW. MFG. CO., INC. NEW YORK N.Y. U.S.A. STAINLESS" with graduations in 32nds, 16ths, and 8ths of an inch.

DATM (Nelson 1999) lists 1887 as the founding date of this company. The wrapper lists the following information: "STK. NO. 8560 41-R-2750" "NOMENCLATURE RULE" "QUANTITY ONE UNIT EA." "PROCESSED LKY AUG 54" "METHOD 1A-1 P9" Stainless steel was not invented until 1917. General Hardware made tools into the 1990s.

http://www.davistownmuseum.org/pics/40408dtm3p1.jpg
http://www.davistownmuseum.org/pics/40408dtm3p5.jpg

Cast Iron Tools and Artifacts

The Industrial Revolution (1865f.): Other Factory Made Tools

Cast Iron Tools and Artifacts

50402A1   **Architectural ornament**   DTM   MH

Cast iron, 9 1/2" high, 7 1/4" wide, unsigned.

This is a nice example of Victorian ironwork.

TGB2206   **Pot**   DTM   MH

Cast iron, 3 1/4" high, 2 3/4" diameter, signed "PAT D APR 16 1872.".

The production of cast iron implements continued throughout the 19th century, characterized by an increase in quality, variety, and durability as forging methods and alloys became more sophisticated.

TTCI3000   **Screw jack**   DTM   MH

Cast iron, 3 1/2" high with a 1 1/2" diameter jack face and a 2" base, signed "C E HOBBS CO BOSTON" and "3/4 X 2".

DATM (Nelson 1999, 387) lists C. E. Hobbs as an individual working in Barre, VT from 1887-1890, but no company in Boston with this name.

Cobbler and Saddler Tools

93012LTC5   **Beating out hammer**   DA   TT (Pub)

Cast steel, wood (hickory), 9 1/4" long, 2 5/8" long head, 2" diameter face, signed "USMC".

This is also known as a toe hammer.

30311T9   **Burnisher**   DTM   TT

Steel, brass ferrules, and wood handles, 15 1/2" long, working area 6" x 7/8", unsigned.

This tool has two handles and is used for burnishing and/or shaping leather.

22813LTC7   **Cobbler and saddlers' hammer**   DA   TT (Pub)

Cast steel, wood (hickory), 12" long, 4 3/4" long head, 1 7/8" diameter face, signed "WARRANTED EXTRA CAST STEEL".

3213LTC1   **Cobbler or leather workers' lasting hammer**   DA   TT (Pub)

Cast steel, wood (hickory), 7 1/2" long, 2" wide head, 1 1/4" x 1 1/8" face, signed "ZTR-B".

102512T11   **Cobblers' beating out hammer**   DTM   TT

Steel, wooden handle, leather, 7" long, 2 1/2" long head, unsigned.

A leather strip was added by the owner to keep the handle secured. Courtesy of Liberty Tool Co.

3312T3   **Cobblers' channel gouge**   DTM   TT

Drop-forged steel, wooden handle, brass ferrule, 6" long, unsigned.

The cutting edge is broken off.

The Industrial Revolution (1865f.): Other Factory Made Tools

Cobbler and Saddler Tools

22411T2   **Cobblers' hammer**   DTM   TT-D30

Drop-forged steel, wooden handle, 11 1/2" long, with a 3 1/4" long, 1 1/2" wide head, signed "S. W. CHRISTENSEN CO." "BROCKTON, MASS." "MADE IN" "U.S.A." and "2".

32412T4   **Cobblers' hammer**   DTM   TT-29

Drop-forged steel, hickory wood handle, signed "REX" and "STEEL DROP FORGED CHAMPION".

Numerous companies have Champion or Rex in their name or as brand names, but DATM (Nelson 1999) does not list any using both. Courtesy of Liberty Tool Co.

102512T1   **Cobblers' hammer**   DTM   TT

Steel, wooden handle, 12" long, 5 3/4" long head, signed "CLARKSON".

Clarkson is an owner's mark. Courtesy of Liberty Tool Co.

42405T10   **Cobblers' hammer**   DTM   MH

Drop-forged steel, 3 5/8" long, 1 1/8" diameter face, signed "USMC D".

USMC stands for the United Shoe Manufacturing Co., Boston and Lynn, Massachusetts, 1873 - 1913. This is a typical generic late-19th century drop-forged cobblers' hammer.

52603T5   **Cobblers' pincers**   DTM   MH

Drop-forged steel, 7 3/4" long, signed "W + C. WYNNE 2 WARRATED STEEL HAMMERS".

These are a type of pliers.

111206T4   **Corn bung**   DTM   MH

Drop-forged malleable iron, 5/8" diameter corn bung, 16 5/8" coupling with a 1" diameter corn bung hole, signed "Lightning Fulton III, Pat. Oct. 12 87".

This is a tool that would be used to impress your shoe with an indentation to make the situating of your corns (on your foot) in your boot or shoe more comfortable. It is an excellent example of a drop-forged malleable iron or low-carbon steel tool.

121412T13   **Curriers' fleshing knife**   DTM   TT

Cast steel, wood (rosewood), 25 1/4" long, 15" cutting edge, 5 1/2" long handles, signed "SNOW & NEALLEY BANGOR - MAINE".

61612T8   **Curriers' fleshing knife**   DTM   TT

Drop-forged steel, rosewood handles, 25 1/2" long, 14" long cutting edge, signed "SNOW & NEALLY CO. BANGOR-MAINE".

71412T1   **Curriers' fleshing knife**   DTM   TT

Drop-forged steel, brass, wooden (rosewood) handles, 12" wide, 12" long cutting edge, 4" long handles, signed "11 P. PIEVS".

The Industrial Revolution (1865f.): Other Factory Made Tools

Cobbler and Saddler Tools

31808SLP15   Curriers' shave

DTM   TT

Steel and wood, 15 1/2" long, 13" curved blade, unsigned.

http://www.davistownmuseum.org/pics/31808slp15-1.jpg
http://www.davistownmuseum.org/pics/31808slp15-2.jpg

102904T20   Draw gauge

DTM   MH

Drop-forged steel and iron, brass, and rosewood, 5 7/8" long slitter with a 5" handle, signed "C. S. OSBORNE & CO" "NEWARK" " N.J." and owner's mark "I BOIS" and "36".

This is a nicely made cobblers' leather slitting gauge. C. S. Osborne & Co. started producing leatherworking tools in 1826 and still makes tools today (www.csosborne.com). This leather slitting tool is a generic form and would be found in every cobblers' toolbox. This tool has a rosewood handle and represents the deluxe version of this implement. It is used to cut reins and straps.

http://www.davistownmuseum.org/pics/102904t20_p1.jpg
http://www.davistownmuseum.org//bioOsborne.html

63001T10   Draw gauge

DTM   MH

Drop-forged steel, brass, and wood, 6" wide, 5 5/8" long pistol grip, signed "Osborne Co Newark NJ Est 1826 Pat Aug 13, 76 Reissued July 7, 1877".

This is a classic example of a factory-made tool from the heyday of the Industrial Revolution. By 1876, Davistown's cobblers were substituting quality factory-made tools for handmade tools. This tool was also used by harness makers to slice leather.

http://www.davistownmuseum.org/pics/63001t10.jpg
http://www.davistownmuseum.org//bioOsborne.html

TJD1002   Hand punch

DTM   MH

Drop-forged iron, 4 3/16" long, signed "EYELET TOOL BOSTON".

This factory-made cobblers' tool is clearly signed. Even in the late 19th century, many shoes and boots were still made at the farm for both home use or for wholesalers.

http://www.davistownmuseum.org/pics/tjd1002.jpg

111001T34   Lace cutter

DTM   MH

Drop-forged iron and steel, japanned finish, 2 1/4" long, unsigned.

This tool is identified as an Elliot Patent (May 3, 1880) lace cutter for cutting shoelaces in Sellens (2002, 270) "Dictionary of American Hand Tools".

http://www.davistownmuseum.org/pics/111001t34.jpg

7612LTC6   Leather eyelet punch

DA   TT (Pub)

Forged steel, 7 1/2" long, 1 5/8" wide, 1/8" diameter punch, signed "FORGED" "4".

Courtesy of Liberty Tool Company.

The Industrial Revolution (1865f.): Other Factory Made Tools

Cobbler and Saddler Tools

090508T10   Leather pliers   DTM   MH

Drop-forged steel, 9 1/4" long, signed "4" and "2B MADE IN U.S.A." with a diamond mark between 4 and 2..

102512T16   Leatherworkers' smoothing tool   DTM   TT

Rosewood, 7 3/4" long, 7/8" x 7/8", unsigned.

Courtesy of Liberty Tool Co.

14302T18   Patterns (3)   DTM   MH

Drop-forged steel, various designs, 4" wide, 5 5/8" wide and 6 1/8" wide, unsigned.

They are marked only with size numeration and are used to cut leather patterns for use by a harness-maker or cobbler.

101412LTC2   Pinking iron   DA   TT (Pub)

Cast steel, 4" long, 1/2" wide, signed "C.S. OSBORNE & CO. 1/2".

http://www.davistownmuseum.org/bioOsborne.html

22612T2   Pliers   DTM   TT

Drop-forged steel, 9" long, signed "EYELET TOOL CO" on one side of the jaws and "E.T.CO BOSTON" on both sides at the pivot point.

This specialized set of pliers is used to cut leather for 1/4" strips. DATM (Nelson 1999, 268) indicates this company worked from 1858 to 1920. However, this tool looks newer, perhaps from the 1940s or 50s. One cutting edge is broken.

42812LTC2   Revolving leather hole punch   DA   TT (Pub)

Steel, 8" long, signed "W. SCHOLLHORN CO. NEW HAVEN, CONN. MADE IN U.S.A." "BERNARD" "LODI".

DATM (Nelson 1999, 697) lists William S. Schollhorn Co. as working from 1873 to 1913 making dividers, pliers, and other tools. Lodi is one of their brand names. William A. Bernard held the July 26, 1904 patent for this punch. View the patent at: http://www.google.com/patents?id=csx9AAAAEBAJ&printsec=frontcover&dq=william+a+bernard&hl=en&sa=X&ei=ejC1T-bWH9Gg-wbw5vWoDg&ved=0CEYQ6AEwBQ. Courtesy of Liberty Tool Co.

8912T5   Round leather punch   DTM   TT

Cast steel, 4 3/4" long, 7/8" wide, 7/16" diameter hole, signed "THOMAS ADAMS 12".

DATM lists a T. Adams of Philadelphia that made leather tools (Nelson 1999, 14).

The Industrial Revolution (1865f.): Other Factory Made Tools

Cobbler and Saddler Tools

3312T2   Shoe lasting pliers   DTM   TT

Drop-forged steel, 9" long, signed "UNION PATENTED OCT 25, 1887" "WHITCHER   3".

There is a crisscross pattern on the hammer face. Hammer pressed fit into body. Frank Whitcher of Boston, MA patented the lasting pinchers, which were made by Union Shoe Machinery Company of Lynn, MA, 1873 - 1913. His patent may be viewed at: http://www.google.com/patents?id=yDhOAAAAEBAJ&pg=PA2&dq=OCT+25,+1887+whitcher&hl=en& sa=X&ei=_mqpT-2qDYPH6AG0qtGzBA&ved=0CDcQ6AEwAA#v=onepage&q=OCT%2025%2C%201887%20whitcher &f=false. Courtesy of Liberty Tool Co.

3312T1   Shoe lasting pliers   DTM   TT

Drop-forged steel, 8" long, signed either "PREETH" or "FREETH".

This is a typical curved pliers w/ hammer but cast as one piece. The end is slightly damaged (the tack remover is broken off.) DATM (Nelson 1999) lists a foreign toolmaker named Benjamin Freeth as working 1770 - 1824. Courtesy of Liberty Tool Co.

52612LTC2   Shoe or saw toothed tack puller   DA   TT (Pub)

Steel, Bakelite, 6 1/4" long, 2 3/8" long blade, signed "USM".

The United Shoe Machinery Company's working dates were from 1873 to 1913 in Boston, MA, however, their factory was in Lynn, MA (Nelson 1999, 808). Courtesy of Liberty Tool Co.

31808SLP25   Shoemakers' hammer   DTM   TT

Drop-forged steel and wood, 8" long, 6 7/8" long handle, 3 1/2" long head, signed "STEEL" "DROP" "FORGED" "CHAMPION" and on the other side of the head "REX".

DATM (Nelson 1999) lists a number of companies named "Champion", several "Champion" marks on tools, and three "REX" marks. However, none of them specifically made cobblers' tools or hammers.

http://www.davistownmuseum.org/pics/31808slp25-3.jpg
http://www.davistownmuseum.org/pics/31808slp25-1.jpg

913108T9   Shoemakers' hammer   DTM   MH

Drop-forged malleable iron and low carbon steel, 9 1/4" long including a 7 3/4" long handle, 4 1/8" wide head, signed "JVIGEANT" "MARLBORO" "MASS" and on the other side "PAT JAN7" "1869" "NO. 2".

DATM (Nelson 1999) states Jacob Vigeant held a hammer patent but it is unknown if he also made the hammers, which are factory-made. His patent 73,141 from 1868 can ve viewed here: http://www.google.com/patents/US73141?pg=PA2&dq=Vigeant+hammer&hl=en&sa=X&ei=nCi1UIuU O4fJswalTw&ved=0CDcQ6AEwAA#v=onepage&q=Vigeant%20hammer&f=false.

The Industrial Revolution (1865f.): Other Factory Made Tools

Cobbler and Saddler Tools

111412T7   Sole gauge   DTM   MH

Alloy steel, 4 1/4" long, 1 1/8" wide, signed "SNELL & ATHERTON" "BROCKTON, MASS." and a star touchmark.

The measure marks 14 13 12 to 3. Snell & Atherton's working dates are unknown. They primarily made leatherworking tools for shoemakers (Nelson 1999, 736).

32313LTC4   Wing calipers   DA   TT (Pub)

Cast steel, 6" long, 3 1/4" wide when closed, signed "W. SCHOLLHORN NEW HAVEN CT. PAT. JAN. 9, 1866".

The patent belongs to Schollhorn & Pfelghar.

Coopers' Tools

102512T21   Coopers' bung   DTM   TT

Wood, steel ferrules, 8 1/2" long, 3 1/3" wide, unsigned.

Courtesy of Liberty Tool Co.

102512T3   Coopers' bung hammer   DTM   TT

Steel, wooden handle, 12" long, 5 3/4" long head, signed "LANG & JACOB" and "BOSTON MASS" on the head, on the handle "THE LA PIERRE SAWYER HANDLES" around "GREEN SEAL HANDLES" inside a circle..

Lang & Jacobs of Boston, MA, made coopers' tools from 1884 to 1890 (Nelson 1999, 470). The "S" in Jacobs appears to have worn off the hammer head. The LaPierre-Sawyer Handle Company was founded in Jackson, MO, in 1902 and is still in business. (http://news.google.com/newspapers?nid=1893&dat=19850417&id=BcwfAAAAIBAJ&sjid=jtgEAAAAIB AJ&pg=1398,5338142). Courtesy of Liberty Tool Co.

102512T22   Coopers' croze   DTM   TT

Oak body, steel edge, 13" long, 5 1/2" wide body, 9" long and 2" wide plane, unsigned.

Courtesy of Liberty Tool Co.

82512LTC1   Coopers' drawshave   DA   TT (Pub)

Cast iron, steel, wood (oak), 18 1/2" long, 6" handles, 3" edge, signed CINCINNATI. TOOL CO.; (on cutter) HARGRAVE 99.

Courtesy of Liberty Tool Co.

101008T2   Coopers' flagging iron   DTM   MH

Malleable iron, 22 1/4" long, 4 1/2" wide, unsigned.

The Industrial Revolution (1865f.): Other Factory Made Tools

Coopers' Tools

31808SLP24   **Coopers' hammer**   DTM   TT

Steel and wood, 14" long, 12" long handle, 4 3/4" long head, unsigned.

http://www.davistownmuseum.org/pics/31808slp24.jpg
http://www.davistownmuseum.org/pics/31808slp24-2.jpg

22512T2   **Coopers' hoop driver**   DTM   TT

Drop-forged steel, hickory, 14" long, 4 3/4" wide, 1 1/4" diameter face, unsigned.

31212T3   **Coopers' scorp**   LPC   MH-O

Forged steel, wood, 7" long, 8" wide, 5" wide cutting edge, signed "SNOW & NEALLEY Co. BANGOR-MAINE".

This c. 1900 tool is specifically for coopering. Courtesy of Liberty Tool Co.

040103T2   **Coopers' shave**   DTM   MH

Cast grey iron with steel blade, 23" long, 2 1/8" blade, signed "Stanley" and "57".

This coopers' shave is a Stanley no. 57, type one, manufactured c. 1870. It signifies the appearance of mass-produced factory made tools. Coopers had been producing their wooden barrels and kegs from time immemorial. This handy coopers' tool appeared just at the twilight of the era of the cooper, whose handiwork was soon superseded by factory-made tin and steel containers.

http://www.davistownmuseum.org/pics/040103t2_p1.jpg
http://www.davistownmuseum.org/pics/040103t2_p4.jpg

33011T1   **Croze**   DTM   TT

Oak with a cast steel cutter, 24" long, 4" cutter, 7" radius area, unsigned.

It includes a three piece set of lance croze irons.

22512T6   **Drawknife**   DTM   TT

Drop-forged steel, wood, 19" long, 12" long blade, unsigned.

The blade is curved; it was probably a coopers' tool. Courtesy of Liberty Tool Co.

31808PC9   **End shave**   DTM   MH

Steel and wood, 6 1/2" long, 4 3/4" wide blade, signed "J.STORTZ&SON PHILA".

John Stortz and his son's company was in Philadelphia, PA from 1853 to 1972 (DATM 1999).

102512T20   **Hoop driver**   DTM   TT

Cast steel, 12" long, 3" diameter round end, 1 3/4" x 3" rectangular end, unsigned.

Courtesy of Liberty Tool Co.

The Industrial Revolution (1865f.): Other Factory Made Tools

Coopers' Tools

72812T2　　**Hoop driver**　　　　　　　　　　　　DTM　MH

Cast steel, 3 3/8" long, 3 1/2" edge, unsigned.

This hoop driver has a socket.

101312T20　　**Hoop set**　　　　　　　　　　　　DTM　TT

Cast steel, cast iron, wood (maple), 7 1/4" long, 2 1/4" wide edge, 1 5/8" long handle, signed "SLOAN".

101312T14　　**Hoop set hammer**　　　　　　　　DTM　TT

Cast steel, wood (maple), 13" long, 5" long head, 1 3/8" wide edge, 1 1/4" diameter face, signed "DAMAGED".

This tool is also called a hoop driver or coopers' driver.

102503P3　　**Keg**　　　　　　　　　　　　　　　DTM　MH

Wood with steel bands, 10 1/2" wide, 16" high, signed "__ Libby & Meke__" in paint. Label: "Swift & Company Wholesale dealers in choice dressed beef, mutton, veal, pork provisions & produce Bath Maine".

This is a typical mid- or late 19th century (1860 - 80) meat keg or "pork barrel" for the Maine coastal trade. It is a nice example of a factory-made keg.

62212T3　　**Leveling plane (sun plane)**　　　　　DTM　MH

Wood (bird's eye maple), cast steel blade, 17" long, 3 1/8" wide, 2 1/8" blade, signed "GREAVES & SONS ELECTRO BORACIC STEEL".

Greaves & Sons is a famous and prolific Sheffield, England, manufacturer. The mark "electro boracic steel" suggests it had a late 19th century manufacturing date.

31811T26　　**Unidentified tool**　　　　　　　　DTM　TT

Wood with a steel bracket, 21" long, unsigned.

This possible coopers' tool has a tapered wood handle with a steel "L" shaped bracket threaded and secured to the handle with a standard sized nut.

31811T25　　**Unidentified tool**　　　　　　　　DTM　TT

Wood with a steel bracket, 22" long, unsigned.

This possible coopers' tool has a tapered wood handle with a steel "L" shaped bracket threaded and secured to the handle with a standard sized nut.

Domestic Utensils

52512LTC1　　**Butcher's steel**　　　　　　　　DA　TT (Pub)

Forged steel, wood (beech), 15" long, unsigned.

Courtesy of Sett Balise.

The Industrial Revolution (1865f.): Other Factory Made Tools

Domestic Utensils

121011T1   Candy roller   DTM   MH

Brass, cast iron, tempered alloy steel, and rosewood, 11 1/2" x 6 3/4" base, 10" crank, 1/2" balls, signed "THE THREE MILLERS CO." "CONFECTIONERS SUPPLIES" and "7".

This is a Thomas Mills Drop Roller, patented 1871, also known as a fruit drop roller. This unusual tool is used for making candies. The crank turns the two cylinders like a wringer. It is missing one of the feed gates. On the gears there will be an arrow or dot to let you line up the two rollers to match exactly. They were machined at the same time, so they only really match at one point. Use this link for a description of how it works. Http://www.akirarabelais.com/v/witchbefooled/candy/make.html (The Candy Maker's Guide 1896, pg. 11). The Three Millers company is listed in Boston, MA, business directories as early as 1890 and as late as 1914 as a purveyor of flavor extracts and confectioner's supplies. Ernest L. Miller was the owner in 1911. Thank you to Greg at www.LoftyPursuits.com for some of the above information. Go to his website to order candies made with similar machines.

http://www.davistownmuseum.org/pics/121011t1-web1.jpg
http://www.davistownmuseum.org/pics/121011t1-web5.jpg

42712LTC1   Cigar box opener   DA   TT (Pub)

Drop forged steel, 8" long, signed "R.G. SULLIVAN'S 7-20-4 CIGAR" "R.G. SULLIVAN, INC. MANCHESTER, N.H.".

This is a twentieth century artifact. Courtesy of Liberty Tool Co.

32708T50   Crimping/pinking machine   DTM   MH

Drop-forged iron and steel, wooden handle, 5" long handle, 5" at the widest point, 6 1/4" high, signed "MFD BY" "SOUTH" "RICHLAND" "MACHINE CO" "PULASKI NY" and on the other side "CLEAN CUT".

http://www.davistownmuseum.org/pics/32708t50-3.jpg
http://www.davistownmuseum.org/pics/32708t50-1.jpg

6712LTC1   Embroidery hoop clamp   NOM   TT (Pub)

Iron and steel, japanned finish, unsigned.

It was patented in 1902. Courtesy of George Short

6712LTC3   Grass shears   DA   TT (Pub)

Drop-forged steel, 12" long, 6" long cutting edges, signed "PAT. AUG. 11,1914 No.4".

They were patented by Patrick F. Ryan of Syracuse, NY. View the patent here: http://www.google.com/patents?id=vl9UAAAAEBAJ&pg=PA1&dq=aug.+11+1914+shears&hl=en&sa=X&ei=yMPpT6O0FZHUsgat1bXCDg&ved=0CDkQ6AEwAg#v=onepage&q=aug.%2011%201914%20shears&f=false. Courtesy of Liberty Tool Co.

The Industrial Revolution (1865f.): Other Factory Made Tools

Domestic Utensils

6312LTC11   Hat brim cutter   DTM   MH

wood and brass, 8" long, 9 1/2" wide, 3/4" thick, signed "ALBERT C. COURTER NEWARK N.J." and "10" with rule markings 1 to 5 inches.

http://www.davistownmuseum.org/pics/6312LTC11_thumb_p1.jpg
http://www.davistownmuseum.org/pics/6312LTC11_thumb_p2.jpg

42012T2   Horologist's screw plate   DTM   TT

Cast steel, 7 3/4" long, 1 5/8" wide, signed "P S STUBS" "19 ENGLAND".

This tool is a watch and clock-makers' screw threading plate.

http://www.davistownmuseum.org/bioStubs.htm

42712LTC2   Ink eraser   DA   TT (Pub)

Forged steel, bone, 6" long, signed "GERMANY".

Courtesy of Liberty Tool Co.

41801T8   Meat saw   DTM   MH

Malleable iron, cast steel, brass, and wood, 22 1/4" long, blade 16" long, 7/16" wide, signed "EDWARD J. HOLDEN & Co NEW YORK CAST STEEL WARRANTED".

DATM (Nelson 1999) lists this company in New York and Brooklyn in 1870 - 1871. This saw has the distinctive American eagle brass also characteristic of H. Disston saws of the period. It is a very rare maker's mark.

32708T66   Mouse trap   DTM   MH

Wood and metal, 3" wide, 2 3/8" long, 1 1/8" high, signed "SOURICIERE A TROUS" REFLEX" "-RESSORTS ACIEL-" and on bottom "galeries Lafeyetto" plus a vertical "ABRICATIO" and "FRANCAIS".

This is a guillotine style mouse trap, made in France.

http://www.davistownmuseum.org/pics/32708t66-1FrenchGuillotineMouseTrap.jpg
http://www.davistownmuseum.org/pics/32708t66-2.jpg

71312T4   Pruning shears   DTM   TT

Cast steel, 10" long, 1 3/4" wide, 3" cutting edge, signed "FRANCE" "MAC".

These shears have a crescent moon shape cut into them that appears when they are closed and locked.

52403T5   Razor   DTM   MH

Cast steel, 6 1/4" long, 3" blade, signed "T. NOONAN & SONS CO BOSTON MASS MADE IN GERMANY".

This is a late example of excellent quality German steel.

ID #		Status	Location

Domestic Utensils

22411T12   Scraper

DTM   TT

Forged malleable iron, 12" long, 5 1/2" wide, 3 3/4" deep, unsigned.

This may have been used as a chicken coop scraper. It is hand-forged and hand riveted.

22411T20   Shears

DTM   TT-D9

Forged steel, 9" long with a 2" blade, signed "W PA____" "& SON" "SHEFFIELD" "ENGLAND" "HERRIC___" and "COMPANY".

These shears have a curved blade.

32708T49   Stapler

DTM   MH

Metal, 7" long, 2 1/2" wide, signed "MADE IN U.S.A." "PATENTED U.S.A. A.2-6-17" "PATENTED G.B. 3.26-15" "EVEREADY MFG. CO" "OF BOSTON" "U.S.A." with another "EVEREADY" in a diamond..

http://www.davistownmuseum.org/pics/32708t49-1.jpg
http://www.davistownmuseum.org/pics/32708t49-3.jpg

6312LTC3   Stove burner handle

DA   TT (Pub)

Grey cast iron, japanned finish, 8 3/4" long, unsigned.

Courtesy of Liberty Tool Co.

110611T3   Straight razor

DTM   TT

Cast steel, pearlite, 8.5" long handle, 3" long razor blade, signed "T. NOONAN & SONS CO BOSTON MASS", the trademark on the leather case reads "Black Demon".

"Timothy Noonan was a Boston Hairdresser from 1871 through 1880. His primary address was on Washington Street: at 723, then 913, and 910. Sometime after 1880, the company became known as 'T. Noonan & Sons'. (http://www.hairraisingstories.com/Proprietors/NOONAN.html).

102904T19   Teapot

DTM   MH

Cast iron, 3" diameter, signed but the mark is obscured.

This is a gorgeous example of the age of malleable cast iron.

http://www.davistownmuseum.org/pics/102904t19_p1.jpg

72712LTC8   Upholsterers' shears

DA   TT (Pub)

Cast steel, brass, 15" long, unsigned.

Courtesy of the Liberty Tool Company.

121412T15   Wall scraper

DTM   TT

Cast iron, steel, 8 5/8" long, 3 3/4" cutting edge, signed "WALL SCRAPER" "USE BROOM STICK ->" "WARRANTEED STEEL".

The Industrial Revolution (1865f.): Other Factory Made Tools

Domestic Utensils

71312T3	**Weavers' shears**	DTM	TT

Cast steel, 4 1/2" long, 1 1/2" wide, 1 5/8" cutting edge, signed "TREAT ENGLAND".

Files

1020T9	**Cabinet file**	DTM	TT

Tempered alloy steel, 8 1/2" long, 1/2" wide, signed 00 NICHOLSON XF MADE IN USA.

102012T5	**Crossing file**	DTM	TT

German steel (?), 11" long, 3/4" wide, signed "MADE IN SWITZERLAND A VALLORBES".

102012T14	**Crossing file**	DTM	TT

Cast steel, 9 3/8" long, 11/16" wide, signed "PS STUBS".

http://www.davistownmuseum.org/bioStubs.htm

102012T12	**Crossing file**	DTM	TT

German steel (?), 9" long, 5/8" wide, signed "B ANTOINE GLARDON VALEORBE MADE IN SWITZERLAND".

102012T11	**Double cut square file**	DTM	TT

German steel(?), 19 1/2" long, 3/4" wide, signed "K&F U.S.A.".

Kearney & Foot of Paterson, NJ and Philadelphia, PA, 1879-1897 used this mark. They made files and handles. Eventually, they were acquired by Nicholson File Co. (Nelson 1999, 437).

92812T1	**Double cut wood file**	DTM	TT

Cast steel, 22 1/2" long, 1 3/4" wide, signed "WARRANTED CAST STEEL" (with a man on a horse) "W.A.T. ZACK & CO. Sheffield".

31811T16	**File**	DTM	TT

Drop-forged and machine cut steel, 6 1/2" long, 3/8" wide, signed "ASHWORTH".

This file is used for the second or fine cut. DATM (Nelson 1999) lists Sager Ashworth & Co. as working in Lowell, MA, 1857-1871.

913108T27	**File**	DTM	MH

Probably German steel, 9" long, signed "FL. GROBETAVALLORBE" "MADE IN SWITZERLAND" and a rabbit trademark.

This is a nice example of a Swiss-made file.

The Industrial Revolution (1865f.): Other Factory Made Tools

Files

72712LTC4   File handle   DA   TT (Pub)

Cast iron, 5 1/2" long, 1" diameter, holds a 1/4" diameter file, unsigned.

This file handle appears to be based on E.C. Stearns' design but is unmarked. Courtesy of the Liberty Tool Company.

31212T9   Files (2)   DTM   TT

Drop-forged tool steel, 8" long, 5/16" wide, signed "00 XF NICHOLSON MADE IN U.S.A.".

William Nicholson founded Nicholson Files and Rasps in Providence, RI. They made files from 1864 to1972 (Nelson 1999). Courtesy of Liberty Tool Co.

http://www.davistownmuseum.org/bionicholson.html

31811T21   Four in hand file   DTM   TT

Drop-forged machine cut tempered alloy steel, 10" long, 1" wide, 1/4" thick, signed with an obscured trademark.

This file can be used for a combination of flat and half round coarse and medium cuts.

102512T19   Rasp   DTM   TT

German steel, brass ferrule, wooden handle, 18" long, 12" long and 1 1/4" wide blade, signed "W. E" on the tang with the rest hidden under the handle and "AOG" owner's mark.

Courtesy of Liberty Tool Co.

102012T8   Riffler file   DTM   TT

German steel (?), 11" long, 1/2" wide, signed with an obscured mark.

102012T10   Riffler file   DTM   TT

Cast steel, 6 1/2" long, 3/8" wide, signed with an obscured mark.

31212T10   Round cut metal file   DTM   TT

Drop-forged tool steel, 8" long, 3/8" wide, signed "A.H. SWISS U.S.A. 00".

Courtesy of Liberty Tool Co.

102012T4   Single cut square file   DTM   TT

German steel (?), 12 1/2" long, 5/16" wide, signed "MCCAFFREY PHILADA".

McCaffrey Bro. was founded by Hugh McCaffrey (born 1843 in Ireland, died 1919). Brothers John, Henry, James, and possibly Arthur were his partners. Founded in 1863, by 1896 they had become the McCaffrey File Company, which stayed open until 1933. They also used the name Pennsylvania File Works (Nelson 1999, 523).

The Industrial Revolution (1865f.): Other Factory Made Tools

Files

102012T13   **Single cut triangle file**   DTM   TT

Cast steel, 7" long, 3/8" wide, signed "PS STUBS".

http://www.davistownmuseum.org/bioStubs.htm

102012T7   **Single cut triangle file**   DTM   TT

Cast steel, boxwood, 5 3/8" long, 2 7/8" long handle, 3/4" wide, unsigned.

30911T2   **Square bastard file**   DTM   TT

Drop-forged tool steel, 17" long, unsigned.

The cut of the file refers to how fine its teeth are. They are defined from roughest to smoothest as: rough, middle, bastard, second cut, smooth, and dead smooth.

31212T11   **Triangle cut metal file**   DTM   TT

Drop-forged tool steel, 8" long, 3/8" wide, signed "F.I. BROBETA FOLLORBE" "2 MADE IN SWITZERLAND" and a running rabbit logo.

Courtesy of Liberty Tool Co.

Fishing Implements

101312T2   **Clam rake**   DTM   TT

Malleable iron, wood (maple), 10" long, 8 1/4" long handle, 12 1/2" wide, unsigned.

This tool is also known as a clam hook.

101312T1   **Clam rake**   DTM   TT

Steel, wood (hickory), 9" long blades, 10 1/2" long handle, 7" wide, unsigned.

This tool is also known as a clam hook.

22512T8   **Eel spear**   DTM   TT

Forged iron, 16" long, 6" wide, signed 'IDEAL'.

This is a very nice example of an eel spear, it has not been damaged through use. A number of different companies used the brand name Ideal, but none are listed as making fishing equipment. Garant Inc. of Montmagny, QU, made various types of tools (Nelson 1999). Courtesy of Liberty Tool Co.

33013T6   **Fishing spool**   DTM   MH

Wood (pine), rope (cotton), 12 1/2" x 13 1/2" x 1 1/2", unsigned.

The Industrial Revolution (1865f.): Other Factory Made Tools

Fishing Implements

112704T1   Flensing knife   DTM   MH

Low carbon steel with wood handle, 9 5/8" long, cutting edge 8 1/2" wide, 30 1/2" long handle, unsigned.

This flesh cutting whaling tool is used to strip or flense a whale of its blubber or skin. It appears to be of relatively modern drop-forged construction. It was found in the New Bedford, MA, area along with other fishing gear. It looks like a common garden edger and was probably locally made by one of the many whalecraft (tool) manufacturers working in the New Bedford area in the 19th century.

112004T1   Handline weight   DTM   MH

Lead with two brass swivels at ends of horse, 7 3/4" long horse with 1 pound lead, signed "H.H. CRIE & CO. ROCKLAND ME.".

The handline weight is also called a Dickinson swivel or Georges Bank sinker. It is used on a handline to fish for cod and halibut, especially on Georges Banks in areas with a strong current. H. H. Crie was a purveyor of hardware of all types. This information is courtesy of Larry Davis, Bath, ME.

http://www.davistownmuseum.org/publications/volume10.html

101312T5   Hoe   DTM   TT

Forged iron, wood (hickory), 42" long, 7" x 6" head, unsigned.

This hoe came from a family of clam diggers and likely served some duty for a marine hunter-gatherer.

102100T24   Mackerel plows (2)   DTM   MH

Wood and slate, 7 1/2" long, 7 1/4" long, signed "J. A. P. 1864".

Only the longer one is signed.

Hammers

12813T3   Adz-eye hammer   DTM   TT

Cast steel, 5" long, 1 3/8" wide, 1 1/8" diameter face, unsigned.

22601T4   Armorers' doming hammer   DTM   MH

Cast steel, 7 3/4" long, 1 1/4" and 1 1/2" diameter peens, signed "MOB" with trademark and marked "40" and "5".

MOB is the mark of the French toolmakers' cooperative that manufactured those tools. An additional description of this hammer can be found in Lynch's catalog of tools in the museum reference area.

http://www.davistownmuseum.org/bioLynch.htm

22411T25   Ball peen hammer   DTM   TT

Drop-forged steel with a wooden handle, 10" long, 3 1/2" x 1 1/4" head, signed "AMES MFG" "DROP FORG".

Ames Mfg. Co. was in Chicopee Falls, MA from 1829-1876. Don't confuse it with the Ames Shovel Co. of Easton, MA.

The Industrial Revolution (1865f.): Other Factory Made Tools

Hammers

041505T9   **Ball peen hammer**   DTM   MH

Drop-forged steel with wooden handle, 13" long including the handle, 3 5/8" long head with 1 1/16" diameter face, signed "1312 PASCHALL" "MADE IN USA 90".

No Paschall is listed as a hammer-maker in DATM (Nelson 1999). Probably this was produced in the early to mid-20th century (c. 1925 - 1940). It is a nice example of a high quality drop-forged steel hammer. It is the center hammer in the photograph.

http://www.davistownmuseum.org/pics/041505t7.jpg

92112T10   **Ball peen hammer**   DTM   TT

Malleable cast iron, wood (hickory), 16" long, 4 1/2" long head, 1 1/2" diameter face, signed "HERCULES FORGED STEEL HAMMER ATHA DEPARTMENT THE STANLEY RULE & LEVEL PLANT STANLEY WORKS MADE IN U.S.A. NEW BRITAIN, CONN.".

http://www.davistownmuseum.org/bioStanley.htm

31311T2   **Ball peen hammer head**   DTM   TT

Drop-forged steel, 3" long, 7/8" wide head, signed "D MAYDOLE" "MADE IN USA".

DATM (Nelson 1999, 520) lists David Maydole & Co. as a hammer manufacturer in Norwich, NY, 1861-1931. Maydole was the inventor of the modern claw hammer.

10112LTC4   **Brass face hammer**   DA   TT (Pub)

Cast steel, wood (hickory), brass, 12 1/2" long, 4 3/8" wide head, 1 3/4" diameter face, signed "N R".

One face of this hammer is covered in brass.

42604T9   **Bung hammer**   DTM   MH

Drop-forged iron, 4 3/4" long, 1 1/2" wide head with a 1/8" bung ridge, 10" long wooden handle, signed "C.DREW & CO".

This is one of the many products of Christopher Drew's factory in Kingston, MA.

http://www.davistownmuseum.org/bioDrew.htm

121412T11   **Caliper chisel**   DTM   TT

Cast steel, wood (rosewood), 18 1/2" long, 8 3/4" long handle, 1/4" cutting edge, signed "BUCK BROS CAST STEEL".

http://www.davistownmuseum.org/bioBuckBrothers.html

TJG1002   **Carriage upholsterers' hammer**   DTM   MH

Drop-forged steel and wood, 7" long handle, 4" long head, 1/2" square face, signed "PATENTED JUNE 76".

The Industrial Revolution (1865f.): Other Factory Made Tools

Hammers

TJG1001A   Carriage upholsterers' hammer   DTM   MH

Drop-forged steel and wood, 5 3/4" long with a 3/4" diameter head, 13" handle, signed "R C CLAY 1874".

No R. C. Clay is listed in DATM (Nelson 1999).

http://www.davistownmuseum.org/pics/tjg1001a.jpg

22311T22   Caulking hammer head   DTM   MH3-D3

Oak body and steel ferrules, 12" long, 1 1/2" wide, signed "C DREW & CO" and "000".

Part of the Robert Sullivan Collection donation.

http://www.davistownmuseum.org/bioDrew.htm

22612T13   Claw hammer   DTM   TT

Drop-forged steel, wood handle, 7" long, 2 3/4" hook, signed "Cheney".

The head has a curved claw with a nail starter/holder, marketed as the "Cheney Nailer." The manufacturer was Cheney Hammer Co. in Little Falls, NY. Courtesy of Liberty Tool Co.

http://www.davistownmuseum.org/bioCheney.html

121412T2   Claw hammer   DTM   TT

Cast steel, wood (hickory), 13" long, 5" long head, 1 1/16" diameter face, signed "STANLEY 5 1/2 16-OZ".

http://www.davistownmuseum.org/bioStanley.htm

6703T18   Claw hammer   DTM   TT

Forged iron and steel, 5" long, 1 1/2" wide, 2" tall, signed WARNER.

The DATM lists I. Warner and Warner & Noble as hammer makers from 1882 to 1894. The stamp is crude, but the hammer is exceptionally hand forged: both the face and claws feature forge-welded laminated steel.

TJD1004   Claw hammer - screwdriver   DTM   MH

Drop-forged steel, wood, 8 5/8" long, 2 1/2" long claw hammer, 3/4" diameter face, unsigned.

This unusual hammer is typical of the mass-produced tools making their appearance in the late 19th century.

123012T1   Claw hammer head   DTM   TT

Drop-forged steel, 3 1/2" long, 1 5/8" tall, face is 13/16" diameter, signed "HAND MADE".

22612T10   Claw hammer head   DTM   TT

Drop-forged steel, 4 1/2" long, unsigned.

This hammer head has a curved claw with a Cheney design nail holder/starter. Courtesy of Liberty Tool Co.

300

The Industrial Revolution (1865f.): Other Factory Made Tools

Hammers

3312T7   Claw hammer head   DTM   TT

Cast steel, 5 1/2" long, 2" tall, 1" wide, 1" diameter face, signed "STANLEY 101 ½ 16 OZ".

Courtesy of Liberty Tool Co.

http://www.davistownmuseum.org/bio#bioStanley.htm

101312T26   Cross peen hammer   DTM   TT

Cast steel, wood (maple), 13 1/4" long, 4 1/2" long head, 7/8" wide edge, 1" diameter face, signed "SNOW & NEALLY CO BANGOR MAINE OUR BEST".

041505T4   Cross peen hammer   DTM   MH

Drop-forged steel and wood, 16" long including wooden handle, 1 3/4" beveled face, 4 1/2" long head, signed "DEFIANCE" on head and "DEFIANCE SOLID STEEL HAMMER" on a paper label on the handle, c. 1930.

The torn label also reads "Atha Department Stanley Rule & Level, Plant _____, New Britain, Conn. USA". The plant name is obscured. This is a nice example of a modern drop-forged steel hammer. It is the bottom right hammer in the photograph. This hammer is part of the hammer study group.

http://www.davistownmuseum.org/pics/041505t4.jpg
http://www.davistownmuseum.org/bioStanley.htm

32802T3   Cross peen hammer   DTM   MH

Drop-forged steel, 4 1/4" long, 15/16" wide peen and head, unsigned.

http://www.davistownmuseum.org/pics/32802t3.jpg

41212T2   Cross peen sharpening hammer head   DTM   TT

Drop-forged steel, 4 3/4" long, 2" wide, 1 7/8" tall, unsigned.

This design is also called a drill sharpening hammer, intended for sharpening rock drilling tools. This example is just the head with no handle. Courtesy of Liberty Tool Co.

102512T7   Doghead saw hammer   DTM   TT

Steel, wooden handle, 14" long, 4 1/4" long head, signed "HENRY DISSTON & SONS" "PHILADA" in a curve and an owner's mark "D.P.M.".

Courtesy of Liberty Tool Co.

http://www.davistownmuseum.org/bioDisston.htm

041505T13   Floor hammer   DTM   MH

Drop-forged steel, 6" long, 1 3/16" octagonal face, unsigned, c. 1875.

This is a typical 19th century hammer. It was used for floor ripping. It is the hammer on the right side of the photograph.

http://www.davistownmuseum.org/pics/041505t7.jpg

The Industrial Revolution (1865f.): Other Factory Made Tools

Hammers

31602T8   **Hammer**   DTM   MH

Drop-forged steel with wooden handle, 11" long with head 4 1/2" long and 5/8" wide, signed with an obscure etched mark: "MOR___S Woburn Mass, Chicago USA" and a logo.

This hammer was found together with the hammer 31602T1. A possibility for the mark is: "Morley Bros" a saddlery and harness company in Chicago. The mark "Woburn Mass" is a mystery.

http://www.davistownmuseum.org/pics/31602t8.jpg

31602T1   **Hammer**   DTM   MH

Drop-forged steel with a wood handle, 15 1/2" long, 4 11/16" wide, signed "4" meaning four pounds.

The hammer head is faceted. The use is unknown.

http://www.davistownmuseum.org/pics/31602t1.jpg

31311T7   **Hammer**   DTM   TT

Drop-forged steel with wood handle, 12" long, 4 3/4" x 1 1/8" head, unsigned.

This type of hammer is used to nail molding.

93011T11   **Hammer**   DTM   MH

Drop-forged steel and wood, 11" long, 4" head, unsigned.

This hammer is tapered on both ends. It could be used by a cooper, tinsmith, or silversmith.

33002T23   **Hammer**   DTM   MH

Drop-forged steel, 4 1/8" long, 2 5/8" long cross peen, 3/32" and 5/16" wide ends, signed "Simonds 333".

It was probably made by George Simonds, Boston, +/- 1889, a hammer- and planemaker. It is similar to a grindstone trimming hammer but is probably for whitesmithing. It is not in the hammer section of Sellens (2002) Dictionary of American Hand Tools.

http://www.davistownmuseum.org/pics/33002t23.jpg

52603T32   **Hammer**   DTM   MH

Drop-forged steel, 9 1/2" long, 5" head, signed "H. K. NIGHT", 1883.

10112LTC6   **Hammer adz**   DA   TT (Pub)

Cast steel, wood (hickory), 14" long, 5 3/4" wide head, 1 7/8" wide edge, 1 1/16" diameter face, signed "CHENEY No. 777".

31811T22   **Hammer head**   DTM   TT

Drop-forged steel, 9" long, 1 1/2" wide, signed "JOHN EA__" "BOSTON MASS".

This could be a stone workers' hammer.

The Industrial Revolution (1865f.): Other Factory Made Tools

Hammers

31311T4   **Hammer head**   DTM   TT

Drop-forged steel, 4 1/2" long, 1 1/8" wide, unsigned.

This broken head shows the metal's porosity. It may have been used by a metal worker or tinsmith.

22211T6   **Hammer head**   DTM   TT

Bronze, 3 1/2" long, 1 1/2" x 1", signed "PAT. 42 43".

The rest of the mark is not legible. It is cast as a goat's head novelty hammer with a claw. Part of the Robert Sullivan Collection donation.

TJG3001   **Hammers (5)**   DTM   MH

Drop-forged steel or alloy steel, signed as described below.

This is a group of five 20th century hammers. The claw hammer is signed "GARDEN CITY". This hammer is unusual because of the amount of wear shown on the handle as well as on the head - it must have been used by somebody over a period of decades to have this much wear on the handle. The tack hammer has a 5 1/4" long head, unsigned but noteworthy for the label on its handle "JEWFL HARTWELL HICKORY MEMPHIS TENN CHICAGO IL". A second tack hammer, 5 7/16" long head, is signed "1419 PLUMB MFG. USA". A claw hammer is signed "CHRO-MOLY MADE IN USA". The rest of the signature is obscured, 5" long head with a 1 1/8" face. This 20th century hammer typifies variations in tool steel that could be used in a special purpose hammer. This one appears to be steel and molybdenum. A body hammer, 4 1/4" long, 1 3/4" round face, and 1 1/2" square face is signed "Blue Point" and "BF 60C USA".

31808SLP2   **Nail holding hammer**   DTM   TT

Drop-forged steel and wood, 13 3/4" long, 11 1/2" long handle, unsigned.

http://www.davistownmuseum.org/pics/31808slp2-1.jpg
http://www.davistownmuseum.org/pics/31808slp2-1.jpg

10112LTC5   **Nailer hammer**   DA   TT (Pub)

Cast steel, wood (hickory), 13" long, 5" wide head, 1 1/8" diameter face, signed "CHENEY".

This Cheney hammer has a built in nail holder that uses ball bearings.

10112LTC2   **Railroad hammer**   DA   TT (Pub)

Cast steel, wood (hickory), 35 1/4" long, 9" wide head, 2" diameter face, signed "N".

This hammer is used for setting and removing railroad spikes.

92812LTC1   **Rawhide hammer**   DA   TT (Pub)

Rawhide, wood (hickory), 14" long, 4 3/4" wide head, 2 11/16" diameter face, signed "GARLAND".

32708T55   **Riveting hammer head**   DTM   MH

Drop-forged steel, 6" long, 1 1/8" wide, unsigned.

http://www.davistownmuseum.org/pics/32708t55.jpg

The Industrial Revolution (1865f.): Other Factory Made Tools

Hammers

121112T3   Rounding hammer   DTM   MH

Drop-forged iron and steel, wooden handle, 32 1/2" long, 8 3/8" long head, 3" diameter circular steel faces at both ends of the head, unsigned.

The use of this hammer is not known. It is in the form of a very large tin knockers' raising hammer, but with two identical, slightly rounded, peens. The weight of the hammer head is 8 to 9 pounds. Possibly it was associated with metalworking at the Bath Shipyards.

102612T7   Saw hammer   LPC   MH

Steel, wooden handle, 14 3/4" long, 6" long and 2" wide head, signed "FISHER".

This is a hammer for working on large circular mill saws to true the blades. There were two Fishers working out of Philadelphia, PA circa early 1800s, who made saws but neither one is listed as having made hammers and this looks more recent than that.

102612T4   Scaling hammer   DTM   TT

Steel, 38" long, 3" wide, 4" circular handle and lever, signed "303" on the handle.

The lever is used to move the pointed end.

http://www.davistownmuseum.org/pics/102612T4.jpg

041505T6   Sledge hammer   DTM   MH

Drop-forged steel, wood, 11 1/2" long including the handle, 5 1/4" long head with two 1 3/16" round faces, signed "ATHA" "CAST STEEL" and "A - 1", c. 1875.

This 19th century tool was probably made long before Atha was purchased by the Stanley Tool & Level Co. in 1913. The mark "CAST STEEL", the early look and the numbers suggests the early years of Benjamin Atha's toolmaking activities in Newark, NJ, when the cast steel mark was still the advertising choice of quality toolmakers. It is in the center of the photograph, under the other hammers. This hammer is part of the hammer study group.

http://www.davistownmuseum.org/pics/041505t5.jpg
http://www.davistownmuseum.org/bioAtha.html

041505T5   Sledge hammer   DTM   MH

Drop-forged steel and wood, 10" long including the handle, 4 1/4" long head with 1 1/8" diameter beveled round face on both ends, signed "CRAFTSMAN" "38311-4803-M" "MADE IN USA" "WEAR SAFETY GOGGLES".

This is an example of a late 20th century drop-forged steel hammer. It is the bottom hammer in the photograph. This hammer is part of the hammer study group.

http://www.davistownmuseum.org/pics/041505t5.jpg

52612LTC1   Sledge hammer   DA   TT (Pub)

Drop-forged steel, wood (hickory), 15 1/4" long, 13 1/2" long handle, 1 3/4" diameter face on the head, signed "4 LB WEAR SAFETY GOGGLES".

Courtesy of Liberty Tool Co.

The Industrial Revolution (1865f.): Other Factory Made Tools

Hammers

913108T16   **Sledge hammer**   DTM   MH

Drop-forged steel, wood, 5 1/6" long with a 3 1/2" long handle, 3" wide and 1 1/2" long head, unsigned.

22813LTC4   **Stone bush hammer**   DA   TT (Pub)

Cast steel, wood (hickory), 13 1/2" long, 8" long head, 2 1/2" edges, 2" wide, unsigned.

101312T15   **Striking sledge hammer**   DTM   TT

Cast steel, wood (hickory), 31 1/2" long, 6" long head, 2" diameter faces, signed "4.".

Ice Tools

52907T1   **Ice ax**   DTM   MH

Drop-forged iron and steel, 13 1/4" long, 1 3/4" wide cutting edge, signed "WM T. WOOD & CO.".

DATM (Nelson 1999) lists William T. Wood & Co. in Arlington, MA, from 1845 - 1905. The text "Town of Arlington, Past and Present" by Charles Symme Parker notes that William T. Wood came there about 1841 and started working with Abner Wyman making and repairing ice tools. He purchased the business in 1845 and ran it by himself until partnering with his brother Cyrus in 1858. He died in 1871. His son, William E. Wood took over retaining the name of William T. Wood & Co. In 1905 the company was consolidated with Gifford Brothers of Hudson, NY as Gifford-Wood Co.

http://www.davistownmuseum.org/bioWood.html

82308T1   **Ice ax**   DTM   MH

Drop-forged iron and steel, 13 1/2" long, 1 5/8" wide, signed "WM.T.WOOD".

http://www.davistownmuseum.org/bioWood.html

91303T11   **Ice ax**   DTM   MH

Drop-forged iron and steel with a wooden handle, 11 1/2" long, 2 1/4" wide blade, signed "Wm. T. Wood & Co".

This is a typical ice ax with an atypical short handle. The Harvard Business School Baker Library has a catalog from this company circa 1895: "Wm. T. Wood & Co. Manufacturers of ice tools, Arlington, Mass."

http://www.davistownmuseum.org/pics/91303t11.jpg
http://www.davistownmuseum.org/bioWood.html

101312T22   **Ice chopper**   DTM   TT

Drop-forged steel, wood (rosewood), 9" long, 2 1/2" wide, 1 1/4" tall, signed "HAMILTON BEACH NO 50".

The Industrial Revolution (1865f.): Other Factory Made Tools

Ice Tools

61512LTC1   Ice chopper   DA   TT (Pub)

Drop-forged steel, brass, rosewood handle, 9 1/2" long, 2 1/4" wide, unsigned.

Courtesy of Liberty Tool Co.

101312T13   Ice chopper and scoop   DTM   TT

Drop-forged steel, wood (rosewood), 10" long, 2 1/4" wide, 2" tall, signed "NORTH BROS. MFG. CO. PHILA. PAT APR 8 1884".

Hermann Albrecht was issued patent 295,501, which he assigned to the American Machine Company of Philadelphia. The North Brothers bought them out in 1892. (http://www.google.com/patents/US296501?pg=PA2&dq=apr+8+1884+ice&hl=en&sa=X&ei=bW19UK aFKMnJtAbxkYHQDw&ved=0CDMQ6AEwAA#v=onepage&q=apr%208%201884%20ice&f=false).

61204T5   Ice hook   DTM   MH

Forged iron with wood handle, 17 1/2" long, 7" wide handle, unsigned.

This ice hook came from the Hardscrabble Ice House, Rt. 97, East Boothbay, Maine, which was active in the late 19th century.

http://www.davistownmuseum.org/pics/61204T5.jpg

12103T1   Ice saw   DTM   MH

Drop-forged iron and steel, wood, 48" long, 6" wide, with 16" long and 2" wide wooden handle, unsigned.

Knives

42712LTC3   Banana knife   DA   TT (Pub)

Steel, hardwood handle, 10 1/2" long, signed "DEXTER SOUTH BRIDGE. MASS.".

DATM (Nelson 1999, 356) lists Dexter Harrington & Son of Southbridge, MA as makers of knives and leather tools from 1873 to 1875. It also lists Harrington Cutlery Co. of Southbridge, MA as using Dexter for a brand name. Courtesy of Liberty Tool Co.

12812T2   Bill hook   DTM   TT

Drop-forged German steel, brass rivets, wooden (hickory) handle, 16 3/4" long, 3" long blade with 5" hook, 5 1/2" long handle, signed "RUBINO" "NETRO".

This brush hook or machete is made with one casting and the hook is protruding from the handle. Rubino Netro is an Italian maker.

22813LTC5   Butchers' cleaver   DA   TT (Pub)

Cast steel, wood (rosewood), 20" long, 9" long handle, 7" wide, signed "FOSTER BROS TRADE MARK 10" with an arrow.

Knives

30911T5   Carriage-makers' body knife   DTM   TT

Cast steel (?), brass ferrules, and wood handles, 17" long, 5 1/2" long handles, 2 1/2" x 1" cutter, signed "J. R. WESTON" twice on one side and "G. ELLISON" twice on the adjacent side.

Both signatures may be owners' marks.

72712LTC5   Cloth knife   DA   TT (Pub)

Drop-forged steel blade, brass, wooden (rosewood) handle, 5 1/2" long without the blade inserted, 3/4" wide, 6" long blade, unsigned.

Courtesy of the Liberty Tool Company.

7712LTC5   Dandelion or asparagus knife   DA   TT (Pub)

Drop-forged steel, wooden (ash) handle, 14" long, 1 3/8" wide, 9 1/4" long cutting edge, unsigned.

Courtesy of Liberty Tool Company.

10112LTC3   Head knife   DA   TT (Pub)

Drop-forged steel, brass, wooden (rosewood) handle, leather sheath, 6 1/2" long, 4 1/2" wide, 1" thick, signed "C.S. OSBORNE EST 1896 NEWARK NJ" with a star touchmark.

http://www.davistownmuseum.org/bioOsborne.html

31311T5   Knife   DTM   TT

Drop-forged steel, iron ferrule, wooden handle, 11" long, 6" long x 1 1/8" wide blade, signed "L. D. LOTHROP" "GLOUCESTER" "MASS.".

This company is listed as a manufacturer of fishing apparatus and tools, such as knives, used to make tackle, in "Participation of the United States in the International Fisheries Exhibition, held at Bergen, Norway, 1898" by Jospeh Collins.

22612T11   Knife   DTM   TT

Drop-forged steel, wood handle, 4 3/4" long blade, 4" handle, signed "CHARLES M&H Co FRANCE NEW.YORK" with double quotes around "CHARLES".

Probably this was used as a fillet knife. Courtesy of Liberty Tool Co.

31611T2   Knife   DTM   TT

Drop-forged steel, brass ferrule, and wood handle, 9" long, 4 3/4" long by 1/2" wide blade, signed "W. WEBSTER".

W. Webster is listed in DATM (Nelson 1999) as working in Brockton, MA in 1872.

31811T15   Knife   DTM   TT

Drop-forged steel with a wood handle, 4 3/8" long, 2 1/8" long and 5/8" wide and 1/16" thick blade, signed "BARTLETT & BUT___" "HARVARD WOR___" and "SHEFELD".

The manufacturer's mark is partially hidden under the handle. This knife might be used for shucking clams.

Knives

33002T22 Knife   DTM   MH

Drop-forged steel, brass ferrule, wooden handle, 8 7/8" long including 4 5/8" handle, signed with Japanese lettering.

Not all tools found in New England tool kits are English or American. The blade shows evidence of grinding.

http://www.davistownmuseum.org/pics/33002t22.jpg

42812LTC3 Oyster knife   DA   TT (Pub)

Steel, wood (beech), 6" long, 2 1/2" long blade, unsigned.

Courtesy of Liberty Tool Co.

72312LTC2 Pruning knife   DA   TT (Pub)

Drop-forged steel, brass fittings, wooden (rosewood) handles, 4 1/2" long, 3 1/4" long blade, signed "KUTMASTER UTICA, N.Y., MADE IN U.S.A.".

Kutmaster was founded in 1910 and is still in business today as a division of Utica Cutlery Company (http://www.kutmaster.com/). Courtesy of Liberty Tool Company.

42012T7 Pruning knife   DTM   TT

Drop-forged steel, rosewood, 4" long folded, 1" wide, signed "NORTHFIELD" "KNIFE Co" "CONN".

It was made by Northfield Knife Co. of Lichfield County, Connecticut (still standing), which was in operation from 1858-1929 (Nelson 1999, 581). Provenance: Northfield, CT.

090508T5 Putty knife   DTM   MH

Drop-forged steel, wooden handle, signed "HENRY SEARS & SON" "1865" and "WARRANTED". There are star marks to either side of the date..

DATM (Nelson 1999) indicates they made cutlery and buttonhole scissors but has no location for them. Uniclectica lists this company in Chicago, Illinois c. 1883 - 1897 (http://www.uniclectica.com/misc/manuf.html).

090508T7 Putty knife   DTM   MH

Drop-forged steel blade, brass ferrule, and wooden handle, 6" long, 3 3/4" blade, 1" wide, signed "J. TYZACK & SON" and "SHEFFIELD" with a trademark on the other side.

Uniclectica lists this company as Joseph Tyzak & Son located at Heely (near Sheffield) c. 1842 to at least 1919 (http://www.uniclectica.com/misc/manuf.html).

52603T39 Scutcheon knife   DTM   MH

Drop-forged steel, wooden handle, 17" long, unsigned.

The Industrial Revolution (1865f.): Other Factory Made Tools

Knives

62112LTC2   Taxidermy and cadaver knife   DA   TT (Pub)

Cast steel, stag horn, ivory, silver trappings, 5" long, 1 1/2" lip, 2 1/2" and 2" long blades, signed "WARREN MUSEUM BOSTON MASS.".

The Warren Anatomical Museum opened in 1847 as an extension of Harvard University. No other example of this rare knife form is currently known with this signature.

http://www.davistownmuseum.org/pics/62112LTC2-5bw.jpg

121805T29   Utility knife   DTM   MH

Drop-forged steel, 6 3/4" long including a 3 1/2" wooden handle, signed "Russell Green River Works", c. 1870.

One of the finest tool factories, John Russell's Green River Works in Greenfield, MA, produced a wide variety of skinning and hunting knives by modern drop-forging techniques after 1837.

http://www.davistownmuseum.org/bioRussel.html

Logging Tools

61204T1   Cant dog   DTM   MH

Drop-forged iron and steel, wooden handle, 40" long including a 26 1/4" long wooden handle, 13 3/4" wide, signed "2 1/2 E. MANSFIELD & Co" "SNOW & NEALLEY CO" "BANGOR MAINE".

http://www.davistownmuseum.org/pics/61204T1_p1.jpg
http://www.davistownmuseum.org/publications/volume10.html

4106T9   Cant dog peavey   DTM   MH

Drop-forged iron and steel, wooden handle, 44" long, 14" shaft point, 9 1/2" curved cant dog, 30" long handle, signed "The Peavey Mfg. Co. Oakland ME" and "2 3/8 Peavey NO. 228".

This peavey is made with drop-forged low carbon steel. The 2 3/8 in the mark refers to the inside diameter that holds the handle. Joseph Peavey of Stillwater, Maine, invented the cant dog peavey c. 1860. This late 19th or early 20th century example of a classic Maine tool was made before the company moved to Brewer in 1928.

http://www.davistownmuseum.org/publications/volume10.html

22211T14   Folding caliper rule   DTM   TT

Boxwood and brass, 24" long (extended), 12" long (folded), 3/4" wide, 1/8" thick, signed "STANLEY RULE" "& LEVEL CO." "No 6".

This is a Stanley No. 6 rule. It has a twofold scale, each leg is 12". There is a brass caliper on one leg and a board foot scale on the other leg. Part of the Robert Sullivan Collection donation.

http://www.davistownmuseum.org/bioStanley.html

The Industrial Revolution (1865f.): Other Factory Made Tools

Logging Tools

71512LTC1   Folding log measure rule   DA   TT (Pub)

Boxwood, brass, 24" long, 11/16" wide, 5/32" thick, signed "THE C-S. CO. PINE MEADOW CONN. U.S.A.".

This unusual four-fold rule, the Chapin-Stephens No. 79 1/2, has a lip on the end of one of the legs and graduations for measuring board feet of lumber in a log of given length. Typically, log measures are not folding. Courtesy of Liberty Tool Company.

http://www.davistownmuseum.org/bioChapin.html

22211T15   Folding rule (board scale)   DTM   TT

Boxwood and brass, 24" long (extended), 6" long (folded), 5/8" wide, 1/8" thick, signed "No 82".

This is a Stanley No. 82 rule. The scale on one side is in inches and on the other it is in board feet for measuring logs. Part of the Robert Sullivan Collection donation.

http://www.davistownmuseum.org/bioStanley.html

22211T13   Folding rule (board scale)   DTM   TT

Boxwood and brass, 24" long (extended), 6" long (folded), 5/8" wide, 1/8" thick, signed "STANLEY RULE" "& LEVEL CO." "NEW BRITAIN, CONN." and on opposite side "No 81".

This is a Stanley No. 81 rule. The scale on one side is in inches and on the other it is in board feet for measuring logs. Part of the Robert Sullivan Collection donation.

http://www.davistownmuseum.org/bioStanley.html

33112T2   Hewing ax   DTM   TT

Cast steel, wood handle, 7 1/4" long, 1/2" wide, signed "J. R. Deering" "Libby and Bolton" and "Warranted cast steel".

Deering is a Saco Maine toolmaker (1849- 1881). He probably made this ax for Libby and Bolton who were also Maine toolmakers in Portland, Maine.

http://www.davistownmuseum.org/publications/volume10.html

51102T1   Log caliper   DTM   MH

Boxwood and brass, signed "Valentine Fabian".

DATM (Nelson 1999) states Fabian made rules, including log rules, in Milo Junction, Maine, starting in 1897. Donated to the Museum by Phil Platt.

http://www.davistownmuseum.org/publications/volume10.html

121412T12   Log marking hammer   DTM   TT

Cast steel, wood (hickory), 31 1/2" long, 11" wide head, 1" x 2" face, signed "GN".

This hammer is used to mark ownership of logs. The "GN" it imprints stands for Great Northern Paper Company of Millinocket, ME.

The Industrial Revolution (1865f.): Other Factory Made Tools

Logging Tools

101312T10   **Multi-use lumber tool**   DTM   TT

Drop-forged steel, 14 1/2" long, 3" wide, 15/16" thick, signed "US TWEAKER US PAT. NO. 4762303".

Phillip G. Thomas of Ashland, OR, received this patent in 1988. Tweaker is a brand name currently sold by Mayhew and Sears.
(http://www.google.com/patents/US4762303?pg=PA5&dq=4762303&hl=en&sa=X&ei=83B9UOjSMJD esgboy4HAAQ&ved=0CDIQ6AEwAA#v=onepage&q=4762303&f=false).

22813LTC2   **Peavey**   DA   TT (Pub)

Cast steel, wood (beech), 56" long overall, 16" head, 9" hook, signed "3/8E. MANSFIELD & Co SNOW & NEALLEY CO.".

93011T5   **Pickaroon**   DTM   TT

Drop-forged iron and steel, wooden handle, 15" long, 5" wide head, signed "SNOW & NEALLEY CO" "BANGOR".

http://www.davistownmuseum.org/publications/volume10.html

4106T11   **Pickaroon**   DTM   MH

Drop-forged iron and steel, wooden handle, 7 3/8" long, 27 1/4" handle, signed "SNOW & NEALLEY Co. BANGOR MAINE OUR BEST" in white letters on the handle.

This is a typical drop-forged example of a Snow & Nealley pickaroon, essential for moving small logs and branches during lumber harvesting.

http://www.davistownmuseum.org/publications/volume10.html

93011T6   **Pickaroon**   DTM   TT

Low carbon steel, 10" long, 6" wide head, unsigned.

112704T6   **Portable chain saw**   DTM   MH

Drop-forged steel and wood, 44 " long, 9 1/2" long handle, signed "DISSTON USA".

This is a portable saw that was used by the military and others in isolated locations where it was not practical to carry stiff one or two man saws.

http://www.davistownmuseum.org/bioDisston.htm

121111T1   **Portable chainsaw**   DTM   MH

Steel, brass, wood, and leather pouch, 48" long, signed "FRANCIS" "WOOD & SONS" "SHEFFIELD" "1917".

This is a World War I era British combat engineers' folding saw.

http://www.davistownmuseum.org/pics/121111t1web1.jpg
http://www.davistownmuseum.org/pics/121111t1web3.jpg

The Industrial Revolution (1865f.): Other Factory Made Tools

Logging Tools

31908T39   **Pulp hook**   DTM   MH

Drop-forged iron and steel, wooden handle (rosewood), 10" long, signed "SNOW & NEALLEY CO" and "BANGOR - MAINE".

http://www.davistownmuseum.org/pics/31908t39p3.jpg
http://www.davistownmuseum.org/publications/volume10.html

12801T17   **Saw set**   DTM   MH

Drop-forged iron, 8" long with 7 set sizes, signed "HOE & CO".

DATM (Nelson 1999) lists R. Hoe & Co.'s working dates as 1828 - 1969 in New York and Boston. It did not list this exact mark. Hoe was a major manufacturer of saws, saw tools, and later, printing presses. This set is probably late 19th century.

http://www.davistownmuseum.org/pics/12801t17.jpg
http://www.davistownmuseum.org/bioHoe.html

32802T13   **Saw set**   DTM   MH

Drop-forged iron and steel, 8" long, signed "Morrell's PAT. Dec 14 88".

This is one of a wide variety of Morrell designs for saw sets. DATM (Nelson 1999) lists two patents, Feb. 24 and Dec. 14, 1880. This may not be the only unrecorded saw set patent. This design is rare; the 1880 patent designs were widely produced. Charles Morrell worked in New York city; DATM gives 1851 - 1920 as the working dates of the company with his name. Saw sets of this size are often associated with setting the teeth on two-man logging saws.

6312LTC7   **Timber scribe**   DA   TT (Pub)

Forged steel blade, brass ferrule, rosewood handle, 7 3/4" long, 1/8" wide channel, 3 3/8" long blade, unsigned.

Courtesy of Liberty Tool Co.

041505T39   **Timber-framing chisel**   DTM   MH

Forged iron and cast steel, 12" long, 1 1/2" wide, signed "PAGE, WHITMAN & CO" " W. FITCHBURG" "CAST-STEEL" and " WARRANTED".

DATM (Nelson 1999, 596) gives the date 1864 for this Massachusetts company, which made chisels. It is an excellent example of welded cast steel with a clear steel-iron transition zone.

http://www.davistownmuseum.org/pics/041505t39_p1.jpg
http://www.davistownmuseum.org/pics/041505t39_p2.jpg

Machinists' Tools

32313LTC7   **Threading tool holder**   DA   TT (Pub)

Drop-forged steel, 6 1/4" long, 1 5/8" tall, 1/2" thick, signed "NO. C-51 WILLIAMS THREADING-TOOL HOLDER" "J.H. WILLIAMS & CO. DROP-FORGED IN U.S.A.".

J. H. Williams & Co. was located in Brooklyn, NY from 1882 to 1909 and later in Buffalo, NY.

The Industrial Revolution (1865f.): Other Factory Made Tools

Machinists' Tools

32313LTC8   Threading tool holder   DA   TT (Pub)

Drop-forged steel, 7 1/4" long, 3" tall, 1/2" thick, signed "Pratt & Whitney Hartford, Conn. U.S.A. M2" "P&W U.S.A. P8HS35".

Measuring Tools

22211T20   Carpenters' rule   DTM   TT

Boxwood and brass, 8" long, 2 1/4" wide, 1/2" thick, extends to 6 feet, signed "EDISON PORTLAND CEMENT CO. NEW YORK - BOSTON - PHILA" "PAT'D 12.13.1910" "PAT'D 7.29.1913".

Other marks include: "EDISON SIGNATURE", "A PRODUCT OF THE EDISON LABORITORIES", "N.Y. APPRD.", "X-4", and a pointing finger touchmark. This rule slides open, it does not fold. Part of the Robert Sullivan Collection donation.

22211T21   Carpenters' rule   DTM   TT

Tempered alloy steel, 6" long, 3/4" wide, 3/32" thick, extends to 6 feet, signed "THE L S STARRETT CO. ATHOL, MASS USA" "PAT. MAR. 14. 1911" "NO. 451" and "TEMPERED".

Part of the Robert Sullivan Collection donation.

http://www.davistownmuseum.org/bioStarrett.html

3213LTC3   Combination rule   DA   TT (Pub)

Boxwood, brass, 12" unfolded, legs are 3/8" x 5/8" thick, signed "No 36" "STEPHENS & CO. RIVERTON, CT. PATENTED JAN. 12. 1858".

Phillip Stanley calls this "The most universal measuring tool ever made in America" in "A Source Book for Rule Collectors" (2004). It can be used as a two-fold ruler, try square, or inclinometer. The level in this particular specimen is missing. An image of this tool in the Chapin-Stephens catalog may be found here: http://www.davistownmuseum.org/bioChapin.html

http://www.davistownmuseum.org/bioChapin.html

31602T3   Cyclometer   DTM   MH

Brass, bronze, and steel, 4 1/4" high, 2" diameter face, signed "Boys & Ruckers signal cyclometer. Patent.".

040103T15   Drill gauge   DTM   MH

Steel, 7 1/2" long, signed "W & M Mfg Co. Worcester Mass".

W & M Mfg. Co. is not listed in DATM (Nelson 1999). This tool has graduations from 0 to 20 -- about a 1/4" at 0 to 1/64" at 20. Is it a wire gauge?

http://www.davistownmuseum.org/pics/040103t15_p1.jpg

041505T30   Drill gauge   DTM   MH

Steel, 5 1/4" long, 1 5/8" wide, signed "T. F. WELCH BOSTON".

Tools by this small, c. 1900, Boston-maker of jewelers' bench drills are very uncommon.

http://www.davistownmuseum.org/pics/041505t30.jpg

The Industrial Revolution (1865f.): Other Factory Made Tools

Measuring Tools

32313T6   **Level**   DTM   MH

Wood (rosewood), brass, glass, 29 1/2" long, 3 1/4" tall, 1 3/8" wide, signed "J.M. DAVIDSON PO'KEEPSIE".

James M. Davidson worked in Poughkeepsie, New York circa 1860 to 1869.

52408T6   **Level**   DTM   MH-O

Wood, brass, and glass, 5 1/2" long, 1 1/4" wide, 1 1/2" high, signed "STANLEY" "RULE & LEVEL CO." "New Britain Ct.".

http://www.davistownmuseum.org/bioStanley.htm

913108T11   **Level**   DTM   MH

Brass and wood, 6 3/4" long, signed "J W HARMON" "BOSTON" "MASS" "HAVERILL".

Leon Robbins of Bath, Maine, made this level out of an old one originally made by John W. Harmon of Boston, MA, whose working dates were 1860 - 1907.

http://www.davistownmuseum.org/bioLeon.html

22311T9   **Marking and mortise gauge**   DTM   TT

Rosewood and brass, 7 1/2" long, 2" x 2" body with a brass adjustment mechanism, unsigned.

Part of the Robert Sullivan Collection donation.

42912LTC5   **Medical calipers**   DA   TT (Pub)

Drop-forged steel, 11 1/2" long, signed "WILLIS, PHILA.".

These unusually designed calipers have a rule mounted on them with both metric and fractional increments. Courtesy of Liberty Tool Co.

6212LTC2   **Miter square**   DA   TT (Pub)

Forged steel, brass screws, rosewood, 9 1/2" long, 3 1/2" long handle, signed "STANLEY RULE & LEVEL CO".

Courtesy of Liberty Tool Co.

http://www.davistownmuseum.org/bioStanley.htm

30311T5   **Plumb bob**   DTM   TT

Steel and brass, 4" long, 1 1/2" diameter, unsigned.

This is a reworked munition from WWI or WWII.

3213LTC4   **Plumb bob**   DA   TT (Pub)

Turned brass, cast steel, 3.5 ounces, 3" long, 3/4" diameter, unsigned.

The Industrial Revolution (1865f.): Other Factory Made Tools

Measuring Tools

32708T60   **Plumb bob**   DTM   MH

Brass, 5 1/2" long, 4 1/2" diameter at top, signed "SUVERKROP INSTRUMENTS" BAKERSFIELD, CALIF U.S.A." "MICRO" "PATS PEND" and "12".

http://www.davistownmuseum.org/pics/32708t60-2.jpg
http://www.davistownmuseum.org/pics/32708t60-1.jpg

51212LTC1   **Plumb bob**   DA   TT (Pub)

Brass, 6 3/4" tall, 2 3/4" diameter, signed "C DREW & CO. KINGSTON, MASS.".

Courtesy of Liberty Tool Co.

http://www.davistownmuseum.org/bio#.bioDrew.htm

22211T8   **Printers' ruler**   DTM   TT

Brass, 8 5/8" long, 3/4" wide, signed "6 & 12 PT INCHES" and an owner's mark "H" on the bottom of the back side.

Part of the Robert Sullivan Collection donation.

8312T6   **Scratch gauge**   DTM   TT

Tool steel, 2 5/8" long, 3/4" diameter, unsigned.

Also called a marking gauge it is used to scribe a line parallel to a surface.

61204T13   **Speed indicator**   DTM   MH

Cast bronze, iron, and steel, 3 3/8" long with a 1 1/4" diameter dial, signed "B. GALLAGHER MFGR" "LYNN MASS".

DATM (Nelson 1999) lists Gallagher as working in Lynn, MA, around 1888.

http://www.davistownmuseum.org/pics/61204T13.jpg

31808SLP14   **Square**   DTM   TT

Steel, 7 3/8" long rule, 4 3/4" long handle, signed "STANLEY" on the handle and "HMC0" on the rule.

http://www.davistownmuseum.org/pics/31808slp14-2.jpg
http://www.davistownmuseum.org/bioStanley.htm

11301T2   **Surveyors' transit**   LPC   MH

Brass and alloy steel in a wood case with leather straps, 14" high, 12" telescope arm, 5" diameter compass dial, signed "Buff & Buff MFG Co 29870 Boston PAT 1674317".

The case has a metal "Buff" label and a paper label on the case door with a photograph of the original Buff & Buff factory on Green St, Jamaica Plain. When it closed in the 1980's, Liberty Tool Co. cleaned out some of the contents of the Buff & Buff factory. One of a number of colored lithographs salvaged at this time is on display with this tool.

http://www.davistownmuseum.org/pics/11301t2.jpg
http://www.davistownmuseum.org/bioBuff.html

The Industrial Revolution (1865f.): Other Factory Made Tools

Measuring Tools

102503T5   Tape measure   DTM   MH

Steel, 2 3/4" long, 2 3/4" wide, signed "TRADE MARK" "THE "ONE-MAN" TAPE" "821" "25 FT" and "CROGAN MFG. CO. BANGOR, MAINE U.S.A.".

It also is marked on the back "Pat. April 6, 1915 Pat. July 10, 1917 Pat. Feb. 20, 1917 PAT. PEND."

http://www.davistownmuseum.org/pics/102503T5_p3.jpg
http://www.davistownmuseum.org/publications/volume10.html

5100T9   Tape measure   DTM   MH

Steel, 3 3/16" diameter, signed "Trade Mark THE 'ONE-MAN' TAPE" and "Crogan MFG, Co. Bangor, Maine USA" and "PAT. APRIL 6 1915 PAT. FEB. 20 1917 PAT. JULY 10 1917, PAT. PEND.".

It measures up to 50 feet. DATM (Nelson 1999, 199) lists this company as making rules with no dates. Anyone with more information about the history of the Crogan Mfg. Co. in Bangor, please contact the Museum.

http://www.davistownmuseum.org/publications/volume10.html

22601T3   Trammels   DTM   MH

Tempered alloy steel, 4" beam, with a 3 1/2" high trammel, signed "L S Starrett Co. Athol Mass USA".

DATM (Nelson 1999, 751) contains historical information on L. S. Starrett Co.

http://www.davistownmuseum.org/bioStarrett.htm

090508T4   Wire gauge   DTM   MH

Steel, 5 1/8" long, signed "MAY & Co" "BOSTON" "WARRANTED" and "HARD".

DATM (Nelson 1999, 520) indicates that S. May & Co. made leather tools, such as curriers' knives and scrapers.

Miscellaneous Items

22612T12   Gate hook   DTM   TT

Drop-forged malleable iron, 7" long, 2 3/4" hook, unsigned.

Courtesy of Liberty Tool Co.

31811T12   Gun barrel   DTM   TT

Forged iron and steel, 9" long, signed "85279" (serial #) and "44 CAL. - BARREL AND LUG FORGED IN ONE.".

The barrel has been cut to shorten it.

The Industrial Revolution (1865f.): Other Factory Made Tools

Miscellaneous Items

3405M1   **Lithograph stone**   DTM   MAG-5

Limestone, 5" long, 6" wide, 3 1/2" high, signed "Rogers Wade Furniture Co. Paris Texas", c. 1915.

The stone is also marked with an engraving of a five story building, other structures, automobiles, and "J W Wade President W C Clark Vice President Secretary T B Revell 2nd Vice President". There are three trademarks; two with Texas maps. This is an interesting example of a lithograph stone used for printing - in this case, for business-related materials. A steel plate engraving appears to have been transferred onto this stone. More information and comments on this item are solicited.

22612T8   **Railroad spike**   DTM   TT

Drop-forged steel, brass, 6 1/4" long, unsigned.

It has a hole drilled into the pointed end and a 1/4" brass insert; perhaps it was used as an ornament? Courtesy of Liberty Tool Co.

22411T9   **Ticket punch**   DTM   TT

Nickel-plated drop-forged alloy steel, 4" long, 2 1/2" wide, signed "R. Woodman" "mf'r" "Boston, Mass.".

DATM (1999) indicates that R. Woodman made machinists' tools from 1878 to 1900.

93011T1   **Troutman's cough syrup**   DTM   MAG-2

Brown bottle in a cardboard carton, 6" high, 2 1/4" x 2 1/4", signed "G. E. LABORATORIES SHAMOKIN, PA." "ROY J. TROUTMAN, PROP.".

TJR3500   **Wine bottle**   DTM   MH

Glass, 23 1/2" high, signed on the label "C. H. Mumm & Co. Reims", 20th century.

It is a full Condon Rouge wine bottle. It is the curator's favorite wine bottle from his college days; it has nothing to do with the Archaeology of Tools.

Miscellaneous Tools

101312T19   **Angle locknut pliers**   DTM   TT

Cast steel, 8" long, 2" wide when closed, signed "UTICA 750-8 PATENTED UTICA N.Y. U.S.A.".

These pliers are used for tightening locknuts in electrical boxes, removing burs from conduits and pipe, and cutting and stripping wire. The Utica Drop Forge and Tool Company of Utica, NY, has a number of plier pagtents that were issued in the early 1900s.

6312LTC5   **Battery pliers**   DA   TT (Pub)

Drop-forged steel, 8" long, signed "PAZZANO WRENCH CO. WALTHAM MASS." "PAT. NO. 19027 MADE IN U.S.A.".

These pliers originally had a nickel finish. The Directory of American Tool and Machinery Patents (DATAMP) has posted a copy of Frederick Pazzano's (Waltham, MA) patent at this link: http://www.datamp.org/patents/search/advance.php?pn=RE19027&id=34068&set=2. Courtesy of Liberty Tool Co.

Miscellaneous Tools

21812LTC5   Bench clamped sheet metal cutter   DA   TT (Pub)

Drop-forged steel, rosewood grip, 30" long, 8" wide, 6" deep, 7" handle, signed "NIAGARA" (with anchor logo).

Courtesy of the Liberty Tool Company.

51012LTC4   Bolt cutter   DA   TT (Pub)

Drop-forged steel, 18 1/4" long, signed "HKP" "Porter's "New Easy." Size No. 0. FOR 5-16 INCH BOLTS. RIGHT. LEFT. LEFT CLIPPER CUT JAW 5/16 SOFT STEEL" "RIGHT CLIPPER CUT JAW 5/16".

Markings continued: "SOFT STEEL. BOSTON. U.S.A. PAT. OCT. 18. 92. OIL THE JOINTS AND CUTTING EDGES. TRADEMARK." John W. Geddes of Watertown, MA, invented a bench cutter and assigned it to H. K. Porter, Inc. of Everett, MA. This patent may be viewed at: http://www.google.com/patents?id=sPlFAAAAEBAJ&printsec=frontcover&dq=2,086,863&hl=en&sa=X &ei=a6OyT6dtkfCyBuSHzJUE&ved=0CDcQ6AEwAA. Courtesy of Liberty Tool Co.

102512T18   Bolt header   DTM   TT

Hand-forged malleable iron, 9" long, 1" and 1 1/2" wide heads, unsigned.

This is an essential tool of the shipsmith. One head has a 1/2" square hole and the other has a 1/2" round hole. Courtesy of Liberty Tool Co.

72312LTC1   Book press   DA   TT (Pub)

Cast iron, japanned finish, 14" long, 18" wide, 16 1/2" high, unsigned.

Courtesy of Liberty Tool Company.

8912T1   Bow drill   DTM   MH

Lathe turned steel, leather, wood, 13 1/4" long shaft, 11" wide, unsigned.

111001T18   Brick chisel   DTM   MH

Drop-forged steel, 8" long, 1 3/4" x 3/16" wide chiseling face, signed "C. Drew & Co".

This provides a reminder that Christopher Drew made more than calking irons, shingle rips, and cat's paws.

http://www.davistownmuseum.org/bioDrew.htm

52603T26   Brick chisel   DTM   MH

Drop-forged iron or steel, 11 3/16" long, 3" wide head, signed "C. S. OSBORNE & CO".

http://www.davistownmuseum.org/bioOsborne.html

The Industrial Revolution (1865f.): Other Factory Made Tools

Miscellaneous Tools

81200M   **Buffalo belt**   DTM   MHC-L

Buffalo hide, 12' long, 3" wide, unsigned, c. 1880.

This belt was used for belt drawn water- or steam-powered machinery. Use of strong buffalo hide instead of cow hide for belt driven equipment quickly led to the near extinction of the buffalo. Interestingly, Louis C. Hunter in his monumental (1985) "A history of industrial power in the United States, 1780-1930. Volume two: Steam power" makes no mention of the use of buffalo belting in the industrialization of manufacturing in the 19th century.

8512LTC1   **Bull leader**   DA   TT (Pub)

Drop-forged steel, 8 1/2" long, 3" wide, unsigned.

Courtesy of Liberty Tool Company.

101701T9   **Bullet mold**   DTM   MH

Drop-forged iron, signed with an obscured maker's mark.

This is another specimen for a classroom whatsit. It has an 1874 patent date.

102100T28   **Burins (5)**   DTM   MH

Steel, brass, and wood, various lengths from 2 3/4" to 4" long, unsigned.

These are generic tools for copper plate engraving. Please visit the print collection for several examples of prints made with these tools.

http://www.davistownmuseum.org/pics/102100t28.jpg

72712LTC1   **Butchers' saw**   DA   TT (Pub)

Drop-forged iron and saw steel, wooden handle, 40 1/2" long, 10" wide cutting edge, unsigned.

This saw has 11 teeth per inch and is designed for cutting through meat, sinew, and bone. Courtesy of the Liberty Tool Company.

122712LTC2 **Butt and rabbet gauge**   DA   TT (Pub)

Brass, wood (rosewood), 7 1/4" long, 2 1/4" x 2" wide, unsigned.

122712LTC1 **Butt gauge**   DA   TT (Pub)

Cast gray iron, nickel plate finish, 2 7/16" x 1 1/2" x 1 1/2", signed "No 95" "STANLEY".

http://www.davistownmuseum.org/bioStanley.htm

319

Miscellaneous Tools

42912LTC11 Button pliers   DA   TT (Pub)

Drop-forged steel, 10 1/2" long, unsigned.

The "button pliers" patent, from 1867, number 67,370, belongs to W. X. Stevens of Waterford, NY but was apparently purchased or reassigned to J. M. King & Company (there's no record of which it was, or when it happened). The 1886 book, "The City of Troy and its Vicinity" by Arthur James Weiss makes reference to an 1867 ad by the company referring to them as "button pliers" and the name stuck. There is another early reference to them named as such with an illustration in the 1897 catalog for Charles A. Strelinger & Company (http://home.comcast.net/~alloy-artifacts/other-makers-p2.html). Courtesy of Liberty Tool Co.

42912T13   Card stretcher   DTM   MAG-5

Steel, nickel finish, 6 1/4" long when wound all the way, signed "PAT'D JUN. 23 1885".

This is "a textile mill tool used for redrawing or taking blisters out of card clothing." (Sellens 2003, 108). Patent 3230,795 was assigned to George E. Kimball of Franklin, MA. View the patent here: http://www.google.com/patents?id=EW5eAAAAEBAJ&pg=PA2&dq=JUN.+23+1885+card+stretcher&hl=en&sa=X&ei=Az-1T4W-OM2a-ga_pZGqDg&ved=0CDcQ6AEwAA#v=onepage&q=JUN.%2023%201885%20card%20stretcher&f=false.

TJD1005   C-clamp   DTM   MH

Drop-forged malleable iron, 6" long, 3" throat, signed "MARK CHICAGO 2 1/2".

It is characteristic of the mass-produced C-clamps of the late 19th century.

111001T24   C-clamp   DTM   MH

Drop-forged steel, 8 1/4" long, 3 1/4" throat, signed "P. S. & W. Co. Southington, CONN USA PAT. June 5. July 10, 88" on the verso "STEEL No 3 SCREW".

P S & W is the abbreviation for Peck, Stow & Wilcox (1870 - 1950). For an extensive description of this important New England tool manufacturer see DATM (Nelson 1999, 610).

http://www.davistownmuseum.org/bioPeck.html

101701T6   C-clamp   DTM   MH

Drop-forged malleable iron, 7" long, 3 1/4" throat, signed "Woodruff 3 Eagle".

Many Woodruffs are listed in DATM (Nelson 1999) but none as clamp-makers.

31611T9   C-clamp   DTM   TT

Drop-forged steel, 8" long, 3 1/2" wide, 4" capacity, signed "14".

33002T11   C-clamp   DTM   TT

Drop-forged steel, 3 11/16" long, 2 5/16" throat, signed "Semi steel Made in USA", c. 1920.

This is another variation in steel terminology on a commonplace generic hand tool.

The Industrial Revolution (1865f.): Other Factory Made Tools

Miscellaneous Tools

33002T10   C-clamp   DTM   MH

Drop-forged malleable iron, 3 3/8" long, 2 1/4" throat, signed "Malleable Iron Unbreakable Made in USA", c. 1950.

This is a generic 20th century tool common to every workshop. The malleable iron in this tool is also called low-carbon steel; the production of malleable iron originates with the puddling process and became a common commodity with specific tool type applications once the Siemens open hearth steel production process allowed controlled mass production of large quantities of durable ductile malleable iron (low-carbon steel).

111001T23   Crimping tool   DTM   MH

Drop-forged steel, wooden handle, 8 3/4" long, 5 1/8" handle, 2 5/8" diameter crimping wheel, signed "Made in USA by Hoggson & Pettis New Haven Conn USA".

Hoggson & Pettis Mfg. Co. are listed in DATM (Nelson 1999, 390) as working from 1890 - 1905. The crimping wheel is smooth with an angled back, no serrations. Would it be used in the leather working trade? This is another whatsit.

92911T11   Crowbar   DTM   MH

Steel, 22" long, 3/4" diameter, unsigned.

It is handmade from rebar stock,

11301T8   Cutting tool for lathes   DTM   MH

Drop-forged steel, 6 3/4" long, 1 1/4" wide, signed "Cooper & Phillips Patented July 3, 1866 4".

This is another tool heralding the arrival of the Industrial Revolution with its new tools that make other tools. Patent 56,141 was assigned to Theodore Cooper of Crompton Mills, Warwick, RI and Thomas Phillips, Providence, RI. View the patent here: http://www.google.com/patents/US56141?printsec=drawing&dq=july+3+1866+cooper&ei=izfjT9XRBtD ntQbi16jEBg#v=onepage&q=july%203%201866%20cooper&f=false.

111412T10   Diagonal pliers   DTM   MH

Alloy steel, 4 1/4" long, signed "U.D.F.&T. CORP." "41-4" ALLOY STEEL" and with three diamond shapes containing "U" "TI" "CA".

They are made by Utica Drop Forge & Tool Corporation, located in Utica, NY from 1895 to 1912 (Nelson 1999, 809). More information on their pliers is here: http://home.comcast.net/~alloy-artifacts/utica-tool-p2.html.

72002T7   Drift   DTM   MH-K

Steel, signed "Scully drift PAT. PEND. No 3 25103".

This is an unusual looking 20th century tool.

The Industrial Revolution (1865f.): Other Factory Made Tools

Miscellaneous Tools

111412T11   Fence pliers   DTM   MH

Drop-forged iron and steel, 8 3/8" long, signed "HELLER BROS. CO." with a standing horse trademark.

http://www.davistownmuseum.org/bioHellerBros.html

72712LTC12   Gasoline blowtorch   DA   TT (Pub)

Drop-forged steel, brass, 6 1/2" long, 5 3/4" diameter tank, 11" tall, signed "GUARANTEED MERIT TORCHES".

Courtesy of the Liberty Tool Company.

81200T6   Glass cutter   DTM   MHC-J

Drop-forged iron and steel, 13" long, unsigned, late 19th century.

21812LTC2   Heavy duty bench clamp with crimpers   DA   TT (Pub)

Drop-forged steel, 22" long, 6" wide, 3 1/4" high, signed "NIAGARA M. & .T WKS. BUFFALO, N.Y.".

Courtesy of Liberty Tool Company.

8312T5   Jackscrew   DTM   TT

Drop-forged steel, 1 11/16" tall, 1" diameter, unsigned.

TBL5009   Jig   DTM   MH

Forged iron and wood, 9 1/2" long, 4" wide, unsigned.

This unusual tool appears to have been recently made (c. 1900 - 1920) out of much earlier components, all of which are hand-forged iron. The nails in the wood as well as the saw marks are contemporary - that is to say early 20th century. We have no idea what this jig would have been used for, what do you think?

10811T1   Knife grinder for reapers   DTM   MH

Cast iron and steel, 28" long, 11 1/2" diameter gear, signed "AYERS PAT JUNE 3 1868".

Frequently mistaken for a hand drill, this high speed tool was used as a grinding sharpener for reapers, mowers, and other edged machinery. This particular example has a threaded mount for stones. The patent was granted to Daniel W. Ayres, of Sheldon, Iroquois county, Illinois, on June 23, 1868 for grinding reaper knives.

http://www.davistownmuseum.org/pics/10811t1web1.jpg
http://www.davistownmuseum.org/pics/10811t1web2.jpg

22411T22   Lasting pinchers   DTM   TT-D30

Drop-forged alloy steel, 9" long, signed "A" "PATENTED" "OCT. 25. 1887" "WHITCHER" "UNION MADE 20" and "KNELL" owner mark on one handle.

Patent 372,246 was issued to Frank W. Whitcher of Boston, MA.

The Industrial Revolution (1865f.): Other Factory Made Tools

Miscellaneous Tools

7712LTC9   **Lead pipe expander pliers**   DA   TT (Pub)

Drop-forged iron painted black, 11 1/2" long, 3" wide, unsigned.

Courtesy of Liberty Tool Company.

6912LTC3   **Lead pipe expander pliers**   DA   TT (Pub)

Drop-forged steel, black paint finish, 11" long, 2 1/4" diameter, unsigned.

These pliers are used for expanding lead pipes. Courtesy of Liberty Tool Co.

102612T11   **Lead pipe expanding pliers**   DTM   TT

Steel, 11" long, 2" long head, signed "PAT. MAY 5th 1896".

These are used by plumbers. This is the same patent, it belongs to John Anderson, as used on the Stanley No. 19.
(http://www.google.com/patents/US559763?pg=PA2&dq=anderson+May+5+1896&hl=en&sa=X&ei=iJ-SUPjDI-GQ0AW7koD4AQ&ved=0CDUQ6AEwAA#v=onepage&q=anderson%20May%205%201896&f=false).

072112T8   **Linemans' pliers**   DTM   TT

Drop-forged iron and steel, 6 1/2" long, 1" wide, signed "THE WAYMOTH CORP., PAWTUCKET, R.I.".

This company made only cutting pliers (http://home.comcast.net/~alloy-artifacts/other-makers-p3.html).

31611T8   **Linemans' pliers**   DTM   TT

Drop-forged German steel, 8" long, 1 1/2" head, signed "FRANCE".

51606T9   **Linemans' pliers**   DTM   MH

Drop-forged steel, 7 1/4" long, signed "Drop forged steel Witherby No 1517".

These early 20th century pliers show some evidence of handwork both in the ground surfaces on the handles and in the double lines separated smoothly from serrated handle surfaces. Soon all such tools would be completely machine-made without any sign of handwork, even handwork with electric grinding tools.

http://www.davistownmuseum.org/bio#bioWitherby.html

7612LTC7   **Linemans' splicing clamp**   DA   TT (Pub)

Drop-forged steel, 11 1/2" long, 2" wide, signed "KLEIN & SONS CHICAGO, U.S.A." "R56" with a small logo of two lineman on a telephone pole.

This tool was made prior to the Chicago fire and was used for splicing several different sizes of wire. Mathais Klein began working in 1855, first specializing in electrical and telephone tools. The company is still in business as Klein Tools and sells many kinds of hand tools (http://en.wikipedia.org/wiki/Klein_Tools#Mathias_Klein_Builds_a_Legacy). Courtesy of Liberty Tool Company.

The Industrial Revolution (1865f.): Other Factory Made Tools

Miscellaneous Tools

72712LTC6   Linemans' splicing clamp   DA   TT (Pub)

Drop-forged steel, 11 1/2" long, 2" wide, signed "KLEIN & SONS CHICAGO U.S.A.".
Courtesy of the Liberty Tool Company.

93011T8   Mechanics' cold chisel   DTM   TT

Drop-forged steel, 18" long, 2" wide, signed "ATHA" "1470" and with a horseshoe enclosing an A.

http://www.davistownmuseum.org/bioAtha.html

5512LTC1   Nail puller   DA   TT (Pub)

Cast iron, 17" long retracted, 22 1/2" extended, signed BRIDGEPORT.

TJR3002   Needle nose pliers   DTM   MH

Drop-forged iron and steel, 3" long, signed "WINCHESTER TRADE MARK".
It is one of the tools produced in Connecticut by the Winchester Arms Co.

http://www.davistownmuseum.org/bioWinchester.html

93011T12   Nippers   DTM   MH

Drop-forged malleable iron and steel, 10 3/4" long, signed "N. S. NENBOOES" "SHEFFIELD".
The signature is difficult to read. This is an example of an English-made and imported tool.

TDJ1009   Oiler   DTM   MH

Sheet metal, 5 3/8" high with a 6" spout, signed "T. Stenau & Co. Pat May 12, 96".
It looks older than it is.

12413T1   Organ tuning cone   DTM   MH

Lathe-turned steel, 7 1/8" long, 1 1/4" diameter, unsigned.

30202T9   Pattern   DTM   MH

Cast steel, 5" long base, 1 1/2" wide at top, 2 3/4" wide at bottom, 5/8" high, signed "5".
The pattern is superimposed on the base. It appears to be a one-piece steel casting of unknown use.

22612T7   Pin vise   DTM   TT

Drop-forged steel, brass, 4 1/2" long, unsigned.
This tool was made in the late 1800s or early 1900s.

101212LTC5   Pinking iron   DA   TT (Pub)

Cast steel, 4" long, 1/2" wide, signed "C.S. OSBORNE & CO. 1/2".

http://www.davistownmuseum.org/bioOsborne.html

Miscellaneous Tools

TJR2201   **Pliers**   DTM   MH

Drop-forged iron, 5 1/4" long, signed "L.A. SAYRE, NEWARK, NJ".

DATM (Nelson 1999) lists this company as working from 1884 - 1916.

31611T7   **Pliers**   DTM   TT

Drop-forged German steel, 7" long, 1" nippers, signed "GARANTIE".

This is a pinch plier with a nail remover. Garantie is the French word for guaranteed or warranted

22411T10   **Pliers**   DTM   TT

Drop-forged German steel, 6" long, 2" wide, signed "HUGONIOT-TISSOT" "FRANCE" and "A. F. & Co".

These are electrician or linemans' pliers. The British Museum has pliers signed "HUGONIOT-TISSOT" that were made by Lucien Hugoniot-Tissot (French 1850 - 1930).

102512T12   **Pliers**   DTM   TT

Drop-forged German steel (?), 11 1/4" long, 2" wide, signed "PAT. JULY. 6. 75" "OUT>>>" "<<<IN" and with owner's mark "ANSON P. MORRILL" stamped several times.

Silas and John W. Sparks held the July 6, 1875 patent 165,266 for pliers (http://www.google.com/patents/US165266?pg=PA2&dq=pliers+July+6+1875&hl=en&sa=X&ei=FfePU LSmLoa-0QXT0oCoDg&ved=0CDIQ6AEwAA#v=onepage&q=pliers%20July%206%201875&f=false). Courtesy of Liberty Tool Co.

31011T6   **Pliers**   DTM   TT

Drop-forged cast steel, 8" long, signed "HUBER PHIL" "C STEEL".

The nose is made to grip round materials. DATM (Nelson 1999, 406) lists Huber H. F. & A. in Philadelphia as manufacturers of leather-making tools in 1836 and Henry Huber of Philadelphia in 1870-1871.

101701T13   **Pliers**   DTM   MH

Drop-forged steel, 8 3/8" long, signed "Wm Hjorth Jamestown NY. Pat Sept 8 1903".

See DATM (Nelson 1999, 386) for more information. It is interesting for its unusual shape -- a tool as a sculpture object.

83102T9A   **Pliers**   DTM   MH

Drop-forged iron and steel, 8" long, signed "PAZZANO PAT RE19027 MADE IN USA".

These curved special purpose pliers were made in the early 20th century. Pazzano Wrench Company was located in Waltham, MA. Frederick F. Pazzano received this patent December 19, 1933. http://www.google.com/patents/about?id=H_0nAAAAEBAJ&dq=pazzano. Also see http://www.datamp.org/displayPatent.php?id=34068.

The Industrial Revolution (1865f.): Other Factory Made Tools

Miscellaneous Tools

6703T8   Pliers   DTM   TT

Drop forged steel, 7" long, 1 1/2" wide, 3/4" thick, signed PATENTED MAY 26-17.

These elaborate pliers have an unknown function.

41302T14   Pliers   DTM   MH

Drop-forged iron and steel, 5 1/2" long, 1 1/8" long and 1/8" wide adjustable steel jaws, unsigned.

This is an unusual design for a special purpose hand tool. Its use is unknown.

52603T10   Pliers   DTM   MH

Drop-forged iron, 9 1/4" long, signed "HUBER" "TOO-WOP".

These pliers are used for gas pipe fitting.

7712LTC2   Plumb bob   DA   TT (Pub)

Drop-forged steel, nickel-plated finish, 5" long, 3/4" diameter, signed "THE L.S. STARRETT CO., ATHOL, MASS. U.S.A." "No 177 PLUMB BOB 5 IN".

Courtesy of Liberty Tool Company.

http://www.davistownmuseum.org/bioStarrett.htm

TK1002   Pressed brick machine (U. S. patent model)   LPC   MH

Bronze, iron, steel, and wood, 11" by 5 1/2" with a 7" diameter wheel kegs that extends 1 1/2" over the frame, unsigned.

The patent was received by Zephirin Vaurier Nov. 6, 1878. It appears that this brick-making machine was never produced, but it is significant, nonetheless, as illustrating machines and machinery that supplant and then replace the more primitive wooden brickmakers' smoothing wheel on display across the street in the Liberty Tool Co.'s second floor Museum annex. Most U. S. patent models were lost in fires in 1836 and 1887.

http://www.davistownmuseum.org/pics/tk1002.jpg
http://www.davistownmuseum.org/pics/tk1002_p2.jpg

31112T23   Pry bar   DTM   MH3-D2

Drop-forged steel, 15 1/4" long, 1" wide, signed "C. Drew and Company".

This is another of the Drew Co.'s more modern tools. Courtesy of Liberty Tool Co.

http://www.davistownmuseum.org/bioDrew.htm

31908T42   Pry bar   DTM   MH

Drop-forged steel, 8 1/2" long, unsigned.

This is a very small pry bar.

http://www.davistownmuseum.org/pics/31908t42p1.jpg
http://www.davistownmuseum.org/pics/31908t42p2.jpg

Miscellaneous Tools

33002T13   **Pry bar**   DTM   MH

Drop-forged steel, 11 1/4" long, 1/2" wide pry, unsigned.

The second pry is offset. This tool is for automotive use, possibly brake related.

http://www.davistownmuseum.org/pics/33002t13.jpg

42801T18   **Pry bar**   DTM   MH

Drop-forged steel, signed with the distinctive Atha and horseshoe trademark enclosing the letter A..

http://www.davistownmuseum.org/bioStanley.htm

TGB2204A   **Pulley (2)**   DTM   MH

Cast iron, cast steel, and wood, pulleys 3 3/4" long, 2" wide with 7/8" by 1 1/2" roller, other item 4 3/4" high, 2" diameter base, signed "31046" and "310 :.." on the two pulleys.

41212T4   **Pulley wheel**   DTM   TT

Wood (probably lignum vitae), 7" diameter, unsigned.

This wheel is well-worn and has three screw-holes through it. Courtesy of Liberty Tool Co.

72712LTC7   **Railroad conductors' punch**   DA   TT (Pub)

Drop-forged steel, nickel-plated finish, 5 1/2" long, signed "MCBEE MADE IN U.S.A. 529 5201".

Courtesy of the Liberty Tool Company.

101312T3   **Railroad shovel**   DTM   TT

Cast steel, wood (maple), 36" long, 9 1/2" wide, signed "MCRR CAST STEEL".

22211T7   **Ratchet screwdriver**   DTM   TT

Brass body, steel point, and wooden handle, 4" long, 1/2" wide body, and 1" long handle, signed "PAT. NO.".

The rest of the mark is not legible. Part of the Robert Sullivan Collection donation.

63001T5   **Ratchet screwdriver**   DTM   MH

Drop-forged iron and steel, brass, wood, 15 1/2" long, 7 1/2" driver, signed "Gay Pat Dec 17 1878".

This is a classic example of George E. Gay's (Augusta, ME. 1878 - 1905) patented screwdriver. It is a truly Maine-made tool.

http://www.davistownmuseum.org/publications/volume10.html

70701T5   **Ratchet screwdriver**   DTM   MH

Drop-forged iron and steel, brass, wood, 10 3/4" long, 5" blade, signed "GAY" the patent date is obscured.

It has the same patent date as the larger Gay screwdriver displayed to the right (ID # 63001T5).

http://www.davistownmuseum.org/publications/volume10.html

Miscellaneous Tools

93011T18 Ratcheting screwdriver   DTM TT

Drop-forged tempered alloy steel, brass, wood, 12" long, signed "DECATUR COFFIN CO." "DECATUR, ILLS." "PAT. OCT. 7-1884".

The oil hole is marked "OIL". This company operated between 1872 and 1943 making spiral screwdrivers. Christopher H. Olson held the patent (Nelson 1999).

33002T12 Recessed head screwdriver   DTM MH

Drop-forged steel, wooden handle, 11 5/" long including a 4 1/2" handle, signed on ferrule "R & P Mfg Co Worcester-Chicago USA"; "Reed & Prince Mfg Co Worcester Chicago recessed reed wood screws machine screws sheet metal screws", c. 1938.

The second signature is on the handle. This tool is an excellent example of the age-old tradition of using a manufactured tool for advertising purposes. Reed & Prince is connected to a spin-off / successor the Reed Small Tool Company which became Reed Rolled Thread Die Co. and is currently known as Reed-Rico, located in Holden, Mass. It is not connected with F. E. Reed or the Reed - Prentice Co., Worcester, MA, 1876 - 1895. Thank you to Alden Reed for the previous information on all the Reeds.

http://www.davistownmuseum.org/pics/33002t12.jpg

41312T1 Ring clamp   DTM TT

Brass, wood, leather, 6 1/4" long, 1" wide, unsigned.

Courtesy of Liberty Tool Co.

72712LTC9 Riveting machine   DA TT (Pub)

Malleable cast iron, japanned finish, 12" tall with handle extended, 6" wide base, signed "FH SMITH MFG CO. CHICAGO USA" "THE UNIVERSAL PAT'D JUNE 1905".

Henry C. Pomeroy's patent 791,724 may be viewed here: http://www.google.com/patents?id=ZaJGAAAAEBAJ&pg=PA2&lpg=PA2&dq=June+1905+riveting+machine&source=bl&ots=LOXnavtPZW&sig=ow9hXmOj0-DFKMi7CbPQWtlwwwQ&hl=en&sa=X&ei=dCwhUOjZlc_itQbIs4DABw&ved=0CDAQ6AEwAA#v=onepage&q=June%201905%20riveting%20machine&f=false. Courtesy of the Liberty Tool Company.

4512LTC1 Rule clamp   DA TT (Pub)

Tempered alloy steel, 2 1/2" long, 1 3/4" wide, signed "No. 604R THE L.S. STARRETT CO. ATHOL, MASS.U.S.A.".

Courtesy of Liberty Tool Co.

22311T13 Saw set   DTM TT

Drop-forged steel, 7" long, signed "NIKE" "ESKILSTUNA" "MADE IN" "SWEDEN".

Part of the Robert Sullivan Collection donation.

ID #   Status   Location

Miscellaneous Tools

102512T13   Saw set

DTM   TT

Drop-forged steel, cardboard box, 8 1/2" long, 2" wide, signed "ATKINS" "MADE IN USA".

It is in the original, damaged, box. This is an Atkins Criterion Saw Set made by E. C. Atkins & Co., Indianapolis, IN. U.S.A. (For more information go to: http://www.wkfinetools.com/hUS-saws/Atkins/pubs/1895-Catalog/1895-Catalog.asp). Courtesy of Liberty Tool Co.

71512LTC2   Saw set

DA   TT (Pub)

Drop-forged steel, nickel finish, 9" long, 3" wide, 7/8" thick, signed "KEEN KUTTER".

E. C. Simmons, the large hardware firm of St. Louis, MO, used the brand name KEEN KUTTER. Courtesy of Liberty Tool Company.

71312T1   Saw swage

DTM   TT

Drop-forged steel, wooden box, 4 3/8" long, 1 3/16" wide, 3/4" thick, signed "J.W. MIXER SAW TOOL CO. PLYMOUTH MASS. PAT'D JULY 2, 83 No 0.".

021812T5   Scraper

DTM   TT

Drop-forged steel, wooden handle, 12" long, 2 1/4" edge, 9" long handle, unsigned.

This is a paint scraper that was commonly used in the early 20th century. The handle has a ball end.

TJR2202   Screwdriver

DTM   MH

Drop-forged iron, wood, 6 1/2" long, unsigned.

31811T5   Screwdriver

DTM   TT

Drop-forged steel, brass ferrule, wood handle, 5" long, 2" blade, unsigned.

111900T11   Screwdriver

DTM   MH

Drop-forged steel, wood, 4 1/8" long, signed "Stanley Hurwood Pat April 01 Made in USA".

"Shortly after George Wood was granted the above patent (no. 671,039) on 2 April 1901, he went into business with John Hurley to manufacture screwdrivers. They set up a shop in Plantsville, Connecticut, and named the new company using their last names. The founding of the Hurwood Manufacturing Company marked the beginning of the 11 solid bar screwdriver." The company was sold to the Stanley Rule & Level Co. in 1904 (Jacob, June 2002, The Chronicle).

30311T7   Screwdriver

DTM   TT

Steel and wood, 12" long, 1 1/2" wide, unsigned.

It is handmade from a file.

The Industrial Revolution (1865f.): Other Factory Made Tools

Miscellaneous Tools

101701T18   Screwdriver   DTM   MH

Drop-forged steel, wood, 7" long, signed "Stanley No 45 Made in USA".

This is a classic example of Stanley's fine 20th century screwdrivers.

http://www.davistownmuseum.org/bioStanley.htm

14302T17   Screwdriver   DTM   MH

Drop-forged steel, 8" long, signed "Mullen Mfg. Co. Boston Mass Patented".

No Mullen is listed in DATM (Nelson 1999) but this tool might be post 1900. It is an interesting design for a screwdriver.

91303T10   Screwdriver   DTM   MH

Drop-forged steel, wood, 10" long, 3/4" wide blade, signed "The H. D. S. & Co Perfect Handle PAT Aug 26 03".

This mark is by H. D. Smith of Plantsville, CT. The patent belonged to William Ward and may be viewed here: http://www.google.com/patents?id=fwtAAAAAEBAJ&pg=PA2&dq=ward+aug+25+1903&hl=en&sa=X&ei=4SzjT--sB8vssgbR9NnBBg&ved=0CDcQ6AEwAA#v=onepage&q=ward%20aug%2025%201903&f=false.

913108T43   Screwdriver   DTM   MH

Drop-forged steel, wood, 14" long, 8 1/2" long blade, signed "HSC 8 ATA" "PERFECT HANDLE" "MADE PLANTSVILLE CONN USA" the company name is obscured.

H. D. Smith worked in Plantsville, CT, 1850 - 1930; the "Co" was added to the mark in 1901. He used the "perfect handle" trademark (Nelson 1999). His heavy duty screwdrivers and wrenches are among the most sought after of all tools by collectors.

81200T10   Screwdriver   DTM   MHC

Drop-forged steel, wood, and brass, signed "Winchester Tradesmark Made in USA".

Note the screwdriver is incorrectly labeled in the photo as 81200T12.

http://www.davistownmuseum.org/pics/tjg1001a.jpg
http://www.davistownmuseum.org/bioWinchester.html

31011T3   Screwdriver bit   DTM   TT

Hand-forged steel, 4 1/2" long, 1/2" wide, unsigned.

The bit has been hand-shaped from steel bar stock and both ground to fit the brace and hand-forged to flatten it to form the screwdriver head.

31311T10   Scribe (?)   DTM   TT

Steel with wood handle, 15" long, 1 1/2" wide, 2 3/4" blade, unsigned.

This tool has a slightly curved handle holding a circular "blade" that was to be sharpened.

The Industrial Revolution (1865f.): Other Factory Made Tools

Miscellaneous Tools

100108T4   Shears' sharpener   DTM   MH

Steel, wood, 3 3/4" long, 1 5/8" wide, 2" long blade, signed on a paper label "MANUFACTURED BY" "C. R. HALEY Milford, Me.".

The paper label includes directions for use. The town name could be Gilford, there is a scratch on the label. A gift from Ed Shaw.

http://www.davistownmuseum.org/publications/volume10.html

102800T2   Slate trimmer   DTM   MH

Drop-forged iron, 17 15/16" long with a 7 7/8" point for cutting holes in the slate, signed with the Belden Machine Co. bell with "DEN" stamped inside the bell.

Belden began marking slaters' tools in New Haven, CT, in 1885 and among slate roofers are famous for their slate hammers.

http://www.davistownmuseum.org/bioBelden.html

63012T2   Slaters' hammer   DTM   TT

Drop-forged steel, wooden handle, 12 1/2" long, 11" long, 3/4" wide head, 4 3/4" long, 1 1/8" wide handle, signed "H. H. HARVEY" "MANDER".

This tool may have been re-forged at some point (see the shaft of the tool at the top of the handle). H. H. Harvey & Co's working dates were 1872-1914, Augusta, Maine with a sales office in Boston, MA.

http://www.davistownmuseum.org/bioHarvey.html

TBL1001A   Slaters' shingle ripper   DTM   MH

Drop-forged iron and steel, 24 3/4" long with 2" wide rip, signed "C DREW & CO KINGSTON MASS".

This tool is on display above the fire exit.

http://www.davistownmuseum.org/pics/tbl1001a.jpg
http://www.davistownmuseum.org/bioDrew.htm

51212T1   Slaters' shingle ripper   DTM   TT

Drop-forged iron and steel, 24 1/2" long, signed "C DREW & CO. KINGSTON, MASS.".

Courtesy of Liberty Tool Co.

http://www.davistownmuseum.org/bioDrew.htm

31112T21   Soldering iron   DTM   MH3-D3

Wood, iron, copper, steel, aluminum ferrule, 11" long, 1 1/4" wide, unsigned.

Courtesy of Liberty Tool Co.

22411T18   Spiral screwdriver   DTM   TT

Drop-forged malleable iron, brass, wooden handle, 10 1/2" long, signed "F. A. Howard" "Maker" and "Belfast Me".

This screwdriver has a special locking feature and a slot type drill bit.

http://www.davistownmuseum.org/bioHowardF.htm

The Industrial Revolution (1865f.): Other Factory Made Tools

Miscellaneous Tools

31602T6   Spiral screwdriver   DTM   TT

Drop-forged steel, brass, iron, wood, 12" long, signed "Goodell Pratt".

Goodell Pratt Co. was located in Greenfield, MA from 1899-1931 (Nelson 1999, 321).

http://www.davistownmuseum.org/bioGoodelpratt.html

111001T27   Spiral screwdriver   DTM   MH

Drop-forged steel, brass, wooden handle, 7 3/4" long, 2 3/4" handle, signed "Stanley Yankee No 4595 Made in USA".

This is another classic Stanley tool from the early 20th century.

http://www.davistownmuseum.org/bioStanley.htm

111412T12   Spiral screwdriver   DTM   MH

Steel, brass, wooden handle, 12" long, signed "MADE * BY" "F. A. HOWARD & SON" "BELFAST, ME. U.S.A." "Pat'd July 23 95".

Patent 543,096 belonged to James W. Jones of Belfast, Maine and was manufactured by F. A. Howard & Son. The patent may be viewed here: http://www.datamp.org/patents/advance.php?inc=1.

http://www.davistownmuseum.org/bioHowardF.htm

121600T2   Spiral screwdriver   DTM   MH

Drop-forged malleable iron, bronze, wood, 13" long, signed "Made by F.A. Howard & Sons, Belfast Me USA Pat. Maf. 1892".

http://www.davistownmuseum.org/bioHowardF.htm

111001T25   Spiral screwdriver   DTM   MH

Steel, brass, wood, 12" long, signed "F. A. Howard Belfast Me Allard Pat. Aug 4 1868 24 Nov 1874".

http://www.davistownmuseum.org/publications/volume10.html

913108T25   Spiral screwdriver   DTM   MH

Drop-forged steel, brass, wood, 14 3/8" long, 4 3/4" long brass section, 5 1/4" long steel tip, signed "MADE BY" "F. A. HOWARD & SON" and "PAT. July 2".

Franklin Augustus and William Russell Howard of Belfast, Maine, worked together from 1895 to 1901.

http://www.davistownmuseum.org/bioHowardFhtm

92112T7   Spiral screwdriver   DTM   TT

Drop-forged steel, brass, wood, 19 1/2" long open, 13 1/4" long shut, 1/4" wide bit, signed "F.A. Howard Pat'd Aug. 4 68".

The chuck is seized so the bit is permanently affixed.

http://www.davistownmuseum.org/bioHowardF.htm

92112T8   Spiral screwdriver   DTM   TT

Drop-forged steel, wood (rosewood), 8 1/2" long closed, 12 1/2" long open, 3/16" wide bit, unsigned.

The Industrial Revolution (1865f.): Other Factory Made Tools

Miscellaneous Tools

32708T59   Spiral screwdriver

Drop-forged steel, brass trim, wood handle, 12 3/8" long, signed "GAY" "PAT. DEC. 17. 1879" and on the other side of the handle "PARSONS" "AUGUSTA" "ME".

This patent is held by George E. Gay and John A. Parsons of Augusta, Maine.

http://www.davistownmuseum.org/pics/32708t59-3.jpg
http://www.davistownmuseum.org/publications/volume10.html

4512T1   Square nail collection

Iron, wooden display mount, 18 1/2" long, 16" wide, unsigned.

This hanging display contains nails ranging from the 18th to 20th centuries. Courtesy of Liberty Tool Co.

TCR1050   Stamp

Cast iron, forged steel, 4" long with 5/8" long arrow, signed "WRIGHT & SON Cin.ti. O.".

This is a stamp used to mark an arrow. An internet search turned up this tidbit: one company "which struck bimetallic tokens is Wright and Sons of Cincinnati, Ohio. Their work was sometimes signed WRIGHT CIN. O. or WRIGHT & SON, CIN. O."

101312T30   Stanley no. 89 sliding clapboard gauge

Cast gray iron, wood (rosewood), japanned finish, 9" long, 1 5/8" wide, 2 3/4" tall, signed STANLEY RULE & LEVEL CO. NEW BRITAIN CONN. U.S.A..

071704T3   Steam gauge

Iron, steel, brass, glass, 8 1/4" long case, 6 5/8 long gauge, signed "Crosby Steam Gage and Valve Co. Boston U.S.A. & London, Eng.".

"Perhaps the most successful of the pre-1914 [steam] indicators were made in Boston, MA, by Crosby Steam Gage & Valve Company. Their first patent was granted Sept. 2, 1879" (John Walter, 2011, "The Engine Indicator"). They made internal-spring and external-spring Crosby indicators until the 1930s (http://www.archivingindustry.com/Indicator/sourceinfo.htm).

61512LTC2   Steelyard scales

Cast iron, 20" long, unsigned.

It is marked with graduations in inches, 1 to 10. Courtesy of Liberty Tool Co.

30911T3   Tapered reamer

Tempered alloy steel, 4 1/2" long, 9/16" wide, signed "REIFF & NESTOR CO" "LYKENS, PA U.S.A.".

This reamer is used in a brace. The Reiff & Nestor Company began in 1912 and is still in existence today http://www.rntap.com/.

Miscellaneous Tools

30911T6   Tapered reamer   DTM   TT

Reforged steel, 15" long, 8" blade, unsigned.

This convex-shaped reamer is handmade from a file.

42912LTC12   Tire pliers   DA   TT (Pub)

Drop-forged steel, 5 7/8" long, unsigned.

Courtesy of Liberty Tool Co.

22311T3   Tool handle   DTM   TT

Rosewood handle with drop-forged malleable iron or steel bits, signed "FRAY'S. PAT. AUG.7.83.".

The following tools are stored in the handle: straight chisel, curved chisel, scribe, small screwdriver, medium screwdriver, large screwdriver, awl, and tack remover. This patent is online at: http://www.google.com/patents/about?id=1OpMAAAAEBAJ&dq=fray+august+7+1883. Part of the Robert Sullivan Collection donation.

30911T9   Trowel   DTM   TT

Drop-forged malleable iron, brass ferrule, and wood handle, 6" long, 2 1/2" x 1 1/2" blade, signed "DDBCON".

The signature is hard to read. This may be a plasterers' trowel.

30911T10   Trowel   DTM   TT

Drop-forged steel, steel ferrule, wood handle, 9" long, 5" x 1 1/2" blade, signed "W. Germany" "83" and "WAG___" "KONSTAN___" possible owner's marks.

The signatures are partly obscured. This may be a plasterers' trowel and is probably made from German steel.

3312T4   Trowel   DTM   TT

Drop-forged cast steel, iron ferrule, wooden handle, 10" long, 3 5/8" wide blade, signed "I.REED" "CAST STEEL", c. 1880.

It is unusual to encounter a mason's trowel made from cast steel. Courtesy of Liberty Tool Co.

102512T14   Unidentified tool   DTM   TT

Steel, 8" long, 2 1/2" wide, signed "W. GILPIN" "WEDGES MILLS" "WARRENTED".

DATM reports a tool made by W. Gilfin Wedge Mills (Nelson 1999, 314). It was a business in England: "Wedges Mill is a hamlet in the south-west corner of the Urban District [of Cannock] dating from the foundation of William Gilpin's edge-tool works in 1790." (http://www.clickityworld.co.uk/cannock/localhistory/tabid/161/Default.aspx). Courtesy of Liberty Tool Co.

The Industrial Revolution (1865f.): Other Factory Made Tools

Miscellaneous Tools

42712LTC4 **Veterinary fleam**   DA   TT (Pub)

Steel, brass, 3 1/2" long handle, 3" long blades, unsigned.

Courtesy of Liberty Tool Co.

22512T3   **Wagon jack**   DTM   TT

Cast iron and steel, wood, 30" high, 14" by 5" wide base, unsigned.

This is a nice complete example of a wagon jack. Courtesy of Liberty Tool Co.

2713T4   **Wagon jack**   DTM   TT

Cast steel, wood (hickory), 28" tall, 18" long handle, 5" x 12" base, unsigned.

42912LTC15 **Washer cutter**   DA   TT (Pub)

Drop-forged iron and steel, 4 1/2" long, 3 1/2" wide largest blade, unsigned.

Courtesy of Liberty Tool Co.

42912LTC16 **Washer cutter**   DA   TT (Pub)

Drop-forged iron and steel, 4 1/2" long, 3 1/2" wide largest blade, signed "C.S. OSBORNE & CO NEWARK, N.J." "16".

Courtesy of Liberty Tool Co.

http://www.davistownmuseum.org/bioOsborne.html

81212LTC6   **Windsor beader**   DA   TT (Pub)

Wood (rosewood), cast bronze, steel cutters, 10 3/4" long, 2" tall, 2" wide, unsigned.

This beader is Windsor's 1885 patent with a revolving cutter mechanism. Courtesy of Liberty Tool Company.

42912LTC10 **Wire cutters**   DA   TT (Pub)

Nickel-plated drop-forged steel, 6 1/2" long, signed "SARGENT & CO. NEW HAVEN, CONN. MADE IN U.S.A.".

Courtesy of Liberty Tool Co.

http://www.davistownmuseum.org/bioSargent.htm

12613T4   **Wooden mallet**   DTM   TT

Wood (hickory), 15" long, 6" long head, 2 1/4" and 1 3/4" diameter faces, unsigned.

12613LTC1   **Wooden mallet**   DA   TT (Pub)

Wood, 12" long, 6" long head, 3" diameter face, unsigned.

Patternmakers' Tools

Patternmakers' Tools

42904T4B   Crane necked gouge   DTM   MH

Cast steel, brass ferrule, wooden handle, 12" long including 5 1/4" handle, 1/12" wide, signed "BUCK BROS" with a buck touchmark.

http://www.davistownmuseum.org/pics/42904t4b-2.jpg
http://www.davistownmuseum.org/bioBuckBrothers.html

42904T4A   Crane necked gouge   DTM   MH

Cast steel, brass ferrule, wooden handle, 12 1/2" long including 5 1/4" handle, 11/16" wide, signed "BUCK BROS" with a buck touchmark.

This is also called a bent gouge or offset gouge (Sellens 1990, 197).

http://www.davistownmuseum.org/pics/42904t4a-2.jpg
http://www.davistownmuseum.org/bioBuckBrothers.html

121600T4   Lifter   DTM   MH

Drop-forged steel, 11" long, signed "Monk".

This is a patternmakers' smoothing tool used in cleaning and finishing the bottom and sides of deep narrow openings in molds used in foundry work. See page 18 of "Founders Work" by Stimpson, Gray and Grennan. DATM (Nelson 1999) lists a Monk as a maker of molders' tools, c. 1894, location unknown.

30202T14   Patternmakers' burnisher   DTM   MH

Cast brass, 4 3/4" long, 1/2" and 3/8" diameter heads, unsigned.

This tool was used by a patternmaker for smoothing the surfaces of sand molds prior to casting.

http://www.davistownmuseum.org/pics/30202t14.jpg

913108T35   Patternmakers' drawshave   DTM   MH

Steel, brass trim, and wooden handle, 5 1/2" wide, 2 3/4" long blade, unsigned.

21013LTC1   Patternmakers' mold   DA   TT (Pub)

Cast bronze, 6" diameter, 1 1/2" deep, unsigned.

2713T2   Patternmakers' mold   DTM   TT

Wood, black paint, 12" diameter, 4" tall, unsigned.

72002T6   Patternmakers' plane   DTM   MH-I

Wood, 7" long, signed "J. Johnson", 20th century.

DATM (Nelson 1999, 429) lists J. Johnson of New York with a working date of 1870 made wooden planes. A exquisite example of an owner-made and signed special purpose patternmakers' plane. It does not have the blade. It was probably made about 1930; recently purchased from the Johnson family of Braintree, MA.

The Industrial Revolution (1865f.): Other Factory Made Tools

Patternmakers' Tools

913108T2   **Router**   DTM   MH

Brass, steel blade, wooden knobs, 4" long, 1/4" wide blade, unsigned.

10910T6   **Shrink rule set (9)**   DTM   MH

Tempered alloy steel, 12" long, 1" wide, signed "THE L.S.S. CO. ATHOL, MASS. U.S.A." "No. 377" "TEMPERED No 4" "SHRINK 1-4 TO FOOT", c. 1950.

Donated by the Swenson family.

http://www.davistownmuseum.org/pics/10910t6web3.jpg
http://www.davistownmuseum.org/bioStarrett.htm

31811T24   **Unidentified tool**   DTM   TT

Lignum vitae, 9" long, 1 1/2" wide, 3/8" high, unsigned.

This tool came from a patternmaker's shop. The curved side with a dovetail cutout is a possible holding fixture.

Patternmakers' Tools - H A Cobbett Group

42801T4   **Center finder gauge**   DTM   MH

Steel, 7 7/8" long, 3 11/16" wide horizontal cross guide, signed "H A Cobbett" by the owner/maker.

Another essential component of the patternmakers' tool kit.

42801T2   **Inside calipers**   DTM   MH

Steel, 4 5/8" long, signed "H A Cobbett" by the owner.

These are distinctively stylized lady leg calipers with a silhouetted head. Possibly they are owner-made, probably from tempered alloy steel. They are an excellent example of an American folk art tradition: American patternmakers' lady legs caliper.

40501T1   **Patternmakers' gouge**   DTM   MH

Cast steel, brass, and wood, 11" long, 1 1/4" wide blade, 5" long handle, signed "Corbett" on handle.

42801T3   **Patternmakers' tools (4)**   DTM   MH

Brass and steel, 3 are 3 1/2" long with 1 1/2", 1 1/8" & 1" cutters; the other is 2" long, 1 1/4" wide, 1 1/2" cutter, unsigned, c. 1865 - 1885.

These are all planes, three are shavers and the other is a spoke-shave type rounding plane. They were all found in the Corbett collection; no owner signatures.

http://www.davistownmuseum.org/pics/42801t3.jpg

Patternmakers' Tools - H A Cobbett Group

42801T1   Shrink rule   DTM   MH

Boxwood and brass, 24" long, signed "Stanley Rule & Level Co., New Britain, CONN USA No 30 1/2 1/4 in per ft shrinkage".

Sets of shrink rules were essential for judging shrinkage as a result of cooling of various metals in molds used in foundry work. Patternmakers constructed the wood molds for the casting the machinery used in the factories. This was found in the Cobbett collection; no owner signature.

http://www.davistownmuseum.org/bioStanley.htm

Quarrying Tools

31112T17   Brick chisel   DTM   MH3-D2

Drop-forged steel, 6 7/8" long, 2 7/8" wide cutting edge, signed "C. DREW & CO.".

Courtesy of Liberty Tool Co.

http://www.davistownmuseum.org/bioDrew.htm

072112T4   Cold chisel   DTM   TT

Steel, 5 1/4" long, 1" wide, 3/4" cutting edge, signed "PINEL TOOL CO, QUINCY MASS".

"The Pinel Tool Company, 242 Water street, Quincy Adams [MA], is composed of Alfred Pinel and his son Alfred P. J. Mr. Pinel, Sr." (http://thomascranelibrary.org/legacy/history/hisch5.htm). It was established in 1908 as a successor to Pinel Brothers.

TCU1006   Facing tool   DTM   MH

Cast iron and forged steel, 6" long, 3/4" wide blades, unsigned.

The 4 inserted blades are held by a nut and bolt. The distinctly knurled handle suggests this quarry tool probably dates after the Civil War.

032103T5   Miners' pick (?)   DTM   MH

Forged iron, 13" long, 3" handle socket, signed "2225".

This turn-of-the-century tool has an unusual form and a Kenneth Lynch provenance indicating he collected it in France or Spain in the early 20th century and brought it to this country with the other tools he collected.

http://www.davistownmuseum.org/pics/032103t5.jpg
http://www.davistownmuseum.org/bioLynch.htm

101312T29   Rock hammer   DTM   TT

Drop-forged steel, compressed leather discs, 12 3/4" long, 7" wide head, signed "ESTWING ROCKFORD ILL. MADE IN U.S.A.".

Estwing of Rockford, IL, has been making hammers since 1923 (http://www.estwing.com/about_us.php).

ID #   Status   Location

Quarrying Tools

31112T4   **Stone chisel**   DTM   TT

Drop-forged iron or steel, 6 1/2" long, 3/4" wide, signed "VAUGHAN & BUSHNELL MFG Co." "AL-O-ITE".

This company made various hand tools in Chicago and Hebron, IL, from 1873 to 1994. Courtesy of Liberty Tool Co.

12801T11   **Stone chisel**   DTM   MH

Drop-forged iron with a welded steel cutting edge, 8 5/8" long, 2" wide, signed "Bicknell Mfg. Co. Rockland Maine".

This company was the premier manufacturer of tools for the quarry industry of coastal Maine. DATM (Nelson 1999) has no listing for Bicknell. The company began manufacturing in 1893 as the Livingston Manufacturing Company. This tool appears to be post 1900, but Bicknell played a key role in supplying the tools for quarrying in Vinalhaven and Stonington once factory production suppressed on-site forges. The company is now named Bicknell Supply Co. and is located in Elberton, GA. More information is sought for our files on Bicknell.

http://www.davistownmuseum.org/bioBicknell.htm
http://www.davistownmuseum.org/publications/volume10.html

52603T20   **Stone chisel**   DTM   MH

Drop-forged steel, 7 3/4" long, signed "AMIESON".

31112T5   **Stone cutter or splitter**   DTM   MH3-D2

Drop-forged steel, 7 1/4" long, 1/2" wide cutting edge, signed "C. DREW & CO.".

Drew is not well known as a producer of stone-working tools. These are probably from around 1950 when Drew expanded into modern style tools such as cat's paws. Courtesy of Liberty Tool Co.

http://www.davistownmuseum.org/bioDrew.htm

31112T6   **Stone cutter or splitter**   DTM   MH3 D2

Drop-forged steel, 6 1/4" long, 3/8" wide cutting edge, signed "C. DREW & CO.".

Courtesy of Liberty Tool Co.

http://www.davistownmuseum.org/bioDrew.htm

31112T7   **Stone cutters' splitting chisel**   DTM   MH3-D2

Drop-forged steel, 5 3/4" long, 1/4" wide cutting edge, signed "C. DREW & CO.".

Courtesy of Liberty Tool Co.

http://www.davistownmuseum.org/bioDrew.htm

Shipwrights', Sailmakers', and Mariners' Tools

Shipwrights', Sailmakers', and Mariners' Tools

91612T3   **Belaying pin**   DTM   MH

turned copper, 10 3/8" long, 9/16" diameter, unisgned.

These pins originally belonged to Joseph A. Pigeon (1908 - 1997). Pigeon was a US Navy Chief Carpenter's Mate and a veteran of World War II. At some point, he did work on the USS Constitution, and owned a boat shop at 58 High Street in Charlestown, MA, later moving to 38 Cottage St., Taunton, MA.

91612T2   **Belaying pin**   DTM   MH

Turned brass, 10 3/8" long, 5/8" diameter, unsigned.

These pins originally belonged to Joseph A. Pigeon (1908 - 1997). Pigeon was a US Navy Chief Carpenter's Mate and a veteran of World War II. At some point, he did work on the USS Constitution, and owned a boat shop at 58 High Street in Charlestown, MA, later moving to 38 Cottage St., Taunton, MA.

91612T1   **Belaying pin**   DTM   MH

Cast brass, 10 5/8" long, 9/16" diameter, unsigned.

These pins originally belonged to Joseph A. Pigeon (1908 - 1997). Pigeon was a US Navy Chief Carpenter's Mate and a veteran of World War II. At some point, he did work on the USS Constitution, and owned a boat shop at 58 High Street in Charlestown, MA, later moving to 38 Cottage St., Taunton, MA.

9912T2   **Belaying pin set**   DTM   TT (Pub)

Wood (lignum vitae, teak, beech), turned copper, turned brass, cast brass, nickel-plated cast iron, Ranging from 10 3/8" long and 9/16" diameter to 19 1/2" long and 1 1/8" diameter, unsigned.

This set of 13 pins includes a cast brass, a turned brass, a nickel-plated cast iron, and three turned copper pins, as well as seven pins made of assorted woods. These pins originally belonged to Joseph A. Pigeon (1908 - 1997). Pigeon was a US Navy Chief Carpenter's Mate and a veteran of World War II. At some point, he did work on the USS Constitution, and owned a boat shop at 58 High Street in Charlestown, MA, later moving to 38 Cottage St., Taunton, MA.

TCX1005   **Caulking iron**   DTM   MH

Cast steel (?), 5 3/4" long with a 2 1/4" wide blade, signed "T. LAUGHLIN Co" and "PORTLAND, ME", c. 1865-1870 (?).

T. Laughlin Co. is listed in DATM (Nelson 1999, 473) as located in Portland, ME, without a date. Wooden shipbuilding and ship repairing continued in Maine despite the decline of maritime industries after the Civil War and the depletion of coastal forest resources. Ocean-going steam ships remained impractical in comparison to the large 4 and 5 masted schooners built in Maine due to the heavy weight and large bulk of the coal necessary for transatlantic travel.

http://www.davistownmuseum.org/pics/tcx1005-2web.jpg

http://www.davistownmuseum.org/publications/volume10.html

The Industrial Revolution (1865f.): Other Factory Made Tools

Shipwrights', Sailmakers', and Mariners' Tools

22813LTC3   Caulking irons   DA   TT (Pub)

Cast steel, Bent one is 8" long, 1/2" wide, other two are 6" long, 2" and 2 1/4" wide, signed "T LAUGHLIN & Co PORTLAND, ME".

This set includes a caulking iron, a butt iron, and a curved spike iron.

102800M9   Compass (mariners)   DTM   MHC-K

Malleable iron or steel, 3" long, signed by owner "W.F. Blake".

http://www.davistownmuseum.org/bioKnoxEngine.htm

31112T2   Fid   DTM   TT-D27

Tropical hardwood, 11 1/2" long, 2" wide, unsigned.

Fids are used by mariners and others to separate strands of rope when splicing. See marlin spike. Courtesy of Liberty Tool Co.

91612T5   Keeper pin   DTM   MH

Wood (teak), 11" long, 1 1/2" diameter, unsigned.

91612T4   Keeper pin   DTM   MH

Cast brass, 12" long, 1 1/4" diameter, unsigned.

9912T3   Keeper pin set   DTM   TT (Pub)

Cast brass, wood (maple, redwood), Ranging from 11" long and 1 1/2" diameter to 14 1/8" long and 1 1/2" diameter, unsigned.

This set includes one cast brass, one redwood, and two maple keeper pins. These pins originally belonged to Joseph A. Pigeon (1908 - 1997). Pigeon was a US Navy Chief Carpenter's Mate and a veteran of World War II. At some point, he did work on the USS Constitution, and owned a boat shop at 58 High Street in Charlestown, MA, later moving to 38 Cottage St., Taunton, MA.

21812T20   Lipped adz   DTM   TT

Drop-forged cast steel, hardwood handle (oak?), 33 3/4" long, 11" long head, 5" edge, signed "COLLINS & CO HARTFORD CAST STEEL WARRANTED MADE IN USA" with hand holding hammer logo.

This is probably a post-Civil War adz. There is some evidence of additional forging on the cutting edge. It was formerly in the collection of George DuPrey and was donated to the Tools Teach program.

http://www.davistownmuseum.org/bio#bioCollins.html

Shipwrights', Sailmakers', and Mariners' Tools

21812LTC1   Lipped adz   DA   TT (Pub)

Cast steel, hardwood handle (oak?), 33 3/4" long, 11" long head, 5 1/4" edge, signed "GUARANTEED PLUMB" (inside a square).

It has a wooden sheath for protecting the edge. This adz was formerly in the collection of George DuPrey.

62406T4   Lipped adz   DTM   MH

Drop-forged cast steel, 10 3/4" long, 2 5/8" peen, 5" wide cutting edge, 31" wood handle, signed "Collins & Co Hartford cast steel warranted legitimus" with a hammer touchmark on the handle.

This is the classic Collins shipwrights' adz, unused, with the original black and gold paper label stating "Look for the stamp if you want the genuine Collins & Co Hartford".

http://www.davistownmuseum.org/pics/62406t4.jpg
http://www.davistownmuseum.org/bioCollins.html

30911T7   Marlin spike   DTM   TT

Drop-forged malleable iron or steel, 12" long, 1" wide, unsigned.

30311T2   Marlin spike   DTM   TT

Drop-forged malleable iron or steel, 15 1/2" long, 1" wide, unsigned.

It is used to splice wire rope. See fid.

71312T2   Marlin spike   DTM   TT

Drop-forged steel, brass, wood (tiger maple), 13 1/2" long, 8" long blade, unsigned.

091909T3   Mast shave   DTM   MH

Forge-welded iron and steel, wood, 20 1/4" long, 5 1/2" wide, signed "J.GREEN".

It is made by a currently unidentified maker.

http://www.davistownmuseum.org/pics/091909t3web2.jpg
http://www.davistownmuseum.org/pics/091909t3web1.jpg

2713T5   Ship block or pulley   DTM   TT

Rope, forged iron, wood (beech, boxwood), 28" long, 13" wide, 9" thick, unsigned.

22211T17   Ships' bevel rule   DTM   TT

Brass and boxwood, 12" long, 5/8" wide, 3/8" thick, signed "No 42", c. 1900.

It has two brass blades, one 6 1/2" the other 3 1/2". Part of the Robert Sullivan Collection donation.

Shipwrights', Sailmakers', and Mariners' Tools

22211T18   **Ships' bevel rule**   DTM   TT

Brass and hardwood, 12" long, 5/8" wide, 3/8" thick, unsigned.

This rule is homemade with a single blade marked with graduations but no numbers. Part of the Robert Sullivan Collection donation.

91312LTC1   **Shipwrights' slick**   DA   TT (Pub)

Cast steel, hardwood handle, 25" long, 3" wide cutting edge, signed "WATERHOUSE" "CAST STEEL" and owner's mark "WM".

The ferrule is missing from this slick. Courtesy of Liberty Tool Co.

31808SLP1   **Slick**   DTM   TT

Drop-forged iron and steel, wooden (maple) handle, 29" long, 16 5/8" long handle, 3" wide blade, signed 'ROCKFORD" "GREENE" "ILLINOIS" "MADE IN USA" and on handle "FM".

http://www.davistownmuseum.org/pics/31808slp1-2.jpg
http://www.davistownmuseum.org/pics/31808slp1-3.jpg

52907T2   **Slick**   DTM   MH

Drop-forged iron and weld steel, 21 1/2" long including a 12 1/2" handle, 3 1/2" wide, signed "DOUGLASS Mfg Co" and owner's initials "S.H.W.".

This slick has a clearly defined steel-iron interface on the bottom. DATM lists Douglass Mfg. Co. in Seymour, CT from 1856-1894. The name is sometimes spelled with one "s". There also is a Douglas Axe Co. in East Douglas, MA. DATM does not describe a clear relationship between the two companies, but the Douglass Mfg. Co. was owned by a number of famed toolmakers, including F. L. Ames (c. 1873), Thomas Douglass and Richard Bruff (c. 1873), Russell Erwin (1874-77) and James Swan (1877 - 1951). James Swan is the famous Seymour, CT edge toolmaker who came to the US from Scotland in 1854. He changed the business name to Swan sometime after 1877 but was still marking tools Douglass Mfg. Co. as late as 1894 (Nelson 1999, 236, 770). This is an excellent example of a fine shipwrights' slick, probably made around 1880.

http://www.davistownmuseum.org/bioSwan.html

Unidentified Tools

31811T23   **Unidentified tool**   DTM   TT

Lignum vitae, 14 3/8" long, 2" wide, 1/2" high, unsigned.

913108T38   **Unidentified tool**   DTM   MH

German steel, iron ferrule, and wooden handle, 6 3/8" long, 3 1/2" long blade, signed "PEGGIANO BAKATTA" and "PARMA".

This is an Italian mark; possibly it is a leather cutting tool?

The Industrial Revolution (1865f.): Other Factory Made Tools

Unidentified Tools

81801T15   Unidentified tool   DTM   MH

Steel with wood handle and metal ferrule, 3/4" diameter blade, signed "Patented 12-5-09".

This small hand tool has a loop attached to a blade and a modern style handle. What was its use?

81801T14   Unidentified tool   DTM   MH

Drop-forged iron with wood handle and brass ferrule, 12 3/4" long, 7 1/2" pistol grip, 9/16" wide, signed "PAT Feb 6 1877".

It has an unknown use, but resembles a curling iron with a wider, flatter iron.

Watchmakers, Jewelers, and Silversmiths' Tools

22512T9   Dapping block   DTM   TT

Cast steel, 2" by 2", unsigned.

This steel block has various diameter half spheres cast in it and was used by a jeweler for shaping purposes. Courtesy of Liberty Tool Co.

32502T36   Divider legs (2)   BDTM   T

Drop-forged malleable iron, 6 3/4" long on 1/16" diameter iron bar stock, unsigned.

http://www.davistownmuseum.org/bioEpstein.htm

32502T16   Gouge   BDTM   T

Cast steel with cellulite handle, 2" long, 5/16" wide gouge, and 3" long handle, unsigned.

http://www.davistownmuseum.org/bioEpstein.htm

92911T14   Hammer   DTM   TT

Cast steel, wood, and brass, 11" long with handle, 4" long by 1 1/2" wide heads, unsigned.

This silversmith's hammer is used for chasing and forming. It has two heads with hand-forged brass caps. The handle is wooden.

31311T1   Hammer head   DTM   TT

Cast steel, 4 1/2" long, 1/2" wide, unsigned.

This is known as a staking, watchmakers, or jewelers hammer.

31011T8   Hammer head   DTM   TT

Cast steel, 3 1/2" long, 3/8" diameter round head with curved claw, unsigned.

32502T19   Hold down screws (2)   BDTM   T

Brass with beech handle, 3 1/4" long handle, unsigned.

http://www.davistownmuseum.org/bioEpstein.htm

344

The Industrial Revolution (1865f.): Other Factory Made Tools

Watchmakers, Jewelers, and Silversmiths' Tools

30202T8   **Jewelers' dies (13)**   DTM   MH

Steel, 1 1/4" x 1/2" up to 2 7/8" x 5/8", one is 1 7/8" diameter, unsigned.

These are associated with the jeweler industries in Providence, RI and Attleboro, MA.

32802T2   **Jewelers' dies (lot of 6)**   DTM   MH

Cast steel, from 2 to 2 3/4" square and 3 to 3 3/8" high, signed (1) "* O NEIL Attleboro Mass * " with eagle touchmark, (1) "MFRS SUPPLY CO PROV RI", (3) "WHM & SONS MFRS PROV RI" and (1) "GD KING & SONS ATTLEBORO".

http://www.davistownmuseum.org/pics/32802t2.jpg

22211T24   **Jewelers' fret saw**   DTM   TT

German steel, steel blade, hardwood handle, 12" long, 5 1/2" wide, 6" blade, signed "MADE IN GERMANY".

Part of the Robert Sullivan Collection donation.

32502T14   **Jewelers' hammer**   BDTM   T

Drop-forged German (?) steel, 2 7/8" x 7/16" diameter face with a 3/8" wide cross peen, signed "France".

http://www.davistownmuseum.org/bioEpstein.htm

71401T8   **Jewelers' saw**   DTM   MH

Steel, brass, and rosewood, 8" long, 4" handle, signed "M F Millers Falls Mass USA".

This is an exquisite example of a rather uncommon early Millers Falls Co. tool from the heyday of New England tool manufactories.

http://www.davistownmuseum.org/bioMillersFalls.htm

22311T10   **Mallet**   DTM   TT

Horn and wood, 10" long, 4" head, unsigned.

It is handmade. Part of the Robert Sullivan Collection donation.

32502T48   **Pliers-type tools (4)**   BDTM   T

Drop-forged German (?) steel, 4 3/8" to 4 3/4" long, signed "Lindstrom Sweden", "Halle IT Co", "T H Brown" and "P S Studeay".

http://www.davistownmuseum.org/bioEpstein.htm

32912T3   **Screw threader**   DTM   TT-48

Cast steel, 6 1/4" long, signed "BLECKMANN".

This would be used by a jeweler, gunsmith, or clock-maker. DATM (Nelson 1999, 24) lists this signature as having been found on bits, braces, drawknives, knives, and vices but has no information on the location or dates of this maker. Courtesy of Liberty Tool Co.

The Industrial Revolution (1865f.): Other Factory Made Tools

Watchmakers, Jewelers, and Silversmiths' Tools

2713T1   Silvermsiths' hammer   DTM   TT

Cast steel, 3 1/2" long, 5/8" peen, 1/2" face, signed "HAMMOND PHILA 0".

TKD1302   Silversmiths' doming hammer   DTM   MH

Drop-forged steel (?), 4 1/4" long with a 1" diameter face, signed "24" with an obscure touchmark on the reverse side, c. 1880-1910.

This is another specimen from the large tool collection purchased from Kenneth Lynch by the Liberty Tool Co.

http://www.davistownmuseum.org/pics/tjg1001a.jpg
http://www.davistownmuseum.org/bioLynch.htm

32413T1   Silversmiths' forming tool   DTM   MH

Cast steel, 18" long, 7/8" diameter, unsigned.

121412T8   Silversmiths' hammer   DTM   TT

Drop-forged steel, wood (hickory), 11" long, 4 1/2" long head, 1 1/4" wide faces, signed "nan mccurrach" owner's mark in script engraved into the wooden handle.

121412T7   Silversmiths' hammer   DTM   TT

Drop-forged steel, wood (hickory), 11 3/4" long, 4 3/4" long head, 1 3/8" wide faces, signed "nan mccurrach" owner's mark in script engraved into the wooden handle.

121412T10   Silversmiths' hammer   DTM   TT

Drop-forged steel, wood (hickory), 12 1/2" long, 6" long head, 1 1/4" wide faces, signed "EXCELSALL GENUINE HICKORY SALEM INDIANA U.S.A. 13" MACHINIST HAMMER HANDLE FOR 8-12 Oz. Hammer Code 413-04 PAT. No. E106-13".

The O.P. Link Handle Co. of Salem, Indiana made this handle.

121412T6   Silversmiths' hammer   DTM   TT

Drop-forged steel, wood (hickory), 12 1/4" long, 4 3/4" long head, 1 1/4" wide faces, signed "nan mccurrach" owner's mark in script engraved into the wooden handle.

121412T9   Silversmiths' hammer   DTM   TT

Forged steel, wood (hickory), 11 7/8" long, 10 3/4" long head, 1/2" wide faces, signed "nan mccurrach" owner's mark in script engraved into the wooden handle.

123012T3   Silversmiths' hammer head   DTM   TT

Cast steel, 4 1/2" long, 3/4" wide, 3/4" face, signed "WARNER & NOBLE CAST STEEL".

This company was a hammer-making partnership of William M. Noble and Marvin R. Warner of Middletown, CT, 1877 to 1884. See this website for information on earlier and later partners (http://www.angelfire.com/wy/mttools/warnernoble.htm).

The Industrial Revolution (1865f.): Other Factory Made Tools

Watchmakers, Jewelers, and Silversmiths' Tools

41302T12   **Thread gauge**   DTM   MH

Drop-forged German steel, 2 7/8" long, signed "GARANTIE" and "MARTIN FILS Made in Switzerland SWISS MADE".

This is a miniature jewelers' tool.

32502T32   **Tweezers**   BDTM   T

Drop-forged tempered alloy steel, 5 7/8" long, signed "L Silverman Germany", c. 1920.

They are double ended.

http://www.davistownmuseum.org/bioEpstein.htm

32502T33   **Wire cutter**   BDTM   T

Drop-forged tempered alloy steel, 4 3/16" long, signed with an obscure mark, c. 1920.

http://www.davistownmuseum.org/bioEpstein.htm

Woodworking: Axes and Hatchets

111412T13   **Ax**   DTM   MH

Forged steel, wood (hickory) handle, 13" long, 5 1/2" wide, signed "COLLINS AXE" "LEWISTOWN, PENN." on a label on the ax head.

This ax has been added to the museum collection to illustrate the dramatic decline in the metallurgical quality of the "Collins Axe". In 1966, Mann Edge Tool of Lewistown, PA bought the Collins Company and continued to use the Collins Axe branding. For more history see: http://woodtrekker.blogspot.com/2010/12/brief-history-of-collins-axe-company.html.

http://www.davistownmuseum.org/bioCollins.html

7409T1   **Ax**   DTM   MH

Drop-forged steel, wooden handle, 14" long, 6 1/2" wide head, 4 1/2" cutting edge, signed "AMERICANAX" "GLASSPORT".

The American Axe & Tool Co. offices in Oakland, Maine, were discontinued on Oct. 15, 1890 and a new Glassport, PA, manufacturing facility was constructed.

http://www.davistownmuseum.org/pics/7409t1.jpg
http://www.davistownmuseum.org/publications/volume10.html

52603T24   **Ax**   DTM   MH

Steel and iron, 7 2/16" long, unsigned.

Woodworking: Axes and Hatchets

102612T16   Ax head castings (4)   LPC   MH

Cast steel, wood, 4 " long, 3" wide to 7" long, 3 3/4" wide, unsigned.

This is a set of four unfinished ax head castings from the Peavey Mfg. factory in Bangor, ME, that burned down. They were evidently in-production when the factory burned, so they're not yet drop-forged to completion, just vaguely ax-shaped cast steel blanks that give a rare look into the manufacturing process. This four piece group shows a progression in size. Previously, they were owned by Ed Shaw.

http://www.davistownmuseum.org/bioPeavey.htm

52907T3   Broad ax   DTM   MH

Drop-forged cast steel, 23 3/4" long handle, 10" long head, 10 1/2" wide blade, 3 1/4" poll, signed "Wm Beatty & Son" "CAST STEEL" "__ESTER" and "MANESKOOTU".

DATM (Nelson 1999) lists the numerous variations of the famous Beatty clan of edge toolmakers of Chester, Springfield, Pottstown, and Waterville, Pennsylvania as working from 1806 - 1899. A son of the original founder, also named William, probably made this ax. It is marked "MANESKOOTU" three times on its opposite side for the name of the island community where it was used and found in northwestern Massachusetts. It is a fine example of a large late 19th century welded cast steel broad ax with a significantly off-set (to the left) handle.

http://www.davistownmuseum.org/bioBeatyson.html

050112T1   Cambodian hatchet   DTM   TT

Drop-forged cast steel, 5 1/2" long, 3 5/16" wide cutting edge, unsigned.

It is made from one piece of cast steel with surface filing throughout. The cutting edge is heavily filed. This tool was purchased by Brett Ciccotelli at the Krakor, Cambodia, village tool market in the winter of 2012 and represents state of the art edge tool manufacturing capabilities of a third world country in 2010-12. The tool is nicely made and looks like it would hold a good edge.

12813T2   Double bit ax   DTM   TT

Cast steel, wood (hickory), 32" long, 29" long handle, 9 3/4" long head, 5" wide edges, signed "32 PLUMB".

Fayette R. Plumb worked from 1887 to 1964 in Philadephia, PA making axes and many other types of edge tools.

10407T6   Double-bitted ax   DTM   MH

Drop-forged steel, wooden handle, 7 1/2" long, 3" wide blades, unsigned.

This is an interesting ax made in one of America's hundreds of small ax factories in the late 19th century.

52707T1   Double-bitted ax   DTM   MH

Forge-welded iron and steel, wooden handle, 35 1/2" long handle, 10 1/2" long and 3 11/16" wide head with a 5 1/2" curved cutting edge, signed "G53 D/W MS".

This is a nice quality, late 19th century example of a heavy duty, double-bitted, felling ax with ground and filed steeled edges.

ID # Status Location

Woodworking: Axes and Hatchets

091909T2 **Felling ax** DTM MH

Forge-welded iron and cast steel, wooden handle, 32" long, 6 1/4" wide, 4" cutting edge, signed "DOUGLAS AXE MFG Co.", "CAST STEEL WARRANTED", and "MFD BY W. HUNT".

Warren Hunt first worked with his father at Oliver Hunt & Co, 1815-1830, then at Warren Hunt & Co., 1831 - 1836 before becoming a partner in the Douglas Axe Mfg. Co., 1836-1897 (Nelson 1999, 235, 410).

http://www.davistownmuseum.org/pics/091909t2web2.jpg
http://www.davistownmuseum.org/pics/091909t2web1.jpg

31311T3 **Hatchet** DTM TT

Drop-forged iron and steel, 3 1/2" long, 2 1/2" wide head, unsigned.

This hatchet has a broad-shaped head and might have been used for shingling as it has a nail puller notch.

041505T26 **Hatchet** DTM MH

Drop-forged steel and wood, 6 1/2" long, 3 5/8" cutting blade, 1 3/16" diameter poll head face, 13 3/8" long handle, signed "COLLINS & CO" HARTFORD" "LEGITIMUS" with a crown hallmark on the head and a red paper label on the handle stating "COLLINS TOOLS".

The Collins Co. was in Canton, later Collinsville, CT from 1826 - 1957. This circa 1950 edge tool is by one of America's most prolific and famous edge toolmakers. It is an excellent example of a modern all-steel edge tool made just before the rapid decline of the quality of their tools occurred after they were purchased by other owners in 1957.

http://www.davistownmuseum.org/pics/041505t26.jpg
http://www.davistownmuseum.org/bioCollins.html

22512T7 **Hatchet** DTM TT

Drop-forged iron and cast steel, 13" long, 4 1/2" wide head, signed "UNDERHILL EDGE TOOL Co" "WARRENTED CAST STEEL".

Courtesy of Liberty Tool Co.

http://www.davistownmuseum.org/bio#bioUnderhill.html

3091112 **Hatchet** DTM TT

Drop-forged steel, wooden handle, 12" long handle, 5 1/4" long, 2 1/4" wide, 1" thick blade, unsigned.

This hatchet was used in a trade, perhaps by a plasterer.

31908T27 **Hatchet** DTM MH

Drop-forged German steel (?), 5 7/8" long, 3 3/4" long blade, signed "JOHN RILEY & SONS" "1186" and an obscured mark beginning with S and ending with D.

This company used the brand name "TRINAX" and made hatchets. No location or dates are listed in DATM (Nelson 1999, 660).

Woodworking: Axes and Hatchets

61204T16   **Hatchet**   DTM   MH

Drop-forged steel and wood, 13 3/4" long including a 11 1/2" handle, 3 1/4" wide cutting edge, 1 3/16" poll, signed "FINDLAY AXE & TOOL CO." "FINDLAY O. U.S.A." "1".

The Findlay Axe & Tool Co. is not listed in DATM (Nelson 1999). This is a rare mark not often found in New England tool chests. Jack Devitt (2000) author of "The Who, What, Where and When of Ohio Toolmakers and Their Tools" states that "Findlay Axe and Tool Co. was in business in the late 1890s." The Grant Motor Company website indicates that "The Findlay Motor Car Co. produced passenger cars from 1910-13, in the old Findlay Axe and Tool plant at the foot of Santee Avenue."

http://www.davistownmuseum.org/pics/61204T16.jpg

32708T61   **Hatchet head**   DTM   MH

Hand-forged steel, 3 1/2" long, 2 1/4" wide, unsigned.

This is an example of a carefully forged edge tool.

http://www.davistownmuseum.org/pics/32708t61.jpg

101511T1   **Hatchet mold**   DTM   TT

Drop-forged steel, 6.5" long, 3 3/4" long blade, unsigned.

This incompletely drop-forged untrimmed hatched is still within its mold. Its casting pattern clearly indicates the drop-forging process prior to the steeling of its edge by quenching and tempering. This is from the Ed Shaw collection of Peavey edge tools.

4105T5   **Hatchet or belt ax**   DTM   MH

Drop-forged cast steel (?), wooden handle, 12 1/2" long including an 11" long handle, 2 1/4" wide cutting edge, signed "L. A. SAYRE & Co. Newark".

This mark does not appear frequently in New England but DATM (Nelson 1999) records Sayre as working from around 1884 into the early 20th century making a wide variety of hand tools.

http://www.davistownmuseum.org/pics/4105t5.jpg

32313T3   **Hewing ax**   DTM   MH

Forged steel, wood (oak), 25" long, 11" long head, 6" cutting edge, signed "H.N. DEAN CAST-STEEL".

H.N. Dean worked in New Bedford, Connecticut, circa 1870-1871.

12900T7   **Hewing ax**   DTM   MH

Drop-forged German steel, 11 5/8" long, 7 1/2" wide blade, signed with an obscured foreign maker's sign and touchmark, c. 1900 - 1910.

This is an edge tool from the Pyrenees or Alps area of France or Spain that was brought to the US by Kenneth Lynch.

http://www.davistownmuseum.org/pics/12900t7-1bw_web.jpg
http://www.davistownmuseum.org/bioLynch.htm

The Industrial Revolution (1865f.): Other Factory Made Tools

Woodworking: Axes and Hatchets

31212T5   Lathing hatchet   DTM   TT

Drop-forged steel, hickory handle, 12 1/4" long, 6 1/2" long and 2 1/2" wide head, signed "STANLEY".

This is a Stanley No. 1 hatchet, marketed as a "half hatchet with nail puller." Courtesy of Liberty Tool Co.

http://www.davistownmuseum.org/bioStanley.htm

31311T8   Packing hatchet   DTM   TT

Drop-forged malleable iron and steel, 11" long, 5" x 3" head, signed "F".

This hatchet is used to assemble wood boxes or crates.

30311T4   Shingling hatchet   DTM   TT

Drop-forged malleable iron and steel, 7" long, 2 1/2" wide blade, unsigned.

42012T1   Single bit hewing ax   DTM   TT

Forged iron and steel, wooden handle, 34 1/4" long handle, 6 1/2" long, 1 1/2" wide, and 3 3/4" tall head, unsigned.

This ax has a clearly forge-welded cutting edge and steel pole. It shows a lot of blistering.

62207T4   Splitting ax   DTM   MH

Drop-forged iron and steel, 6 13/16" long, 3 3/4" wide blade, unsigned.

Woodworking: Axes and Hatchets Made in Maine

121600T1   Ax   DTM   MH

Drop-forged steel, 6 3/4" long, 3 3/4" wide cutting edge, signed "J P Billings Clinton Me".

A John P. Billings worked in Clinton from 1869 - 71. Other J. P. Billings worked in Saco as early as 1825 and Hallowell in 1841. No lap marks are visible on this ax between the steel blade and iron poll. It is accompanied by a framed advertisement from the Clinton Advertiser illustrating a small man cutting down a large tree. "I cannot tell a lie, father. I did it with one of Billing's Axes. All kinds of edge tools manufactured by J.P. Billings, Clinton, Me." It is a gift to the Museum from Rick Floyd, Newport, ME. The frame also contains an advertisement for "Chas. Jaquith general Blacksmith, Manufacturer of Axes and all kinds of edge tools."

http://www.davistownmuseum.org/publications/volume10.html

92911T12   Broad ax   DTM   MH

Forged iron and steel with wood handle, 33" long, 8" wide cutting edge, 6 1/2" long head, signed "PEAVEY" "BANGOR, ME".

http://www.davistownmuseum.org/bioPeavey.htm

The Industrial Revolution (1865f.): Other Factory Made Tools

Woodworking: Axes and Hatchets Made in Maine

062207T3   Double-bitted ax   DTM   MH

Drop-forged iron and steel, 9 1/4" long, 3 7/8" wide blade, signed "The New Little Giant" "King Axe & Tool Co." and "Oakland Maine" on a paper label, on the tool "KATCO" and "3 1/4".

43006T9   Lathing hatchet   DTM   MH

Drop-forged steel, wooden handle, 13" long, 2 1/4" wide blade, 1" diameter poll, signed "C. A. Williams & Co.".

C. A. Williams worked in Skowhegan, Maine, c. 1860 - 1870. This is the second Williams tool to enter the museum collection.

http://www.davistownmuseum.org/pics/43006t9_p2.jpg
http://www.davistownmuseum.org/publications/volume10.html

6112T2   Maine pattern single bit ax   DTM   TT

Drop-forged iron and steel, hickory wood handle, 30" long, 9 1/4" wide head, 4" long cutting edges, signed "E & S" "3 1/2".

This ax was made by Emerson & Stevens of Oakland Maine in 1941. Courtesy of Liberty Tool Co.

12801T12   Offset hewing ax   DTM   MH

Forged iron and steel, 6 1/2" long, 5 5/8" wide cutting edge, no handle, signed "JOHN KING" "OAKLAND, ME.".

A nice example of a welded steel ax, this is our first example of a John King ax with the imprint in the iron rather than on a paper label. King may have made axes as early as 1877. For comments on John King and the John King Ax Co. see the Registry of Maine Toolmakers (Brack 2008). This ax was located by Dana Phillippi of Liberty, Maine at a Burnham auction, October, 2001.

http://www.davistownmuseum.org/pics/12801t12_p1.jpg
http://www.davistownmuseum.org/publications/volume10.html

6112T1   Ship carpenters' broad ax   LPC   MH

Forge-welded iron and steel, hickory wood handle, 30" long, 9" long head, 7" long cutting edge, signed "LIBBY & BOLTON".

Libby & Bolton worked in Portland, ME, from 1857 to 1886. Courtesy of Liberty Tool Co.

Woodworking: Boring Tools

31811T19   Adjustable drill bit   DTM   TT

Drop-forged alloy steel, 8 1/2" long, 1" wide, signed "L H GIBBS" "NY" "PATENT" "JUNE 17 1885".

DATM (Nelson 1999) lists Gibbs in Washington, DC when he received his patent. He later moved to NY.

101312T23   Adjustable hollow auger bit   DTM   TT

Malleable cast iron, steel, 6" tall, 5" x 3 1/4" base, signed "E.C. STEARNS & COL. SYRACUSE, N.Y.".

This company operated from 1877 to 1941.

Woodworking: Boring Tools

52712LTC1   Adjustable hollow auger or spoke pointer   DA   TT (Pub)

Cast iron, steel, 7" long, 6" wide, 2 1/8" high, 1" cutting edge, signed "The A.A. Wood & Sons Co. Cuts 1/4 to 1 1/4".

The Albert A. Wood & Sons Co. was in Atlanta, Georgia in 1896. They were patent attorneys and their augers, grinders, and shaves may have been produced by March Machinery Co. or Atlanta Machinery Co. (Nelson 1999, 875). Courtesy of Liberty Tool Co.

22311T7   Archimedean drill   DTM   TT

Tempered alloy steel, brass, and copper with a wooden handle, 13" long (extended), 8" long (closed), signed "Goodell Bro's Greenfield, Mass." "Patented, July 22, 1890. Nov. 17, 1891".

The drill has a slot type screwdriver bit. The patent is online at: http://www.google.com/patents/about?id=JRBhAAAAEBAJ&dq=goodell+nov+17+1891. Part of the Robert Sullivan Collection donation.

5212LTC4   Archimedean drill   DA   TT (Pub)

Tempered alloy steel, 10 3/4" long, signed "PAT APP. FOR G.M. MFG. Co. INC. N.Y. CITY N.Y.".

Courtesy of Liberty Tool Co.

5512LTC4   Archimedes twist drill   DA   TT (Pub)

Steel, 10 3/4" long, signed PAT APP. FOR G.M. MFG. Co. INC. N.Y. CITY N.Y..

914108T7   Auger   DTM   MH

Steel, 7 1/2" long, signed "J. T. PUGH" and "PHILA PA".

Job. T. Pugh worked in Philadelphia, PA, from 1876-1891 making flour testers, augers, bits, and other tools.

914108T3   Auger bit   DTM   MH

Steel, 10" long, 7/8" diameter cutting size, signed with a partially obscured signature "PETEROR".

Information on this maker's mark is welcomed.

101909T3   Box of six ship auger drill bits   DTM   MH

Tempered alloy steel, cardboard box, 7 3/4" long, 7/16" diameter bits, signed "THE JAMES SWAN Co." and "SEYMOUR, CONN. U.S.A." with their trademark on the bits.

The box is also marked "7/16 1-2 Doz. No. 40 Auger Bits The James Swan Co. Seymour, Conn."

http://www.davistownmuseum.org/bioSwan.html

The Industrial Revolution (1865f.): Other Factory Made Tools

Woodworking: Boring Tools

40408DTM6　Box of six ship auger drill bits　　　　　DTM　MH

Drop-forged steel with cardboard box, 9 " long, 15/16" diameter bits, signed "THE JAMES SWAN Co." AND "SEYMOUR CONN USA" with their trademark on the bits.

The wooden dovetailed box reads on a blue paper label: "1-2 Doz. No. 30 7 1/2 - 8 SWAN'S SHIP AUGER BITS (FINEST HAMMERED STEEL) WITH SCREW Manufactured by THE JAMES SWAN CO. Seymour, Conn., U.S.A."

http://www.davistownmuseum.org/pics/40408dtm6p1.jpg
http://www.davistownmuseum.org/bioSwan.html

40408DTM9　Box of six ship auger drill bits　　　　　DTM　MH

Drop-forged cast steel with wooden box, 8 5/8" long, 7/16" diameter bits, signed "THE JAMES SWAN Co. JENNINGS PATTERN" on the bits.

The wooden dovetailed box reads on a blue paper label: "1-2 Doz. No. 80. SUPERIOR CAST STEEL BITS JENNINGS' PATTERN Manufactured by THE JAMES SWAN COMPANY, Seymour, Conn., U.S.A."

http://www.davistownmuseum.org/pics/40408dtm9p1.jpg
http://www.davistownmuseum.org/bioSwan.html

40408DTM7　Box of six ship auger drill bits　　　　　DTM　MH

Drop-forged steel with wooden box, 8" long, 1/2" diameter bits, signed "THE JAMES SWAN Co. SEYMOUR CT" on the bits.

The wooden dovetailed box reads on a RED paper label: "1-2 Doz. No. 30 4-8 SWAN'S SHIP AUGER BITS. (FINEST HAMMERED STEEL) Manufactured by THE JAMES SWAN CO."

http://www.davistownmuseum.org/pics/40408dtm7p1.jpg
http://www.davistownmuseum.org/bioSwan.html

40408DTM11　Box of six ship auger drill bits　　　　　DTM　MH

Cast steel with wooden box, 9 1/4" long, 11/16" diameter bits, signed "THE JAMES SWAN Co. SEYMOUR CT" on the bits.

The wooden dovetailed box reads on a red paper label: "1-2 Doz. No. 80. SUPERIOR CAST STEEL BITS JENNINGS' PATTERN Manufactured by THE JAMES SWAN COMPANY, Seymour, Conn., U.S.A."

http://www.davistownmuseum.org/pics/40408dtm11p1.jpg
http://www.davistownmuseum.org/bioSwan.html

40408DTM10　Box of six ship auger drill bits　　　　　DTM　MH

Tempered alloy steel, wooden box, 7 3/4" long, 5/16" diameter bits, signed "THE JAMES SWAN Co." and "SEYMOUR, CONN. U.S.A." with their trademark on the bits.

The wooden dovetailed box reads on a red paper label: "1-2 Doz. No. 30. 2 1/2-8 SWAN'S SHIP AUGER BITS (Finest Hammered Steel.) With Screw. Manufactured by THE JAMES SWAN COMPANY, Seymour, Conn., U.S.A."

http://www.davistownmuseum.org/pics/40408dtm10p1.jpg
http://www.davistownmuseum.org/bioSwan.html

The Industrial Revolution (1865f.): Other Factory Made Tools

Woodworking: Boring Tools

40408DTM8   Box of six ship auger drill bits   DTM   MH

Tempered alloy steel with cardboard box, 9 1/8" long, 5/8" diameter bits, signed "THE JAMES SWAN Co." AND "SEYMOUR CONN USA" with their trademark on the bits.

The wooden dovetailed box reads on a red paper label: "1-2 Doz. No. 30 5-8 SWAN'S SHIP AUGER BITS (FINEST HAMMERED STEEL) WITH SCREW Manufactured by THE JAMES SWAN CO. Seymour, Conn., U.S.A." These bits were manufactured during the last decade of the Swan Company production, probably just before or during WWII. This lot was part of a stash located by the Liberty Tool Co. in a Boston hardware store. Most of the James Swan tools in the museum collection were obtained from this lot.

http://www.davistownmuseum.org/pics/40408dtm8p1.jpg
http://www.davistownmuseum.org/bioSwan.html

101909T2   Box of ten ship auger drill bits   DTM   MH

Drop-forged steel, 7 3/4" long, 1/2" diameter bits, signed "MADE IN GERMANY" on the base and "Jrwin - Schlagenbohrer 10 Stck. M 328 8/16" on the box.

The mark on the bits is identical to the mark on some bits in this collection that are also marked with the James Swan logo.

http://www.davistownmuseum.org/bioSwan.html

41203T3E   Center bit   DTM   MH

Steel, signed "Walter & Co. Cast Steel".

This company is not listed in DATM (Nelson 1999); it is probably a Sheffield, England, manufacturer.

3312T6   Center bit   DTM   TT

Steel, 5 1/4" long, 1 1/2" wide, signed "EARNSHAW BRO SHEFFIELD".

This is an English company. Courtesy of Liberty Tool Co.

41203T3F   Center bit   DTM   MH

Steel, signed "Stortz & Son".

DATM (Nelson 1999) lists this company's working dates from 1853 - 1972 in Philadelphia, PA.

41203T3D   Center bit   DTM   MH

Steel, signed "Thiele & Quack".

DATM (Nelson 1999, 782) lists this company as making bits and dies with no location or date.

41203T3C   Center bit   DTM   MH

steel, signed "Bagshaw & Field".

DATM (Nelson 1999, 47) lists this company's working dates from 1881 - 1931 in Philadelphia, PA. Walter Bragshaw was working in Philadelphia as early as 1866.

Woodworking: Boring Tools

41203T3B   Center bit   DTM   MH

Steel, signed "H. Boker".

DATM (Nelson 1999, 98) lists this company's working dates from 1837 - 1969, no location given. Most Boker tools were imported from Germany.

32313LTC6   Continuous motion two-speed ratcheting breast drill   DTM   TT

Cast iron, steel, wood (rosewood), 17 1/4" long, 7" tall, 12 1/4" wide, signed "MILLERS FALLS CO. NO 97 MILLERS FALLS MASS. PAT. AUG.***1911 PAT AUG 6 1912".

http://www.davistownmuseum.org/bioMillersFalls.htm

81212LTC8   Corner bit brace   DA   TT(pub)

Nickel-plated steel frame with wood (cocobolo) handles, 10" long, 7 1/4" long head, 2 1/2" diameter rear handle, signed "STANLEY NO. 984".

Courtesy of Liberty Tool Company.

http://www.davistownmuseum.org/bioStanley.htm

93012LTC1   Corner bit brace   DA   TT (Pub)

Cast iron, nickel plated finish, wood (cocobolo), 20 1/4" x 12", signed "MILLERS FALLS CO. MILLERS FALLS MASS. MADE IN USA NO 502".

http://www.davistownmuseum.org/bioMillersFalls.htm

31701T2   Countersink   DTM   MH

Drop-forged steel, 4 1/4" long, 5/8" cutter at a 45° angle, signed "_B WHEELER PATD APR 12 1870".

DATM (Nelson 1999, 864) lists George B Wheeler of Brattleboro, VT, 1870, as having received this patent from his father, Asa Wheeler (Warwick, MA, 1849; moved to Brattleboro the same year.)

32405T1   Countersink   DTM   MH

Drop-forged steel, 5 5/8" long, 3/4" wide, signed "PATENDED" "JAN 23, 1877." "D.J. ADAMS" "KITTERY,
ME." and "R.L. MARKS".

The Directory of American Machinery and Tool Patents lists this as patent number 186,513 for an improvement for countersinks and also shows the patent diagram at: http://www.datamp.org/displayPatent.php?number=186513&type=UT. It is unknown who manufactured the countersink. R.L. Marks was probably an owner. A countersink is a tool used to make a hole with the top part enlarged so the head of a screw or bolt will lie flush with or below the surface.

914108T9   Countersink   DTM   MH

Drop-forged iron and steel, 4 1/8" long, signed "G. B. WHEELER".

George B. Wheeler worked in Brattleboro, VT, from 1870 - 1873 making axes, bits, and machinists' tools. His father, Asa, held an 1870 patent for countersinks and a countersink depth gauge that he assigned to George.

The Industrial Revolution (1865f.): Other Factory Made Tools

Woodworking: Boring Tools

31611T1   Countersink bit   DTM   TT

Drop-forged cast steel, 4 3/4" long, 1/2" countersink, signed "C. STEEL".

This bit is made for use with a brace.

8912T8   Diamond center gimlet bit   DTM   TT

Cast steel, 3 7/8" long, 5/8" wide, signed "S" in a diamond.

31908T38   Double twist auger bit   DTM   MH

Drop-forged steel, 15 1/4" long, signed "JAMES SWAN" "COOK" "PATENT" with the swan trademark and "16" on the bit point.

http://www.davistownmuseum.org/pics/31908t38p1.jpg
http://www.davistownmuseum.org/bioSwan.html

62212LTC1   Doweling bit   DA   TT (Pub)

Cast steel, 5 1/2" long, 3/4" diameter, signed "RUSSELL JENNINGS".

The Russell Jennings Mfg. Co. was located in Deep River, CT from 1853 to 1944 and Chester, CT from 1865 to 1890. The company was sold to Stanley in 1944 and they continued to use the name until 1960 (Nelson 1999, 426). Courtesy of the Liberty Tool Co.

21812T2   Expansion bit   DTM   TT

Drop-forged steel, 7 1/4" long, 1/2" diameter bit and 7/8" diameter bit, signed "GENUINE" "MUR MAC" "W. A. CLARK".

William A. Clark patented an expansive bit on May 11, 1858 (Nelson 1999, 171). He patented an improvement in 1873. See ID# 021812T1 for a version of his bit patent that was manufactured by R. H. Brown & Co.

22612T5   Expansion bit   DTM   TT

Drop-forged steel, vinyl case with printed instructions, 7" long, 2 sizes of bits, small from 5/8" to 1", large 1" to 1 3/4", signed "IRWIN No 21A US of A".

These were manufactured around the 1980s; courtesy of Liberty Tool Co.

Woodworking: Boring Tools

021812T1   Expansion bit

DTM   TT

Drop-forged steel, 10 1/2" long, 1/2" diameter, signed "THE CLARK BROWN MODEL" "MADE BY R.H. BROWN & CO".

William A. Clark patented an expansion bit on May 11, 1858 (Nelson 1999, 171). Reuben H. Brown bought the patent and manufactured it. The 1873 patent is one of Clark's improvements on the1858 bit here: http://www.google.com/patents?id=kLVQAAAAEBAJ&pg=PA1&dq=141324+1873&hl=en&sa=X&ei=c gFRT4efMcXn0QHvyYmEDg&ved=0CDQQ6AEwAA#v=onepage&q=141324%201873&f=false. By 1894, R.H. Brown was the sole manufacturer of the bits and was patenting improvements on them himself: http://www.google.com/patents?id=SJ9WAAAAEBAJ&pg=PA2&dq=Brown+expansive+bit&hl=en&sa= X&ei=9QBRT9uYOOSs0AHEzrD8DQ&ved=0CDIQ6AEwAA#v=onepage&q=Brown%20expansive%2 0bit&f=false.

040103T14   Expansion bit

DTM   MH

Drop-forged steel, 9 1/4" long, signed "DAVIS THE HARDWARE MAN".

Who is Davis the hardware man?

3312T11   Expansion drill

DTM   TT

Drop-forged tempered alloy steel, 10 1/2" long, bit from 7/8" to 1 3/4", signed "THE CLARK, BROWN MODEL" "MADE BY R.H.BROWN & CO.".

DATM (Nelson 1999, 119) lists R. H. Brown & Co. as making machinist tools, bits, braces, and screwdrivers in Westville, CT, from 1873 to 1905. Courtesy of Liberty Tool Co.

111412T1   Expansive bit

DTM   MH

Drop-forged steel, 7 1/2" long, 1" wide, signed "W. A. IVES" "MFG. CO.".

William A. Ives had 12 patents between 1868 and 1917 for augers, bits, braces, etc. This specific mark is thought to have come into use after 1900. He was reported working in New Haven, Wallingford, and Hampden, CT. (Nelson 1999, 419).

33013LTC1   Expansive drill bit set

DA   TT (Pub)

Drop-forged steel, Two bits, one is 8" x 5/8", the other is 7 1/2" x 7/16", signed "C.E. JENNINGS STEERS' PATENT APR ** '84 DEC 19, 1905 MAR 1 1910" "MADE IN U.S.A. 1922".

112400T1   Hand drill

DTM   MH

Drop-forged tempered alloy steel, wooden handle, 14" long, signed "MADE IN USA No. 2A MILLERS FALLS TOOLS GREENFIELD, MA", c. 1950.

http://www.davistownmuseum.org/pics/112400t1_p1.jpg
http://www.davistownmuseum.org/bioMillersFalls.htm

The Industrial Revolution (1865f.): Other Factory Made Tools

Woodworking: Boring Tools

22411T17   Hand drill
DTM   TT

Brass with wooden handle, 9" long, unsigned.

This is an Archimedean style drill with a fine drill holder end.

52612LTC3   Hand drill
DA   TT (Pub)

Cast iron and steel, 7 7/8" long, unsigned.

This tool is pictured in Sellens (2002) under "Hand Drill" with a Hammacher & Schlemmer maker's mark. Courtesy of Liberty Tool Co.

3312LTC1   Jennings patent auger bit set
DA   TT (Pub)

Drop forged steel, wood box, signed Russell Jennings STANLEY AUGER BITS.

This three-tiered box holds a set of Jenning pattern auger bits. Courtesy of Liberty Tool Company.

102100T22   Mortising bit
DTM   MH

Drop-forged steel, 8 1/2" long, 3/4" diameter, signed "Greenlee Rockford ILL MADE IN USA".

DATM (Nelson 1999, 333) indicates Greenlee Bros. & Co. moved from Chicago to Rockford, IL, in 1905. This modern mortising bit is almost 50 years newer than the Miller's Falls mortising machine that can still utilize this distinctive wood bit. Notice the two circular indentations for securing this type of bit in a mortising machine.

http://www.davistownmuseum.org/bioGreenlee.html

82500T3   Mortising machine
LPC   MH

Cast iron, drop-forged malleable iron, signed "M.F.Co. Millers Falls Mass", c. 1885.

This is a prototypical mortising machine of the late 19th century. It was used in shipyards and for barn building to cut the mortise for tenons. This tool dates from before the age of electric powered hand tools.

http://www.davistownmuseum.org/pics/82500t3.jpg
http://www.davistownmuseum.org/bioMillersFalls.htm

31908T32   Pod auger
DTM   MH

Drop-forged iron and steel, 17 1/8" long, signed "MATHIGSON" with an M inside a circle.

It is Scottish.

31908T36   Single twist auger bit
DTM   MH

Drop-forged steel, signed "THE JAMES SWAN CO" "SEYMOUR, CT. U.S.A." with swan trademark and "18" on the bit point.

The James Swan Co.'s working dates were from 1877 to 1951.

http://www.davistownmuseum.org/bioSwan.html

The Industrial Revolution (1865f.): Other Factory Made Tools

Woodworking: Boring Tools

8912T7   Snail countersink bit   DTM   TT

Cast steel, 3 3/8" long, 5/16" wide, signed "HAWESWORTH CAST STEEL".

This bit has a square shank for a bit brace. DATM (Nelson 1999) does not list any Hawesworths.

42812LTC1   Star bit   DA   TT (Pub)

Drop-forged steel, 7 3/4" long handle, 5/8" diameter, signed "UTICA USA 5/8".

DATM (Nelson 1999, 809) lists Utica Drop Forge & Tool Co. in Utica, NY from 1895 to 1912. Courtesy of Liberty Tool Co.

101212LTC1 Three bit gang drill   DA   TT (Pub)

Cast iron, cast steel, 8 1/4" long, 4 1/2" wide, 1 1/8" thick, bits are 1" wide, signed "GRAND RAPIDS SASH PULLEY CO".

This company was located in Grand Rapids, Michigan (http://vintagemachinery.org/mfgindex/detail.aspx?id=1955).

31811T9   Twist drill bit   DTM   TT

Drop-forged steel, 8" long, 1" diameter, unsigned.

It is used with a brace.

Woodworking: Edge Tools

102612T6   Adz   LPC   MH

Steel, wooden handle, 35" long, 10" long and 4" wide head, signed with an owner's mark "T R" using punched dots and including a diamond between the T and R.

3312T13   Adz   DTM   TT

Malleable iron, forged steel tip, wooden handle, 8" long, 1 3/4" wide blade, unsigned.

This commonplace contemporary tool was purchased in a Nairobi, Kenya flea market in 2011 and donated to the museum by Judith Bradshaw Brown. It's curved handle form is from natural tree growth. It is notable in that the design of this adz is a perpetuation of the now obsolete model of socket hole edge tools, which characterized tool forms during the European Bronze Age. See "Steel and Toolmaking Strategies and Techniques Before 1870" (Brack 2008, 15) for commentary on the modern design of the shaft hole ax, which first appeared in the toolkits of Sumerians c. 3000 BC. Also see Goodman (1964).

Woodworking: Edge Tools

32808DTM5   Box of six outside bevel socketed firmer gouge chisels   DTM   MH

Drop-forged steel, wooden handles, 13 1/2" long, 1/4" wide, signed "THE JAMES SWAN CO" on the chisels.

The chisels are fitted loosely with wooden handles. A blue label on the cardboard box reads: "1-2 Doz. SWAN'S No. 1230 OUTSIDE BEVEL SOCKET FIRMER GOUGES WITH LEATHER TIPPED HANDLES MANUFACTURED BY The James Swan Company, Seymour, Conn., U.S.A."

http://www.davistownmuseum.org/pics/32308dtm5p3.jpg
http://www.davistownmuseum.org/bioSwan.html

31011T5   Box scraper   DTM   TT

Drop-forged tempered alloy steel with wood grip, 10 1/2" long, 5" wide, 3" high, 5" blade, unsigned.

It has an adjustable blade. It is used to remove paper labels from wooden boxes.

14302T19   Box scraper   DTM   MH

Drop-forged steel, wood, and brass ferrule, 12 1/2" long, 8 1/2" long handle, 1 9/16" wide cutting blade, signed "Patd July 26 1870" on ferrule.

It is used for removing paper labels on fruit, etc., boxes.

42812LTC5   Box scraper   DA   TT (Pub)

Cast iron, steel blade, wood (beech), 13" long, 2" wide cutting edge, signed "STANLEY SW MADE IN U.S.A.".

Courtesy of Liberty Tool Co.

81602T18   Box scraper   DTM   MH

Drop-forged cast iron with steel blades and brass adjustment nut, 9 7/8" long, 3" wide, 2 1/2" wide blades, signed on nut "Holmes PATENT May 6 1868".

Many Holmes are listed in DATM (Nelson 1999, 392) but none with this patent date or listed as making box scrapers. This is an early form of this tool. It could be Elijah Holmes of Lynn, MA.

31908T28   Carving chisel   DTM   MH

Steel, brass trim, and wood, signed "C. MAIERS" and two stars.

DATM (Nelson 1999, 504) lists C. Maiers as making chisels with no date or location.

041709T3   Chisel   DTM   MH

Drop-forged steel, 13 1/4" long, 2" wide, 5/16" thick, signed "THE JAMES SWAN CO" "SEYMOUR, CT. U.S.A." "DOUGLASS MFG. Co", 1859 - 1877.

This chisel is double marked with both Charles Douglass and James Swan's marks. Douglass was operating in Seymour from 1859 to 1877 when Swan bought him out.

http://www.davistownmuseum.org/bio#bioSwan.html

The Industrial Revolution (1865f.): Other Factory Made Tools

Woodworking: Edge Tools

041709T2   Chisel   DTM   MH

Drop-forged steel, 12 1/4" long, 1 3/4" wide, 1/4" thick, signed "THE JAMES SWAN CO" "SEYMOUR, CT. U.S.A." "DOUGLASS MFG. Co", 1859 - 1877.

This chisel is double marked with both Charles Douglass and James Swan's marks. Douglass was operating in Seymour from 1859 to 1877 when Swan bought him out.

http://www.davistownmuseum.org/bio#bioSwan.html

31811T31   Chisel   DTM   TT

Malleable iron and steel, 9 1/2" long, 1 1/2" wide, signed "BY" "_____ HARDWARE CO" and "____ CONN".

The marks are very worn and difficult to read. This chisel is broken. It has been saved to study its microstructure.

22612T4   Chisel   DTM   TT

Drop-forged steel, wooden handle, 12" long with 8" long and 11/16" wide blade, 4" long handle, unsigned.

52603T14   Chisel   DTM   MH

Tool steel, signed "TOOL STEEL" "MADE IN USA" "HARDENED AND GROUND".

Contemporary tool steel has a carbon content of 0.7% and above. The mark "TOOL STEEL" is another way of saying tempered alloy steel.

33002T14   Chisel   DTM   TT

Hardened tool steel with wood handle, 7 3/4" long, 3 3/4" handle, 15/16" wide blade, signed "Hardened tool steel _____ MADE IN USA", c. 1900 (?).

This is a generic early 20th century tool.

93011T17   Chisel   DTM   TT

Drop-forged iron and steel with a broken wooden handle, 7" long, 1/4" wide blade, signed "RUBBARD Y___".

Could this be Hubbard Hardware Company of Middletown CT, which used the mark "HUBBARD H. W. CO." and made chisels?

41302T4   Chisel   DTM   MH

German steel, wooden handle, 8 3/4" long, 4 3/4" long blade, 1/2" wide, signed "Peugeot Frère" with a cartouche of a hand, probably c. 1900 - 1920.

This French chisel is a reminder that not all edge tools in American carpenters' tool chests were made in England or America.

Woodworking: Edge Tools

091309T2   **Chisel set (3)**   DTM   MH

Steel and wood, signed "F. Stones".

1) 11 3/4" long, 1" wide, 3/16" cutting edge; 2) 12" long, 1 1/4" wide, 1/4" cutting edge; 3) 12 1/2" long, 1 1/2" wide, 5/16" cutting edge.

31808SLP16   **Corner chisel**   DTM   TT

Drop-forged iron and steel, 11 1/4" long, 1 1/4" wide blade, signed "WITHERBY".

http://www.davistownmuseum.org/pics/31808slp16-3.jpg
http://www.davistownmuseum.org/bioWitherby.html

72612LTC1   **Deck or ship scraper**   DA   TT (Pub)

Forged malleable iron and steel, 12" long, 1" wide, 2 1/2" wide cutting edge, unsigned.

Courtesy of the Liberty Tool Company.

22411T15   **Drawknife**   DTM   TT

Drop-forged iron and steel, steel ferrules, wooden handles, 12" long, 6" wide and 6" long blade, 6" long handles, signed "HART M___".

Some of the signature is obscured. DATM (Nelson 1999) lists a Hart Mfg. Co. as a maker of drawknives but has no other information on it.

102612T9   **Drawknife**   LPC   MH

Steel, wooden handles, 16" long, 5 3/4" long handles, 9 1/2" long cutting edge, signed "C. J. KIMBALL".

The Caleb Jewett Kimball company was in Bennington, NH from 1894 -1900.

http://www.davistownmuseum.org/bioKimball.html

102612T8   **Drawknife**   DTM   TT

Steel, wooden handles, 20" long, 5" long handles, 13 1/2" long cutting edge, signed "J. P. DAVIS" "UNION" "WARRENTED".

It looks like Davis is an owner's mark.

12112T2   **Drawknife**   DTM   MH

Forged steel, wood (rosewood) handles, 16 1/2" long, 11" cutting edge, 4 3/4" long handles, signed "A. FENTON & SON".

This is a previously unrecorded maker.

22411T5   **Drawknife**   DTM   TT

Drop-forged iron and steel with wooden handles, 17" long, 6 1/2" wide, 11" long blade, unsigned.

This drawknife has a slightly concave blade.

The Industrial Revolution (1865f.): Other Factory Made Tools

Woodworking: Edge Tools

31811T2   Drawknife   DTM   TT

Forged iron and steel, 19" long, 4 3/4" wide, 12" long by 1 5/8" wide blade, signed "B GORDON".

B. Gordon looks like an owner's stamp. The wooden handles are missing.

22311T16   Drawknife   DTM   TT

Drop-forged iron and steel with a wood handle, 12" long, 6" long blade, unsigned.

This drawknife is factory-made. Part of the Robert Sullivan Collection donation.

41302T2   Drawknife   DTM   MH

Forged iron and steel, wooden handles, 19" long, 12 5/8" blade, signed "L. Palmer".

This maker is not listed in DATM (Nelson 1999). This tool is a nice example of a finely forged 20th century drawknife with a distinct welded steel blade and modern appearing handle attached by threaded bolts and nuts. It serves as a reminder that 20th century craftsmen can still fashion a drawknife the old fashioned way.

121412T1   Drawshave   DTM   TT

Cast steel, wood (hornbeam), 19" long, 13 1/2" cutting edge, 6" long handles, signed "SNOW & NEALLEY Co BANGOR MAINE".

31808SLP17   Drawshave   DTM   TT

Drop-forged steel, wooden handles, 9 3/4" long, 4" long blade, signed "C. E. JENNINGS" "MADE IN USA" with a "J" in a triangle.

Charles E. Jennings is believed to have possibly worked under his own name for a few years before adding "& Co." in 1878. The company headquarters was located in New York City (DATM 1999).

http://www.davistownmuseum.org/pics/31808slp17-1.jpg
http://www.davistownmuseum.org/bioJennings.html

110611T2   Drawshave   DTM   TT

Forged iron and steel, wooden (ash) handle, 14" long cutting edge, 5" long handles, signed "T.H. WITHERBY" and "T. ERSKINE" owners mark.

This drawshave has a distinct forge-welded steel blade.

http://www.davistownmuseum.org/bioWitherby.html

31808SLP6   Drawshave   DTM   TT

Drop-forged steel, wood, 15 1/4" long, 10" long blade, signed "WITHERBY" and "10".

http://www.davistownmuseum.org/pics/31808slp6-2.jpg
http://www.davistownmuseum.org/bioWitherby.html

The Industrial Revolution (1865f.): Other Factory Made Tools

Woodworking: Edge Tools

31808PC14   Drawshave   DTM   MH

Steel and wood, 21 1/4" long, 14" blade, signed "HARRIS" and "& ALLAN" with "CS" on either side.

Harris & Allan worked in St. John, NB from 1860 - 1888. James Harris eventually bought out his partner.

32808DTM2   Firmer chisel   DTM   MH

Drop-forged steel, 11" long, 5/8" wide, signed "JAS SWAN CO. U.S.A.".

It has a beveled socketed style.

http://www.davistownmuseum.org/bioSwan.html

52403T4   Folding drawknife   DTM   MH

Forged iron and steel, wooden handle, 10 1/2" long, 6" blade, signed "A. J. WILKINSON & CO." "MAKERS - BOSTON MASS." "PATENTED JULY 6.1895" and "6".

DATM (Nelson 1999) lists Wilkinson with the working dates of 1842 - 1893, but they continued working later than this date. The July 16, 1895 patent was issued to John G. Young of Hyde Park, MA. It may be viewed here: http://www.datamp.org/patents/displayPatent.php?pn=542721&id=12867.

http://www.davistownmuseum.org/pics/52403t4_p4.jpg
http://www.davistownmuseum.org/pics/52403t4_p3.jpg

111209T1   Framing chisel   DTM   MH

Tool steel and white oak, 17 1/4" long, 1 1/2" cutting edge, signed "BARR" with a bear trademark.

Barr Specialty Tools of McCall, Idaho (www.barrtools.com) is a contemporary toolmaker. This chisel is hand-forged with a wooden handle. It is used by timber framers for mortise and tenon work.

51606T3   Framing chisel   DTM   MH-O

Drop-forged steel, 16 1/4" long including a 4 1/2" handle, 1 3/8" wide, signed HART MFG CO..

Three Hart Mfg. Companies are listed in DATM (Nelson 1999); the only edge toolmaker (drawknives) is listed without a known location. More information on this maker is sought.

http://www.davistownmuseum.org/pics/51606t3_p1.jpg

The Industrial Revolution (1865f.): Other Factory Made Tools

Woodworking: Edge Tools

51606T4   Framing chisel   DTM   MH

Drop-forged steel, 16 3/8" long with a 4" wooden handle, 1 3/4" wide, signed "BIGELOW & DOWSE" "BOSTON".

Clarence Blanchard of the Fine Tool Journal thinks this mark is that of a hardware store in which case this tool would have been made by a New England edge toolmaker (e.g. Underhill or Witherby) and then sold to this hardware company for resale. A poster for Worth Tools was for sale on eBay that came in an envelope marked Bigelow & Dowse Company, Boston & Springfield Mass. The company published a hardware catalog in 1906 and is referenced importing nails in 1896. The book "Geneology of the Bigelow Family" lists Samuel A. Bigelow (b. 1838) as a senior member of the firm Bigelow & Dowse. This company also sold bicycles. DATM (Nelson 1999, 503) reports that Bigelow & Dowse marked metal planes with the brand name "Worth" circa 1925-45. More information on this company and touchmark is solicited.

http://www.davistownmuseum.org/pics/51606t4_p3.jpg
http://www.davistownmuseum.org/pics/51606t4_p4.jpg

31808SLP20   Froe   DTM   TT

Drop-forged iron, wooden handle, 13" long blade, 15 1/2" long handle, unsigned.

Its cutting edge has probably been carburized (+/- 0.5 % carbon content).

http://www.davistownmuseum.org/pics/31808slp20-1.jpg

31311T12   Gouge   DTM   TT

Drop-forged steel, steel ferrules, and wood handle, 17 " long, 11" long and 1" wide blade, 6" long handle, unsigned.

93011T14   Gouge   DTM   MH

Drop-forged iron and steel, wooden handle, signed "HIBARD SPENCER" "& CO WINOOKS".

The last part of the signature (WINOOKS) is difficult to read. In 1865 - 1871 there was a hardware company called Hibbard, Spencer & Co. at 92-94 Michigan Ave. in Chicago. After the Chicago fire it relocated and in 1882 became HSB (Hibbard, Spencer, Bartlett & Co.) (http://www.thckk.org/history/hsb.pdf)

110611T5   Paring chisel   DTM   TT

Steel, wood, 3 1/4" long blade, 4 1/2" long wooden faceted handle, 1/4" diamond shape edge, signed "BUCK BROS" "JAMES CAM".

Possibly it was reforged into a diamond shaped edge tool. The signature sequence is particularly significant showing Buck Brothers utilizing English steel. This is the first edge tool we've encountered with a James Cam (steelmaker) mark on the verso.

http://www.davistownmuseum.org/bioBuckBrothers.html

ID #   Status   Location

Woodworking: Edge Tools

31501T4   Peen adz   DTM   MH

Drop-forged iron and steel, 33" long, 4 3/4" wide blade, signed "A DRAUDAY" or "A DRAUBAY" "PAT JUNE 8, 1875" (?).

No such maker is listed in DATM (Nelson 1999). This adz has a very distinctive fitted peen and handle ferrule. The ferrule attachment, which protects the wooden handle, is 8" long and is fitted over the adz peen. The patent was assigned to John Pinkerton of Philadelphia (http://www.google.com/patents?id=2hhEAAAAEBAJ&pg=PA2&dq=june+8+1875+adz&hl=en&sa=X&ei=4W-QT6-YCab06QHDhpCoBA&ved=0CDIQ6AEwAA#v=onepage&q=june%208%201875%20adz&f=false).

31112T16   Plugging chisel   DTM   MH3-D30

Drop-forged tool steel, 8 1/4" long, 3/4" wide blade, signed "C. DREW & CO.".

Courtesy of Liberty Tool Co.

http://www.davistownmuseum.org/bioDrew.htm

12413LTC1   Razor edge spokeshave   DA   TT (Pub)

Drop-forged steel, wood (boxwood), 11" long, 2 1/2" wide cutting edge, signed "STANLEY SW No. 85".

http://www.davistownmuseum.org/bioStanley.htm

120907T1   Slick   DTM   TT

Steel, iron, wooden handle, unsigned.

There is a clear suggestion of either a welded steel-iron interface or differential tempering. The iron shaft is probably low-carbon steel and shows signs of forge-welding.

http://www.davistownmuseum.org/pics/120907t1.jpg

102512T15   Socket chisel   DTM   TT

Steel, 3 3/4" long, 1" wide cutting edge, signed "ERIK ANTON BERG" "ESKIL__UNA__" "SWEDEN" plust a shark trademark.

Erik Berg worked in Eskilstuna, Sweden. Go here for a history of E. A Bergs Fabriks AB (E.A. Berg MFG. Co. LTD) (http://straightrazorplace.com/razors/26475-erik-antonberg-short-history.html). Courtesy of Liberty Tool Co.

121805T15   Socket chisel   DTM   MH

Forged-welded German steel, 9 1/2" long, 1 1/2" wide, signed "HR 1861" with three trademarks and a fleur de lis.

There are signs of hand-filing but no evidence of steeling - uniform microstructure throughout the tool and socket. Possibly it is made of puddled steel.

http://www.davistownmuseum.org/pics/121805t15_p2.jpg

Woodworking: Edge Tools

030910T1   Socket chisel   DTM   MH

Drop-forged iron and steel, 11" long, 1 1/2" wide, signed "W. C. BAILEY" and "SAG HARBOR TOOL Co.".

The book "Sag Harbor - The Story of an American Beauty" by Dorothy Ingersoll Zaykowski states "In the Spring of 1892 Mr. Bailey of Southington, Connecticut showed an interest in starting a cut tool factory in Sag Harbor. He met with village officials and proposed to subscribe $1000 and run the business for three years, asking no profit until the 8% per annum was paid to the stockholders. Bailey was notified that his offer was acceptable. Additional capital of $17,000 had to be raised and the enthusiasm was so great that within two weeks half of the money had been collected. By-laws were adopted and officers elected: George C. Gibbs, President; George C. Raymond, vice-president, George Kiernan, secretary and treasurer; and C.A. Parsons, J.M. Hildreth, B. Lyon and Charles Watson Payne, directors. The first floor of the old mill property was rented for five years at $500 per year. For the first four years the tool company grew and prospered. An order for 700 dozen chisels from a Philadelphia company was filled. The company prided itself on being the only tool factory that stayed in operation during the hard times of 1895. Unfortunately the situation was not to last, for in July 1896 the factory closed its doors and remained shut until May 1897 when Superintendent Bailey bought all the stock of the company and completed manufacturing tools that had been left unfinished when the plant closed."

http://www.davistownmuseum.org/pics/030910t1web4.jpg
http://www.davistownmuseum.org/pics/030910t1web3.jpg

62202T4   Socket chisel   DTM   MH

Drop-forged iron and steel, wooden handle, 13" long including a 4 5/8" long handle, signed "Bailey" and "SAG HARBOR TOOL CO".

DATM (Nelson 1999) notes W. C. Bailey as manufacturing chisels and drawknives in Sag Harbor, NY, c. 1896.

http://www.davistownmuseum.org/pics/62202t4_p1.jpg
http://www.davistownmuseum.org/pics/62202t4_p2.jpg

71401T20   Socket chisel   DTM   MH

Drop-forged steel, wood, and brass, 8 3/4" long, 9 1/2" blade, signed "Charles Buck".

This is an excellent example of the craft of one of New England's foremost edge toolmakers.

http://www.davistownmuseum.org/bioBuckBrothers.html

913108T18   Socket chisel   DTM   MH

Iron and steel with a clearly laminated steel base, 10 1/2" long including an 8" long blade, signed "G. S. WILDER".

According to DATM (Nelson 1999, 860), George Sheldon Wilder worked with his uncle Pliny Merrill as Merrill & Wilder (c. 1860), then was part of Wilder & Thompson (c. 1868), and Wilder & Hopkins (1870-73). He also worked alone and sold his business to the Jennings & Griffin Mfg. Co. in 1883 and worked for them. C. E. Jennings used his name on tools until 1901.

The Industrial Revolution (1865f.): Other Factory Made Tools

ID #

Status   Location

Woodworking: Edge Tools

32808DTM21 Socketed firmer chisel
DTM   MH

Drop-forged tool steel, 9" long, 5/8" wide, signed "THE JAMES SWAN Co." and "SEYMOUR CONN. U.S.A." with their trademark.

By the late 1920s, the Swan Co. is probably using tempered alloy steel smelted in an electric arc furnace as are many other tool companies. Steel alloy composition will vary according to the function of the tool, with calipers and precision machinists' tools having a slightly different composition than edge tools.

http://www.davistownmuseum.org/bioSwan.html

40408DTM5 Socketed framing chisel
DTM   MH

Drop-forged tool steel, 10" long, 1 3/4" wide, signed "THE JAMES SWAN CO. SEYMOUR, CONN. U.S.A.".

http://www.davistownmuseum.org/pics/40408dtm5p1.jpg
http://www.davistownmuseum.org/bioSwan.html

40408DTM2 Socketed inside bevel gouge chisel
DTM   MH

Drop-forged tool steel, 9 1/4" long, 1 1/4" wide, signed "JAS. SWAN CO. U.S.A.".

http://www.davistownmuseum.org/pics/40408dtm2p1.jpg
http://www.davistownmuseum.org/bioSwan.html

40408DTM1 Socketed inside bevel gouge chisel
DTM   MH

Drop-forged tool steel, 9 5/8" long, 1 1/2" wide, signed "JAS. SWAN CO. U.S.A.".

http://www.davistownmuseum.org/pics/40408dtm1p3.jpg
http://www.davistownmuseum.org/bioSwan.html

101909T1 Socketed paring chisel
DTM   MH

Drop-forged tool steel, 11" long, 5/8" wide, signed "THE JAMES SWAN CO".

http://www.davistownmuseum.org/bioSwan.html

12413LTC2 Spokeshave
DA   TT (Pub)

Cast steel, wood (boxwood), 13 1/4" long, 2" wide cutting edge, unsigned.

22211T30 Spokeshave
DTM   TT

Drop-forged tempered alloy steel, steel blade, signed "No 45" on body, "STANLEY" on the plane blade, and "MADE IN USA" on the handle.

Part of the Robert Sullivan Collection donation.

http://www.davistownmuseum.org/bioStanley.html

The Industrial Revolution (1865f.): Other Factory Made Tools

Woodworking: Edge Tools

7712LTC6   Spokeshave

DA   TT (Pub)

Drop-forged steel, wooden (rosewood) handles, 10 1/4" long, 3/4" diameter, 2 1/4" long cutting edge, signed "MILLERS FALLS CO. MILLERS FALLS MASS. MADE IN U.S.A.".

This is the No. 1 spokeshave from Miller's Falls, patented by Albert D. Goodell on February 19, 1884. View the patent here: http://www.google.com/patents/US293651?printsec=drawing&dq=Goodell+February+19,+1884&ei=m 9AOULKQIcfZ0QWsz4GgAQ#v=onepage&q&f=false. Courtesy of Liberty Tool Company.

http://www.davistownmuseum.org/bioMillersFalls.htm

913108T13   Spokeshave

DTM   MH

Steel and boxwood, 9 1/2" long, 2 3/4" long blade, signed "JOHN BOOTH & SON" and "PHILA".

This prominent company was in Philadelphia, Pennsylvania, from 1874 to 1890, where they made edge tools, bits, and braces (Nelson 1999). This spokeshave is made in the English style.

6204T5   Tang chisel

DTM   MH

Iron and steel with a wood handle, 14" long including 7 3/8" long chisel and 6 5/8" long handle, signed "A MAHANT GARANTIE".

This is a typical late 19th century edge tool made in France using German steel, i.e. the continental method of fining cast iron.

41308DTM6   Tanged chisel

DTM   MH

Drop-forged tool steel, 7 1/4" long, 1/2" wide, signed "THE JAMES SWAN Co." and "SEYMOUR CONN. U.S.A." with their trademark.

http://www.davistownmuseum.org/bioSwan.html

41308DTM3   Tanged firmer chisel

DTM   MH

Drop-forged tool steel, 8 7/8" long, 3/8" wide, signed "THE JAMES SWAN CO USA".

http://www.davistownmuseum.org/bioSwan.html

32808DTM15 Tanged gouge

DTM   MH

Drop-forged tool steel, 9 7/8" long, 3/4" wide, signed "JAS. SWAN Co. U.S.A.".

http://www.davistownmuseum.org/bioSwan.html

32808DTM16 Tanged gouge

DTM   MH

Drop-forged tool steel, 9 1/8" long, 9/16" wide, signed "JAS. SWAN Co. U.S.A.".

http://www.davistownmuseum.org/bioSwan.html

32808DTM22 Tanged gouge

DTM   MH

Drop-forged tool steel, 10" long, 1/4" wide, signed "THE JAMES SWAN Co.".

http://www.davistownmuseum.org/bioSwan.html

The Industrial Revolution (1865f.): Other Factory Made Tools

Woodworking: Edge Tools

32808DTM1   **Tanged inside bevel edge gouge**   DTM   MH

Drop-forged tool steel, 9 1/2" long, 1 1/4" wide, signed "THE JAMES SWAN CO.".

http://www.davistownmuseum.org/bioSwan.html

32808DTM13 **Tanged inside bevel edge gouge**   DTM   MH

Drop-forged tool steel, 9 1/4" long, 1 1/2" wide, signed "THE JAMES SWAN CO. U.S.A.".

http://www.davistownmuseum.org/bioSwan.html

41308DTM2   **Tanged mortising chisel**   DTM   MH

Drop-forged tool steel, 9 1/2" long, 1/8" wide, signed "THE JAMES SWAN CO".

http://www.davistownmuseum.org/bioSwan.html

41308DTM4   **Tanged mortising chisel**   DTM   MH

Drop-forged tool steel, 7 1/2" long, 1/8" wide, signed "THE JAMES SWAN Co." and "SEYMOUR CONN. U.S.A." with their trademark.

http://www.davistownmuseum.org/bioSwan.html

32808DTM12 **Tanged mortising chisel**   DTM   MH

Drop-forged tool steel, 9 3/4" long, 1/8" wide, signed "THE JAMES SWAN Co." and "WARRANTED" with their trademark.

http://www.davistownmuseum.org/bioSwan.html

40408DTM12 **Tanged outside bevel edge chisel**   DTM   MH

Drop-forged tool steel, 8 1/4" long, 1" wide, signed "THE JAMES SWAN CO. U.S.A.".

http://www.davistownmuseum.org/pics/40408dtm12p2.jpg
http://www.davistownmuseum.org/bioSwan.html

32808DTM19 **Tanged outside bevel edge chisel**   DTM   MH

Drop-forged tool steel, 7 1/2" long, 3/4" wide, signed "THE JAMES SWAN CO. U.S.A.".

http://www.davistownmuseum.org/bioSwan.html

32808DTM14 **Tanged outside bevel edge gouge**   DTM   MH

Drop-forged tool steel, 11" long, 1 3/8" wide, signed "THE JAS. SWAN CO. U.S.A.".

http://www.davistownmuseum.org/bioSwan.html

41308DTM1   **Tanged paring chisel**   DTM   MH

Drop-forged tool steel, 7 " long, 7/16" wide, signed "THE JAMES SWAN Co." and "BEST TOOL STEEL" with their trademark.

http://www.davistownmuseum.org/bioSwan.html

The Industrial Revolution (1865f.): Other Factory Made Tools

Woodworking: Edge Tools

41308DTM7   Tanged paring chisel   DTM   MH

Drop-forged tool steel, 7 1/2" long, 3/8" wide, signed "THE JAMES SWAN Co." and "SEYMOUR CONN. U.S.A." with their trademark.

http://www.davistownmuseum.org/bioSwan.html

41308DTM5   Tanged paring chisel   DTM   MH

Drop-forged tool steel, 7 1/4" long, 7/16" wide, signed "THE JAMES SWAN Co." and "BEST TOOL STEEL" with their trademark.

http://www.davistownmuseum.org/bioSwan.html

32808DTM18 Tanged paring chisel   DTM   MH

Drop-forged tool steel, 7 3/4" long, 1/2" wide, signed "THE JAMES SWAN Co." and "SEYMOUR CONN. U.S.A." with their trademark.

http://www.davistownmuseum.org/bioSwan.html

32808DTM7   Tanged skewed turning chisel   DTM   MH

Drop-forged tool steel, 10 3/4" long, 3/4" wide, signed "THE JAMES SWAN Co." and "SEYMOUR CONN. U.S.A." with their trademark.

http://www.davistownmuseum.org/bioSwan.html

32808DTM8   Tanged skewed turning chisel   DTM   MH

Drop-forged tool steel, 9 1/2" long, 1 1/16" wide, signed "THE JAMES SWAN Co." and "SEYMOUR CONN. U.S.A." with their trademark.

http://www.davistownmuseum.org/bioSwan.html

32808DTM3   Tanged timber framing chisel   DTM   MH

Drop-forged tool steel, 9 3/4" long, 1 3/4" wide, signed "THE JAMES SWAN CO. BEST TOOL STEEL" with a swan touchmark.

http://www.davistownmuseum.org/bioSwan.html

32808DTM10 Timber framing socket chisel   DTM   MH

Drop-forged steel, 7 7/8" long, 1 1/2" wide, signed "THE JAMES SWAN CO. SEYMOUR, CONN., U.S.A." with a swan touchmark.

It has a beveled socket.

http://www.davistownmuseum.org/bioSwan.html

22311T4   Veining tool   DTM   TT

Walnut and drop-forged tempered alloy steel, 9" long, 1 1/2" wide, 1 1/8" deep, unsigned.

The steel cutter is probably factory-made. It has a homemade wooden holder. Veining tools have the smallest sizes of straight gouges, with narrow yet deep "U" shaped cutting edges designed for roughing-out, and grooving small lines or areas. Part of the Robert Sullivan Collection donation.

The Industrial Revolution (1865f.): Other Factory Made Tools

Woodworking: Edge Tools

121412T14   Wedge   DTM   TT

Cast steel, 5" long, 2 3/4" cutting edge, 5/8" thick, signed "SNOW & NEALLEY Co BANGOR MAINE".

31112T15   Wood chisel   DTM   MH3-D2

Drop-forged tool steel, 7 1/4" long, 5/8" wide cutting edge, signed "C. DREW & CO.".

Courtesy of Liberty Tool Co.

http://www.davistownmuseum.org/bioDrew.htm

31112T19   Wood chisel   DTM   MH3-D2

Drop-forged steel, plastic handle, 9 1/4" long, 1" wide blade, signed "C. DREW & CO.".

Courtesy of Liberty Tool Co.

http://www.davistownmuseum.org/bioDrew.htm

31112T18   Wood chisel   DTM   MH3-D2

Drop-forged steel, plastic handle, 7 1/2" long, 3/4" wide blade, signed "C. DREW & CO.".

Courtesy of Liberty Tool Co.

http://www.davistownmuseum.org/bioDrew.htm

41203T2C   Wood chisels (2)   DTM   MH

Drop-forged steel, 1/2" wide and 1 1/2" wide, signed "C. Drew & Co.".

These have a yellow plastic handle c. 1960.

http://www.davistownmuseum.org/bioDrew.htm

Woodworking: Edge Tools - American Made Cast Steel

92112T5   Beveled butt chisel   DTM   TT

Cast steel, leather, 6" long, 2" long handle, 1/2" wide cutting edge, unsigned.

This full tang chisel has a grip constructed of compressed leather washers.

92112T4   Beveled butt chisel   DTM   TT

Cast steel, leather, 6" long, 2" long handle, 5/8" cutting edge, unsigned.

This full tang chisel has a grip constructed of compressed leather washers.

22411T1   Box scraper   DTM   MH3-D3

Drop-forged malleable iron, steel blade, wooden handle, 14" long, 4" wide, signed "C DREW & CO" and "CAST STEEL".

http://www.davistownmuseum.org/bioDrew.htm

The Industrial Revolution (1865f.): Other Factory Made Tools

Woodworking: Edge Tools - American Made Cast Steel

92112T2   Carpenters' socketed gouge   DTM   TT

Cast steel, wood (boxwood), 13" long, 8 5/8" blade, 7/16" cutting edge, signed "A W CROSSMAN".

This outside bevel curve edge gouge has a turned round handle. The mark belongs to Amory W. Crossman, who worked out of West Warren, Massachusetts, circa 1850-1866.

30911T8   Chisel   DTM   TT

Drop-forged iron and cast steel, wooden handle, 13" long, 7/8" wide, 6" long blade, signed "CHARLES BUCK" "CAST" "STEEL".

http://www.davistownmuseum.org/bioBuckBrothers.html

TTDA3000   Drawknife   LPC   MH

Forged iron and cast steel, wood, 18" long with a 12 1/2" blade, signed "TINKHAM & CUMMINGS WARRANTED CAST STEEL" with a very unusual eagle and flag touchmark.

http://www.davistownmuseum.org/pics/TTDA3000.jpg
http://www.davistownmuseum.org/bioTinkham.htm

3312T8   Firmer chisel   DTM   TT

Drop-forged iron and cast steel, aluminum ferrule, wooden handle, 8 1/2" long, 7/8" wide, 4 1/2" long handle, signed "E. PARKER, CAST STEEL 3709".

DATM (Nelson 1999, 600) lists E. Parker as a chisel-maker with no other information. Courtesy of Liberty Tool Co.

12112T1   Floor chisel   DTM   MH

Cast steel, 9 1/2" long, 3" wide cutting edge, 1" diameter, signed "BENJAMIN O. PAINE SUPERIOR EDGE TOOLS MILLBURY, MASS.".

31212T13   Framing chisel   DTM   TT

Drop-forged iron and cast steel, 9 3/4" long, 1" wide blade, signed "A.G. PAGE CAST STEEL".

This is the Page from Page, Whitman & Co. It was made sometime before 1959 (http://www.simonds.cc/company/history4.php?menu=../mnu/mnuCompanyHistory). Courtesy of Liberty Tool Co.

42904T1   Framing chisel   DTM   MH

Drop-forged cast steel, iron ferrule, 12 1/8" long, 2" wide, 4 1/2" long handle, signed "T. H. WITHERBY".

http://www.davistownmuseum.org/bioWitherby.html

31311T6   Gouge   DTM   TT

Drop-forged cast steel with wood handle, 8" long, 1 1/8" wide and 5" long blade, 3" long handle, signed "GORFIELD" "CAST STEEL".

The Industrial Revolution (1865f.): Other Factory Made Tools

Woodworking: Edge Tools - American Made Cast Steel

93011T13   **Gouge**   DTM   MH

Drop-forged cast steel and wood, 14" long, 1 1/2" wide blade, 4 1/2" long handle, signed "BUCK BROS" "CAST" and owner's mark "EWEEK".

http://www.davistownmuseum.org/bioBuckBrothers.html

42904T2   **Gouge**   DTM   MH

Drop-forged cast steel, brass ferrule, wooden handle, 5 3/4" long with additional 5 7/8" handle, 1" wide, signed "BUCK BROS" "CAST STEEL" with a buck touchmark.

http://www.davistownmuseum.org/bioBuckBrothers.html

22512T12   **Mortising chisel**   DTM   TT

Drop-forged iron and cast steel, wood (beech), 13" long, 1/2" wide blade, signed "H.T BLODGET" "CAST STEEL" and "TBF" owner's mark.

DATM (Nelson 1999) lists a number of Blodgett companies and toolmakers but none with a spelling of one "T" or these initials. Courtesy of Liberty Tool Co.

101212LTC3   **Socketed corner chisel**   DA   TT (Pub)

Cast steel, 11 3/8" long, 1" x 1" edges, signed "T.H WITHERBY WARRANTED".

http://www.davistownmuseum.org/bioWitherby.html

92112T6   **Socketed firmer chisel**   DTM   TT

Cast steel, 5 7/16" long, 7/16" wide cutting edge, 3/4" diameter socket, signed "HUBBARD H.W. CO".

Hubbard Hardware Company operated out of Middletown, Connecticut circa 1864 to 1872 with Charles C. Hubbard as President (http://http://www.angelfire.com/wy/mttools/hubbardhw.htm).

113004T1   **Timber framers' socket chisel**   DTM   UNK

Malleable iron and cast steel, 11 3/8" long, 1" wide, signed "C. A. WILLIAMS & CO" "CAST STEEL".

The Williams family were Skowhegan, Maine, edge toolmakers working after the Civil War. This chisel appears to be of welded cast steel construction where the cast steel edge is welded onto the iron handle portion.

http://www.davistownmuseum.org/publications/volume10.html

93011T7   **Timber framing socket chisel**   DTM   TT

Forged iron and cast steel, wood, 15 1/2" long, 1 1/2" wide, 4 1/2" long handle, signed "UNDERHILL" "EDGE TOOL CO" "WARRENTED" "CAST-STEEL".

http://www.davistownmuseum.org/bio#bioUnderhill.html

Woodworking: Edge Tools - Imported Cast Steel

Woodworking: Edge Tools - Imported Cast Steel

92112T1   Carpenters' tanged gouge   DTM   TT

Cast steel, wood (beech), 9" long, 4 3/4" long blade, 1/2" wide cutting edge, signed "G W & T * EADON" "CAST STEEL".

This outside bevel straight edge gouge has an octagonal handle.

090109T4   Chisel   DTM   MH

Cast steel, brass, and wood, 11 1/2" long including a 5 1/2" long handle, 1 1/4" wide cutting edge, signed "J.B. ADDIS & SONS", "ARCTIC WORKS", and "SHEFFIELD" on one side; "9PRIZE MEDALS" and "61 & 62" on the other.

By 1872 "James Bacon was articulating in advertisements
that the only true Addis-made carving tools carried the 'J. B. Addis & Sons' brand. Ads from this period state the valid imprints on tools and enable us to date many of the J. B. Addis tools made after 1872. The Hawley Collection lists 1874 as the most likely date for a split between James Bacon Addis and Ward & Payne. The company was still working at the Arctic Works at least past 1881...The principles of J. B. Addis & Sons were listed as James Bacon Addis, James Bacon Addis, Jr., and George Allkins Addis." (http://swingleydev.com/archive/get.php?message_id=157681).

121805T14   Chisel   DTM   MH

Cast steel and wood, 9" long including 3 3/8" tanged chisel, signed "IBBOTSON SHEFFIELD PAT CHRYSTALIZED CAST STEEL".

This has an anomalous mark by a prolific maker. The significance of chrystalized is yet to be explained.

http://www.davistownmuseum.org/pics/121805t14_p2.jpg

51606T15   Chisel   DTM   MH

Cast steel and a brass ferrule, 1 1/4" long including a 5 1/4" long handle, signed "BOB SORBY SHEFFIELD" with two cartouches on one side and "CAST STEEL" on the other.

This is a typical late 19th century imported English edge tool by one of England's major toolmakers.

3312T10   Chisel   DTM   TT

Drop-forged iron and cast steel, 13 1/2" long, signed "INo/ CUTLER" "CAST STEEL" and a stamped crest with "V" on the left side, "R" on the other side.

It has a tang type shank. Courtesy of Liberty Tool Co.

3312T9   Chisel   DTM   TT

Forged steel and iron, wooden handle, 12" long, signed "W.GRAVES & SONS" "SCMSAFWORKS" "ELECTRO" "EDRACIL" and "STEEL".

Some of the marks are hard to make out. This appears to be a late 19th century example of steel produced in an early electric arc furnace. Courtesy of Liberty Tool Co.

The Industrial Revolution (1865f.): Other Factory Made Tools

Woodworking: Edge Tools - Imported Cast Steel

92112T3   **Firmer chisel**   DTM   TT

Cast steel, wood (hardwood with a very dark patina, possibly teak), signed "T. SYER WARRANTED".

Thomas J. Syer wroked out of 21 Finsbury St., London, circa 1880 - 1890 and 45 Wilson St, Finsubry Square circa 1890-1911. They made cabinets, vices, chisels, planes, and offered other services. Syer ran the Finsbury Practical School of Amateur Mechanics (Goodman 1964, 422).

42904T5   **Gouge**   DTM   MH

Cast steel, wood, brass, 8 1/2" long including a 4 1/8" wooden handle with brass ferrule, signed "H. TAYLOR" "SHEFFIELD" "9" on the front and "MADE IN ENGLAND" on the back.

31908T23   **Mortising chisel**   DTM   MH

Cast steel, copper, and wood, 16 1/2" long, 9 1/2" long blade, 1/2" wide cutting edge, signed "J. N. CUTLER" "PIONEER" and "CARBONIZED CAST STEEL", there is also a crossed x mark.

The term "carbonized cast steel" suggests a late 19th century production date. The Historical Society of Geauga County, Ohio, lists John Cutler as a plane and chisel maker ("Pioneer and General History Geauga County" 1880, 640), but this tool could also be English.

http://www.davistownmuseum.org/pics/31908t23-1.jpg
http://www.davistownmuseum.org/pics/31908t23-2.jpg

31212T8   **Paring chisel**   DTM   TT

Cast steel, hardwood handle, 8 1/4" long, 1/4" wide edge, signed "BARTON BROS. SHEFFIELD CARBONIZED CAST STEEL".

Courtesy of Liberty Tool Co.

121805T19   **Tang chisel**   DTM   MH

Cast steel, wood, and brass ferrule, 4 5/8" long with a 5" handle, signed "J. N. Cutler" and "Electric cast steel" and a pioneer on the reverse with "TM", c. 1890 (?).

See the comments on the chisel, ID# 31908T23.

http://www.davistownmuseum.org/pics/121805t19_p2.jpg

Woodworking: Edge Tools Made in Maine

TJC1001   **Drawknife**   DTM   MH

Forged iron and steel, wooden handles, 14 1/4" long, 8 3/16" long blade, signed "L. WEBB BANGOR".

Probably it was made by Lester Webb, 1867-1871, who DATM (Nelson 1999) lists as having an association with Higgins and Webb.

http://www.davistownmuseum.org/publications/volume10.html

Woodworking: Edge Tools Made in Maine

22411T6   Drawknife   DTM   TT

Forged wrought iron and steel, brass ferrules, and wooden handles, 13 1/2" long, 5" long handles, 7 1/2" long blade, signed "J. T. BUDGE".

This drawknife is handmade from an old file. Possibly Budge was the maker/owner. The Penobscot County ME Archives History - Businesses listings for Lee in 1883 has J. T. Budge as a blacksmith. The Maine Register of 1889 lists J. T. Budge & Son as blacksmiths in Lee, Maine.

41212T6   Drawknife   DTM   TT

Re-forged steel file, rosewood handles, 16 1/2" long, 9 1/2" long cutting edge, signed "T.C. JACKSON" "STINSON".

This tool was made in Bath, Maine circa 1869 or earlier from a recycled steel file or rasp. Courtesy of Liberty Tool Co.

http://www.davistownmuseum.org/publications/volume10.html

92901T1   Drawknife   DTM   TT

steel, wood handle, 14" long, 8 3/4" blade, signed "L Webb Bangor".

This drawknife is an especially interesting example of a drop-forged steel tool that is the product of a sophisticated factory system where machine work replaces hand work. It has an unusually elegantly shaped cutting surface. A gift to The Davistown Museum from Rick Floyd.

http://www.davistownmuseum.org/pics/92901t1_p1.jpg
http://www.davistownmuseum.org/publications/volume10.html

070705T2   Drawshave   DTM   TB

Forged steel, possibly German steel with wooden handles, 15 3/4" long with 9 7/8" long cutting blade and 5" long handles
long with 9 7/8" long cutting blade, signed "C. DAGGETT".

C. Daggett is listed in the 1879 Maine Business Directory as an ax maker in Sherman, Maine.

71903T5   Drawshave   DTM   MH

Forged iron and steel, 16 1/4" wide, 10 3/8" long blade, signed "I Haskell".

It was made by Isaac Haskell of Garland, Maine. This tool has the appearance of being made of cast steel, but the back of the shave shows clear evidence of a weld steel cutting edge. Haskell was a blacksmith who also made tools. This may be the only known shave by this maker, as this is a previously unrecorded maker's mark. It was donated to The Davistown Museum by Rick Floyd.

http://www.davistownmuseum.org/pics/71903t5_p3.jpg
http://www.davistownmuseum.org/publications/volume10.html

111711T1   Lipped adz   DTM   MH

Forged iron and steel, wooden handle, 7 3/8" long, 4 1/2" wide cutting edge, 27 1/2" long handle, signed "STINSON", second line is obscured.

The "Registry of Maine Toolmakers" (Brack 2008) lists three Maine Stinsons: John F. Stinson worked in Bath in 1869, J.F. Stinson worked in Springfield from 1879-1882, and R.G. Stinson worked in Bath from 1874 - 1879. All of them made axes and edge tools.

The Industrial Revolution (1865f.): Other Factory Made Tools

Woodworking: Edge Tools Made in Maine

121311T3   **Ships' adz**   DTM   TT

Forged iron, steel, and wood, 2' long curved wood handle, 4 3/4" long edge, 2 1/2" long spike, signed "STINSON" and an indecipherable mark.

The shipbuilders' adz tapered spike is used to drive nails below the surface. J. F. Stinson worked in Bath, ME, 1869-1871. This is a good example of weld steeling.

111512T1   **Spokeshave**   DTM   MH

Brass body, steel blade, 6 3/4" long, 1 3/8" wide cutting edge, signed "LIE-NIELSEN" on both the blade and body.

This is a brand new tool with a box and instructions. The instruction sheet indicates it is copyright 2002.

http://www.davistownmuseum.org/bioNielsen.html

Woodworking: Other Tools

111001T10   **Bit brace**   DTM   MH

Drop-forged iron and steel, brass, iron, rosewood handle, 15 3/8" high, 7 1/2" swing, signed "Miller's Falls Mfg Co." on upper arm and "Pat'd Apr. 10 67 no 0".

DATM (Nelson 1999) lists Miller's Falls Mfg. Co. working from 1868 - 72 (formerly the Levi J. Gunn and Charles H. Amidon Co.) In 1872 they dropped the Mfg. to become Miller's Falls Co. (1872 - 1931). DATM also notes an 1877 patent hand brace for them but no 1867 brace. The patent date on this brace clearly states 67.

http://www.davistownmuseum.org/bioMillersFalls.htm

032203T12   **Bit brace**   DTM   MH

Drop-forged iron and steel, brass, wood, 14" long with a 5" swing, signed "The Davis Level & Tool Co Springfield Mass" "Pat April 17, 1883 Oct 14, 1884".

Davis Level & Tool Co. made levels, dividers, machinists, and other tools in Springfield, MA, from 1875 to 1892. Prior to 1875, their tools were marked "Davis Co." (1867 - 1875). These tools are considered among the finest produced by American toolmakers in the 19th century.

http://www.davistownmuseum.org/pics/032203t12_p2.jpg
http://www.davistownmuseum.org/bioDavis.htm

22601T1   **Bit brace**   DTM   MH

Drop-forged grey cast iron and steel, 12" high, 6 1/2" wide wheel, 1/4" chuck, signed "The Jacob Mfg Co. Hartford Conn USA" and "Patented Sept 16 1907".

DATM (Nelson 1999) lists a Jacobs Mfg. Co. in Danielson CT, with no dates. This is an unusual bit brace with a very large wheel and a twisted stock. Possibly it is one-of-a-kind or a limited edition never seen before by the curator.

22311T6   **Brace**   DTM   TT

Drop-forged steel with wooden handle and grip, 10 1/2" long, 4 1/2" wide, unsigned.

This brace has a 3/8" square lever style chuck. Part of the Robert Sullivan Collection donation.

Woodworking: Other Tools

22311T5   Brace   DTM   TT

Drop-forged steel, 10 1/2" long, 6" wide, signed "SPOFFORD'S PAT." "MAR. 23. 80.".

This is an all steel brace with a 3/8" square lever style chuck. The patent holder is Nelson Spofford of Haverhill, MA. Patent 225,768 is online at: http://www.google.com/patents/about?id=PV1kAAAAEBAJ&dq=SPOFFORD+Mar+23+1880. Part of the Robert Sullivan Collection donation.

3312T5   Cabinet-makers' screwdriver   DTM   TT

Drop-forged cast steel, copper ferrule, wood, 11 3/4" long, 6 1/4" long and 5/8" wide blade, signed "W.E. THAYER" "CAST STEEL".

DATM (Nelson 1999) lists William E. Thayer as a maker of screwdrivers in Williamsburg, MA, from 1870 - 1883. Courtesy of Liberty Tool Co.

3312T15   Cabinet-makers' screwdriver   DTM   TT

Drop-forged steel, wooden handle, 12" long, 5 1/2" long handle, 1/4" bit width, signed "MATHIESON & SON" "GLASGOW" with a stamped crescent moon with star within; also owner's mark "H.D.J.".

Courtesy of Liberty Tool Co.

31212T2   Carpenters' multitool handle   DTM   TT

Nickel plated steel, cocobolo wood handle, 6" long, signed "MILLERS FALLS CO. MILLERS FALLS MASS.".

This pocket sized tool handle is hollow with a threaded wooden butt cap that houses six different tools which can be fitted into the chuck, including a chisel, various screwdrivers, and a saw. Courtesy of Liberty Tool Co.

http://www.davistownmuseum.org/bioMillersFalls.htm

61612T7   Carpenters' square   DTM   TT

Forged steel, brass, wood (cocobolo), 4 1/2" long blade, 3 1/2" long handle, unsigned.

12801T16   Cat's paw   DTM   MH

Drop-forged steel, 11 1/8" long, signed "C. Drew CAT'S PAW - 277".

This is a (later) 20th century production.

http://www.davistownmuseum.org/pics/12801t16.jpg
http://www.davistownmuseum.org/bioDrew.htm

31112T22   Cat's paw   DTM   MH3-D2

Drop-forged steel, 10 3/4" long, 5/8" wide, signed "C. Drew cat's paw-277-".

Courtesy of Liberty Tool Co.

http://www.davistownmuseum.org/bioDrew.htm

Woodworking: Other Tools

31811T20   **Cat's paw**   DTM   MH3-D2

Drop-forged steel, 11 1/4" long, 1 1/8" head, signed "DREW CATSPAW - 277B".

http://www.davistownmuseum.org/bioDrew.htm

33002T7A   **Cat's paw**   DTM   TT

Drop-forged steel, 10 1/2" long, signed "C. Drew & Co.".

31112T24   **Cat's paw pry bar**   DTM   MH3-D2

Drop-forged steel, 12" long, 1/2" wide, signed "Drew No. 12".

Courtesy of Liberty Tool Co.

http://www.davistownmuseum.org/bioDrew.htm

100108T5   **Clamp**   DTM   MH

Wood, 3 3/8" long, 3 1/4" wide, 3" wooden screw, signed "PATENT PENDING" "by" "W.W.WYMAN" and "W. Waterville Me".

This is a gift from Ed Shaw, who notes that Walter Wyman was an engineer and one of the original founders of Central Maine Power Company. Could he have applied for this patent?

http://www.davistownmuseum.org/publications/volume10.html

6312LTC10   **Crosscut saw set**   DA   TT (Pub)

Cast iron, 15" long, 8" wide, unsigned.

Courtesy of Liberty Tool Co.

22311T11   **Dowel pointer**   DTM   TT

Malleable cast iron and steel, 5" long, 2 3/4" wide, unsigned.

This tool is also called a dowel trimmer. It is used by a chair-maker for tenon chamfering. Part of the Robert Sullivan Collection donation.

31112T20   **Flathead screwdriver**   DTM   MH3-D2

Drop-forged steel, plastic handle, 9" long, 3/4" wide blade, signed "C. DREW & CO.".

Courtesy of Liberty Tool Co.

http://www.davistownmuseum.org/bioDrew.htm

52403T6   **Framing clamp**   DTM   MH

Drop-forged iron, 7 3/4" long, 4 5/8" wide when closed, unsigned.

This is an excellent example of late 19th century tool designing ingenuity. This tool appears very useful as a frame clamp, but this design is no longer manufactured.

ID #   Status   Location

Woodworking: Other Tools

41212T7   Framing square   DTM   TT

Drop-forged steel, 24" long, 16" wide, signed "MITER CUTS FOR POLYGON PAT APR. 23-1901".

This framing square is marked with metric measurements but has no maker's mark. The measurements include "HEXAGON 24-14 HEPTAGON 24-11 1 2 OCTAGON 24-10 NANAGON 24-8 5 8 DECAGON 24-7 3 4 UNDECAGON 24-7 DODECAGON 24-6 1 2". The patent was assigned to Moses Nicholls of Glenwood, Iowa and may be viewed here: http://www.google.com/patents?id=tu5IAAAAEBAJ&printsec=frontcover&dq=672455&hl=en&sa=X&ei=hyC1T63qO8-IhQenroHwDQ&ved=0CD0Q6AEwAg. Courtesy of Liberty Tool Co.

61612T1   Hand vise   DTM   TT

Drop-forged steel, 4" long, 2 3/8" wide, 1 1/8" wide clamp jaws, signed "H. BOKER" "W.P. WENTWORTH".

H. Boker was the US affiliate of a German company. Its working dates were 1837-1969. William P. Wentworth, Seneca Falls, NY, held patent 214,071 for the clamping device for this vise, which is used for filing saws. View the patent here: http://www.google.com/patents?id=bEdRAAAAEBAJ&pg=PA1&dq=wentworth+apr.+8+1879&hl=en&sa=X&ei=p8zpT_CiE4nXtAbd-YH7DQ&sqi=2&ved=0CDMQ6AEwAA#v=onepage&q=wentworth%20apr.%208%201879&f=false.

121112T8   Mason's joint filler   DTM   MH

Drop-forged iron, 10 1/4" long, 1/2" and 5/8" wide curved beaders, signed "C Drew & Co.".

http://www.davistownmuseum.org/biio#/bioDrew.htm

41801T9   Miniature brace   DTM   MH

Cast iron, steel, and wood, 7 7/8" long, takes at most a 1/8" diameter bit, unsigned.

This is probably a Miller's Falls product. It is a collectable tool from the classic period of the Industrial Revolution.

http://www.davistownmuseum.org/bio#bioMillersFalls.htm

72712LTC3   Miter jack   DA   TT (Pub)

Wood (various hardwoods), 32" long, 10" wide, 7 1/4" high, unsigned.

Courtesy of the Liberty Tool Company.

31808SLP26   Nail puller   DTM   TT

Drop-forged steel, 6 3/4" long, signed "THE BRIDGEPORT HDWE MFG. CORP" "MADE IN U.S.A" and on the other side "BABY TERRIER" "WARRANTED FORGED STEEL".

DATM (Nelson 1999) states that this company was located in Bridgeport, CT. Baby Terrier was one of their brand names.

http://www.davistownmuseum.org/pics/31808slp26-1.jpg
http://www.davistownmuseum.org/pics/31808slp26-2.jpg

The Industrial Revolution (1865f.): Other Factory Made Tools

Woodworking: Other Tools

5212LTC1   Nail puller

DA   TT (Pub)

Drop-forged steel, 17" long retracted, 22 1/2" wide, signed "BRIDGEPORT".

Courtesy of Liberty Tool Co.

52712LTC4   Offset slip-joint pliers

DA   TT (Pub)

Drop-forged tool steel, 7 1/8" long, signed "THE H.D. SMITH & CO. PLANTSVILLE, CONN. PAT. JUNE ____".

This is the patent, which was assigned to H. D. Smith by William S. Thomson: http://www.google.com/patents?id=BW5PAAAAEBAJ&pg=PA2&dq=PLANTSVILLE+smith&hl=en&sa=X&ei=yArqT-ufOIKI8gOU2sAE&ved=0CDIQ6AEwADgU#v=onepage&q=PLANTSVILLE%20smith&f=false.
Courtesy of Liberty Tool Co.

22411T13   Pinch dog

DTM   TT

Forged malleable iron, 5" long, 3 1/4" wide, signed "F C RAND" possibly an owner's mark.

This dog has three points. Pinch dogs are used like clamps to draw two pieces of wood together for gluing.

111412T16   Planemakers' float

DTM   MH

German steel, brass ferrule, hardwood handle, 15 1/2" long, 10" long blade, signed "F G S" owners' mark.

This is a nice example of a finely crafted edge tool utilizing German steel.

041505T19   Saw jointer with original box

DTM   MH

Sheet metal, 4 3/8" long, signed "PIKE".

The box is also labeled with a logo containing "PIKE" and the following: "PERFECT SAW JOINTER Joints The Teeth Absolutely True An Excellent Skate Sharpener Fine for Meat Block Scrapers PIKE MANUFACTURING CO. PIKE, NEW HAMPSHIRE U. S. A." The Pike Co. was the East Haverhill, NH, clan of Alonzo (1860 - 1889) and Joseph Pike (1870 - ?), whetstone makers. The Pike Mfg. Co. went out of business in 1932.

http://www.davistownmuseum.org/pics/041505t19.jpg

32512LTC1   Saw set

DA   TT (Pub)

Cast steel, cocobolo, 8 1/2" long, 1" wide, signed "WYNN & TIMMINS CAST STEEL".

This tool has an unusual maker's mark. DATM (Nelson 1999, 884) lists Wynn & Timmins as making a hammer with no location or dates. It also lists C. Wynn as a maker of saw sets. This is the Wynn, Timmins & Co. of Birmingham, England working from 1787 to 1937. Courtesy of Liberty Tool Company.

The Industrial Revolution (1865f.): Other Factory Made Tools

Woodworking: Other Tools

30202T3   Saw set   DTM   MH

Drop-forged steel and brass, 6 3/4" long, signed "E. C. Sterns & Co. Syracuse N.Y. USA".

DATM (Nelson 1999, 752) indicates the Edward C. Stern Co. made saw vises, sets, wrenches, shaves, clamps, and other tools in Syracuse from 1877 to 1891. This saw set has small brass adjustment knobs. It is very similar to a Morrill patent saw set (1880).

http://www.davistownmuseum.org/pics/30202t3.jpg

6312LTC4   Saw set   DA   TT (Pub)

Drop-forged iron, japanned finish, 12" long, unsigned.

Courtesy of Liberty Tool Co.

42912LTC7   Saw set   DA   TT (Pub)

Drop-forged iron, 6 1/2" long, unsigned.

Courtesy of Liberty Tool Co.

102503T4   Saw swage   DTM   MH

Drop forged steel, 4" long in a 4 3/4" long wood box, signed "The Simonds swage Fitchburg Mass No 8" also stamped "48".

This tool comes with paper directions for use (with advertising on the back). It is also called a "ripset" on the paper label. It is used for shaping or spreading hand saw teeth.

112303T1   Screw box and screw tap   DTM   TT

Wood and steel, 3/4", signed "Imhoff & Lange" "Germany" "8" and "7/8".

The screw box is accompanied by a 3/4" screw tap marked "3/4", "19", and "West Germany". It was received in November, 2003, from an anonymous donor. It is an excellent modern example of an age-old woodworkers' tool. The purpose of this tool is to cut threads onto 7/8" dowels to be used as handles, etc. to be screwed into holes that have been threaded with a tap made to cut threads in a wooden hole. For example, it could be used for making wooden clamps with wooden screws.

122303T1   Screw box and screw tap   DTM   MH

Wood screw box and cast steel tap, 9 1/2" long, 2 1/16" wide, 1 3/4" deep box, 5 7/16" long, 7/8" wide tap, signed "IMHOFF &LANGE GERMANY" and "1" and "7/8" on box; "7/8" and "1" on tap.

22211T1   Spirit level   DTM   TT

Mahogany with brass vial cover, 24" long, 3 1/8" x 1 3/8", signed "WINCHESTER" "TRADE MARK" "MADE IN USA" and "#9811-24IN".

It has a decorative routed hand grip. Part of the Robert Sullivan Collection donation.

http://www.davistownmuseum.org/bioWinchester.html

The Industrial Revolution (1865f.): Other Factory Made Tools

Woodworking: Other Tools

22211T4   Spirit level

Mahogany with brass vial cover and end caps, 24" long, 3 1/8" x 1 3/8", signed "STANLEY" "RULE & LEVEL CO" "NEW BRITAIN, CONN. USA" "PAT'D 5-8-06" "No 30" "TO ADJUST REMOVE PLATES" and "STANLEY ADJUSTABLE" on side sights.

The sight is adjustable on all 3 level sights. Part of the Robert Sullivan Collection donation.

http://www.davistownmuseum.org/bioStanley.html

22211T3   Spirit level

Mahogany with brass vial cover and end caps, 26" long, 2 5/16" x 1 1/4", signed "SARGENT & CO" "NY" in a circle with "PAT. MAR" and "12 1878".

The vial is protected on the sides with brass. Part of the Robert Sullivan Collection donation.

22211T2   Spirit level

Mahogany with brass vial cover and end caps, 26" long, 3 1/4" x 1 3/8", signed "J. W. HARMON" "BOSTON" "MASS" in an arch.

The brass end caps are only on the corners. The vial is protected on the sides with brass. Part of the Robert Sullivan Collection donation.

42912LTC18 Spofford bit brace

Drop-forged iron, 10" long, signed "BRIDGEPORT CT. U.S.A." "JOHN S. FRAY & CO.".

John S. Fray's working dates were from 1886 to 1900 (Nelson 1999, 294). There are a number of bit brace patents assigned to Spofford. Courtesy of Liberty Tool Co.

041505T25   Spoke pointer

Drop-forged steel and cast iron, unsigned.

This is a typical factory-made tool of the late 19th century. This pointer is used by chair-makers and wagon wheel-makers.

http://www.davistownmuseum.org/pics/041505t25.jpg

22311T12   Tack or nail remover

Drop-forged malleable iron, 6" long, signed "BI-PED." "PAT. APLD. FOR".

This tool has a plier-type lever action. Part of the Robert Sullivan Collection donation.

52712LTC5   Tack puller

Drop-forged steel, Bakelite, 7 1/8" long, signed "THE H.D. SMITH & CO. PLANTSVILLE, CONN. PAT. JUNE *****".

Courtesy of Liberty Tool Co.

51312LTC1   Teardrop plumb bob

Brass, 6 3/4" tall, 2 3/4" diameter, signed C DREW & CO. KINGSTON, MASS..

The Industrial Revolution (1865f.): Other Factory Made Tools

Woodworking: Other Tools

22211T36   Two speed hand drill   DTM   TT

Drop-forged malleable iron, steel, and a wooden handle, 12" long, signed "MILLERS FALLS CO." "MADE IN USA" "MILLERS FALLS, MASS" "No 5" and their triangle logo.

This drill has two gears, which allow changing it to different speeds. The drills can be stored in the handle. Part of the Robert Sullivan Collection donation.

http://www.davistownmuseum.org/bioMillersFalls.htm

3312T17   Wood carving mallet   DTM   TT

Lignum vitae head, oak handle, 12" long, 5" long and 2 1/2" wide head, unsigned.

This factory-made mallet has a well worn head from use. Courtesy of Liberty Tool Co.

Woodworking: Planes

100400T1   Bailey plane   LPC   MHC-K

Grey cast iron, cast steel blade, 7 1/2" long, 2" wide, signed "BAILEY TOOL CO. Woonsocket RI DEFIANCE".

The Bailey Tool Company was in operation from 1872 to 1879 and was founded by Selden A. Bailey. Leonard Bailey of the Stanley Rule and Level Company joined Selden Bailey in Woonsocket in 1878, and introduced his own line of Defiance Metallic planes. This plane is illustrated in Patented Transitional and Metallic planes in America, Volume 2 (Smith 1960) and is identified as a number F block plane. For more information see volume 1, pages 61 - 68 and volume 2, page 32. Both volumes of Smith's important references are in the visitor tool examination area and available for hands-on reference.

http://www.davistownmuseum.org/pics/100400-1.jpg

31808SLP11   Beading plane   DTM   TT

Grey cast iron with nickel-plating, 11 1/4" long, signed "STANLEY No 66" and "PAT. FEB. 9 86".

The patent is to Justustraut 2/9/1886. The size dates this plane to post-1909.

http://www.davistownmuseum.org/pics/31808SLP11.jpg
http://www.davistownmuseum.org/bioStanley.htm

100400T2   Bedrock smooth plane   LPC   MHC-K

Grey cast iron, wood, steel blade, 7 1/2" long, 1 15/16" wide with a 1 9/16" blade, signed "BEDROCK" on the cap iron and the casing, "3 607" also on the casing, "STANLEY MADE IN USA" and "PATENDED APR 2, 85 APR 19, 10".

This No. 2 plane illustrates the Stanley Tool Company at the height of its plane-making artistry.

http://www.davistownmuseum.org/pics/100400-2.jpg
http://www.davistownmuseum.org/bioStanley.htm

Woodworking: Planes

6312LTC2   Belt-makers' plane   DA   TT (Pub)

Grey cast iron, wood (beech), cast steel blade, japanned finish, 6" long, 3 3/8" wide, 3" high body, 2 3/8" wide cutting blade, 11 1/4" long handle, signed "STANLEY NEW BRITAIN CONN. U.S.A." "No 11".

Courtesy of Liberty Tool Co.

http://www.davistownmuseum.org/bioStanley.htm

TJE1002   Birmingham smooth plane   LPC   MH

Gray cast iron, steel, 6 3/8" long, 1 3/4" wide, blade 1 1/2" wide, unsigned.

Birmingham Plane Co. no.1 or no. 2 smooth planes are very rare. This specimen is a no. 1; the handle overlaps the bottom of the plane by 1/2". The penultimate classic cast iron plane. It is one of the most sculptural designs in late 19th c. patented planes.

http://www.davistownmuseum.org/pics/TJE1002_p1.jpg

51201T2   Blind nailing plane   LPC   MH

Steel, 2 1/4" long, takes a 1/4" wide blade, signed "STANLEY" on side, verso "PAT. AP'L 10-88".

The blade is missing. This plane is very rare; the smallest of all Stanley's planes.

http://www.davistownmuseum.org/bioStanley.htm

31808SLP13 Block plane   DTM   TT

Grey cast iron with nickel-plating, 3 1/2" long, 1" wide cutting blade, signed "STANLEY".

http://www.davistownmuseum.org/pics/31808slp13-3.jpg
http://www.davistownmuseum.org/bioStanley.htm

42812LTC4   Block plane   DA   TT (Pub)

Grey cast iron, steel blade, rosewood knobs, 7" long, 1 7/8" wide, signed "STANLEY" "No. 140".

The side of this plane is removable for rabbeting functions. Courtesy of Liberty Tool Co.

62202T2   Block plane   DTM   MH

Wood (beech), steel blade, 5 5/8" long, 2 1/8" wide, 1 3/8" wide blade, signed "Fred Craven, Sheffield" on nose and blade.

Although later than most of the planes in the Museum collection, this specimen from a New England tool chest is English-made, with the same signature on the nose and blade. The nose also has additional illegible information including a street address. Did Craven make both the blade and the plane? Craven is not listed in Goodman (1993) as a plane blade manufacturer.

http://www.davistownmuseum.org/pics/62202t2.jpg

The Industrial Revolution (1865f.): Other Factory Made Tools

Woodworking: Planes

31808SLP4   Bull nose plane   DTM   TT

Grey cast iron, nickel-plated, steel blade, 5 1/2" long, 1" wide cutting edge, signed "STANLEY" "MADE IN USA" and "92".

This is a cabinet-makers plane.

http://www.davistownmuseum.org/pics/31808slp4-2.jpg
http://www.davistownmuseum.org/bioStanley.htm

31808SLP31   Bull nose rabbet plane   DTM   TT

Grey cast iron, Japanned, nickel-plated thumbscrew, 4" long, 1" wide blade, signed "STANLEY" and "MADE IN USA".

It is plane no. 12-975.

http://www.davistownmuseum.org/pics/31808slp31-3.jpg
http://www.davistownmuseum.org/bioStanley.htm

31808SLP22   Carriage-makers' curved rabbet plane   DTM   TT

Wood (maple), steel blade, 6" long, 1" wide blade, unsigned.

122712LTC3   Carriage-maker's plane   DA   TT (Pub)

Wood (maple), cast steel blade, 7" long, 1 1/2" wide, 3" tall without peg or cutter installed, signed with the remnants of a "Moulson Brothers" logo on the blade, which has been recut from a block plane blade to fit the plane.

31808PC3   Circular plane   DTM   MH

Grey cast iron, Japanned, nickel-plated trim, 10 1/2" long, 1 3/4" wide blade, signed "STANLEY RULE & LEVEL CO." "PATENTED SEPT. 25, 1877".

This is a Stanley model 113.

http://www.davistownmuseum.org/pics/31808pc3-4.jpg
http://www.davistownmuseum.org/bioStanley.htm

31808SLP9   Circular plane   DTM   TT

Grey cast iron with Japanned and nickel-plated trim, 10 1/4" long, 1 3/4" wide cutting blade, signed "STANLEY" and "NO 113".

The size dates this plane to after 1936. It has ornate knob decoration.

http://www.davistownmuseum.org/pics/31808slp9-2.jpg
http://www.davistownmuseum.org/bioStanley.htm

22211T29   Combination plow and beading plane   DTM   TT

Grey cast iron, tempered alloy steel, steel blades, brass nuts, with a wooden handle, 11" long, 1/8" straight cutter, signed "No 45" "STANLEY" "RULE & LEVEL CO" "NEW BRITAIN CONN." "USA" and "TRADE45MARK"on fence.

Part of the Robert Sullivan Collection donation.

http://www.davistownmuseum.org/bioStanley.html

Woodworking: Planes

83102T3   Combination plow and beading plane   DTM   MH

Grey cast iron, tempered alloy steel, steel blades, stored in an oak box, 12" long, 5 7/8" wide box, 10 1/4" long plane, signed "Stanley No 45".

This plane was owned by a New Bedford, MA, shipwright and boat builder. It was never used; all the parts are like new with the blades in the original box. Other box contents: 18 blades and depth stops, adjustable cam, extra fence extension, 2 1/2" long screwdriver for adjusting the depth stops, torn directions, and a small tool catalog. One of the illustrations on the catalog shows a newly designed frog on a smooth plane with a 1902 patent date. This dates the catalog to 1902 - 1908. This plane is a survivor from the twilight of New England's maritime era.

http://www.davistownmuseum.org/bioStanley.htm

22211T26   Compass plane   DTM   TT

Grey cast iron, tempered alloy steel, steel blade, 10" long, 4 1/2" x 2 3/8", signed "No 113" on body, "STANLEY RULE & LEVEL Co." on the knob, "STANLEY" and "MADE IN U.S.A." on the plane blade with the sweetheart logo (SW in a heart).

Part of the Robert Sullivan Collection donation.

http://www.davistownmuseum.org/bioStanley.html

31808PC5   Compass plane   DTM   MH

Grey cast iron, cast steel blade, brass trim, and wood, 8 3/4" long, 1 3/4" wide blade, signed "MOULSON BROTHERS" "WARRANTED" and "CAST STEEL" trademark on the blade.

Moulson Brothers of England's working dates were 1824 - 1912.

7712LTC4   Dado plane   DA   TT (Pub)

Grey cast iron, japanned finish, steel blade, 9 3/4" long, 7/8" wide, 4 3/4" high, 3/8" wide blade, signed "No 39. 3/8 In STANLEY".

This is Stanley's number 39 dado plane with a "sweetheart" mark, indicating a manufacturing date of 1923-1932. Courtesy of Liberty Tool Company.

http://www.davistownmuseum.org/bioStanley.htm

2713LTC3   Double low angle block plane   DA   TT (Pub)

Grey cast iron, steel, japanned finish, rosewood knob, 8" long, 2 1/16" wide, 1 5/8" wide blade, signed "STANLEY" "No. 130".

http://www.davistownmuseum.org/bioStanley.htm

72812LTC2   Fillister and rabbet plane   DA   TT (Pub)

Cast grey iron, 10 1/2" long, 5" wide, 5 1/4" high, signed "Stanley No. 289" "PAT'S 6-7,&8-23-10".

Courtesy of Liberty Tool Company.

http://www.davistownmuseum.org/bioStanley.html

Woodworking: Planes

31808SLP3   Fillister plane   DTM   TT

Wood (beech), steel blade, brass fittings, 9 5/8" long, signed "AUBURN TOOL CO" and "AUBURN, NY".

Auburn Tool Co.'s working dates were 1864 - 1893. They used many other names on their markings. DATM (Nelson 1999) indicates this might be Empire Tool Co. or Owasco Tool Co. Gray and Dudly were hardware dealers who marked planes made by Auburn.

http://www.davistownmuseum.org/pics/31808slp3-2.jpg
http://www.davistownmuseum.org/pics/31808slp3-1.jpg

22211T25   Fillister rabbet plane   DTM   TT

Drop-forged grey cast iron, steel blade, 10" long, 2 1/4" x 1 1/2", signed "STANLEY" "No. 78" and "MADE IN U.S.A.".

The plane blade is also marked "STANLEY" and "MADE IN U.S.A." Part of the Robert Sullivan Collection donation.

http://www.davistownmuseum.org/bioStanley.html

102512T23   Fore plane   DTM   TT

Wood body, Swedish steel cutting edge, 18" long, 2" wide, 2" high, 5" long and 1 3/8" wide blade, signed "B & O LIBERG" "ROSENFORS" "GARANTERAR".

This maker is Bernard and Oskar Liberg of Rosenfors, Sweden, who began making corkscrews, knives, axes, and plane irons in 1861. For more information go to (http://www.vintagecorkscrewcenter.com/story-of-some-famous-corkscrew-makers/the-story-of-bernard-and-oskar-liberg,-rosenfors-sweden-12232249). Courtesy of Liberty Tool Co.

2713LTC2   Horned scrub plane   DA   TT (Pub)

Wood (beech, hornbeam), steel, brass, 9 1/2" long, 1 15/16" wide, 32 mm wide blade, signed "ULMIA QTT" "Made in Germany" "SCHUTZ ULMIA MARKE OTT" "33 m/m".

8180T7   Howell   DTM   MH

Wood (beech), steel, 13 1/2" long, 6 1/2" wide, 3 1/4" thick, unsigned.

22211T34   Jack plane   DTM   TT

Drop-forged grey cast iron, wood bottom, brass fittings, steel blade, 15" long, 2 5/8" wide, 1 1/2" high, 2" wide blade, signed "BAILY" on the body and "STANLEY" "MADE IN USA" on the plane blade.

Part of the Robert Sullivan Collection donation.

http://www.davistownmuseum.org/bioStanley.html

22211T35   Jack plane   DTM   TT

Drop-forged malleable iron, wood bottom, brass fittings, steel blade, 15" long, 2 3/4" wide, 1 1/2" high, 2" wide blade, signed "BAILEY" on the body and "STANLEY" on the plane blade.

This is a Stanley No. 5 jack plane. Part of the Robert Sullivan Collection donation.

http://www.davistownmuseum.org/bioStanley.html

ID #

Woodworking: Planes

7512LTC1   Jack plane

DA   TT (Pub)

Grey cast iron, wood (rosewood), brass knobs, japanned finish, 14" long, 2 7/16" wide, 5 1/4" tall, 2" wide cutting edge, signed "STANLEY" "No. 5" "MADE IN U.S.A.".

This is a standard Stanley No. 5 metal bench plane. Courtesy of Liberty Tool Company.

http://www.davistownmuseum.org/bioStanley.html

TJE4002   Jointer plane

LPC   MH

Grey cast iron, cast steel blade, 22" long x 5 1/2" high x 2 3/4" wide, signed "The Birmingham Conn Plane MFG. Co".

It is a No. 7 size, but the size is unmarked.

112806T1   Jointer plane

DTM   MAG-3

Malleable iron, rosewood handle and knob, and brass adjustment nut, 23 1/2" long, 2 15/16" wide, signed on the brass adjustment nut "Patented Aug 3, 1875".

This is one of the most interesting planes in the Davistown Museum collection. The day before its purchase from a Civil War period Somerville, MA, workshop, it was dropped on a cement floor and broken in half by its owner. When purchased, this broken plane was missing its lever cap and blade. Other than its rarity, its significance lies in the fracture of the metal frame of the plane. The appearance of the metal structure of the plane is that of white cast iron, much coarser than the fracture exhibited along the cleavage lines of the many chipped and broken malleable iron planes that turn up in every tool chest. The distinctly white fracture of the iron in this plane suggests that during its manufacture, some mishap occurred in the annealing process, which resulted in a failure of transition from rapidly cooled white cast iron to correctly annealed malleable grey cast iron. This metallurgical failure, along with the new designs for plane frogs and adjustment mechanisms being introduced by Leonard Bailey at this time, may explain both the rarity of this tool and its failure to become widely used. Extensive discussion and illustration of the Bailey Tool Company's products (Woonsocket RI, 1872 - 1879, Seldon A. Bailey, president - no relationship to Leonard Bailey) is contained in Volume I, pg. 61 - 68 of Roger K. Smith's (1960) Patented Transitional and Metallic Planes in America, 1827 - 1927. Smith makes this comment about the recent history of the design of this particular piece: "A design variation of this plane eliminated the cap screw adjustment for the iron but incorporated the cutter adjustment as patented by David F. Williams, No. 166,240 on August 3rd, 1875... the lever clamp device [on the earlier planes] was soon replaced with a screw held cap, which was also specified in William's 1875 patent." (pg. 65). Smith notes in 1879 the Bailey Tool Company was absorbed by the Bailey Wringing Machine Company and in January of 1880 by the Stanley Rule and Level Co. The Bailey Tool Company planes manufactured in Woonsocket, MA, can often be clearly distinguished from the planes Leonard Bailey designed for the Stanley Rule and Level Co. by the large letters cast into their ornate lever caps (BAILEY TOOL CO). Bailey Tool Co. planes are now fairly uncommon and were produced in much smaller quantities than those designed by Leonard Bailey for the Stanley Rule and Lever Co. This tool is available for hands on examination in the Center for the Study of Early Tools first floor tool cataloging area.

The Industrial Revolution (1865f.): Other Factory Made Tools

Woodworking: Planes

7512LTC2   Jointer plane   DA   TT (Pub)

Grey cast iron, wood (rosewood), brass knobs, japanned finish, 22" long, 3" wide, 5" tall, 2 3/8" wide cutting edge, signed "STANLEY" "No. 7" "MADE IN U.S.A.".

This is a standard Stanley No. 7 metal bench plane. Courtesy of Liberty Tool Company.

http://www.davistownmuseum.org/bioStanley.html

6312LTC6   Match plane   DA   TT (Pub)

Grey cast iron, nickel plated finish, 9" long, 1 1/2" wide, 5" high, signed "STANLEY" "PAT'D JAN 20-03" "7/8 INCH" "No 148".

Courtesy of Liberty Tool Co.

http://www.davistownmuseum.org/bioStanley.htm

31811T4   Molding plane   DTM   TT

Wood (beech), steel blade, 10" long, 1 7/16" wide, 3" tall, signed "FANNING" with an obscured word underneath it and "N. PACK" owner signature.

22211T32   Molding plane   DTM   TT

Wood (beech), steel blade, 9 1/4" wide, 3 3/8" x 2", plane blade 1 1/2" contour, signed "S. DALPE" "BOXTON POND".

S. Dalpe was a prominent Quebec planemaker in the second half of the 19th century. Part of the Robert Sullivan Collection donation.

22211T31   Molding plane   DTM   TT

Wood (beech), steel blade, 10" wide, 3 1/2" x 2 1/4", unsigned.

It cuts a 1 7/8" concave radius. Part of the Robert Sullivan Collection donation.

31811T3   Molding plane   DTM   TT

Wood, 10 1/2" long, 2" wide, 1 3/4" high, signed "AYMAR".

This plane is damaged, the front has been sawed off. It has a radius iron design. Aymar may be the owner's name.

22211T33   Plane   DTM   TT

Lignum vitae body and cast steel plane blade, 9 " wide, 2 1/4" x 2 1/4", plane blade 1 7/8", signed "MOULSON BROTHERS" "WARRENTED" "CAST STEEL" on the blade and "ATR" owner's mark three times in a circle on the body..

Part of the Robert Sullivan Collection donation.

The Industrial Revolution (1865f.): Other Factory Made Tools

Woodworking: Planes

31808SLP5   Plane   DTM   TT

Wood (beech), steel blade, 9 1/4" long, 1/4" wide cutting edge, unsigned.

This plane has two double bead curved cutters.

http://www.davistownmuseum.org/pics/31808slp5-1.jpg
http://www.davistownmuseum.org/pics/31808slp5-2.jpg

30311T8   Plane blade   DTM   TT

Tool steel, 7 3/4" long, 2 3/8" wide, signed "FORSMAN" "TOOL MFG CO" "QUINCY MASS".

DATM (Nelson 1999, 397) lists Horsman Tool Mfg. Co. of Quincy, MA as making plane irons with no dates.

10112LTC1   Plow plane   DA   TT (Pub)

Cast iron, cast steel, japanned finish, 9 3/4" long, 5 1/2" tall, 1" wide, unsigned.

This unusual plow plane was patented by Russell Phillips, who was originally from Gardiner, Maine, and worked out of Boston in the 1870s.

31808SLP10   Plow plane   DTM   TT

Wood (beech), cast steel blade, brass fittings, 8 3/4" long, 1/4" wide cutting blade, signed "3" "WARRANTED" "CAST STEEL" and on the wood "C.F.W".

http://www.davistownmuseum.org/pics/31808slp10-2.jpg
http://www.davistownmuseum.org/pics/31808slp10-3.jpg

32708T54   Plow plane   DTM   MH

Wood (beech), steel blades, brass fittings, 8 1/2" wide with 1 1/4" and 1/4" wide blades, signed "HILDICK" on the wide blade and "DICK" on the small blade.

DATM (Nelson 1999, 382) reports on a family of Hildicks working from 1860-1879 (Aaron, I & H, John, and R).

http://www.davistownmuseum.org/pics/32708t54-1.jpg
http://www.davistownmuseum.org/pics/32708t54-2.jpg

42607T7   Plow plane blade   DTM   MH

Cast steel, 8 1/2" long, 5/8" wide, signed "Humphreysville Mfg. Co. Warrented Cast Steel".

Humphreysville Mfg. Co. is listed as being in Seymour, CT (1852 - 1904). This is probably a Civil War period blade. Is this cast steel imported from England or made in the USA (Pittsburg)?

Woodworking: Planes

7602T1   Razee Plane   LPC   MH

Ebony with cast steel blade, 22" long, 2 5/8" wide, 1 7/8" wide blade, signed "Made by P Marshall" on the toe and "Buck Brothers Warranteed Cast Steel" on the blade.

This plane was one of three in a collection of tools formerly owned by a ship caulker who worked in the 19th century in the shipyards of Boston and Chelsea. It was found with associated caulking tools in a dark corner of 3 Derby, Chelsea, June 2002 by the Liberty Tool Co.

http://www.davistownmuseum.org/pics/7602t1-1bw_web.jpg
http://www.davistownmuseum.org/bioBuckBrothers.html

6312LTC9   Router   DA   TT (Pub)

Grey cast iron body, nickel plated finish, hardwood handles, cast steel blade, 7 5/8" long, 4 1/2" x 3 3/4", signed "STANLEY No 71 MADE IN U.S.A.".

Courtesy of Liberty Tool Co.

http://www.davistownmuseum.org/bioStanley.htm

22211T28   Scraper plane   DTM   TT

Grey cast iron, steel blade, brass nuts, with a wooden tote and handle, 9" long, 3 1/2" wide, signed "No 112" on body.

This is a Stanley No. 112 plane. Part of the Robert Sullivan Collection donation.

http://www.davistownmuseum.org/bioStanley.html

31808SLP12   Side rabbet plane   DTM   TT

Grey cast iron with nickel-plating, 5 1/4" long, 1/2" wide cutting blade, signed "NO 79" "STANLEY" and "MADE IN USA".

http://www.davistownmuseum.org/pics/31808slp12-2.jpg
http://www.davistownmuseum.org/bioStanley.htm

81212LTC9   Side rabbet plane   DA   TT(pub)

Cast iron, wooden (rosewood) knob, 4" long, 1 7/8" tall, 1 5/8" wide, signed "No 98" "STANLEY".

This is Stanley's No. 98 side rabbet plane. Courtesy of Liberty Tool Company.

http://www.davistownmuseum.org/bioStanley.htm

TJE4001   Smooth plane   LPC   MH

Gray cast iron, cast steel, wood (rosewood), 8" long, 4 3/4" high, 2 1/8" deep, signed "The Standard Rule Co. Patented Oct. 30, 1883 __ntonville, Conn".

http://www.davistownmuseum.org/pics/TJE4001.jpg

101400T4   Smooth plane   LPC   MH

Rosewood, cast steel blade, 4 5/8" long, 1 1/2" wide, with a 15/16" wide blade, signed on blade "Jacob Reisser New York".

The blade maker is not listed in DATM (Nelson 1999). This is an exquisite late 19th century plane.

The Industrial Revolution (1865f.): Other Factory Made Tools

Woodworking: Planes

42904T9　　Smooth plane
DTM　MH

Grey cast iron, steel blade, rosewood handles and knobs, brass adjustment knob, 9 1/2" long, 2 1/2" wide, 5" high, signed "BAILEY" "No 4" "PAT'D" "MAR-25-02" "AUG-19-02".

This is a nice example of a Stanley smooth plane at their peak of production.

http://www.davistownmuseum.org/bioBaily.html

TAL1001　　Smooth plane
LPC　MH

Drop-forged steel and wood, 2" long, signed "STANLEY NO. 2".

Loaned to the Museum by Thom McKee.

http://www.davistownmuseum.org/bioStanley.htm

122912LTC1　Stanley no. 43 adjustable plow plane
DA　TT (Pub)

Cast gray iron, brass, wood (rosewood), 10 1/2" long, 6 1/2" wide, 5 1/4" high, signed "STANLEY RULE & LEVEL CO." and on slitter "PAT OCT. 24,82".

http://www.davistownmuseum.org/bioStanley.htm

81212LTC10　Tailed block plane
NOM　TT (Pub)

Cast iron, japanned finish, steel blade, 4 3/4" long, 1 1/4" wide, 2" tall, 1" wide cutter, signed "STANLEY SW".

This pattern was used between 1923 and1932.

http://www.davistownmuseum.org/bioStanley.htm

6312LTC8　　Tongue and groove plane
DA　TT (Pub)

Gray cast iron body, nickel plated finish, rosewood handle, cast steel blade, 11" long, 1 3/4" wide, signed "STANLEY No 48".

This plane has a swinging fence. Courtesy of Liberty Tool Co.

http://www.davistownmuseum.org/bioStanley.htm

22211T27　　Veneer scraper
DTM　TT

Grey cast iron, steel blade, brass fittings, wooden handle, 6 1/4" long, 3 1/2" wide, 3" high, 11" wide handle, signed "No 12" on body, "STANLEY RULE & LEVEL Co." "NEW BRITAIN, CONN USA" on the knob.

Part of the Robert Sullivan Collection donation.

http://www.davistownmuseum.org/bioStanley.html

12112T3　　Wooden jointer plane
DTM　MH

Wood (beech), cast steel, 21 1/2" long, 3 1/4" wide, 6 1/2" tall, 2 1/2" cutting edge, signed "J.L. LEE".

The mark is probably an owner's mark as it appears several times and upside down.

Woodworking: Planes Made in Maine

The Industrial Revolution (1865f.): Other Factory Made Tools

Woodworking: Planes Made in Maine

52408T1	**Bench plane**	DTM	MH-O

Tiger maple, steel blade, 13.5" long, 2.5" wide, 6.5" high, unsigned.

Made by Leon Robbins of Crown Plane in Bath, Maine.

http://www.davistownmuseum.org/bioLeon.html

42607T3	**Convex block plane**	DTM	MH

Wood (beech) with an iron and cast steel blade, 7 5/8" long, 2 1/2" wide with a curved 2 1/8" wide blade, signed "Orin Hardin" and on the blade "warrented cast steel" with an obscured signature.

The blade is clearly steeled (steel welded on iron), showing the use of cast steel as a weld steel. At least 20 of Orin Hardin's planes were recovered in 3 tool chests accompanied by eight J. C. Jewett planes. Both were Waterville, Maine, planemakers.

http://www.davistownmuseum.org/publications/volume10.html

TJE1001	**Evan's circular plane**	BDTM	MH

Malleable cast iron, cast steel blade, 10 3/8" long, 2 3/16" wide, with a 1 5/8" wide blade, signed "Moulson Brothers cast steel" on the blade.

One of the earliest of American-made circular planes, this Maine-made tool pre-dates most Stanley Rule and Level Company circular planes. It is noteworthy that while this tool was produced either in Norway, ME or Hudson, NY, the blade was produced in England, reflecting the continued U.S. reliance on imported British edge tools as late as c. 1870. See the Registry of Maine Toolmakers (Brack 2008) for the entry on George F. Evans, who worked 1862 - 1864.

http://www.davistownmuseum.org/pics/TJE1001.jpg
http://www.davistownmuseum.org/publications/volume10.html

030206T1	**Evan's circular plane**	DTM	MH

Grey cast iron, steel blade, 10 " long, 4 1/8" high, 2" wide, unsigned.

This plane is identical in appearance to planes made from the Evans Patent Jan. 28, 1862 (no. 34,248) March 22, 1864 (no. 41,983), but is not marked. George F. Evans of Norway, Maine filed the patent. Most planes made with this patent were by R. H. Mitchell & Co. of Hudson, NY. Prior to them purchasing the patent, some were made by Darling & Schwartz of Bangor, Maine. The Mitchell Co. soldered a brass nameplate to the side and perhaps this is missing? Some were also sold with paper labels (Smith 1960, vol. I pg. 145-6; vol II, pg. 156).

http://www.davistownmuseum.org/pics/030206t1_p1.jpg
http://www.davistownmuseum.org/publications/volume10.html

70701T6	**Molding plane**	DTM	MH

Wood, steel blade, 8" long, 1/4" diameter blade, signed "Use this tool for fitting BURROWES Patent sliding screens. E.T. BURROWES CO., MANUFACTURERS, PORTLAND MAINE".

Also on the side of the plane is printed "If screens do not run easily groove or follow groove a little with this plane". Burrowes made screens, and planes for use in their installation, from 1878-1928.

http://www.davistownmuseum.org/publications/volume10.html

Woodworking: Planes Made in Maine (Contemporary)

Woodworking: Planes Made in Maine (Contemporary)

103102T1   Bench plane   DTM   MH

White bronze with rosewood handles, 6" long, 1 1/2" wide, 3 1/2" high, blade is 4 1/2" high, 1 1/4" wide, signed "LIE-NIELSEN USA" on blade and "Lie-Nielsen" "USA" "2002" "No 1" on base of plane.

This plane is modeled after a No. 1 Stanley; No. 284 of 500 produced.

http://www.davistownmuseum.org/pics/103102t1.jpg
http://www.davistownmuseum.org/publications/volume10.html

52408T7   Bench plane   DTM   MH-O

Wood (three hardwood types), steel blade, 4 3/4" long, 1 3/4" wide, 2 3/4" high, signed "L.R." over a flying bird inside a shield on one end and a crown inside a horseshoe on the other end.

It was made by Leon Robbins of Crown Plane Co. in Bath, Maine.

http://www.davistownmuseum.org/bioLeon.html

52408T3   Coffin plane   DTM   MH-O

Etched maple, steel blade, 8 3/4" long, 2 1/2" wide, 4 3/4" high, signed "Buck Brothers" on the blade.

This plane was made by Leon Robbins of Crown Plane in Bath, Maine. The blade was made by Buck Brothers of Millbury, MA.

http://www.davistownmuseum.org/bioLeon.html
http://www.davistownmuseum.org/bioBuckBrothers.html

90502T1   Coffin plane   DTM   MH

Wood (curly maple), steel blade, 8 1/4" long, 2 1/8" wide, 2 1/2" high, 1 3/4" wide blade, signed on the wood "J W" with a crown emblem, 2002.

This plane and its blade was made special for the Davistown Museum by Jim White of Crown Plane Co. in S. Portland, Maine. It is the museum's only specimen from this planemaker.

http://www.davistownmuseum.org/publications/volume10.html

52408T5   Coffin plane   DTM   MH-O

Wood (maple), steel blade, 11" long, 2 1/2" wide, 5 1/4" high, unsigned.

It was made by Leon Robbins of Crown Plane Co. in Bath, Maine. It has stripes burned into the wood and a hand-etched curly pattern.

http://www.davistownmuseum.org/bioLeon.html

41302T1   Convex block plane   DTM   MHC-K

Wood (type unknown) with steel blade, 4 1/2" long, 2 3/16" wide, signed "L.R." with a crown touchmark, c. 1990.

This is the handiwork of Leon Robbins, Crown Plane Co., Bath, Maine, now operated by Jim White in South Portland, ME.

http://www.davistownmuseum.org/publications/volume10.html

The Industrial Revolution (1865f.): Other Factory Made Tools

Woodworking: Planes Made in Maine (Contemporary)

52408T8   Hollowing plane   DTM   MH-O

Wood (tiger maple with maple core), steel blade, 9" long, 3/4" wide, 5 1/2" high, signed "LR" over a crown.

It was made by the late Leon Robbins, founder of Crown Plane of Bath, Maine.

http://www.davistownmuseum.org/bioLeon.html

52408T2   Molding plane   DTM   MH-O

Wood (tiger maple), steel blade, 9 3/4" long, 6" high, 1 1/4" wide, unsigned.

It was made by Leon Robbins of Crown Plane in Bath, Maine.

http://www.davistownmuseum.org/bioLeon.html

112508T1   Scrub plane   DTM   MH-O

Wood, steel blade, 5 7/8" long, 1 23/32" wide, 3 1/4" tall with cutter, and 1 11/32" cutting edge, signed "L.R." with a flying bird inside a shield.

This plane was made by Leon Robbins.

http://www.davistownmuseum.org/bioLeon.html

6405T5   Smooth plane   DTM   MH

Wood (curly maple), cast steel blade, 8 1/4" long, 1 1/2" wide, 2" wide blade, signed "L. R." with a crown hallmark, blade signed "W. Greaves & Sons warranted cast steel", c. 1985.

This plane was made by Leon Robbins of Bath, Maine. The blade is a typical 19th century imported Sheffield blade.

http://www.davistownmuseum.org/bioLeon.html

52408T9   Smooth plane   DTM   MH-N

Wood (tiger maple with maple core), 8 3/8" long, 2 5/8" wide, 4" high, signed "L.R." over a crown.

It was made by the late Leon Robbins, founder of Crown Plane of Bath, Maine.

http://www.davistownmuseum.org/bioLeon.html

Woodworking: Saws

30311T6   Backsaw   DTM   TT

Saw steel, steel, brass rivets, and wooden handle, signed "KENYON" and "J. D." owner's mark.

DATM (Nelson 1999, 445) lists Kenyon as a saw-maker with no location or dates.

Woodworking: Saws

040103T6   Backsaw
DTM   MH

Saw steel, brass, and apple wood handle, 15" long, 10" blade, signed "C. H. BILL & SON WALTHAM MASS" "SPRING STEEL WARRANTED" and an eagle medallion.

This mark is not listed in DATM (Nelson 1999) nor has the curator, who was born in the town adjacent to Waltham (Newton), ever seen this mark in 33 years in the tool business. A finely made backsaw with a beautiful applewood handle.

http://www.davistownmuseum.org/pics/040103t6_p1.jpg
http://www.davistownmuseum.org/pics/040103t6_p3.jpg

2213T3   Backsaw
DTM   TT

Spring steel, cast steel, wood (rosewood), 18 1/2" long, 14 1/4" long cutting edge, 5" wide, signed "S. JOHNSON CAST STEEL".

DATM (Nelson 1999) lists a Samuel Johnson of Jewett, NY as an edge toolmaker.

92911T15   Backsaw
DTM   TT

Cast steel, brass, and wooden handle, 10" long blade, 6" wide tapering to 1" wide, signed "R. GROVES & SON" "SHEFFIELD" "CAST STEEL" "ELASTIC SPRING TEMPER" "WARRENTED".

It's blade stiffener is made of brass. The saw is made of specially tempered cast steel (saw steel).

92911T16   Backsaw
DTM   TT

Tempered alloy steel, brass, and wooden handle, 13" long blade, 8" wide tapering to 2 1/2" wide, signed "R. GROVES & SON" "BEE HIVE WORKS" "SHEFFIELD" "SILVER STEEL" "ELASTIC SPRING TEMPER" "WARRENTED GOOD".

This saw has hardwood handles with brass screws. Silver steel is another variation of tempered alloy steel and may be an early product of the electric arc furnace, which was used to make tool steel beginning in the 1880s.

8612T1   Backsaw
DTM   TT

German steel, hardwood, brass rivets, 12" long, 1" wide, 2 1/2" cutting edge, signed "SPEAR GERMAN STEEL".

92911T17   Backsaw
DTM   TT

Cast steel, wooden handle, 18" long blade, 14" long cutting edge, 3 1/2" wide, signed "I COLBECK" "CAST STEEL".

We have heard from one other person who has a backsaw marked "I COLBECK". This mark could be "J COLBECK". Erwin Schaffer's "Saw Makers of North America" lists Colbeck as American, with no known information.

Woodworking: Saws

31602T15   Buck saw
DTM   MH

Steel and pressed wood, 34 1/2" long with 32" blade, signed "Lumber Products Co. Lewiston Maine" "Patented USA Jan 15 1918" "Patented Canada Jan 22 1918".

This is an interesting early 20th century Maine buck saw. Donated to The Davistown Museum by Michael Ross.

52512LTC3   Buck saw
DA   TT (Pub)

Saw steel, wood (maple), 31" long, 27" cutting edge, unsigned.

Courtesy of Liberty Tool Co.

22311T20   Cabinet saw
DTM   TT

Saw steel, 24" long, 12" long handles, 1" wide blade, signed "SCHMIDT PACKSAW" "BY" "CURTIS-STEBBINS" "DENMARK, MAINE".

This saw is in an oak frame. Part of the Robert Sullivan Collection donation.

102612T14   Carpenters' saw
DTM   TT

Saw steel, wooden handle, 25" long, 4 1/2" wide, signed "68009" on handle, owner's marks "A P" on handle and "Pigeon" using a pencil and cursive script..

This saw was used in work done on the U.S.S. Constitution at 58 High St., Charlestown, MA. The owner was J. A. Pigeon of 38 Cottage St, Tauton, MA.

102612T15   Carpenters' saw blade
DTM   TT

Saw steel, 18" long, 5 1/2" wide, unsigned.

This saw was used in work done on the U.S.S. Constitution at 58 High St., Charlestown, MA. The owner was J. A. Pigeon of 38 Cottage St, Tauton, MA.

31808PC2   Crosscut saw
DTM   MH

Steel, brass, and wood, 30" long, 25 1/2" long cutting blade, signed "C. H. TUPPER" on handle and "SUPERIOR TEM__ WARRANTEE" on brass.

The saw's handle is handmade. This could be C. H. Tupper & Martin who worked in Vermont in 1885.

7712LTC7   Dovetail saw
DA   TT (Pub)

Saw steel, brass fuller, wooden (beech) handle, 11" long, 3" wide, 6" long cutting edge, signed "WM MARPLES & SONS LTD SHEFFIELD, ENGLAND".

Courtesy of Liberty Tool Company.

41302T3   Hacksaw
DTM   MH

Steel, brass, and wood, 19 1/2" long, 14 5/8" adjustable frame, signed "No 6 Millers Falls Co. Millers Falls Mass USA" with their star cartouche.

This is an uncommon example of an unusual, early Millers Falls hacksaw design.

http://www.davistownmuseum.org/bioMillersFalls.htm

ID #   Status   Location

Woodworking: Saws

12813T1   **Hand saw**   DTM   TT

Spring steel, wood (beech), 24" long, 20" cutting edge, 6" wide, 11 teeth per inch, signed "WHEELER MADDEN & CLEMSON".

Wheeler, Madden & Clemson worked out of Middletown, NY from 1860 to 1893 (Nelson 1999).

2213T2   **Hand saw**   DTM   TT

Spring steel, wood (beech), brass, 24" long, 20" long cutting edge, 5 3/4" wide, signed "USE R. GROVES & SONS SHEFFIELD DOUBLE REFINED SPRING STEEL WARRANTED" "ESTABLISHED 1770" with crown trademark.

92911T18   **Hand saw**   DTM   TT

Cast steel and wood, 25" long blade, 5" wide, signed "_WECL & GR___HS" "BOSTON" "CAST STEEL" "WARRENTED".

The signature was poorly stamped and not very legible. Possibly this is Welch & Griffiths, who made saws in Boston from 1830 to 1871.

7712LTC8   **Keyhole saw**   DA   TT (Pub)

Brass, wooden (beech) handle, 7 1/2" long, 1/2" wide blade, unsigned.

Courtesy of Liberty Tool Company.

41801T12   **Keyhole saw**   DTM   MH

Cast steel and brass, 19 1/2" long, 14" blade, signed with an obscured mark on the blade followed by "Warranteed Cast Steel".

There's nothing unusual about this run-of-the-mill keyhole saw except the early eagle brass (H. Disston style) and the obscured mark.

913108T28   **Saw**   DTM   MH

Silver steel, brass trim, wooden handle, 22" long, signed "CHANDLER & BARBER" "SILVER STEEL WARRANTED" "BOSTON , MASS." and with a circle with an eagle in the middle and "WARRANTED SUPERIOR".

Chandler & Barber were hardware dealers who marked this saw with their trademark. It was made by Henry Disston, whose eagle trademark is also on the saw. Silver steel is another name for saw steel.

http://www.davistownmuseum.org/bioDisston.html

101312T27   **Veneer saw**   DTM   TT

Cast iron, cast steel, lacquered wood, 8" long, 2 7/8" edge, signed "DISSTON USA".

http://www.davistownmuseum.org/bioDisston.htm

Wrenches

The Industrial Revolution (1865f.): Other Factory Made Tools

Wrenches

32708T63   Adjustable box wrench   DTM   MH

Drop-forged steel, 8" long, signed "WAKEFIELD WIZARD" "No 120" "PATENTS PENDING" "IN U.S.A." "AND FOREIGN COUNTRIES" "MADE IN WORCHESTER. MASS U.S.A.".

This company's working dates were from 1891 - 1900.

http://www.davistownmuseum.org/pic/32708t63-3.jpg
http://www.davistownmuseum.org/pic/32708t63-1.jpg

31212T6   Adjustable nut wrench   DTM   TT

Drop-forged tempered alloy steel, 8" long, signed "W.J. LADD No. 77 NEW YORK".

This is similar to a Coes patent nut wrench. Courtesy of Liberty Tool Co.

121412T18   Adjustable pipe wrench   DTM   TT

Cast steel, red paint, 13" long when closed all the way, signed "RIDGID HEAVY DUTY 1" " "THE RIDGE TOOL CO. ELYRIA, OHIO U.S.A." "ALLOY STEEL".

This company, which uses the Ridgid brand, began in 1923 and is still in operation (http://www.ridgid.com/).

52603T23   Adjustable pipe wrench   DTM   MH

Drop-forged steel, wood (rosewood), 7 1/4" long, signed "F.E. WELLS & SON CO." "GREENFIELD MASS. USA" "8" "2ND".

"In 1900 Frederick E. Wells left the Wells Brothers Co. and, with his son, formed the F. E. Wells & Son Co. to manufacture pipe threading tools." (http://vintagemachinery.org/MfgIndex/detail.aspx?id=877)

7612LTC2   Adjustable tractor nut wrench   DA   TT (Pub)

Drop-forged grey cast iron, 8 3/8" long, 2 1/2" wide, 3/4" thick, signed "78G, IHC".

This wrench was made by International Harvester Company for servicing their agricultural machines. Courtesy of Liberty Tool Company.

TCZ1001   Adjustable wrench   DTM   MH

Drop-forged steel, 6" long, signed "B&C" and "6 IN.".

This wrench has an "S" type handle. Bemis & Call Co. manufactured wrenches in Springfield, MA, c. 1860-1875. This tool signals the arrival of the Industrial Revolution and the mass production of tools.

http://www.davistownmuseum.org/pics/tjg1001a.jpg

The Industrial Revolution (1865f.): Other Factory Made Tools

Wrenches

TCZ1002   **Adjustable wrench**   DTM   MH

Drop-forged steel, 6" long, signed "BUFFALO" and "BARCALO" and marked "6".

It has a "S" type handle. DATM (Nelson 1999, 56) reports these marks on an adjustable crescent style wrench and that the "Buffalo" might be a brand name rather than referring to Buffalo, NY. The website "http://www.alloy-artifacts.com/barcalo-buffalo.html" indicates that there was a Barcalo Manufacturing in Buffalo, NY, 1896 - 1960s. Eventually, this company became more famous for the Barcalounger chair.

http://www.davistownmuseum.org/pics/tjg1001a.jpg

TCZ1003   **Adjustable wrench**   DTM   MH

Drop-forged steel, 8" long, signed "ROBINSON" and "DROP FORGED STEEL".

Robinson is listed in DATM (Nelson 1999, 665) as a wrench-maker with a patent of June 16 1885. Squire Robinson lived in Southington, CT when the patent was issued. A copy of the patent is here: http://www.google.com/patents?id=cmBdAAAAEBAJ&pg=PA1&dq=June+16+1885+robinson&hl=en&sa=X&ei=SMOWT_F2qd7pAdX72LcO&ved=0CDQQ6AEwAA#v=onepage&q=June%2016%201885%20robinson&f=false.

http://www.davistownmuseum.org/pics/tjg1001a.jpg

TCZ1006   **Adjustable wrench**   BDTM   MH

Drop-forged steel, 8 3/4" long, signed "PENNEY & THURSTON MECHANICS FALLS ME PAT OCT 11 __".

This is a very uncommon wrench made by a very obscure, yet historically important, Maine wrench-maker not listed in DATM (Nelson 1999). Thank you to the Missouri Valley Wrench Club Newsletter for the following: "The Penney & Thurston wrench is patent No. 44,653 issued Oct. 11, 1864. It was described in the Nov. 26, 1864, Scientific American". Follow the link to see more photographs of this wrench.

http://www.davistownmuseum.org/pics/tcz1006p2.jpg
http://www.davistownmuseum.org/bioPenney.htm

032203T6   **Adjustable wrench**   DTM   MH

Drop-forged steel, 5" long, signed "ACME MADE IN USA PAT. FEB 27, 83".

This nifty little wrench is typical of the American factory-made tools that were appearing in great quantities after the Civil War. With the Industrial Revolution underway at full blast by 1880, a typical ships' carpenter or shipyard worker needed a wide variety of hand tools to execute a much broader range of work assignments than just building a wooden ship. Modern navigation instruments and marine fittings might necessitate the use of a mundane wrench such as this.

http://www.davistownmuseum.org/pics/032203t6_p3.jpg
http://www.davistownmuseum.org/pics/032203t6_p2.jpg

111206T2   **Adjustable wrench**   DTM   MH

Forge-welded and drop-forged steel, unsigned.

This mid- to late nineteenth century wrench illustrates the juxtaposition of a hand-worked, twisted handle with the drop-forged jaws characteristic of machine-made fabrication.

The Industrial Revolution (1865f.): Other Factory Made Tools

Wrenches

30202T5   Adjustable wrench   DTM   MH

Drop-forged steel, 5 1/4" long, signed "TRIMO EMERGENCY" "Pat'D Drop Forged" on handle and "TRIMONT MFG CO ROXBURY MASS" "188997" "TRIMO 6".

This is a rare and unusual Tremont wrench. DATM (Nelson 1999) lists Tremont Wrench as in business 1889 - 1920. This example is not pictured in Cope's (1993) "American Wrench Makers".

http://www.davistownmuseum.org/pics/30202t5.jpg

041505T16   Adjustable wrench   DTM   MH

Drop-forged steel, 8" long, signed "Walworth Company Made in USA" and "WALCO PIPE WRENCH".

This is the bottom wrench in the photograph. Walworth was a prolific manufacturer of pipe wrenches.

http://www.davistownmuseum.org/pics/041505t15.jpg
http://www.davistownmuseum.org/bioWalworth.html

101400T13   Adjustable wrench   DTM   MH

Drop-forged steel, 12" long, unsigned.

This is a typical S-curved adjustable wrench.

http://www.davistownmuseum.org/pics/tjg1001a.jpg

32708T47   Adjustable wrench   DTM   MH

Drop-forged steel and wood, 11" long, signed "BEMIS & CALL H & T" and "SPRINGFIELD, MASS USA".

This wrench is also marked with two figure 8-like marks.

http://www.davistownmuseum.org/pics/32708t47-2.jpg
http://www.davistownmuseum.org/bioBemis.html

041505T20   Adjustable wrench   DTM   MH

Drop-forged steel, 7 1/4" long, signed "GORDON" "AUTOMATIC" "PAT'D USA".

Gordon is listed in DATM (Nelson 1999) with no dates or location. It is not listed in Cope (1993) and Schultz (1989).

http://www.davistownmuseum.org/pics/041505t20.jpg

072512T1   Adjustable wrench   DTM   TT

Drop-forged iron and steel, 5" long, 1 1/2" wide, 7/16" thick, signed "Billings & Spencer Co." "Hartford, Conn" and "B" in a triangle; "C. E. Billings" "Pat'd Feb. 18th 1879"; also "B" on the bottom section.

Charles Billings was issued patent 212,298 for an improvement in wrench design. View it here: http://www.google.com/patents?id=UJdOAAAAEBAJ&printsec=frontcover&dq=Feb.+18+1879+Billings &source=bl&ots=xnN2JWONAh&sig=CIThXq-dPeZ90tctjaxTMrdFlo8&hl=en&sa=X&ei=sS4QUN3WKaaW0QX2yIDIAQ&ved=0CDEQ6AEwAA.

http://www.davistownmuseum.org/bioBillingspencer.html

The Industrial Revolution (1865f.): Other Factory Made Tools

Wrenches

52603T38   Adjustable wrench   DTM   MH

Drop-forged steel, 4 1/4" long, signed "HAWKINS DERBY. CT".

DATM (Nelson 1999) states that Hawkins Hdw. Mfg. Co. made wrenches patented by William Baxter Dec. 1 1868. A copy of the patent is here:
http://www.google.com/patents?id=JW8_AAAAEBAJ&pg=PA2&dq=Baxter+Dec.+1+1868&hl=en&sa=X&ei=MsKWT8bNEu3G6AHuzd3PDg&ved=0CDQQ6AEwAA#v=onepage&q=Baxter%20Dec.%201%201868&f=false.

32708T52   Adjustable wrench   DTM   MH

Drop-forged steel, brass, 6 7/8" long, head 2" long and 1 3/8" wide, signed "EVANS WRENCH CO." "FALL RIVER" "MASS." and "PAT NO. 1728282".

The Evans Wrench Company started in 1880.

http://www.davistownmuseum.org/pics/32708t52-1.jpg
http://www.davistownmuseum.org/pics/32708t52-2.jpg

51201T1   Adjustable wrench   DTM   MH

Drop-forged steel, 3 3/8" long, signed "J. R. Long Wrench Co. PAT. APR. AKRON, OHIO 17, 1906".

This is the patent:
http://www.google.com/patents?id=WZJOAAAAEBAJ&pg=PA2&dq=apr+17+1906+long+wrench&hl=en&sa=X&ei=tr6WT_roFJD06AGelf2cDg&ved=0CDQQ6AEwAA#v=onepage&q=apr%2017%201906%20long%20wrench&f=false.

62202T6   Adjustable wrench   DTM   MH

Drop-forged steel with cast lead handle, 5 7/8" long, signed "Goodell Pratt Company TOOLSMITHS Greenfield Mass USA".

This is the only example of this wrench we have encountered in 30 years.

http://www.davistownmuseum.org/pics/62202t6.jpg
http://www.davistownmuseum.org/bioGoodelpratt.html

52603T1   Adjustable wrench   DTM   MH

Drop-forged German steel, nickel plated finish, 4 1/2" long, 2" wide, signed "Avaokra".

31908T40   Alligator wrench   DTM   MH

Drop-forged steel, 8 1/4" long, signed "THE K & B CO." and "NEW HAVEN CT" on one claw and "SAXON" on the other claw.

This mark is from the Kilburn & Bishop Co.

http://www.davistownmuseum.org/pics/31908t40p4.jpg
http://www.davistownmuseum.org/pics/31908t40p1.jpg

Wrenches

101212LTC4 Alligator wrench   DA   TT (Pub)

Drop-forged steel, 6" long, jaws are 1 1/8" apart, signed "SHAW" "S" "SHAW PROPELLOR CO BOSTON MASS, U.S.A." "DROP-FORGED 6 PAT'D APRIL 26 1910. OTHER PAT'S PENDING".

The patent on this wrench belongs to George Bryant of Boston, MA.

52603T13   Alligator wrench   DTM   MH

Drop-forged steel, 8" long, signed "THE S. and T. WRENCH".

52603T12   Alligator wrench   DTM   MH

Drop-forged steel, 9 3/4" long, signed "MADE IN USA" "TWIN" and with a W in a diamond.

6703T3   Alligator wrench and pipe threader   DTM   TT

Cast steel, 5 1/4" long, 2" wide, 5/16" thick, signed 1/4; 3/16; 5/16; MADE IN U.S.A..

101312T18   Alligator wrench and screw threader   DTM   TT

Cast steel, 8" long, 2 1/4" wide, 1" and 1 1/2" jaws, signed "BONNEY VIXEN ALLENTOWN PA. MADE IN U.S.A.".

The brand name Vixen was used by Bonney Vise and Toolworks of Philadelphia and Allentown, PA., operating from 1886 to 1910.

TJF1005   Box wrench   DTM   MH

Drop-forged steel, 19 1/2" long, 1 3/8" box, 1/58" box, signed "Hinckley Myers J 602", c. 1900.

"The Hinckley-Myers Company operated in Chicago, Illinois as maker of automobile specialty equipment and tools." (http://home.comcast.net/~alloy-artifacts/other-makers-p2.html).

31908T41   Box wrench   DTM   MH

Drop-forged chromium vanadium steel, 9 3/4" long, signed "11/16 PERFECTION NoP-27 5/8" and on the other side "CHROMIUM VANADIUM".

Chromium vanadium is one of the many variants of tempered alloy steel.

http://www.davistownmuseum.org/pics/31908t41p1.jpg
http://www.davistownmuseum.org/pics/31908t41p2.jpg

040103T13   Claw wrench   DTM   MH

Drop-forged steel, 13 1/2" long, signed "LeClaw Wrench Co. Chicago USA Pat'd Feb 6 1912".

This is a hefty tool with great sculptural qualities. It's not an early tool, but is too interesting to sell at Liberty Tool Co.

http://www.davistownmuseum.org/pics/040103t13_p1.jpg
http://www.davistownmuseum.org/pics/040103t13_p3.jpg

The Industrial Revolution (1865f.): Other Factory Made Tools

Wrenches

7612LTC4   Combination alligator wrench with thread chasers   DA   TT (Pub)

Drop-forged steel, 8 1/4" long, 2 1/4" wide, 3/8" thick, 1" and 1 3/8" wide jaws, signed "PAT. NO. 720554 PAT'S PENDING" "THE HAWKEYE WRENCH CO. MARSHALLTOWN, IA".

This appears to be an example of Hawkeye Wrench Co's combination wrench for model T Ford automobiles. Charles Benesh of Wahpeton, ND's 1903 patent may be viewed here: http://www.google.com/patents/US720554?dq=720554+wrench&ei=rboOUKaiOOTF0QXH-4GAAw. Courtesy of Liberty Tool Company.

2713LTC5   Combination pipe and nut wrench   DA   TT (Pub)

Cast steel, wood (rosewood), black paint, 12 3/4" long, 4" wide, signed "B&C TRADEMARK" "BEMIS & CALL COMPANY SPRINGFIELD, MASS. MADE IN U.S.A.".

http://www.davistownmuseum.org/bioBemis.html

30202T12   Combination wrench   DTM   MH

Drop-forged steel, 6 3/8" long, 1/8" wide, signed "Ryder's Combination Pat'D Nov 10 1896".

Ryder is not listed in DATM (Nelson 1999) or Cope's (1993) "American Wrench Makers". The patent was given to Josiah F. Ryder of Attleborough, MA. The patent may be viewed here: http://www.google.com/patents?id=KZVBAAAAEBAJ&pg=PA2&dq=ryder+nov+10+1896&hl=en&sa=X &ei=EcyWT8mKNsyw8QPVjrXuCQ&ved=0CDQQ6AEwAA#v=onepage&q=ryder%20nov%2010%201 896&f=false.

http://www.davistownmuseum.org/pics/30202t12.jpg

7712LTC3   Combination wrench and cutter   DA   TT (Pub)

Drop-forged steel, 6 7/8" long, 2 5/8" wide, 1 1/4" thick, unsigned.

The patent belongs to Edward Tryon. This wrench is an earlier version of 52712LTC2. Courtesy of Liberty Tool Company.

52712LTC2   Combination wrench and cutter   DA   TT (Pub)

Drop-forged steel, nickel plating, 8 1/4" long, 2 5/8" wide, signed "PAT. JAN. 29 1901".

This tool was manufactured by the Hartford Hardware Co. and invented by Edward E. Tryon, Hartford, CT, patent number 667,143 on January 29, 1901. View the patent here: http://www.google.com/patents?id=QKA_AAAAEBAJ&printsec=frontcover&dq=667,143&hl=en&sa=X &ei=ilnsT-XhHI3itQbWw8TOBQ&sqi=2&ved=0CDkQ6AEwAg. Courtesy of Liberty Tool Co.

913108T21   Crescent wrenches (4)   DTM   MH

Drop-forged steel, 7 1/4" long with 3/4" opening; 8" long with 1 1/4" opening; and two 9 1/4" long with 1 1/2" opening, signed "<- 3/4" C. DREW & CO. 3/4" ->", "<-7 3/16"- DREW NO. 15 -1 1/4" ->", and two "1 7/16" DREW NO. 19 - 1 1/2"->", c. 1930.

These four wrenches are an uncommon product of this factory: Christopher Drew & Company, Kingston, MA, 1837 - 1937.

http://www.davistownmuseum.org/bioDrew.htm

The Industrial Revolution (1865f.): Other Factory Made Tools

Wrenches

42912LTC4   Cycle wrench
DA   TT (Pub)

Drop-forged steel, 5" long, signed "DIAMOND No. 10" "Frank Mossberg Co. Attleboro Mass. U.S.A. PATENTED NOV. 13 '00 Mar. 11 '02.".

The patent may be viewed here:
http://www.google.com/patents?id=_i1IAAAAEBAJ&pg=PA2&dq=nov+13+1900+wrench&hl=en&sa=X&ei=ODi1T8e5KIq2-wbx0sXwDQ&ved=0CEQQ6AEwBQ#v=onepage&q=nov%2013%201900%20wrench&f=false.
Courtesy of Liberty Tool Co.

041403T1   Double jaw buggy wrench
DTM   MH

Drop-forged steel, wooden handle, 5 3/8" long, unsigned.

This wrench was patented by H A Thompson on Nov. 2, 1880 and produced by the Portland Wrench Co. in Maine. In 1886, Portland Wrench was reorganized as the Diamond Wrench Co. In 1893, the company went bankrupt. In the interim, these companies produced some of the most interesting small and medium sized buggy wrenches of any American companies. These Portland-made wrenches are among the most sought after specimens of 19th century wrench producers.

http://www.davistownmuseum.org/pics/041403t1.jpg
http://www.davistownmuseum.org/publications/volume10.html

041505T34   Drain plug wrench
DTM   MH

Drop-forged steel, 10" long, signed "DROP FORGED" "DRAIN PLUG WRENCH" "MADE IN USA".

This is a combination wrench with sockets for up to 3/4 plugs. The maker is not identified.

http://www.davistownmuseum.org/pics/041505t34.jpg

42801T16   Elgin wrench set
DTM   MH

Drop-forged nickel-plated steel in wood box, signed on box label "Boxed sets of Elgin Wrench & Attachments (etc) Stan Manufacturing Co. Carpentersville ILL, USA".

The tools are inscribed "extra jaw 25¢". DATM (Nelson 1999) lists Stan Mfg. as working from 1897 f.

7612LTC3   Horseshoe calk wrench
DA   TT (Pub)

Cast iron, 7" long, 2 1/4" wide, 3/8" thick, signed "NEVERSLIP NO.1" "5/8" "9/16".

Possibly this was made by the Neverslip Calk Co. of New Brunswick, NJ. Or the Neverslip Horseshoe Co. of Boston, MA (Nelson 1999, 570). Horseshoe calks are traction devices screwed into the bottom of a horseshoe, also commonly called shoe studs or screw-in calks. Courtesy of Liberty Tool Company.

The Industrial Revolution (1865f.): Other Factory Made Tools

Wrenches

7712LTC1   Jointed socket wrench with extension   DA   TT (Pub)

Drop-forged steel, 7 1/4" long, 3/4" wide, 1/2" square socket, 3/8" extension, signed "WHEATON" "PATENTED" "7HW" "FEB. 5, 1918".

Abram W. Wheaton received patent 1,255,370 for a "self closing faucet and wrench or handle thereof" and assigned it to A.W. Wheaton Brass Works of NJ. View the patent here: http://www.google.com/patents/US1255370?printsec=abstract&dq=FEB.+5,+1918+wheaton&ei=rscO UOaLGqXD0QHkxoCYAw#v=onepage&q=FEB.%205%2C%201918%20wheaton&f=false. Courtesy of Liberty Tool Company.

6703T35   Locking combination box wrench   DTM   TT

Cast iron, 8 3/4" long, 1" square closed socket, 3/4" open square socket, signed 1; HOOD; PAT'D (illegible).

7612LTC1   Multi-socket box wrench   DA   TT (Pub)

Drop-forged steel, 6" long, 1 1/2" wide, 3/8" thick, signed "FITS-ALL * 1/4" TO 1" "TRADE MARK PAT. PEND. RAST PROD. CORP. MADE IN NEW YORK U.S.A.".

This box wrench has a novel stepped socket design allowing for a wide variety of bolts to fit each socket. The hex bolt sizes are 15/16", 1 1/16", 3/4", 13/16", 1/2", 3/8", 9/16", and 7/16". Courtesy of Liberty Tool Company.

121412T4   Offset crescent wrench   DTM   TT

Cast steel, wood (rosewood), 6 1/2" long, 1 3/4" wide, signed "THE HD SMITH & CO 6 IN" "PERFECT HANDLE PATENTED".

"The H.D. Smith Company was founded in 1855 in Plantsville, Connecticut. The company operated as a foundry and merchant drop-forger, and in the latter role was possibly the first of many such businesses. After 1900 tool production became an important part of the company's business, and their best known products became a line of wood-handle tools sold under the 'Perfect Handle' brand" (http://home.comcast.net/~alloy-artifacts/other-makers-p3.html).

7612LTC5   Offset six point box wrench   DA   TT (Pub)

Drop-forged steel, 8 1/4" long, 1 3/8" wide, 1 3/4" tall, 1" and 15/16" box ends, signed "OF&CO QUALITY".

Courtesy of Liberty Tool Company.

7612LTC8   Offset tractor nut combination box wrench   DA   TT (Pub)

Forged steel, 10" long, 1 3/4" wide, 1 1/2" tall, signed "BARCALO-BUFFALO,U.S.A. PATENT No 1,870,612".

It has sockets for 5/8" square, 1" six point, 1 3/16" six point, 5/8" eight point, and a 5/16" square male extension. Barcalo Manufacturing began in Buffalo, NY in 1896. Alex de Schebeko's 1932 patent may be viewed here: http://www.google.com/patents/US1870612?printsec=description&dq=1,870,612&ei=jsQOUNqtGYe6 0QGT24CoDA#v=onepage&q=1%2C870%2C612&f=false. Courtesy of Liberty Tool Company.

The Industrial Revolution (1865f.): Other Factory Made Tools

Wrenches

31112T25   Open ended wrench   DTM   MH3-D2

Drop-forged steel, 7 1/4" long, 1/2" wide, signed "3/4" C. Drew & Co. 3/4"".

Courtesy of Liberty Tool Co.

http://www.davistownmuseum.org/bioDrew.htm

11301T11   Open ended wrench   DTM   MH

Drop-forged iron, 5 1/2" long, 5/8" and 3/4" openings, signed "Ford" in the earliest of known Ford scripts.

This must be among the oldest of Ford Motor Co. wrenches.

32708T48   Piano tuning wrench   DTM   MH

Drop-forged steel, rosewood, 9 1/4" long, 4 1/4" wide, signed "GERMANY".

It is probably made of German steel.

http://www.davistownmuseum.org/pics/32708t48-2.jpg
http://www.davistownmuseum.org/pics/32708t48-1.jpg

041505T15   Pipe wrench   DTM   MH

Drop-forged steel, 18" long, signed "Walworth Company Made in USA" "WALCO PIPE WRENCH" "PATENT NO 1862002" and "18".

Walworth was a Boston manufacturer and the first maker of the Stilson wrench (1882), of which there is a later variation. See the acrylic on canvas artwork of Alan Magee for a c. 2000 interpretation of this tool. This is the top wrench in the photograph.

http://www.davistownmuseum.org/pics/041505t15.jpg
http://www.davistownmuseum.org/bioWalworth.html

93011T10   Pipe wrench   DTM   TT

Drop-forged steel with wood handle, 6" long, signed "WALWORTH" "MADE IN USA" and their trademark "GENUINE STILSON" in a diamond shape, on jaw "STILSON C1" "REG. U.S. PAT. OFF. C".

http://www.davistownmuseum.org/bioWalworth.html

42801T20   Pipe wrench   DTM   MH

Drop-forged steel, 7" long when closed, signed "Genuine Stilson Wrench Walworth Mfg. Co. Boston Mass Automobile 8 inch".

This is a fine example of a circa 1910-1915 wrench by one of America's most prolific wrench-makers.

http://www.davistownmuseum.org/bioWalworth.html

Wrenches

52603T37   **Pipe wrench**   DTM   MH

Drop-forged steel, 7" long, signed "WALWORTH COMPANY" "MADE IN USA" "PATENT NO 1711083".

This patent belonged to Alphonse O. Brungardt, Scituate, MA, and has to do with the process of making the wrench (http://www.datamp.org/patents/advance.php?id=22386&set=8).

http://www.davistownmuseum.org/bioWalworth.html

93011T9   **Pipe wrench**   DTM   TT

Drop-forged steel with wood handle, 7" long, signed "WALWORTH MFG. CO." "BOSTON, U.S.A." and their trademark "REGISTERED STILLSON" in a diamond shape.

http://www.davistownmuseum.org/bioWalworth.html

31811T14   **Pocket wrench**   DTM   TT

Drop-forged steel, wood handle, 6 1/2" long, 1 1/2" x 1/2" head, signed "WORCHESTER" with two preceding lines that are obscured.

This style of wrench is also called a screw wrench or monkey wrench.

TCL1001A   **Ratchet wrench**   DTM   MH

Drop-forged steel, 10 7/8" long, 5/8" ratchet, signed "TRUTH TOOL CO. MANKATO MINN.", c. 1920.

This is an unusual wrench. This company began in the early 1900s as Arthur E. Cowden's blacksmith shop in Ellendale, MN and is still operating as Truth Hardware. (https://www.truth.com/main/generalinfo/history.cfm).

11301T8A   **Ratchet wrench**   DTM   MH

Drop-forged alloy steel, 6 3/4" long, 1/2" diameter socket, unsigned.

This is a primitive, single ratchet socket wrench with a simple peened mechanism.

6312LTC1   **Screw adjusted nut wrench**   DA   TT (Pub)

Drop-forged steel, rosewood, 21" long, unsigned.

Courtesy of Liberty Tool Co.

7512LTC4   **Six-way box wrench with square extension**   DA   TT (Pub)

Drop-forged steel, 7 1/4" long, 1 1/4" wide, 13/16" thick, signed "CHAMPION No. 175".

The wrench has a 7/16" male square extension and the following ends: 1 3/16" six point end, 1" six point end, 13/16" six point end, 13/16" eight point end, 1 1/16" eight point end, and 11/16" eight point end. It was made by International Harvester Company but was never listed in any of their company catalogs. Courtesy of Liberty Tool Company.

The Industrial Revolution (1865f.): Other Factory Made Tools

Wrenches

32412LTC1   Slide adjust pipe wrench   DA   TT (Pub)

Drop-forged steel, 12" long, signed "H & E WRENCH CO. U.S.A. NEW BEDFORD MASS.; PAT. MAR. 27 1923 TRADE HANDE MARK REG. U.S. PAT. OFF.".

This "HandE" wrench employs a sliding screw adjustment mechanism. The H & E Wrench company was founded by G.E. Hemphill and E.J. Evans. Courtesy of Liberty Tool Company.

7512LTC3   Sliding jaw adjustable wrench   DA   TT (Pub)

Drop-forged steel, 5 7/8" long, 3/8" thick, jaws go from 1/4" to 7/8" wide, signed "DROP FORGED STEEL PATENTED APR 17, 1923 6 IN. NO. 61" "GELLMAN WRENCH CORPORATION ROCK ISLAND ILL. U.S.A. Polly".

This wrench design was originally patented in 1921 by I.C. Gellman, patent #1,451,906. This particular example has a badly torqued handle. Courtesy of Liberty Tool Company.

22512LTC2   Sliding wedge bicycle wrench   DA   TT (Pub)

Drop-forged steel, 8" long, signed "TRADE MARK FITZALL" (in a diamond) "PATENTED JUNE 9.1908 APR.26.1910" "2B ROGERS PRINTZ & CO WARREN PA." "DROP FORGED STEEL".

Information on John R. Long's patent may be viewed here: http://www.datamp.org/patents/search/advance.php?pn=955974&id=14725&set=1. Courtesy of Liberty Tool Co.

21812T21   Slip adjust nut wrench   DTM   TT

Drop-forged steel, 28 5/8" long, 5 1/8" long head, unsigned.

The adjustment mechanism is seized.

42801T19   Socket wrench   DTM   MH

Drop-forged steel, 4 3/4" long, 1/2" socket, signed "WHR21711".

This is an unusual wrench as well as an interesting sculpture object.

21912T1   Spring adjusted diamond wagon wrench   DTM   TT

Drop-forged steel, brass spring, 9" long, 1" wide, signed "Reed & Co. Higgaum CT".

This wrench was patented by T. H. Remington on May 21, 1878. There is a photo of the patented wrench in Cope (1993, 206). Courtesy of Liberty Tool Co.

TCZ1004   Stillson wrench   DTM   MH

Drop forged steel, 9 1/2" long, signed "RED-HEAD" and "MADE IN U.S.A.", c. 1920 (?).

The maker is not listed in DATM (Nelson 1999). There is a modern company named Red Head Brass that makes wrenches for firefighters.

The Industrial Revolution (1865f.): Other Factory Made Tools

Wrenches

22612T9   Tap wrench   DTM   TT

Drop-forged steel, 2 1/2" long, 1/4" diameter, 3" long handle, signed "The Dikeman Mfg. Co. Norwalk, Conn".

The Dikeman Mfg. Co., Norwalk, Conn. was founded in 1906 in Norwalk by two bothers, Charles and Joseph, after both had worked in Torrington, Conn at a bicycle factory. Dikeman Mfg made mechanics tools and metal goods. (Bacheller 2000). Courtesy of Liberty Tool Co.

50402T8   Tap wrench   DTM   MH

Drop-forged steel, 7" long, signed "C. E. Billing's PATENT MAY 6 1879. Billings & Spencer Co. Hartford CT USA", "B" in a triangle and owner's signature "A. E. Wright".

DATM (Nelson 1999, 86) lists Billings & Spencer as working in Harford from 1873 to 1950. Christopher Spencer was the inventor of the Spencer rifle and Charles Ethan Billings apprenticed with the Robbins & Lawrence Co. Armory in Windsor, VT. For more information go to the American Precision Museum website (http://www.americanprecision.org/).

http://www.davistownmuseum.org/bioBillingspencer.html

8612T2   Tractor nut box wrench   DTM   TT

Malleable cast iron, 6 1/4" long, 13/16" open end, 7/16" closed square end, signed "IRON ACE".

IRON ACE is cast into the body of the wrench.

021812T3   Wagon wheel wrench   DTM   TT-D5

Hand-forged malleable iron, 9" long, unsigned.

This is a two ended wrench.

101212LTC2 Wagon wrench   DA   TT (Pub)

Cast steel, rosewood, 5 1/2" long, 1 3/4" wide, 9/16" thick, signed "DIAMOND WRENCH CO STEEL FORGED PORTLAND, ME.".

31908T31   Wagon wrench   DTM   MH

Drop-forged iron and steel, brass trim, wooden handle, 10 1/2" long, signed "PAT. NOV. 2, 80".

This wrench is similar in design (revolving nut slide) to the wagon wrenches made by the Diamond Wrench Co. in Portland, ME, also in 1880. It is otherwise not illustrated in Cope's "American Wrench Makers" (1993, 99). The patent was given to Henry Thompson of Farmington, ME. It may be viewed here:
http://www.google.com/patents?id=kGJxAAAAEBAJ&pg=PA2&dq=NOV.+2,+1880+wrench&hl=en&sa=X&ei=KdCWT6iLMYmg0QWb-MCGDg&ved=0CDQQ6AEwAA#v=onepage&q=NOV.%202%2C%201880%20wrench&f=false.

http://www.davistownmuseum.org/pics/31908t31p2.jpg
http://www.davistownmuseum.org/pics/31908t31p2.jpg

Wrenches

31808SLP21   **Wagon wrench**   DTM   TT

Drop-forged iron, 8 1/4" long, unsigned.

http://www.davistownmuseum.org/pics/31808slp21.jpg

42912LTC3   **Wagon wrench**   DA   TT (Pub)

Drop-forged iron, 4 3/4" long, unsigned.

Courtesy of Liberty Tool Co.

91312T1   **Wagon wrench**   DTM   MH

Cast steel, wooden (rosewood) handle, 10 1/2" long, 3" long and 1" wide head, 13/16" nut socket, signed "PATT NOV. 2'80 OCT. 16 '83" "DIAMOND WRENCH CO. STEEL FORGED ***RT".

Link for the 1880 patent 234,091of Henry A. Thompson:
http://www.google.com/patents/US234091?pg=PA1&dq=nov+2,+1880+thompson&hl=en&sa=X&ei=UCxSUOqYGpHmtQb6nYHwDQ&ved=0CEAQ6AEwBg#v=onepage&q&f=false.

http://www.davistownmuseum.org/pics/91312T1-2_thumb.jpg

41801T5   **Wagon wrench**   DTM   MH

Drop-forged iron, wooden handle, brass ferrule, 12" long, takes a 5/8" square nut, signed "PAT. NOV. 2. 80".

See wrench ID#: 31908T31 for information on this patent.

TCZ1003A   **Wrench**   DTM   MH

Drop-forged steel, signed "DROPPED FORGED STEEL".

This is a typical one piece drop-forged tool.

TCZ3001   **Wrench**   DTM   MH

Steel, 6 5/16" long, signed "A J".

This is a combination alligator open ended wrench. It is probably shop made by the owner who used it.

102904T18   **Wrench**   DTM   MH

Drop-forged steel, 6" long, signed "W.--W. MFG. CO. INC." " WORCESTER, MASS." " PAT 7-9-20".

This is an uncommon wrench. This maker is not related to the current W. W. Manufacturing Company, Inc. of Bridgeton, NJ, which began business in 1964.

http://www.davistownmuseum.org/pics/102904t18_p1.jpg

913108T3   **Wrench**   DTM   MH

Drop-forged steel, 6 1/4" long, signed "BLUEPOINT" BOXOCKET" "PATENT APPLD FOR" "CHICAGO" and "ILL".

Bluepoint is an early mark of the Snap-On Tool Corporation.

The Industrial Revolution (1865f.): Other Factory Made Tools

Wrenches

42801T22   **Wrench**   DTM   MH

Drop-forged alloy steel, 5 1/2" long, signed "1/4 Brake Eccentric Wrench 3/16 Herbrand Van Chrome No. 195 Made in USA".

This is an unusual wrench utilizing alloy steel characteristic of tools made beginning in the early 20th century with the advent of electric blast furnaces.

33002T9   **Wrench**   DTM   MH

Drop-forged alloy steel, 10 3/8" long, signed on handle "Heller Brothers Newark. NJ. USA 4-14-25. 11-12-29" and on verso "10 MASTERENCH CHROME 7-11 VANADIUM 41".

Heller & Brothers was one of America's foremost manufacturers of blacksmith tools, 1866 - 1899. DATM (Nelson 1999, 374) indicates they changed their name in 1899 to the Heller Brothers Company. In 1955 they became the Heller Tool Co.

http://www.davistownmuseum.org/pics/33002t9.jpg
http://www.davistownmuseum.org/bioHellerBros.html

32912T4   **Wrench**   DTM   TT-46

Drop-forged steel, 11" long, signed "WELLS BROS & CO" "7/16" "1/2".

A Wells Bros. Co. located in Greenfield, MA is listed in DATM (Nelson 1999, 840), but this tool does not bear one of the listed marks and appears to be earlier than the 1887 to 1912 operation dates listed. Courtesy of Liberty Tool Co.

Bibliography

Bacheller, Milton H., Jr. 2000. *American marking gages, patented and manufactured.* Plainville, MA: Self-published.

Barraclough, K. C. 1984. *Steelmaking before Bessemer: Crucible steel, the growth of technology.* Volume 2. London: The Metals Society.

Brack, H. G. 2008a. *Art of the Edge Tool: The ferrous metallurgy of New England shipsmiths and toolmakers.* Hulls Cove, ME: Pennywheel Press.

Brack, H. G. 2008b. *Registry of Maine Toolmakers.* Hulls Cove, ME: Pennywheel Press.

Brack, H. G. 2008c. *Steel- and Toolmaking Strategies and Techniques before 1870.* Hulls Cove, ME: Pennywheel Press.

Cope, Kenneth L. 1994. *Makers of American machinist's tools: A historical directory of makers and their tools.* Mendham, NJ: Astragal Press.

Dane, E. Surrey. 1973. *Peter Stubs and the Lancashire hand tool industry.* Altrincham, UK: John Sherratt and Son Lt.

Devitt, Jack. 2000. *Ohio toolmakers and their tools.* Anderson, SC.: Tavenner Pub Co.

Diderot, Denis and d'Alembert, Jean Baptiste le Rond. [1751-65] 1964-6. *Recueil de planches sur les sciences, les arts libéraux, et les arts mechaniques avec leur explication.* Volumes 1-6. Paris, France: Au Cercle du Livre Precieux.

Goodman, W. L. [1968] 1993. *British planemakers from 1700.* Mendham, NJ, Astragal Press.

Jacob, Walter W. 2011. *Stanley woodworking tools: The finest years: Research and type studies adapted from The Chronicle of the Early American Industries Association.* Hebron, MD: Early American Industries Association.

Jones, Robert S., The 'Plane' Gentleman, 3042 Conchise Circle SE, Rio Rancho, NM 87124-2271, personal correspondence.

Moxon, Joseph. [1703] 1989. *Mechanick exercises or the doctrine of handiworks.* Morristown, NJ: The Astragal Press.

Nelson, Robert E., Ed. (1999). *Directory of American Toolmakers* [DATM]:*A listing of identified makers of tools who worked in Canada and the United States before 1900.* Early American Industries Association.

Pollak, Emil and Pollak, Martyl. 2001. *A guide to the makers of American wooden planes, fourth edition.* Mendham, NJ: Astragal Press.

Schulz, Alfred and Schulz, Lucille. 1989. *Antique and unusual wrenches.* Malcolm, NE: Self-published.

Sellens, Alvin. 1990. *Dictionary of American hand tools: A pictorial synopsis.* Augusta, KS: Self-published.

Smith, Roger K. (1981-1992). *Patented transitional & metallic planes in America 1827 - 1927.* 2 vols. Lancaster, MA: North Village Publishing Co.

Stanley, Philip E. 1984. *Boxwood & ivory: Stanley traditional rules, 1855 - 1975.* Westborough, MA: The Stanley Publishing Co.

Timmins, R. & Sons. 1976. *Tools for the trades and crafts: An eighteenth century pattern book.* Fitzwilliam, NH: K. Roberts Pub. Co.

Yeaton, Donald G. 2000. *Axe makers of Maine.* Unpublished, Donald Yeaton, 51 Strafford Rd., Rochester, NH 03867-4107.

www.ingramcontent.com/pod-product-compliance
Lightning Source LLC
Chambersburg PA
CBHW081147090426
42736CB00017B/3214